THE COLLEGE
A History of Queen's/University College Cork,
1845–1995

Frontispiece: Civil engineering class (1912–13) with Iris Ashley-Cummins, who became the first female BE graduate in Ireland, in 1915

THE COLLEGE

A History of Queen's/University College Cork, 1845–1995

JOHN A. MURPHY

CORK UNIVERSITY PRESS

First published in 1995 by
Cork University Press
University College
Cork
Ireland

© John A. Murphy 1995

Reprinted 1996

British Library Cataloguing in Publication Data
A CIP catalogue record for this book is available from the British Library.

ISBN 1 85918 056 6 hardcover

Typeset by Seton Music Graphics, Bantry, Co. Cork
Printed by ColourBooks, Baldoyle, Co. Dublin

To the unknown student

CONTENTS

ABBREVIATIONS

AC   Academic Council
ACM   Academic Council Minutes
AMA   American Medical Association
APDC   Academic Planning and Development Committee
BWLB   Board of Works Letter Book
BU   (archival material relating to) Buildings
BOW   Board of Works
CC   College Council
CC   *Cork Constitution*
CCM   College Council Minutes
CE   *The Cork Examiner*
Comm. Rep. *Commission Report*
CS   Chief Secretary
CSO   Chief Secretary's Office
CSORP   Chief Secretary's Office Registered Papers
CTM   Comhairle Teachta na Macléinn
CUP   Cork University Press
CUR   *Cork University Record* (title from 1944 to 1956: thereafter *University College Cork Record (UCCR)* to 1980)
CWE   *Cork Weekly Examiner*
D   (Cork Archives Institute) Dowden Papers
DÉ   *Parliamentary Debates Dáil Éireann*
DNB   *Dictionary of National Biography*
EE   *Cork Evening Echo*
FC   Finance Committee
FCM   Finance Committee Minutes
FP   *Cork Free Press*
FJ   *The Freeman's Journal*
GB   Governing Body
GBM   Governing Body Minutes
GMC   General Medical Council
HEA   Higher Education Authority
II   *Irish Independent*
ILN   *Illustrated London News*
IP   *The Irish Press*

IT	*The Irish Times*
ITS	Irish Texts Society
JCHAS	*Journal of the Cork Historical and Archaeological Society*
JGAHS	*Journal of the Galway Archaeological and Historical Society*
MG	*Manchester Guardian*
MP	Munster Pamphlets (Special Collections, Boole Library)
MUP	Munster University Pamphlets (Special Collections, Boole library)
n.d.	no date
NFBT	National Food Biotechnology
NLI	National Library of Ireland
NMRC	National Microelectronics Centre
NUI	National University of Ireland
OHA	Oral History Archive
OPW	Office of Public Works
PO	(archival material emanating from) President's Office
PR	(UC) Property Register
PR	*President's Report*
PRONI	Public Record Office Northern Ireland
QCB	Queen's College Belfast
QCC	Queen's College Cork
QCC	*Queen's College Cork* (Student magazine)
'QCC'	Ph.D. thesis (see Pettit in Bibliography)
QCG	Queen's College Galway
QUB	The Queen's University of Belfast
QUI	The Queen's University in Ireland
RCI	Royal Cork Institution
RDS	Royal Dublin Society
RIA	Royal Irish Academy
RUI	The Royal University of Ireland
SI	*Sunday Independent*
SRC	Students Representative Council
T	*The Times*
TCD	Trinity College Dublin
TES	*Times Educational Supplement*
U	(Cork Archives Institute) Unofficial papers
UC/	University College Cork, generic archival term, followed by creating office e.g. PO (President's Office)
UCC	University College Cork
UCCR	*University College Cork Record* (title of *Cork University Record*, 1956–80)
UCD	University College Dublin
UCG	University College Galway
UNREG	Unregistered (Papers, in Chief Secretary's Office)
VEC	Vocational Education Committee
WEA	Workers' Educational Association

ILLUSTRATIONS

Front endpaper: Part of Ordnance Survey Map (1841) indicating the western boundary of Cork City. The County Gaol and Gillabbey border the site which was finally selected for the college. The other significant landmark on this side of the city is the City Gaol situated north of the northern channel of the Lee. Otherwise the vicinity is mainly pastoral. (Based on the Ordnance Survey by permission of the government, permit no. 6109.)

Back endpaper: Map showing chronological growth of the Western Road site from the original area selected by Thomas Deane in 1846 to the modern campus. Not included are college lands at the Mardyke (1918), the Lee Maltings Complex (1968) and properties on Dyke Parade, Muskerry Villas, Presentation Brothers College, Eye Ear and Throat Hospital, Good Shepherd Convent; University Dental School and Hospital and the Munster Institute, all acquired in the 1980s and early 1990s. Although adjoining the college campus the Honan Chapel is not owned by UCC.

Frontispiece: Civil engineering class (1912–13) with Iris Ashley-Cummins, the first female BE graduate in 1915. She is seated to the left of Professor Alexander. (College Archives, UCC)

FOREWORD

WHEN PRESIDENT MICHAEL P. MORTELL asked me to undertake a history of the college to be published in the sesquicentennial year of 1995, my hesitation was brief. Though I hankered after a *dolce far niente* retirement, I quickly realised that I would have to 'scorn delights and live laborious days' since I had no real choice in the matter. With the exception of some interludes and offstage diversions, the college has been my life since I registered as a first-year student in October 1945. I owe a great deal to the institution and this labour of love is a partial repayment of the debt. Besides, Caribbean cruises apart, I could hardly have chosen a more appropriate activity at this stage of my life.

UCC graduates I have met abroad recall sentimentally features of college that touch a perennial chord – the great redwoods, the worn stone steps, the ritual of 'signing on' in registration week, theodolite displays by engineering students, nine o'clock maths lectures, the eternally optimistic fishermen on the banks of the south channel, and (long since stilled) the ringing of the clock-tower lecture bell as well as the matter-of-fact tone of the examinations officer reading out results like a court martial list, from the judgement doorway in the North Wing. While all this, and more, is a vivid memory for me also, *my* nostalgia is controlled and balanced by my experience of the diurnal realities of the place, by a somewhat acerbic temperament and, I would hope, by a historian's objectivity. I raise these points by way of countering the argument that the insider academic is not the most appropriate person to write the history of his alma mater. On the contrary, it is the insider who most keenly scents the various trails of a familiar institution and who most intensely experiences the presence of academic ghosts, recent and remote, within its hallowed walls.

Over these last few years, I have repeatedly emphasised that I was not working on 'the' history of the college, and I have used the less ambitious 'a' in the title of the work. I have a number of reasons for this disclaimer, none of them having to do with modesty on my part. In the first place, it may be questioned philosophically whether there can be anything so comprehensive and definitive as *the* history of a 150-year-old institution, in all its complex ramifications. But if such a thing could be accomplished, it could not be encompassed in an 'overview' book of moderate size, requiring rather the work of a team of researchers spread over several volumes. A project for another anniversary, perhaps? Moreover, if 'the' history is thought of as a complete tapestry, 'a' history consists of major threads which interest the author and which he interweaves as skilfully as he can. My final reason for insisting on 'a', not 'the', is the calculated self-interest of fire-proofing myself against the inevitable accusations of sins of omission. At the same time, I hope that I have dealt with every important development, issue, episode and personality in the (!) history of the college.

That history is full of human interest, throwing light not only on educational, religious and social issues, but on the subtleties of gown/town relations on various planes. Of the three Queen's Colleges, perhaps Cork had the most interesting and varied history. Belfast was almost bound to be a success, with its designated Presbyterian and Protestant student community; the small Galway college had dismal experiences and was frequently on the verge of extinction; in its fluctuating fortunes, Cork was just strong and large enough to meet challenge with response, according to the classic formula for survival and eventual success.

In a letter to *The Cork Examiner* on 14 September 1899, R. J. Smith, a Cardiff-based QCC graduate, deplored the college's failure to mark the fiftieth anniversary of its opening, the only celebrations for the occasion being organised by the Old Corkonians graduates club in London. Perhaps the college had little to celebrate in 1899 but it was a lost opportunity, in Smith's opinion, to mobilise graduate loyalty for practical purposes. College's omission or oversight was a slight on those graduates 'scattered throughout the globe, proud to be sent forth the bearers of its name, the custodians of its honour and to be associated with its traditions'.

In 1945, some articles and booklets were published dealing with early college history, but it is by no means clear that they were written to commemorate the 100th anniversary of the 1845 Colleges Act and of the incorporation of Queen's College Cork. Echoes of old ecclesiastical thunderbolts rumbled in the *Cork University Record* where a priest ringingly endorsed, nearly a century afterwards, the Catholic bishops' condemnation of the Queen's Colleges.[1] The college itself totally ignored its 1845 origins, though it made quite a fuss that year about the centenary of the death of Thomas Davis. A few years later, there was some talk[2] about celebrating the centenary of the college's opening in 1849, but it seems to have come to nothing in the end, apart from an honorary degree conferring ceremony in the college.[3] Plans for a more general commemoration apparently fell foul of Catholic/nationalist opposition.[4] The president of the Cork Chamber of Commerce, deploring the lack of public benefaction of the college over the hundred years, seemed to have a keener sense of the centenary's significance than the president of UCC.[5] Alfred O'Rahilly crowed over his QCC

[1] Rev. W.J. Hegarty, 'The Irish Hierarchy and the Queen's Colleges', *CUR*, no. 5 Christmas 1945.
[2] E.g. *CE*, 16 June 1948; *II*, 11 July 1949, Alfred O'Rahilly's concluding address.
[3] *CE*, 20 July 1949; *CUR*, no. 17, Christmas 1949. Galway had celebrations of a sort: *IP*, 11 November 1849.
[4] Hearsay and anecdotal evidence for this appear to get more substantial support in Fleischmann correspondence December 1948–January 1949: Fleischmann Papers, UC Archives.
[5] *CE*, 17 November 1948.

predecessors, condemning their 'secularist and neutral' ethos and giving thanks that the college had 'moved a long way from the barren and negative ideas of 1849' and had 'escaped the decrepitude of a centenarian'.[1]

Thus in the 1940s UCC was both ashamed and scornful of its beginnings. In contrast, the college in 1995 was prepared to embrace all of its history as a continuum and not to reject a part of its past with which it was ideologically out of tune. In short, it had reached that stage of civilised maturity where it was content to read the pages of its history and then turn them over instead of tearing them out. It was in the same sesquicentennial spirit of accepting the college's total heritage (despite changes in constitution and title) that I was glad to write my history.

Some miscellaneous points of comment and explanation about the book are called for. First, I have highlighted the personalities and policies of college presidents, since the role of the chief executive has been vital in shaping the college in successive phases. Secondly, I can well anticipate the purist objection that the period from the 1960s is much too close for comfortable assessment. Indeed, it is, and my treatment of it must inevitably be myopic in places, but I would be shirking my 'overview' brief had I not attempted, however tentatively and impressionistically, to come right up to date. Thirdly, if a 'National University of Ireland, Cork' will have been created by amending legislation before the end of the sesquicentennial year of 1995, as promised, then 'The College' of this book's title will have a purely historical significance, though one suspects it will not go out of circulation for a very long time. Finally, I have used the term 'staff' throughout to include academic members of staff: the equivalent transatlantic usage of 'faculty' is one of the few Americanisms not yet adopted here.

By the way of an introduction to acknowledging my debts, I must say that I made fruitful use of work already done on different aspects of college history. In undertaking a comprehensive survey stretching over 150 years (and this is the first such overview to be published), I was glad to avail, greedily and gratefully, of the more specialised studies that had already appeared. The reader will see how liberally I have mined Moody and Beckett's monumental *Queen's Belfast* work (for the general university background); Seán Pettit's thesis on the origins and early years of the college; Des MacHale's biography of Boole; Monica Taylor's *Windle*; and J. Anthony Gaughan's study of Alfred O'Rahilly.[2] UCC colleagues like Pettit and MacHale – and at an earlier period, people like Ronan O' Rahilly and Deasmhumhan Ó Raghallaigh – deserve praise for taking on aspects of college history long before its archives were professionally organised. Now that there has been such a bright change in this respect, it is to be hoped that numerous features of the college's past – personalities, episodes, issues, departments or whatever else may be prompted by the present book – will be investigated in depth in the years ahead, and that interest will not flag once the UCC 150 fever subsides. I am also grateful to Frederick O'Dwyer for letting me see the draft text of his *Architecture of Deane and Woodward*.

[1] *CE*, 10 November 1949. O'Rahilly also said (*CUR*, no. 14, Christmas 1948 p. 31) that QCC in 1849 did not represent 'the ideals of the Irish nation'.
[2] See bibliography for details.

In the first place, I want to thank President Michael P. Mortell for his help and encouragement. Both he and Mr Michael F. Kelleher (finance officer and secretary) willingly facilitated the progress of the work in various ways. Mr Edwin McCarthy, the college planning officer, was similarly helpful. So were the staffs of various college offices, but I owe a particular debt to the Boole Library staff, especially in the Special Collections area, for their expert, friendly and patient assistance at all times. Further afield, I have to thank the staff of the Cork City Library, the Cork County Library, the National Library of Ireland, Trinity College Library, NUI Archives, UCD Archives, and most particularly the National Archives of Ireland which is the repository of the bulk of the Dublin-based material used in this history.

However, the richest and most significant sources are in the UCC archives, and I discuss their importance in the bibliography. The expertise of the college archivist, Virginia Teehan, was constantly and unstintingly at my disposal, and her suggestions, supplemented by historical intuition and good sense, were invariably helpful. I am additionally obliged to her for her advice on illustrations and help in supplying captions.

Without research assistance, I could not have hoped to deal adequately with such voluminous and variegated source material covering a span of 150 years. At the outset, Mary Harris surveyed the sources in Cork and Dublin, and drew up informative reports which were a fruitful basis for much of my subsequent work. Paul Rouse was my research assistant in 1994, working in the National Archives in Dublin (particularly on the Chief Secretary's Registered Papers, essential material for QCC history) and subsequently rendering me valuable service through his researches in UCC and in the Cork City Library. The efficient and committed labour of these two young scholars was indispensable.

Patricia McCarthy drew my attention throughout to items of interest at the Cork Archives Institute. While engaged in his own research in Cork newspapers, Colman O'Mahony generously kept an eye out for items of college relevance. During our long country walks together, my colleague and companion Seán Teegan gave me the benefit of his own long and intimate knowledge of UCC, in the course of informed reminiscences that were at once enchanting, disenchanted, loyal and affectionate. Eilís Caffrey of the UCC Secretarial Centre arranged for the typing of the manuscript, since I myself am a pre-computer quill *primitif*: Niamh Spillane and Sinéad Mahony typed most of the work with skill and patience. I am particularly grateful to Tom Dunne who read the typescript and who suggested a re-arrangement of the material which I was glad to implement. In seeing the book through to publication Cork University Press was extremely helpful and encouraging. I also have to thank Paul Williams for supplying the composite map.

Within college and among graduates generally, the project aroused widespread interest, a reflection of people's affection for the institution. Many individuals contributed by supplying information, offering suggestions, lending material, agreeing to be interviewed, or helping in other ways. The acknowledgement list includes: Patrick D. Barry, Andy Bielenberg, Maeve Bradley, Suzanne Buckley, Cornelius G. Buttimer, Vincent Carmody, Áine Ní Chonaill, Mary B. Cotter, Patrick A.J. Cronin, Edmond C.

Dillon, Teresa Dowling, John Fahy, Diarmaid Ferriter, Raymond J. Fielding, Ruth Fleischmann, Brian Girvin, Dick Haslam, Charlotte Holland, Finbarr Holland, John J. Lee, Donal Lehane, J.C. Lehane, C.J.F. MacCarthy, Bernard MacDonagh, Matthew J. McDonnell, Ruth M. McDonnell, Walter McGrath, Áine McNeely, Maurice Moynihan, Deirdre Mortell, Brian S. Murphy, Ted Nevill, Bill Nolan, Seán Ó Coileáin, Madoline O'Connell, Essie O'Donoghue, Donal O'Donovan, Cornelius O'Leary, David O'Mahony, Diarmuid Ó Murchadha, Pádraig Ó Riain, Fergus O'Rourke, Kieran O'Shea, Eoin O'Shea, Mícheál P. Ó Súilleabhain, Charles O'Sullivan, Colm O'Sullivan, Noreen O'Sullivan, Anne Skally, David Slattery, Katherine Weldon and Gerry Wrixon.

When all acknowledgements are duly made, this book remains my own, in concept, approach and style. I alone am responsible for its flaws (which will be gleefully proclaimed) and for whatever insights and illumination it may offer. It will have done its job if it gives the reader, particularly perhaps the graduate of the diaspora, a historical feel for the college over its one hundred and fifty years.

Finally, I must thank my wife Cita, as always, for her love, tolerance and sound advice.

University College Cork
September 1995

CHAPTER ONE

THE BEGINNINGS

Cork, the principal city of a Province whose population
nearly equals that of all Scotland, presents peculiar
advantages for such a Collegiate Institution . . .

memorial to lord lieutenant, 1831

WHY AND HOW did Queen's College Cork come into being? It owed its existence to a combination of state, national, regional and local factors. The period of its foundation was one of intense and wide-ranging debate about education.

In the general United Kingdom context, the great cry was for reform and an end to privilege in the rarified preserves of university education. The new professional and commercial middle classes were protesting against aristocratic dominance in the academic as well as in the social and political order. The cry of reform, however, did not resound in the unwashed ears of the lower orders.[1] It would be a long time, longer in Ireland than in Britain, before anything like equality of opportunity beckoned to the masses. The belief persisted into the twentieth century that, in the words of Cardinal Cullen to the Powis Commission in 1870, 'too high an education will make the poor oftentimes discontented . . . [they] ought to be educated with a view to the place they hold in society'.[2]

The admission of the middle classes to higher education was seen as a guarantee of political and social stability. Reform, not revolution, was in the air. There would be necessary adjustments to, but no radical changes in, the existing scheme of things. As Thomas Wyse (who was to play a prominent part in the move to set up a Munster college) put it: 'to a well-educated and middle order, the State must mainly be indebted for its intellectual and moral progress'.[3] Such prudential, conservative considerations applied with particular force to Ireland, always potentially unstable. A related Victorian belief informing the education debate was that the social conditions of Ireland might be improved by diffusing the benefits of education among 'the middle and higher class of society'.[4]

While the middle classes demanded their place in the higher educational sun, they did not aspire to a takeover of the hallowed halls of the old universities. Oxford and Cambridge were seen as decrepit and stagnant, and their ethos a fusty and outmoded one. The new models – the University of London and the Scottish universities – were not Oxbridges writ large. They would satisfy the longing, not just for higher, but for a different form of, education. Thus there would be an end to restrictive religious tests, though the place of religion itself in the new education remained to be resolved. Moreover, the dusty curriculum of the traditional universities

1.1 Sir Thomas Wyse who played a prominent part in the move to set up a Munster college.

1.2 Sir Robert Peel introduced the Colleges Bill partly as a conciliation measure to appease Catholics.

was regarded as part of the privileged and discredited ivory tower. Middle-class reform and ambition embraced the idea of 'useful knowledge' as central to the new curriculum. On one occasion Sir Robert Kane encouraged a young audience to emulate 'the Paladins of industry . . . the true heroes of the present age'.[5] University students should be no longer gentlemen of leisure but serious pursuers of active careers. The Queen's College in Cork was to reflect these popular new values.

In Ireland, the spirit of reform and anti-privilege was influenced by national factors. At one level, the Queen's Colleges initiative was in line with the 'mixed' educational philosophy which gave us the national schools. More immediately, the Roman Catholic middle class, at once emboldened by the achievement of Emancipation in 1829 and disenchanted by its failure to shake ascendancy privilege, determinedly pursued the goal of higher education facilities. Sir Robert Peel's initiative was due, *inter alia*, to a realisation that conciliation of the Catholic bourgeoisie was a social and political imperative, if social order *and* the Union were to be preserved. Since nationalism and Catholicism were so intertwined, effective British rejection in 1843–44 of the nationalist demand for repeal of the Union made an important conciliation measure for Catholics all the more necessary. The grudging admission since 1793 of non-Anglicans to second-class status in Trinity College Dublin was certainly not the answer, though it was availed of perforce by a substantial number of Catholics.

However, meeting Catholic demands could not and did not take the form of establishing a Catholic university. Increasing the Maynooth grant raised a severe storm but it could be justified on logical lines extending back to its foundation in 1795. Using public funds for a new lay Catholic university was politically unacceptable to Irish Protestants and to public opinion in the United Kingdom as a whole, whatever the militants in the Irish Catholic hierarchy might say.

Irish Protestants were also determined to keep an exclusive Anglican grip on Trinity perks, prizes and professorships, as well as dog-in-the-mangerishly opposing a second non-denominational college within the University of Dublin.[6] In this stand-off situation, the Queen's Colleges proposal was a compromise that never really flourished in the nineteenth century, except in Belfast where by and large the college was in harmony with its religious and cultural catchment area.

The campaign for a college

Reinforcing and overlapping the various other pressures for an extension of third-level education, there were specific Cork[7] and Munster demands for a provincial college. Apart from all other considerations, it was inherently unbalanced and unjust to have only one university college in Ireland to serve the needs of eight million people, as Sir Thomas Wyse pointed out in the House of Commons in July 1844.[8] (A university, however, was not high on the priority list for the army of paupers in the Irish population nor for the four million women who simply did not count in the higher educational scheme of things.)

Queen's College Cork (QCC), possibly more so than University College Cork (UCC) later on, was always to see itself clearly as a college for Munster as well as the city of Cork. An event which stimulated interest in the new scientific learning was the lecture tour (including Cork) undertaken in 1837 by the professors of the Royal Dublin Society, including Sir Robert Kane.[9] A closer focus on the need for provincial colleges was provided by the sittings and report of the Select Committee on Education (Ireland), 1835–38 (the Wyse Committee). That report recommended the setting up of provincial colleges which would have no religious tests. Thomas Wyse MP, the secretary of the committee, and William Smith O'Brien MP went on to organise the popular agitation for a Munster college.

The Munster Provincial College Committee was under the chairmanship of a Catholic, James Roche, the Cork banker and so-called 'father of Queen's College Cork'. Roche, who circulated potential college supporters on National Bank note-paper, was present, to acclaim, at the opening ceremonies of the Queen's College on 7 November 1849 (he was then almost eighty), and his portrait hangs today over the stone staircase in the North Wing.[10] There was a reasonably good response from Catholics and Protestants alike to requests for popular support and, some years before views were to polarise around the 'godless colleges' issue, the organisers received the enthusiastic backing of Daniel O'Connell (who in October 1838 was 'ready to devote my best energies for the purpose – the plan of Provincial Colleges, in conjunction with, and subordinate to, a National University') and Bishop Cornelius Egan of Kerry.[11]

1.3 James Roche, chairman Munster Colleges Committee
and so-called 'father of Queen's College Cork'.

Since land and business were then and long thereafter dominated by the Protestant interest, the complexion of influential supporters reflected that reality: otherwise, the committee was as representative as could reasonably be expected. It included various MPs such as William Fagan who was to reject eloquently the 'godless' allegation where QCC was concerned; the businessman Richard Dowden who was active in Cork cultural circles; and the influential Beamish family. It was Major North Ludlow Beamish who was to hand over symbolically the Munster College Committee's records to Sir Robert Kane on opening day on behalf of the committee's surviving members who were also present. Other committee members of interest were the secretary, Dr Denis Brenan Bullen, who wrote a pamphlet as early as 1829 on the need for a 'secular Collegiate' institution and who was to have a controversial career in QCC; and Thomas Jennings, part of whose family land was to be acquired by the college.[12]

The enthusiasm of the committee was expressed at big meetings in Cork and Limerick towards the end of 1838. Resolutions were passed, petitions were organised, a deputation met the lord lieutenant, and MPs were instructed to promote the cause in parliament. But the political situation was unfavourable, and the prospects of a government-sponsored colleges scheme remained slight despite the prestigious support of Thomas Spring Rice, Lord Monteagle, a former Chancellor of the Exchequer. Thomas Wyse found he was being referred from pillar to post, and he ruefully informed Dr Bullen that the petitions he had formally laid before the Commons had 'produced little or no effect'. Yet he doggedly persisted with the cause and his efforts finally seemed to have borne fruit in July 1844. When he raised the issue in the Commons, Sir Robert Peel admitted the inadequacy of 'academical education' in Ireland, and promised early action 'or we shall have to notify to the honourable gentleman that our efforts have been unsuccessful, and there we must leave him to bring on his plan'.[13] Wyse reviewed the whole situation at a great meeting of the revived Munster College Committee on 13 November. Six months later, Peel introduced the Colleges Bill, for reasons of state rather than for reasons of pressure. Nevertheless, the great debate generated by the committee over the previous years had made its own contribution, and the surge of support in Cork showed that, for Catholic and Protestant laymen if not for clergy, localism was stronger than sectarianism.

In the late 1830s, Thomas Wyse (MP for Waterford City) and William Smith O'Brien (MP for Limerick County) formed an appropriate partnership in leading the agitation for a Munster college.[14] Both were liberals and landed gentlemen. Wyse was a Catholic and Smith O'Brien a Protestant, but both ardently believed in the principle of united or mixed education. Wyse had made a significant contribution to the national education scheme and he prophetically believed that third-level colleges would not prosper unless a secondary system ('county academies') was instituted. The two men reflected a north–south Munster balance or perhaps tension. Although they never fell out on the issue, Wyse and O'Brien differed, not surprisingly, on the preferable location of the new Munster college. Wyse believed there would and should be only one college for each province, at least initially, and that should be in Cork. Smith O'Brien's view was that, in a one-college-only situation, Limerick was an appropriate centre for the west as well as the south of Ireland, but he felt that colleges for both Limerick and Cork should be sought. What amounted to virtually rival committees were formed in Limerick and Cork, but the latter was much more assertive. Eventually, of course, the final decision in 1845 was made for its own reasons by government. Limerick had to wait a long time for its day.

According to Wyse,

> Cork is a more central situation for the Province than Limerick but, independent of position, it has other advantages, large opportunities for Medical study, for instruction in navigation, the Fine Arts etc. The existence of the Royal Cork Institution has produced good fruits, and the materials for Scientific and other collections, especially the casts from Rome,[15] appear to be good.

James Roche, writing to Smith O' Brien (26 November 1838) bluntly claimed that the case for Cork 'may be considered as determined'.

> Of the six counties, four, constituting three-quarters of the population – Cork, Kerry, Waterford and Tipperary are in favour of Cork, and a claim therefore on behalf of any other site, at a moment when union is our surest ground of success, would, I fear, be injurious to our common object.

Dr Bullen, the committee's secretary, argued that:

> to secure a prosperous result the first trial should be made in that position where the greatest number of essential elements were in existence to secure its success. The Medicine Faculty *alone* in Cork would afford 100 students tomorrow to the Infant college, and as Inspector of Anatomy I can undertake to provide the means of Anatomical Studies to three times that number.

And one of the resolutions passed at the November 1844 meeting in Cork claimed that

> Cork, the most populous and commercial city in the south of Ireland, is the appropriate site for such an establishment, as in addition to many other advantages, there already exist several Scientific and Literary institutions which present a suitable basis for the formation of a Provincial College in Munster.[16]

The general economic and social climate in Cork was conducive to a lively interest in the arts and sciences which in turn stimulated the agitation for a college. The prosperity deriving from the provisioning, butter, brewing, distilling and related trades provided the basis and the means for middle-class intellectual pursuits, which were particularly concentrated on the fashionable area of scientific experiments. 'Useful knowledge' was the great cry of the day, and in 1829 goodly numbers of women (or, more accurately, ladies) attended lectures on scientific topics. Catholics and Protestants alike manifested an eager appetite for knowledge, which augured well for the success of 'mixed education' in a provincial college.

The reminiscences of Denny Lane, Cork nationalist and businessman, evoke a cultured middle-class milieu in the city of the 1830s and 1840s. Allowing for smugness and self-deception (perennial Cork traits, it might be suggested), there seems to have been a genuine thirst for learning waiting to be slaked. Rev. Thomas Dix Hincks (Unitarian minister, whose son William was to be the first professor of natural history, 1849–53, in QCC) was emphatic that the Cork middle classes 'would willingly embrace' opportunities offered 'for scientific study'.[17]

One of the most interesting contributions to the Wyse Committee, 1835–38, especially in the light of his subsequent career at QCC, was that of Dr Denis Brenan Bullen who was at that time lecturer in chemistry at the Royal Cork Institution which he wished to see achieving collegiate status. Giving extensive evidence to the committee, Bullen (who incidentally did not believe in free lectures for people able to pay for them) made some highly individual observations about the scholarly disposition of Cork people:

> I do not know any city where there is a greater anxiety for really useful knowledge than in Cork. I attribute it very much to the domestic habits of the people of Cork who are fond of staying at home in the evening and reading: and to the existence of the Cork Library which I think has been a great advantage, and also to the existence of the Cork Institution library so that they have therefore had a very ample supply of books, and made a good use of them.

Interestingly he confirms a trend noted elsewhere: 'The ladies of Cork have a great taste for scientific reading'. The people of Cork, Bullen attested, wanted all this interest in knowledge fulfilled in 'a proper system of academical or collegiate study' for arts, classical literature, law and medicine. He outlined his ideas on the governance of a Cork provincial college which should be modelled on London University and the Scottish colleges. Theology spelt trouble, in Bullen's opinion, and religious instruction for students should take place away from the college (as was the practice in London University).[18] It should be said that Bullen's views were reflected in the committee's report, which in turn found expression in the Queen's Colleges legislation.

One of the strongest arguments used by the proponents of a Cork location for a provincial college was that there was already a well-established tradition of medical training in the city. (As things turned out, QCC was to be little more than a medical school for a considerable part of its history.) Bullen, in his evidence to the Wyse Committee, made the medical case forcefully. He referred to the success over twenty-five years of the medical school established by Dr Woodroffe, in spite of lack of grants and 'in defiance of the colleges that wanted to crush it'. Dr Woodroffe's institution was connected with the South Infirmary and the House of Industry Hospital; there was ample clinical instruction and there were twenty-eight students in the average class. Sounding a note discordant to modern ears, Bullen mentioned as a considerable advantage the plenitude of paupers who offered ample opportunity for the study of anatomy and various aspects of pathology.[19] In the context of medicine, we should mention a memorial from 'the Members of the Cork School of Medicine' to the home secretary in the spring of 1845, which noted that Cork's claims to be given a college 'are enhanced in the eyes of Her Majesty's Government by the circumstances of its containing a complete School of Medicine in full operation' which they hope will become 'a Medical Faculty in the Munster College'.[20]

Of Cork's libraries and learned societies in pre-QCC days, two institutions in particular were precursors of the college – the Royal Cork Institution (RCI, 1807–61) and its offspring, the Cuvierian Society (1835–78). The RCI, which was housed first in the South Mall and then in the old Custom House, was primarily concerned with the provision of public lectures. It loomed large in the intellectual life of the city – in Sean Pettit's phrase it was 'a civic centre of public education'. Modelled on the Royal Institution in London, the RCI was incorporated by charter in 1807 and received a state grant until 1830. Its cross-denominational members were enthusiastic amateur scholars and many of them were active in the campaign for a provincial college. Its distinguished guest lecturer list included Robert Kane. The RCI fostered an interest in agriculture which was to be a special concern of QCC from the beginning. It was the RCI that got the British Association to come to Cork in 1843 for a celebrated meeting. And the RCI was the first custodian of the ogham stones collection under the antiquarian John Windele's direction; these were later donated to QCC and became part of the display in the Stone Corridor.[21] Incidentally, Windele, who has left us a detailed description of the RCI, its location and its assets, argued for its development into 'a collegiate form, with adequate endowment, under the sanction of government'.[22]

Indeed, after the RCI lost its parliamentary grant in 1830 (paradoxically because of its limited activities and local scope) and was consequently obliged to reduce drastically its lecture courses, its logical role was to press for a complete collegiate institution. The case for a full-blown, degree-awarding college was made to Thomas Spring Rice when that influential politician visited the institution in 1832. The year before, a memorial from the RCI to the lord lieutenant desired that the institution would become the nucleus of a college, and in this connection the non-denominational character of the RCI was stressed. The memorial asserted

> that Cork, the principal City of a Province whose population nearly equals that of all Scotland, presents peculiar advantages for such a Collegiate Institution not only as being remote from the Metropolis and surrounded by a number of large and populous towns but being besides provided with most of the requisites essential for giving immediate effect to its operations.

Though the RCI was to survive until 1861, its historical justification was complete when the Queen's College opened, and some of its actions at this period symbolise a co-operative transition. On 4 April 1849, the newly appointed Professors Alcock (anatomy and physiology, 1849–54), Boole (mathematics, 1849–64) and Fleming (materia medica, 1849–58)[23] were admitted as subscribers to the institution's library. At a meeting of the RCI on 5 November 1849, two days before the opening ceremony of Queen's College, with James Roche in the chair, a gratuity of £5 was given to the institution's porter, William Cunningham, whom President Kane had appointed as steward in the new college. Finally, on 4 November 1850, in the context of QCC's initial equipment difficulties, the institution's minute book records that apparatus was lent to, and doubtless gratefully received by, the college.

Names associated with the Royal Cork Institution included those of the Earl of Bandon, William Beamish, James Roche, Sir Thomas Deane and Thomas Jennings, all of whom were closely involved in the college's beginnings. Moreover, the RCI had a considerable common membership with the Cuvierian Society. For example, James Roche was vice-president of the institution for some time, as well as being the first president of the Cuvierian Society.[24]

The Cuvierian Society was named in honour of the French anatomist and zoologist, Baron George Cuvier (1769–1832) who died a few years before the Cork society was founded. It was thought desirable to give the society an extended title –

the Cork Cuvierian Society for the Cultivation of the Sciences – since Cuvier's name, though much better known then than later, was apparently regarded with some suspicion in conservative Cork circles. The spirit of the society was pioneering, and its interests ranged over the sciences, statistics, political economy, antiquities and the fine arts. Sadly, one of the phenomena that required its investigative attention was the potato blight. The society's activities both prefigured and contributed to the work of the Queen's College. In particular, it had a preparatory role in the assembling of material for the museums of the college. In turn, the first professors at the college lectured to the society. It held its meetings in the premises of the Royal Cork Institution and had as active members such familiar names as Col. Portlock (the director of the Ordnance Survey), Denny Lane, George Boole, John Windele, William H. Crawford, Richard Caulfield (later to be librarian at the college) and Robert Day.[25]

The Colleges Act

The Wyse Committee report (1838) could be considered the 'green paper' which eventually led to the concept of the Queen's College, the first venture by the state into the university area. The really decisive debate took place within government, the most significant contributors being the prime minister, Sir Robert Peel; Sir James Graham, the home secretary; and Lord Lieutenant Heytesbury. The core questions – the number and location of colleges, the co-ordinating university, the method of professorial appointment, the place of religion in non-denominational institutions – were still being discussed as legislation was being drafted. These were political as well as academic preoccupations. Peel, for example, had reservations about the Crown's absolute right to appoint to chairs: '. . . a bad government with absolute and direct power of nominating all the professors might greatly abuse it!' Nonetheless, Peel and Graham were at one on the issue, even if only on the piper–tune principle. Graham felt that Crown appointments, combined with periodic and influential visitations, were a necessary check on any tendency on the part of academics 'to tinge general instruction with peculiar religious tenets'. And, of course, Crown appointments would put a premium on the loyalty of academics to the Crown, that is to say, to the Union.

The choice of Cork emerged inevitably from the logic and justice of the situation. (Incidentally, Graham believed the colleges at Cork and Belfast in the end would have to be independent universities to which other provincial colleges could be affiliated.) Maynooth was being given an increased grant, the Synod of Ulster was being helped with a college for the education of the Presbyterian clergy, the Belfast (secular) Institute was getting a grant and so, wrote Graham to Peel in November 1844, 'in justice we ought to extend this aid to the South of Ireland; and thus we may arrive at the Foundation and Endowment of a College at Cork'.[26]

The first reading of the Colleges (Ireland) Bill ('Queen's' was not in the bill's title) took place on 9 May 1845; the second reading was passed by a large majority on 30 May; and after amendments in committee, the final draft was approved on 10 July 1845 by 177 votes to 26, becoming law with the royal assent on 31 July 1845.

The Colleges (Ireland) Act 1845[27] provided public funding not exceeding £100,000 'to found one or more new colleges' (locations unmentioned), and it enabled the Commissioners of Public Works to do the necessary business of purchasing sites and contracting for buildings (sections I–IX). Statutes and rules of governance would have to be approved by the Crown, which would also appoint the college presidents and vice-presidents, as well as professors 'until the end of the year 1848, and afterwards as shall be otherwise provided by parliament' (X). The president, vice-president, bursar, registrar and librarian as well as holders of prizes and exhibitions would be paid out of public funds 'not exceeding in any one year the sum of seven thousand pounds for every such college' (XII). Students would

1.4 Sir James Graham, the home secretary, who believed that colleges at Cork and Belfast in the end would have to be independent universities.

pay 'reasonable fees' to the professors 'for attendance on their lectures' and to the bursar 'for matriculation and other collegiate proceedings' (XIII).

With regard to religion, the Act stipulated 'that it shall be lawful' for the college authorities, in order to enable every student 'to receive religious instruction according to the creed which he professes to hold', to assign lecture rooms 'within the precincts' for the use of recognised religious teachers. Such religious instruction was not to interfere with the general discipline of the college, no student would be compelled to attend any 'theological lecture or religious instruction other than is approved by his parents or guardians' and there would be 'no religious tests' for staff or students, 'but this proviso shall not be deemed to prevent the making of regulations for securing the due attendance of the students for divine worship at such church or chapel as shall be approved by their parents or guardians, respectively' (XIV).

The colleges were to be non-residential. Students not living at home would have to stay with some relation or friend selected by parents, or in a boarding-house licensed by the college president (XV). The boarding-house master would be responsible, *inter alia*, for making arrangements facilitating student attendance at worship and religious instruction (XVI). Students might also be accommodated in halls of residence built by private endowment. Such halls could be incorporated, be deemed public works and thus be eligible for loans 'for the extension and promotion of such foundations' (XV, XVII, XVIII). Similarly, private benefactors could fund 'lectures or other forms of religious instruction' (XIX). Finally, every college was bound by the Act to make an annual report to the Crown, and lay a copy thereof before parliament (XX).

The non-denominational, non-residential nature of the Queen's Colleges was a matter of *realpolitik*. The colleges at Cork and Galway were intended to cater for Catholics, but they would not be Catholic colleges. The Protestant establishment, shaken by Catholic Emancipation, the 1833 ecclesiastical retrenchment, the collapse of the tithe system and the general liberal drift of the 1830s, had to be protected against nascent Catholic power – at least for some time yet. The sensibilities of Trinity College were respected by not putting the new colleges within the University of Dublin framework, as Wyse had hoped, or not creating the embarrassing presence of a new Queen's College within the Dublin area. (Catholics did not like, in the phrase of Anthony Blake, a prominent layman, being 'relegated to the provinces'.) Again, the government would hardly consent to the demands of Catholic bishops (made to Lord Lieutenant Heytesbury in May 1845) for a degree of control that would make the Queen's Colleges system tolerable to them – principally, the denominationalisation of key subjects, and the right to oversee the appointment of professors in these areas.[28]

On the other hand, the studied avoidance by the state of the suspicion of proselytism and its taking up of a neutral stance, combined with a proper concern for the rights of religion on a voluntary basis, were welcome features to such liberal prelates as William Crolly of Armagh and Daniel Murray of Dublin. These aspects were also in tune with the whole debate stimulated by the Wyse Committee report, with the cross-denominational climate of middle-class pre-college Cork, and with

1.5 Thomas Davis, the Young Irelander,
supported 'combining the education of
youth to secure the union of men'.

the liberal view of such notables as the Rev. Reuben John Bryce[29] who had been closely associated with the Royal Cork Institution before moving on to Belfast.

Only high Tories and crusading Catholics came out against the Colleges Act initially: it 'pandered to everlasting damnation' warned Fredrick Lucas of *The Tablet*. The 'godless' epithet was first coined by Sir Robert Inglis, MP for Oxford University, whose overlooked god was Anglican and who described the Act as 'a gigantic scheme of godless education'.[30] Ironically, militant Catholics were virtually to monopolise the catchword later, after the Synod of Thurles definitively pronounced against the colleges in 1850. Archbishop John MacHale opposed the colleges from the beginning, applying to them his religious and nationalist hostility to the national schools system. The Act also provoked the opposition of the ageing and increasingly pious Daniel O'Connell, and his furious debates with the Young Irelanders on the subject raised issues in Irish life that still reflect opposing national philosophies. For Thomas Davis and Young Ireland, the 'mixed education' spirit of the Colleges Act seemed to be the realisation of at least one of their idealistic aspirations – 'combining the education of youth to secure the union of men', as Davis's utopian aphorism expressed it.

Birth of QCC: Kane and the Colleges Board

The 1845 Act laid down the broad educational lines, providing for provincial colleges on what had been called the 'Gower Street' model of London University (and of the Scottish colleges also) – non-sectarian, non-residential, low-fee, systematic lecturing institutions – rather than the Oxbridge tutorial system. As yet, however, the Queen's Colleges were established only on paper. There now had to be supplied the specific locations, buildings, academic structures – and personnel. Cork, Belfast and Galway had clearly emerged from the nebulous legislative background as the definite college centres by the autumn of 1845. Each college had to be incorporated[31] before it could exist, so to speak, and the names of the president and vice-president would be mentioned in each charter. In turn the choice of these officers would help to shape the character and direction of each college in its formative period. Queen's College Cork formally came into existence on 30 December 1845 by a charter of incorporation which was a royal, not a parliamentary, document. This ordained that

> in or near the City of Cork in our province of Munster in Ireland there shall and may be erected and established one perpetual College for students in Arts Law Physic and other useful Learning which College shall be called by the name of 'Queen's College Cork' and shall consist of one president, one vice-president and such number of professors in Arts Law and Physic not exceeding Twelve in number . . .

The president, vice-president and professors (later finalised at twenty) were to constitute 'one distinct and separate Body politic and Corporate in Deed and name', who together with the students, 'office-Bearers and Servants' would be 'regulated and governed according to the Statutes, rules and ordinances of the said College'.

The charter named Robert Kane as the 'first and modern president' of the college, and John Ryall as vice-president. Kane was designated for Cork in the lord lieutenant's nominations of 15 October 1845. Apparently there was some consideration given to Dr Daniel William Cahill, a prominent Dublin cleric and seminary head, for the Cork presidency but it can hardly have been serious or prolonged. Nicholas Wiseman, future archbishop of Westminster and cardinal and in 1845 president of Oscott College, was also mentioned as a possibility. In any case, the government was not going to appoint an ecclesiastic as president. The observation has been rightly made that the presidency was 'earmarked' for Kane. Archbishop Murray thought it was an 'excellent' appointment. Lord Lieutenant Heytesbury obviously believed that such a distinguished lay Catholic would have the best chance of 'selling' the whole Queen's Colleges project to official Catholic Ireland in general, and to Catholic Cork and Munster in particular. Kane, then only thirty-eight, was a chemist of international renown and the author of the recently-published *The Industrial Resources of Ireland* (1844), a work which endeared him to economic nationalists then (Young Irelanders) and thereafter (Sinn Féin and Fianna Fáil). As professor of natural philosophy to the Royal Dublin Society (RDS), he had given public lectures in various centres; at Cork, for example, to the Royal Cork Institution. He was president of the new Museum of Irish Industry in Dublin

1.6 Sir Robert Kane, the first president of QCC, 1845-1873

(afterwards the Royal College of Science).[32] At the time, this position conferred additional prestige on his new presidency of QCC, but the implications of double-jobbing and divided residency contributed to his multiple tribulations later.

For the moment, however, he was seen as a considerable catch and it is significant that Peel thought his appointment would 'rally science around us – no bad ally'.[33] The selection of John Ryall as vice-president was seen as balancing the ticket to some extent: Ryall was an Anglican, a Trinity College Dublin (TCD) graduate and principal of Birmingham and Edgbaston Preparatory School. Later, Archbishop Cullen was to remark that the government would have made Rev. D.W. Cahill vice-president, only that 'Sir Robert Kane would not act with a priest'.[34] The president's and vice-president's salaries were fixed from the date of incorporation at £800 per annum and £500 per annum respectively.[35]

Kane, who was knighted in February 1846, had to devote his attention for a time to the grim realities of the Great Famine, the sombre and overwhelming context of all other happenings in the mid-1840s. He was a member of the scientists' commission investigating the failure of the potato crop and he served on the Famine relief commission as well as on the health board set up to deal with the typhus outbreak. However, his continuing task, for which he was entrusted with primary responsibility by the government, was the promotion of the great academic enterprise – putting flesh on the bare bones of the Colleges Act. The presidents and vice-presidents of the three colleges – Queen's College Cork, Queen's College Belfast (QCB) and Queen's College Galway (QCG) – comprised a board, headed by Kane, which was charged with hammering out a common academic structure. Kane's role was a dominant one. Already by November 1845 the Colleges Board had drafted a memorandum as a broad educational guide which the colleges might follow. This put particular emphasis on the undergraduate Arts curriculum. The 'useful knowledge' philosophy was reflected in the place given to modern languages and in the initial recommendation (later changed) that Greek should be optional because of the 'practical wants of the middle classes'. The board also drafted statutes as a constitutional basis for the colleges. It is of interest that Sir James Graham's general observations on these included a comment that the 'authority of president must be upheld' and an insistence that there must be one overall university to give the colleges a federal framework. In fact, the Queen's University was instituted in 1850, the first university examinations being held in 1851.

From July 1846 to October 1847, the board suspended its work as the Famine crisis swept other items off the agenda. However, the change of government from Tories to Whigs did not mean any reconsideration of the colleges scheme. Kane was requested by the government, on Archbishop Murray's suggestion, to visit Belgium, Germany and France to see how academies based on a 'united education' principle worked out in a Catholic environment. Kane was satisfied with what he saw, and confirmed in his belief in the value of non-denominational colleges.[36]

The board resumed its deliberations in October 1847, the month in which a Propaganda rescript from the Holy See condemned the Queen's Colleges for their 'grievous and intrinsic dangers'. Statutes, salaries (humanities professors were to be the

highest paid), rules of discipline, provision of scholarships, distinctions between matriculated and non-matriculated students, the plan for visitations – all these were still being
finalised while the building of the colleges was proceeding apace. The Crown in the
form of the Dublin Castle government was the ultimate controller of fortunes, literally
and figuratively. With no community representatives on the college administration, and
with the colleges in many respects at odds with the majority community, it was hard to

1.7 Declaration of Professors, QCC, 7 November 1849. This volume
records the signature of each college officer, professor, statutory staff member
and student upon their declaration that they will abide by the duties as
outlined in each relevant declaration.

gainsay the allegations over the decades that the Queen's Colleges, at least in Cork and Galway, were governed by alien, autocratic and elitist forces.

Of all the statutes, Ch. VI, 9 contained the most significant and controversial clauses. These required every professor to promise that

> in lectures and examinations and in the performance of all other duties connected with my chair, I will carefully abstain from teaching or advancing any doctrine, or making any statement derogatory to the truths of revealed religion, or injurious or disrespectful to the religious convictions of any portion of my class or audience. And I moreover promise . . . that I will not introduce or discuss in my place or capacity of _____ any subject of politics or polemics, tending to produce contention or excitement.

This declaration, which in modified form is still a statutory requirement of National University of Ireland (NUI) professors and lecturers about to take office, was clearly intended to cool the heated religious and political atmosphere of mid-nineteenth-century Ireland.[37] It was also meant to take divisive religious issues out of the classroom, to head off charges of godlessness and proselytism by the opponents of the Queen's Colleges, and to maintain an ethos of benign neutrality. For the first two (Catholic) presidents of QCC, Kane and Sullivan, minimising features objectionable to Catholics was an obvious priority and it was a source of satisfaction to both that there were no complaints about this statute being violated, though this did not diminish episcopal opposition. General good sense saw to it that the requirement was not insisted upon in any pedantic or literal fashion: otherwise, it would have had an extremely stultifying impact on mature academic discussion.

The Colleges Board had to concern itself with a surprisingly wide range of matters, not all of them of direct educational interest. Resolutions of 24 January 1846 specified requirements for great halls, lecture rooms, laboratories and museums as well as botanic gardens (later a repeated demand by QCC authorities). A 'corridor' or 'cloister', for exercise in wet weather, was sensibly recommended. (The UCC corridors became cluttered up with offices in the 1920s, but were cleared in the 1970s by direction of President McCarthy.) The reasonable comfort of the staff was being planned ahead – 'there should be attached to each lecture room a private room for the professor with a water closet'. However, there might be no money for such frills. The government was simultaneously warning the Board of Works that the colleges must stay within the £100,000 capital sum allotted by the Act: apparently there were fears that the 'apartments' (of the three presidents and the three vice-presidents) described in the resolution, however desirable, might incur extra costs which would not be permitted in any circumstances.[38] There would, of course, be no chapels.

The charters were also drawn up and were ready for discussion by January 1846.[39] In the same month, in reply to a query from the board about seals, arms and 'costumes' for each college, the lord lieutenant said that expensive recourse to the Ulster King of Arms was unnecessary: the board should devise 'a suitable seal for each College with the date of the foundation of the College and an appropriate motto either in Latin or English'. Also, 'the forms of gown may be taken from Trinity College' with suitable alteration.[40]

Among the other matters dealt with was the question of 'connecting' the existing medical schools in Cork and Belfast with the new colleges,[41] entrance examinations and the planning of the academic year. Here the board followed established practice, and made an arrangement that still obtains, in UCC at any rate. From early October until the end of June, there were to be three study terms, averaging three months each, with a recess for July, August and September.[42] In its emphasis on modern languages, the board struck the contemporary utilitarian note – and one increasingly familiar in our own day:

> for the practical wants of the middle classes, too much has been hitherto sacrificed to their [ancient languages] exclusive study, and that for a community busily occupied with practical science, with Commerce, with Agriculture and with manufactures, the study of modern languages should hold an important place.[43]

All students were obliged to study a modern European language and follow a course in English language and literature.[44]

The Queen's University in Ireland

Since the beginning, the Cork college has existed in successive university frameworks, all of them constructed to a political design and in varying degrees unsatisfactory. When the Queen's Colleges were being planned in 1844, it was obvious that university degrees would have to be made available, though there was no immediate hurry. There were, theoretically, a number of possible university contexts. The first was a non-starter, and was to remain so: affiliating the colleges to the University of Dublin was unacceptable to Protestant opinion. Sir James Graham, the home secretary, favoured the option of two new universities at Cork and Belfast, to which other provincial colleges might be affiliated: after all, five universities co-existed beneficially in Scotland, another small country. But in the end it was Peel's idea of a federal university with constituent colleges that won favour: it would give a national character to the system, transcend local prejudices and heighten standards through competition. Graham eventually followed this line when the Colleges Bill was going through parliament, expressing his preference for a London-type central university where 'the youth of Ireland may assemble, and contend, in honourable and honest rivalry' rather than for three provincial universities.[45]

It was the board of presidents and vice-presidents which largely helped to plan, in 1848–49, the shape and substance of the new university. Undeterred by *The Freeman's Journal* jibe that the 'provincials', instead of getting Dublin University degrees, were to be fobbed off with the 'gingerbread' degrees of a university made to order, the board considered whether there should be a strong federated university entrusted with full control over degrees like the University of London (Sir Robert Kane favoured this model) or a loose association of independent colleges, which would conduct degree examinations in the colleges. Prince Albert, who of all people had shown a keen interest in the subject during the recent royal visit to Ireland, was reported to have expressed himself very forcefully by claiming that if the colleges got the degree-granting power they would become 'common nuisances and nests of jobbery[46] and sectarianism', degenerating into a Presbyterian school in Belfast and Catholic seminaries in the south, 'but the competition of the three for university honours and scholarships will create a stimulus which will keep up every one of them to the highest state of efficiency'.[47]

In September 1849, Lord Lieutenant Clarendon chose the Dublin-centred model, independent and centralised, conducting degree examinations and conferring degrees. Apart from the three constituent colleges, there would be no college affiliated to the Queen's University in Ireland: the feeling here was that, say, a Roman Catholic institution so affiliated would irreparably damage the 'mixed education' of the Queen's Colleges. The only students eligible to take the university's examinations were those who had completed prescribed courses in one of the colleges. Even medical students, partly exempt, would have to attend at least one-third of their lectures in their college. Thus close organic links were established between colleges and university. Though the colleges as independent corporations were free to prescribe their own entrance requirements and make their own arrangements for matriculation and scholarships, their educational system overall was determined almost entirely by the Queen's University.[48]

The Queen's University in Ireland was incorporated by charter on 3 September 1850. The chancellor, the three college presidents and seventeen others – including, appropriately, Sir Thomas Wyse – comprised the Senate, all appointed for life by the Crown. The vice-chancellor, on the other hand, was elected annually by the Senate from its own members. From 1851–52 onwards, the Senate met eight times a year on average, with an effective attendance of nine. More than a third of the senators were Roman Catholic and of these only two, Sir Robert Kane and Dominic Corrigan, a leading Dublin physician, were regular attenders – Kane, ironically, because he was an absentee Cork president! After his retirement from QCC, Kane continued to serve on the Senate as a Crown appointee until the dissolution of the Queen's University in 1882. The university's secretary or chief administrative officer from 1857 to 1882, and in many ways its personification, was the distinguished scientist, George Johnstone Stoney.

The university never had a permanent home, having its headquarters until 1877 in Dublin Castle and after that in a nearby building. Its public meetings were always held either in the Council Chamber or in St Patrick's Hall until 1877, and thereafter in the Exhibition Building in Earlsfort Terrace. Students experienced the university as a separate entity only when they went to Dublin for examinations and for conferrings in St Patrick's Hall.[49] Limited as these contacts were, they made the university much more of a reality to, say, QCC students in the 1870s than the NUI was to their UCC successors a century later.

Convocation, meeting annually from 1866 to 1881, gave graduates a voice on university affairs – including representation on the Senate – and on the politics of the controversial university question. But they never succeeded in their proposal to get parliamentary representation for the Queen's University. Total membership of Convocation never exceeded 450 and the usual attendance was 30 to 50. Belfast, by far the most vigorous of the three colleges, appears to have dominated the assembly.

Professors complained that the Senate was unrepresentative and that, in consequence, courses and regulations were being drawn up by men out of touch with the teaching work of the colleges. A new charter in 1864 extended the corporation of the university beyond the chancellor and the Senate to include the professors, graduates and students. Professors were to be represented on the Senate. At the same time, new charters were also drafted for the colleges making their councils more representative of the professors. The academics of the three colleges maintained continuous and vital contact through the involvement of the professors in university examinations and in meetings of the board of examiners. And the presidents, of course, sat *ex officio* on the Senate, amicably and co-operatively.[50]

Like its successor, the Queen's University in Ireland was the subject of political controversy, the nub being the Roman Catholic Church's hostile attitude. Controversy bred uncertainty which in turn inhibited both public funding and private benefaction or investment, and the problem was aggravated rather than improved by replacing the Queen's University with the Royal University of Ireland in the 1880s. For all its limitations, however, the Queen's University in Ireland, as Moody and Beckett observe,

> quickly acquired a prestige that the colleges could hardly have attained individually, and the isolation from which they would otherwise have suffered was counteracted by their share in the common life of a national institution. Under the Royal University system this common life, though it did not wholly disappear, was seriously weakened. The Queen's Colleges lost their exclusive position, and were, in practice, subject to a university policy in which their interests were submerged by other considerations.[51]

In a prize-distributing address at QCC on 27 November 1856, Sir Robert Kane stoutly defended the performance to date of the university and the college, claiming their success was definite evidence that the country was recovering from the ravages of the Famine.[52] Despite the perception in some quarters of the Queen's University as a failure, he argued that it had more matriculated students and more graduates than London University had had at a corresponding stage (seven years) of development. That performance was all the more creditable given that the class from which the colleges had expected to draw most of their students had been impoverished by the Famine.

The Roman Catholic clergy continued to vilify the Queen's University and its colleges as citadels of infidelity and indifferentism. In fact, the Queen's Colleges' 'middle' or 'neutral' position on religion was regarded as being even more objectionable than Trinity College's Protestantism. There were loud complaints about the public monies spent on the Queen's Colleges in contrast to the total absence of funding for the Catholic University. What was being demanded was not only financial support for the Catholic University but the denominationalising of the Queen's Colleges. For British governments for the remainder of the century, the great dilemma (in education as in national issues at large) was how to satisfy the demands of a resurgent and ever more self-confident Irish Catholicism without injuring and undermining the Protestant interest.[53]

A supplemental charter scheme in 1866 empowered the Queen's University to hold matriculation examinations distinct from those of the Queen's Colleges, and to grant degrees to those thus matriculated who had completed appropriate studies not necessarily at the colleges. This arrangement, which would have weakened the connection between the Queen's University and the Queen's Colleges, prefigured the later Royal University scheme, but it remained inoperative because of the opposition of Queen's University graduates.[54]

Location of the college

To return to the origins of QCC, in the case of all three Queen's Colleges a number of sites 'were pressed on their attention', explained Daniel Conville of the Board of Works to Sir Richard Pennefather, the under-secretary at the Castle, on 7 February 1846. The most desirable situations in both Cork and Belfast were 'rather more than one statute mile from the centre of each town', and 'in the immediate space there is considerable population of the respectable class, and with every probability of an increase'. It was felt that 'a cheerful and healthy site, with a good approach' should not be passed up for a less desirable site just because it might take 'a few hundred yards less for the students to reach the College'.[55] (This comment assumes that, in the case of Cork, most students would come from the city direction.) It had been decided at an earlier stage that no existing building in Cork was suitable for adaptation as a college. The old Custom House, the only building considered at all seriously, was in disrepair and of limited size, with little possibility of getting adjoining ground. Other sites were rejected as being too close to such undesirable locations as the poor house, the lunatic asylum and the shipbuilding yards. Moreover, the high aesthetic sensibilities of the citizens had to be kept in mind. Sites could not be considered where buildings would not

> be ornamental to the city generally . . . . there seems to be at Cork more attention paid to the choice of sites and to the embellishment of public buildings than at most other towns in Ireland and there is also more attention paid to the promotion of science and the encouragement of fine arts by the inhabitants, than what is generally met with in provincial towns.

So wrote Henry Paine to the Chief Secretary, Sir Thomas Freemantle on 30 August 1845.[56]

On 9 March 1846 the architect, Sir Thomas Deane, received a letter from Thomas Somerville Reeves that was decisive in finalising the QCC site. Reeves had been anxious to sell his interest in a Gillabbey location but one of his tenants, Rev. Charles Leslie, had refused to leave his residence on the property. Now, as Reeves explained to Deane, because of Leslie's unexpected death 'I am able to offer you Gilabbey as a site

1.8 Sir Thomas Deane (below)
and Benjamin Woodward
(left), QCC architects. Deane
is pointing at the ground plan
of the college.

for the new College'. The lot comprised all of Leslie's premises with a portion of the holding of another Reeves tenant, a Mr Julius Gibbings. 'You are aware', Reeves concluded, 'of the beauties and advantages of this lot and I have only to say in addition that it meets the wishes of the Citizens by being within the Borough Boundary'.[57]

Sir Thomas lost no time in informing the Board of Works of Reeves's proposal and in conveying his own opinions. Incidentally, he described Reeves as 'an eminent merchant of Cork'. (The letter, from Cork on 9 March, bears the receipt stamp of the

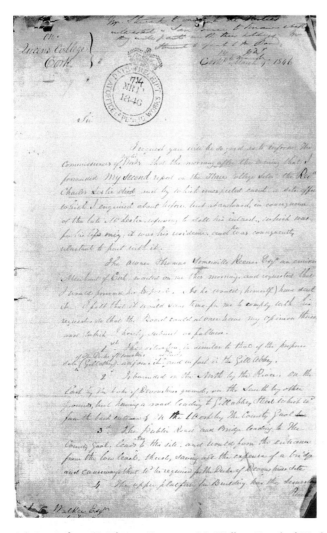

1.9 Letter from Sir Thomas Deane, to Mr Walker, Board of Works, 9 March 1846, strongly recommending that the board sanction the purchase of the Gillabbey site as '. . . it is most beautiful for a public building, and being had for a reasonable sum will enable us with the remainder of the grant to accomplish much more in every way than on the other sites'.

1.10 Pencil sketch of the Gillabbey site by Deane indicating Leslie's house on the cliff edge upon which he sited the building.

Board of Works with the note that Mr Stewart is to write to the parties interested, to find out if they will 'part with their holdings'.) Referring to his first report 'which gives the relative advantages as above and below the City' and his second report 'on the three Colleges sites', Deane went on to give details of the proposed site. It was bounded on the east by the property of the Duke of Devonshire, which 'in fact is the Gill Abbey', and which had also been considered as a site. Reeves's site was bounded on the north by the river Lee, on the west by the county gaol, and on the south by other grounds 'but having a road leading to Gillabbey Street which is from the back entrance'. (Three years later, there were discussions about a right of way to college from the remaining land owned by Reeves.[58]) The road and bridge leading to the gaol would form a ready-made and expense-saving entrance, which would not be so in the case of the Devonshire site. Also,

> the upper platform for building has the Limestone Rock nearly to the surface and is level or nearly so for a space of about 600 feet by 300 feet deep, exclusive of the Rock and low ground to the River over which a Terrace in front of the building could be looking to the City. The foundations would be inexpensive.

Deane noted other advantages. There would be 'little expense, for Boundary Wall only required to the side'. The site 'is within the Borough Boundary', and as a situation for a public building is 'excellent and commanding', and it is 'within the limit of distance'.

Reeves owned the property subject to annual rent payable to the Ecclesiastical Commissioners, and Deane stated the total cost of purchasing the site would be £2,560 (£1,680 to Reeves, and £880 to the commission). Deane enclosed a 'rough' sketch which was meant to give an impression of 'the scenery and nature of the ground' and which incidentally shows Leslie's large house (subsequently demolished) situated on the cliff edge or limestone escarpment on which the new building was to be erected.

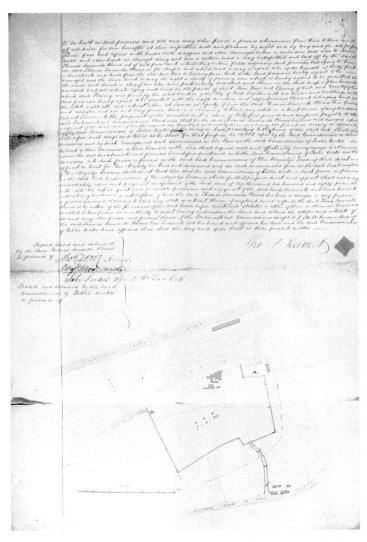

1.11 Articles of Agreement, Gillabbey site, 6 July 1846.
The document is signed by Thomas Deane and
Benjamin Woodward on behalf of the Board of Works
and vendor, Thomas S. Reeves and includes a site plan.

Deane also sent a coloured plan to the Board of Works (again dated 9 March 1846), 'a Tracing from the Ordnance Map', which shows the limited extent of the site.

In a letter to Alex Stewart of the Board of Works, dated 10 April 1846, Deane went into further details about the site. 'The Road leading at the rear to the back entrance is to be widened to 30 feet.' He mentioned 'the present principal carriage entrance' by the gaol, and discussed possible road developments to the east. (A road would run citywards on the south bank of the south channel of the river.) Deane hoped the commissioners would approve of various particulars and conclude the deal. Once more, he urged the advantages of the site, 'by far the cheapest as the saving of foundations, Boundaries, convenience of materials will be very considerable. . . .'

> The site is most beautiful for a public building and being had for a reasonable sum will enable us with the remainder of the grant to accomplish much more in every way than on the other sites. . . . I now have some hope that I shall be soon permitted to commence my plan as this fortuitous offer of a site requires new thought and new arrangements.[59]

There was a complication about the continuing interest of the Ecclesiastical Commissioners in the site – they could not be compelled by law to sell it – and the release of rent was not effected until 1873, four years after the disestablishment of the Church of Ireland.[60]

The deed of agreement between Reeves and the Board of Works was finally signed on 6 July 1846, with the formal assignment of the premises following on 28 November 1846. The map accompanying the agreement shows the area in question to have been 7 acres 0 roods and 33 perches in extent. All parties appeared relieved and satisfied. Reeves was 'most anxious for his money', and Sir Thomas Deane was 'desirous of getting possession of the ground, so as to manage my levels and get on with the awful labour before me in preparing the working plans'.[61]

Six weeks after the deed was signed, a Northside resident (motivated perhaps by a mixture of begrudgery, ambition and public concern) made an ineffectual attempt to scupper the deal. Mr Denis Hayes of Blackpool Nurseries wrote to the lord lieutenant (Earl of Bessborough) on 22 August 1846, asking for a competent architect to be sent to Cork to examine

> the contemplated, very ineligible and bad sites selected for building the Provincial College and the District Lunatic Asylum on.[62] The college site at Gillabbey is the property of a wealthy man, and has been a dead weight on him for many years. Both he and the wealthy Architect[63] who advised the selection will be greatly benefitted, not only by the building but also by a new road which must necessarily be made there.

Hayes claimed that it was the worst watered site in the vicinity of the city and that the sewers of the two new institutions emptying into the Lee would corrupt drinking water supplies. He recalled 'the profligate jobbing practised in the selection of the site for the Cork Barracks', which had access problems and was a source of disease through water contamination. Hayes concluded by commending the merits of an alternative site, 'the ground adjoining the Blackpool Nurseries', and he enclosed the names of three doctors and a bank clerk who could vouch for the validity of the site and 'who can have no interested motives'.[64]

Mr Hayes was wasting his time, however. The Board of Works reminded Under-Secretary Redington that the Gillabbey site had been thoroughly investigated, and the decision to acquire it had been taken in the teeth of various pressures. Not only did the Board of Works consider it a preferable site to that named by Hayes, but the title had been approved and the board was to get immediate possession. Accordingly, Redington informed Denis Hayes that, the plan for building 'having been already decided on, His Excellency cannot now interfere'.[65]

Thus ended this early opportunistic attempt to secure the college for the northside! Certainly, the decision to build on the Reeves site near Gillabbey had important long-term consequences for that part of Cork. (This was a particular detail of the larger picture of the implications for the city as a whole of having a university college.) The Western Road area was largely undeveloped in 1846, the Doric portico of Pain's Gaol (designed in 1818) being its sole architectural feature, and the road itself was new.[66] Within a few years, the splendid college edifice on its imposing site was to dominate and transform the whole area. For a time, the gaol was an embarrassing neighbour, and the first professors expressed their distaste for other insalubrious residents in the vicinity. Eventually, the physical presence of the college influenced the development of a pleasant and sedate middle-class inner suburb.

The building

The building of Queen's College Cork began early in 1847 and was completed within two years.[67] This was all the more remarkable in that construction was suspended for a period because of disagreement between the architect and the builder, John Butler of Dublin, over the manner of completing the masonry.[68] The work was finished barely in time for the opening ceremony on 7 November 1849. The manpower involved was considerable and at least some of the workers must have been drawn from the Co. Cork countryside, thus finding some work relief from the devastating consequences of the Famine in those wretched years of the late 1840s. (The building of the lunatic asylum, completed in 1852, provided a further extension of work relief.) There was plenty of work available at the Gillabbey site, though there is no suggestion that the project was in any way *intended* as relief work. Rather, the Board of Works was anxious to have the work expedited so as to meet the proposed opening date in 1849, and to have it done at a reasonable cost. And so, more labourers and craftsmen were to be employed. 'The Board', complained the secretary, Joseph Walker to Sir Thomas Deane on 27 October 1847, 'find much fewer men employed at Cork College than at either of the others and they request you will report if the contractor is pushing on the work as he ought to.' Six months later, on 18 March 1848, Walker was warning contractor John Butler directly that 'without greater exertion, the building cannot be completed within the time limited by the specification'. Walker even worried about the impact of foreign wars on building progress: as he informed the architect on 11 August 1848, 'the ship containing the timber for the flooring of the College [has] been detained at Mesnel, by the breaking out of the war between Denmark and Prussia'.[69]

The Cork Examiner kept a close eye on the final stages of the building process. After all, such a major construction on a spectacular site was of considerable interest to its readers, who must have avidly read the paper's account on 3 August 1849 of Queen Victoria's flying visit. As she passed along the Western Road, she was gratified (and perhaps amused) at the spectacle enacted for her benefit at the almost-completed Queen's College.

> At the moment the carriages passed the College, the sustaining wedges were withdrawn and amidst the discharge of cannon, a statue of her Majesty, presented to the College authorities by Sir Thomas Deane was suddenly erected[70] to the apex of the most conspicuous gable. By the removal of the wedges, obstacles that interfered with a distant view of this structure were, to a certain extent, removed and the Royal Standard was seen waving in the air, and under it the various trades employed in its erection.[71]

1.12 The visit of Queen Victoria to Cork, August 1849. Illustration shows the royal carriage on Western Road passing the recently completed Queen's College.

The *Illustrated London News* (11 August 1849) tells us that Sir Thomas was present to direct the operation.

Some weeks later, the *Examiner* undertook a detailed visit of the college and published a comprehensive report of developments. (This appeared on the same day, 26 September 1849, that an editorial denounced 'the signal and disgraceful ingratitude' shown to William Kelleher whom 'we might almost call the founder of the Queen's College in Cork'. The writer went on to castigate those responsible for not offering Kelleher a post in QCC.) The report on the new college was most enthusiastic – a 'rave' preview, in fact. The 'splendid structure' was a credit 'to the artistic genius and mechanical skill of our city'. In a room-by-room account, the Examination Hall (or Aula Maxima) stood out: 'when finished [it] will be one of the most magnificent rooms in Ireland'. The writer was obviously aglow with local patriotism, awarding the palm to the architect, Sir Thomas Deane. 'It gives us a satisfactory feeling of pride to say he is a Corkman and a man of a very high order of ability'. Moreover,

> almost every Master Stonecutter of the city has been engaged on the stonework. The artisans are almost all of this city and . . . there could not be found a body of men of better habits and general bearing, or more capable. . . . It is with pride we record this testimony to the decent, hard-working and self-respecting Trades of Cork.

Though the beautiful view 'justifies the selection of the site', it 'cannot, we must say, make amends for its unhappy proximity to the County Jail from which dismal structure the ground attached to the College is only separated by a wall'.

No lyrical description of the Queen's College would have been complete without the customary invocation of the hallowed (though today demonstrably dubious!) Finbarrian tradition, here contrasted with contemporary secularism:

> The Queen's College of Cork now stands upon the very site upon which, in the seventh century, a Catholic Bishop of Cork – Gilleda – founded a monastery: not one of those hybrid institutions which Sir Harry Inglis would call a 'Godless College' but a seat of pious seclusion and learned zeal.

The *Examiner* concluded its pre-opening account of the college by notifying access arrangements: 'The Public will enter the Examination Hall from the Terrace at the East End; the students from the Cloisters at the south side; and the Professors from the library on [to] the dais'.[72]

As we know, Sir Thomas Deane was involved from the site-acquisition stage in early 1846 but the Deane architectural firm also included his younger brother, Kearns Deane, and Benjamin Woodward. The Deanes designed some of the city's most important buildings in the first half of the nineteenth century, including the Cork Savings Bank and St Mary's Church. Although these edifices were in the classical style, Gothic had also come into fashion and was particularly acceptable for colleges, traditionally following Oxford and Cambridge models. Thus the architectural style of

1.13 Early view of the North Wing from lower grounds.

QCC has been variously described as neo–Gothic, Tudor Gothic and Victorian Gothic. Sir Thomas Deane is known to have borrowed a collection of drawings of Oxford colleges from a fellow architect and it seems that Deane's plan was influenced by Magdalen College in particular.

The persistent tradition that there was a mix-up in the plans of the Queen's Colleges, and that Cork got the building intended for Belfast or Galway, belongs to a genre of similar legends and is inherently improbable. Not only did Deane nurse his project from its inception in 1846 but the indigenous limestone quarried on the site confirms that the college authentically belongs to its environment.

Why is the quadrangle an unfinished symphony? There is a rather far-fetched and chronologically inappropriate suggestion that the original plan was scaled down when it transpired that opposition to the 'godless' colleges would mean fewer students than originally expected. It is possible, however, that the fourth side was not proceeded with because of inadequate funds, as happened to Pugin at Maynooth. Contemporary newspapers (*CE* 8 November, *ILN* 17 November 1849) spoke of a 'future extension'. But the most likely explanation is that Deane, like Schubert, felt it neither necessary nor desirable to compose a closing movement. And so the light was let flow in from the south, making the quadrangle a place of soft brightness and tranquillity and, in sunshine, of basking warmth. The high-quality limestone which has never had to be cleaned contributed to the overall effect.

1.14 Elevation, east window, Aula Maxima. The drawing, dated 1847, is signed in the lower right hand corner by Thomas Deane.

Eve Blau has described the quadrangle atmosphere as 'one of soft sunlight, peace and regularity, a marked contrast to the large jutting mass of the exterior'.[73] And a decided contrast, too, one might mischievously add, to the acrimony, intrigue and skullduggery which occasionally marked the relationships of the academic denizens.

From the Western Road below, in 1995 as in 1849, the view of the battlemented pile is spectacular, even stunning. Nowadays, discreet and subtle floodlighting lends the

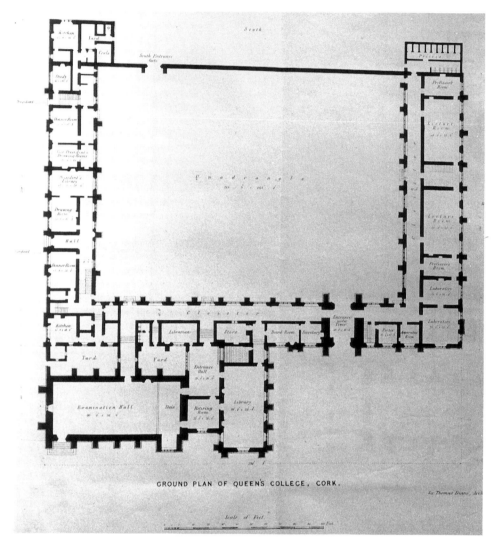

GROUND PLAN OF QUEEN'S COLLEGE, CORK.

1.15 Architects' plans of ground floor (above) and first floor (opposite) of North, East and West wings, indicating room functions.

old stone a special nocturnal beauty. The stone-carved ornaments are also shown to advantage by the artificial lighting. These were executed to the design and under the supervision of Woodward who was strongly influenced by the stonework at Holy Cross and at Cashel, with its 'seaweed' forms, and human and vegetarian heads.[74]

Macaulay's reference to 'a Gothic college worthy to stand in the High Street of Oxford'[75] has appeared *ad nauseam* in guides to, and notices of, the college. (Interestingly, the remark used to be misapplied in Belfast guidebooks to the Queen's College – now university – there![76]) Macaulay meant well, no doubt, but the remark was (not surprisingly, in its time and from such a source) unintentionally condescending. In turn its

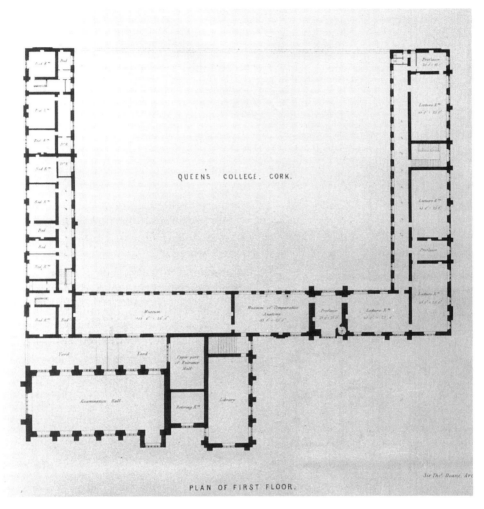

QUEENS COLLEGE. CORK.

PLAN OF FIRST FLOOR.

reverential repetition smacks of cultural cringe. It should be sufficient to observe that the college is worthy to stand imposingly over the elegant western approaches to Cork city.

Jobs for gentlemen and scholars

A famous *Dublin Opinion* cover cartoon, 'The day the Treaty was signed', depicts the excited interest of the living and the dead in the job opportunities about to open up under native government.[77] Similarly, when the Colleges Act was passed, applications for new posts immediately flooded in, though the scramble was rather more sedate. The creation of three new colleges was an academic phenomenon, and for many applicants there was the novel attraction of freedom from a religious test. Late in 1848, when the buildings were well advanced and the college openings were less than a year away, the professorships in the three institutions, as well as the offices of librarian and bursar, were advertised (with a 30 December closing date) for the benefit of possible candidates who had not already applied off their own bat. There were in all about five hundred and eighty contenders for the sixty chairs and the six administrative offices in the three colleges. Although the applications were sent to the chief secretary's office, the positions being Crown appointments, it was the Colleges Board that made the selection, which was completed in May 1849.[78] The lord lieutenant then made the final appointments. *The Cork Examiner* claimed editorially that the choice in some instances meant that the college could not 'claim the confidence of the parents and guardians of Catholic youths'.[79]

The hopeful applicants put in for their preferred position without specific reference to a particular college. Frequently, indeed, they were prepared to accept an appointment in a cognate (or even unrelated) department if they could not have their first choice. On 24 August 1846, the great autodidact, George Boole, applied for 'a professorship of mathematics or natural philosophy in one of the colleges'[80] but over two years later (22 December 1848) as the institutions took shape (literally), he indicated: 'I should prefer Cork or Belfast'.[81] Francis Albani, QCC's first registrar, had initially applied in 1845 for the chair of logic and metaphysics 'in one of the Colleges about to be established in this country',[82] then for the post of librarian, for which he claimed he was very well qualified, and finally in March 1849 for the position of registrar.[83] Henry Hennessy's first choice was any of the three chairs of natural philosophy in the colleges,[84] but he wound up as librarian in Cork. Richard Caulfield, the distinguished antiquarian, also wanted to be librarian (application, 14 August 1845)[85] but was disappointed and had to wait until 1875. Raymond de Vericour applied on 13 December 1848 for modern languages or history.[86] Though he was appointed to the former, it was his historical work that was to cause controversy in the context of the 'godless' colleges argument.

Candidates submitted numerous, elaborate, and often fulsome testimonials. In those early years of the Queen's Colleges, chancers were to the fore. The Rev. Samuel Greer, curate of Celbridge, was refreshingly frank and to the point: 'several friends and respectful parishioners interested in my welfare and advancement in life have signified their desire that I should offer myself as a candidate for the vice-presidency or a first professorship in the college to be established in Belfast'.[87] D.J. Murphy of Cork was the assertive type. In applying for an administrative office, he stated that he had considerable newspaper experience and he felt he deserved well of the government.[88]

When the names of the successful professors for the three colleges were published, it transpired that forty-two were Irish, fifteen were English or Scottish, two were German and one was French.[89] Local men tended to be well represented in the medical faculties, because of links with pre-existing hospitals. The Englishmen appointed to QCC included George Boole (who was to die prematurely) to the chair of mathematics and Bunnell Lewis, a fellow of University College London, to the chair of Latin (1849–1905). Lewis, a 'character', lived on until Windle's time ('very old, but quite all there', noted Sir Bertram[90]), and does not seem to have belonged to that large category of English academics who, then and later, took up a post in Cork only because they had failed to secure an appointment at home and who hurried back to the 'mainland' at the first available opportunity. A jaundiced Corkman complained in 1859 of the poor

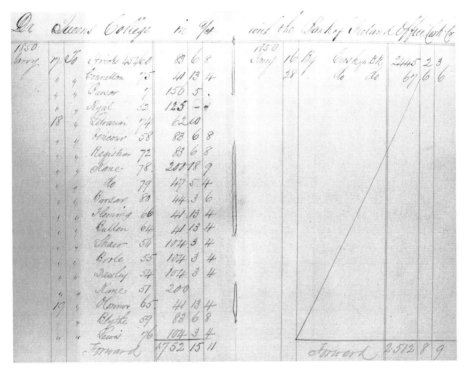

1.16 From the first extant college bank book, January 1850, indicating monies paid to various professors and officers. The account was with the Bank of Ireland.

quality of some professors, and grumbled '. . . an able Irishman with the highest testimonials will have little or no chance against a mediocre Englishman or Scotsman who had never been previously heard of'.[91] This allegation was not borne out by the nationality breakdown of the original appointments.

The government and the Colleges Board claimed that all the appointments were made on academic merit, and were uninfluenced by influence![92] *The Freeman's Journal* (8 August 1849) complained that very few Catholics had been appointed to chairs – seven out of sixty overall, and only three, it seemed, in Cork (two in medicine, Professors Bullen and D.C. O'Connor, and one in law, Professor Francis A. Walsh).[93] The paper bitterly recalled Lord Lieutenant Clarendon's assurance in 1848 to Archbishop Murray that the Catholic religion would be 'fully and appropriately represented' in the council and on the academic staff of each college.[94] The government had particularly broken faith, *The Freeman's Journal* felt, in appointing Protestants to the history professorships in the three colleges, and a Socinian (William Hincks) to the chair of natural history in Cork.[95] The newspaper believed (and probably correctly) that this pro-Protestant bias alone would destroy the already slim chance that Catholics would accept the Queen's Colleges. Young Irelanders, the colleges' natural allies, were considerably disenchanted. The Protestant press did not enter into the argument, but the implicit defence was that the handful of Catholic appointments simply reflected the fewness of sufficiently qualified Catholic applicants.[96] At any rate, it is of interest that over the years QCC president's reports, while constantly publicising Catholic *student* figures, studiously avoided drawing attention to the denominational imbalance in the staff.

And so the first professors took up their appointments at Queen's College Cork at annual salaries varying from £100 to £250,[97] excluding such variables as class fees[98] and, in the case of professional schools, private practices. In this regard, Professor Alexander Fleming considered himself financially hard done by. In a memorial to the lord lieutenant on 14 November 1850 (supported by his colleagues), he complained that his inadequate salary (£100 per annum, plus £10 in class fees for the 1849–50 session) did not allow him to maintain his proper station. His emoluments were lower than 'any one of the five officers'. Materia medica did not lend itself to private practice; besides (and here we have the outsider's perennial complaint of being excluded by Cork clannishness, real or perceived), he was a 'stranger', and did not have the advantages of the 'natives of Cork closely connected with its community'![99]

Various appointment files of the early decades give an impression of intense lobbying, invocation of influence and barefaced self-promotion. Bishop Francis Haly of Kildare and Leighlin wrote to President Kane, successfully pushing Edward Fitzgerald's claims to be bursar at QCC. Fitzgerald, who had not succeeded in being appointed as manager of the Carlow district lunatic asylum (though 'in every respect qualified') despite – or perhaps because of – the support of Haly and the soon-to-be notorious John Sadleir, was now lauded by the bishop for his 'Whig principles'. His principles did not prevent him from making off with the college's money in 1871![100]

When the chair of mineralogy and geology fell vacant in 1853 because of James Nicol's departure to Aberdeen, Rev. William Hincks, the professor of natural history, wrote (in April) to the lord chancellor of Ireland, backing Wyville T.C. Thomson and opposing another candidate, Henry Hennessy, who apparently had not found happiness as librarian. Hennessy's appointment to the chair, Hincks feared, would only aggravate tensions ('uneasinesses') in college. Hincks hastily added that he would not dream of trying to influence the outcome, being concerned only to give information 'in the public interest'. Of course! He added, diplomatically, 'it is a delicate thing to hint a word of depreciation in such a case'. The president, it appears, was also *parti pris*: in a private letter (to Mayor Ponsonby, 7 April 1853), Kane expressed support for Henry B. Medlicott, 'an Irishman of a good Kildare family and thoroughly liberal in mind'. To complete the lobbying circle, Medlicott wrote to Kane unabashedly recommending himself as fresh and vigorous in thought. There were things the Castle did not understand, he implied, and he referred enigmatically to 'provincial savants'. In the event, Robert Harkness (1853–78) was appointed to mineralogy and geology and had a distinguished career. (Thereafter, geology lapsed until 1909.) A stained-glass window in the Aula Maxina commemorates Harkness.[101]

In 1854 there were several candidates for the chair of anatomy and physiology, made vacant by the dismissal of Professor Alcock.[102] Applications were made directly to Lord Lieutenant Granville, with copies being sent occasionally to the under-secretary and to Kane. There were private representations as well as extensive open testimonials, with copies of articles being sometimes submitted.

Dr Thomas S. Holland, lecturer in anatomy and histology, QCC, included the printed text of a course-introductory lecture with his application. Delivered at the Royal Cork Institution in 1853, it was entitled 'The Irish School of Medicine as it is and ought to be'. Holland emphasised the right of students to complain if the professor was not doing the job properly, and the triennial visitation provided for such complaints to be heard. Holland observed that, while Cork students could be as good as others elsewhere, 'they do not, as a general rule, apply themselves to study with the same untiring zeal and self-reliance'.[103]

In his application for the vacant chair, Nathaniel J. Hobart, who had been unjustly dismissed by Alcock in 1852 from his post as demonstrator of practical anatomy and who had been exonerated by the college authorities, now turned to good account the favourable comments of Kane and the College Council.[104] Another candidate, Henry Augustus Caesar, included testimonials from the mayor, Andrew Roche, and from a number of Catholic clergymen in the city. Caesar also deemed it good canvassing politics, apparently, to submit a statement from some Catholic former students to the effect that he had never offended anybody's religious beliefs, inside or outside of class![105] The evidence of impartiality was to no avail, since J. Henry Corbett (1855–75) was appointed.

When Bullen was removed from the chair of surgery in 1864, following the collapse of his unsubstantiated allegations against Kane of involvement in the 1862 fire,[106] one of the hopefuls, and certainly the most brazen applicant for the succession, was Dr Thomas Crofts Shinkwin, lecturer in practical anatomy, who had been an unsuccessful contender ten years previously for the chair of anatomy and physiology. Students of Shinkwin's practical anatomy class of 1863–64 took an advertisement in May 1864 in *The Cork Examiner*, the *Cork Constitution*, the *Southern Star* and the *Munster Reporter* singing his praises as a lecturer, and Shinkwin graciously replied. This shameless electioneering campaign was brought to a climax by the newspapers themselves who took up the theme editorially.[107] Perhaps it was all a bit too much for the Castle, which in the end appointed William K. Tanner (1864–80).

The candidature for the professorship of materia medica in 1875 further illustrates some of the points already made. The successful candidate, Matthias O'Keeffe, had been an applicant for the chair of surgery in 1864 and on this occasion he had a testimonial from Sir Robert Kane, now ex-president. Another candidate was the celebrated Henry Macnaughton-Jones, who among other claims to fame is reputed to have composed the college motto, 'Where Finbarr taught, let Munster learn' (in fact, he just popularised it in verse), and whose loyalty to QCC was to be expressed later in his involvement in the Old Corkonians graduate club in London. In October 1875 he requested Under-Secretary T. Burke to return the original testimonials he had submitted. 'I sent in 30 letters to your office.'[108] Though disappointed on this occasion, he soon became professor of obstetrics and gynaecology (1878–83).

Given the goldfish-bowl character of these academic contests, it is hardly surprising to discover that 'the public in Cork have the deepest interest in the appointments in the College'. Our informant here is Rev. William Magill of Trinity Church who was testifying in June 1864 to the worth of Dr William Peebles, another unsuccessful applicant for the chair of surgery. Peebles, according to Magill, had that combination of character and 'professional abilities'

> which the public here are loudly demanding in the instructors of their sons. Everybody feels keenly that it is the Professors who make the College. If they desire to give confidence to parents and to make the hall of Science attractive to the young men of Munster, the College Authorities must needs appoint men to the great trust of professorships who combine genius in the Science they teach with academic tastes and habits − cultivated minds with high moral excellence and conscientiousness in the discharge of their duties.[109]

CHAPTER TWO

CELEBRATIONS AND A HEADACHE

*Here, after nearly a thousand years, we open now
the portals of this edifice and accept the
task of training the youth of Munster.*

Sir Robert Kane, speech on opening day

QUEEN'S COLLEGE CORK was officially inaugurated on 7 November 1849.[1]
The 'imposing and, indeed, splendid ceremonial' (*CE*, 9 November 1849) began
at noon in a crowded Aula Maxima where the hundreds of invited guests had waited
patiently, crammed together even more tightly than the relations and friends at modern
conferrings.[2] The 'magnificent' Examination Hall (*CE*, 7 November 1849) with its great
neo-Gothic hammer beam trusses already looked mellow, it was observed, even though
the building was just completed. It still remains today the symbolic and ceremonial heart
of the college. By the time the various dignitaries had taken their place and the professors,
led by President Kane and Vice-President Ryall, had filed in from the library, there was
little space on the crimson-clothed dais. The *Illustrated London News* (17 November 1849)
described the building style as 'the Collegiate or Domestic Architecture of the 15th
century' and published an artist's sketch of the platform party which vividly conveys the
flavour of the occasion. *The Cork Examiner* (7 November 1849) mentioned the youthful-
ness of the professors and remarked that they were 'well-developed in the frontal region',
a description which might be understood differently today but which then referred to the
fashionable 'science' of phrenology.

The attendance was richly representative of Cork civic and commercial life and
particularly of the movement that had long agitated for the establishment of a
Munster college. In a letter to city councillors, the mayor had stressed the importance of accepting the college's invitation to the ceremony ('of so much local and
general interest') and of a full attendance in official robes.[3] For many in the assembly,
this was the *dies iam expectata*. They included the octogenarian father-figure of the
Munster Provincial College Committee, James Roche; the mayor, Sir William
Lyons; Major Beamish; William Egan, MP; Thomas Ronayne Sarsfield, the high
sheriff; Sir Thomas Deane, contemplating the great hall of the building he designed
on the site he had favoured; patriot, businessman, poet and scholar Denny Lane; and
antiquarian John Windele. As well as Protestant clergymen, there were twelve
Catholic priests, including Rev. William O'Connor, PP, Courceys, having a brief
outing as dean of residence, before the synodal axe of Thurles would fall the
following year. Also there was the prominent Dublin priest, John Ennis, who had

2.1 The ceremony to mark the opening of Queen's College, Cork, 7 November 1849 from an article in the *Illustrated London News*.

been representing Archbishop Murray of Dublin in Rome in an effort to prevent papal condemnation of the Queen's Colleges. Ennis's presence in Cork incurred the displeasure of Paul Cullen, archbishop-elect of Armagh, and foremost promoter of the anti-colleges policy.[4] Another visitor at the opening ceremony was the prominent Catholic layman, Dr Dominic Corrigan, first Catholic president of the Royal College of Physicians of Ireland.[5]

The proceedings and the speeches reflected the civic origins of the college and projected its philosophical and educational ethos. After the college charter was read by the registrar, Francis Albani, the president, Sir Robert Kane, declared before the mayor that he would discharge his duties 'zealously, faithfully and to the best of my ability for the honour of the College and the promotion of education in Ireland'. The professors, led by D.B. Bullen (who had been so prominent in the Munster college agitation and whose son's name was the first to be entered on the student register), made a similar declaration, and promised they would have regard for the religious sensibilities of their students and avoid political controversy in accordance with Ch. VI, 9 of the statutes.

After this, Major Beamish, as vice-chairman of the Munster Provincial College Committee, by way of introducing an address from the committee to the president, traced the history of the agitation and proudly claimed the committee was responsible for the foundation of the college.[6] Now, they were resigning into the president's hand 'a trust which they have held untarnished for twenty years'. This concept was developed in the address which in flowery fashion evoked the ethos of the new institution – offering 'to all creeds and classes' an education at once scientific, literary, practical and having an 'industrial element' in the image of Kane himself. Having invoked the potential for harmony of mixed education, the address concluded: 'We have sown the seed; we have watched its development; we have awaited the growth of the plant, and now we triumph in the fullness of its produce. It is for Ireland's youthful sons to reap the mental harvest'.

The president's speech was, of course, the *pièce de résistance*, though *pièce* is an understatement since it took over two hours to read.[7] Recalling this aspect exactly a century later at a conferring ceremony, President Alfred O'Rahilly commented wryly that no one would listen to *him* for two hours![8]

Kane pointed out that the charter made the college an independent institution, with the right to present candidates for degrees. It would be reforming, progressive and honest in its philosophy of education. It would 'educate young men . . . for the active age and world in which we live'. Engineering and agricultural courses would provide for 'sound industrial education among the middle and higher classes of this province'. Not surprisingly, the religious issue was highlighted in the speech: after all, in the deceptive calm before the storm of synodal denunciation, there was still hope that the Catholic Church might accept the college's credentials. And so the president stressed the built-in provisions for respecting and protecting religious beliefs, and even for promoting religious practice, such as deanships of residence and the supervisory role of licensed boarding-house keepers. The Catholic dean, he stressed, would voluntarily extend instruction and supervision to students who lived at home. Finally, in invoking the legend of a flourishing monastery on the Gillabbey site in Ireland's golden age, and in linking the Queen's College to a thousand-year-old tradition, the president deliberately struck a supra-denominational and transcendent religious and cultural chord, appealed to powerful local emotions and firmly identified the *genius loci* from that day to this, from Queen's College to University College:

> Fin Barra, the patron saint of Cork . . . left to his followers the charge of founding a seat of learning in this place: here, after nearly a thousand years, we open now the portals of this edifice and accept the task of training the youth of Munster.[9]

In the 'rather vain' hope that his sentiments might soften Roman intransigence, Kane had his speech translated and sent to the Holy See. The translator, Basilio Angeli, professor of Spanish and Italian at TCD, botched the job and his rendering of 'ladies and gentlemen' as 'gentlemen of both sexes' allegedly led an amused cardinal to remark that Cork must be indeed a queer city! Angeli was subsequently dismissed for incompetence.[10]

The inauguration auspiciously set the scene for the college's first year of work and also for continuing celebrations. There was a high consciousness both of the goal that had been achieved and of the challenges that lay ahead. New gown and old town mingled again later in November 1849 when the flourishing Cuvierian Society held a soirée at the premises of the Royal Cork Institution. Many of the distinguished figures who had attended the opening ceremony – John Windele, Denny Lane, Richard Dowden et al. – warmly welcomed the professors of the fledgling college.[11]

In an address to the students and their parents in March 1850, Kane once more emphasised the provisions for religion made by the college. An hour's religious instruction weekly for the various denominations would be compulsory for students living away from home, and strongly recommended to others. The college's first five months had given the lie, the president said, to those who alleged disregard of religion and morality, and subversion of religious principles. 'Whilst the student is taught to respect the honest convictions of his neighbour, he shall be furnished with the most ample means of strengthening and sustaining his own.'[12]

Kane returned obsessively to this theme in other addresses, desperately trying to make the Queen's Colleges acceptable, even after the thunderous condemnation by the Synod of Thurles. His prize-distributing address at QCC on 25 October 1850, some weeks after the conclusion of the synod, was almost entirely devoted to rebutting the 'godless' colleges argument. Once more he pointed to inbuilt college safeguards for religious faith, to the encouragement of religious practice and religious instruction, and to the glowing testimony of the deans of residence in this regard. Invoking the support of a strong minority of Irish bishops, Kane argued that the Queen's Colleges represented the highest potential of Catholic emancipation, offering Irish people the chance to get on equal grounds the best available education, and to attain the highest reaches of the professions without the old penalties against conscience. Like Thomas Davis, Kane claimed that 'equal intercourse in early youth' was a powerful antidote to the divisive effect of religious differences in Irish society. 'Yes, I support mixed education; not as a state official, but as an Irishman.'[13]

The brilliant highlight of that celebratory first year was the glittering banquet in honour of Sir Robert Kane, held in the Imperial Hotel on 8 April 1850.[14] It was attended by the notables of Cork and Munster – *maithe agus móruaisle na Mumhan*, in the traditional Irish phrase. The company foregathered at 6.30 p.m., ate a dinner, drank countless toasts and dispersed shortly after 1.00 a.m.! The nearly two-hundred-strong all-male attendance (the ladies' health being toasted almost as an afterthought) included the usual dignitaries who showed up throughout the year: William Fagan MP, Major Ludlow Beamish, Denny Lane, Sir Thomas Deane, Thomas Ronayne Sarsfield, St John Jefferyes, Aldermen Richard Dowden, Francis M. Jennings, John Windele, etc. In a show of collegial support, Vice-President Ryall and seven professors attended. Among them were the prominent and ubiquitous Bullen and a man who was shortly to be in hot water, Raymond de Vericour. But the shadow of distressing things to come (including Kane's myriad troubles) did not diminish the euphoria of the evening. The mayor of Limerick represented the Munster dimension, the mayor of Waterford pleaded 'pressing engagements', while the mayor of Clonmel published his rejection of the invitation in a local paper. However, Kane must have been especially comforted by the presence of Fr William O'Connor, the Catholic dean of residence and, by implication, the (at least provisional) approval of the new bishop of Cork, William Delany.[15]

The toast of the evening was proposed by Mayor John Shea to Sir Robert Kane. Voicing characteristic Victorian educational sentiments, the mayor asserted that QCC was 'for the middle-classes of society' whose objectives were 'peace and prosperity', the latter element making Kane's choice as president truly appropriate in view of his authoritative work on Ireland's resources. Kane (greeted with 'loud and continuous cheering') took up the class theme in his reply. University education was indispensable 'for the upper and middle classes' if they were to promote industrial development and employment, and if they were not to be 'found ignored and inactive in face of a highly instructed and energetic population of poor'. 'Those who know most will govern.' Expressing another period sentiment, Sir Robert talked of classes being educated 'befitting their respective ranks'. His other views would have gone down well with his audience, especially the flattering references to 'this important city' and 'this great province'. Deploring the 'barbarous' laws that not so long before had deprived 'the mass of the Irish people' of education, he claimed that 'practical education' was the key to 'the prosperity of my native land', which was his cherished objective. He praised the Christian Brothers and the national schools in equal measure, claiming that the latter had benefitted those emigrating to England.

Judge Stock said they were celebrating 'the nativity of our National University' and described TCD as 'a foreign institution'. The mayor conveyed the citizens' gratitude to the professors for generously throwing open 'several of their interesting and instructive lectures to the public'. Professor Francis A. Walsh (English law, 1849–52), who had been a member of the Provincial College Committee, said the two things that had to be done in Ireland were 'cultivating the neglected soil and educating the neglected mind'. Sir Robert Kane, he added, makes learning 'a delightful enjoyment to those under his care'. Vice-President Ryall testified to the success of the new institution 'in its infancy', despite much 'well-meaning and ill-meaning opposition'. He stressed that all students of the college were receiving proper spiritual guidance and he raised 'great laughter' when he assured his audience that the students' time was not 'devoted to peg-tops, sugarsticks and marbles'.[16]

James Roche was an absentee subscriber to the banquet, pleading the burden of his eighty years. He was eulogised by Major Ludlow Beamish for never having

> left our ranks until we had planted the standard of free, full, unfettered academic education upon its fitting depository – the classic summit so long appropriated to the didactic labours of the Gilla of Finbar (great applause) bearing upon its lofty gable the effigy of our gracious Queen and casting its broad shadows upon a landscape aptly harmonising with its classic guise.

But there was more than festive self-congratulation in the evening's speeches. Scientific or practical education was one serious theme, but the dominant one was mixed education. The threat presented to the Queen's Colleges by the rising tide of Catholic ecclesiastical opposition was in the minds of all, and was referred to in varying degrees of obliqueness. Some speakers struck a Thomas Davis-like note in praise of mixed or united education, though they might be poles apart from the Young Irelanders on other issues.[17] There was a brotherhood of students in QCC, claimed Professor Walsh, the professors were scrupulous in observing religious impartiality, there was no 'wall of separation' between Protestant and Catholic. 'Are they not destined to co-operate for the good of this country?' This theme was echoed by St John Jefferyes and M.J. Barry (responding to the toast of 'the press') and most eloquently developed by the friend and biographer of Daniel O'Connell, wealthy Cork butter merchant William Fagan MP. He claimed that united education was quite simply a necessary reflection of a multi-denominational society and asserted that the Cork college held no 'danger to the faith of any', and indeed provided safeguards for faith and morals not to be found in British universities, old or new, nor in Trinity College. He also lavished high praise on the educational standards of the Cork college and the good conduct of the students. Fagan, a Catholic who had a son in QCC, added solemnly, if not ominously, that he had hoped the Roman Catholic Church would listen to his words 'before it is too late', by which he meant presumably a total polarisation of the pro- and anti-colleges camps, with Catholics defying Church disapproval. On what would strike us as a lighter note (but frequently mentioned and earnestly meant), Fagan suggested that an additional reason for sending offspring to QCC was to have them 'under your own eyes' and avoid 'the vicious allurements' of Dublin or London.

The *Cork Southern Reporter* enthusiastically endorsed the sentiments of the evening.[18] This was hardly surprising, given that its editor was M.J. Barry, poet, former Young Irelander and author of the marching song 'Step Together'. Pointing out that the assembly could hardly be more distinguished or representative, with two-thirds of the participants practising Catholics, the paper claimed the function proved that the Catholic laity backed the colleges system. That show of support was the real purpose of the evening – 'a demonstration in favour of the Queen's College system' and the principle of 'united education'. It was a morale-boosting rally against stiffening ultramontanist opposition, which was to culminate in the decrees of the Synod of Thurles within a few months.

Fr O'Connor's presence at the banquet reflected his active involvement in the college in that opening year. He gave an account of his stewardship in the president's report for 1849– 50. He said he was a supporter of mixed education, 'a system . . . which I conscientiously believe to be well suited to the peculiar circumstances and wants of this unfortunate and hitherto distracted country'. He was enthusiastic about the first year's experience which convinced him that the student body was free from sectarian prejudice. Having supervised the moral behaviour and religious practice of his own Catholic students,[19] he expressed his pride in their conduct under the inspection of the 'jealous and scrutinizing eyes of the citizens of Cork'. This suggests that student behaviour was seen by Cork Catholics as one of the tests of the acceptability of the Queen's College.

The 'godless' college: polarisation

The experimenting days were over for Fr O'Connor as soon as the Synod of Thurles pronounced on the colleges issue and the *Acta* were approved by Rome. An erstwhile sympathetic Bishop Delany could no longer co-operate with the college, and Fr O'Connor resigned his deanship: his first report was also his last.[20] Delany had been unwilling to accept successive Propaganda rescripts against the Queen's Colleges, referring to an April 1850 document as 'most imprudent'.[21] The basic attitude of Delany and his colleagues in the Murray camp was that, whatever the defects of the Queen's Colleges, they offered a valuable educational opportunity (indeed, all things considered, the *only* opportunity) for Catholics which it would be irresponsible to spurn. They regretted the Church's rejection of the government offer in the summer of 1850 to give each college a Catholic president or vice-president, and a Catholic professor of metaphysics.[22] And so while they now reluctantly accepted that the clergy could have no part in the colleges' governing structures, the bishops of Cork and Galway were slow to withdraw their priests as deans of residence, and slower still to condemn the attendance of Catholics as students.[23] Indeed, Church disapproval of the Queen's Colleges, though ruling out priestly participation, never extended to the explicit prohibition of lay involvement and of attendance under pain of mortal sin, because such an extreme step would have had disastrously divisive consequences.

It is significant that when Archbishop Slattery of Cashel and Bishop Delany of Cork replied to the announcement of their appointments as visitors to Queen's College Cork, their respective refusals (7 and 15 September 1850) were quite different in tone. Slattery's curt response ('obviously impossible') denounced the Queen's Colleges as 'pregnant with danger',[24] whereas Delany, whose sympathetic leanings were now constrained by the synodal decrees, was more conciliatory, saying he 'greatly regrets that existing circumstances' prevented him from accepting.[25]

Even in the aftermath of the Synod of Thurles, *The Cork Examiner* was still cautiously supporting the Queen's Colleges or at least the general idea behind them.[26] The paper was not enamoured of certain appointments at QCC but it hedged its bets pending a final pronouncement from the Holy See. It condemned John O'Connell's attack on Catholic supporters of the Queen's Colleges as 'injudicious, impolite and injurious', and it claimed that many Cork citizens 'other than place expectants and mere government hacks' had 'creditable and honourable' motives for backing the colleges.

The *Examiner* claimed that 'the great majority of the Roman Catholic laity of the middle-class' and 'a large proportion of the clergy within the City' favoured the colleges as affording 'a cheap and valuable education' and approved of the principles of mixed education. There was, obviously, a hostile Catholic opinion which feared that the colleges would lead to religious indifference and, the paper significantly conceded, 'in the county, so far as we have the means of knowing, the majority against them is beyond question very great'. Aware of looming polarisation, the paper lamented that 'the principle . . . of mixed education in secular matters is not likely to be allowed such a trial as would demonstrate either its advantage or its injury'. But there was no doubt about the side the Catholic *Examiner* would take in the end. If the pope finally outlawed the Queen's Colleges, every attempt must be made to get a Catholic university going (this idea had been backed unanimously by the Synod of Thurles two months before) and 'those Catholics who have said they will not be bound by this or the other decision should reflect on the danger to religion of any division between the Church and any portion of the flock'. Still, a month later, the paper was praising Kane for his 'temperate and moderate tone' in these difficult circumstances.[27]

Cullen and the ultramontanists, who demanded instant compliance with Roman diktats, remained bitter about Cork and its recalcitrant clergy. Cullen wrote in January 1851:

> In Cork I believe they are ready to resist the Pope. They are exerting themselves in every possible way to get pupils for the College – and they have been too successful. I believe there are now 100 Catholics there. The greater part consists, however, of apothecaries' boys and attorney's [sic] clerks. Were it not for the bishops and clergy the schools would be empty.[28]

Cullen had a nice line in caustic insults where Delany was concerned. All three candidates for the vacant Killaloe diocese in 1851 were unfit, he believed. 'The first is the best but he is said to be ignorant. The other two are only editions of Dr Delany.'[29] A Cullen supporter stigmatised the pro-colleges middle classes as *aristocratic* and *respectable* . . . conceited, ill-informed and . . . subservient to . . . government'.[30] But the hard fact was that the ambitious Cork middle classes, determined to promote their sons' professional careers, were not going to be deterred, then or thereafter, by ecclesiastical disapproval.

For Cullen, Sir Robert Kane, as president of QCC, personified the disloyal and contumacious lay Catholic opposition to the Holy See, and the cardinal was splenetic in his remarks in October 1867 about Kane's membership of the Royal Commission on Primary Education – 'a bitter opponent of Catholic education, though himself a Catholic . . . however he will not be able to do much harm as he is a layman . . .'[31] And when Cullen gave evidence to the commission in February 1868, he observed that, while the Protestant commissioners were courteous, 'the only one who was a little insolent was a Catholic [Kane] who is a declared Freemason, but nothing can be expected from that breed'.[32]

Cork continued to have a renegade reputation during Delany's episcopate. Archbishop P.F. Moran of Sydney wrote to Mgr Tobias Kirby, rector of the Irish College in Rome, on 9 March 1884 that Catholic Cork had become estranged from the rest of the Irish Church because of its patronage of the Queen's College. And one of the reasons why Dean Henry Neville, a very prominent Cork cleric, failed to be appointed co-adjutor to Delany in 1884 was because he also supported the College and, from the Holy See's standpoint, was far from sound on the education question.[33]

De Vericour

The de Vericour affair, happening at such an early date, made things that much harder for Delany and the college's supporters, while it further encouraged the college's opponents, only too pleased to have their worst suspicions confirmed.[34]

In 1850, Raymond de Vericour (modern languages, 1849–79) published his *An Historical Analysis of Christian Civilisation*, with 'Queen's College, Cork' on the title-page under his own name, and he recommended the work as a historical textbook. Since the book was critical of the papacy's political role, it was immediately placed on the Index. The College Council was understandably supersensitive to the religious implications of this development, particularly in the first critical year and at a time when the colleges question was on the Synod of Thurles agenda. Accordingly, it reacted strongly, expressing its

> opinion that the form in which the name of the author appears on the title-page is likely to mislead with regard to the nature of the Professorship, such being purely Philological, and not in any way embracing History; that the preface is written in a manner to convey an impression that this work might be received as a text-book in this College, which its subject totally precludes; that the address of the book being dated from Queen's College, Cork implies a connexion and sanction which this Council disclaims; and that without entering into any detailed judgement upon the contents of this work, the Council finds that, being written in his capacity of Professor, it is calculated to produce polemical contention and excitement, to retard the progress of the College, and injure the cause of United Education in Ireland.[35]

De Vericour was in Bonn for the summer of 1850, 'cultivating a more intimate acquaintance with modern languages', and in his absence he was suspended from his professorship and from the deanship of the Arts Faculty (Literary Division).

Predictably, the issue was hotly debated among staff and students.[36] There was controversy in the Cork papers, de Vericour supporters arguing that his offence was merely technical and that he was being made a scapegoat to appease the Catholic bishops. The College Council (despite individual professors' friendships with their errant colleague) wanted the president to recommend to the Crown that de Vericour be removed from office, as having violated his terms of office. The council also made it clear – and this was incorporated into the statutes – that where a professor used his title or the authority of an office for a publication, he was responsible for ensuring that the work was not in conflict with the welfare of the college and the principles of his statutory declaration. De Vericour was summoned before the council (10 September 1850) where he was both co-operative and contrite.[37] He was prepared to remove his professorial designation and the college address from the next edition, as well as his recommendation of the work as a textbook: in return, he was assured there was no intention of interfering with his private independence and he was reinstated in his chair, though he thought it prudent not to take up the deanship again. The 1857–58 Royal Commission on the Queen's Colleges, reviewing the case, felt it was an isolated one, that QCC professors had scrupulously avoided giving religious offence before or since, and that de Vericour 'did everything in his power to remove any just grounds of dissatisfaction in this matter'.[38]

However, the affair had done damage from the outset to the image of 'mixed education' in QCC. The college could now be castigated not only as 'godless' in a neutral, secular sense but as a proselytising institution, to boot. Kane's repeated assurances about religious safeguards could be scoffed at. Archbishop Cullen, in a pastoral in November 1850, denounced de Vericour's 'anti-Catholic' work, criticised the soft treatment he had received, and asked rhetorically 'where now were the securities so often guaranteed'.[39]

Appointments such as de Vericour's were long kept in mind as a warning that government control was highly dangerous. When the Gladstone administration sought episcopal support for the 1873 University Act and the lord lieutenant promised there would be Catholics on the governing body and on the academic staff, Cardinal Cullen retorted that similar promises had been made when QCC was founded 'yet one of the first professors appointed was Vericour, a French infidel'. And Cullen told Archbishop Manning in February 1873 that Gladstone would appoint Frenchmen and Germans as professors who would bring 'Hegelism and infidelity with them as Mr Vericour, a nephew of Guizot, did to the Cork College'.[40]

CHAPTER THREE

THE EARLY YEARS

The several departments of the College will open for
public instructions on Wednesday, the 7th November, 1849.

QCC's first prospectus

The new academic community

IN HIS PHD thesis on the origins and early history of the Queen's College Cork Seán Pettit paints a vivid picture of working conditions during the opening year, 1849–50.[1] First of all, college operated under statutes that were already amended by opening day. The president, officers and professors (increased from twelve to twenty – thirteen arts, five medicine, two law) formed the body corporate. Within the arts faculty, there were two divisions, literary and science. Science included agriculture and engineering as well as science proper. Deans (one literary, one science, one law, one medicine) were elected annually by their respective faculties. The president, the vice-president, and the four deans formed the College Council, which was the central agency of college administration. Four members constituted a quorum, but the president's signature was essential for all resolutions. (The small council theoretically made for efficiency but it also intensified academic tensions.) The council arranged courses, prescribed examinations, supervised student discipline and approved running expenses.

The president had considerable powers – excessively so, in the opinion of turbulent professors, as they were to make plain from time to time. He was entitled to preside at all college meetings, dissolve committees, determine leave of absence for staff, prescribe duty hours of the registrar and bursar, license boarding-houses and, not least, he was bound to prepare an annual report for parliament to be submitted to the lord lieutenant. As real and formal head, he was more of a strong constitutional monarch than *primus inter pares*. As chief executive, he hired and fired college servants.

In the governance of college, the vice-president was second only in importance to the president, with whom he shared the residential East Wing. He could visit any hall, lecture room or office at any time. However, the vice-presidency did not survive the stormy Kane-Ryall relationship, and John Ryall was the first and last vice-president (1845–75), until the office was revived in a milder form a century later. After Ryall, the registrarship came into its own in the formidable person of Alexander Jack (1876–1906) who consolidated his ascendancy under the weak post-Sullivan presidencies of James Slattery (1890–96) and Sir Rowland Blennerhassett (1897–1904). Originally, the registrar ranked behind the vice-president and had more responsibility than power: he was required to attend his office daily, take the minutes at meetings of the College Council (of which he was not a member), keep a list of students' names and addresses, preserve attendance rolls and other records, and accept responsibility for the security of the college premises during the long vacation.

The three faculties were to function – and hold meetings – under the control of the president and council. Professors were to 'lecture, teach and examine', assist in the holding of examinations, maintain order and discipline in class, attend faculty meetings and act on committees. This pattern of activity would be familiar to the modern academic, who would, however, hardly be interested in having students as boarders with the president's sanction.

Matriculated students were the serious students, as it were, being more closely bound in to college discipline than non-matriculated students, who were not obliged to pass any preliminary examination in order to attend lecture courses on an à la carte basis but who could not be candidates for scholarships. Fees were paid not only to the college but also, as a supplement to their salaries, to the professors (class fees), both sets of payments being made through the bursar. College fees for matriculated students averaged £2–3 per annum, with class fees of similar amounts. Fees were slightly higher in such areas as engineering, physics, anatomy and physiology.

On paper, at least, discipline was strict. Matriculated students under twenty-one not living with a parent or guardian, or approved relation or friend, had to reside in licensed boarding-houses. These had to be morally suitable and provide adequate health and comfort standards for their students. In the event, neither the boarding-houses nor their proprietors came up to the expected standards. The regulations for licensed houses were preoccupied in considerable detail with the religious and moral, as well as the material, welfare of the student.[2] The president was empowered to license exclusively denominational houses of residence. The various deans of residence were to arrange for religious instruction and regular observance of religious duties. More mundanely:

> The proprietor shall in all cases arrange that each Student have a separate Bed, and separate means of cleanliness, and shall in case of more than one person sleeping in the same room lodge with the Bursar of the College a plan of such room with the arrangements of the beds proposed.

Students had to be indoors by 9 p.m. in the winter and spring terms, and 10 p.m. in the summer term. The proprietor was required to report to the registrar any student misdemeanours such as intoxication ('the introduction of spirituous liquors by students into licensed houses is strictly forbidden'), 'Quarrelling or Political or Polemical Disputations or any acts of immorality or misconduct', and 'the frequenting of Smoking-rooms, Taverns or Public-houses'. In general, students could be punished, even expelled, for habitually neglecting attendance at divine worship or at religious instruction classes; immoral or dishonest practices; treasonable or seditious conduct; drunkenness; grievous offences against college rules or discipline; and wilful and serious damage to the property of the college.

In practice, however, students were not prepared to submit to a draconian code of discipline and, as we shall see later, they showed solidarity in resisting excessively harsh

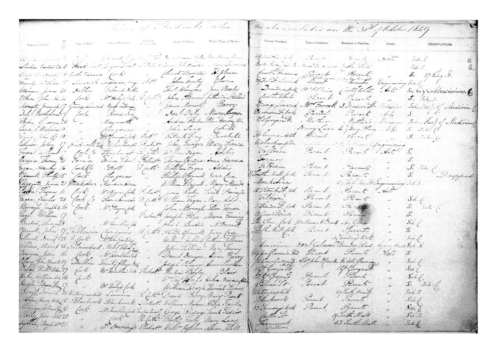

3.1 Admission register, 1849-1862. The first name on the register is Richard Bullen, son of Denis Bullen, first professor of surgery at QCC. The second name is Edmund Larken from Lincoln, who was encouraged to come to Cork by Professor George Boole.

treatment of their fellow students by the college authorities. Student resistance could be by way of public protest (in college or in town) or of an appeal to the Board of Visitors. Records of various visitations show that the students were not at all inhibited in airing their grievances before the august personages who formed the board. 'Ordinary' visitations were held triennially to monitor the general situation in the college. The visitors could inspect various departments, inquire into the general state of discipline and hear appeals from any staff or student member who felt aggrieved by college treatment. An extraordinary visitation could be held at any time on a particular matter either on the initiative of the visitors or on foot of an application from a professor, office-bearer or student. A visitation, then, could be a kind of court of human rights.

'The several departments of the College will open for public instructions on Wednesday, the 7th November, 1849', announced the college's first prospectus.[3] Thus, it would appear that work began on the day of the colourful inauguration ceremony. The professors must have had a busy 'marking' weekend since, according to the prospectus, the matriculation examination was held on Tuesday and Wednesday, 30 and 31 October, and the scholarship examination on Friday, Saturday and Monday, 2, 3 and 5 November.

Of the 115 students enrolled in that first year, 70 were matriculated, with access to the very generous range of scholarships on offer. Of the 115, there were 64 (50

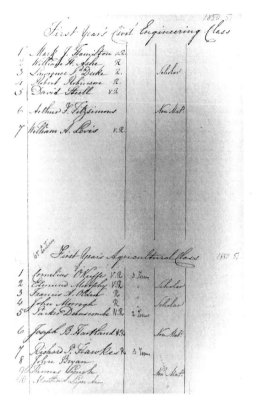

3.2 Roll Book, recording names of students in
the first year civil engineering and agricultural
classes, for the session, 1850-51.

matriculated and 14 non-matriculated) in arts, including science; 21 (6 and 15) in medicine; 12 (10 and 2) in engineering; 5 (4 and 1) in agriculture; and 13 (all non-matriculated) in law.[4] The high proportion of non-matriculated students in medicine and law indicates only a tentative interest in QCC at this stage by these professions and their continuing commitment to outside licensing institutions.

Obviously, many of the students were drawn from schools in Cork city and county but others had more exotic backgrounds – the Irish College, Rome; Trinity College, Dublin; Belfast Institution; Maynooth College; Clongowes Wood College; Wesleyan Collegiate School, Dublin; Carlow College; the Irish College, Paris; Wolverhampton; and the elite Catholic nurseries in England: Stonyhurst, Oscott and Downside. Ages of students ranged from 13-year-old John Stopford, a Wesleyan Methodist of 60 South Mall to 26-year-old Patrick Sullivan, Kilmichael, Co. Cork. In arts, the average age was 17, in medicine 19, in engineering 18 and in agriculture 20. The denominational breakdown of the 70 matriculated students (non-matriculated had a similar distribution) was: 38 Roman Catholic, 26 Anglican, 4 Wesleyan, 1 Church of Scotland Presbyterian and 1 Irish Protestant(!).[5]

In his first president's report (14 July 1850), Sir Robert Kane gives us the feel of that opening year when he refers to the 'premature occupation of an unfinished building', though its architecture had won widespread praise. The College Council minutes (as well as those of different faculties) reflect various aspects of unfinished business. The year's experience revealed numerous deficiencies. Very sensibly, the bursar was instructed in December 1849 not to take over possession of the college buildings from the Board of Works until ordered to do so by the council, which appointed a subcommittee of deans to inspect the condition of the buildings. Matters were sufficiently satisfactory by the following April for the necessary authorisation to be given to the bursar.

The architect continued to be involved in developments. In a letter to Sir Thomas Deane in May 1850, the registrar (Francis Albani) urged the completion of laboratory gas and boiler-fittings in order to end the serious inconvenience being experienced by the Department of Chemistry. The registrar further accused Deane of having done nothing (despite repeated representations from the president and council) about the gaol drainage discharged into the river near the college gate[6] 'and conducted by the stream along the entire front of the building producing almost daily a noisome stench'. Albani argued that, since the architect had chosen the college site, he was responsible for removing the nuisance of the 'Gaol ordure'. On the same day, the registrar also complained to the committee of management of the gaol about 'the very offensive and insalubrious nuisance' of the discharge and the 'putrescent smell' along the front of the college: an elongated sewer pipe; the registrar suggested; would direct it away, or it could be made into manure.[7] Meanwhile, the council requested Sir Thomas Deane to have a paling made in the avenue[8] from the gate to the college as the approach was very dangerous.[9] The Board of Wide Street Commissioners was to be asked to lay down 'a footpath from the Western Road to the Gate of the College' – an indication of unpleasant conditions underfoot.

When Albani informed the Board of Works on 18 May 1850 of various college requirements, he gave the impression of an institution underequipped in numerous respects.[10] Safety was again a priority. 'The precipitous and exposed face of the cliff in front of the College and at the Porter's lodge' was a risk to everybody walking and driving even in the daytime, and an iron wire fence and coping wall needed to be erected. Also, for the health and comfort of staff, students and public, 'the great Entrance under the Tower should be provided with a gate and a small wicket, and that for marking the hours a Tower clock should be provided'. Some months before, at a meeting of the arts faculty (science division), a motion was passed on the proposal of Professor Lane (civil engineering) 'that it be recommended that a porter be directed to announce the conclusion and commencement of each lecture hour by ringing of a bell'.[11]

The professors' rooms – that is, the few 'private' rooms they shared in common for preparation, robing, and keeping rolls and books – lacked items such as carpets, towels and basin stands, all of which had to be requisitioned. However, it seems that in a noble gesture of community solidarity, the professors were willing to waive the carpeting of their 'preparation rooms' and to settle for strong hempen cloth floor-covering and a rug (not a far cry from the 1990s!) in order that students might have additional tables in the lecture rooms.[12] By May 1850, 'the President's office still remaining totally unfurnished, it is required that it be provided with carpet, fire irons, office table with desk and drawers, a press, six black hair chairs and some shelves'.[13] As things turned out, it would have taken a very luxurious office indeed to tempt Sir Robert Kane to stay permanently in residence.

The council had to deal with complaints about uncomfortable working conditions – cold, billowing smoke, rain from the south forming pools and driving into the cloisters.[14] The smoke was caused by great quantities of fuel burning in unsuitable grates which radiated heat inadequately. The council blamed the Board of Works though there was a hint that the architect was not entirely without fault. In any case, it was essential, if injury to college property was to be avoided, that the grates should be changed and the chimney tops properly capped, though it was also accepted that time was needed for the building to become dryer. It was regarded as absolutely indispensable, no matter what the effect on the architectural appearance, that the Board of Works should glaze the lower cloisters because of flooding in southerly wind and rain. And to emphasise the point that life was far from odourless in QCC, and that the neighbouring prisoners were not the sole generators of nuisances, there was a complaint that the water supply for the closet on the lower corridor was inadequate, thus causing an offensive smell in dry weather.[15]

The most serious accommodation difficulty in that first year was caused by the absence of a custom-built medical building. In 1849–50, practical anatomy was carried on in a basement of the science division, and dissections were conducted by medical students in a senior class of engineers, to the mutual embarrassment of both! Other classes were taught in the Cork School of Medicine in the South Mall.[16] However, there were educational compensations: medical students studied Greek and Latin, and the dean of the faculty sang the praises of a curriculum that transcended the merely clinical:

> Without a proper preliminary education, not only in the Departments of Science which are the groundwork of Medical knowledge but also in the Ancient and Modern Languages, candidates for the Degree of Doctor of Medicine cannot acquire those external and varied attainments which are necessary to form a truly educated physician.[17]

Among the numerous and varied matters receiving academic and administrative attention in the inaugural year were: a decision on the student cap-and-gown design, an attire which then became compulsory;[18] the avoidance of timetable clashing;[19] the presidential appointment of porters, including head porter William Cunningham who had a drink problem which ultimately resulted in his demotion;[20] the renting of a field in the neighbourhood for playing cricket;[21] the problem of echoes in some lecture rooms;[22] and library acquisitions, including the purchase of second-hand books.[23]

In his first president's report, Kane tried to pull together the manifold threads of that bewildering first year. The president thanked the Board of Works for its 'hearty co-operation', and paid tribute to the vice-president, officers and professors (all were still in the honeymoon phase!) for their help in overcoming 'extreme difficulties'. These difficulties had ranged from dampness causing staff and student illness to 'ignorance', 'opposition' and 'misrepresentation'. Professors lectured three to thirteen hours per week, five professors in the arts faculty giving a total of forty-seven hours per week, and students averaged twenty-three lecture hours weekly (they were obliged to attend at least two-thirds of all lectures). 'The general diligence of the students was excellent', and 'no complaint of immorality or neglect of religious duty has been made against any student'. Kane also noted with satisfaction that a course of public lectures delivered by R. Horner Mills, the professor of jurisprudence and political economy (1849–93), had been fully attended. The president doubtless felt that this augured well for future fruitful contributions by the college to the community. He also referred to the 'committee of gentlemen'[24] working to procure land near the college for a 'model farm and garden' which would not only complete the work of the school of agriculture but educate 'working agricultural pupils' for employment as stewards or bailiffs, or as managers of their own farms. Finally, Kane asserted that the deans of residence were fully in touch with the students and that weekly religious instruction meetings were being very well attended.

Early administration

After the celebratory glow of opening ceremonies and banquets had dimmed, Kane had to tackle the demanding job of running a new college – indeed, a new kind of college – which was faced with various problems ranging from inadequate facilities to the hostility of the Catholic Church. These were compounded by the distraction of Kane's other main preoccupation – his involvement in the Museum of Irish Industry – and by the tensions to which his periodic absences gave rise.[25]

His correspondence[26] shows the wide range of matters calling for his attention during the first decade of the college's existence. Most of them related to teething problems – the stocking of the library and museums, standards of boarding-houses and renewal of their licences, recognition of (especially medical) degrees, protocol for visiting dignitaries, staff appointments and difficulties, relations with the public and with institutions and scholarly societies in the city. In regard to additional building work, progress was sometimes delayed until vacations, so as not to inconvenience students.[27] Plans had to be discussed for a gate lodge at the south entrance in 1863,[28] and there were recurrent problems about water supply from Cork Corporation.[29] There was tiresome and endless correspondence with the Board of Works, which was constantly warning the college authorities that only essential fitments and repairs could be effected and that the money was running out.[30] Much of the president's work was administrative detail, surprisingly so even when we take into account the small size of the college. Today it would be taken care of – as a matter of course – in the accommodations office or in the library. Other college officials had their problems: the registrar, Francis Albani, wished to acquire a good Turkish carpet at a reasonable price.[31] In general, the impression is that every detail was scrutinised by the Board of Works, if not by the Treasury.

The licensed boarding-houses, as provided for in the Colleges Act, never worked well in practice. Administrators and deans of residence expressed general disappointment with them over the period of the Queen's College, and their failure to serve the needs of the students and of the college was one reason why presidents like Sullivan and Windle were anxious to see halls of residence established. Some of the Cork boarding-houses were surprisingly far from college, in the travel and transport terms of those days.[32] Landlords did not seem to be highly motivated. Samuel Morony of 5 King Street, who applied for a licence to Kane in September 1849 and who was involved in farming as well as teaching, sounded like a man who would chance his arm at anything.[33] Jeremiah Morony, 33 King Street (related to Samuel), was in trouble with the college authorities in early 1860 over student-lodgers who were not obeying the regulations. He wrote ingratiatingly to Kane, obsequiously apologising for taking up the president's time and claiming he had recruited many students for the college: 'I think there was never any man worked so hard as I have done to support the College'. Drink was obviously involved in the mismanagement, since Morony assured the president that he kept only a little drink in the house, and that he himself would frequent public houses only as a last resort if there were no other place of refreshment available while travelling. Kane was prepared not to remove Morony's licence if he promised to keep his boarders under strict supervision in future.[34]

Kane accepted gifts and loans for the new museums and laboratories: for example, scientific apparatus from the Royal Cork Institution; duplicate specimens from the Royal Dublin Society; gifts from Sir Charles Thomas Newton, distinguished archaeologist, and keeper of antiquities at the British Museum; an antique sundial from John Faulett of Lincoln through his friend George Boole. Some gifts were not properly appreciated, apparently: Francis M. Jennings (a prominent citizen who was a founder-friend of QCC, a member of the Farm Committee and whose family owned land acquired by the college for expansion) expressed his shock and dismay that a Peruvian mummy donated to the college through his good offices was lying in an unsuitable box exposed to decay.

Kane was particularly pleased with gifts from Corkmen who had won fame abroad but who were still fond of their native city or county and anxious to be associated with the new college. Sir Redmond Barry, the Australian legal luminary, was sorry he missed Kane on a recent visit to Cork and sent him books and catalogues relating to Melbourne and Victoria.[35] General Daniel O'Leary (1800–54), the comrade-in-arms and adviser of Simón Bolívar, the 'Liberator' of South America, wrote several letters in 1852–53 relating to various gifts – silver ores and fossils in a handmade box of rare wood.[36] O'Leary recalled Cork as his birthplace and said he still took an interest in life there. He was especially pleased to hear of the foundation of the college.

In the sphere of public relations, Kane had to deal with such matters as corporation attendance at conferrings and prize-givings,[37] protocol for an 1854 visit from the lord lieutenant (the mayor would arrange 'to prevent any inconvenience from a crowd outside')[38] and contacts with learned societies downtown. In 1857, the Royal Cork Institution needed the loan of scientific apparatus for a lecture of 'popular instruction', which would after all stimulate an interest of long-term benefit to QCC.[39]

There were hopeful letters from various people who expected the college would help them to turn an honest penny. Batsford, who already supplied the Royal Cork Institution and the Cork Library, applied during the 1849–50 session to be appointed college booksellers and stationers.[40] A Southampton doctor wished to sell his collection of pathology specimens to the college 'at a great sacrifice'.[41] A Penzance lady sought an advance subscription, which she felt would be forthcoming if there was any QCC interest in oriental languages, for her brother's forthcoming dictionary of Pushto (Afghan tribes' language).[42] And a Mr James Brenan would design a border for the college certificate for £5.[43]

The theme of financial constraints runs through this early Kane correspondence. Reminders are sent by the Stationery Office[44] and by provincial newspapers[45] of unpaid bills. The Education Office explains that they are prevented by regulations from supplying maps at special rates.[46] Significantly, there was correspondence with the mayor's office about the water supply in 1859.[47] There must have been further difficulties after the 1862 fire, since the water was turned on again only after the College Council agreed to the corporation scale of charges in October 1862.[48]

The Farm Committee 1849

In his first president's report, 1849–50, Kane recommended that 'land near the College be procured and adapted for the purposes of a Model Farm and Garden which will afford practical exemplification of improved Agriculture and Horticulture'.[49] The college's lively and enduring interest in what might loosely be called an agricultural dimension should be seen in its post-Famine context and was evident, literally, from day one. A minute book in the college archives charts the progress of this movement from an initial meeting in the museum of the Royal Cork Institution on 17 November 1849 to May 1851.[50] But the committee was actually formed on the opening day of QCC (7 November 1849), with the president, Sir Robert Kane, in the chair. The 'Farm Committee' was representative of the landed, financial and political establishment but also included ubiquitous college 'activists' like Ald. Dowden, Francis M. Jennings, the highly vocal Major Beamish, Viscount Bernard, Sir Thomas Deane and, nominally at least, the 'father of the college', James Roche. The professor of agriculture, Edmund Murphy, who had four students in 1849–50, became centrally involved in the committee's work, apparently on a full-time basis, and Kane himself was available to give shrewd advice. The committee met frequently, for some periods on a weekly basis. At an early stage, it was agreed that an income of at least £500 per annum would be needed 'to keep up a Botanic Garden and Model Farm', of which £250 per annum was to be raised in local subscriptions. The objective of the committee was declared (24 November 1849) to be

> the establishment of an Agricultural School of Industry in Munster, in connection with the Queen's College, by the formation of an Agricultural, Botanical, Horticultural, Arboricultural Garden and Experimental Farm, and also a Museum of Materials con-

nected with these important subjects, so as to secure to this locality the appropriation of
the £5,000,[51] as set forth in the 2nd Section of the 11th and 12th Victoria, Cap. 116.

There were different opinions as to the relative importance of the horticultural/
botanic gardens/experimental plot model (closely tied to college study) on the one
hand, and the large agricultural school (or farm attached to the college) on the other.
The emphasis soon shifted to the latter, and this became clear at a public meeting on 11
January 1850. This development would call for support by country gentlemen rather
than, or as well as, city businessmen. There was a view that botanical gardens were a
luxury (in any case they did not qualify for the £5,000 appropriation mentioned above)
and that a model farm on an extensive scale was needed to instruct the farming classes.
Murphy suggested the successful Templemoyle farm near Derry as a possible model. As
T.W. French said at a meeting on January 1850: 'no common farmer received
advantage from what any gentleman in his neighbourhood did, for he charged all the
benefits not to the amount of increased skill or attention, but to capital'. Viscount
Bernard expressed a robustly philistine view – with which Dublin Castle would not
necessarily disagree – that the proper business of expert and well-paid professors of
chemistry and agriculture was to test the soil and lay out the farm, otherwise their
appointment was anomalous. It was absurd to have Latin and Greek professors while
the agricultural population was allowed to starve! Real education was about drawing
from the soil the necessaries of life.

Murphy drew up the plans for the farm, and these were discussed with Kane, who
felt the school should provide both for the education of the working classes, to which
he attached great importance, and also 'for that of the Students of the College'. It
would also be a centre of agricultural instruction and information for 'the South of
Ireland'. A site was soon selected (bearing in mind the contemporary concern that
students should be shielded from the temptations of the city) at Inchigaggin,[52] despite
worries about winter flooding. St John Jefferyes on behalf of the committee assured the
attendance at the Kane banquet in April 1850[53] that all the omens looked favourable for
the school and there was a reasonable expectation of 'means of affording a sound,
practical agricultural education to at least 50 youths of the middle classes'.

It was arranged that Murphy should be resident in a house at nearby Ballygaggin.
Plans for school structures and finance proceeded, and proposals for scholarships to
fund suitable young men were sent to the lord lieutenant's office. Local help was
solicited but the appeal for subscriptions proved disappointing. However, the
cultivation of the farm went ahead, seeds were sown and shrubs planted. In this
connection, help was forthcoming from the botanic gardens at Glasnevin and at
TCD and from the Dublin Agricultural Museum. Five hundred admission cards
were printed for visitors. Professor Murphy's own students were being instructed
on the farm in the 1850–51 session, but there was something of a crisis of financial
confidence in the spring of 1851. There were fears of not qualifying for the £5,000
balance; the Treasury wanted more subscriptions to be raised but potential
subscribers were afraid that the farm would not be 'kept up'.

3.3 The Model Farm School in the 1880s.

Further details on the school are given in 'Agricultural School for Munster' where published plans include an informative sketch map of the school and model farm.[54] In an appeal for funds, the 'self-evident' advantages of such a school are spelt out:

> As a nursery for the training of scientific and practical farmers, gardeners and foresters, it will be invaluable. The experiments with manure, and on various modes of cultures, conducted under the guidance of the Professors of Agriculture and Chemistry, cannot fail to impress in the minds of the pupils, the principles of correct practice – whilst the arrangement of trees, shrubs and plants, correctly named and classified, will, it is confidently hoped, materially promote a taste for Natural History. The more important breeds of cattle, sheep and swine, being maintained pure, will be obtained by farmers, on reasonable terms. Nor will the advantages of instruction be confined to the resident pupils – intelligent farmers, who may visit the Model Farm, and who will have access to the simple system of Agricultural book-keeping there adopted, will obtain a large amount of valuable information, and the students in the agricultural class of Queen's College, will be here rendered familiar with the details of practical husbandry, for which no amount of theoretical teaching can ever prove a sufficient substitute.

The Munster Institute or 'Model Farm' came into being in 1853. The project was abandoned for a time but was revived in 1880, and a committee under QCC president, W.K. Sullivan, took over management of the farm and the new dairy school, the first of its kind in the United Kingdom. One of the benefactors of the institute was the eighth Duke of Devonshire, whose family owned the site. (He was also the main sponsor of the Crawford Observatory.) The institute became a flourishing centre of research and learning in veterinary surgery, dairying, poultry, cheese-making and domestic economy.

The Farm Committee, initiated on college opening day in 1849, had about it the confident and exciting air of new beginnings. For many of those involved, there was a heightened consciousness, in the wake of the Famine, that agriculture was quite literally a matter of life or death. The enterprise also exemplified the quintessential QCC educational philosophy of 'useful knowledge', and for Sir Robert Kane personally it offered the opportunity to exploit the country's primary natural resource in accordance with his own views. It also showed a gratifying solidarity of town and country interests with the college. Above all, it marked the first stage of a college commitment to the scientific promotion of agriculture and dairying. Over the years, research in this area has reflected and contributed to changes in the regional and national economy and today it is spectacularly successful.

The 'Litera'

The college's first year was a honeymoon period for town–gown relations, as the citizens of scholarly interests expressed their expectations of the new institution. Of particular significance in this connection was a letter to the president and council of QCC from 'the President and Council of the Cork Scientific and Literary Society', a society which survives today as the doyen of Cork's scholarly bodies.[55] Affectionately referred to in Cork parlance as 'the Litera', it still observes the meeting times of 150 years ago: 'every Thursday evening in the Session which period commences the first week of October and terminating the last week of April in each year'. The letter, or memorial, explained that the members were largely business or professional people who could not pursue their (mostly) scientific interests by day 'but who perceive the value of even the slight popular knowledge obtained [at the society's meetings] and also for the benefit of the younger members of their families, both males and females'. The society was

> well aware of the advantages which many of the inhabitants of Cork and its vicinity have derived from attendance at the introductory lectures at last Session given in College, and feel that to those who could attend these, it partly supplied those utilities which the extended courses of popular lectures in The Cork Institution used formerly to afford.

Yet the college's 'intelligent and observant Board' (a little cajolery would do the society's cause no harm!) would be aware that many city residents could not enjoy 'the benefits of the College free lectures' because they simply could not afford to take the necessary time off from the day's business 'going there and returning home . . . in addition to the Lecture hours'. So, the society was now requesting the college authorities to allow 'those Professors whose subjects may be fitted for popular lectures or demonstrations, to deliver such in town occasionally at the meetings of the above Society', on the first Thursday of each month, it was suggested, 'from 8 to 10 o'clock'.

3.4 The city of Cork from Shanakiel.

The memorial concluded with another piece of flattery difficult to resist:

> That the Council of the Scientific Society know from beneficial experience that the College authorities are ready to afford to the public every Scientific and Literary facility which a judicious guardianship of the interests of education confided to their care, will permit; they are also assured of the anxiety of the Professors individually to promote the general spread of well-informed intelligences.

The society's council members who signed the memorial included prominent citizens like Thomas Crosbie, William Dowden, and Francis M. Jennings, who was involved in various college-linked activities at the time of its foundation. (The recurrence of the same names in various segments of the Cork scholarly circle underlines the inter-dependence, then as now, of all those involved in a small community of learning: *ar scáth a chéile a mhaireann na daoine*.)

The memorial illustrates the eagerness of interest in popular scientific knowledge at the time (members of the society would have attended the public lectures organised by the RDS in 1837 and given by, among others, Sir Robert Kane) and the confident expectation that the college (and individual professors) would respond to popular demand. The memorial also suggests that, while a form of free 'university extension' lecture was on offer in the Queen's College from the beginning, the attendance rate was limited by, *inter alia*, the fact that the college was, relatively speaking, quite a distance from town in terms of available transport. In the event, the College Council was reluctant to make a general commitment to the society, but gave its blessing to any professor willing to offer his services (CCM 29 Oct. 1850).

Since learned activities of town bodies such as the Cuvierian Society and the Royal Cork Institution had been among the antecedents of the college in the first place, it was appropriate that the college should help substantially to maintain the town–gown culture link. The active role played by college staff in the town's learned societies over the past 150 years has been particularly notable in the case of the offshoot of 'the Litera', the Cork Historical and Archaeological Society, founded in 1891.

The gaol: a new college entrance?

The proximity of the gaol was a problem for the college authorities from the beginning. And twenty-five years after the opening, the professors were complaining that the principal entrance to the college

> is by the road leading from the Western Road to the County Jail, and quite close to the latter and is in every way an unsuitable one. It also adds considerably to the distance of the College from the town and may, it is said, be closed up at any time by the authorities of the Jail.[56]

3.5 View of Cork County Gaol from Shanakiel c1840, prior to the erection of the Queen's College.

The general ambience of this entrance area was perceived as highly undesirable. Class squeamishness as well as concern over public order were frequently and frankly expressed by middle-class Victorians. At an early stage the college professed itself shocked by the spectacle of a public hanging on its doorstep. (Executions were held in public until the late 1860s.[57]) On 7 May 1850, the College Council adopted a resolution requesting the president to inform the lord lieutenant that on 24 April

> the Academical business of the Queen's College was suspended in consequence of a public Execution taking place at the Entrance of the College . . . and the Council consider it extremely detrimental to the character and interest of the College that the students and public should be exposed to contact with such scenes . . .

The council felt that the Board of Works should consider constructing 'a new approach' to the east of college which would not only obviate 'such a painful and shocking interruption to the Collegiate duties' but considerably shorten the distance from the city. The consciousness of excessive distance from town, surprising perhaps to modern ears, was frequently expressed by gown *and* town, and must be understood in terms of unsatisfactory vehicles and poor roads, as well as the psychological effect of the entrance being at the far western end of the college.

Kane, in a covering letter dated 13 May 1850, endorsed the council's views, adding that apart from the executions the gaol entrance to college was undesirable because 'certain classes connected with prisoners' were habitually loitering there. Doubtless Sir Robert might have added that this was particularly embarrassing on the occasion of visits by dignitaries, or on gala days such as the ceremonial opening in 1849.

The lord lieutenant's office forwarded the president's letter and the council resolution to the Board of Works, asking about the feasibility and cost of a new entrance, and whether funds were available.[58] The Board of Works's reply (17 June 1850) was that, at the time the college site was purchased, it had been contemplated that a new road linking the Western Road with the Old Macroom Road (now College Road), and with it of necessity a new bridge, would be built for better access to the college. Nothing had been done and the cost would be considerable, but perhaps a 'footbridge and causeway' (presumably from the Western Road) for the use of students could be constructed for £400. This apparently was Sir Thomas Deane's estimate, but the Board of Works had no money available. Mr Radcliffe, one of the commissioners of public works, had discussed the execution issue with the governor of the gaol, who said he intended to bring the matter to the attention of the gaol authorities with a view to changing the site of executions to the rear of the gaol, looking towards the Old Macroom Road.[59]

But there was no action on the issue, and the College Council sent another resolution to the lord lieutenant on 3 April 1851, with reference

> to the pending execution of female prisoners immediately adjacent to the entrance of the Queen's College . . . and the execution of the sentence thus in view of the College and the great crowd that would probably be collected on the occasion must both shock the students and greatly interfere with the proceedings of the College.

The council added that an execution site at the rear of the gaol would be satisfactory for the college and the populous Sunday's Well area.[60] Needless to say, a rear-of-gaol site would also be public, being viewable from the road there, but perhaps the denizens of that area were not expected to have such refined sensibilities. At any rate, the reply to the council's resolution said in effect that the lord lieutenant had no authority to interfere in the matter.[61] The gaol was a nuisance in other, if lesser, ways. For example, the prisoners had the ill-bred habit of gazing down through the dissecting room windows, so that in 1867 the professor of anatomy wanted shutters to be erected to shield professors, students and the dear departed from the vulgar gaze.[62]

But the college agitation for a new approach road had a rationale independent of the gaol problem. There was disappointment early on when the corporation turned down (January 1850) a request from the college for a footway from the Western Road, because the land was privately owned.[63] Professor D.B. Bullen was to the fore on the issue of building a new bridge and road to the college, in order to shorten the distance from town. On 20 April 1855, John Gordon, mayor of Cork, wrote to the lord chancellor enclosing a letter he had received from Bullen. The latter felt that the people of the city were no longer keenly interested in an institution which they (and he!) had worked so hard to found. (This lack of interest, or at least of support, certainly would be evident at the time of the 1862 fire.) Bullen felt that the lack of accessibility was the root cause of this apathy: 'The manner in which the Queen's College stands isolated from our local community has been most injurious to the interest of education in Cork and is a cause of profound regret to the professors'. The mayor, anxious to co-operate and to promote the project, enclosed a map drawn by a student called Fogerty under the direction of Professor Christopher B. Lane (civil engineering, 1849–53) in November 1850. This map sketched a proposed new road (from a bridge to be built opposite Mardyke Street), with a branch to the Protestant Cathedral and the Bishop's Palace, and continuing on to the college with the entrance behind the Quadrangle. Disappointingly, a note on the file simply said 'no funds available'.[64]

The proximity of the county gaol presented a new security hazard in the 1860s, as the Fenian agitation developed. In the context of the 1862 fire, Professor Bullen expressed fears about the consequences of political subversion.[65] In the aftermath of the Fenian rising of 1867, the college authorities were particularly worried about the security implications of the two institutions having a common wall. Vice-President Ryall wrote anxiously on 13 January 1868 to Under-Secretary Sir Thomas Larcom about the unprotected state of college property. College could easily be used for an attack on the gaol, and men had been seen acting suspiciously in the vicinity.[66] The College Council forwarded a resolution (14 January 1868) to Larcom, requesting that the college be included in any arrangements for the exterior defence of the gaol.[67] Connellan, the local magistrate, added his voice, urging Larcom to take extra precautions and stating he himself was taking measures, with the help of the constabulary, to 'guard against attempted outrage'.[68]

CHAPTER FOUR

A TROUBLED PRESIDENCY

'. . . disfigured by such a mass of personal altercation . . .
unhappy notoriety . . . acrimonious contention among a body of
learned men of mature years . . . '
                    1857–58 Commission report on QCC quarrels

Quarrels

IN 1853 THE PRESIDENT, Sir Robert Kane, sought guidance from Dublin Castle on a basic question:

> I had always considered the purchases [property, books etc.] as being made on the public account, with public money and the object bought to be the property of the Crown deposited in the College in charge of the proper officer for the use of the Professors . . . but still belonging to the public.

Professor Benjamin Alcock, whose quarrels with all and sundry were soon to lead to his enforced resignation, had claimed that specimens bought for his museum of anatomy belonged to the college and not to the state and had refused to sign a receipt for the state. Would items purchased under future parliamentary grants, Kane asked, be legally owned by the college or the state? The ruling of the Crown's legal adviser was that all apparatus, instruments and so on were Crown property, 'though intended for the benefit of the College'.[1]

As we shall shortly see, Alcock was at loggerheads with Kane but was only one of a number of professors with whom the president crossed swords. (Various combinations of disgruntled professors tended to emerge in support of any given colleague who was in the wars.) Bad relations with the academic staff bedevilled Kane's presidency, in particular during his first ten years. Highly personal and public in their manifestation, these clashes mainly turned on differences in interpretation of the statutes which Kane had been largely instrumental in forming and on which he regarded himself as the true authority.[2] Naturally enough, the professors' reading of their statutory rights was more flexible than that of their president, whose double jobbing and lengthy absences, in their view, diminished the moral force of his pronouncements. Part personality clash, part legal wrangle, part power struggle, these internal disputes were fought out in the public press, before the visitors, and finally before a royal commission. They made QCC's early years extremely turbulent.

One of the earliest[3] of these disputes concerned Owen Connellan, the professor of Celtic languages and literature, 1849–63.[4] Connellan complained that Celtic courses were cramped by restrictions (for example, Celtic could not be taken to degree level) and by a lack of prizes and scholarships.[5] For whatever reasons, the numbers taking Celtic until its abolition as 'practically useless'[6] in 1862–63 were risibly few. They increased only a little in the late 1850s and early 1860s, but in the first seven years the registration read, respectively, 0, 1, 2, 1, 2, 1, 0.[7] Compared to these non-figures, the honours Greek classes of the writer's student days were overcrowded.

Connellan submitted his resignation in January 1851 on health grounds, since the delivery of public lectures (held to be an indispensable part of his duties) would 'incur the risk of injuring my health and by promoting a nervous affliction . . . probably endanger my life'.[8] It was hardly surprising that Connellan should not have relished the prospect of facing even a moderate crowd. On 13 February 1851 he withdrew the resignation[9] whereupon Kane tartly informed Sir T.K. Redington that 'Mr Connellan has never discharged any professional duties whatsoever since his appointment', despite being given a year off for ill-health. And Kane emphasised that only the introductory lectures of the first week were required to be given in public 'for the benefit of the College'. What was involved in Connellan's withdrawal of resignation was a crucial issue, since he was being supported by two or three other professors who, according to Kane,

> hold peculiar opinions with regard to their statutory obligations. Their views, so far as they have been discussed in my presence are: that the College has nothing to do with the public but is a Corporation which should be administered only for the private benefit of the individuals composing it; . . . that he [Connellan] is not bound to take any pains to form a class and that if his position falls into the position of a sinecure he is not to be in any way responsible or bound to take any steps to prevent it from so doing.[10]

Kane's opinion of apologists for ivory-tower sinecures is very clear. Connellan's backers – Professsors Alcock, R. Horner Mills, and George Sidney Read (logic and metaphysics, 1849–83) – in asking for Connellan's restoration, informed the lord lieutenant on 11 March 1851 that he was willing after all to give the introductory lectures in public. They insisted that this was a voluntary function and not a statutory duty, and they denied they viewed college only as a private corporation.[11] After further representations and promises from Connellan, the lord lieutenant accepted the withdrawal of the resignation.[12] Though the 1857–58 Commission recommended the abolition of the Celtic chairs in the Queen's Colleges, Connellan remained in what was effectively a sinecure until his retirement in 1862–63.

The Connellan controversy intensified the atmosphere of academic hostility to Kane.[13] Hard on its heels came the Lane row. This concerned Professor Christopher B. Lane of civil engineering, a supporter of Connellan who was viewed by Kane as defending the 'sinecure' interpretation. On 7 February 1852 Kane sent to the lord lieutenant a 'Statement of Circumstances of Neglect of Duty and Inattention to official Remonstrance upon the part of Christopher B. Lane'.[14] The president's charge was that the professor had failed to give his students adequate field work and practical instruction. (Kane's own emphasis on applied science would help to explain his concern.) Sides were quickly taken. The science division of the arts faculty adopted a motion proposed by Boole, which supported Lane's view 'that field practice to some extent is a necessary part of instruction but chiefly so in order to illustrate the principles which the student has learned in class lectures'.[15] Moreover, Lane was a minimalist in interpreting his work obligations and he maintained he was not getting paid for field instructions! Despite faculty support, the dean, Professor Edmund Murphy of agriculture (1849–68), took an anti-Lane stance at the College Council meeting for which he was censured by his science colleagues.[16] Meanwhile, what made Lane's offence worse in Kane's eyes was that the Queen's University would not admit students to diplomas in engineering or agriculture if they had not received practical instruction.

The nub of the statutory position was that Lane rejected the president's right to interfere in the educational concerns of departments (though conceding the council's authority in this area), while Kane charged Lane with violating the rights of students and the public, and neglecting his statutory duties.[17] As the stand-off continued, Lane was asked by Sir Thomas Redington to reply to the president's allegations. He did so in detail, spiritedly and quite plausibly claiming that, although 'a few occasional excursions are desirable', the important thing was to teach students scientific principles of surveying during their time in college: it was impossible in a short course to make them expert practical surveyors. Lane also accused Sir Robert of exceeding his constitutional authority as president.[18]

The fact that Lane's reply was in the form of a printed (and public) memorial (dated 28 February 1852) was seen as further proof of his recalcitrance. Finally Dublin Castle starkly ordered him to obey the president and council or resign.[19] After some stalling,[20] Lane agreed to give the practical instruction required. The president saw the outcome as having satisfactorily established 'the valid responsibility of Professors'.[21] It was, however, a Pyrrhic victory for Kane since it further exacerbated his relations with the staff. Lane, in the end, resigned on 9 April 1853,[22] shaking the dust of QCC off his feet with finality and taking up a new post as far away as Brazil, where he discovered various minerals and reputedly became very wealthy.

Even as Kane exulted in May 1852 in the lesson taught to Lane, the science professors were in open revolt against the president. They appealed to the triennial visitation against Kane's action in cancelling minutes of certain faculty meetings, as having been held without satisfying conditions required by statute. While the visitors ruled that the charter required the president's permission for such meetings, which were in consequence void, nevertheless they obviously felt Kane had gone too far in not making 'some entry or memorandum' instead of complete erasure.[23]

Meanwhile the most acrimonious dispute to date was under way. It was also the most complex in that Professor Alcock's quarrels were conducted on various fronts and his eventual dismissal was the result of his alienation from virtually all parties.

He had been appointed professor of anatomy and physiology in QCC in September 1849. The combined chair gave rise to difficulties in terms of acceptance of certificates of attendance by the Royal College of Surgeons. To meet the situation the college appointed a demonstrator in practical anatomy.[24] Alcock complained that the president and council had prevented him from conducting courses in practical anatomy, had imposed a demonstrator against his will and in general were usurping the Crown's prerogatives. The president, he claimed, had failed to supply him with extra staff and had even withdrawn the porter from the practical anatomy course, and 'students were compelled to light with their own hands the fires of their class rooms'.[25] At a later stage, after a series of departmental thefts, he had asked for a new porter, which made him an object of enmity amongst the servants of college.[26] Moreover, he asked the council to take disciplinary action against the registrar, Francis Albani, for allegedly failing to inform him (as was the registrar's statutory duty) of the holding of a college meeting.[27] He complained throughout about his financial position with regard to entitlement to fees.

The president pulled no punches about Alcock, referring to his 'temper', 'rude interference with Colleagues' and 'very violent' conduct. He had, said Kane, incited the medical students against president and council, 'placarded' an inflammatory notice to his class, urging them to defend their rights against the college authorities.[28] However, the visitors in May 1852 upheld Alcock's case against the president and council, at least in respect of entitlement to fees.[29]

A very serious situation developed when there was a shortage of bodies supplied from the poor house for dissection at QCC. This sad necessity was a controversial, not to say a squalid and slightly illegal, business at the best of times, causing much public unease (Professor Bullen referred to 'the several occasions the populace in Cork have attacked dissecting rooms'[30]). The shortage of supply in 1852–53, causing some students to leave, was blamed on Alcock's attitude and on his refusal to pay the money demanded by the poor house.[31]

Sir John Young in Dublin Castle was exasperated by Alcock – 'a perfect pest',[32] 'Ecce Aeternum – Alcock!!! Another misunderstanding!'[33] The professor himself protested his innocence, and his suffering: 'my classes have been injured – my time wasted – and my health broken'.[34] Nonetheless, Dublin Castle was the ultimate authority and, as happened throughout the history of the Queen's Colleges, it did not hesitate to apply the axe to the neck of a professor it regarded as impossibly recalcitrant. By December 1853, the college dissecting rooms were still without bodies, and Alcock was informed by Dublin Castle:

> the difficulties which exist at Cork are caused by yourself and originate in the unhappy infirmities of your temper. . . . and his Excellency cannot think your remaining in the College beneficial . . . [he] requests you to send in your resignation. . . . otherwise it will become his painful duty to recommend your formal removal.[35]

Alcock tried to defend himself, but in vain. He was forced to resign in February 1854 though he continued to plead his innocence to the lord lieutenant, asking him for some other appointment.[36] He also fired a parting shot against the President:

That Her Majesty's statute has been repeatedly violated by the President of the College, Sir Robert Kane MD FRS, preferring grave charges against me to her Majesty and her executive, without communicating them to me, and my appeals were disregarded.[37]

Explaining the absence of presidential reports for 1853–54 and 1854–55, Kane explained that 'a very serious legal question' was raised in March 1853 about his power as president to make such reports.[38] He was referring to the rapid deterioration of relations between president and council and in particular to the memorial sent to the Crown by the council, signed by the chairman, Vice-President John Ryall, on 4 March 1853.[39] This memorial was tantamount to an impeachment of Kane. It was adopted by a council meeting held while Kane was in Dublin, a procedure subsequently condemned by the 1857–58 Commission which found Vice-President Ryall's behaviour 'quite inexcusable'. Professor J.R. Harvey (midwifery, 1849–78), was also culpable according to Kane.[40]

The College Council accused Kane of negligence because of his protracted absences, and of dictatorial intervention when in residence. (A letter – from Kane to the council, 28 February 1853 – deemed to be threatening, was included with the 4 March memorial.) Kane was accused, in effect, of double standards, insisting on rigid compliance by the professors with the statutes while he permitted himself flexibility and mobility. The president's defence was that the government knew from the beginning that his directorship of the Museum of Irish Industry would necessitate absences from Cork. He also claimed that he had to act authoritatively at various times because of the council's fractious opposition, and the wilfulness of professors in interpreting the statutes to please themselves.

During the dispute Kane refused to attend council meetings and alleged 'violent and insulting letters' had been sent to him by some professors, who denied the charges.[41] Home Secretary Lord Palmerston was informed that, overall, the legal advisers tended to favour Kane's account of events but that 'the warmth of expression and unfortunate tone which pervade the correspondence on all sides afford indeed a matter for regret'.[42] The second half of 1853 saw some improvement in relations between Kane and his opponents, helped by behind-the-scenes negotiations. On 3 December 1853 the council resolved that memorials be withdrawn all round in order to lower personality confrontation and so allow the government to devote much-needed attention to the disputed statutes.[43]

Since students had no inhibitions about complaining to visitors, a surprising feature of these years was their tolerance of the irresponsible behaviour of the staff, which must have been to the detriment of study and scholarship. At any rate, three professors – Hincks, Nicol and Lane – took their departure in 1853;[44] by 1865, nearly half the original professors had resigned or been dismissed.

4.1 George Boole, first professor of mathematics, QCC, 1849-64.

Kane versus Boole

The bitterest college quarrel of the 1850s, that between the president and George Boole, was aggravated by the eminence of both men and by the glare of publicity. Boole was active on the administrative side of college affairs, serving at different periods on the library committee and as dean of science. His singular absence from the public banquet in Kane's honour (8 April 1850) may have been a sign of an early rift between the two men.[45] The president's precipitate action against Raymond de Vericour would not have pleased Boole: apart from the issue involved, the professor of modern languages was an old friend and at one period the two had shared lodgings at 5 Grenville Place, Cork. In the Lane affair, it was Boole who proposed the faculty motion endorsing Lane's viewpoint, and this must have annoyed Kane. Boole also got caught up, as dean, in the Alcock controversy and there was a confrontation at the visitors' inquiry (May 1852) between him and the president over the faculty's attitude to the College Council. By now Boole was clearly identified with Kane's opponents, and of significance here was his close friendship with Vice-President Ryall to whom he dedicated his *Laws of Thought*, published in 1853. The friendship was intensified by Boole's marriage to Mary Everest, Ryall's niece. As a 'faculty wife', Mary's comments are revealing:

> The affairs of the College had been in a very uncomfortable condition and the maladministration and general misdoings of the authorities formed, as I have observed in my visits there, the stock subject of conversation among the professors and not one conducive to health or harmony.[46]

Kane's frequent absences and Ryall's influential presence aggravated tensions between president and vice-president. As for differences between Boole and Kane, they took a personal turn for the worse when Kane implied that Boole in his teaching was neglecting the elements of geometry. Boole resented Kane's intrusion into his departmental business: besides, the criticism stung him. In December 1855, because of his disapproval of Kane's conduct and policy, he declined to sign a memorial inviting the president, among others, to a dinner in college.[47] In November 1856 the quarrel found explosive expression in rancorous public correspondence which scandalously entertained the citizens but which was a sad reflection on QCC's leading academics.

This started with a letter from Kane (addressed, tellingly, from Dublin) to *The Cork Examiner* (7 November 1856) by way of answer to recent criticisms of his administration voiced by Dr D.C. O'Connor (medicine, 1849–88), dean of the medical faculty. The *Cork Daily Reporter* had also blamed Kane for the fewness of public lectures delivered under university auspices in Cork and for devoting his time to his more favoured institution in Dublin.[48] Kane claimed that he had inspected departments and consulted with professors before returning to Dublin a week after the beginning of the session. The college had never suffered any damage, he claimed, because of his absence in Dublin.

This was too much for Boole. As one who regarded himself as an exile in an outpost of the empire, he must have personally resented Kane's absenteeism: if Boole had to stick it out in Cork, so, *a fortiori*, should the president of the college. In close association with Ryall, Boole went on the offensive in a long letter to the *Cork Daily Reporter* (10 November 1856), signing himself 'A Professor' but enclosing his name and address. The reason for this half-hearted anonymity is not clear, and it certainly did not deceive Kane. Boole attacked the president for a snide implication that Vice-President Ryall's long vacation had imposed additional work on Kane. Then he went straight to the heart of the matter, as he saw it – Kane's 'habitual absence' from the college and the consequent neglect of areas for which he was solely responsible, in particular the control of college servants and porters. Rooms were less than clean, and 'disorders, connected with the presence of a most unfortunate family in charge of the College' had become intolerable. In general, university growth was stunted: 'Scholarships and bounties may preserve in it a languid existence, but that is all'.

Kane's response – this time from QCC – on 18 November to *The Cork Examiner* makes it clear that he had no doubts about his assailant's identity. He claims that he had saved Boole 'the mortification of formal censure' at a time 'when his neglect of Professorial duty had seriously compromised the interests of our students and the character of the College'. Kane then went on to rebut Boole's charges but digressed into a bitter attack on Vice-President Ryall for manipulating a council caucus into composing a memorial, publicly and widely circulated, full of 'misstatements and exaggerations', and 'accusing the President of the abuse of power and the neglect of duty'. Kane concluded that, while QCC was successful due to the zeal and co-operation of the professors, 'the only department of the College in which students have been found to fail' was Boole's own.

The tone of Kane's letter suggests a desperate awareness that the case he was making for his double appointment was untenable, causing him to overcompensate by bludgeoning his opponents. Boole now responded in the *Cork Daily Reporter*, convincingly refuting Kane's attack on his academic competence. Moreover, he developed his argument that Kane's 'maladministration' was 'a very important cause' of the college's troubles:

> The time, thought, and energy that have been expended in quarrels between him and the Professors – in enforcing Presidential rights Sir Robert Kane would perhaps say, in resisting despotism and oppression, others might say; but I prefer an unexceptionable word and say, quarrels – the time, thought, and energy thus expended would have suf-ficed to establish the College in a far higher and securer position than it now occupies. Add to this the loss of *esprit de corps*, of proper Academic feeling, of united, cordial and generous supervision over discipline and morals, and the amount of injury for which Sir Robert Kane is, in my opinion, in a very serious degree accountable, cannot be esteemed slight.[49]

The 1857–58 commission

At the conclusion of his letter, Boole called for a government inquiry and the government indeed had decided that it was time to inspect the dirty linen indoors. There was now established a 'Royal Commission to inquire into the Progress and Condition of the Queen's Colleges at Belfast, Cork and Galway'.[50] It looked searchingly at the Cork situation, as well as comprehensively reviewing a ten-year-old experiment. Boole, Kane and others (Bullen, for example, spoke of friction with the president) gave evidence before the commission. Boole claimed the college was suffering from the president's continued absence, and from the lack of any defined authority, and this had a deleterious effect on student morale. Kane attempted to justify his absence from Cork by saying he was serving the college's interests in attending Queen's University Senate meetings held in Dublin. This was hardly a plausible point, given the infrequency of these meetings. Even more unconvincing was his argument that permanent residence in Cork would create an embarrassing situation for the professor of chemistry (John Blyth, 1849–72) because Kane would be research-ing in that area. It may well be that Kane's absenteeism was also escapism, that is, a respite from the complex administrative and human problems of the presidency. Particularly depressing was the government's failure to meet the challenge of chron-ically inadequate accommodation.

Kane conceded that Boole's newspaper letters were written from high motives, and the president also paid surprising tribute to Boole's diligent discharge of his duties and to his eminence as a mathematician. Furthermore, Kane admitted that the wife and daughter of the head porter might be described as an 'unsuitable family' and that it was inappropriate to have a 'dressy fifteen-year-old girl' in the cloisters of an all-male establishment.

In terms, then, of a confrontation between Kane and Boole, the president seemed to be backing down but the commission berated both men for resorting to the public press and thereby giving their differences an 'unhappy notoriety'. The commissioners also regretted the negligence of government in not intervening earlier in the controversy. They lamented that the Cork college should be 'disfigured by such a mass of personal altercation', in contrast to the good relations prevailing in the academic communities in Belfast and Galway.

The College Council was condemned for its March 1853 memorial to the Crown complaining of Kane's conduct. The vice-president, in particular, was 'highly blamable' and his conduct 'quite inexcusable'. Though the commissioners' report 'entirely disapproved' of Boole writing to the press to attack the president, there were nonetheless 'circumstances of mitigation'. The report distributed blame all round, finding it deplorable that 'since October 1854, no amicable discourse appears to have existed between the President and the Vice-President'. The former's conduct in resorting to the public press was 'particularly inexcusable'. Had he resided in Cork, personally discharging his college duties and 'kindly offices' to his colleagues (just as important as 'mere administrative duties'), then 'these calamitous occurrences . . . could never have arisen'.

On the central issue of residence, the commissioners' report was unambiguous. They totally rejected Kane's 'view of non-continuous residence': 'We therefore consider that residence should be a condition of holding the office of President, and residence in the sense that the College shall be the President's home'. Only thus could the president properly oversee the workings of the various departments and their harmonious intercourse; 'guide, exhort and advise the students'; assess 'the Academical wants of the Province'; and 'take a leading position in the society of the great town in which the College is situated'. In short, Kane's non-residence was a serious bar to the progress and well-being of the college.

After the commission had declared it was imperative that presidents should reside in the colleges, Kane assured the chief secretary (letter of 13 September 1858) that 'it is my intention to make the College my home during the College session'.[51] But this promise was hugely qualified by the statement that he would still have to spend time in Dublin, especially in the last term because of the requirements of his directorship of the Museum of Irish Industry. Thus the problem of presidential absenteeism was never really solved, despite the firm language of the 1857–58 Commission, and it raised its head again notoriously in end-of-the-century presidencies.

The *Evening Post* (27 July 1858) was caustic about the reasons Kane had given for his non-residence:

> Some of them are so puerile as to excite a smile at the simplicity of this learned gentleman. Others are so extraordinary and so suggestive that they cannot fail to excite the interest of our readers . . . strangest of all [the reasons given is that] because if he lived in the College no clergyman of his church would visit his family inasmuch as that institution is under the interdict of the Pope.[52]

It is hardly surprising that after the buffeting storms of the 1850s Kane should have been investigating the possibilities of retirement in 1860, though in the end the financial conditions on offer were not sufficiently enticing. After the 1857–58 commission's report, he was asked by the Lords of the Committee of Council for Education to choose finally between the two roles he had attempted to fill since 1849, or indeed since late 1845 when he had begun planning the shape of the Queen's Colleges.

Writing to Under-Secretary Larcom on 28 July 1860, Kane asserted his first interest was in the Museum of Irish Industry and implied that he had agreed to take the QCC post only out of a sense of public duty. He claimed he had given up a substantial professional practice with potentially lucrative contacts, as well as academic positions, in order to serve the government in Cork. In all these circumstances, before making a decision, he wished to know what retirement pension he would get from the presidency. The chief secretary was sympathetic to Kane's position, making a favourable case on his behalf to the Treasury in London, which however gave the unsympathetic civil service response that Kane would get no compensation on departing from Cork: after all, he would still hold a government-funded office, he was still under sixty years, and the retirement would not be a saving since the position of president would still have to be filled.[53]

And so Sir Robert Kane stayed on as president even though the strong-minded Lady Kane wished to live permanently in Dublin. After 1860 the pressure on Kane to resign one of his offices appears to have eased. Nevertheless, rumours about his impending resignation continued to circulate, particularly at the time of the 1862 fire. *The Cork Examiner* (26 April 1864) reprinted a 'Cork Correspondent's' article in *The Freeman's Journal* which claimed that, despite the chief secretary's denial, 'people here' had no doubt it was 'a mere matter of time'. Speculation as to his successor centred on two QCC personalities, Vice-President Ryall and Professor O'Connor of the medicine department, and on President Berwick of QCG. However, the speculation was premature by almost a decade.

On the thorny religious issue, the 1857–58 commissioners consoled themselves that since the opening of the colleges there was no evidence of interference with the religion of any student: that being so, they hoped that Catholic Church hostility to the colleges would in time diminish, when

> experience proves that the duties of religion can be attended to without raising up barriers of exclusiveness at the entrance of life between those who will have to spend their lives together as citizens of a common country. . . . We believe that the Colleges are calculated to soften feelings of party antagonism and sectarian animosity. . . . and that they are rapidly generating a feeling of local self-reliance and self-respect and exciting an interest in . . . literature and science throughout the community at large.

The commissioners were satisfied that Professor de Vericour had removed any reasons for dissatisfaction, and expressed their 'warm approbation' that the professors in general had carefully avoided giving any religious offence. They also noted Kane's assurance that not a single student had complained on this score since the college opened. They made the interesting comment that students did not take deans of residence (there were no Roman Catholic deans at this stage) seriously because 'as these services were not worth being paid for, they were not worth being attended to'.

Notwithstanding the commissioners' pious hopes for a softening of Catholic Church attitudes, the harsh fact was that, if anything, positions had hardened. Kane's impassioned exasperation with the ecclesiastical intransigents was expressed in an 1859 prize-giving speech in which he denounced their uncompromising mentality. Perhaps, he sarcastically commented, 'those aspirations after an ideal monastic perfection' might be entitled to some consideration

> if we had not to deal with the practical realities of professional and business life; if we did not live in communities of mixed and often jarring interests and ideas; . . . if we had not before us our country torn asunder and paralysed for centuries by the hatreds and antagonisms of religious feuds . . . But . . . it is incumbent on us as Roman Catholics to make use of and improve what is practically at hand; to appropriate the substance rather than risk its loss, by clutching after a shadowy ideal, a splendid phantom. Such has been, after ten years' experience, the verdict of the Roman Catholic laity of this province.[54]

In the same year, Archbishop Cullen showed how unbridgeable the ultramontane–liberal gap was when he once again outlined the Catholic agenda. After ten years, in his view, the Queen's Colleges in Cork and Galway had been 'a complete failure, and have entailed an enormous expenditure on the Country without any good result'. It was time to reconstruct or suppress them altogether. 'Catholics will never cease to oppose the system on which they are founded.'[55]

Despite the various difficulties experienced, the commissioners expressed 'unqualified satisfaction' with the 'Educational Progress of the Colleges'. 'Although but a short time in operation, they have distinguished themselves in those public contests in which even the most distinguished students of the old Universities are proud of success.' And the commissioners applauded the success of Cork students in securing 'the most important appointments that are disposed of in these countries – the Writerships in the East India Company's Service'. QCC authorities throughout its history made much of its graduates' achievements in the colonial public service, particularly in the areas of medicine and engineering.

A progress report

The 1857–58 commission report – an important progress report on the first decade of the Queen's Colleges – ranged far and wide in its comments and offered optimistic observations wherever the situation was palpably gloomy.[56] The report suggested various answers to the central criticism that the Cork and Galway colleges were expensive failures. It was unfortunate, for example, that at the time of the colleges' foundation, conditions were not favourable:

> When the Colleges were opened the country had hardly recovered from the effects of the terrible calamity of famine, which crippled the means of an important proportion of both the higher and middle classes of the Irish people, and also, temporarily at least, changed the social circumstances of the country.

(The sufferings of the lower orders were not the commissioners' priority.)

The commissioners were compelled to admit that one important reason for disappointing progress was the colleges' lack of prestige and the low market-value of their degrees and diplomas, where qualifications from Trinity College Dublin, for example, were perceived to have social status as well as academic worth. The colleges presented no competitive threat to Trinity, as far as the sons of the gentry and of professional men were concerned. Trinity's advantages impeded the growth of the Queen's Colleges, and much of the time this meant Cork, since QCB was sturdily successful (its ethos being quite acceptable to the majority population of its catchment area) and QCG was struggling for survival in any case. Since the colleges offered no divinity education, aspirants to the Church of Ireland ministry naturally went to Trinity. More generally, students who might otherwise have gone to QCC were attracted by Trinity's non-residence regulation: all the necessary terms could be kept by examination alone. For example, in 1851–52 when the total Queen's Colleges' student population was only 411, half of Trinity's 1,200 undergraduates did not reside in Dublin or its neighbourhood. In general, it would take the Queen's Colleges considerable time to acquire prestige and a reputation.

Notwithstanding Thomas Wyse's emphasis in 1838 on the need for 'county academies', the lack of an intermediate or secondary system (not supplied until 1878 and after) was undoubtedly a serious obstacle to the progress of third-level education, and this was an oft-repeated contemporary observation. It was to Trinity's advantage that there were close links between endowed schools and that college. However, there were wider social factors at work outside the commissioners' terms of reference. Despite the clamorous demand of the 1830s and 1840s for provincial colleges, middle-class Catholics did not rush to take up the offer when it became available.[57] Apart from the religious dimension, university education was not seen by many of them as a pressing necessity for their material advancement. Nor were the universities in any way central to economic development. Businessmen then and thereafter showed little interest in commercial courses in the groves of academe. Academic agricultural courses, for example, were theoretical and dilettantish, and at best availed of by small numbers of prospective estate managers, in the shape of sons of gentry and large farmers: more practical agricultural education was available elsewhere. The 1857–58 commissioners recommended the abolition of the agricultural chairs: this was put into effect in the new 1863 charters, and the department of agriculture ceased to exist in QCC when its first head, Professor Edmund Murphy, died in 1868.[58]

4.2 Photograph presented by three engineering graduates of QCC, to Professor Jack. Annotation on back reads 'To Alex. Jack Esq., with C. J. Burke's kind regards and best wishes Aug. 29th 1868'.

Low student numbers were also due to the absence of a requirement, in some areas, of a university qualification for professional practice. Law lectures were attended by only a sprinkling of professional students, since there were few advantages in doing so: the reduction of the solicitor's apprenticeship period from five to four years was hardly a major incentive, as the 1857–58 commissioners noted. On the other hand, arts students took law as a general education subject.

Medicine and engineering were relatively flourishing areas, particularly in QCC. Engineering responded to various building and construction developments in imperial parts like India and to the demands of the new railway age at home, which coincided with the early years of the colleges. The great majority of engineering students taking the three-year course were in Cork, reaching a peak of forty-eight in 1863–64, whereas the numbers in Belfast and Galway remained in the ten to fifteen range. As for medicine, then as now, the prospects it held out of generous monetary rewards and social esteem attracted substantial numbers of students. Such was the case in pre-college Cork and continued to be so after 1849. Professional ambition was much too powerful to be frightened off by ecclesiastical disapproval. As early as 1854–55, there were more students in medicine than in arts. By the end of the nineteenth century, the QCC medical school was second only to QCB in medical graduate output.[59] (The lack of adequate medical accommodation was noted by the 1857–58 Commission which recommended new medical buildings as essential for QCC.) The association of the skull-and-crossbones symbol with the college shows how medicine came to dominate the other disciplines at QCC.[60]

Competition for scholarships in arts declined at Cork and Galway. By 1876, scholarships were there for the taking by all attaining a certain examination standard! Not surprisingly, this situation provoked Catholic taunts that students were being bribed to attend the Queen's Colleges. But certain standards prevailed: over the 1871–76 period, fifty-seven scholarships at Cork were withheld because of lack of merit.[61]

Though Sir Robert Kane was insistent that the success of the Queen's Colleges was not to be judged by the small proportion of students who graduated, nevertheless he must have been concerned by the situation.[62] In fact, there were two separate causes for anxiety: the low attendances and the small numbers graduating from the Queen's University. Over the 1851–56 period, only 208 degrees and diplomas were awarded (more than half of them to QCB students), even though a total of 734 matriculated students had entered the colleges for the corresponding undergraduate years. The degree failure rate (14 per cent) was fairly low, so why did so many students simply not bother to graduate, or even to matriculate? (The number of part-time non-matriculated students was large: the General Medical Council was concerned at the low level of matriculation in Cork and Galway in 1857–58, and most medical schools required no matriculation.[63])

Students left the colleges without graduating for a variety of reasons – family circumstances, taking up appointments in the public services or in commercial life, lack of staying power, or the severity of a particular course. Sitting for the degree examination was a big commitment, involving an expensive and troublesome three-weeks visit to Dublin. But the principal reason for non-graduation was the low value and status of Queen's University qualifications, as has been already mentioned. Medical students got their licences not from the Queen's University but from medical and surgical corporations which acted as examining bodies and whose requirements were not very rigid. This was the common pattern in the United Kingdom. Students could become members of the Royal College of Surgeons, England by studying for three years in a Queen's College and doing a single examination in London. They were thereby qualified not only to become dispensary doctors in Ireland but for work in the army and navy, and in the Indian medical services. A Queen's University medical degree did not give them this entrée, which was an anomaly that concerned the 1857–58 commission and on which it recommended reform. Moody and Beckett sum up the position succinctly: 'It was Queen's Colleges education, not Queen's University degrees that mattered to them [medical students]'.[64] In general, then, it was a major disincentive both to student recruitment and to the pursuit of degrees in the Queen's University that graduation even in the professional schools was not an essential qualification for professional employment.

The 1857–58 report depicted poor conditions and low morale in the QCC medical school:

> It has been stated the students hold the opinion that the Clinical Instruction is uncertain and defective; and one of the Medical Staff . . . stated the attendance of the students is occasionally very irregular, as sometimes they did not come for half an hour, or three quarters of an hour after the appointed time, and sometimes not at all.

The report called for this 'very unsatisfactory state of things' to be rectified. It also noted that 'the Medical School has increased so much latterly that it [the Clarendon Building] does not suffice for the convenient accommodation of the students. The Theatre also is stated to be injurious to their health'.

The commission dealt with a number of other college matters. In response to a complaint from the science division of the arts faculty that it had only the same representation on the College Council as the law faculty (which was 'of comparatively inferior importance'), the commission recommended that the literary division of the arts faculty combined with law should elect two members to serve on the council for two years (one of these to retire annually), that the science division should similarly elect two members, and medicine one. All retiring members were eligible for re-election.

The commission felt that the president–council balance had worked well in the colleges. Though the presidents of Belfast and Galway believed their office tended to have 'despotic power', because the presidential signature was necessary for a council resolution to become effective, Sir Robert Kane did not think this requirement conferred on him an 'absolute power of veto'. (The issue was to become very contentious in President Slattery's time.) At any rate, the commission recommended no change here.

The commissioners' report also referred to the Committee of Discipline set up in QCC by the College Council. The committee, which included Alexander Jack (engineering) and Alexander Fleming, complained that the existing rules did not provide for supervision of student behaviour beyond the college grounds (a vexed question in the student disturbances of 1884), and that there was no mechanism whereby an officer or professor could impose an on-the-spot fine. The commission recommended that a system be introduced of assigning every student for supervision to a professor, and that professors be given the power of fining students up to ten shillings for such offences as riotous or disorderly behaviour, smoking, neglect of college notices, and absence from class.

The commissioners gave some attention to the matter of student lodgings. The average total cost of board and lodgings for an academic year (three terms) was only £22–23 in Belfast and, inexplicably, almost double that (£42) in Cork and Galway. This was 'much beyond the means of the large majority of the class from which the students came'. The report referred to this as the 'middle class', not in the affluent connotation it would have today but in the almost opposite sense of a segment of society with access for the first time to a hitherto exclusive upper-class privilege. The commissioners noted that:

> in Cork, the President states that none but persons of a rather inferior class have ever proposed to keep Boarding houses, and that in several instances gentlemen who visited the College, for the purpose of seeing where they could place their sons, on finding that no suitable lodgings were to be had in Cork, were reluctantly obliged to send them elsewhere; and he considers the establishment of Residences, where students of a respectable rank in life could be boarded and lodged to be of the most essential importance towards the further success of the Cork College.

Presidents Sullivan (1873–90) and Windle (1904–19) were to share Kane's views on the desirability of halls of residence, and to see them realised to some extent.

The commissioners noted the parlous state of Celtic in the colleges and the fact that it attracted few students or none. In QCC, during the commission's inquiries, only one student was taking the subject. Since the college opened, there had never been more than two students of Celtic in any session. The QCC and QCG professors tended to put the blame on the lack of scholarships or adequate prizes but the commissioners were pessimistically inclined to write the subject off. In their opinion, the chairs were 'practically useless' and did not justify their existence: the professors would be better employed, at higher salaries, doing antiquarian research under Royal Irish Academy auspices, or otherwise.

In his evidence, Kane had agreed that the chair of Celtic was not, strictly speaking, necessary but he considered 'that as the National Language of the country, though nearly extinct it should have a representative in our University'. The professor himself, Owen Connellan, offered his opinion to the commission on the state of the language:

> I dare say that in consequences of railways and the National Schools, the numbers who speak it will be reduced very much. Perhaps in half a century the reduction will be very great, but still there are parts of Ireland, particularly along the coasts and in the mountains, where it may continue . . . for another hundred years.

Medical accommodation

One of the many problems clamouring for Kane's attention in the busy, if not frantic, lead-up to opening day was that of accommodation and facilities for the medical faculty. Indeed, this was to be a perennial problem. On 5 February 1849 Kane (writing, as he often did, from 51 St Stephen's Green, Dublin) stressed the urgency of having buildings made ready for 'delivery of medical courses' in the opening session. He identified the basic difficulty:

> Owing to the plan upon which the buildings of the Cork College were originally arranged, not contemplating the immediate organisation of the medical faculty, there has been no prospect made therein for the more specifically medical lectures, nor for the anatomical dissections and demonstrations.[65]

In reply (13 February 1849) the Board of Works rather tartly pointed out that there had been no mention of dissecting rooms, or rooms for lectures in medicine, in the original instruction. Residences for the president and vice-president had been added after the original estimates were approved. The buildings Kane now wanted for the medical courses could be considered only if there was money left over from the estimates.[66]

It is curious that such inadequate provision was made at the outset for medical faculty accommodation considering the flourishing nature of Cork medical education, which indeed had been adduced as a powerful reason for placing a college in Cork. In fact, the Cork School of Anatomy closed in 1845, since it seemed to be no longer necessary. Yet under the Queen's College accommodation arrangements, anatomy was to share classrooms with botany and geology! Botany, in particular, seems to have had a disproportionate importance. What made the original arrangement bizarrely haphazard

4.3 The Medical Building, originally called the Clarendon Building, c1880.

was that one out of the three wings of the building was allocated to residential space for the president and vice-president.

Medicine needed a whole area to itself and this was provided through the good offices of Lord Lieutenant Clarendon (1847–52), after whom the medical building was called.[67] W.K. Sullivan, the second president, wished to unite this building, completed in his time, to the North Wing, and so create an overall E-shaped structure.[68] As usual, lack of funds prevented the implementation of such a plan. (Perhaps this was just as well, since a connected structure would have compounded traffic problems in modern times.) Of course, uncertainty about the future of the college (in part, created by fluctuating student numbers) would have aggravated the natural parsimony of the Treasury.

As is clear from successive president's reports, anatomy in particular suffered from grievous overcrowding. In 1865 the College Council complained in a memorial (14 May) that demonstration and dissection facilities were grossly inadequate (presumably worsened by the consequences of the 1862 fire). Ventilation was 'positively prejudicial to health, being about one-tenth of the amount absolutely required'. The council wanted a new lecture theatre built and existing rooms upgraded.[69] The response from the Board of Works was predictable – there was scarcely enough money for essential maintenance and repair and certainly not for a project costing at least £2,600.[70] Kane was looking for an immediate grant of £1,200 to build the theatre, but insisted that anatomy needed a new building. The number of medical students had soared in 1864–65 from 27 to 133. The overcrowding had facilitated the spread of typhoid fever and tubercular consumption, and the fatal illness of two students was directly attributed to 'the unhealthy atmosphere of the Anatomical rooms'.[71] Kane kept up the pressure on Under-Secretary Larcom during the summer of 1865, and the Treasury finally agreed it was 'urgently necessary' that 'a new Lecture Room . . . should be forthwith proceeded with'.[72]

The great fire

> *Amongst the lower order of people here, there*
> *is no feeling of regret felt at the occurrence,*
> *some say it is a pity any of the building escaped.*
>
> Investigator's report on the fire

The fire which gutted the West Wing on 15 May 1862 was a dramatically lurid episode in the history of Queen's College Cork. It received intensive press publicity, it was discussed in the House of Commons and it inspired a number of conspiracy theories, ranging from the probable to the bizarre. In the end, nobody was charged with what was almost certainly arson on a large scale, and the failure to bring the culprit(s) to book kept a sense of mystery alive about the fire. Moreover, the question of compensation gave rise to, or perhaps intensified, antipathy towards the college on the part of the citizens.

For a time the finger was pointed at President Kane himself. There was a visitors' inquiry and the fire became part of the vexed question of Kane's relationship with

4.4 Fire in the West Wing, from the *Illustrated London News*, 24 May 1862.

the staff of QCC: indeed, the fire may possibly have been fuelled by academic grudges and ambitions. In turn, the groundless allegations against Kane rebounded on his accuser, Denis Brenan Bullen (who, as we have seen, was prominently associated with the origins of the college, ever since the Wyse Committee and the colleges agitation of the late 1830s where he was at the forefront), forcing him to resign from the chair of surgery and effectively ruining his career.

The fire was a grave material and psychological blow to an infant institution already struggling with severe problems of lecture-room and laboratory accommodation: in the years after 1862, the embers of the fire still smouldered through annual departmental reports. In short, the fire scarred the college's psyche as well as its structure, and became part of its folklore.

About 5.45 a.m. on the morning of Thursday 15 May 1862, smoke and flames were observed gushing from the roof and chimneys of the West Wing. Those who first spotted the blaze included the local quarrymen Denis and Michael Shea who were quickly at the scene; some women in Sunday's Well who were early risers, and observant to boot; and the turnkey of the adjoining county gaol who raised the alarm. President Kane, Vice-President Ryall and their families were roused from their apartments in the East Wing.[73]

Porters, students, college officers, 'the military under Col. Smith', the constabulary, 'and the officers of the county Gaol' – all did their utmost to arrest the flames. So Kane informed Under-Secretary Larcom, writing on the evening of the fateful day,[74] but

14077

Queen's College,
CORK.

THE President, Vice-President, Professors, Officers, Graduates, and Students of the QUEEN'S COLLEGE, CORK, hereby offer

A REWARD
OF

One Hundred & Fifty
POUNDS,

In addition to the Reward of One Hundred Pounds offered by the Government,

For such information as shall lead to the discovery and conviction of the Person or Persons guilty of the late Malicious Firing of the Queen's College, Cork.

Signed, by order of the President,

MAY 19th, 1862.   **ROBERT J. KENNY, Registrar.**

PURCELL & CO., Steam Press Printers, Cork.

4.5 A reward was offered for information leading to the apprehension of the arsonist(s).

despite all exertions, the conflagration spread so rapidly that 'the entire of that wing of the College was destroyed only the walls being left standing'.[75] The roof, woodwork, and much of the contents went up in the blaze. Fortunately, the gate-tower masonry halted the advance of the inferno so that the North and East Wings were unharmed, and the library and Natural History Museum were unscathed. The medical building was also untouched and the collection of physical and chemical apparatus was removed from the burning wing to safety.

The College Council launched an inquiry on the same day. There was no doubt, said Kane, but that the fire was 'malicious and contrived with elaborate ingenuity'. Efforts had been made to ignite four separate doors in the cloisters of the West Wing which is 'open and accessible to the College square'. (A later report from the two local quarrymen who were early arrivals on the scene gives a more plausible explanation – that the fire began from a planned bonfire inside the materia medica quarters.[76]) The ignition attempts failed at three doors but succeeded at the fourth which led to the materia medica room, and 'the ceiling being continuous from end to end of that wing, the extension of the fire was extremely rapid'. There was great difficulty in getting water but engines and water were eventually obtained and worked effectively.[77] It was suggested that a large reward, say £500, be offered 'to provide for a family out of this country' in order to get evidence leading to a conviction of the authors of the outrage.[78]

The college property destroyed or damaged included the materia medica, pathology, surgical and midwifery museums; the collection of classical arts objects (the Bunnell Lewis plaster casts); models, instruments and drawings from the engineering school; specimens belonging to the professor of agriculture; and the herbarium, considered to be one of the finest in the United Kingdom.

In preparing claims for compensation for malicious injury, the council estimated overall losses of the contents at £2,020. That figure, according to *The Cork Examiner* (15 May) included the cost of 'a collection of cichone plants made for the late Emperor Napoleon'. One consolation was that last-term lectures were coming to a close, so there would be 'no material interference' with the work of the college. Later in his annual report, Kane was to express gratification that, due to the co-operation of the Board of Works and the professors, repairs effected during the long recess enabled business to be resumed in time for the next session (1862–63). But the individual departments went on counting their losses. The president's report for 1861–62 recorded several professors' responses to the routine presidential enquiry about the 'general condition' of their departments. The laconic response from Professor William Rushton (history and English literature, 1858–71) was 'Burnt'. Professor Bunnell Lewis's (Latin) class roll was destroyed, which must have been a relief to at least some of his students! More seriously, Professor D.B. Bullen (surgery) – who was shortly to step centre-stage in the drama – reported that his 'supplies and fitments' were destroyed. The library, being situated in the North Wing, was not affected but the librarian gave details of the books on loan which were destroyed in the general conflagration.[79]

The Treasury would not pay for the immediate restoration of the West Wing but gave a grant for temporary arrangements. Thus, the chemistry laboratory was housed in the president's kitchen, and natural history and philosophy in his dining-room. Latin and modern languages were catered for in his drawing room, and the medical department was located in his bedroom.[80] Whatever about the appropriateness of the individual allocations, they can hardly have left much room (literally) for Sir Robert Kane – but then his critics would doubtless remind us that he was not in Cork all that much.

In the following two years, some departments were still showing the effects of the fire (materia medica, obviously, and medicine) but others were coping well, and even recovering (for example, civil engineering, logic and chemistry). The vice-president was upbeat about this: considering the dire condition of the college buildings after the fire, the various departments were now functioning efficiently.[81]

Nevertheless, the impact of the destruction on the work of various departments continued to be noted. In 1865–66, George Sidney Read, professor of logic and metaphysics, complained that since his old lecture room was destroyed by the fire, great inconvenience had resulted from the allotment rooms 'in the new building'. Professor J.R. Harvey's (midwifery) department was 'deficient in many respects' because of losses not yet made good. Professor Purcell O'Leary (materia medica, 1858–74, where the fire originated) stated that only a 'very small sum' had been allocated to cover the total loss, so that his department was 'insufficiently supplied'.[82] Even as late as 1874–75 Professor D.C. O'Connor (medicine) drew attention to 'a great want of pathological specimens since the burning of the College'.[83]

There was general agreement that the deed was malicious but who was the culprit? The strangest and most startling development was the charge made by one of the professors that the president was involved! J. Pope-Hennessy, MP (a former student of the college), stated in the House of Commons in June 1863 that a QCC professor had declared there was strong circumstantial evidence to suggest that the fire was the work of a college official.[84] As this was a reflection on every officer 'from the President to the humblest porter', President Kane called on Pope-Hennessy to identify his 'authority' – which he did, naming Professor D.B. Bullen after some show of reluctance. Kane commented that newspapers and 'public opinion' in Cork had already guessed as much.[85]

Bullen had visited the materia medica museum the day before the fire and had noticed, on an open shelf over the door, a dozen large glasses containing pathological specimens preserved in spirits of wine with some in methylated spirits. Bullen made a detailed examination of the ruins after the fire and eventually came to the conclusion that the incendiary was 'some person intimately acquainted' with the layout of the college buildings and having access to the materia medica museum without fear of being detected. Moreover, according to Bullen, the person being aware of the inflammable nature of the liquid stored there, poured this over manuscripts taken from presses, then applied matches and exited, locking the door. The culprit had also placed combustible material at the corridor doors, as a diversionary ploy to suggest an outsider was responsible.[86]

Bullen (who was anxious to succeed Kane should the latter take over the presidency of a proposed fourth Queen's College in Dublin[87]) went to visit the president in the college on the day before the fire. He left details of his version of the visit both in his 'commonplace book'[88] and in a deposition. Bullen said he was visiting Kane 'to take leave of him, it being generally understood throughout the College that he was about to resign the Presidency'. At their meeting, Kane confirmed that he was resigning because of government failure to support him, particularly in the context of a Commons motion attacking his double-jobbing. According to Bullen, Kane ranted against the 'miserable coquetting' 'between Lord Lieutenant Carlisle and Dr Cullen about the Catholic University; that Lord Carlisle and his party wanted to get him [Kane] out of the way'.

The talk then turned to the dominant education issue, Bullen asserting that if he were president of QCC he would try to effect a reconciliation between the government and the bishops on the matter of the Queen's Colleges. Kane replied that Bullen might do as he pleased but he (Kane) would not 'concede an inch to the Ultramontanes'. Kane ended their meeting, according to Bullen, in the same bitter vein:

> When I was leaving the room he said – Bullen, if you want the Presidency, get the Rev. Dominick Murphy[89] to write a line to the Castle, hinting it would be agreeable to have you appointed. That is the way things are done by the Castle people. A priest calls there and says Doctor Cullen would be pleased if the Lord Lieutenant would do so and so, of course, the thing is done. Such is the way in which Ireland is governed.

Bullen then recorded that as he returned from the college after this conversation he reflected that Kane was bent on confrontation with the ultramontanes, which would have the effect of making an amicable settlement between the government and Catholic MPs impossible. And so Bullen hurried home and dashed off a communication to Lord Lieutenant Carlisle, assuring him that he would implement a reconciliation policy, if he were to become president of Queen's College, an office which Kane had informed him he would be vacating immediately. The West Wing went up in flames on the following morning, 15 May. On 16 May, Under-Secretary Larcom wrote to Bullen informing him that there was no intimation from Kane of an impending resignation.

It was against this background that Sir Robert and Lady Kane called on the Bullens on the evening of 19 May, 'to take leave of Mrs Bullen and the girls'. (Kane obviously thought of the Bullens as friends, despite the divergent views of the two men.) Discussing the dramatic event, Kane, according to Bullen, 'said he was sure the fire was the act of some fanatic, influenced by the Ultramontane priests', a view from which Bullen dissented. Kane then suggested to Bullen that they should draw up a joint report to government upon the origin of the fire, and attribute the crime to ultramontane influence. But Bullen refused to do any 'such thing' and strongly advised Kane not to convey any information to government except what he could swear to from his own knowledge.

Bullen said he had no further private communication with Kane. (Neither did he incriminate the president in his sworn statement in July 1862 concerning the fire.[90]) In July 1863, he forwarded to the Castle correspondence published by Kane in the Cork newspapers. Allegations in these letters and 'recent proceedings in the House of

Commons' rendered it imperative for Bullen to place before the Castle all his correspondence with Kane relating to the fire. Bullen was prepared 'to state on oath' his conviction that 'the incendiary is an official of the College, and the conduct of Sir Robert Kane with reference thereto demands inquiry'.

On receipt of Bullen's communications, Larcom wrote to Kane inviting him, in effect, to respond to the charges. Kane (whose letters at this period are addressed from a number of Dublin and continental locations) responded in no uncertain manner, apparently with the support of the College Council. He strongly denied that he had ever spoken disparagingly about Lord Carlisle. Equally emphatically, he rejected Bullen's allegation about suggesting the joint drafting of a report blaming the fire on ultramontane influence as 'utterly false'. The charge was mischievous and absurd. Kane particularly denounced Bullen for writing down a calumny in a commonplace book, being disloyal to his president as well as calumnious, and communicating that libel to government fourteen months later.[91]

In the event, Bullen's charges against Kane totally collapsed. Though as late as 22 March 1864 he declared it his 'duty to tender criminal informations against Sir Robert Kane and William Williams[92] for having maliciously burned the Queen's College at Cork',[93] he soon changed his tune with dramatic suddenness. At the triennial visitation on 12 April 1864 (which was crowded to capacity by 'the gentry of the city, ladies and gentlemen, and the students and officials of the College'[94]), the lord chancellor, presiding, said that Bullen's statements 'gravely affected the discipline of the College' and 'reflected seriously' on Kane, alleging as they did 'a great breach of discipline' on his part. The president again repeated his utter denial of the allegations, demanding the fullest investigation and leaving his case to the legal team. At this point, Bullen, who did not attend the visitation, caved in completely while unconvincingly trying to put the best face possible on his position. According to a letter read out by his counsel, Bullen said his deposition to the lord lieutenant (9 July 1863) was not written until a 'considerable interval afterwards', when time and other events had effaced an 'accurate recollection' and substituted an 'erroneous impression' of what passed between him and the president. At the time he made the deposition, he believed his recollections were accurate but he was now satisfied he was completely mistaken, and entirely withdrew what he had said. The excitement surrounding the public discussion about the fire had misled him to prefer charges against Kane which were totally unfounded and which he now retracted without qualification. He expressed his deep regrets and profuse apologies. The lord chancellor commented that, if the charges had been true, Kane could not have presided over QCC 'for one hour' after verification. The visitors expressed gratification that Kane had been cleared, hoped there would not be a recurrence of such unpleasantness, complimented the president for dealing promptly with the fire outbreak and conveyed their good wishes for the future of the college.[95]

The sequel was predictable. The head of the now disgraced Bullen was for the chop. Larcom wrote to the Home Secretary[96] immediately after the visitation saying Bullen should be removed from his chair: 'Dr Bullen must have been influenced by malice in making these charges, or have been labouring under some insane delusion'.[97]

Larcom informed Kane on 29 April that Bullen was to be removed,[98] and the decision was conveyed to Bullen himself. Before that, however, in a letter (31 March 1864) to Larcom, he had come up with another justification for his extraordinary conduct. From the landing of the papal brigade in Cork in November 1860[99] to the Fenian showpiece funeral of Terence Bellew MacManus in November 1861, he felt he had grounds for believing that a political intrigue was on foot in Cork to upset Palmerston's ministry. 'When the fire occurred on the 15th, I suddenly found myself . . . brought face to face with a fearful crime, pregnant, as I suspected, with danger to the British Empire and shrouded by an impenetrable mist.'[100] Subsequently, Bullen wrote to the government asking for a full investigation into the circumstances of the fire, and for a personal meeting to discuss his own case, but a deaf ear was turned to his entreaties.

In fact, the Castle authorities had never taken Bullen's charges seriously. Their private investigator, Constable Peter Goulden reported (8 July 1862) that, apart from Bullen,

> I cannot find that any other person here suspects the President but there are some here who know him well and who say that he was not at all sorry at the occurrence having taken place.[101]

When Bullen made his deposition in July 1863, the recipient Sir Henry Browning commented:

> the statement is of so vague and indefinite a character – charging no-one with any specific offence – that I doubt very much whether any magistrate would feel himself warranted in adopting it as an information at all.[102]

Larcom, writing to Bullen on 4 August 1863, endorsed Browning's assessment of the charge:

> there appears to be no evidence to sustain it except your own statement . . . His Excellency [the lord lieutenant] does not feel that any benefit would be likely to result from any further enquiry into the matter.[103]

That would probably have been the end of the matter only for the Pope-Hennessy reference in the House of Commons. But even when Bullen dramatically, if belatedly, named Kane as the arsonist, Browning's response was casually dismissive, saying that if Bullen had information he should tender it to the local justices.[104]

Why should a senior QCC professor, with a high standing in the academic and civic community, have pursued such charges, at once grave and grotesque,[105] against his president? And, moreover, why should he have persisted to his own detriment to the point where, in the face of visitation demands to substantiate his claims, his only option was a humiliating backdown, with ruinous consequences for his own career?

The general context of the answer may lie in the strained relationship that had developed between Kane and the professors, in particular over the issue of his dual positions and his non-residence. The fire, which compounded his difficulties, afforded a welcome opportunity to any colleague bent on stirring up trouble, for whatever reason. Was Bullen, who saw himself as having borne the burden of the pre-1845 colleges agitation, envious of Kane? And was there, as well, 'vaulting ambition' which in the end was indeed destined to 'o'erleap itself'?

Bullen obviously wanted very badly to be president of QCC and, when Kane was not obliging enough to move out, he may have decided that audaciously desperate measures were called for. But Bullen was also filled with crusading zeal to square the circle of mixed education and Catholic orthodoxy. This was evident in a long letter to Bishop Delany, written in September 1850 after the Synod of Thurles had pronounced against the Queen's Colleges. (Bullen described himself as 'the person who first originated the movement in favour of the foundation of these collegiate institutions'.[106]) He believed the Church was favourable to the colleges movement before 1845, and was surprised at the extent of ecclesiastical antagonism thereafter.[107] He may well have sincerely believed that Kane's attitude was only making a bad situation worse and that, as president of QCC, he himself could really bring about a reconciliation, or at least a *modus vivendi*, between Catholicism and the Queen's Colleges.[108]

From the flames and smoke there was a fallout of rumours, speculations and theories. According to *The Cork Examiner* (19 May 1862),

> where there is least known, assertion is loudest and most vehement. All sorts of statements, accusations, proofs and disproofs are flying about in the most complete confusion.

Constable Peter Goulden, sent to Cork to investigate the occurrence and reporting back privately, observed at an early stage (31 May) that

> there are many even very respectable persons who entertain the idea that the fire was accidental while others equally responsible consider it malicious.[109]

The *Morning News* was convinced

> that the fire arose from a purely accidental cause . . . The destruction of that handsome wing of the Cork College with its valuable (but to students almost useless) museum, we regret.[110]

This piece also referred to the practice of students (waiting for professors to arrive at the West Wing) of diverting themselves by 'shying cinders' at one another. But hardly at 5.45 a.m!

However, accidents are not nearly as exciting as conspiracies, and among the proliferating theories there was a favourite speculation that the West Wing (which contained the pathology laboratory) was set on fire in order to get rid of forensic evidence relating to one or more murder cases. Goulden reported (31 May) that

> others consider that the object in motive was to destroy some matters in connection with the Clogheen poisoning case or the Glenbower murder, which were in the laboratory of Dr Blythe for analysis.[111]

'A Ratepayer' writing to *The Cork Examiner* (20 May) wondered if the fire was connected 'with a blood-stained knife which was in the buildings to undergo a chemical analysis'.

The most widespread story in this category was given prominence in T.M. Healy's *Letters and Leaders of my Day*[112] and copied elsewhere.[113] This concerned Richard Burke, clerk of the Waterford Poor Law Union, who was suspected of poisoning his wife in 1860, in collusion with a nurse with whom he was having an affair and who obligingly supplied him with arsenic from the union pharmacy. The dead woman's stomach was sent in a jar to QCC for analysis, poisoning was confirmed, and the jar was accidentally discovered intact during the reconstruction of the West Wing. His love affair turned out unhappily for Burke who was found guilty of murder and whose public hanging was said to have been attended by thousands.[114] Unfortunately for this morality tale, in which truth will out to confound murderous adulterers, the chronology simply does not fit the episode. The forensic analysis had been completed, evidence given thereon, and Burke charged, before the fire took place. The Burke story obviously belongs to a popular category of modern folk-tale murder mysteries.

Another class of suspects comprised those who were said to have grievances against college. Constable Goulden's first report (31 May) allowed for the possibility that the fire was caused 'by some troublesome discontented students'.[115] More specifically, Goulden (13 June) mentioned that a college professor had been involved in the suppression, because of irregularities, of Dr Cosar's dissecting hospital and that 'there is a suspicion that the parties or some of them who felt angered at the suppression of Dr Cosar's establishment employed some party to burn the College'.[116]

More and more, however, the view took hold that the fire was an 'inside job', which indeed was also Bullen's conviction. A *Cork Examiner* article on 16 May 1862 asserted that the perpetrator was a 'habitué' of the college and could therefore select from 'the vast number of rooms it contains those which were practicable for fire'. For a time the finger of suspicion pointed at John Reynolds, a porter in the department of surgery and 'a man of indifferent character' according to Goulden. The motivation would have been a grievance over a recently refused pay increase and the sacking of his wife as a college charwoman. Goulden was informed that Reynolds was 'very much addicted to drink' and that some time previously he had stolen some spirits of wine (mixed with chemical compounds) from the very room where the fire started. It was believed that he had been there again the night before the fire. But Goulden also admitted that he had no real evidence against Reynolds, who was soon ruled out of consideration once it was clear he had an alibi.[117]

The prime suspect then was William Williams, the college steward, a powerful and influential figure. He was very much in Kane's confidence, according to Goulden, being the president's eyes and ears, indeed, and keeping him informed of college happenings during his frequent absences. (The services of similar informants have been available to presidents in the recent past.) For that very reason, Williams was not popular with the academic staff and it was believed he would be sacked if Kane resigned the presidency, as seemed likely at the time.[118]

A number of professors believed Williams was the culprit and in July 1862 Goulden expected charges to be laid against him very soon.[119] Williams was reported to have remarked on the day before the fire that the college would be burned and would be rebuilt by the Board of Works.[120] When a turnkey at the gaol called Sweeney informed Williams and his wife of the fire, Mrs Williams allegedly made the memorable comment: 'Let it burn away, there is nothing in it belonging to us'. Goulden observed (2 August):

> The conduct of Williams when the fire was reported to him was most extraordinary. He was told by Tobin the porter the very room where the fire was, yet he did not open it.[121]

All those who witnessed the beginning of the fire agreed that,

> had Williams exerted himself as he should have done, and opened the door of the room where the fire was, that it would have been extinguished with a few buckets of water which were at hand in the same room where the fire was.[122]

In fact, there was a rainwater tank nearby, with a pipe hose, but Williams claimed he had forgotten about its existence.[123] Nevertheless, all the evidence – much of it biased – against the steward was circumstantial, and no clear motive to justify his arrest could be established, as Philip O'Connell, the Crown solicitor in Cork, informed Under-Secretary Larcom on 2 August.[124] Ironically, Williams was one of those who later put out a small fire in the West Wing 'at some personal risk'.[125]

Towards the end of his investigation, Goulden reluctantly admitted (27 September):

> the offender will never be discovered but they all agree in the opinion that it was done by either Williams the steward or John Reynolds the porter.[126]

That opinion was influenced, it would appear, by dislike of the porters and their life-style. Mr Orme, RM, who helped the college with its inquiries into the fire, thought the porters 'were all a bad lot', according to Goulden's report of 9 August.[127] Some porters apparently feared they would face instant dismissal if Kane ceased to be president.[128] (Porters, incidentally, had to be between twenty and thirty-five years at appointment, a process which involved an examination.[129])

Religious controversy was never far away from the Queen's Colleges, and there were rumours (but no more) that the fire was connected with the Catholic Church's denunciation of the 'godless' colleges. Goulden reported on 13 June:

> There are many here, even very respectful Roman Catholics, who attribute the burning of the College to the frequent denunciations of these institutions by the clergy. Some of the students, as well as their parents, were refused the sacraments of the church as I am informed.[130]

Two Cork priests had preached against the colleges in the fortnight before the fire,[131] and one view was that under their influence ultramontane zealots had torched the college. Indeed, a student claimed that the culprit was one of the preachers themselves!

An absurd claim, said the *Morning News*,[132] and sensible people like Goulden thought clerical denunciation was not a crucial factor.[133] An outlandishly Machiavellian variation on the ultramontane theme was that the fire was the work of anti-Catholic elements whose motive for burning the college would have been to make Catholics appear guilty, so preventing any rapprochement between government and the Catholic clergy at a time when the education question was being considered by parliament.[134]

The town appears to have had precious little sympathy for the badly singed gown. There was civic irritation at college negligence of basic fire security (in particular, the College Council's failure to instal a hydrant) and civic determination not to shoulder responsibility for the expensive consequences. And,

> it is scarcely worthy of remark that a building so extensive, and so accessible, and so costly, was in the habit of being left without a night watch of any sort.[135]

The outrage report of 15 May 1862 confirmed that the fire engines had been summoned early on but the work was hampered by lack of a water supply and the absence of hydrants on the premises.[136]

The College Council was naturally anxious to get compensation and it filed a claim immediately. It urged the president to go to Dublin to look for reparation to save QCC from ruin.[137] The reason why the college authorities avoided making any serious investigation was probably because the prospects of compensation would be diminished if there was definite confirmation that the culprit was a college employee, something widely suspected. Apparently there was strong feeling in Cork against payment of compensation because of perceived college negligence and suspected employee involvement. *The Cork Examiner* pressed the point home: 'We understand that neither the College itself nor any of the property in it had been insured' (15 May 1862). And:

> An aside has got abroad that the enormous loss incurred . . . is to be made good out of the funds of the city, under the law relating to malicious burning. This idea, however, we cannot countenance. That law was intended for the private protection of individuals against the malice of enemies; but it never contemplated the destruction of such concerns as government buildings.[138]

Subsequently, letters from readers endorsed the editorial view.

Nearly two years later, a *Cork Examiner* editorial (13 April 1864) reacted cynically to the visitation which resulted in Bullen's resignation. The outcome of the visitation, the editorial claimed, was essentially a whitewash, containing a mass of contradiction. The people of Cork had little interest in the Kane–Bullen dispute, but they

> did want to know if possible, how the College was burnt and, what certainly seemed quite capable of discovery, who were the parties who so persistently attempted to fix the shame and responsibility of the act upon the citizens of Cork.

The hostility of the local paper to Kane and QCC (in contrast to the co-operative note struck when the college first opened and before the battle lines were drawn on the 'godless' issue) was editorially expressed in another context in 1866.[139] The *Examiner* caustically observed that QCC students were hardly a good advertisement for the much-vaunted system of secular education, judging by their role in disturbances at a recent Queen's University meeting: 'No, not even manners. We should certainly hope that no ecclesiastic or denominational seminary in Ireland would have made a display as indecent as interrupted the delivery of the address of the Vice-Chancellor.' However, the editorial did add that QCB students were equally to blame. *The Cork Examiner* was to have a long tradition of reprimanding college students for high-spirited behaviour. On the other hand, the paper could publish a lyrically favourable account of a college sports meeting.[140]

Not surprisingly, the Treasury was unwilling to send money to QCC for a restoration project since it shrewdly suspected that the Grand Jury would not award compensation at the September assizes.[141] Philip O'Connell, the Cork Crown solicitor, told Larcom (23 August 1862) that he needed the best counsel for the assizes since ratepayers were strongly opposed to paying compensation and their strongest card was the widespread belief that somebody connected with college had committed the crime.[142] Goulden referred (30 August) to the 'general opinion' that compensation would be refused,[143] and reported on 9 September that this indeed had happened even though it was based on the technical grounds that the college and the Board of Works had failed to post up notices of claim in the usual places around the city. Appeals against the decision were also lost.[144] Because of the absence of restoration funds (apart from an increased annual grant to aid rebuilding) the new West Wing, though externally a fine piece of reconstruction, lacked the finish (for example, the splendid oak rafters) of the original.

Finally, one of the two remarkable things about the whole melodramatic episode was that, despite all the excitement and intense speculation, there was never a thorough investigation of the fire, either by college itself or by the government. The College Council was more concerned (4 Jan 1863) about the absence of preventative measures against a recurrence, a concern heartily endorsed by Vice-President Ryall who lived in the other wing![145]

The second notable feature of the affair was the coolness, if not the antipathy, of the citizens to the college in its hour of tribulation. As we have seen, there were hard-headed reasons for this attitude on the part of the ratepayer: at the same time, it revealed a remarkable lack of civic appreciation, or awareness, even on the part of the propertied classes, of Cork as a university city. As for the unpropertied, the college was a remote and incomprehensible institution in class terms and, in the increased religious and nationalist excitement of the early 1860s, the alien and 'godless' college was simply part of the oppressor's world. And so Goulden's observation (31 May 1862) should hardly surprise us: 'Amongst the lower order of people here, there is no feeling of regret felt at the occurrence, some say it is a pity any of the building escaped.'[146]

Kane's resignation: assessment

It was unfortunate that the closing stage of Kane's presidency should have been attended by another of those unpleasant rows which had marred relations with his professorial staff throughout much of his presidency. This time, however, no blame was attached to him, as a visitors' report (22 May 1872) made clear.[147] He had called for a visitation, as was his duty by statute, to consider the case of Professor J. Reay Greene (natural history, 1858–77) whom the president had charged with neglect of duty. Greene had not lectured for much of the first term in the 1871–72 session, and had insolently countered Kane's queries by saying he could not promise 'his health would be invariably good, as seemed to be required'. The natural history course was in abeyance, in effect.

Before the visitors, Greene said he had 'a nervous affection' which prevented him from lecturing. The visitors found that Kane had acted correctly throughout, and reprimanded Greene: 'It is a manifest if a professor in this college can treat the head of it in the manner that Professor Greene did . . . that all discipline of the College must cease and that the interests of the students must be neglected'.[148] Acting on the visitors' report, the lord lieutenant made it clear that Greene would have been fired if he had not 'made up' the missed lectures. Indulgence was being shown on this occasion, but any further neglect of duty would result in removal.[149] The incident illustrates how easily the president was able to secure a visitation to deal with awkward business; how expeditiously the visitors could act, when so minded; and how effective and decisive the Castle could be in firing, or threatening to fire, a troublesome academic. In this case, Greene must have mended his ways as he remained in his post for several more years.

In the college folklore, such as it is, there is a vague story that one president 'made off with the money'. Perhaps this is a confusion of two different people – the president whose bankruptcy was a major reason for his dismissal in 1896, and the bursar who absconded with some funds in 1871. Edward M. Fitzgerald had been bursar from the beginning, having been recommended for his 'Whig principles' by Bishop Haly of Kildare and Leighlin. He had been highly praised by Kane in his 1855–56 president's report. However, in March 1871, Kane (for whom this incident was a further headache during his final years at QCC) reported to the Castle that there were 'very serious defalcations' in the bursar's accounts, amounting to £1,100 (which was nearly one-and-a-half times the president's salary). Fitzgerald was dismissed, and a warrant was issued for his arrest. He succeeded in evading capture at least for a period,[150] and apparently died a short time later.[151]

Details are scarce on the Fitzgerald affair but it caused government and college to take precautions when appointing a successor. In May 1871, Professor John England (natural philosophy, 1855–94, ultimately sacked from his chair because of deafness) was made bursar (1871–86), receiving £75 per annum in addition to his professorial salary. On taking up appointment, he had to provide personal security of £1,000, together with two independent sureties of £500 each.[152] The largeness of these sums suggests that the college had learned a very serious lesson from the Fitzgerald affair.

Sir Robert Kane finally resigned from the presidency of QCC on 5 August 1873, having served twenty-eight years.[153] (He also resigned from the deanship of the Royal College of Science which had replaced the Museum of Irish Industry in 1867.) He pointed out – in his resignation letter to the Lord Lieutenant – that he was over sixty (in fact, he was nearly sixty-four, having been born on 24 September 1809). A strain of ill-health in his family made it necessary for him to winter in a mild climate.[154] Cork's purgatorial climate was a recurrent complaint by presidents and was partly the reason, or the pretext, for prolonged absences or, in Blenner-hassett's case, even for resignation. It was a factor in the illnesses of Slattery and Windle and it could be said to have contributed to George Boole's death.

Kane left QCC on a surprisingly comfortable pension. His salary had been £800 per annum (unchanged since 1845), in addition to free accommodation and £71 per annum for lighting and heating. The lord lieutenant recommended (15 August 1873) that he be accorded a good pension, and the Treasury agreed to pay a sum of £595 per annum (that is, 75 per cent of salary).[155] He enjoyed an active retirement in Dublin, up to his death on 16 February 1890. He was a commissioner of national education, a member of the council of Dublin University, and vice-chancellor of the Queen's University during the last two years of its existence. He was a foundation member of the Senate of the Royal University, and president of the Royal Irish Academy (1877–1882).[156]

His significance in Irish industrial history is immense, and he has a special niche in the pantheon of economic nationalism despite the anti-home rule opinions of his later days. It is more difficult to assess his presidency of QCC. His period of office was controversial, even stormy. Much of the trouble he experienced seems to have been the consequence of a temperamental difficulty in establishing good relations with his staff, and of a rigid approach to statutes and regulations. He only belatedly and reluctantly conceded the virtual impossibility of directing two institutions, and of a bilocational mode of existence. A revealing report in the year of his retirement showed that of the 302 College Council meetings held between 1859 (just after the 1857–58 commission had been so emphatic about absenteeism) and 1873, Kane attended only 112 (37 per cent), compared with 168 out of 195 for the QCB president (86 per cent) and 254 out of 453 for the Galway head (56 per cent).[157]

Yet Kane had taken the lead in planning the whole colleges system. He brought his great prestige and abilities to bear on bringing Queen's College Cork into existence, and on overcoming the numerous obstacles in the path of not only a new university college but of an experimental educational institution. Inspired by a well-defined philosophy, he gave the college a clear educational direction. He courageously upheld, indeed salvaged, the principle of united or mixed education against sustained assault. He also established the college's intellectual independence in the face of widespread condescension towards, even disparagement of, the Queen's Colleges as government-controlled institutions, on the part of hostile elements in TCD, Kane's alma mater.[158]

THE SULLIVAN YEARS

*In learning profound, in science a master, he devoted to the
intellectual and industrial progress of Ireland, the fruits of his deep
study of her history, language and character, and a knowledge
unparalleled of her resources.*

SO RUNS THE inscription on the Celtic cross over the grave in St Finbarr's
Cemetery, Cork of William Kirby Sullivan, the only Cork-born president
(1873–90) of Queen's College Cork. The memorial, funded by public subscription,
was unveiled by the mayor of Cork on 25 June 1894, and for once there was
substance in the rhetoric of the epitaph.

Sullivan was born in 1822 in Dripsey, Co. Cork, where his father James
Bartholomew Sullivan was the proprietor of a paper mill, which was the largest of the
many paper mills in Co. Cork and was said to have employed over 2,000 people. When
the mill workers set fire to the plant, in an angry Luddite reaction to the introduction of
machinery, the child William Kirby, so the story goes, was rescued in a blanket by a servant. (The traumatic incident did not inhibit the adult Sullivan from having an industrial
scientist's interest in the paper trade.) Thereafter the family moved to Cork city, where
Sullivan was educated by the Christian Brothers before going on to study chemistry
under the illustrious German chemist Liebig at Giessen, where Kane had also trained.
Sullivan delivered some of his first lectures in the old Cork Mechanics' Institute in Cook
Street. His career developed in Dublin in the Museum of Economic Geology, afterwards the Museum of Irish Industry, where he was private assistant to Robert Kane and
subsequently chemist to the museum. Kane and Sullivan continued to be associated for
many years, both serving on the senates of the Queen's University and the Royal University, and both dying within a few months of each other in 1890. Sullivan's work in
Dublin included teaching and research for government departments and public bodies.

He was sympathetic to the Young Ireland movement (incidentally, Kane's father
had been a supporter of the United Irishmen) and he became one of the registered
shareholders of the *Irish Tribune*, which replaced the *United Irishman* after John
Mitchel's deportation in 1848. At this time, Sullivan had an attack of rheumatic
fever which was a blessing in disguise since it prevented him from further political
involvement. Whatever the seriousness of his commitment to nationalism, it certainly did not damage his subsequent career and it gave him a common bond with
the Cork patriot Denny Lane with whom Sullivan shared scholarly interests and
developed a friendship during the presidential years, and whose own Young Ireland

5.1 William Kirby Sullivan, president, QCC, 1873-1890.

past (including a spell in jail) did him no harm in Cork society. Perhaps Sullivan's nationalist dalliance also made him wary, when he became president of QCC, of student political activities and fearful of their possible adverse impact on the college, given vigilant Crown supervision.

Continuing his researches, he and Kane showed that sugar beet could be successfully cultivated in Ireland but this was an idea before its time. Many decades later, it attracted further research attention in UCC and developed into a successful food industry in the protectionist era and after. In 1856, at Newman's invitation, Sullivan became professor of chemistry in the Catholic University of Ireland. He helped to develop its medical school, as well as organising its laboratories and museums. He edited and published in *The Atlantis*, which was founded by Newman in 1858 and which won prestige as an academic journal during its five-year life, enhancing Sullivan's reputation. His articles included contributions on philosophy as well as chemistry, and he was particularly interested in the influence of geography on European languages. He was a good linguist and was highly regarded as a philologist and as an antiquarian. His impressive book-length introduction to O'Curry's *On the Manners and Customs of the Ancient Irish*,

published in 1873, exemplified his scholarly brilliance and versatility.[1] He later contributed, co-operatively with Dr George Sigerson, the volume on the eighteenth century
to *Two Centuries of Irish History*, edited by James Bryce. Jeremiah Curtin, the celebrated
Irish-American anthropologist, spent some days with Sullivan in Cork in 1887 and
described him as one of Ireland's celebrated scholars. However, there seems to be no
basis for T.S. Wheeler's assertion that Sullivan was probably a native Irish speaker.[2]

Sullivan was held in high esteem by the Catholic University authorities. 'His views
were large and bold, and I cordially embraced them', said Newman. He was one of the
Catholic members of the Powis Commission,[3] he actively pushed university claims for
Catholics and he expounded a positive *raison d'être* for the Catholic University against
those (particularly in the press) who dismissed it as merely a reaction to the Queen's
Colleges. It was, he claimed, in an arresting image, 'an inevitable necessity . . . for five
millions of people could not remain in receipt of the educational outdoor relief which
the other colleges afforded them'. In 1858, Cardinal Wiseman referred with approval to
Sullivan's argument that

> the time was come when, as a matter of right, the people of this country should
> demand that recognition of its University which would so much contribute to its
> success and to the development of the intellect of the country.[4]

It was against this image of Sullivan that his 'defection' to QCC seemed to conservative bishops to be such a betrayal.[5] He had begun to consider Cork on the very day
that he read of Kane's resignation, as he explained to his friend William Monsell[6] in the
summer of 1873, in letters which reflect his disenchantment with the Catholic
University and lay-ecclesiastical relations in Catholic education:

> My position here is so precarious that I am forced to look about to see what I can do.
> The University is all but defunct, and I do not believe enough will be collected this
> year to pay the salaries of the professors who are still attached to it. I believe too that it is
> the desire of the Authorities to get rid of the lay professors, at least that is the only
> situation that seems to me to explain the state they have reduced the institute to.

He feared that the Royal College of Science, where he also taught, might be closed in
the following year. Because of 'this state of things' and the unlikely prospect of any
change in the university question following the defeat of Gladstone's Irish University
Bill, the whole situation was so serious that he was now asking Monsell bluntly if he
could find out whether the QCC vacancy had already been 'given away'; 'whether in
the event of my applying for it, I would have any chance of getting it'; and what was
Monsell's opinion generally. Monsell in fact thought the chances were favourable but
he did not approve of Sullivan's applying for the Cork presidency. However, Sullivan's
mind was already made up, as was evident from his reply:

> The conspicuous leadership with which you have invested me is a brevet rank and that
> not even acknowledged by the ruling powers who as you will know would not

bestow the humblest educational office on a layman for which they could find an ecclesiastic fitted.

He argued further that any objection to his going to a 'mixed' Queen's College should logically mean that he should quit the mixed Royal College of Science, the Agricultural Training Department (the more objectionable because it was a boarding establishment) and the Senate of the Queen's University. Sullivan then gave the interesting explanation that he joined the Catholic University not because he was opposed to mixed education in principle, as he had informed Newman,

> but because I believe all progress must emanate from within a people and cannot be impressed upon them by external means, and consequently that a great Liberal Catholic University could do more for the advancement of learning and the intellectual and political training of Irish Catholics than any number of government institutions, I believed that such a university was possible in the hands of Newman.

He had worked hard for the institution, still hoping to see a Catholic university in which 'the ideas and idiosyncrasies of the Irish people would find a genial nursery. That hope has alas! vanished'. Sullivan recalled that his pamphlet published nearly ten years before singled out the exclusion of Roman Catholics from chairs as his chief objection to the Queen's Colleges.[7] Had Clarendon's promises[8] been fulfilled in this respect and Catholics given their fair share of posts, the Catholic University would probably never have been heard of. Sullivan considered that the present position of the Catholic University absolved him from all reservations about accepting the Cork presidency.

He then vigorously attacked the bishops who 'want a Seminary or rather a number of Diocesan Seminaries under their absolute control'. For them, science and secular learning were secondary – in fact, they were suspicious of science because of its 'supposed dangers to faith', and their own education did not equip them to understand the importance of science as an element of secular education. 'They wish besides to impose upon University Students the discipline which in my opinion is even unsuited to a Seminary.' Sullivan then detailed the manifold deficiencies of the Catholic University. Besides the lack of endowments, buildings and facilities, there was the hostility or at least indifference of many clerics. The bishops, he thought, might really prefer a purely examining university which might be offered in the following year, 1874 (in fact, the Royal University was established in 1879).

> As a scientific man, I cannot consent to see young Catholics – my own sons – deprived of the means of competing with their Protestant fellow-countrymen. As a layman, I cannot consent to allow the office of teacher to become among Catholics the exclusive privilege of priests.

Even if the university were well endowed, there would be no openings for laymen: 'Even a Pro-Vice-Rectorship can only be filled by a priest'. If he were to go for Cork, his 'antecedents' and present position would not be a bar. He added the tongue-in-cheek comment: 'I am further strengthened in this view by the remarkable unanimity with which public opinion – the opinion of all parties in T.C.D., the Royal Irish Academy etc have bestowed the office on me'. He would have left the Catholic University long since, if he could, not primarily because he had to think of 'the interest of my family', but because his two great ideas were further away than ever from realisation – 'a great technological Institute, and a great free Liberal Catholic University'. In another letter to Monsell (n.d.), Sullivan sketched his wider educational philosophy, which has an interesting contemporary ring:

> The real difficulty of Ireland is not want of Capital, or incapacity for skilled work . . . . it is rather financial and social. Our banks do not encourage manufacturers, our middle classes do not give a practical education to their children. Even a moderate farmer with £500–1,000 laid by, never thinks of educating his son for trade – his only idea is to make a lawer [*sic*] a priest or a doctor.[9]

It was mid-September 1873 before a surprised Bartholomew Woodlock, rector of the Catholic University, was informed by Professor Thomas Hayden (anatomy and physiology) that Sullivan's imminent departure was common knowledge. Hayden thought the loss would be so great that efforts should be made (a vice-rectorship, with a salary increase?) 'to avert the evil'. However, Sullivan was already gone. He wrote to Woodlock on 19 September, saying he was accepting the lord lieutenant's invitation to become president of QCC. Woodlock informed Archbishop Leahy of Cashel who was distressed: 'a great blow to the Catholic University, to Catholic Education, to the Catholic Church of Ireland'. The Dublin Protestant paper, the *Evening Mail*, had the news in capital letters 'because the Mail knows it is a heavy blow to us', observed Leahy. Commenting to Cullen on the news, Leahy remarked bitterly: 'It is one other instance of the deserter going over to the enemy for filthy lucre'.[10]

Musing over other staff problems in the university, Cullen noted: 'You see what problems there are with laymen'. Leahy was right in his analysis: Sullivan's departure, though it stiffened espiscopal resolve to sustain the Catholic University at any cost, was nonetheless a shattering blow to morale and to an already impaired public image of the university. The episode further increased the Church animus against the Queen's Colleges and it did not augur well for reconciliation prospects during Sullivan's presidency. But above all perhaps it intensified the clerical neurosis about laymen: lacking adequate disinterested 'dedication', they simply could not be trusted with positions of influence or power in Catholic education. That attitude persisted at second-level education down to our own day when, with the collapse in vocations, ecclesiastics finally had no other recourse but to 'put their trust' in laymen.

Sir Robert Kane on his retirement as QCC president suggested that Sullivan be appointed to succeed him. When Lord Lieutenant Spencer offered the position to Sullivan, he emphasised the need for a permanently resident college head, given the trouble caused by Kane's absenteeism, or at least attempted bilocation. Sullivan, appointed on 27 September 1873, readily concurred, pointing out (with a native's fervour) that living in Cork was an added inducement to accepting the presidency. His residence in college was the key to his grasp of college issues, his commitment to the institution and his vigorous direction of its multifaceted development, making him one of the outstanding presidents.

Since Kane had only been intermittently resident at best, spending ever shorter periods in Cork in his later years, the president's house was in a state of some neglect. This considerably annoyed Sullivan since he had given up his residence in Dublin in order to move to Cork with his large family. He wrote to Under-Secretary Burke[11] on 28 October 1873 requesting money to repair the dilapidated house and an allowance for fuel and lodgings while refurbishment was proceeding. 'The President's house had not been permanently occupied by my predecessor Sir Robert Kane for many years past and . . . I found the acting steward of the college and his family living in it.'[12] But the Board of Works and the Treasury were dilatory as usual, and even after the Sullivan family returned to the house early in the new year of 1874 repairs remained uncompleted and the fitments asked for had not yet been provided, as the president complained to Burke on 11 February 1874. Moreover, he had had to pay for the maintenance of his family in lodgings for three months, and had yet to receive the £1 per diem expenses which he had requested the previous October. Eventually the Treasury reimbursed him with these expenses in May 1874 though they were unwilling to pay rates and taxes on the house while Sullivan was not living there, stating that such money must come out of the lodgings allowance.[13]

When he tried to get Dublin Castle to provide a stable as well, he drew a blank. He told Burke (5 February 1875) of his surprise at finding no stable attached to the president's house. This was a matter of great inconvenience, discomfort and even danger to his family: because of the wet climate, he had to send for a car every time one of the family wished to visit the city.

> It is well known that the public vehicles in Cork are wretched and are frequently wet inside, so that delicate persons face much danger in them . . . . My wife and eldest daughter have been confined to the house for nearly a month owing to a severe attack of Bronchitis caught in a wet car.[14]

But the Treasury was callously impervious to this *cri de cœur*, and the Board of Works pointed out that there was no stable for the president in QCB, while the one in Galway had come with the college site there. Some kind heart at the Board of Works commented, 'I think it hard, but you know the Treasury'.[15]

The 1874 memorial

'The Memorial of the President and Professors of Queen's College, Cork,' sent on 13 March 1874 to the lord lieutenant, the Duke of Abercorn, is an unusual document in that it is a (printed) comprehensive state-of-the-college survey, twenty-five years after the opening, though there is no indication that it was a formal anniversary review.[16] More relevantly perhaps, it was composed shortly after Sullivan's appointment as president, and we may see it as an instance of that illusory surge of expectation which marks the accession of a new president. Indeed, Sullivan's particular concerns were evident in the emphasis on the practical requirements of the sciences, in particular the need for a new chemistry laboratory. The memorial also reflected renewed hope in the future of the Queen's Colleges, following the abortive Irish University Bill of 1873. The failure to secure Catholic acceptance for a new university settlement could be seen as a blessing in disguise for the Queen's Colleges, which felt they could now look forward to assured government support rather than the uncertain metamorphosis or indeed downright extinction with which they might otherwise have been faced. But there was another development that powerfully helped to concentrate the minds of the memorialists: the throwing open by Trinity College in 1873 of its privileges and opportunities to members of all denominations without restriction. That could well have been a threat to the future student intake of Queen's College Cork. More immediately, however, increasing student numbers made increased accommodation imperative. Overall, therefore, quite a number of factors accounted for the 1874 memorial, with its far-reaching plans for personnel, buildings, facilities and extended and improved college premises.

The memorial suggested that, since there was now an assurance of permanence about the Queen's Colleges, it was timely for the academics to put forward their own plans for the college in the larger context of supplying the 'educational wants of the South of Ireland'. They added that the cost of implementing their proposals 'if extended to the three Queen's Colleges . . . might be drawn from the surplus resulting from the disestablishment of the Church of Ireland' and the total amount would only be half the sum proposed to be withdrawn from that surplus for similar purposes in the recent, and failed, Irish University Bill.

The proposals were detailed in a lengthy appendix. First of all, the professors were concerned that the colleges lacked the necessary incentives to zealous learning and higher standards, in the shape of fellowships. The absence of such inducements had not encouraged parents to send their sons to the Queen's Colleges and had therefore tended to diminish the number of arts students. This had now become a particularly compelling consideration in view of the Trinity open-doors policy. Accordingly, the foundation of ten fellowships in the arts faculty was suggested, each tenable for five years at £200 per annum. There should also be a travelling fellowship in medicine, with the requirement of study 'at some celebrated School of Medicine on the Continent'.

The professors then moved on to the not unimportant matter of their own remuneration. Here their thinking was imaginative and generous. The highest level of salary, they pointed out, was only £322 per annum and this applied to only six chairs. The salaries of other professors ranged downwards from £292 to £130 per annum. Class fees, which were supposed to supplement salaries, were kept small by statute. (A table of annual average class fees income in the early 1870s showed an astonishing range – from £522 in anatomy, from which admittedly the salaries of two demonstrators had to be deducted, through £268 in chemistry and £140 in natural philosophy and modern languages to £12 in logic and metaphysics.) The majority of professors in QCC, it was claimed, had incomes inferior to their counterparts in most other colleges and to those in 'a similar class in the Civil Service' (there is a familiar ring about this comparison). This state of affairs, it was alleged darkly if vaguely, 'tends to cramp the energies of the present occupiers of chairs' and would make it difficult to attract good candidates to vacant posts (again, a familiar argument down the years). It was therefore proposed that, in the case of professorships whose holders did not practise a profession and had only small class fees, the salary should be not less than £500 per annum, with other professorships enjoying a proportionate increase. The proposed amalgamation of some chairs was deplored, it being self-evidently absurd that one professor should be expected to lecture on zoology, botany, geology, physical geography and mineralogy. Other recommendations were that class fees should be taken into account when estimating superannuation, that the 'antedating' granted to professors in the Queen's Colleges should be extended from seven to ten years as in the Scottish colleges, and that the bursar, registrar and librarian should enjoy the same advantages as regards salary increase and antedating as the professors. In all of this, it is interesting to observe the professors deploying their considerable argumentative skills in promoting their own salary and status claims. However, in fairness it should be noted that there was a steep increase in the cost of living in the early 1870s.[17]

The second half of the memorial dealt with the problems of running the college, and of improving and extending the college premises. College running costs (purchase of books and apparatus, printing and stationery, heating and lighting, botanic garden and college grounds, miscellaneous expenditure such as postage, advertising, uniforms of servants, brushes, etc.) came from the annual parliamentary grant – £1,000 – and from college fees. The income available was insufficient, and this was reflected everywhere – in shortage of equipment and instruments but above all in the library situation:

> The Library is deficient in most of the large expensive sets of books and in scientific periodicals. Many of the Scientific and Literary Journals and Proceedings of Societies . . . had to be discontinued. The result of this is that any one engaged in scientific, historical or literary research must often wait to consult many books that ought to be in the Library until he can visit Dublin or London . . . It may be added that the Library of Queen's College, Cork is the only Public Library in the whole of the south of Ireland available to scholars or inquirers in any branch of knowledge.

The inadequacy of the parliamentary grant was felt very severely due to 'the rise in the price of fuel, gas and of every article of consumption'. In 1871–72, heating and lighting cost £182: in 1873–74 it was likely to exceed £325, or nearly one-third of the total maintenance cost. In comparison with the Royal College of Science in Dublin, which did not have QCC's wide range of faculties and which had considerably lower running expenses, the Cork college was being particularly badly treated. The wages of college stewards needed to be improved and their number increased, and a properly qualified and well-paid curator of museums should be appointed.

The next section of the document dealt with the need for more accommodation to take into account the greatly increased importance of physical science, its paramount value in medical education and the new emphasis on practical instruction. Sullivan's hand is clearly discernible here, and the need for better and bigger accommodation is a constant theme of presidential reports throughout the second half of the century. The college was suffering, it was pointed out, from the deficiencies of the original plans. No provision had been made for anatomy, and the medical building had been enlarged around the nucleus founded by the Earl of Clarendon. He had funded the dissecting room and the Board of Works had subsequently added lecture rooms and a museum. Now the accommodation was insufficient, and in other respects the building was inconvenient and unsuitable. Different lecturers had to use the same room in successive hours, and the setting up and removal of specimens and so on resulted in much delay and prevented students from properly examining the displayed material. 'The Professor of Natural Philosophy has no means whatever of teaching his subject practically' and this made nonsense of the simplest scientific research, so essential for staff and students alike.

The chemical laboratory could accommodate only half the practical chemistry class, so that there had to be much duplication of instruction, with students doing insufficient practicals. Extra accommodation was also necessitated by the expected increase in the number of chemistry students over the coming years. Medical students needed a physiological and pathological laboratory, an enlarged dissecting room and a reading room nearby. The professors of natural history and of materia medica needed more

5.2 The Quad, c1890.

accommodation. College also required a comprehensive, all-purpose museum and a glasshouse such as was provided in the Botanic Garden at Glasnevin and in TCD. A better botanic garden and a glasshouse for tropical and sub-tropical plants could be made available 'if the vacant ground to the east of the College grounds were purchased'. (The repeated request for a glasshouse was to be granted through W.H. Crawford's generosity in the 1880s.) The various extensive accommodation requirements could be provided by connecting the present college buildings 'with the Medical Building, so as to form a second quadrangle'.[18]

Finally, the library was becoming overcrowded with books and students, and there seemed no way in which it could be extended. (In fact, an extra floor was added, in more modern times, thus doubling the floor space.) It had been proposed to use the examination hall as a reading room (which was also eventually done) but this would involve 'the employment of an additional Library porter, which cannot be afforded'! Museums with improved facilities and a new glasshouse could be opened to the public at times that would not interfere with college work: 'If this could be done a taste of Science would probably be created and fostered, and the advantages of the College brought more fully before the people of Cork'.

In a rare display of larger concern for the college's environment and its long-term future, the academic community then proposed an extension of the college grounds and the improvement of existing boundaries.[19] They wished to acquire 'the land lying between the Eastern College boundary and Love Lane . . . the natural complement of the present College ground [which] should have been included when the College was being built'. This eastern strip beyond the President's Garden, part grass, part market gardens, was 'the only side on which the College grounds can be added to'. It would provide an excellent site for a botanic garden (which, in fact, it did) and could be used for other purposes. One very good reason for acquiring the land was to pre-empt house building there

> of a very low class, like those in the adjoining lanes, owing to the only approach to it being by College Road. No greater blow could be inflicted on this College than the erection of lanes or courts of small houses in the fields to the east of the College, and some of which would be within 200 feet of the College buildings.

College Road was described as 'a back road, through an impoverished district . . . very inconvenient and dirty, especially in winter'. Social undesirables were not confined to one particular section:

> The state of the upper gate – properly speaking the principal gate – also affords an argument for rectifying the Eastern boundary of the College grounds. At one side of the gate, *and in fact forming part of the gateway*[20] are several old cottages occupied by cottiers who keep pigs and fowl, and the yards of which are filthy and full of manure and cess-pools, besides being active fever nests. The close proximity of such cottages to the gateway . . . is injurious in many ways to the reputation of the College. Their purchase and removal is strongly recommended.

Further social horrors on the northern boundary required similar decisive action. The 'islands and land'[21] bordering Western Road were not college property, and in summer 'are frequented by boys and girls from the neighbouring part of the City for the purpose of bathing. Persons of low character also congregate there, and in Gill Abbey Lane . . .' Moreover,

> the principal walk in the President's garden overlooks the filthy yard and rear of the . . . houses underneath [the cliff] while the end of the lane is a convenient haunt for idlers who gamble or flay dead animals or occupy their time at other like amusements. Everything done in this lane can be witnessed from the garden and everything said can be heard . . . The place must be seen to enable one to judge of the shocking effect which this corner has on the appearance of the College from the Western Road . . . Clearly this state of things should not be allowed to exist in the neighbourhood of such an institution.

The document refrains from making the usual contemporary complaint about the gaol being a nuisance: perhaps the professors felt grateful that at least the riff-raff on the college's western side were securely locked up! Most of the land referred to, 'formerly held by different proprietors and under complicated tenures', was in the possession of Messrs Jennings so that there was now a rare opportunity for the Board of Works to acquire the various pieces for the use of the college, remove the objectionable residences and abate the various nuisances.

There were two other legitimate and laudable reasons for acquiring pieces of land by, and in, the river. One was based on the familiar argument that the college entrance close to the county gaol was distant, unsuitable and dependent on the gaol authorities, thus making it necessary to construct 'a direct and handsome entrance to the College nearer to town' on the Western Road ('the road almost exclusively used by persons coming to the College'), which would be 'connected by a bridge and road with the College'.

While collegians today would be appalled (or at least would affect to be appalled) by the brutally frank class attitudes of the 1874 memorial, the concern of the professors to preserve 'the chief public view of the College', the other reason for land acquisition, would be strongly endorsed by the present environmentally-conscious generation. The professors were worried that the 'best view of the College' from the Western Road, 'much injured' by the very recent construction of Home Rule Terrace (now Home-ville Place), might be 'shut out' altogether 'by forming, as has been proposed, a continuous piece of land between Western Terrace [still Western Terrace] and Home Rule Terrace, and building a terrace of houses on it'. Hence the importance of purchasing the relevant portion of land and planting it with trees.

The 1874 memorial was a useful exercise. It clarified various college objectives at the outset of a vigorous presidency which saw many of them achieved. The salary aspirations were rather fanciful, as is frequently the case, but there was considerable progress during Sullivan's time in library stocking, laboratory expansion, and the development of a botanic garden. Advances on many fronts were due in no small measure to the benefactions of W.H. Crawford, Sullivan's wealthy and public-spirited friend.

5.3 The Botanical Gardens, c1890.

Finally, the boundaries of the college were pushed out under Sullivan, and several portions of land added.[22] Already in the mid–1860s the land between the Quadrangle and College Road had been acquired by the commissioners of public works. In March 1878 a beginning was made in the acquisition of the 'lands and islands' bordering Western Road, and owned by the Jennings family. As we shall see shortly, the memorial's hopes for a 'handsome entrance' nearer town were fulfilled under Sullivan. The fears that Western and Home Rule Terraces might be joined were never realised, and the superb 'chief view' of the college over Perrott's Inch continues to be enjoyed. The land east of the President's Garden was also acquired and a botanic garden and glasshouse were developed there. The college grounds thus took on the dimensions they were to maintain up to the middle of the twentieth century. In the acquisitions process, the whole area was 'gentrified'. Academic gentility was no longer offended by the rough children who disported themselves where Perrott's Inch now smoothly stands, or by the unspeakable denizens of Gillabbey Lane enjoying their dissolute pastimes. The lower orders obligingly moved out of sight and out of earshot.

Progress report

Meanwhile, Sullivan threw himself into his work for the college, and the wide range of his concerns is reflected in the president's reports from 1873–74 to 1887–88 (the brevity of the 1889–90 report foreshadowed his terminal illness). The reports, which incorporate reports from departments, give us a comprehensive picture of the developments of these years and of what were regarded as the main issues and problems. Like his predecessor, Sullivan was concerned to show that QCC was not the failure its opponents depicted it to be, and to underline the welcome evidence provided by student numbers. Thus, the 1875–76 report recorded Catholics as 52.4 per cent of the student body overall, and 59 per cent of the medical school.[23] The year 1878–79 was 'in every respect the most prosperous the College has had', and there were 146 Catholic students out of 280, the largest number in any year since the college opened. Sullivan thought it very satisfactory, all things considered, when the student body reached 300 in 1879–80. The college, in his opinion, was now comparable in numbers to the smaller German universities. In 1882–83, he was proud to contrast the 61.2 per cent Catholic student statistic with the 34.4 per cent of 1870–71.

Sullivan was more diplomatic than Kane in that he did not stress the Catholic 'ban' as the main obstacle to the college's growth. He preferred to emphasise other factors such as the lack of 'good intermediate schools' and the deplorable cramming which was caused by the 'examination craze'. One consequence of this was the small number of entrance scholarships awarded because of the weakness of the candidates. Another was that first-year students followed their courses only 'in a limping and unsatisfactory manner' and that they 'lose much of the first year at College from not knowing how to work'.[24] (*Mutatis mutandis*, university heads in different periods tend to lecture second-level schools on their shortcomings.) The other major damaging factor was the 1879 Act replacing the Queen's University by the Royal University, which substituted 'mere examination' for the collegiate system, greatly weakened the disciplinary powers of the college authorities and left the students to their own devices 'free to attend lectures or not as they please'.[25]

Certain themes recur in the president's reports. Overcrowding in the chemistry department was often referred to, and a new chemistry laboratory was demanded, although progress was not made here until the physics and chemistry building (now civil engineering) was opened in 1911. Library needs were mentioned in Sullivan's first report in 1873–74 and frequently thereafter. The books and journals stock needed to be increased, and accommodation to be enlarged. In fact, Sullivan came around to thinking (prophetically) that an entirely new library was the solution, and that it should have been a separate building from the beginning.[26] At the triennial visitation in May 1876, Sullivan defended an increased charge on book borrowing by graduates on the grounds that long-term borrowing was an abuse and that the college had an obligation to give equitable treatment to all readers, not only its own students but also general users.[27] The concept of the college library as a resource for researchers from all over Munster was a favourite one for Sullivan and his successors.

His wish that anatomy and physiology should be separated, with a view to a new chair for the latter,[28] was not to be fulfilled until Windle's time. In a very different area, he expressed satisfaction that 'fine casts of old Celtic crosses' had been placed 'in one of the corridors, alongside the three or four Ogam [*sic*] stones which form the beginning of a series of inscriptions (originals or casts) illustrative of such monuments of early nations'. He appealed for donations to fund this project.[29]

Successful botanic developments on newly acquired land were a cause of great satisfaction. In 1881–82, the botanic garden was 'in excellent order'. The 1883–84 report noted:

> This year the islands and grounds along the river Lee have been laid out with a view of adding to our Botanic Gardens collections of wood and water plants, and at the same time of improving the College grounds and given shelter by planting and better protection to the whole place.

The 1885–86 report stated that 'the Botanic Garden is . . . now practically co-extensive with the College grounds' and that the pond, with its aquatic plants, was completed. The wider significance of such developments was pointed out: 'year by year, such a College will become more and more indispensable to the people, and its value be more appreciated'. A piece of ground had also been set apart for a 'mythological garden' for the benefit of ancient classics and arts students.[30]

Sullivan's pragmatic – and progressive – philosophy of education can be inferred from his approach to a number of issues. A new omni-collections museum could be opened to the public in off-hours, thus fostering an interest in matters scientific and so benefitting art and industry in Cork.[31] Referring to the fact that the chair of agriculture had been allowed to lapse on the death of the first occupant (Professor Edmund Murphy), Sullivan remarked that it had been 'by no means unsuccessful under the circumstances', the value of scientific training for agriculturalists not then being properly appreciated. That being so, there was a strong case for its re-establishment, a case supported by tenant farmers and landed proprietors alike. (In fact, re-establishment had to wait until the early 1920s.) Sullivan also felt that the school of engineering should be adapted so as to provide scientific instruction for those going into manufacturing industry and those involved in agriculture and veterinary medicine.[32] Moreover, the college should keep pace with advances in medical science and establish a lectureship in psychological medicine, while local authorities should require all applicants for medical appointments to have certificates in mental diseases and sanitary medicine.[33] Sullivan urged Cork hospitals to share expensive clinical resources such as instruments and so improve the quality of their service to the community, especially the poor. As his successors were to do regularly, he reminded the citizens of the economic importance of the college, in this case the injection of more than £10,000 per annum into the city's economy by a medical school of 250 students.[34]

As noted already, one of Sullivan's chief objectives was to push out the physical boundaries of the college. He was concerned to give it more breathing and building space for the future, as well as with establishing suitable entrances. There was substantial

5.4 Biology Building and Plant Houses c1890.

acquisition of land to the east and north, amounting to eight acres in all, an area slightly greater than the original site.[35] Sullivan was clear about what he had in mind. In his first report he referred to:

> the defective and very objectionable character of the modes of access to the College and the necessity of providing a direct entrance nearer the city, and also to earnestly recommend the purchase of some adjacent land, so as to save the College from being shut in between the County Gaol and a number of lanes of small houses, of which there is immediate danger.[36]

Progress was reported in the 1877–78 report where it was stated that land was acquired (using money from 'unappropriated balances') for three purposes: to secure 'free space about the College' before adjoining land should be built on, to develop a small botanic garden and a good site for plant houses, and to make a direct entrance to the college from the Western Road. W.H. Crawford, the college's great bene-factor, had promised £1,500 for the erection of tropical plant houses in the botanic garden if parliament would provide the money for enclosing and laying out the new botanic ground and making the new entrance.[37] Crawford subsequently increased his offer to £2,750, which was half the estimated cost of these works. The Treasury accepted this arrangement, which was then sanctioned by parliamentary vote.

Sullivan was jubilant: 'Thanks to Mr Crawford and the bounty of Parliament, the College will, at length, have a proper entrance opening upon the highway that will bring it within a moderate distance of town . . .' Access from the Western Road over a proposed bridge was facilitated by the generous co-operation of the owners of the portions of land where the entrance was to be built, namely, Cork Corporation and Francis M. Jennings, part of whose land had been involved in the original purchase in the 1840s.[38]

The president's report for 1878–79 noted that the new entrance, bridge and road had been completed and opened to the public on the occasion of the recent visit of the British Medical Association to Cork.[39] The entrance 'had much shortened the distance from town'. *The Irish Builder* (1 May 1879) remarked on the new road 'carried to the front of the College, with a gradual sweep and incline' and on the 'great advantage' of all this, 'instead of the present unsightly, and inconvenient entrance'. Thus, a hope entertained for over two decades was realised at last.

A QCC Maecenas

The provision of money for the erection of plant houses is only part of the story of W.H. Crawford's remarkable generosity to the college. Crawford was a wealthy brewer who admired Sullivan's qualities, his dedication to the college and his courage in pursuing its interests in the face of opposition and adversity. Their friendship was a fruitful source of Crawford's liberality. He was one of the very few substantial benefactors in the history of the college (despite countless appeals over the decades for public donations), and his patronage was particularly timely at a critical phase in its development.

He made successive and munificent donations to the library, his 331 volumes in 1877–78, including many costly historical works, enhancing the library's function as a reference resource for the south of Ireland.[40] When the residential Berkeley Hall was finished, 'with his usual liberality' he furnished all its chambers in an elegant and comfortable manner.[41] His ready and apparently boundless patronage, as well as his strong friendship with Sullivan, were indicated by a casual statement in the 1886–87 report that, on the president's 'mentioning the matter to Mr Crawford', the latter agreed to put up more money to enable the college to join a celestial photography and mapping programme. This would be undertaken from the observatory which he had already equipped and which still bears his name. Later improvements to the telescope were again funded by Crawford and completed by Sir Howard Grubb in 1901.[42]

The observatory project reflected the intense contemporary interest in astronomy and meteorology. The buildings and revolving dome cost about £800, of which £500 was contributed by a very interested Duke of Devonshire and much smaller sums by the Earl of Cork, A.H. Smith Barry and the Marquis of Lansdowne. Crawford gave £1,000 towards the purchase of astronomical instruments, and Sullivan enthused about the prospect of practically every branch of physical science being taught in the college at an early date.[43] In his 1883–84 report, he promised that the observatory would be in full working order before the end of 1884.

The college commissioned Howard Grubb of Dublin to make the instruments, the most important of which was an 8½" telescope, equatorially mounted, which had been exhibited at the Paris Exhibition in 1878 where it had won a gold medal. Grubbs was the only Irish scientific instrument company to achieve international status. A recent report recommends that UCC should give the conservation of the Crawford Observatory 'a high priority', and underlines its significance:

> At Cork, Howard Grubb built a complete observatory including the telescope dome, clocks, three major astronomical instruments and their ancillary equipment. This Observatory though small is unique in Ireland, if not in Europe, for the remarkable state of preservation of its instruments and the original condition of its buildings. . . . Howard Grubb was proud of his achievements in Cork and detailed the many improvements he first introduced there in an article published by the Royal Dublin Society. . . . All in all, the Crawford Observatory is a monument to the ingenuity and craftsmanship of its builders and is of exceptional interest both for the history of the sciences in Ireland and for the technological achievements it incorporates.[44]

The building is in harmony with the main structure and is rare among observatories in having Gothic architectural features. Sullivan and Crawford were justifiably proud of it and would have been dismayed if they could have foreseen its sad story of neglect. The appointment of an observatory assistant to oversee the celestial mapping programme became part of an unseemly row between President Slattery and the College Council in 1894.[45] Subsequently, though the citizens at large enjoyed indulging their bent as amateur astronomers when visiting the observatory,[46] its intramural importance gradually declined. Although attention was devoted to it from time to time by some members of

5.5 Crawford Observatory c1890.

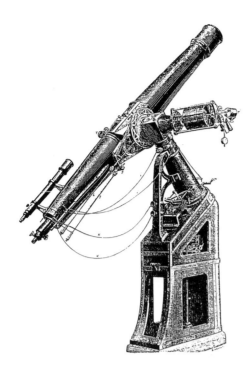

5.6 Grubb Equatorial Telescope, as
illustrated in 1879, was made by Howard
Grubb at his Dublin workshops and won
the Gold Medal award at the Paris
Exhibition in 1878.

the physics department,[47] it had only a very marginal place in courses of study, and in the
end it was nobody's responsibility. The virtually unimpeded celestial view originally
commanded by the main telescope, at least south of the zenith, was gradually restricted –
by the physics and chemistry building from 1910–12 – and eventually obscured at all
points. (However, the writer recalls enjoying – courtesy of Dr Joe Lennon of physics –
the splendid spectacle of Jupiter and its moons, viewed in the eastern sky sometime in
the 1960s.) Even in the 1930s, part of the observatory was being used as a music room,
though it barely had space for a piano and two chairs: Professor Aloys Fleischmann later
recalled the outrage of Professor J.J. McHenry (physics, 1932–64) at the removal of an
obtrusive column which was the bedrock contact of a seismograph. However, according
to Fleischmann, the protests became more muted when it transpired that sensational
registerings on the Richter scale were in reality reactions to the mundane trundlings of
College Road buses.[48] In 1913 there had been a similar false alarm when an apparent
bout of seismic hyperactivity was caused by a bluebottle in a machine.[49]

Though postgraduate and staff research in physics has been carried out intermittently
in the observatory which still attracts the occasional visiting specialist, its future now

obviously lies, paradoxically, in preserving and exhibiting its past, that is, in showing its valuable instruments *in situ* in a proper museum setting to students and public alike. Such a development would also be welcomed by observatories and astronomical museums elsewhere.

A hall of residence

In his first report (1873–74), President Sullivan commented that there were 'no Licensed Boarding Houses in connection with the College', and no application for a licence had been made to him during the session. In fact the idea of licensed boarding-houses, which had been part of the planning for the Queen's Colleges, had been a failure, as Sir Robert Kane quickly found out. Students discovered that such accommodation where available was inferior and expensive, and less suitable for study than ordinary lodgings.[50]

Sullivan was keenly interested in the concept of residential halls, 'a valuable factor in Collegiate education' which, he felt, might be built in the immediate neighbourhood

5.7 Berkeley Hall (later Honan Hostel), the first residential hall under the Colleges Act, was intended for Church of Ireland students and was opened at the beginning of the 1884-85 session.

of the college. (While at the Catholic University, he had suggested to Newman the desirability of a hostel for medical students.) The Colleges Act had stated that such halls could be built by local enterprise, with Board of Works loans. They could have a denominational ethos and their own dean of residence, and thus would be popular with parents and guardians, according to Sullivan. Residents who might find lectures in the college itself offensive to their religious sensibilities (though Sullivan denied there were any such) could have congenial supplementary lectures in their hall. This was particularly feasible under the new Royal University system where attendance at college lectures was not obligatory.[51]

The first such institution to be erected, Berkeley Hall, was intended for Church of Ireland students. The site was in the south-east corner of the college premises formed by College Road and the more recent Donovan's Road. Construction work in the early 1880s was delayed for various reasons, some of them having to do with the political turbulence of the period. However, the first residential hall under the Colleges Act opened at the beginning of the 1884–85 session. A board of governors was incorporated by royal charter. W.H. Crawford once again showed a generous interest and saw to the furnishing of the rooms, so that the residents had only to provide linen. Sullivan, who suggested Berkeley[52] as a more suitable name than Whately[53] (the original proposal), hoped very much that the Roman Catholics – 55.4 per cent of the student body in 1885–86 – would follow suit and build their own hall, getting a charter and borrowing money from the Board of Works as the Colleges Act provided and as the Berkeley Hall governors had done. There was ample room for building such a hall 'in close proximity' to the college. Such a development would contribute to 'a practical solution of the vexed question of Irish university education'.[54] In other words, Sullivan hoped that a residential hall for Catholics would help make the Queen's College acceptable to the Catholic Church authorities. In the event, Berkeley Hall foundered as a Church of Ireland enterprise. The 1886–87 president's report pointed out that the hall needed 'a moderate endowment', its only income being low-level chamber rents.

Ten years later it was closed. As the registrar, Alexander Jack, informed the under-secretary at the Castle, the hall had been managed successfully by the Rev. George Webster (d. 17 December 1890) and his son, G. Arthur Webster. Thereafter it had deteriorated under the direction of W.E. Flewett and William Connolly, and students simply did not go there any longer, leading to its closure in 1897. Jack said the college believed it to be vital that the hall should be bought and he asked for a £1,200 loan, but to no avail.[55] A decade later again, President Windle told Chief Secretary Birrell (14 May 1907) that the 'ugly building' could be purchased for use as 'an excellent residential hostel'.[56] He also informed Birrell (23 May 1907) that the owner, Thomas Donovan, had developed the area, constructing a new road (hence Donovan's Road) and building a bridge at the northern end of that road across the Lee. However, since he now proposed to convert Berkeley Hall into a terrace of houses, it was imperative that the building and the ground be bought as soon as possible.[57] There was no prospect, said Windle, of any local contribution to the purchase money. 'The relations of the College to the district must be adjusted' before that could happen. But pending a popular settlement of the university question (thus opening the floodgates of local generosity!), the government should purchase 'the only piece of property near the College which is likely to be in the market for years to come'.[58] However, the Treasury, as usual, were not impressed: they were 'not aware that there is at the present moment any need for increased accommodation; and, in any case, having regard to the present position of University Education in Ireland, they do not think it desirable to acquire further property at Cork'. It was little consolation to Windle that the under-secretary noted that he thought 'the Treasury's reasons for refusing are feeble in the extreme'.[59] But providence was soon stirring in an unexpected quarter.

After a long period of closure and disuse, the hall was acquired from Thomas Donovan by the Franciscan order, and opened in 1909 as a Franciscan student house and as a hostel for lay Catholic undergraduates. By now, the new UCC in the new NUI was acceptable to the Catholic Church authorities. It was President Windle, following the example of Sullivan in his time, who suggested a new name, this time St Anthony's Hall. Parts of it were derelict but repairs were carried out. It had a private chapel which could be used by college staff and students. For Windle, the hall made it easier to attract Catholic students to the college. Much to his chagrin, the Franciscans decided to close the hall in 1912, since the order was divided from the beginning about the whole project, extremist reformers objecting to their clerics attending a secular university. The day was saved, however, when the hall was sold to the Honan bequest in 1914, thus entering a new phase of its existence as the Honan Hostel, a residence for Catholic students. It survived in this guise until 1991, by which time it had become antiquated in terms of both ethos and economics. It was acquired by the college and demolished in 1995 to make way for an applied business/languages building.[60]

The persistence of George Webster

The guiding spirit behind the building of Berkeley Hall was an indefatigable Church of Ireland clergyman, the Rev. George Webster, rector of St Nicholas church and dean of residence for Anglican students at QCC from 1857.[61] His zeal for the religious welfare of QCC's Church of Ireland students had been frustrated for years by the attitude of the college authorities, or so he claimed. It was only when he finally despaired of their co-operation that he undertook the Berkeley Hall project, as an alternative means of providing an acceptable moral and religious environment for his students.

Webster had undertaken a sustained one-man campaign against the 'godless' college. He maintained that as dean of residence and as catechist he was bound by statute to instruct his Protestant students and that they were obliged to attend his religious instruction classes. He argued that the 1863 charter had made deans of residence *ex officio* religious teachers and given the college the power to assign lecture rooms for their use. Visitors in 1864 agreed that, in the light of his arguments, the college should grant him the use of a room, and Sir Robert Kane promised to do so. But two subsequent visitations, in 1867 and 1870, ruled that the 1864 decision should be interpreted as permissive rather than obligatory. In 1873 visitors also held that students absenting themselves from religious instruction were not committing an offence. Webster stubbornly maintained that the college was responsible for 'this evil' – the non-attendance of students at religious instruction classes in his own house or parochial school house.

Webster relentlessly but fruitlessly pestered Kane, Sullivan and successive College Councils to accommodate him, not only with a room but also with a timetable slot. He put his case before numerous visitations which clearly had no intention of reversing the college ruling in the matter. At the ordinary triennial visitation of May 1876, recorded in the president's report of 1875–76, Sullivan testified that the College Council had to interpret the statutes in a practical sense and did not wish to pass theoretical resolutions which might bind their successors or hamper their actions. The visitors confirmed the 1870 ruling that the college was not obliged to assign rooms for the purpose of religious instruction. Students were not bound to attend such classes outside the college walls: really, the question of religious instruction should be left to the good sense of students and their parents.

Though the 1876 visitors praised Webster for the conscientious discharge of his duties and their 1879 successors also clucked sympathetically, they gave him no satisfaction and clearly regarded him as a nuisance. Crank or zealot, however, he embarrassed the college

5.8 Rev. George Webster, the guiding spirit
behind the building of Berkeley Hall.

into facing the realities of its relationship with the dean of residence of one denomination and, by extension, with the religious situation in general. College seemed to have arrived at the logical conclusion that, if it was to be perceived as impartial, it had to be 'godless', at least on its own premises. Giving Webster a lecture room would expose it to the charge of proselytism which was worse, if anything, than godlessness![62]

The Royal University of Ireland

The disestablishment of the Church of Ireland in 1869 created an entirely new situation in that religious denominations were no longer state funded and were therefore (in theory at least) on an equal footing. In 1872, G.J. Stoney, the secretary of the Queen's University, proposed a grand new solution to the university question, in memoranda supplied to the prime minister, W.E. Gladstone. There would be one big university in Dublin, embracing both Trinity College and the Catholic University as separate component entities and drawing on the best professorial talent in the country, which would serve an academic institution 'brimful of intellectual energy'. The Queen's Colleges of Cork and Galway would have to go if this extravagant centralised scheme were to be effected. Stoney's sentiments, with their condescending assumption of the superiority of centralism, are characteristic of the philosophy of Victorian planning in Ireland:

> It is a mistake to suppose that local colleges in such places are a great benefit to their neighbourhoods. The actual town is too small to supply many students, and when once a student's home is sufficiently distant to oblige him to reside away from it, it would be better for him, whether poor or rich, and would lead to less expenditure in the case of a poor student, to come to such a place as Dublin.[63]

Had Stoney's proposals been taken seriously and implemented, what would have become of the abandoned Queen's College Cork?

Gladstone's ill-fated 1873 measure was obviously influenced by Stoney's memoranda to the extent of proposing a new national and non-sectarian university of which the University of Dublin would be the centrepiece, and to which would be affiliated the colleges of Trinity, Belfast, Cork, Magee College in Londonderry and the Catholic University of Ireland. Galway would be abolished but Cork would be spared. (QCG was generally regarded as not viable, situated as it was in a poverty-stricken area with a declining population, and with little demand for higher education.) Gladstone's bill simply succeeded in antagonising everybody, and its defeat led to the fall of his government.[64]

Prime Minister Benjamin Disraeli's Irish University Education Act of 1879 was another attempt to square the circle and it established an uneasy, unsettling and embittered compromise for nearly thirty years. In the light of the failure of previous experiments, this Act left the three Queen's Colleges and the University of Dublin (including Trinity College) untouched but replaced the Queen's University with the Royal University of Ireland (RUI), which was empowered to confer its degrees on all who had matriculated in it and passed its prescribed examinations. Residence in any college or attendance at lectures was not obligatory on candidates for RUI degrees, except in the case of medicine or surgery. There was to be a senate of not more than thirty-six persons of whom six were to be elected by convocation and thirty appointed by the Crown. Parliament would provide funds for university buildings, and for scholarships, exhibitions and fellowships.[65] The Queen's University was dissolved on 3 February 1882.

A major objective of the exercise was conciliation of the Catholics (though it failed to conciliate them sufficiently). One-half of the Royal's fellowships were assigned to professors in the arts faculty of the Catholic University (known from 1882 as University College Dublin), and the remainder to Magee and to the Queen's Colleges. In effect, public money was being used to subsidise denominational colleges: the Catholic University was rescued from near extinction and began a new career. But to the Catholic bishops the Queen's Colleges were still godless, and they had to be reformed or transformed.

Though Queen's University graduates were now to become Royal University graduates, they had no enthusiasm for this strange and untried 'examination-only' institution.[66] To compound their sense of grievance, the legislation had been passed during the long vacation of 1879 and had come as an unpleasant surprise to the 'Queensmen'. Convocation strenuously protested against the extinction of the university which, they argued, had served the cause of higher education well and had formed an integrated teaching and examining whole with the Queen's Colleges, which were now certain, they predicted, to be considerably weakened.[67]

And indeed from the 1880s, the Queen's Colleges came under increasing political and educational pressure. Their opponents included the Irish Parliamentary Party, who promoted the Catholic episcopal line on the education question and whose stance had to be taken into account by British governments, disinclined in any case to court trouble by lavishing money on the Queen's Colleges with their uncertain future. The Catholic bishops resented state endowment of the Queen's Colleges and demanded equal treatment for University College Dublin. The Queen's Colleges, no longer organic university colleges, so to speak, had to make substantial adjustments to come to terms with the new university, which was mainly an examining board with examinations open to all comers. Contacts between the colleges diminished, though some members met regularly as university examiners. In the Senate of the Royal University, the Queen's Colleges representatives were in the minority. A student from a Queen's College might, in any subject, be examined by a board of professors entirely external to his college. QCC medical students felt particularly aggrieved in that one of the two examiners they had to face was *always* a Dublin man, which gave students in Dublin hospitals a considerable advantage.

In itself, however, and considered apart from its impact on the Queen's Colleges, the Royal University benefitted the cause of higher education in Ireland, especially since it more or less coincided with the operation of the 1878 Intermediate Education Act. (The absence of an organised second-level system had been long and frequently deplored by third-level educationalists like Sullivan.) The Royal's degree standards were high, the range of available degrees was extensive and the curricula content was progressive, reflecting the new priorities of the intermediate system. In the Royal's matriculation examination, for example, Greek was one of a number of language alternatives, and physics was added to the list of subjects. Progressive, too, was the principle that all its degrees, honours exhibitions, prizes and scholarships were open to women on equal terms with men (a gender equality principle which continued into the National University of Ireland structures). Another welcome feature of the Royal University was the relatively lavish provision of prizes and exhibitions on a competitive basis for good candidates at its examinations.[68]

Sullivan, students and politics

W.K. Sullivan, it seems, had a pleasant and affable personality, combining *grámhaireacht* with *gravitas*, as his Aula Maxima portrait suggests. Unlike his predecessor, he got on well with the staff and had a good rapport with the students because, living on campus, he was close to them and, being Cork born and bred, he shared a certain sense of identity with them. In his first report (1873–74) he praised their conduct in college and outside it. When he got to know them better, he sang their praises even higher. Their behaviour was without reproach, he assured the 1879 visitation, and the public had a favourable opinion of them. The visitors were pleased to hear it.[69]

There was a minor brush with students in 1882 when, on the occasion of the dissolution of the Queen's University, they proposed to have a mock funeral procession through the streets of the city. It never took place for want of money, and the ringleaders were rebuked but, very sensibly, not punished by the College Council.[70] The foremost agitator, Stephen Moxley, had previously been rusticated for twelve months.[71]

The sudden deterioration of relations between the president and a section of students in 1884, then, was all the more surprising because of this earlier harmony. The trouble was foreshadowed in 1880 when pro- and anti-Parnell factions clashed and 'some disturbances arising out of the excitement created by the General Election . . . imposed the unpleasant duty upon the Council of rusticating for twelve months two students'.[72] In December 1882, Parnell paid a visit to Cork and, in an episode long remembered, a student deputation presented an address to him at the new observatory and expressed their hope there would be a later opportunity to inform him of their great and numerous grievances, which apparently Parnell promised to redress.[73] It seems that Sullivan invited the 'Chief' to meet the college staff in 1885 but only one professor (John England, natural philosophy) came to the reception.[74] This was hardly surprising: Sullivan's QCC colleagues did not empathise with the national aims of land revolution and home rule, much less with the cult of the uncrowned king.

Sullivan tried to play down the 1884 trouble when he referred to it in his 1883–84 president's report but the bitterness of his tone is unmistakable. Discipline had been good, he claimed, until the excitement which usually accompanies a parliamentary election everywhere afforded an opportunity to a small number of students, apparently desirous of injuring the College in every way they could, to commit breaches of discipline themselves and lead others astray.

The College Council, he continued, failed to convict all the culprits: a few, including two of the most culpable, evaded justice. The chief promoter of opposition to the college authorities was rusticated for twelve months. The culprits had appealed the College Council decisions, and the consequent extraordinary visitation of 16–17 May 1884 upheld the council rulings, with some variations. Thus, according to Sullivan, the disciplinary authority of the president and council was confirmed.[75] In reality, it is hard to see how president–student relations after 1884 could ever have enjoyed 'glad confident morning again'.

Visitations were a regular feature of the Queen's College experience. They were held in public, and adjudicated on the grievances of staff and students. In contrast to the autocracy of the College Council, they were remarkably democratic, even egalitarian, in that students were apparently allowed to confront and cross-examine the president and professors. The events investigated by the extraordinary visitation of 15–16 May 1884 occurred in an atmosphere charged with the political excitement of the middle 1880s, a period of heightened nationalist feeling. There was, accordingly, intense public interest in the visitation proceedings[76] which were reported in considerable detail in *The Cork Examiner* on 16 and 17 May, with an interesting editorial comment on the latter date.

The context of the events discussed at the visitation was the Cork by-election of 23 February 1884, a hotly fought contest between John Deasy, the Home Rule candidate, and William Goulding, the Conservative representative. (In the event, Deasy was an easy winner – 2,125 votes to 1,153.[77]) In a huge eve-of-the-poll rally in Patrick Street, 'a formidable contingent of College students' was prominent. 'Impassioned addresses were delivered by certain of the students which were received with demonstrations of enthusiasm.' More significantly from the standpoint of the college authorities, the students held their own meeting at the Barrack Street Band Room (the 'Barracka' enthusiastically espoused the nationalist cause) where they declared their support for Deasy, demanded reform of the Queen's College constitution and determined to confer with the Irish Parliamentary Party to that end. They then participated in tumultuous demonstrations in the city centre against Goulding.

President Sullivan and the College Council regarded these proceedings as grievous breaches of discipline, claiming that the college's jurisdiction over the students extended to the town area. The student activists, on the other hand, maintained they were never informed such politicking violated the statutes, and emphasised the fact that no disciplinary proceedings had followed the student address to Parnell on 19 December 1882. The students' relations with Sullivan worsened further on 7–8 March when at a stormy meeting with J.J. Lynch, the ringleader of the student demonstration, the president described him as the chairman of the 'mob'. As a result, the students refused to join the president in a common college tribute to Jerome J. Collins (1841–81), the

Cork-born explorer, whose 'longest funeral in the world' was then being completed to Curraghkippane graveyard. Another development in the Sullivan–students row was the election of a recalcitrant nationalist student, James F. Magner, to the vice-presidency of the Philosophical Society, in defiance of the president's wishes.[78]

There was a bizarre revelation during Lynch's aggressive cross-examination of Sullivan at the visitation when he accused the president of trying 'to capture a Chinese lantern' at a downtown demonstration. Sullivan admitted that he had 'tried to get hold of the face of the person who held it to see who he was', and then went on to defend passionately his presence at that meeting:

> Information was given to me that a procession was to be organised and that there was danger of a collision with the police and I went into town on a wet night to make enquiries – what many Presidents of Colleges would not do – entirely in the interests of the students.

In appealing the council's sentence, Lynch claimed that the president as well as Professors George F. Savage-Armstrong (history and English literature, 1871–1905) and J.J. Charles (anatomy and physiology, 1875–1907) were motivated by a personal animus against him and other students, but the visitors rejected this allegation – 'it is almost inconceivable that men in positions of authority in a College could be actuated by motives so very unworthy as personal pique towards a student to work out his destruction by gratifying feelings of that description'. It was admitted that the students should have been more clearly informed about rules and regulations by the council, and the visitors would not accept Sullivan's sweeping contention that *all* extramural meetings of students – even one to discuss founding a cricket club – were illegal.

Mitigating circumstances were conceded in the case of one or two students, and their penalties were modified. By and large, however, the visitors substantially upheld the council's rulings, and confirmed the rustication of Lynch whom they branded as insubordinate and defiant. In his evidence, Professor Bunnell Lewis said the council had explained repeatedly to the students that they were *in statu pupillari* which, he remarked, they regarded as a strange idea. The visitors obviously shared Lewis's patriarchal opinions, chiding the students for prematurely dabbling in politics and for being so presumptuous at their tender age in discussing college reforms – all that was for 'wiser heads'. They were reprimanded for refusing to answer questions or disclose information when asked to do so by the council, and the visitors stated they would expel the student (if they knew who he was!) who wrote to the newspapers alleging Professor Charles was charging excessive fees for anatomy. In conclusion, they expressed the pious hope that the students would settle down and stop defying the council, and that good relations would prevail and discipline be restored.

There were various subtexts and side issues to the 1884 controversy but the most striking feature was the cultural, religious and political gap, indeed confrontation, between the students involved and a hostile council. The stark contrast between the native names of those in trouble – Lynch, Hennessy, Kearney, McSweeney, O'Callaghan – and the colonial appellations of their punitive judges – Malet, Charles,

Jack, Lewis, Armstrong – is illuminating and symbolic. The perception of the college as an alien institution was strengthened by the whole episode.

There was no doubt which side *The Cork Examiner* supported though its views were not expressed in overtly nationalist or political terms.[79] It did not find the visitors' judgements surprising – 'the natural tendency of authority is to back up authority'.

> But we think that it is impossible to fail to see that for the Council it is a pyrrhic victory. It is impossible to avoid contrasting the effects of the *laissez faire* policy of 1882 with the too vigilant demeanour manifested in 1884. The masterly inactivity of the former period was followed by peace; the interference on the later occasion has been productive of anything but tranquillity or probable advantage to the College.

The college should enforce discipline within its walls, but it was counterproductive to follow the students inquisitorially out of doors:

> The country has often been scandalised by the Orange freaks of Trinity College yet what serious effort has ever been made to discover the perpetrators? A similar judicious ignorance of events which were not brought formally under the notice of the Council of the Queen's College would have spared them from an adverse judgement on the part of the public which is quite independent of the judgement of the Visitors.

It was a sensible assessment which Sullivan must have perused attentively.

A brief remark made at the visitation by the president had repercussions in an unlikely quarter. With reference to the student meeting in the Barrack Street Band Room (in fact, the premises belonged to the Barrack Street Temperance Society, founded by Fr Mathew in 1838, of which the band was a dominant feature), the visitors rather snobbishly gave the impression that while the band room might be all right for working class men, it was *infra dig.* for students to frequent it. Sullivan, unfortunately, was much blunter, describing the band room as 'one of the rowdiest places in the town', a remark which was greeted with hisses by some of his hearers at the visitation. The Barrack Street Temperance Society was outraged and a largely-attended protest meeting was immediately held at the premises. The attendance included the mayor; John Deasy, the recently elected MP; city notables; and the 'Barracka' fraternity.

It was an occasion for letting off much self-righteous steam, with resonances of class and locality. There was particular indignation that President Sullivan had neither explained nor retracted his offensive remark. The meeting found it hard to accept that he could have confused the distinguished band with 'one of the fife and drum bands so often brought before his worship the Mayor at the Police Office'. The secretary of the society said the members 'might be humble but they always tried to the best of their ability to make themselves free from the charge of rowdyism, always trying to act respectably'. This unctuous class tone was maintained by another speaker who said 'it was not because a man wore a fustian jacket that his ideas would not be as exalted as those who wore purple and fine linen and drove in carriages'. There was applause also for those who vindicated the good name and 'respectability' of the neighbourhood: did it not include the residences of the Protestant Bishop Gregg, and indeed by a little extension, of President Sullivan himself? Apparently, the whole matter ended with the meeting, but the extensive coverage was a further embarrassment for Sullivan who must have regretted the gaffe as soon as it was uttered.[80]

The events of 1884 reveal Sullivan in a surprisingly harsh and disciplinarian light, and this calls for some explanation. As he explained to the visitors, he was responsible for the behavioural standards of students in a non-resident, relatively new college with little tradition. He was excessively apprehensive about their downtown conduct in such a highly volatile political environment, and his concern was dramatically illustrated by his presence and his actions in the middle of a demonstration, and by his rigidly logical but absurd conclusion that all unauthorised meetings were a breach of discipline. Indiscipline, if overlooked or tolerated in one case, would break out everywhere. The confrontation with the aggressively defiant Lynch simply aggravated the president's authoritarian approach. He was also part of the Cork establishment which expected students to abstain from nationalist activism. Moreover, Dublin Castle, controlling the purse-strings and the appointments system, was ever vigilant and it behoved heads of educational institutions to ensure there would be no unpleasant enquiries about alleged subversive behaviour. Sullivan also suspected the Irish Parliamentary Party, so enthusiastically backed by his delinquent students, of making trouble for the Queen's Colleges and, in common with the bishops, conspiring to destroy them in the Catholic interest. Finally, it may well be that proceeding as he did went against Sullivan's natural, and national, instinct and perhaps the students were aware of this. Nevertheless, he was determined not to provoke a quarrel with the council and the staff, being well aware of the disastrously divisive effects of the strife in his predecessor's time. A similar disinclination to confront his colleagues was evident in the Margaret Tierney Downes case in 1889,[81] though his illness was an important factor at that stage.

Corporation supports the college, 1884

An interesting motion (passed unanimously) before Cork Corporation on 9 May 1884 shows the city's awareness of the college as a vital educational resource which might well be at risk from current developments and which it was essential to support.[82] Councillor J. Hooper, who proposed the motion at some length, was a Roman Catholic and in the course of his speech he made an oblique appeal for necessary changes to make the college acceptable to Catholic sentiment. This seemed to go down well with his Protestant colleagues.

The motion expressed Cork's claim to 'the retention of its rights as a Collegiate Centre in the Irish University System' and the corporation's support for the preservation 'of the grants at present enjoyed by the Queen's College, Cork'. Hooper's main concern was that, if the scholarships and prizes of the Queen's College were thrown open through competition to all the students of the Royal University, the whole idea of a state-supported college in Cork would be undermined. 'Poorish' people would no longer be able to have their sons educated. The establishment of the Royal University had already damaged QCC's stability – the student numbers had fallen from over four hundred to under three hundred – and the number of arts students would fall further if the college could no longer offer them the incentive of prizes and scholarships. There would be a further deterioration of morale, 'a complete paralysis of the energies of the professors who cannot be expected to display much energy or enthusiasm for a dying institution'. In these circumstances, the public would be told that there was no need for an arts faculty, and when that disappeared, law and engineering would inevitably go with it, leaving only the medical school which would not last long as a stand-alone state-endowed school. (In any case, doctors so trained 'would be simply so many Sawbones'.)

The medical school would come under intensified attack from the private medical schools of Dublin which had strongly objected to the Cork medical school all along, and its demise would be 'nothing short of a disaster for the city, the county, and the greater part of the South of Ireland (applause)'. It was therefore the corporation's duty to avert this dire scenario and 'to take measures in time not only to prevent the ultimate loss of the grant to the city, and the province, but to make it more available for the people at large than it has been hitherto'. Perhaps, Hooper suggested, there could be 'two denominational halls for the two great religious bodies', with duplicate chairs for teaching disputed subjects, and even 'a new title, Cork University College (hear, hear)'. Properly reformed, the college could have a thousand on its rolls, with the new intermediate schools sending a plentiful supply of students. In any case, the grant must be preserved to continue the work of university teaching which 'can only be carried on within the walls of properly endowed institutions possessing costly appliances'. Is it, Hooper wondered, 'because every other place in Ireland outside Dublin cannot possess an educational establishment so equipped, that, therefore no one place shall have it?' Hooper referred to the movement for the 'extinction of the Cork College'. As a Munsterman and Corkman, his duty was to preserve it. He went on to describe the medical school in Cork as 'one of the largest, if not the largest in Ireland'. It was popular because the fees were low (only about half the Dublin fees), the teaching good, and the equipment – laboratories, museums, library, botanic garden, plant house – satisfactory and compactly located.

Hooper made the strong point against the Royal University arrangement that 'under the examining system students never display that average of high academic culture that those do who pass through a well-digested undergraduate course in a properly-equipped University College'. He also listed various continental examples to show that Ireland had too few universities, and Cork was fully entitled to a college 'with University powers'. And 'it is a well recognised fact that a diversity of University systems in a country . . . has the happiest results in producing intellectual power and originality'. In claiming that Cork was 'eminently suited for a University or University Centre', Hooper pointed out – striking a note of great contemporary concern – that 'it possesses the minimum of disadvantages as regards dangers that beset youth in populous centres and great cities, and the maximum of advantages as regards central position and accessibility by rail (hear, hear)'. He referred to the munificent benefactions of William Crawford, and hinted that they had halted because of 'the uncertainty of the fate of the College'. The professors would be very well compensated if the college were disestablished (obviously, a very real fear in 1884), 'but', Hooper concluded, 'I am sure none of them and especially the Corkmen who are among them (with the President at their head) take this selfish view of the matter'.

The admission of women

In 1885–86, herstory began in the college! It could be argued that in the long term the most significant development of Sullivan's presidency was the admission of women students. Earlier in the century, it had been remarked that women were prominent attenders at lectures and demonstrations on scientific matters, for which there was a great vogue in polite Cork society in pre-college days. The presence of women in

5.9 Early female graduate c1890. Women were first admitted to QCC for the 1885-86 session but they did not enter in significant numbers until the advent of the NUI (1908) when Catholic clerical pressures eased.

visitation audiences was also noted,[83] but they were otherwise conspicuously absent from the college community which was exclusively a fraternity.

The question of admitting women to Irish universities first arose in the 1870s in Belfast, which had a strong radical tradition.[84] Though the Senate of the Queen's University, by a small majority, was favourable (Sullivan as a Senate member was opposed), in 1876 the QCB College Council turned down Mary Edith Pechey's request to attend medical courses.[85] The issue was discussed on 15 November 1876 by the QCC College Council which agreed with its Belfast counterpart that the idea was 'inexpedient'. A group called The Ladies Association for the Promotion of Higher Education of Women in Cork organised courses of literary and scientific lectures to be delivered by QCC staff and other experts. This obviously increased the pressure on the college authorities who by 1878 allowed the Ladies Association use the Aula Maxima as a lecture venue. After some years of activity, the women, encouraged by developments, arranged for an application to be submitted to the College Council for admission to courses of lectures in arts. This was discussed at council meetings on 1 and 6 November 1883, and the following historic motion was adopted:

> That the Council have no objection to ladies attending courses of lectures delivered by the Arts Professors of the College, either as Matriculated or non-Matriculated students of the College, on their paying the usual fees . . . . the Council will not require any Professor to alter his Courses of Instruction, or to divide his classes, or to deliver any additional course or courses of lectures in consequence of the admission of any lady to the College.

And no special classes would be formed for women to assist them prepare for Royal University examinations.[86]

In his report for 1886–87 Sullivan noted the admission of women to QCC:

> The Act of Parliament founding the Royal University of Ireland, having opened its examinations, honours and prizes to men and women alike, the College Council decided that the time had come to extend to women the full benefits of collegiate education, so as to enable those who desired to obtain University degrees, to get the necessary teaching for the purpose. A separate cloakroom having been provided last year, we were able to admit women to the classes during the past Session.[87]

He went on to praise those first women students for having obtained high honours grades. Sullivan then made a comment which no doubt was intended to be complimentary but which today would be seen as patronising, if not sexist: 'The presence of ladies in the classrooms and in the Library greatly contributed to the preservation of order; and I expect their example will stimulate the men to more attentive and regular work.' Returning to this theme in the following year's report, Sullivan commented – perhaps recalling the turbulence of 1884 – that discipline had been 'very well maintained' and 'the presence of ladies among the students has, I think, contributed in some measure to this excellent result'.

The admission registers of the 1885–86 session list the names of the first women students: Mary Tierney Downes (age 26) and Adelaide M. Stuart (25). In 1886–87, Jane Roche (17), Sarah Walker (19) and Barbara C. Denroche (21) were registered. Of these five, only Downes was a Roman Catholic. The number of women students in pre-UCC days was tiny – only a total of thirty registered during the years from 1885 to 1896, and of these only six were Catholics. The Catholic woman student was truly a *rara avis*! Catholic women were particularly pressured by their Church authorities not to attend the college.[88]

Admission to arts was the first step and the next breakthrough was into the privileged world of medicine. Dora Elizabeth Allman, a nineteen-year-old Protestant from Bandon, and Lucy Elmarie Smith, a twenty-year-old Presbyterian from Midleton, became the first women medical students, graduating in 1896. A special (men's) pressure group – including Professor Marcus Hartog and Dr P.T. O'Sullivan – had to agitate for women to be allowed attend practice and clinical lectures at Cork hospitals. The Association of Women Graduates, formed in Cork in 1902, helped in the further promotion of women's interests. The 'Ladies Column' in the student magazine *QCC* indicates the active role of women students in college life in the opening decade of the new century, including spirited participation in debates, frequently on 'gender' topics.[89] However, the path to progress was not without its obstacles, with some professors being more accommodating than others. In the first year of women's admission to medicine, Professor Charles told the College Council that he had no objection to women students attending classes in anatomy, physiology or practical anatomy but:

> There are obvious reasons why ladies should not dissect alongside the other students; but if the ladies themselves do not object, I shall not. On the other hand, if they should require a 'separate' room with a subject for themselves, special arrangements will have to be made.

The registrar, Professor Jack, was informed by Queen's College Belfast that the presence of women in the dissecting room there was not conducive to disorder but the opposite.[90] Nevertheless, a new dissecting room was provided in QCC in 1907 for the exclusive use of women medical students – 'our fascinating scalpel-wielders', as they were referred to by the student magazine of the period.[91] Women medical graduates faced another struggle in the years ahead in getting access to, and equality of treatment in, the posts of house doctors.

President Sullivan's favourable attitude to women students (despite his initial opposition in the Queen's University Senate) helped to weaken male resistance within the college. Some Canutes, nevertheless, vainly tried to stem the female trickle, correctly sensing that one day it would become a flood. President Slattery was opposed to the admission of women to medicine. Professor R. Horner Mills refused to admit women to his class.[92] Mills would doubtless have appreciated the story of the literary eminence Arthur Quiller-Couch resolutely addressing his one-man, many-women Cambridge class as 'Sir!' In the late 1940s, classics lecturer

William Porter, renowned eccentric and splendid teacher, was reputed to have had recourse to telling risqué stories to drive women from his class.

'I-told-you-so' misogynists had their prejudices strengthened by the stream of indignant letters sent to the College Council in February–March 1889 by Margaret Tierney Downes, one of the two trail-blazers admitted in 1885–86. Her experience of college was not a happy one. She complained that she was 'persecuted' by fellow students in the logic class, that the professor, George J. Stokes (logic and metaphysics, 1884–94), was both indifferent and insolent to her, that President Sullivan treated her with 'marked discourtesy', that she was obliged 'to absent myself from the Logic class for nearly a week while Professor Stokes was lecturing on Cardinal Newman's "Grammar of Assent"', and that a majority of the council were 'bitterly hostile' to her. And the reason she had been subjected to such victimisation? Not, as we might expect, because she was a woman but 'solely because I am a Catholic'. Downes, who was obviously a *mulier fortis* (a term that has died out with the passing of Latin and patriarchy), threatened that 'Dr Sullivan may rest assured that after his base shuffling conduct he has not heard the last word from me yet'. Her letters included two interesting disclosures: first, Sullivan had told her 'the majority of the Professors had been at first against his view of the advisability of admitting female students'; and secondly, Sullivan's daughter (the president was quite ill at this stage) 'in evident consternation' implored her not to communicate with the press because 'no ladies would attend the College any more if the truth be known'.[93] The College Council eventually rebuked her and refused to accept any further letters from her (9 April, 1889).

In the happier days of the early stages of Bertram Windle's presidency (1904–19), the general position of women students improved, together with the facilities available to them in the college. More significantly, women began to be appointed to the staff. Miss Martin became lecturer in methods of education in 1905 and Miss Bowen-Colthurst was appointed demonstrator in mineralogy in 1907. A major milestone was reached in 1910 when Mary Ryan, lecturer in German, was appointed professor of romance languages (1910–38), the first woman in the United Kingdom to hold a chair. But the college continued to be ruled by a male establishment which insisted that women students, being 'ladies', had to observe extra regulations made specially for them, like being required 'to wear their College gowns whilst they are inside the College Boundaries',[94] not to smoke in public or, much later and most famously, not to lie *about* on the grass.

With regard to student numbers, the presence of women was insignificant from their first admission to the end of the QCC period. They reached a peak of ten in 1893–94 and again in 1895–96. The provision of a course of lectures on education stimulated a little growth, so that women numbered seventeen in 1906–07. With the establishment of the NUI in 1908, clerical pressures ceased and, for the first time, there was a really significant increase in the numbers of women students. By 1917–18 they totalled 113 out of 566 overall, in particular filling wartime male vacancies in the medical school. In 1934–35 women accounted for 296 out of a total of 906; by 1948–49, the figure was

5.10 Professor Mary Ryan, professor of romance languages,
UCC 1910-38 was the first woman professor in Ireland,
and in the United Kingdom.

306 out of 974. After a static (percentage-wise) 1950s, the number of women increased at a higher rate than men in the 1960s. In 1969–70, there were 1,165 women out of a student body of 3,181. The pattern was maintained over the next two decades, and by the late 1980s women students outnumbered men, a century after they were first admitted to the college.

This development was in sharp contrast to the tiny number of women on the professorial staff, a situation which proportionally worsened, if anything, as the twentieth century wore on. The principle of gender equality impressively enshrined in NUI legislation remained largely a dead letter. Women were employed in relatively generous numbers in the sub-professorial grades but for a long time non-statutory women lecturers had to retire at marriage. Even in the more enlightened age of equality committees in the 1980s and 1990s, the men in power in UCC had no intention of sharing it with women, while deeming it expedient to pretend the contrary.

End of vice-presidency

The most far-reaching administrative change of Sullivan's presidency was that the office of vice-president was allowed to lapse on the death of the first incumbent, and oldest QCC professor, John Ryall.[95] The vice-presidents had a central role in the planning and establishment of the Queen's Colleges from 1845 onwards, and the corporate body in each college was initially defined as 'the president, the vice-president and the professors'.[96] The registrarship was a relatively inferior office, and the 1857–58 commission report stressed the importance of the vice-presidency. The vice-president, moreover, was a residential officer in Cork, sharing the East Wing with the president. (The 1857–58 report rejected a complaint by the three registrars that it was unfair to charge them with the responsibility for the premises during the summer vacation, since they did not enjoy college residence.) The 1857–58 report described the vice-president's role as follows:

> During the absence or illness of the President he is entitled to exercise the powers and discharge the duties of the President in the internal administration of the College . . . . He is bound to attend the meetings of the College Council and the public meetings of the College, and to exercise a constant supervision over all the departments of the College and direct his particular attention to order and discipline therein . . . . The only difficulty that appears to have arisen in the exercise of the functions of Vice-President has been at Cork, where subtle distinctions have been taken as to what is included in the word [*sic*] 'internal administration'.

The 1863 statutes heralded a radical change in the initial arrangements. Revoking the letters patent of 1846 and 1849, the 1863 statutes declared that the corporate body would now consist solely of 'the president and the professors'. Specifically, the new statutes ordained that

> John Ryall shall be vice-president of the College and that until the office of vice-president shall determine[97] he shall be ex-officio, the deputy of the president . . . . that if we should hereafter deem it expedient to appoint future vice-presidents, that they shall also be appointed by writing under the sign manual of us, our heirs or successors from among the professors for the time being.

The office of vice-president was thus put on an optional footing, post-Ryall, and was not filled on his death in 1875. When it was revived a century later in UCC, it was in a different and less important form. Meanwhile, the most striking effect of the termination of the office was to enhance the importance of the office of registrar who now replaced the vice-president as occupant of the East Wing and as the president's second-in-command. More particularly and immediately, the change initiated the personal ascendancy of Professor Alexander Jack (civil engineering, 1855–1906) who was appointed registrar (1876–1906) in succession to Robert J. Kenny. Jack became a power in the land during the weak and often nominal presidencies of James Slattery (1890–96) and Sir Rowland Blennerhassett (1897–1904): he was a kind of regent

5.11   Professor Alexander Jack, registrar QCC, 1876–1906.

acting *in loco praesidis*, and was to be found exercising such presidential functions as corresponding with Dublin Castle about matters like property acquisition.[98]

Appointments

Ryall's death in 1875 also meant that the chair of Greek was vacant for the first time since the foundation of the college. Curiously, President Sullivan confessed his ignorance of procedures to be followed in filling the chair (the first professorial vacancy since his own appointment as president).[99] It also seems odd to have the president of Queen's College Cork requesting the chief secretary's office to show him the list of candidates and testimonials and hoping his opinions will be taken into consideration. This reminds us again of the powerful role of the Castle in making appointments to the

Queen's Colleges. At any rate, the list of candidates and the testimonials were forwarded to Sullivan. He was asked to select 'three who in your opinion would be best qualified for the office', and to offer his observations.[100] There were eighteen candidates for the position, including the scholar and antiquarian, Richard Caulfield, who had already unsuccessfully applied for the vacant chair of history and English literature in 1871 and who wound up as the college librarian (1875–87). This scattergun approach to applying for vacancies was not unusual at the period. Another candidate, James J. Hynes, was recommended to the lord lieutenant by a host of Cork notables, including the mayor, three MPs, the high sheriff, the Earl of Cork and Orrery, and Sir George Colthurst.[101] However, the successful candidate was Vaughan Boulger (1875–83).

During the vacancy, lobbying of a different kind was carried out by 150 graduates of Queen's University in a memorial to the lord lieutenant on 28 August 1875. With reference to the vacant chair of Greek in QCC, their concern was that 'so few' Queen's University graduates had been made professors in the Queen's Colleges. This was a 'reproach to the talent' of such graduates or 'an admission of the failure of the system' if after thirty years it was necessary to go outside the university to find a 'fully competent' candidate. Elsewhere, fellowships and similar awards help to create 'a body of illustrious scholars', and the lack of such incentives militated against the success of the Queen's Colleges. The prospect of professorial promotion for university graduates would infuse a sadly-needed 'vitality and energy' into the colleges, make the professors more representative of university talent and 'thus conduce to the realisation of the hopes of its founders'.[102]

The memorial exemplified a widespread perception that TCD and British applicants were given preference for chairs and that Queen's University candidates were being discriminated against. The resentment this generated was reflected in the nativist view that, all other things being equal (a delightful saving clause!), preference should be given to the graduates of the college where the post was being filled. A common feeling in post-independence UCC was that the jobs should be given to 'our own' wherever possible. Long before NUI days, however, this sentiment was frankly expressed in the petition (150 signatures) sent to the lord lieutenant from a public meeting of students and graduates in the Aula Maxima, QCC, on 15 January 1889:

> We . . . desire respectfully to impress upon the authorities who have the power of filling its [QCC's] vacant chairs and offices, the justice and importance of giving the preference, *ceteris paribus*, to candidates who have pursued their studies in the College.[103]

The nationalist undertone in this petition was to be heard again in a *Cork Examiner* editorial of 1895.[104] This demanded that in deciding on a successor to Professor Owen O'Ryan (modern languages, 1879–95), Chief Secretary John Morley should ensure that the successful candidate should not only satisfy 'the educational and collegiate requirements of the Chair' but also 'have the approval of the Catholic and Nationalist population which may avail of his teaching directly or otherwise'.

> The Queen's Colleges [in Cork and Galway] are supposed to subserve mainly the
> interests of a Catholic and Nationalist population . . . While in Belfast the
> professoriate has run, it may be said, arm-in-arm with popular feeling, not of Ulster
> but of Belfast, that of the Colleges in the two Catholic centres has been kept, if not
> actually hostile to, at least in a different plane from the public feeling and sentiment.

The *Examiner* was clearly saying that Queen's College Cork, particularly in its staffing
policy, was still an alien institution. However, in the particular instance of a successor to
Owen O'Ryan, 'the Catholic and Nationalist population' would have had no cause to
complain at the appointment of W.F.T. Butler (professor of modern languages,
1895–1909; registrar, 1906–09), historian of the Gaelic lordships and of land
confiscation.

Sullivan under siege

Sullivan considered the student disturbances of February–March 1884 to be part of a
wider assault on the college. In his president's report for 1884–85, he complained of the
'useless yet harassing inquiries and attack', the 'never-ending discussions on the Queen's
Colleges', the 'continuous agitation' creating uncertainty and halting promising
developments. It may well be that, after twelve years, Sullivan was experiencing the
symptoms of fatigue, stress and disenchantment which affect even the best of presidents
– perhaps *particularly* the best of presidents – during the later stages of their administration. His cardiac illness was to become increasingly troublesome from 1887. He was
particularly upset by criticisms (emanating from, among others, the formidable John
Pentland Mahaffy of Trinity College) about the low standards of QCC's entrance
examinations, when the real fault lay, so Sullivan claimed, with the country-wide
cramming system.[105]

He elaborated on his 'conspiracy' theory of attacks on QCC when he replied in
1885 to a request from the assistant under-secretary in Dublin Castle for his comments on a Queen's Colleges motion in the House of Commons tabled by the
nationalist MP, Justin McCarthy. Sullivan's answer was unambiguous. The motion
was obviously

> part of the system of attacks persistently made in letters and articles in a Dublin
> newspaper,[106] and vexatious questions put in the House of Commons to which in
> the case of Queen's College Cork has been added the fomentation of political
> dissensions among the students for the purpose of disorganising the College
> discipline and interrupting the teaching.

The strategy, Sullivan went on, was even more sinister. The ultimate objective was

> to destroy the Queen's Colleges and hand over their endowments to the Catholic
> bishops for the benefit of their seminaries and schools, and failing this to hand over the
> colleges of Cork and Galway to them to be converted into denominational institutions.

The government should act quickly to end the uncertainty surrounding the education issue. What was at stake for Cork was a major stage in the physical development of the college:

> Mr W.H. Crawford of this city wished to provide houses for the arts professors . . . and a Hall for senior students engaged in teaching, and for assistants. With this in view, he purchased nearly 8 acres of land adjoining the College and at his expense I enclosed it, made a road through it and partially laid it out for the purpose of joining it to the College grounds . . . As this land and the buildings to be erected on it are to be given to the College only so long as it remains undenominational, Mr Crawford hesitates to complete his gift until the existing uncertainty as to the future of the College shall have ceased . . . This state of suspense does irreparable injury to the College, paralyses the energies of the professors and my own exertions for its benefit, and involves the risk of losing altogether the gift of Mr Crawford.[107]

While Sullivan may have exaggerated the impact of 'this state of suspense' on professorial morale and also may have been rather fanciful in seeing the student demonstrations of February–March 1884 as part of a grand design, it would be a mistake, nevertheless, to dismiss his anxieties as neurotic. There *was* a question mark over the future of the Queen's Colleges (excepting Belfast) during this period. There *was* an emerging consensus between the Catholic bishops and the Irish Party of which a central component was the party's recognition of education as being in the bishops' sphere of influence and its willingness to promote Catholic interests in this area. (Emmet Larkin notes that Parnell's conciliation of the Catholic clergy included a demonstration that he was sound on the education question by voting in the House of Commons against money for prizes in the Queen's Colleges.)[108] It was not alarmist to fear the consequences of this arrangement, given the party's leverage in the power balance of parliamentary politics.

College business, extramural activity

Quite independently of all this, Sullivan had his college eye on another piece of desirable property. In a memorandum to Courtenay Boyle in the lord lieutenant's office on 15 February 1885, the president said he had succeeded in obtaining all the land necessary for the protection and development of the college (he had concluded an expansionist phase), except for a small peninsula of river land on the western side. This parcel had just come on the market, and Sullivan was opposed to a proposal to build ten small houses which would seriously affect the appearance of the college and moreover make it impossible to protect the grounds from trespassers, especially because the river ran dry in places during the summer. Besides, such a development would interfere with the college's freedom to take gravel from the river for its walks and roads. Sullivan wanted the lord lieutenant's help in acquiring the land, in spite of the uncertainty on the education question. The lord lieutenant's response was that while it was a cause worthy of support, he could not interfere with the decision of the Board of Works.[109] Nevertheless, by the end of August, a substantial acquisition had been made in the 'weirs and islands' area.[110]

In his last year or two, among the items Sullivan was anxious to tidy up was that of the college arms. He told the under-secretary on 2 February 1889 that in building the gate lodge on the Western Road (by then the main entrance to the college) a stone was inserted over the wicket, the face of which was boasted[111] for the purpose of carrying the arms of the college on it: 'The College has, however, no proper arms. The form used as a seal, book plate, etc, is wholly incorrect and was never authorized by the Office of Arms . . .' Application had been made to Sir Bernard Burke, Ulster King of Arms, for a correct seal. Though this had arrived, the college could not afford the patent! He requested the Treasury to meet the costs: the distinction of proper arms had become more vital since the dissolution of the Queen's University. That event 'has tended to lower the status of the College and allow us to be confounded with intermediate schools of every kind'.[112] In these circumstances the Treasury softened and agreed to pay the costs, and quickly too (22 February).[113]

In the Kane tradition, Sullivan made Irish industrial development his foremost public concern. He had been involved in the Dublin Exhibition of 1853, and brought a lifetime's interest and experience to the Cork Exhibition of 1883, where he was a judge and served on committees. (Bertram Windle was to perform a similar public service in his time as president.) Sullivan wrote a lengthy report on the exhibition, which was in fact a comprehensive review of the various factors affecting the growth of Irish industry, its potential and its prospects. He paid particular attention to the paper trade, to fisheries and (an old interest) to the possibilities of a sugar beet industry. The emphasis throughout was on practical education through technical instruction, and this was the tenor of his submissions to parliamentary commissions and committees over the years.

In the best tradition of gown service to town, Sullivan was active in the life of the city, reviving the Cork Scientific and Literary Society (still flourishing today) of which he became president. He helped found and develop the Munster Dairy School, and his scholarly interests in antiquities, social history, and philology were lifelong.[114] In spite of all this, however, the college remained a place apart from the community.

Able administrator, imaginative initiator, energetic director, Sullivan's was a creative presidency which witnessed museum extensions and expansion in many departments, particularly in the progress of the medical school, the advance of clinical teaching, and the forging of closer links with local hospitals. The acquisition of extra land, the growth of the botanic garden, the building of the plant house, the new entrance on the Western Road, the Biological Institute, the observatory, the construction of Berkeley Hall, the opening of the college to the public – all this amounted to a transformation of the college and (in conjunction with the munificent Crawford) to a remarkable phase of physical expansion, completed by 1885 and not to be recommended until Windle's time.[115]

It has been suggested that the Kane–Sullivan emphasis on practical education and applied science was excessive, and that it contributed to a long-term utilitarian bias in such departments as chemistry, thereby militating against the emergence of high-quality pure research which was to be observed, for example, in QCG. Be that as it may, Sullivan's achievements in so many areas were considerable and, by any standards, he must be rated an outstanding president. Unfortunately for him, he had to work in an increasingly unfavourable environment – the dissolution of the Queen's University and its replacement by the purely examining body that was the Royal; the consequent loss of prestige for the college; the lowering of entrance standards; the school cramming system; the distracting political fever of the 1880s; the pressures exerted by a hostile Church and the powerful Irish Party. None of this was any fault of Sullivan's. And though his presidency ended in some disenchantment, ushering in a period of decline, it was nevertheless the strong foundations laid by him that ensured the college would survive the two placemen who followed him and the vicissitudes of the next fifteen years.

Sullivan's health deteriorated in 1887 but he stayed on as president at the government's request, giving up his involvement in public affairs and confining himself to the duties of his office, working and sleeping in his study. His wife predeceased him in 1888 and on 12 May 1890, after a long illness, William Kirby Sullivan died and was widely mourned – from all the evidence, genuinely so.[116] Speaking at the unveiling of the grave monument to President Sullivan on 25 June 1894, his 'oldest friend', Denny Lane, said: 'There was not an Irish town he did not know; there was not an Irish shire through which he had not walked. The history, the geography, the geology, the botany, the agriculture, the industries of Ireland were familiar to him'.[117]

CHAPTER SIX

FIN DE SIÈCLE DECLINE

Slattery, 1890–96

> *I am to be more pitied than blamed . . .*
> President James Slattery to lord lieutenant, July 1896

AT A CONFERRING CEREMONY some years ago, President Michael Mortell referred humorously to the array of presidential portraits on the wall behind him (where he too would one day hang) as a rogues' gallery. The third (James W. Slattery) and fourth (Sir Rowland Blennerhassett) presidents of the college were conspicuously missing from the gallery, largely because college tradition long regarded them *as* rogues and consequently no serious effort was made to locate their portraits.[1] Both of them are perceived as creatures of government, rewarded with the presidency as political hacks for services rendered, and treating the office as a sinecure, to the total detriment of the college which reached the nadir of its fortunes under their negligent stewardship. And there is a vague but persistent impression in college folklore that one of them was in particular disgrace, since he made off with the college money! In the case of Slattery at least, it is now possible to penetrate this fog of garbled tradition and reveal something of the historical figure.[2]

Slattery was a Co. Tipperary Catholic who, after a period in Maynooth, had a brilliant undergraduate career as a classical scholar in TCD.[3] He got a senior moderatorship and gold medal in history, political science and English literature. He was appointed Whately professor of political economy at TCD in 1866 while also becoming one of the professors of law at King's Inns from 1868. He wrote a Victorian-style novel or romance, entitled 'Francis Rowan'. It remains unpublished and in the possession of his great-nephew, Professor David Slattery. Apparently, it has autobiographical elements though these are not immediately or explicitly evident beyond the outline story of a young man who goes to Maynooth but discovers he has no vocation and that celibacy is not for him, whereupon he attends TCD. When Slattery consulted his friend, Edward Dowden, about the possibilities of publication, he received the diplomatic advice that the novel was unlikely to have a large readership.

When W.K. Sullivan died, Slattery applied on 2 June 1890 to the lord lieutenant for the vacant presidency of QCC, and submitted 'testimonials in evidence of qualifications for that office'.[4] Curiously, however, none of these related to his suitability in 1890 for the vacancy since they were tributes to his earlier distinctions, and none was later than 1873. Thus his fitness to fill chairs of ancient classics, history and English literature was

6.1 James Slattery, president QCC, 1890-96.

variously attested. Interestingly, the providers of these open and somewhat dated enco-
miums included mathematician and theologian – and Corkman – George Salmon;
Edward Dowden, the renowned TCD critic who was also a native of Cork and an
alumnus of QCC; John Kells Ingram, better known as the author of the ballad 'Who
fears to speak of '98?' than as a Trinity don; and Christopher Palles, chief baron of the
Irish Exchequer. Impressive as these testimonials seem in respect of Slattery's scholarly
activities and of his character, they lose considerable force because of their antiquity and
the absence of any attestation to his specific qualifications for the business in hand.
Perhaps Slattery regarded the evidence of his wide scholarly interests and accomplish-
ments as sufficient for this purpose. He did state in his letter of application that 'on the
ground of general character and ability I may refer with confidence to the Provost and
Fellows of the Dublin University and to the Heads of the legal profession in Ireland'.

But the questions remain. Why did not Slattery seek and submit more updated and relevant references? Why did the government recommend his appointment and with such speed? The lord lieutenant made his recommendation on 16 June, within two weeks of Slattery's application, and the warrant of appointment was dated 27 June 1890. Why was the consensus of opinion in favour of Professor John England eventually ignored? Did the government have other reasons for appointing Slattery, and was he given a specific brief? Was his liberal loyalism a factor in his appointment, as well perhaps as his membership of the St Stephen's Green Club, and his influence with the charmed circle within it? Why did Slattery, in calling at Dublin Castle soon after the news of his appointment, expect from the chief secretary '*instructions as to the duties of this office that may require immediate attention*'?[5] Did the government have its own reasons for removing him in 1896, apart from the obvious ones? Whatever the answer to these questions,[6] Slattery's short presidency was a disaster. It was marked, or marred, by illnesses, frequent absences and violently disagreeable relations with the academic staff, and it was to culminate – uniquely – in ignominious dismissal. The Slattery presidency was at once a reflection of, and a contribution to, the sickly condition of QCC at the end of the century.

As president, his accounts of his stewardship were perfunctory to a degree. The annual presidential reports from 1890–91 to 1894–95 are ludicrously skimpy, averaging little more than a page in length. They briefly mention developments relating to the Crawford Observatory and repeatedly take up Sullivan's constant plea for a new chemistry laboratory. Otherwise, there is little until 1895–96 which turned out to be Slattery's last report. It is a reasonably substantial survey, with the kind of information people had come to expect from the reports presented by Kane and Sullivan – staff changes, student statistics, even an account of university extension lectures on English poetry, delivered under the auspices of the Cork Society for the Extension of University Teaching. These were, Slattery said, 'a great attraction to the people of Cork and a great benefit to the University Extension Society' (this is a very early reference to extension lectures).

The 1895–96 report also mentioned his 'severe illness which had lasted seven months', his leave of absence for that period, and the deputising by Professors Savage-Armstrong and Stephen O'Sullivan. It is ironic that Slattery should have presented the only decent report of his tenure at this late stage, when he was seriously ill, in deep financial trouble, and experiencing the unpleasant attentions of Dublin Castle. Perhaps he was desperately anxious to make some sort of impression at this point, and that may also be the reason why the report of the extraordinary visitation of 1894 was now belatedly presented: pressure may have been brought to bear on him to publish it. He had rather airily glossed over it in his 1893–94 report, saying it had been placed in the college registry.

The lengthy report of the extraordinary visitation of 16–17 May 1894 is a revealing insight into Slattery's personality and attitudes, and his tense relations with the professors.[7] The Court of Visitors comprised Mr Justice Holmes and the presidents of the College of Physicians and the College of Surgeons. The visitation arose from charges preferred against their president on 16 February 1894 by all six members –

that in itself was significant – of the College Council. These were Professors Alexander Jack, Owen O'Ryan, Marcus Hartog, W. Ridgeway, Henry Corby, and G.J. Stokes. Corby, O'Ryan and Ridgeway, as disappointed presidential candidates, would not have been enamoured of Slattery. The lengthy charges were tantamount to an impeachment of the president. It is interesting that, in seeking to have it determined whether Slattery had acted against the statutes, the council had not looked for an *extraordinary* visitation: the Castle's decision to give that form to the visitation showed the urgency with which the government regarded the matter.

According to the charges, Slattery interfered with the council's rights by personally appointing an assistant to help with the new Crawford Observatory's contribution to the international 'photographing the heavens' scheme, and by failing to make reports of work in progress available to the council, which he asserted was 'only a consultative body'. He had acted dictatorially at council meetings, refusing to put resolutions, ruling motions out of order, wanting to use minutes for his own purposes, dissolving meetings while important business remained uncompleted. He had several times ignored the council in dealing on his own with public service correspondence. He would not allow college correspondence to be conducted by the registrar, in accordance with the statutes, and to be accessible to the council. (The role of the registrar in college correspondence was again to be an issue in the dairy science row in the early 1930s.) He had granted the use of rooms without council sanction. He had habitually omitted to appoint a deputy when ill or absent for weeks, thereby making much of college business impossible. At a meeting of the Corporate Body on 24 March 1893 to elect two members to the council, he had taken away the ballot papers instead of destroying them. He had negotiated the purchase of a portion of ground from Mr Perrott, for the purpose of erecting additional college buildings on it, without reference to the council. He kept valuable college records in his house, which were inaccessible to the professors. In addition to these council charges, the registrar (Professor Jack) complained that the president had tried to use him as the non-appointed, non-existent deputy; as an informant during his absences; and also as a researcher in the college records to supply him with ammunition, 'converting the College Registrar into his private secretary'. Professor Hartog's additional grievance was that the president used threatening language, tried to intimidate him and threatened him with court proceedings.[8]

The Court of Visitors, which Justice Holmes ruled should be held in public, was interrupted once or twice by noise and applause, causing the justice to call for decorum and to threaten to clear the room. Feelings were obviously running high: 'If any gentlemen wish to make a noise, they can find ample liberty in the spacious grounds I see around these buildings'. Counsel for the professors emphasised that Slattery's language and demeanour had been of such 'a very insulting character' to each member that in the end they had to take action. At a meeting on 2 March 1892 'the President lost all control, shook his fist in Professor Ridgeway's face and used some language of a character which I [counsel] am not going to mention having regard to the nature of this assembly'. At another meeting, he allegedly took a paper from Professor Stokes. 'Give me that', he said and put it in his pocket. We may observe that, unlike later and larger bodies, the small size of the College Council facilitated such ill-tempered gestures and antics. (There were stormy academic sessions even in the sedate days of Bertram Windle, as when Professor Pearson [surgery] fired an ink bottle at the president – and missed!⁹)

The really crucial charge against Slattery was that he misconstrued the clause 'no resolution of the Council shall come into operation until it shall have received the signature of the President, or in his absence, of his deputy acting by his authority' as a presidential veto rather than a sign of legality and formal completeness. This issue had been discussed at the 1857–58 commission, as had the perception of the presidents having despotic power. Counsel for the president held that Slattery had exercised his power reasonably as 'a brother professor', not as 'a dictator'.

Slattery defended himself well before the court, anxious to explain away certain matters, promising others would not happen again, and giving some revealing examples of his firm thinking on meetings of the College Council. It was not desirable 'that more Councils should be held than are required for the transaction of any real practical business'. Such meetings were 'a waste of time, of my time and of everybody's time'. They 'make the Council a place for debating hypothetical impractical useless questions'. Why, he asked, should QCC have needed sixteen or seventeen council meetings in a session compared to QCB's six or seven? (Incidentally, he made a reference at one point to the long vacation of '4½ months'.) Obviously, Slattery lacked a keenly developed sense of collegiality and was brutally frank on the propensity of academic bodies to refine debating points exquisitely, so as to take up much more than the time available.

On the thorny question of the registrar dealing with college correspondence, Slattery permitted himself a mild outburst: 'Surely I am not to understand that I should call in the Registrar to write a letter. Was that done by Dr Sullivan? Was that the system?' The president also defended his action in handling the Perrott land purchase on his own in June 1892. The land was 'in the market' and 'we could not live as a botanical school without it'. It took a long time to get the government sanction – and cash. In the meantime there really was nothing to report to the council. (At council meetings on 24 February, 23 March and 19 October 1893, Slattery kept his colleagues informed of the various stages in the acquisition of Perrott's Inch – a 'piece of ground at the north-west angle of the College boundary, and lying between the river, the Western Road and the old mill stream'. Since the Board of Works was unable or unwilling to advance the money, it was to be purchased out of 'lapsed balances'. The lord lieutenant gave his consent, and the property came into college hands on 29 August 1893.)

On a rather lighter note, the president had been accused of allowing the attendant in the refreshment room to sleep and live there at the commencement of the 1891–92 session. The attendant was a college 'character', an old woman called Mrs Jolley. Slattery said he had kindly permitted her to put a chair in the refreshment room ('she made a poor mouth') and afterwards found she had changed the chair to a 'chair bed (laughter)', at which stage the president instructed the steward to remove her.

In his judgement, Justice Holmes said the most serious issue in the whole case was the president's claim to render council resolutions inoperative by withholding his signature. Though the cases in point had been fairly trivial, it was 'a matter of supreme importance in the government of the College', and it had much to do with the other controversies as well as with the mutual 'general feeling of antagonism and jealousy'. Justice Holmes noted that the argument about the presidential discretion to refuse signature went back to the 1850s, being discussed by the 1857–58 commission, but it was a tribute to past presidents and professors that differences had been 'amicably settled' on the point, and a visitation had been avoided. Regrettably, 'President Slattery has now for the first time in fifty years raised the controversy by claiming the right to nullify the unanimous resolutions of his colleagues' not on high principle but on matters 'not worth five minutes discussion'. Chapters III and IV of the statutes made it clear, Justice Holmes said, that the council was no mere consultative body: it had independent legislative and administrative functions in the governance of the College. 'The Council, alone and uncontrolled, is the governing body.'

The supposed presidential veto had no substance: it only represented the president's obligation to ensure that all was in order. If a college resolution was legal, proper and under the council's jurisdiction, it was the president's duty to sign it. With regard to the specific complaints, the judgement stated:

> Most of them would probably never have arisen were it not for a disposition on the part of the President to assert in a somewhat aggressive and pedagogic way his personal authority and position – and the hostility thus engendered in his colleagues who, it is to be feared, have occasionally shown themselves deficient in the reasonableness that sweetens Counsel.

The visitors' report also condemned Slattery for his insupportable demand to have written statements inserted in the council minutes; for his 'authoritative and somewhat condescending tone' in one lengthy memorandum on a trivial subject; for not having appointed a deputy during his absences; and for his reluctance in unreservedly admitting the rights of the council and thereby revealing 'a difficulty of disposition which we trust the President will endeavour to control in his dealings with his colleagues'.

But the visitors' reproofs were by no means reserved exclusively for Slattery, and he was vindicated in some respects. The council was described as being 'hypercritical' in one instance, and some of its charges against Slattery as frivolous. The complaint that he had withheld public service communications from the council 'utterly fails'. Indeed, 'on several occasions investigated we find that the President acted with zeal and agility on behalf of the College, and carried out the wishes of the Council in a faithful and proper manner'. In conclusion, the visitors, who saw themselves as having a supervisory as well as a judicial authority, expressed some pious hopes for 'more friendly and harmonious relations' in the college in the future. They deplored the 'spirit of hostility and recrimination', and, in a spirit of gentle chiding, they looked forward to the cultivation of mutual tolerance and charity for the sake of the college. It is doubtful if these anodyne counsels of perfection had any effect.

The importance of the 1894 visitation is that it defined and limited the president's jurisdiction in his relations with the College Council, and it put paid to the notion of a despot with a discretionary veto. Beyond that, the visitors' report did not so much find against Slattery as berate president and professors alike for their pettiness and their malice. The visitation had uncovered a sorry story of an academic community involved in endless wrangling about trivialities, and wasting precious time necessarily filched from research or teaching. What would the students have had to say about all this?

There was no indication in the 1894 report that any drastic action was contemplated against Slattery. But hopes of improved relations between president and council were soon dashed. Before the end of the year there was a row about their rival claims to controlling pension and superannuation matters, and on 4 December 1894 the chief secretary wrote to Slattery deploring the 'further indication of want of harmony between you and the Council . . . His Excellency sincerely hopes that you and the other members of the Council will see the absolute necessity in the interests of the College of harmonious action without appealing to the Government'.[10] Meanwhile, although Slattery had professed interest in promoting popular lectures for the benefit of the citizens, he outraged public opinion by closing the college gates at certain times so that a right of way would not be established. Moreover, he quarrelled with the librarian, Owen O'Ryan, accusing him to the chief secretary's office of negligence, so that 'a spirit of disorder' prevailed in the library which 'has almost ceased to be a place of study and has become a scene of gossip'. The librarian defended himself, saying he had often been complimented by the late President O'Sullivan 'whom we every day get fresh reason to regret'.[11]

During the 1894 visitation, reference had been made to Slattery's ill-health. This increasingly dogged him from early in 1895 when he requested six months' leave of absence, which was eventually granted when he forwarded certificates attesting to cardiac weakness and a general nervous disposition. At the end of this period, the president requested a further six months because he had contracted a kidney disease – in fact he also suffered from diabetes. In May 1896 he applied for an extension of one month to his sick leave. At this stage, not surprisingly, the Castle began to jib, and a note on Slattery's application from David Harrell, a CSO official, to the chief secretary said: 'It is believed that Dr Slattery will never be able to resume his duties as President. I would suggest that his present application be granted and that when he makes another application for leave his case be considered'.[12] He was, of course, no longer running the college at this stage, and Alexander Jack, the registrar, was the saving and dominant administrative presence then and thereafter. His ascendancy during weak presidencies was grounded in the respect he earned through the punctilious discharge of his duties, without any ambition to supplant or succeed presidential incumbents. It is also of considerable interest that the poor relationship (ranging from contempt to antagonism) between a president and his second-in-command is seen in the cases of Kane–Ryall, Slattery–Jack, Merriman–O'Rahilly and Mortell–Moran.

In the summer of 1896, Slattery's sea of trouble extended to bankruptcy. He was adjudged bankrupt on 31 July 1896.[13] Some days before, he promised to explain the matter to the lord lieutenant, pathetically commenting: 'I will merely say that I am to be more pitied than blamed in this transaction'.[14] The Crown held its hand for the moment, partly because the president of a college did not fall into the category of a civil servant who would have been suspended without pay for bankruptcy.[15] Eventually, on 18 November, Slattery told his story to the under-secretary.[16] As far back as 1868 he and a friend, Mr D.C. O'Keeffe, had invested a large sum to establish his brother John Vincent Slattery as a bacon commission agent. The business eventually collapsed, much of the capital in the investment was lost and Slattery, feeling responsible for introducing O'Keeffe to the investment, voluntarily executed a bond in May 1877 'in the penal sum of £10,000 to secure the principal sum of £5,000'. O'Keeffe died in July 1895, and a nephew, Stephen Lanigan O'Keeffe, his residuary legatee, now claimed the bond, refused Slattery's offer of an annual sum of £300 in reduction of the liability, and moved to have the president adjudged bankrupt. On 3 November 1896 the Court of Bankruptcy allocated a sum of £350 per annum out of his salary towards payment of the debt. Slattery claimed that such allocation would not affect 'my means of maintaining my position as President', since his wife's independent income of 'more than £300 a year' would make up the shortfall. He added:

> I have incurred no more responsibility nor been guilty of any act of which I have reason to be ashamed and that the Bankruptcy which had overtaken me is not the consequence of any misconduct or extravagance on my part, but of circumstances which when investigated will show no breach of the laws of honesty or good faith.

The government was unmoved by this *cri de cœur*. An internal Castle minute on 25 November posed a rhetorical question: 'Is it possible for a President who has been publicly declared bankrupt to discharge the duties imposed on him by the College Statutes?'[17] Slattery desperately tried to stay in office and made every effort to avert his impending doom, moving in early December to have his bankruptcy annulled and to avoid the necessity of having any part of his salary allocated to his creditor. But the government had already decided he could not continue in office. The Castle might move slowly at times but it could as surely exercise its power of dismissal, for the first and only time in the case of a president. It now closed off another possible escape hatch:

> Apparently Dr Slattery contemplated the assignment of his wife's fortune to his creditor. If this was carried out he might lose both fortune and salary and be left penniless. This might be a convenient arrangement for the creditor but hardly for Dr Slattery.[18]

It was also pointed out that if he resigned voluntarily, he would be given favourable pension terms but that if he had to be dismissed, he would get nothing.

His solicitors made one last attempt, claiming that as the bankruptcy would shortly be annulled his official salary would be left untouched. They claimed to be 'altogether at a loss to understand on what grounds his contemplated dismissal can possibly be rested'.[19] The chief secretary refused to correspond with the solicitors, noting that 'Dr Slattery's tenure of the Presidential Chair has, I fear, been prejudicial to the College from the outset; his health seems shattered; and now on top of other disqualifications comes the bankruptcy'.[20] By the end of December 1896, a Queen's letter was sent to Slattery, telling him he was being dismissed because of ill-health, bad relations with the QCC professors, and bankruptcy. His presidency was to end on 31 December 1896. The dismissal letter referred to the 'spirit of hostility and recrimination' in QCC which was 'detrimental to the best interests of the institution'; to Slattery's 'practically continuous absence from active duty for a period of nearly two years'; and to his refusal to tender his resignation. Professor Jack, the registrar, assumed responsibility for the college in the brief interregnum between Slattery's dismissal and his successor's accession, pointing out that he was thus charged under the statutes.

There was a sad final twist to the Slattery saga. On Christmas Day 1896, a week before Slattery's dismissal date, Drs O'Sullivan and Hobart wrote to the chief secretary from QCC, saying 'that it would be dangerous to his life if he were obliged to leave his residence in the College before a decided amelioration of his present condition has taken place'.[21] But there was to be no amelioration, and in April 1897 a further medical certificate from the same two doctors informed the chief secretary that

> Dr James Slattery is dangerously and, in our opinion, hopelessly ill. It would not be possible to remove him at present from the President's residence in the Queen's College, Cork and judging from his condition we do not think his life will be prolonged beyond a month.[22]

The new president, Sir Rowland Blennerhassett, was clearly annoyed at this bizarre situation. He informed the under-secretary on 8 April 1897 that he had taken up his duties but not his residence which was otherwise occupied. Though he had not doubted, of course, that Slattery was seriously ill, still:

> I thought it advisable to procure a medical certificate which I now forward. The position is exceedingly unpleasant; and it will be seen from the certificate that it may remain for some time uncertain. Up to the end of the present term which closes on Saturday next, I shall be able to fulfil my duties, although with very considerable inconvenience, not only to myself, but to others. I hardly think that I can obtain the residence of the President for some time, even if it were free from a month hence; it is manifest that after the protracted illness of Mr Slattery, the house will require considerable scrutiny before I could occupy it.[23]

It was blackly ironic that the authorities, having deposed Slattery from office, could not move him out of QCC. On 25 April 1897 he died, aged sixty-five, in the president's house in the East Wing (one of three presidents to do so[24]) and he was buried in St Finbarr's Cemetery, near the grave of his predecessor, W.K. Sullivan. He had been married to Virginia Wolfe, a wealthy American woman who had connections with the schnapps business. After his death, she returned to the United States. It was she who devised the inscription on his headstone which refers with proud precision to his 'six-and-a-half years' as president of Queen's College Cork. (Only J.J. McHenry, 1964–67, had a shorter presidential tenure.) Unlike the nearby W.K. Sullivan memorial, the Slattery headstone records only the duration of his presidency. A trust fund established by Mrs Slattery and administered by Chemical Bank, New York, arranges for the regular checking of the grave and headstone and pays Cork Corporation for any upkeep.[25] Consequently, they are extremely well maintained.

The unfortunate Slattery was an unsuitable appointment from the beginning. It may well be that the professors, accustomed to an agreeably loose rein during Sullivan's final and unwell years, actively resented the attempted reimposition of discipline by a president who had such an authoritarian view of his functions, and who, in their eyes, represented centralised Dublin authority as against local and Munster interests. Slattery made some attempt to expand the college premises and to encourage extension lectures before being overwhelmed by a complication of illnesses, desperately bad relations with his staff (in part, a reflection of his poor health and, in part, a consequence of their provocation) and a bankruptcy in which he seems to have been the victim of circumstance, and guilty of imprudence rather than nefarious intent.[26]

He may have been his own worst enemy but his dismissal from the presidency in ignominious circumstances was deeply demoralising for an already troubled college, and the embarrassing situation of a discredited ex-president too ill to vacate the premises further worsened the general image. That image was not refurbished by Slattery's successor.

Blennerhassett, 1897–1904

> *I think that Sir Rowland Blennerhassett's attention should be called to the necessity of his residence in College during term.*
>
> under-secretary, Dublin Castle, 1904

Sir Rowland Blennerhassett is categorised simply as 'politician' in a dictionary entry which makes no mention of his Queen's College presidency.[27] We might more accurately describe him as a politician with academic inclinations which he got an opportunity to indulge at the expense of Queen's College Cork.

He was born to a Catholic gentry family in Blennerville, Co. Kerry on 5 September 1839. Educated at Downshire, Stonyhurst and Oxford, he also studied at Continental universities and developed a facility for cultivating the acquaintance of celebrities (Bismarck and the famous chemist, Liebig, for example). His admiration for German scientific achievements strongly influenced his views on education. With the help of Lord Acton, he founded *The Chronicle*, a political and literary journal for liberal Catholics. In 1870, he married the Countess Charlotte de Leyden, who was honoured by the French government for her historical scholarship.[28]

His politics were Liberal, and he was MP for Galway City (1865–74) and for Co. Kerry (1880–85). Standing in the Dublin Harbour one-seat constituency in the 1885 general election, he was trounced by the prominent Nationalist, T.C. Harrington.[29] At one time a lukewarm supporter of home rule, Blennerhassett came to oppose it vigorously. He supported the Irish Loyal and Patriotic Union (ILPU), founded in 1885 to oppose home rule and the Land League. Moreover, it appears that he contributed

£70 to Edward C. Houston, secretary of the ILPU, who was raising money to buy the notorious Pigott letters which purported to show that Parnell and his colleagues were involved in criminal conspiracy during the land war but which were dramatically revealed to be forgeries. Blennerhassett's subscription was small compared to those of other ILPU enthusiasts but it verified his true-blue loyalism which a Tory government may have felt was deserving of recognition and reward when the opportunity arose.[30] It is a plausible explanation of his appointment to the QCC presidency, though as well as being a government placeman, he could claim to be a considerable authority on educational matters in a wide comparative setting. He was also a commissioner of national education, and an inspector of reformatory and industrial schools, 1890–97. At all events, he was the stereotype of the 'Cawstle Cawtholic'.

No other name being put forward for the vacancy, apparently, Blennerhassett was appointed by the Crown as president of Queen's College Cork: he was to hold office until seventy years of age, with five years' extension at the discretion of the lord

6.2 Sir Rowland Blennerhassett, president QCC, 1897-1904.

lieutenant (in fact, he resigned at sixty-five). His appointment (which had been decided on from the moment of Slattery's dismissal on New Year's Day 1897) took effect from 20 March 1897, and he was entitled to his salary as inspector of reformatory and industrial schools up to 19 March.[31] He presented himself as president to the College Council on 26 March 1897.[32]

As presidencies are wont to do, Blennerhassett's began with a flourish, and it appears that he gave an excellent inaugural address which was so well attended that the Medical Students' Association complained to the College Council (18 January 1898) of the unsatisfactory accommodation arrangements at the venue.[33] Blennerhassett's president's reports started off most impressively but became successively shorter and more cursory. The initial enthusiasm soon flagged. But the first two reports (1896–97 and 1897–98) afford evidence of original, vigorous, even visionary thinking on educational matters, if one ignores the pedantry and the name-dropping. Indeed, the 1896–97 report, where Germany is the model for many of his ideas, was as much a disquisition on his philosophy of education, richly rooted in the Continental scene, as a statement of QCC's wants and needs.

He enthusiastically proclaimed the need for chairs in Celtic and agriculture, the former vital in the context of comparative philology, the latter in the development of scientific farming in the Munster region. (In fact, the young Cork scholar Osborn Bergin began to lecture in Celtic studies in 1897–98, thereby restoring a link missing since Owen Connellan's professorship of Celtic languages and literature had ended in 1863). Chairs like these, Blennerhassett claimed, should not have been abolished just because the subjects attracted too few students: a handful of students was by no means a barrier to thriving research in a subject. Deploring the prevalence of cramming and the emphasis on examinations, he asserted that in too many cases conditions in QCC militated against serious scholarship, since professors also had to be schoolmasters, willy-nilly. He condemned the impossibly wide spread of departments such as modern languages. The concept of a hold-all modern languages brief was absurd, especially since the then incumbent, W.F. Butler, was librarian as well.

Again, not only should history be separated from English literature, but there should be separate chairs for the scientific study of Irish history and of European history: 'A separate chair for the modern history of Europe is an absolute necessity in any educational establishment of pretensions to culture'. The area of work for which Professor George F. Savage-Armstrong (history and English literature), was responsible was divided in Harvard among sixteen people, and in the University of Berlin among three times that number. Professor Marcus Hartog (zoology) had to deal as well with botany and geology when it was obvious that independent chairs were needed in those three disciplines. Interestingly, Blennerhassett also called for a chair of Russian. In short, only through financial investment in new areas of teaching and scholarship could a university hope to become great, as Europeans had realised. And Queen's College Cork had been chronically underendowed from the beginning, Blenner-hassett asserted: the money available was 'not sufficient to work a single Faculty in a manner suitable to the requirements of the age'.[34]

Once again, a pathology laboratory was demanded and the lack of a pathology chair was declared to be 'a national scandal'.[35] The library, absurdly underfunded, was 'constructed in defiance of all the theories of ventilation'.[36] There was no money to operate the excellent observatory properly, and QCC needed an astronomer.[37] A new chemistry laboratory (for long, a presidential demand) would eventually mean the application of scientific principles to business and industry in the Cork region.[38] Blennerhassett doubtless secured the plaudits of his colleagues when he argued that professors should be properly remunerated, pointing out approvingly that the salary of the celebrated German chemist Viktor Meyer, as a Heidelberg professor, was equal to that of Prince Hohenlohe, chancellor of the German empire![39] The president was also aware of the unacceptable denominational imbalance at staff level: in recommending George C. Green for the chair of English law, Blennerhassett mentioned in his favour that he was from Cork, practised on the Munster circuit, and was a Catholic – 'so few of the professional staff are Roman Catholic'.[40]

If only all its deficiencies could be remedied, the Cork college could become a great university, or so Blennerhassett predicted with a flamboyant optimism. Such a university 'on the confines of the old world' – and there is a prophetic note in this observation – could link the cultures of Europe and America. If the college could be made sufficiently attractive, it would be the Mecca for American professors on sabbatical, as well as their students. As a location for a great university, Cork had considerable potential, being a flourishing town with a bright commercial future, 'situated in a province remarkable for the intelligence of the people'.[41]

Blennerhassett subscribed to the then fashionable opinion, conditioned perhaps by travellers' tales of Kerry shepherds chattering animatedly in Latin, that south Munster people were intellectually talented beyond the norm. (After all, Blennerhassett was himself one of this privileged group, and the conceit was harmless enough.) His personal experience, he believed, had borne out this view, in that he had invited those attending his university extension lectures on modern French history to write commentaries on the subject matter:

> and, for my part, I can truly say that, highly as I rate the mental capacity of the people of Cork, I was simply amazed at the critical power and intelligence shown in the essays sent to me by those who did me the honour to attend my lectures.

Elsewhere in the same report, he had commented:

> I have never known anyone of any nationality well acquainted with these islands that has not been struck by the extraordinary and quite exceptional ability of the people of the South of Ireland, particularly those who inhabit the counties of Cork and Kerry.[42]

Difficult as it is to understand by today's standards, the Blennerhassett administration complained in time-honoured fashion about lack of accommodation, even though in the year of his appointment student numbers were at their lowest (106 in 1896–97) since the foundation. Still, laboratories as well as rooms for students and professors were badly needed. Students had nowhere to assemble between lectures (the college being a distance from their homes or lodgings) or to wash and change after athletic activities[43] except 'a wretched cellar' which they described to the visitors as a 'coal-hole'. Blennerhassett's proposed solution to the accommodation problem would not have met with universal satisfaction. Berkeley Hall, which was a conspicuous failure as a hall of residence, should be purchased, he suggested, and made an integral part of college property. (It took another century for that to happen.) More radically, 'an entire wing of the College remains uncompleted making an unsightly gap in an otherwise handsome structure'.[44] Whether he meant joining the West Wing to the medical building thus forming an E-shaped total structure as Sullivan had suggested in 1879, or enclosing the Quadrangle on the south side, is not clear. (In October 1897, for example, the College Council declared itself in favour of completing 'the western quadrangle'.)[45] In either case, it was truly an academic aspiration. Visitors expressed pious goodwill but the Treasury turned a deaf ear.

Though Blennerhassett claimed that he impressed on government again and again the need to finance extra accommodation and new chairs and that he repeatedly visited Dublin to argue the case, his supposed friends in high places paid no heed. A long letter to *The Cork Examiner* on 14 September 1899 from R.J. Smith, a QCC graduate living in Cardiff, claimed that Blennerhassett 'has a good deal of influence with members of her Majesty's Ministry' but was not exerting himself sufficiently to capitalise on his connections. Smith was in the habit of offering an annual public commentary on the president's report. In regard to the 1898–99 report, Smith asserted that the president had understated the appalling 'changing' conditions the students had to put up with in 'the dark, draughty, dirty and comfortless subterranean passages of College'. Smith saw Blennerhassett's presidency as a disappointment in that there was a failure to push for change in various areas – academic, administrative and operational. There was a pressing need to introduce electric light; 'it is high time that the College was put in connection with the telephone system of the city'; no serious effort had been made to urge the division of the chair of anatomy and physiology; the library, as ever, was short of accommodation and funds, and graduates who availed themselves of its advantages should contribute to its support. Finally, Smith deplored the college's failure to commemorate its jubilee year (apart from the celebrations organised for the Old Corkonians in London by Dr Macnaughton-Jones). The lack of interest in this matter on the part of the college authorities was a slight on its graduates 'scattered throughout the globe, proud to be sent forth the bearers of its name, the custodians of its honour and to be associated with its traditions'. A jubilee should be a time for focusing the loyalty of alumni to their alma mater and for getting them to express that loyalty in practical ways. Overall, in Smith's view, Blennerhassett had failed to be an agitator for the college's advancement, and the lack of development of QCC under his direction compared unfavourably with the situation of QCB and with medical schools elsewhere. Incidentally, it is obvious that Smith, himself a doctor in all probability, saw the college as primarily a medical school and with good reason: in the academic year in which he wrote his letter there were 137 medical students in QCC with only 34 in arts (including science), 17 in engineering and 7 in law.

Medical matters, indeed, loomed large in the proceedings of the ordinary visitation of 6 June 1903, 'a beautiful day', as Blennerhassett observed to the visitors, 'when the grounds are looking so well'.[46] The general opinion on the state of the medical school was favourable. Professor W.E. Ashley-Cummins (medicine, 1897–1923) had no complaints about the clinical facilities available in the city hospitals – the North and South Infirmaries, the District Hospital, the Victoria, the Eye, Ear and Throat. It was stated that professors were appointed primarily because of the position (physician, surgeon, gynaecologist) they held in one or other of the clinical hospitals. Professor Henry Corby (midwifery, later obstetrics and gynaecology, 1883–1924) summarised for the visitors' benefit the evidence he had given some time previously to the Royal Commission on University Education when it held sittings in the college. QCC medical students, according to Corby, distinguished themselves in clinical examinations, winning in their finals 'nearly double the honours as against all the other candidates'. It would be a pity, added Corby, if such talent 'will not be further developed by the foundation of a Cork university'. The visitors endorsed the professors' laudatory assessments. Having made their tour of inspection, they declared themselves well satisfied, with the usual regrets about the missing pathology dimension. The medical school was 'large', 'successful' and 'exceedingly well equipped'. (It should be noted that of the three visitors, one was a judge, another was the president of the Royal College of Physicians and the third was the president of the Royal College of Surgeons.)

After four or five years in office, Blennerhassett seemed to be taking an extraordinarily roseate view of the state of QCC, and attributed much of its perceived good condition to his own leadership. In his skimpy president's report for 1901–02 (one and a half pages) he predicted a brilliant future for the college, if only the proposals he had advocated were implemented. He pointed to a small increase in student numbers, and believed they were at a turning point. In the event, his optimism on this point was justified. He was also correct in stating that the arts faculty would not flourish as long as degrees were given to students who did not attend college lectures: there was a tripling of arts numbers after the NUI replaced the Royal University, but of course the ending of ecclesiastical disapproval was also a great stimulus to growth. The other major problem in Blennerhassett's time, as he mentioned in the 1903–04 report, was the reluctance of QCC medical students to read for honours in the Royal University, because of the dominance of Dublin and Belfast professors on the examinations board. Hence the tendency of a large number of students to seek qualifications from the royal colleges of physicians and surgeons in Dublin and Edinburgh. It was especially regrettable, for example, that the distinguished Augustus E. Dixon (chemistry, 1891–1924) was not an examiner in chemistry in the Royal University.

But otherwise all was well in QCC, Blennerhassett told the 1903 visitation. He spoke about 'solid College work', the 'utmost harmony', excellent student behaviour inside and outside the college and the success of graduates especially in the Indian civil service and medical establishment, including professorships in Calcutta and Bombay.[47] When he resigned from the presidency in 1904, he gave this self-satisfied assessment to the chief secretary's office:

> I am glad to say the College is in a very different state as regards general tone, the
> relations of Professors with each other, and with the students, and the spirit among the
> students themselves from what it was when I first went there. The change for the
> better has been most marked.[48]

How do we reconcile Blennerhassett's complacent appraisals with the general perception that the college had touched rock bottom in the pre-Windle years? Blennerhassett
apparently ignored unpleasant realities, shutting his eyes, for example, to the scandal of
his own absences, to deep-seated student discontent and to the ineffectual handling by
his administration of riotous and destructive student misconduct during the 1899
disturbance (which is discussed in detail below). Allowing for all that, however, it could
be argued that (all things being relative) Blennerhassett's term of office was an
improvement on that of his unfortunate predecessor, James Slattery; that in terms of
student numbers, at least, a corner had been turned; and that Queen's College Cork,
considered as little more than a glorified medical school, was modestly prospering.

Blennerhassett's absences from duty are the stuff of legend but are also borne out by
the records. Michael Cahill, a lifelong member of the library staff still serving in the
early 1950s, clearly recalled Blennerhassett's presidency. According to Cahill, the
registrar, Alexander Jack, did much of the president's work while the president himself
paid a visit in October and May, spending a fortnight on each occasion, but otherwise
living in London and on the Continent.[49] (The minute book of the College Council
shows Blennerhassett's attendances to have been at once more irregular and rather
more frequent than Cahill's neat account.) Another anecdote is that of Blennerhassett
appearing from time to time on horseback in the Quadrangle for the purpose of
discussing college business with the professors.[50]

Fortunately, we do not have to rely only on the oral tradition. Blennerhassett chaired,
and signed the minutes of, council meetings only at irregular intervals (increasingly so
during his later years), and numerous deputies did duty for him. (He went off to Dublin
'on public business' on the day the council discussed the notorious 1899 riot.[51]) We also
find him applying for leave of absence in early 1901, at first on 'urgent business'[52] and
subsequently on grounds of illness.[53] He had not applied for leave since his appointment,[54] so that he must have helped himself to generous leave of the French variety. On
20 February 1904, as Blennerhassett's presidency was coming to an end, Professor Jack
reported to the chief secretary that between 1901 and 1904 the QCC president had
attended only twenty-two out of fifty-six council meetings. This compared with
twenty-six out of twenty-seven and fifty-four out of fifty-six for his counterparts in
Belfast and Galway, respectively. The under-secretary made the rather mild
recommendation (was the president still an influential figure in government circles?): 'I
think that Sir Rowland Blennerhassett's attention should be called to the necessity of his
residence in College during term', adding the very obvious comment that in institutions
with a resident head 'much closer attention is paid to discipline and academical work'.[55]

Blennerhassett finally decided to absent himself from Cork for health reasons on a
full-time and permanent basis (though he was to return occasionally as a visitor

between 1905 and 1909). Once again, Cork's climate was invoked, though its effect on Blennerhassett could not have been all that debilitating given his frequent absences. Accompanying his resignation letter to the chief secretary's office on 6 September 1904 was a note from his physician, W. Bezleythorne, which said that '. . . the climate in Cork encourages in him catarrhal affections, leading to weakness of the heart's actions, and that on that and general medical grounds, including recurrent rheumatic affections, I advise him to resign his official position . . .'[56] The Treasury decided (26 January 1905) to grant him a pension of £231 7s 9d per annum, an amount about which he could hardly complain, given the shortness of his service and the sporadic performance of his duties.[57]

On 19 October 1911, the Governing Body thanked Mrs Slattery and Lady Blennerhassett for the respective portraits of their husbands.[58] Neither of these was subsequently displayed on the portrait wall of the Aula Maxima, presumably because their subjects were, in different ways, *non grata*. In Blennerhassett's case, an additional factor has been adduced: as a recruiter for the forces of the Crown, he was particulary unacceptable in militant nationalist quarters, and exhibiting him might have provoked retaliation on college property.[59] In 1995, thanks to the kindness of Professor David Slattery and to his persistence in rehabilitating his great-uncle's name, a John B. Yeats painting of James Slattery joined the other presidential portraits. Blennerhassett is now the only blank in the presidential gallery. Perhaps it is appropriate that in art as in life he should be a conspicuous absentee.

Students: conduct and misconduct

> . . . *grievous breach of discipline* . . .
>
> student riot, 25 November 1899

Student behaviour, like human nature in general, is a constant, at least in its public aspect. It does not fluctuate wildly from one age to another but at any given period it ranges widely over a behaviour spectrum. Some students are altruistically motivated, some nurse real or imagined grievances against staff, more protest against perceived academic or political injustice, some are lotus-eaters, others steal books and deal in stolen books, and others again riot downtown out of passion or from an exuberant sense of fun, or from a mixture of motives. Queen's College students exhibited all these variations and combinations.

As we have already illustrated, students were remarkably independent-minded, being prepared to make full use of the mechanism of visitation to express their grievances, and being quite uninhibited in arguing the issues with their president or professors who, of course, were also complicated creatures. Perhaps Catholic students who had braved clerical disapproval to go to college were thereby disposed not to be overawed by secular authority. At any rate, the strong impression is that UCC students in the conformist decades after independence were considerably more timorous and deferential than their QCC predecessors.

The Cork Examiner gave a condescendingly approving pat on the head to QCC Dramatic Club for a production in the (Cork) Theatre Royal in March 1875, in aid of the Cork Maternity Hospital. The students performed Goldsmith's *She Stoops to Conquer* as well as two shorter sketches, and the 8th Regiment band also contributed.

> The object for which the performance was given and the fact that this is only the second appearance of the society, to a certain extent disarms criticism. However, we must say that the evening's entertainment, without showing any high histrionic abilities on the part of any of the performers, was still very good.[60]

These amateur thespians were not always so philanthropically engaged. Individual students were quick to protest if their sensibilities were wounded, and could in turn be quite severely punished for their impertinence. Sometimes, a student–professor row was charged with cultural antagonism, increasingly so as a spirit of nationalism pervaded the student body in the 1880s and 1890s. Moreover, small student numbers meant that student–professor relations were correspondingly personal.

A pungently-phrased letter from a student to Vice-President John Ryall was read at a meeting of the College Council on 25 January 1870:

> Permit me to inquire into the accuracy of a report at present circulating through the College to the effect that you have, in class this day,[61] sneeringly alluded to me as a 'credit to Dungarvan'. For my part, I have, Sir, as yet carefully avoided giving credence to the rumour which ascribes to a dignitary of the College, and a gentleman, language equally impertinent, ungentlemanly and undignified.

Hamilton Williams was called before the council but refused to say if he had written the letter. Silence was obviously equated with guilt, and Williams paid severely for what was seen as *his* gross impertinence. He was rusticated for two years for 'addressing a most unbecoming letter to the Vice-President'.[62] A protest demonstration was held in the Quadrangle within days and was attended by a majority of the student body. (A strong sense of solidarity was a notable student characteristic.) A unanimous if disingenuous resolution condemned the College Council for rusticating Williams who, after all, had only requested an explanation for Ryall's offensive remark.[63] The vice-president's unpopularity (he was responsible for student discipline) had been attested several years before when 'a number of those young gentlemen assembled in the quadrangle hooted and groaned at him as he passed, and one very young lad . . . put out his tongue at him' (*CE*, 6 Feb. 1857). For his insolence, he was rusticated for six months, which the *Examiner* considered severe.

Two other incidents were variations of the Williams episode. A medical professor wrote a facetious letter to the newspapers, excusing himself for not attending a function because he had been 'engaged in an impious attempt to fathom the depths of human ignorance – examining pass candidates'. The pass men in question were not amused by the caustic witticism at their expense and got the Royal University to reprimand the offender.[64] On another occasion, a professor who had castigated a whole class for the bad manners of one student was compelled to withdraw his remarks when requested to do so by a class deputation. Student feelings were inflamed by the incident, according to a newspaper report.[65]

A more substantial complaint was made by students (mostly medical) in March 1872. They had met in the Opthalmic Hospital to censure the College Council for making a particular temporary appointment to a vacant post in anatomy and physiology. The council's response to the censure was to fine some of the censurers. A second student meeting condemned this as severe and unjust. The least any man could expect, said the proposer of the motion, was freedom of opinion. It was asserted that those who attended the first meeting were unaware they were breaking the rules and that, since the College Council arbitrarily determined rules for students, almost anything could be branded as a breach of discipline. (This comment is of particular interest: the students who were embroiled in controversy with President Sullivan and the College Council in February–March 1884 made substantially the same point about student ignorance of a council ruling that seemed quite arbitrary to them.) A proposal was made at the meeting that practical solidarity be shown by setting up a subscription fund to defray the fines imposed on their colleagues.[66]

Students sometimes complained other students to the council. Charles Porter, who had been in college for 'several years', alleged that he was 'unwarrantably assaulted in the Hall of Medical Buildings by . . . Randall McCarthy' on 7 December 1888. The fact that McCarthy was a freshman was seen as literally adding insult to injury. The council told Porter to take the matter up with the president in person.[67] Books were occasionally stolen and disposed of in a pattern familiar to later generations of students. W.E. Fox informed the council on 22 April 1902 that a book of his, Loney's *Dynamics*, had been stolen from his desk in the drawing school. Acting on a suggestion, he tried Massey's Bookshop, Cook Street, where he found his book for sale in the second-hand section: 'It is not the first time since Christmas that things have been taken from my desk'. Norcott d'Esterre Harvey sought compensation from the council (5 November 1897) for the theft of a case of instruments from 'my locker in the College' which had been 'broken open'.[68] Students did not hesitate to 'shop' their fellows, when guilty. Sometimes they had no choice. Clubs and societies had to return a copy of their annual accounts to the council. The honorary secretaries of the athletic and cycling clubs (J.E. English and W.J. O'Regan) informed President Windle on 22 May 1907 of 'the irregularities of Messrs. Dillon and McCarthy in collecting for last year's sports'. They had collected £15 17s 6d on 'the King [now MacCurtain] Street beat' but 'failed to account for any of this to the treasurer'.[69]

The 'Miscellaneous Letters' in the college archives from the 1897–1908 period deal with, *inter alia*, incidents of student indiscipline coming before the College Council. There are many letters from professors informing the council of fines they had imposed on students. Professors Marcus Hartog, William F. Butler, William Bergin (natural philosophy, later physics, 1895–1931) and J.J. Charles were stern disciplinarians, if frequency of fining was any yardstick. Most professors, however, do not seem to have exercised their prerogative in this regard. Fines (generally, six pence or one shilling) were imposed for a variety of petty misdemeanours – singing or smoking in the corridor, failure to do work prescribed, lack of punctuality, inattentiveness in class, absences, name-engraving on desks (a perennial form of aspiration to immortality) and 'insubordination and insolence', such as that displayed by Richard J. Ahern for which he was fined a shilling by Professor Charles in December 1906. If fines were not paid within a fortnight, students could be debarred from lectures.

Professor Charles complained to the council on 27 November 1903 of the loutishness of his medical students and their unhygienic habits:

> I have tried to prevent smoking and spitting in the Upper Corridor of this Building, but some students persist and argue that the rules of the College allow 'smoking in the Medical Building'. I do not object to smoking in the Dissecting Room, but I am very much opposed, for the sake of cleanliness and decency, to smoking in the Laboratory, the Class Room or the Corridor. Occasionally there are pools of offensive material on the landing at the top of the stairs.[70]

The council responded by ordaining 'that a notice be affixed on the medical notice board stating that spitting in the Buildings is a breach of discipline'.[71] The students Professor Bergin complained about to the council (20 March 1902) were boisterous to the point of vandalism. (The observatory was in Bergin's area of responsibility.)

> . . . the movable part of the roof of the transit room cannot be raised, it has been so strained by students climbing up it. I would also direct your attention to the smashing recently of the thermometer which, I may remind you, is placed some yards in front of the observatory. Some days ago two of the lower windows were found broken in.[72]

On one occasion, Professor Hartog fined a whole class which refused to attend one of his lectures rescheduled from earlier in the week to 3 p.m. on Friday, 15 December 1905. Students from the class had been due to go to a lecture by Professor Bergin who, however, found his lecture room empty and (according to Hartog)

> . . . a notice on the door headed 'Esprit de Corps' calling on students to abstain from attending his lecture as well as Professor Hartog's 'which is given at an illegal hour', on the ground that a football match between two teams of the College Club had been arranged: students of the class, I am informed, hung about the corridors, but none entered Professor Bergin's room.[73]

Sometimes the professors took time off from complaining about students to complain about their colleagues or about college shortcomings. Hartog wrote to the council (8 February 1899) concerning

> the unfairness of the regulation against cycling in College. My colleagues who drive have no need to waste time walking up and down the avenue: those who cycle are compelled to [walk] by the College regulations.

An undated statement (probably 1899) drawn up by the College Council lists professorial grievances. For example, fifty years after the opening of the college an entire wing remained unfinished leaving an unsightly gap in the Quadrangle! Students had nowhere to sit or meet between lectures (Windle was to give priority to the provision of a students' club). Because of shortage of lecture-room accommodation, lectures sometimes had to be held in 'professors' private rooms', so-called:

> These . . . consist in several cases of a single small apartment with a single writing desk common to four professors. As there are no residences for Professors at the College, the want of privacy in their 'private' rooms is an extreme inconvenience for men occupied in intellectual work.[74]

The most spectacular student demonstration in the history of Queen's College Cork occurred on Saturday, 25 November 1899, and had the dimensions of a riot. The occasion, or perhaps the pretext, was the mainly ineffectual and negative response of a visitation (held in the examination hall) to various student complaints.[75] Perhaps the wider background was a frequently absent president, low student numbers, uncertainty about the future of the university question, and poor morale overall. In 1899–1900, there were 135 medical students out of a total of 185. The visitation heard demands for a recreation ground and a students' room. The Medical Students' Association drew attention to unsatisfactory conditions in the dissecting room, where they wanted an improvement in opening hours. Moreover the lack of a pathology professorship and laboratory was frequently deplored in successive president's reports, to no avail. (The first professor, A.E. Moore, was not appointed until after the 1908 transformation.)

After the visitation, over a hundred students started their protest by smashing the furniture in the examination hall and throwing it on a fire. They then took over the college fire engine and, showing 'a marked antipathy to anything in the shape of glass', directed the water-hose at a window in the president's house where the visitors were lunching. The table conversation doubtless faltered when the window broke. The rampage continued around the college grounds with the breaking of gas lamps and signposts and the destruction of shrubs. There was an attempt to storm the council room, but it was secured from the inside. The note of student insurrection continued to be sounded on a tin whistle.

This intellectual elite then headed out of the college with a red fan on a stick as a bannerette. Or, as the newspaper account colourfully put it,

> . . . having secured everything of a portable nature in the grounds, including wheelbarrows, shovels and other garden implements they proceeded from the back entrance in the direction of the Western Road, headed by one of their number carrying a banner that could scarcely be recognised as the emblem of any nationality by even the most critical observer.

A prison-van which they had commandeered overturned under their weight, seriously injuring the driver to whom however they medically attended (being the professionals they were) before bringing him to the North Infirmary hospital. That night (the newspaper account did not consider it necessary to dwell on their whereabouts in the intervening hours) the students went to the Palace Theatre where they passed the evening shouting, cheering and singing:

> . . . once or twice things looked like taking a nasty turn but the presence of a large force of policemen scattered around the pit where the students were located, prevented anything in the nature of a conflict.

In any case, the citizens, or at least some of them, enjoyed the diversion. Afterwards the students, followed by a large crowd, marched through the city streets singing such national and, at the time, highly popular airs as 'God Save Ireland' and 'The Boys of Wexford'. (The Manchester Martyrs, in whose honour T.D. Sullivan had written 'God Save Ireland', were commemorated annually on 18 September, and nationalist Ireland was still basking in the afterglow of the 1798 centenary celebration.) The college was the destination of the return march but the police lined the road and most of the crowd dispersed. Some scuffles broke out later between 'local ragamuffins' and a small group who sang such songs as 'Rule Britannia' and 'The Soldiers of the Queen'. Otherwise, the students went to bed, tired but happy (as they were wont to write in their school compositions) after their exciting day.

Strangely, *The Cork Constitution*, having reported this major riot at length, proceeded editorially to 'offer to the students of the Queen's Colleges our sympathy with their very reasonable demand'.[76] Some students, however, regretted the means used to achieve the end. The council permitted John O'Leary and twelve others to hold a meeting to express regret for the accident involving the prison-van driver and to organise a subscription fund in order to make amends to him.[77]

The 'disorderly proceedings' (end-of-the-century madness?) were investigated by the College Council over three days. Newspaper reports were studied and evidence was heard from students, porters and others: the council concerned itself only with the disturbances in the college grounds. Incredibly, only one or two of those responsible for the destruction of college property could be identified. Six were, in effect, found not guilty, J.G. Harty was fined ten shillings for being one of the riotous crowd and C.S. McDermott was fined £5, a substantial sum, for being a ringleader of the disturbance and committing a 'grievous breach of discipline'. Professor George J. Stokes (mental and moral science, 1894–1909) dissented from the council's decision, possibly because he thought McDermott was being made a scapegoat.[78]

The failure to remedy the causes of grievances leading to the demonstration, the mentality of the participating students, the unchecked destruction of college property, the carry-on downtown, the ineffectual attempts at apprehension and punishment – all speak volumes for the disordered state of the college in the closing years of the century and, above all, for the poor quality, or rather the absence, of its leadership.

A new university structure

The dissatisfaction of the Queen's Colleges with various aspects of the Royal University, on the one hand, and Catholic complaints that the Queen's Colleges (with their alleged low standards and low student numbers) did not justify public expenditure, on the other, led to the setting up in 1884 of yet another commission of inquiry into the Queen's Colleges. In a majority report, the three Protestant commissioners found standards of education in general satisfactory, but recommended certain improvements in the medical schools, including separate chairs for anatomy and physiology, both at Belfast and at Cork. The two Catholic commissioners (one of them the rector of University College Dublin) predictably condemned the scanty and inferior student material in Cork and Galway, claiming the colleges' failure was due to their unacceptability, on religious grounds, to the great majority of the people whom they were intended to serve. The standard of education in QCC, according to the minority report, 'must in some measure come down to the level of an Intermediate School'. Matriculation standards there were abysmal, and the principals of two large city boys' schools had allegedly testified that the few pupils who 'went up' to the college were the backward boys of the class.

Significantly, all the commissioners were in agreement that QCB was a success, the Catholic commissioners drawing a straight and simple conclusion that Cork and Galway had failed because they were non-denominational while Belfast had succeeded because it served the Presbyterian community (a conclusion strenuously disputed by the QCB president). Therefore, reasoned the Catholic commissioners, the Cork and Galway colleges should be made acceptable to Catholics, and public funding for university education should benefit not a small minority but the whole population.[79]

Falling numbers in the Queen's Colleges in the 1880s and 1890s was commonly attributed by contemporaries to the dissolution of the Queen's University and, under its successor the Royal, the non-requirement of attendance at the colleges. Though there were other reasons for declining attendances (numbers fell at Trinity over this period and there were two successive disastrous presidencies at QCC, 1890–1904), the depressing and dominant mood of higher education was uncertainty about a final solution to the university question, or even about financial support in the short term.

Still, the Cork Medical School did fairly well during the Royal regime – increasingly, until the renaissance of the college under Sir Bertram Windle, QCC *was* the medical school. Among the medical schools in Ireland as a whole at the turn of the century, it ranked second only to Belfast, at least in graduate output.[80]

QCB, in the person of its president J.L. Porter, complained in 1886 of the money being spent on QCC and of the niggardly treatment of Belfast which had twice as many students and much greater needs. The interesting answer of the chief secretary, Sir Michael Hicks Beach, was that government grants to Cork were a response to the liberal benefactions of Cork citizens. The generous gifts of W.H. Crawford (ironically a Belfast native) to QCC for buildings and equipment had no parallel in Galway or Belfast, despite the latter city's industrial prosperity. President Porter, ardently wishing to have halls of residence in Belfast, was particularly envious of Crawford's liberality to Berkeley Hall.[81] QCB, however, was to be much more successful in eliciting financial support from its graduates in general.[82]

The new century ushered in yet another royal commission (under Lord Robertson) to inquire into higher education and to report on what reforms were needed to make 'that education adequate to the needs of the Irish people'. The four reports it produced between November 1901 and February 1903 only contributed to the general sense of insecurity and uncertainty, the last report in particular reflecting a serious divergence of views. The commissioners had seen their brief as devising a system of university education acceptable to the Catholic bishops. They felt that the Royal University should be reconstructed as a teaching university comprising four constituent colleges – the three Queen's Colleges and a new Catholic college in Dublin. Each college would have a representative governing body. Once again doubts were expressed about the future of QCG. The commissioners recommended that QCC be brought under some form of Catholic control, with the new governing body there empowered to duplicate certain professorships, 'such as those of mental philosophy and modern history . . . on the principle recognised by several foreign universities'. Thus, the college might be made 'such as to secure the sympathy and support of the Roman Catholic population'.[83]

Disagreement and failure did not end the perennial search for an acceptable compromise. The Earl of Dunraven proposed in January 1904 that the University of Dublin should be reorganised to include (the Catholic) University College Dublin, as well as Trinity College and the Queen's Colleges of Belfast and Cork, with the unfortunate QCG becoming a technical school.[84] The Dunraven proposal at least kept the ball rolling.

Keeping government purse-strings closed was a form of psychological pressure on the academic community to move things along to a solution. Thus, Chief Secretary Bryce informed the QCB president in December 1906 that there would be no further grants in the present uncertain situation, and that

> no further grants . . . can be made to Belfast unless something is at the same time done for Cork whose needs are not less urgent. But the question of giving assistance to Cork has a special connection with the large question of university education as it affects the Roman Catholics of Ireland.[85]

And so a solution had to be found if the money was to start rolling again. Incidentally, there was no mention of Galway here.

The Fry Commission, 1906–07, on Trinity College was also expected to contribute to the general enlightenment. The Liberal government was now determined to solve the problem once and for all. The trick was to come up with a scheme which seemed non-sectarian enough to allay the fears of Nonconformists in England and of Presbyterians in Ulster, and yet not *too* non-sectarian if the Catholic bishops were to be kept on board. The cabinet-approved scheme drawn up in January 1907 by Chief Secretary Bryce (and very similar to the earlier Dunraven proposals) appeared at first sight to meet these delicate criteria. The proposal was for one national university which was to be an enlarged University of Dublin comprising Trinity, QCB, QCC and University College Dublin, with Galway, Magee and Maynooth colleges as 'affiliated institutions'. Despite the apparently favourable omens, the scheme perished on the rocks of QCB opposition to an arrangement in which it feared Trinity would be the predominant partner. This was matched by Trinity's vocal objection to the partnership, and the abandonment of the scheme was inevitable.

6.3 Augustine Birrell, chief secretary, architect of the
1908 university settlement.

However, one thing was now crystal clear: an all-Ireland framework was simply
not feasible, and Augustine Birrell, the new chief secretary, acted on that fundamental
premise. By leaving Trinity alone (a mercy for which it was profoundly grateful) and
making QCB a university in its own right, it was politically safe to establish a
'Southern' university under Catholic influence, if not indeed Catholic control. The
government insisted that the new National University of Ireland (with constituent
colleges at Cork, Dublin and Galway) was non-sectarian but everybody knew it was
acceptable to the Catholic bishops, though they might grumble that it did not fully
satisfy Catholic claims. Ulster unionists were opposed to what they saw as a Roman
Catholic university but it was a pill which the establishment of the new independent
Queen's University of Belfast (QUB) made palatable.[86]

Once more, educational considerations had been subordinated to political imperatives. The Irish Universities Act 1908 had not only a political but a partitionist rationale.
Partition was prefigured, educational apartheid prevailed and sectarianism was institu-
tionalised in the two new universities, North and South, despite their ostensibly non-
denominational basis.

CHAPTER SEVEN

THE WINDLE ERA[1]

I hope not alone to identify myself with your College, but
also with the city as far as possible.

Windle in 1904, on taking up the presidency

. . . wasted fifteen years in Cork, but I suppose God had
some good reason for sending me there . . .

Windle in 1920, having relinquished the presidency

BERTRAM ALAN COGHILL WINDLE[2] was descended on his father's side from a Shropshire family but had strong Irish connections through his mother, Sydney Catherine Coghill. The writer Edith Somerville was his first cousin and close friend, and he was a frequent visitor to Castletownshend during his years at Cork.[3] He was born on 8 May 1858 at Mayfield, Staffordshire, where his father was the vicar. When Windle was four, the family moved to Kingstown, Co. Dublin, where he spent his early school years. He was educated at Repton in England (1871–73) and then at Trinity College Dublin (1875–82) where, having first distinguished himself in English literature and natural science, he went on to graduate brilliantly in medicine. The family circumstances became somewhat straitened with the early death of his father when Windle was halfway through his medical studies, so that he had to have recourse to coaching and tuition to supplement his living expenses. It seems that the memory of those experiences made him particularly anxious as president years afterwards to help Cork graduates secure employment. When he left UCC, Professor Marcus Hartog commented that 'there was no need for an employment bureau as long as he was President'.[4]

Windle pursued his medical career in Birmingham where he became a fervent convert to Catholicism, got involved in social and charitable work, married one Madoline Hudson in 1886, and took up Liberal politics, supporting home rule and land reform. He became the first full-time professor of anatomy at Queen's College, Birmingham. He was foremost in the development of the Birmingham Medical School and worked eagerly for the establishment in 1900 of the new University of Birmingham, England's 'first civic university', and the prototype of many others. 'Birmingham, I may say with all modesty, I made', he wrote long afterwards in 1927.[5] He was the first dean of its medical faculty. His first wife having died during his last years in Birmingham, he married Edith Mary Nazer, who was related to Madoline.

7.1 Sir Bertram Windle, president
QCC\UCC, 1904-1919.

Meanwhile, he had established a reputation as a brilliant anatomist and he later developed a deep interest in archaeology, which he pursued while at Cork where he was to set up the department of archaeology and become the first professor of the subject. (A later professor of anatomy, Micheal A. Mac Conaill, 1942–73, also had a lively interest in archaeology.) Windle was something of a polymath though not on so diversified a scale as Alfred O'Rahilly, his successor but one as president of UCC whose initial career in the college Windle was to promote and whose Sinn Féin faction was to make his position in Cork ultimately untenable. Windle wrote and lectured on English literature (notably Shakespeare and Hardy), on anthropology, on education and, like O'Rahilly, on the relationship between Catholicism and science.

In Birmingham, he made a distinctive mark as a lecturer, evincing those formidable qualities which made him such a forceful personality as a college president. Elegantly austere in appearance, he was a stern disciplinarian, and students in Birmingham and Cork, as well as some of his colleagues, stood rather in awe of him:

> You remember the rather stony stare of the blue eyes and the rapid way that stare was turned upon anyone unlucky enough to make . . . a slip.[6]

7.2 Letter from Charles McCarthy (a porter), South Lodge, to Sir Bertram
Windle, President, QCC. The letter, probably written in March 1905,
reminds us of socio–economic differences within the college community.

Another student recollection is of

> the hush that used to fall upon the most turbulent as his apocalyptic eye ranged over the
> class . . . He never appeared to bother much about our personalities. He rarely spoke
> to us and hardly ever had a word of encouragement or of praise; but in after years one
> awoke to the fact that he had always taken a keen interest in the performance of his
> men, and the realization dawned that behind his singularly undemonstrative manner lay
> innumerable springs of kindness and of loyalty. He was just and fierce and self-sufficing,
> and he was the greatest teacher I ever knew.[7]

And yet another:

> Who does not remember the swift passage from the chattering impatient crowd
> without to the calm sanctum sanctorum [the dean of medicine's office] where the
> searching eyes of the Dean and the extreme brevity of his remarks made the chill
> comfort of the armchair by his desk peculiarly unattractive?[8]

The initial impression (afterwards reversed) that Windle made on Dr Magner, a junior
member of the academic staff in Cork, was that of a 'cold and unapproachable' person.
When Dr Magner went to see him about a possible increase in his demonstrator's salary,
adducing cogent reasons for his case, the president 'listened in silence and immobility to
my halting utterances and then, "fixing me with his glittering eye", said, "That may be
all true but we haven't got the money. Good morning".'[9] A warmer picture is drawn
by an observer early in 1905, as Windle was taking up his duties in Cork:

In his prime of life, tall, keen-featured and fresh-complexioned, Dr Windle is a
remarkable man to meet. An alertness in his look and an elasticity in his gait attest his
activity, while his face, clean-shaven, is intensely intellectual, and strongly stamped
with character. To talk to Dr Windle is to be attracted by his earnest but easy,
unassuming disposition, and by his cultured, clear-cut style of conversation.[10]

His correspondence was peppered with tart witticisms. His comment on one of the
candidates for the QCC registrarship (eventually secured by W.F. Butler in 1906, was:
'Professor [Arthur H.] Anglin [mathematics, 1887–1913] is quite impossible. He would
create and maintain chaos in office'.[11] Conscious that, in looking for government funds
to improve QCC, he might be fobbed off with the excuse that the university question
was as yet unresolved, he observed: '. . . the horse should not be altogether starved
while the stable is being provided for him'.[12] Again, while the details of his presidential
salary under the new NUI dispensation were still being finalised, he noted that 'all
argument with the Treasury is like conversing with a deaf adder which does not listen,
but does sting'.[13] When Windle became friends with the Dr Magner whose application
for an increase in his demonstrator's salary the president had so glacially rejected, they
would meet frequently in Magner's laboratory during the final disenchanted years of
Windle's presidency:

[He] would freely discuss college affairs. He had a marvellous power of semi-
humorous invective, and could pulverize some unfortunate individual with a flow of
sonorous phrases almost biblical in their construction.[14]

When Windle was appointed (through the influence of George Wyndham, the chief
secretary) president of Queen's College Cork in 1904 in succession to the egregious
Sir Rowland Blennerhassett, his immediate task was one of reform, as President M.D.
McCarthy's was to be in 1967.[15] At this stage of its existence – the nadir of its fortunes –
QCC was a high-quality medical school, and little more. Rugby was the sole social
expression of its students. Windle's appointment was a signal that the meagerly
endowed college was not to be downgraded to a technical school, as had been feared:
the fear indicated the prevailing poor morale. In the wider context, the Irish university
question remained unsolved despite numerous attempts.

The *Irish Independent* felt that the passing over of Professor Henry Corby for the
presidency would create great disappointment in QCC, making it difficult for Windle
to gain the staff's loyalty. But the real objection to his appointment came from
nationalist sources (for example, *The Freeman's Journal*) which regarded him as an
Englishman, and a 'Cawstle Cawtholic' Crown hack. The perception of Windle as a
West Briton was to be strengthened during World War I and after 1916 with the
resurgence of Sinn Féin. In fact, he regarded himself not only as Irish but as a nationalist
to boot, despite his part-English ancestry: 'I attach much more importance to the
amount of interest a man feels in [Ireland] than to the exact composition of his
genealogical table'.[16] As we have mentioned, he had championed the causes of land
reform and home rule, and he strongly believed in the Gaelic League as a social and

moral as well as a cultural and national force, though later on his enthusiasm did not extend to supporting compulsory Irish for NUI matriculation.

His appointment was defended against his detractors by, among others, *The Tablet* ('the best man is the best choice') and the *Catholic Times* ('no man has a more genuine sympathy with the aspirations of the Irish people, and the suggestion that "the appointment is the reward of political services" is far, far wide of the mark'). However, the enthusiasm of English Catholic organs was unlikely to mollify the indignation of Irish nationalists. More 'native' was the reaction of a Munster doctor, M.G. McElligott, who castigated *The Freeman's Journal* for its derogatory article on Windle's appointment:

> Professor Windle will no doubt raise the Cork College to a position of which, up to the present moment, its most ardent alumnus can never have dreamed. What a pity, therefore would it be if your sub-leader should effect a chilling reception for such a man!

But Windle's most impressive champion was his friend Dr Douglas Hyde, Irish scholar and co-founder of the Gaelic League, who emphatically vindicated the new QCC president:

> I know that for many years he has kept closely in touch with Irish thought and Irish literary movements. He *believes* in the *creation* of an Irish Ireland with ideals of its own and not of any other country. He is a member of two different branches of the Gaelic League, and I have heard him expressing himself strongly on the necessity for Irish education following Irish lines. I think that a man holding these (to my mind) absolutely sound views on Irish education should be set free to practise at home.

While nationalist Ireland disapproved, and his English colleagues expressed their congratulations, acclaim and regret at their loss, the students of Queen's College Cork gave Windle a boisterous and warm-hearted welcome ('probably unparalleled in the history of the institution', said the *Examiner*) when he arrived in the city by train on the fine morning of 8 November 1904.[17] Three hundred students assembled in the Quadrangle and went in procession to the railway station, under a banner of the college colours emblazoned with the skull and crossbones (symbolising the dominant role of the medical school). When the train arrived, there were ringing cheers, renderings of 'He's a jolly good fellow' and a display of that kind of chaotic enthusiasm which students have enjoyed generating from times medieval. The Windles were greeted by Mr John J. Horgan who introduced a number of prominent students to them.[18] A bouquet was presented to Mrs Windle, and D.L. Kelleher, afterwards a well-known London-based journalist and essayist, read an address of welcome from the students. When it ended, the (presumably slightly apprehensive) Windles were 'literally hustled' into their waiting carriage, and the procession swept back to the college. When the carriage passed under the arch into the Quadrangle, another bouquet was presented to Mrs Windle by the women students (still a mere handful at the time[19]) who had patiently awaited the arrival of the procession. The whole student body, we are told, then surrounded the carriage and there were seemingly endless rounds of cheers before

Windle could get a hearing. He and Mrs Windle must have been relieved that an end was in sight to an occasion which, though gratifying for them, was primarily designed for student entertainment, allowing them a certain amount of licence, not to be repeated, with olympian figures.

In his address, Windle said he appreciated 'the magnificent reception' all the more because of the controversial things the newspapers had been saying about him. (He addressed the students throughout as 'gentlemen' and spoke as to an all-male audience – which it virtually was.) He assured his listeners that

> I can honestly say I have never forgotten the country to which I belong . . . I have never once relinquished the hope of coming back . . . And my hopes with regard to my work here were intensified when I read . . . a statement . . . made by a gentleman from Belfast that Cork could claim to contain the cleverest portion of the population of Ireland.

That was certainly calculated to endear him to his audience! He concluded by saying he hoped 'not alone to identify myself with your College, but also with the city as far as possible'. *The Cork Examiner* (9 November 1904) noted that the new president had 'a great capacity for municipal work, an earnest sympathy with democratic progress and with more than an academic interest in the Gaelic League'.

The day's events and the speeches enabled Windle's Birmingham medical students to have some valedictory fun at the expense of their Cork counterparts and indeed of their own departing dean and professor. A writer in their house organ, the *Queen's Medical Magazine*, hoped that 'with the advent of their new President, the number of "chronics" will become a diminishing quantity' in Cork. Referring to the Cork students' address with its reference to Windle's various scholarly interests, the Birmingham magazine indulged itself in some Lewis Carroll-like verses depicting their polymath dean:

> He said: 'I leap the barrier of vile Anatomy,
> And take the road which I prefer
> Called Archaeology.
> I wander with the ancient Gael
> Through old and dirty barrows,
> These flints and stones I have for sale –
> A trifle for these arrows'.[20]

With the farewells and the frolics over in Birmingham and Cork, it was time for Windle to get down to the daunting and formidable task awaiting him at QCC.

The early period

One indispensable quality that Windle had in common with other outstanding presidents of the college was a capacity for hard work and a willingness to serve the college and the community in any way his versatile talents might be of use. The priority was the college itself with its low numbers, poor morale, lack of finance for development, the absence of any real university context, the unrepresentative nature of its ruling body, the interference in its administration by Castle officials (despite its nominal status as an independent corporation), continuing ecclesiastical disapproval, and general public indifference, if not hostility.

The new president sought to restore, or perhaps to create anew, a sense of *esprit de corps* and loyalty among students and graduates alike. He became a well-known figure at social gatherings and public meetings, and he established strong links with the city. With graduate support, he started a students' club. This was a major development, since student facilities were previously non-existent. A College Council committee (including three student members) was successful in raising funds.[21] The controlling committee of the club had two council members (one of whom served as treasurer[22]), five medical students (once again reflecting the faculty's importance), and one student each from arts, law and engineering. The annual membership subscription was fixed at the fairly stiff sum of ten shillings, and 'card playing and the sale of intoxicating liquors' were forbidden.[23] The women students wished to avail of these facilities, as was indicated by their desire to attend a 'proposed smoking concert' in February 1908.[24]

Windle enlivened the social side of college life by initiating a series of dances with staff participation, and by holding soirées in the president's house for staff, students and leading citizenry. This was certainly a new departure and created a pattern that endured at least into O'Rahilly's time, even if the culinary foundation of such events was no more substantial than a cup of tea and a bun.

Windle's diary apparently mingled reflections on personal, family, college and public activities in such detailed richness that its unavailability is most regrettable. We are dependent on the extracts in Monica Taylor's book for an impression of its contents and its flavour.[25] *Inter alia*, the diary chronicled Windle's (fervent) performance of his religious duties and the charitable works incumbent upon him as a member of the Society of St Vincent de Paul. References to his beloved archaeological research included the listing of artefacts found and brought home: he would have been horrified by accusations from latter-day environmentalists of heritage violation and vandalism! He tabulated, for each of his years in Cork, the annual total of letters written (maximum: 4,845 in 1910), books read (maximum: 387 in 1907), meetings attended (maximum: 204 in 1917, the year of the Irish Convention on which Windle served), and visits to Dublin (maximum: 112 in 1909). The numerous meetings in Dublin in 1909 arose out of the founding of the National University of Ireland, the new University College Cork's role therein, and the general transformation effected by the Irish Universities Act 1908. Over the period of his presidency, the number of visits to Dublin annually on average was only one-third of the phenomenal peak of 1909, but the travel burden overall was extraordinarily taxing. He returned repeatedly to the theme that such a waste of presidential time and such an expenditure of energy were intolerable, which powerfully strengthened the case (though there were other arguments) for an independent Munster university at Cork.

The day-by-day entries in Windle's diary for the first three months of 1905 show him settling in at the college and at the appropriate levels of Cork society, generally middle-class Catholic. Significantly, the Windles saw a great deal of the Horgans, family of his future son-in-law, John J. Horgan. It was at a dinner in their house that Windle began an acquaintance, which ripened into firm friendship, with the novelist, Canon Sheehan. As early as October 1905, Sheehan told Windle that he had 'leaped, at one bound, into a position never reached by any of your predecessors, not even Dr Sullivan'.[26] The president did his best to develop contacts with the students. He had them to his house, which was an official as well as a personal residence. On one occasion, thirty or forty repaired to the East Wing for tea, after he had chaired a meeting of the Philosophical Society. He attended a students' ball on 24 February, staying until 3.30 a.m. and on the following day 'didn't get up till late and then felt a wreck'. A social event involving the wider community was a big reception in the college on 24 June, attended by about four hundred people who were entertained 'by Irish pipers'.

On college business, he was also very accessible: 'shoals of people called in afternoon' is not an untypical entry. Windle had particularly frequent discussions with the registrar, Alexander Jack, who was a significant college figure since Sullivan's time, providing an element of continuity and stability throughout a period of decline and low morale. Windle clearly relied on Jack's counsel on matters such as finance and proposed new buildings and he was invaluable to the president during these first years. Windle was glad to see C.W. O'D. Alexander taking over Jack's old chair of engineering in 1906. He was coming to QCC, Windle thought, because he preferred 'a small income with time for research and study to a large fortune made at the expense of work and thought'.[27] When Jack died, Windle noted (16 October 1908) that 'he did a man's work for this place'.[28] The well-known Marcus Hartog seems to have been another confidant. Windle also talked to, and expressed his affection for, Bunnell Lewis, professor of Latin who remarkably had been in that chair since 1849 and was only just then retiring after fifty-six years – 'very old but quite all there . . . nice old gentleman'.[29] QCC professors retired of their own volition, and often at leisure: Bunnell Lewis bowed out at eighty-four, and the influential Alexander Jack at eighty-one.

The matters preoccupying Windle at this early stage of his presidency were reflected in the diary entries as well as in the College Council minutes, the presidential reports from 1904–05 onwards, and in his correspondence with government. Dominating everything else was the unresolved university question, of which two aspects in particular concerned Cork: would there be such changes in the constitution of the college as to make it acceptable to the people at large? And would there be an independent university for Munster at Cork?

Meanwhile, more immediate problems had to be dealt with – separate chairs for anatomy and physiology; improved laboratory facilities for physics, chemistry and pathology; extra library space; an extension to the porter's lodge at the east gate; and the chronic problem of timetabling which occupied an inordinate amount of the College Council's time.[30] Windle also vaguely speculated about a possible school of architecture in QCC, but this never became a matter for serious consideration. He seemed doubtful at this early stage about the feasibility of 'University Extension Science Courses held before at Crawford Schools. Did well for some years, people coming in from a distance – Cork a small place, thought it well to give it a rest. Thought short course in Archaeology would be interesting and well received'.[31]

In February 1905, the new broom got the council to support him on a number of proposed improvements, some of which have familiar echoes. They included a reduction on periodicals expenditure to allow for more book purchases; the creation of more library shelf-space by removing outdated books; the refurbishing of the Aula Maxima with a view to arranging public lectures by the staff; and the building of a pavilion, with club and dressing rooms, on a bank at the southern side of the Quadrangle.

The provision of a new football ground was the welcome if belated answer to a frequently expressed student grievance at the turn of the century. A visitation had recommended the acquisition 'of a suitable field for football, etc' and in April 1898 the Medical Students' Association put pressure on the College Council to follow this up.[32] The council agreed that facilities were dire: the students 'have no lavatory' and no changing room. In May 1905, a student told the registrar, Alexander Jack, that some students did not 'join in football practices' because of dressing room conditions.[33] The real breakthrough in the sports side of college life came in 1911 with the acquisition of the Athletic Grounds.

The growth of student societies (literary, social and athletic) was stimulated in June 1910 by a Governing Body endorsement of a Finance Committee proposal to raise the college fee by £1 to £2 with the sole purpose of subsidising student associations

> in order that they may be placed on a perfectly sound footing. These associations form a most important part of the student's education, and experience has shown that they cannot be carried on in institutions like ours without substantial aid from College funds.

A committee consisting of the president and faculty deans would distribute the funds which were really the result of a student levy. Six months later the GB accepted a Student Representative Council suggestion that students paying the increased £2 fee be given free membership of four athletic clubs and the Philosophical Society – *corpus sanum* evidently taking precedence over *mens sana!*[34]

Windle also fostered the publication of college journals, not surprisingly since he promoted the study of journalism as a degree subject. On 29 March 1905, the College Council sanctioned the publication of *QCC*. The first committee/editorial board included D.L. Kelleher, who was to become a celebrated journalist. The council insisted that the board bear all the costs, and that it should avoid 'all subjects of religious or political controversy' and 'everything which is inconsistent with the maintenance of good order and discipline in the College'.[35] Incidentally, in 1908, the College Council turned down a request from the Philosophical Society that the ban on political discussions be lifted.[36] At a GB meeting on 19 October 1911, Windle referred to a small net loss (£4) on the *UCC Official Gazette*, probably to be made good by advertising revenue due. He was convinced that the free distribution of 2,500 copies of the *Gazette* was a great advertisement for the college.[37] It is interesting to find a president in 1911 so alert to the importance of promoting UCC's image.

Within two months of Windle's arrival in Cork, he permitted himself some hope that Catholic hostility to Queen's College Cork might be lessened at least at diocesan level: 'Dr F. Maher O.S.F. (Fr Minor) called in afternoon – very pleasant and evidently learned – says Ep.[bishop] very favourable and would like to come to some arrangement'. Another priest – Windle had many clerical friends and acquaintances in Cork – Fr O'Sullivan 'thinks everyone would like to utilize Q.C. more and the Ep. made error in v. beginning in not taking over the thing'.[38] The scene brightened towards the close of 1905 when Bishop O'Callaghan gave official leave for the formation of a students' association, and appointed two priests as chaplains.[39] Yet in his 1905–06 president's report, Windle spoke of the 'extreme pressure' brought to bear on young people not to attend arts courses, 'though the objections raised to attendance upon courses of Medicine and Engineering which are "bread" studies have not been nearly so great'. He observed to the chief secretary that the medical school was flourishing but 'there can be no question that . . . the comparative want of success of this college on its Arts and pure Science side is due to the religious difficulty'.[40] This most interesting distinction helps to account for the success of the two professional schools of medicine and engineering and for the 'wretchedly small' dimensions of the arts faculty. This may be attributed, on the one hand, to the relative imperviousness to clerical pressure of the kind of families who were determined their sons would become doctors, and, on the other hand, to an ecclesiastical attitude that regarded the ambience of the professional schools as less hazardous to eternal salvation than the humanities.

At any rate, we have independent evidence around this time of clerical pressure on would-be QCC students. Michael Davitt, whose doughty championing of undenominational education brought him into conflict with Bishop O'Dwyer of Limerick, received allegations about clerical intimidation. A Cork mother indignantly complained that Bishop O'Callaghan and other clergy had intimidated two sets of parents 'by terrifying them by excommunication' into withdrawing two girls from arts courses in 1906. She herself had stood firm in the face of clerical blackmail because she would not surrender her independence and because she believed QCC 'is everything a Catholic parent would ask for':

> The Queen's College in Cork would be filled with Catholic students if they were allowed use their individual consciences . . . Secular education would be the firmest cement to unite North and South or English to Irish in fraternal unity.[41]

Apparently, the Church authorities regarded the presence of the few women in the college as particularly indecorous and obnoxious, in much the same way as the bishops had fulminated against the Ladies Land League in 1881. In the spring of 1905, when Windle, at the request of the Munster branch of the Irish Women Graduates Association, proposed setting up a course of lectures in education for trainee teachers (the forerunner of the Higher Diploma in Education), there were six women anxious to enrol but 'I am sorry to say that they are all Protestants and there does not seem any prospect of any Catholics being allowed take part in this instruction'.[42]

The presidential reports from 1904–05 onwards show Windle getting to grips with a number of college questions. (He did not go through any pretence of paying tribute to his predecessor, who incidentally returned to the college as a visitor in the 1907–08 session.) Even with a student body of two hundred and fifty, there were the perennial problems of cramped library and laboratory accommodation, and 'there is no other institution in the UK accomplishing the work . . . with so small a staff of teachers'. A 'more generous provision' was needed for museums which were of educational benefit to the citizenry as well as to the students. Windle would also like, when accommodation improved, to have consultancy facilities available 'for a small fee' to manufacturers and agriculturalists. Like his predecessor, he was unhappy with the situation whereby medical students got their qualifications from licensing bodies, being unwilling to face strange examiners under the RUI system.

There were some achievements to be listed – the eminence achieved by former medical students in various parts of the UK and the empire, notably India; the separation at last of anatomy and physiology, with Windle himself becoming professor of the independent chair of anatomy for a brief period, and giving four lectures a week;[43] publications by the staff, the president himself foremost; the success of the Old Corkonians Club (a graduates' association) in London, under former midwifery professor, Henry Macnaughton-Jones; the donation of the Nunan Cup (by Dr Joseph Nunan) for inter-varsity soccer competition; and, cheerfully, the new sounds of music in the college.

F. St John Lacy was the college's first lecturer (1903–09) in music, and first professor, 1909–34, with the institution of the NUI. According to his successor, Aloys Fleischmann, Lacy owed his appointment mainly, if not solely, to Mrs Windle's desire to avail of his expert services as a singing instructor and to her success in persuading her husband to employ Lacy in the college. The really piquant point about this story is that Windle himself 'had neither taste nor liking' for music. Before long, Lacy founded a 'glee and madrigal union' which performed at a well-attended concert. Over the years, however, there were few music students, or none, and Lacy's post was a virtual sinecure.[44]

Windle cherished the eternal hope that generous benefactors would fund college buildings and have their names immortalised in the process.[45] He was unduly optimistic in hoping that some donor would give £20,000 for a separate library block.[46] He was also concerned to provide a modicum of creature comforts for the students, and as already stated, the Students' Club, funded by private subscription, was open by the 1906–07 session. Student meals were available and this was important because of 'the distance from the town'. Though it was a men's club, the few women in the college could also get their meals there. The women were provided with a new 'retiring room', in which connection Windle made an unwittingly sexist comment. Their previous room, he explained, was 'entered from the Library, and though our students are no more talkative than others of their sex, their presence near a reading-room was sometimes obvious'.[47]

The university question

When the Liberals came to power in an overwhelming election victory in 1906, there was a quickening prospect of an imminent solution to the long-standing Irish university question. This issue, and its applications to Cork and Munster, was Windle's foremost concern for the next couple of years. Within the desired overall framework of a university settlement acceptable to Catholics, there was a strong push for an independent university at Cork, and Windle orchestrated this drive in the newspapers and at public meetings. In his president's reports for 1905–06 and 1906–07, he argued the case for transforming the college constitutionally by making its ethos and its governance 'acceptable to the district to which it belongs', that is, to Cork and Munster political and public opinion as well as to the Catholic Church authorities. The way in which 'the great and progressive University of Birmingham' had come into being to popular acclaim (a development in which, as has been mentioned, Windle played a prominent part), was a model for what might be done at Cork. If nothing were done, 'the present disastrous state of affairs' – disastrous for the south of Ireland as well as for the college – could result in closure of the college, or at least of the 'wretchedly small' arts faculty. On the other hand, the number of arts students could be increased tenfold, if the 'difficulties in question' were removed.[48] A large meeting of the Catholic laity at the Cork courthouse on 6 February 1904 had demanded that 'local facilities for university education entailing no sacrifice of conscience should be provided'. Windle also ruminated half-heartedly in his 1905–06 president's report that, if the college had been properly funded and equipped over its sixty years, it 'might at least have attracted a number of students from distant parts, even if those of the locality refused to enter its class-rooms'. However, it is clear that he found his own speculation unconvincing.

Meanwhile, the chief secretary was strongly impressed by Windle's argument for carrying out structural improvements at QCC, and made a recommendation accordingly to the Treasury.[49] The latter commented that, while QCB had raised considerable supplementary funds in the locality, '. . . in the case of Cork . . . there is no promise of any local support towards the cost of the new buildings'. The Treasury's strictures were noted with scepticism in the chief secretary's office:

> The community of Cork is comparatively poor compared with Belfast: but it is to be punished for its poverty. If I do not err this matter will be made the subject of strong opposition in parliament – and rightly so, in my opinion.[50]

In his president's report for 1906–07, Windle claimed that the desired constitutional changes could be effected 'by alterations in the Charter and without direct legislation'. He was also able to indicate the level of public support for reform by appending the texts of resolutions in the autumn of 1906 by the city councils of Cork, Waterford and Limerick, and by Cork County Council.[51] These praised Windle's initiatives in Birmingham and Cork and called for the requisite changes in the constitution of the college. Cork County Council expressed the ultimate fear – that in a new university settlement Catholic students from Cork might have to go to Dublin for an acceptable

Catholic institution! The aspirations of the four public bodies were summed up in one clause in the Cork Corporation resolution:

> That we are convinced the conversion of the Queen's College into a properly constituted and equipped University centre would tend in like manner to elevate the whole standard of education, develop the intellectual life, and promote the general prosperity of Munster and, in due time, exercise a potent influence in the uplifting of the nation.

Also in the autumn of 1906 a representative Munster Higher Education Committee summed up its deliberations by asserting that an acceptable university institution in Cork must have a representative governing body rather that an internal academic ruling committee; the ideal future institution was 'an independent university of Munster'; and failing that, the Cork college must have 'the largest amount of autonomy' possible in respect of curriculum, examinations and degrees.[52]

Windle made extensive use of the press in promoting his campaign. Much interest was stimulated by his 'A Call to Action' article in the *Examiner* (11 September 1906), and by subsequent pieces clarifying the terms 'federal' and 'autonomous' in respect of universities. There was also public awareness that he gave evidence on 9–10 November to the Fry Commission which was investigating the university question. The culmination of all this was a great public meeting at the city hall on 17 November 1906, with the lord mayor in the chair. The meeting 'was attended by delegates of all creeds, and from every part of Munster', though there were no clergy present, unsurprisingly. While the resolutions predictably reiterated the standard condition of popular acceptability of a reformed Cork college, the novel development was the extravagant offer made by the redoubtable maverick politician, William O'Brien MP, who had been a QCC student and whose Russian-Jewish wife, Sophie Raffalovich, was reputedly very wealthy.

O'Brien apparently offered 'the entire of his own and his wife's fortune, at their death, for the foundation of a local University or for the support of a truly autonomous College'. Independently of this promise, he would make £10,000 a year for five years available if the borough and county councils would levy half a farthing in the pound on the rates (to be replaced out of their fortunes on the deaths of the O'Briens). This publicly-raised money together with the college grant, as well as the generosity of the O'Briens and other benefactors, could start the university at once, said O'Brien, even if the state came up with nothing more. In reporting O'Brien's offer, Windle stressed the importance of not looking such a gift horse in the mouth: 'any coldness or hesitation in the reception of such offers is likely to check the natural enthusiasm which they elicit', with damaging effects on the institution concerned.[53] In the event, O'Brien's 'most magnificent promise' turned out to be just that – a characteristically flamboyant gesture: the college never benefitted from the O'Brien fortunes.

In the increasingly expectant atmosphere of 1907, Windle continued to publicise the university issue. He stressed that whatever educational settlement was made for Dublin, the people of Munster must be primarily concerned with the local and regional

7.3 Dublin Commissioners, responsible for drafting and overseeing the Irish Universities Act (1908)
Back row (L-R): Stephen Gwynn, MP; J. P. Boland, MP; President Anderson, President, UCG; Sir
Bertram Windle, President UCC; President Coffey, President, UCD;
Front row (L-R): Rt. Hon. Sir W. Butler; Most Rev. Dr Walsh, Archbishop of Dublin; Rt. Hon. L.
Palles, Lord Chief Baron and Chairman Dublin Commissioners; Sir J. Rhys; Dr Jackson OM.

question.[54] Cork irritation with, or resentment of, Dublin dominance was a recurring feature of Windle's attitudes to university issues, and it was even more noticeable under his successors as president, especially Alfred O'Rahilly. On 7 February 1907, Windle's presidential address to the Cork Literary and Scientific Society was on the theme 'The City and the University'. Augustine Birrell, the new chief secretary and soon-to-be architect of the university settlement, visited Windle in March and toured the college. Later on, in October 1907, Birrell wrote to Windle, outlining the settlement he had in mind. He then discussed his plans with a QCC deputation, and Windle commented succinctly on developments in a diary entry on 12 December:

> Long interview with Birrell – will give Governing Body and Autonomy – says enemies
> will try and prevent more money – and Treasury likely to play the waiting game, say,
> wait till Cork gets students – then. I said wait to go into sea till you can swim.[55]

In April 1908, as the Irish Universities Bill was being debated in the House of Commons, Windle appeared reasonably satisfied:

> The University Bill promises, I think, well. It does not give us all we want here, but is
> a decided advance, and will put me in a position to make a really big thing of this
> place, as I hope to do if I live and remain here.[56]

He kept the Cork public informed of the course of events through his letters to *The
Cork Examiner* and *The Freeman's Journal*, in which he continued to make the case for a
separate university for Cork. However, his practical concern now was to ensure a
smooth transition to the new dispensation (University College Cork as a constituent of
the federal National University of Ireland), to get adequate financing and an acceptable
governing body, and to secure continuing tenure of office for existing professors.

Windle addressed a large and enthusiastic public meeting in the city hall on 25 April
1908.[57] There was a great turnout of local and regional notables, including such well-
known MPs as William O'Brien, D.D. Sheehan and Thomas O'Donnell. Windle
stated that 'the creation in Cork for Munster of a separate and independent university'
was still his chief goal. Nevertheless, he welcomed the bill as a great step forward.
There would be three definite advantages in the new college situation: a governing
body representative 'of the several districts [and] . . . all classes and all creeds and all
interests'; 'Cork students would be examined in Cork by their Cork teachers with the
supervision of external examiners provided by the University'; and there would be
'some measure . . . of control over the subjects we are going to teach'. Windle did
not believe 'that we are going to be crossed and hampered and harassed by the Dublin
members' of the new Senate. Experience was to teach him otherwise. Windle also
appealed to local public bodies to 'found maintenance bursaries for the poor boys of
their own district' to enable them to attend the new university college. He went on to
outline his 'idea of a modern university . . . one which will turn out high class men
of business and persons able to pass their living in a variety of ways and instructed to
that end'.

The resolutions passed unanimously at the meeting demanded adequate financing,
expressed disappointment that Cork had not got its long-desired 'separate university',
and hoped the bill would not impede the attainment of that final settlement. Even the
'temporary settlement' of a federal university would be unacceptable

> unless the local college has complete autonomy, an effective voice in the appointment
> of its future teachers, and the management of its own finances, and is given an
> adequate representation on the Senate of the new University . . .[58]

The birth of UCC

In May Windle explained the draft charter for the enlightenment of *The Cork Examiner*
readers. There was nothing in it, he explained, which could prevent the evolution of
the college into a university. Moreover, the charter allowed for the private endowment
of any post in the college and independent arrangements for making such an appointment. For example, the Governing Body could allow the Catholic bishop of Cork the

power to hire and fire a privately-funded professor of theology, without any reference to the university Senate:

> . . . whereas at present we cannot create a chair or even a lectureship without the permission of Dublin Castle, even if we find the money for it ourselves, in the future we can do what we like, so long as we do not do it out of Crown money . . .[59]

Ecclesiastical reaction to the bill was obviously crucial, and in Cork at least the omens were favourable, as Windle noted on 6 and 22 June. Bishop O'Callaghan was well disposed:

> . . . Bishop has acceptance of the College in his pocket and will use it if the Bill fails. This is great intelligence. He thinks everything would go to smash if I left, for the Bishop has only gone this length on my account . . . [he] said he could not stand having to treat me as he had to.[60]

Windle put all doubts aside in making a joyful entry on 9 June:

> Meeting of Temporary Governing Body of the College to consider Charter. Wonderful day in the history of the College and most amicable. I put down the names of those here, it was so remarkable. Archbishop of Cashel, Bishop of Cork, Bishop C. Cloyne and Ross (Protestant Bishop), Dr Barrett, Mr Butler, M. (Christian Brother), C. (Presentation Brother), Lord Mayor, Chairman County Council, Cork, Maurice Healy, Stanley Harrington, Hill, Dale, Townshend, M. Murphy, Butler, Hartog, Bergin, Corby, Pearson.[61]

(The charter incorporated the principle of gender equality,[62] and UCC professors and lecturers were obliged not to 'make any statement or use any language that would be disrespectful to the religious opinions' of any of their students'.[63]) Windle's euphoria continued into the autumn. On 1 October:

> To see the Bishop – most cheerful. Tutors – approved Residences. Lectures – Thomistic Philosophy – Yes. Catholic students this time? If new Charter could be got, he would do thing at once.[64]

For the next two months Windle was busily occupied as one of the commissioners drafting the statutes for the National University and the constituent colleges. Then the charter, issued on 2 December 1908, arrived in the college on 9 December and, true to form, Windle wrote an explanatory article for *The Cork Examiner*.[65] The statute-drafting, which involved Windle in numerous journeys to Dublin, was not completed until the early summer of 1909 (it was the hardest-working year of his life[66]). When the statutes were published on 17 May, Windle noted the momentous occasion – '12.15 CORK signed; then Dublin, Galway, and lastly the University. The Meeting broke up in great amity and I caught the 3pm train home'.[67]

The college had entered the second phase of its history, its future now assured. It had a new name, a representative constitution, and a greatly extended range of disciplines. Ecclesiastical disapproval, which perhaps had been the major factor in the college's stunted growth, was now lifted. The hardline Catholic position was that the National University and UCC, still technically non-denominational and therefore falling short of the Catholic ideal, were being tolerated rather than endorsed. But such fine distinctions did not worry Catholic parents who could now send their children to the college (if they could afford it) with a clear conscience. In respect of religion at least, the college was no longer an alien institution. Indeed, it was to be increasingly Catholicised during the next five decades. A symbolic milestone on that road was the first celebration in the history of the college, on 15 November 1909, of a votive mass of the Holy Ghost (a 'red' mass, so called from the colour of the vestments worn).[68]

What impact did the constitutional transformation actually have on the life and working of the college? It seems that there was surprisingly little disruption, and continuity was as noticeable as change. For example, the minutes of the first UCC Governing Body meeting appear in the same volume as the last QCC College Council meeting, separated only by a page![69] Windle himself powerfully personified the smooth transition, with his status greatly enhanced by the central role he had played in developments and with his leadership position in the new college confirmed. The office of president was as important as ever. The College Council had expressed its full confidence in him when it decided he should be requested to remain in London to monitor the progress of the Irish Universities Bill through the committee stage.[70] The council members were aware that Windle could be depended upon to safeguard the interests of the professors during the changeover. He was gratified and surprised – in academic life, one can never predict where the next compliment or insult will come from – by a private remark of Professor Charles H. Keene (Greek, 1895–1914) at a council meeting on 3 December 1908, that 'we all feel how fortunate we are in having a man whom we can really trust to organize things for us'.[71]

Continuity was indicated by a resolution passed at the first meeting of the Governing Body of UCC 'that the Governing Body . . . hereby confirm all the orders made on December 3 1908 by the Council of Queen's College, Cork'.[72] But there was considerable change also, of course, most obviously in the growth of student numbers. There were new professorships: archaeology – Windle himself held this chair until 1915; economics; education – a chair which women were to dominate; German; hygiene; Irish; mathematical physics; medical jurisprudence; music; ophthalmology; pathology – its institution had been long desired; old professorships writ new (natural philosophy being replaced by experimental physics; natural history by zoology; modern languages by romance languages; mental and social science by philosophy; midwifery by obstetrics and gynaecology); QCC officers and professors surviving into the new order; a new faculty – commerce; and professorships emerging from the break-up of former combined chairs (botany including agriculture up to 1920; English; history; geology and geography; law, common; law, real property; law, jurisprudence). All things considered, this was a revolutionary expansion of academic disciplines, confidently inviting a corresponding growth in student numbers.

Windle, we are told, went to endless pains to secure Irish candidates for the new posts, and he was obviously influential in the appointments process. While in Portrush in the summer of 1909 on an archaeological flint-discovering trip, he met Isaac Swain, who was about to become professor of geology and geography (1909–44) as well as superintendent of examinations. Windle observed that it was an appropriate place to find a geologist.[73] He had previously (2 October 1908) commented rather laconically on a man who was to have a distinguished academic and diplomatic career: 'Saw Smiddy, who wants Chair. Might do for Commerce'.[74]

The 1908 transformation involved a considerable change in college governance. The College Council had been an all-purpose body in a small and declining institution. Now, with growth confidently expected, the council was replaced not only by the Governing Body and the Academic Council – the assembly of professors responsible for academic business and student discipline – but by a number of committees. The most important of these was – and still is – the Finance Committee which had to meet at least once before every Governing Body meeting. Other committees were responsible for grounds, buildings and athletic grounds (acquired in December 1911[75]). The president was entitled to sit on all the committees and proposed most of the initiatives coming from them. In a modernising move Windle in 1909 suggested the introduction of a college telephone system, though its operation remained uncertain and primitive down to the 1970s.[76] It is worth noting that Windle remarked to the chief secretary on 22 April 1911, apropos of the GB, that 'it is not always easy to get a quorum as some of the members rarely attend'.[77]

In his first president's report under the new dispensation, Windle expressed general satisfaction, noting that the number of students was greater than it had been for twenty-five years (that is, since the dissolution of Queen's, and the creation of the Royal, University) and a 'much greater increase' was expected. A considerable burden of work had been thrown on him and others because of the changes, but the loyalty, solidarity and *esprit de corps* of the staff was 'above all praise'.[78]

The 'Munster university' aspiration did not really catch fire again until 1918–19, at the end of Windle's presidency, though it flickered from time to time, as in Windle's address at the first NUI degree conferring ceremony on 25 May 1910.[79] He felt it could still be achieved if Cork people wanted it badly enough and he deplored the waste of time and energy involved in the federal system.[80] It is interesting to note his reaction when the matter was raised by a governor, James M. Burke, on 2 May 1913. Burke himself referred to the difficulties which stood in the way, inasmuch as certain bodies still refrained from extending their support to University College Cork. The president endorsed this observation, saying it was useless putting any 'university' proposal to government until the local authority showed a real interest in the college: so far, Cork Corporation had not funded any scholarships to be held in the college.[81] Funding university scholarships was to be a bone of contention in local bodies for quite some time, and the college authorities were particularly dissatisfied with what was seen as an inadequate Cork city contribution.[82]

The change of name in the 1908 charter and legislation was not universally welcomed, and mostly for the same nostalgic reasons that were to cause middle-aged graduates in foreign parts to deplore the 'desecration' of the Quarry site in the 1980s by building a new library thereon. Windle recorded in his diary (21 February 1909) that a Dr Porter, medical officer of health in Johannesburg and graduate of QCC, visited him in the college 'and much resents change of name'.[83] Protest against the name-change was conveyed in a letter to the chief secretary's office from Col. Thornhill, the secretary of the Old Corkonians graduates club in London. The letter recounted the proceedings of a club meeting held at 20 Hanover Square, London on 21 January 1909, chaired by the surgeon-general, Sir Thomas Gallwey. The meeting unanimously passed a resolution:

> That this meeting of old Queen's College Cork students has learned with deep regret of the change in the name of their Alma Mater from that of Queen's College Cork to University College Cork. They desire to put on record their indignation at an act which was as uncalled for as it was unjustifiable.

The proposer was retired Professor H. Macnaughton-Jones, founder of the club, who confidently asserted that the citizens of Cork as well as the professors and students did not want the change. The seconder, J.D.A. Johnson, made a rather irrelevant contribution wherein he claimed there was never a quarrel about religion in the college. What he said next, as reported by Thornhill, suggests that there was some political resentment as well as nostalgia involved in the protest:

> They [the graduates] were not cattle drivers and they did not go behind hedges with guns. If they did these things they would be respected by the Chief Secretary. But being mere law abiding citizens of the Crown who had tried to lead fairly respectable lives and not make acquaintance with the interior of prisons, he did not suppose notice would be taken of their protest.

During the discussion, it was suggested that ecclesiastical influence (a popish plot?) had been in some part responsible for the name-change.

The file containing this letter also includes a newspaper report (25 March 1909) of a House of Commons exchange on the topic.[84] Lord Robert Cecil (whose interest was surely political rather than nostalgic) asked why the change had been made and whether Chief Secretary Birrell was aware of the deep regret and indignation felt by QCC graduates. Birrell replied he was so aware, but the name-change was part of the process of creating a federal university with constituent colleges. When Sir James Craig (representing unionist opposition to the Irish Universities Act) tried to be smart by asking whether the new institution would be known as the National or the Nationalist University, Birrell replied tartly 'The hon. Member can read, I suppose'.

Windle and the Irish language

Windle's attitude towards the place of the Irish language in the college and the university was rather complicated. As an Irishman, a scholar and antiquarian he had an obvious interest in the ancient tongue of the country, as he would think of it. That interest was clearly indicated by his membership of the Gaelic League and his friendship with Douglas Hyde (who, as we have seen, testified to Windle's 'Irishness'). On the highly controversial question of compulsory Irish for NUI matriculation, he had decided at an early stage to oppose it.[85] Nonetheless, in the end he gave in and voted for it. Archbishop Healy of Tuam spoke of Windle's surrender in this respect 'with withering contempt', claiming he was bribed by the prospect of support for the college from county councils (scholarships and otherwise) 'with their baked meats smoking on the board'.[86]

In private correspondence, Windle referred scathingly to the 'wild priests' of the Gaelic League whose ignorant blather was enough to make any man a heathen.[87] His view of the viability of Irish as a university subject was influenced, doubtless, by its poor performance in the college where, according to Windle's presidential report 1908–09, its history was 'most disappointing' from the start. For the previous two years, the new department had no students at all. There was no enthusiasm for the subject as was obvious from the fact that nobody took it for the entrance scholarship examination.

In April 1919, just before the government decided to drop the Munster university scheme (thereby provoking Windle's departure from UCC), he wrote a memorandum on the subject of 'Compulsory Irish at Matriculation' for the information of the chief secretary who knew nothing about the matter. Though the UCC Academic Council voted five to one against compulsory Irish, Cork was in a small minority at the NUI Senate and in any case Windle felt 'the experiment has to be made'. He believed that

> it is ridiculous to say that it has kept Protestants out of Cork and Dublin, for Irish is neither Catholic nor Protestant. What does, I think, deflect Protestants from Cork to Trinity (and very naturally) is the fact that one has a more Catholic and the other a more Protestant 'atmosphere'.[88]

Windle was concerned lest the chief secretary might listen to 'unwise' persons seeking to have a clause inserted in the charter of the proposed university of Munster forbidding compulsory Irish. Such a provision would be counterproductive and would raise a destructive storm. While he himself favoured an 'open' matriculation (selection by the candidates of, say, any five subjects from a long list) there should be no outside interference, by way of prescription or exclusion, with a university's right to frame its own matriculation regulations. He set out his own views reflectively and critically on the 'compulsory' dimension or perhaps on the compulsory exclusion of Irish:

> . . . gravely to set it down that whilst the University may require a knowledge of the ancient tongue of Greece . . . or of Rome, it is strictly forbidden to require a knowledge of the tongue, yesterday spoken by many and today by not a few, of its own country. It may make anything else compulsory but not what many call 'its own language'. It is really only necessary to put this in words in order to see its absurdity . . .
> . . . It cannot possibly be argued that to require knowledge of the language which is the original tongue of the country and a knowledge of which is essential if persons desire to understand that large part of the history of a country which is embedded in its place-names, is to impose a political disability.

> Finally, the argument that Irish is not taught in certain schools is wholly beside the mark. As well might a parent who had put his son into the modern side of a school complain that it made him unable to enter a university which required Latin or French or both at its matriculation.[89]

In the light of the above, whatever Windle's Sinn Féin enemies might say about his politics, they had no justification for dubbing him a West Brit or a shoneen in cultural terms.

Windle and ogham stones

Windle appeared to come under a cloud in unusual circumstances late in 1913. The antiquarian, Philip G. Lee, publicly deplored the destruction of the rath at Knock-shanawee in mid-Cork through the removal of the great ogham stones supporting the sides and roof of the chamber. They were taken away by 'two learned gentlemen, one from Cork, the other from Dublin' to the 'museum at the Cork University' as he supposed. 'For educated archaeologists to commit such an outrage is unpardonable'.[90] The two responsible were R.A.S. Macalister, distinguished archaeologist and ogham expert, and Bertram Windle. Macalister defended the action as 'a scientific necessity' and praised Windle for developing such a collection of national antiquities at UCC.[91] No less a scholar than Eoin MacNeill vindicated the removal, arguing in the course of a long article that Cork was the best centre for an ogham collection.[92] The controversy continued, with one critic accusing Windle of 'scientific vandalism', a Gaelic League deputation protesting to the county council and the brothers P.S. and Seán Ó hÉigeartaigh (well known later in the nationalist resurgence) ranging themselves on the anti-removal side.[93] P.S. argued, in a characteristically trenchant letter, that the episode demonstrated the arrogant and elitist attitude of 'the Chosen university People' and their disregard for the common man who quite reasonably expected Windle to justify his actions: '. . . a university which divides itself from the populace becomes barren and purposeless'.[94] Though the Royal Irish Academy (RIA) thanked Windle for transferring the stones,[95] a hostile article in the *Free Press* suggested that Windle's record of removing inscribed stones from Co. Kerry spoke for itself . . .'[96]

UCC – early years

In his president's report for 1911–12, President Windle was glad to note that, under the new 1908 constitution, despite some dire predictions of 'serious quarrels and unpleasantness between the Academic and non-members of the College' in the Governing Body, harmony prevailed notwithstanding differences of opinions.[97] In fact, the first *elected* UCC Governing Body was not formed until December 1912/January 1913. The election of four representatives of the graduates, and of six of the professors (Alexander, Corby, Harty, Molohan, Pearson, Ryan), presented no problems[98] but there was acrimonious uproar at the special Cork County Council meeting to appoint a representative, and the matter became a Redmondite/O'Brienite brawl.[99] There seemed to be some momentary doubt as to whether the government would appoint the Protestant and Catholic bishops as two of their three nominees. Not only was this done in the end, but four religious were co-opted so that, all told, the first elected Governing Body included one bishop of each denomination, two Catholic and one Protestant clergymen, one Christian Brother and one Presentation Brother (the celebrated Brother Connolly, otherwise known as 'The Man').[100]

As far as the day-to-day work of the college was concerned, there was a remarkable degree of continuity in the transition from QCC to UCC, but the new dispensation made for a radical change in the public perception of the college and in college–community relations in the years after 1908. It provided not only a kiss of life to a moribund institution but a keen stimulus to development. As letter-writer Daniel Daly from nearby Inniscarra put it, 'for sixty years, the old Queen's College stood apart in pompous and gloomy isolation from the current of life around it' and there were great things expected of the new order, 'a Munster University as the bountiful mother'.[101] Though (as Daly himself was well aware) the sober reality was somewhat different, there was unprecedented public interest in the new UCC and a reciprocal eagerness on the part of the president and staff to advertise their wares attractively.

The length and spread of press coverage of college affairs (detailed reports of conferring addresses and Governing Body meetings, for example) were remarkable. Naturally, there was special attention from the Cork newspapers – the 'Protestant' *Cork Constitution*, the idiosyncratic and sometimes abusive *Free Press*, and above all *The Cork Examiner*. The attitude of 'de Paper' to 'de College' is an interesting research theme in its own right: suffice it to say here that the college provided a rich vein for the *Examiner* to mine over the years – in its news pages and editorials as well as in its advertising columns.

For their part, academics wrote frequent letters to the editor, explaining college courses and services and replying (with surprising speed) to points of criticism.[102] Windle, in particular, was an indefatigable correspondent. Though still deploring the drawbacks of the federal university framework and still pressing for an 'independent' university, he seemed to be in generally sanguine and buoyant mood at this early period. Relatively speaking, he was both respected and popular, winning golden plaudits on the occasion of his knighthood in 1912.[103] Councillor J.J. Goggin's honest and independent opinion was that if anyone could get a dental school for Cork it would be the 'justly popular' Bertram Windle, in whose lexicon there was no such word as fail.[104] More robustly, another councillor said at a corporation debate that Windle 'lived amongst the people and was not like some of his predecessors who spent their time in Continental drawing-rooms'. However, Alderman Beamish primly observed that this remark was in bad taste.[105] Windle, incidentally, deplored the newspaper practice of referring to UCD as the 'National University': the people of Cork spoke of 'the Cork University', 'prophetically', he hoped.[106]

7.4 The College Library c1900. More than half a century later, flooring-in created two storeys and today the lower chamber is the Staff Common Room and the upper, the New Council Room.

The new University College had to go through a lengthy and complex legal process of appeal and counter-appeal before its exemption status in respect of rateable valuation was confirmed. In the course of this process, the legal continuity between QCC and UCC was demonstrated. The old Queen's College had been exempt from ratepaying, as having been founded for public purposes. But Cork Corporation availed of the 1908 transformation to press for their pound of flesh, and the Commissioner of Valuation took UCC out of the exempted category. Thereupon the Governing Body appealed to the recorder of Cork who accepted the 'public purposes' argument and reinstated UCC in the exempt category. Further hearings were held in the King's Bench division and the Court of Appeal. The UCC victory also benefitted the Queen's University of Belfast and University College Galway (UCG) as well as UCD.

On the corporation's behalf, it was argued that payment of fees modified the college's charitable and public status, and that the college was vested in the Governing Body 'as their own private property'. But the points made by the college's counsel eventually carried the day. 'Public purpose' was clearly indicated by the 1908 Act, 'to enable His Majesty to endow a new college for the advancement of learning in Ireland', 'for the better advancement of learning among all classes' of his subjects, and not just for the benefit of one denomination. It was also emphasised that the new charter did not dissolve the old QCC but continued its corporate existence. 'It remains and continues one body corporate with a perpetual succession', though that corporation was now extended from the president and professors to a larger entity on which the public bodies of Munster were represented.[107]

The public was suitably impressed by the post-1908 growth in UCC student numbers, a development emphasised by Windle in his president's report for 1910–11 and in a subsequent letter to the *Examiner*. The average first-year student entry for the previous fifteen years had been 50. There were 102 freshmen (the largest intake so far) in 1909–10, and 181 in 1910–11. The whole student body in 1900–01 was only 171. In 1910–11 it stood at a record 404. The previous highest had been 402 but that was in the early 1880s when students were entering in order to take the 'last advantages' of a dying Queen's University, which was being replaced by the Royal.[108] The *Cork Constitution*, in a wide-ranging review, was also impressed by the figures and the general prospects for progress but (not surprisingly) was inclined to think that non-Catholics and many well-to-do Catholics tended to go to TCD because of the deterrent effect of compulsory Irish in the NUI matriculation, though there might be many other causes, the paper admitted. It also pointed out that UCG, because of its weakness and inability to stand alone, would frustrate Cork's aspiration to independence.[109]

Because the ecclesiastical ban had borne particularly heavily on female students (of whom, as a consequence, there was only a handful at QCC) there were high hopes, warmly expressed by Windle[110] among others and in the event realised, that the number of women at the college would increase substantially. In 1909 Mary Ryan (who the following year would become the first woman appointed to a chair – romance languages – in the UK) and Dr Lucy Smith were made women officers of residence.[111] The mildly feminist tone of a UCC address given by the formidable Countess Aberdeen must have further raised women's morale.[112] And notwithstanding the innocuously universal use of 'boys', girls were eligible to compete on equal terms for local authority scholarships to the college.[113]

There was much admiration for the new chemistry and physics laboratory, which was opened in 1911 and was a most impressive reflection of the college's physical development under Windle in the post-1908 period. The building (now civil engineering) in brickwork with rough casting on the face, was well removed from – and so did not clash with – the main structure. What particularly met with public approval – and conformed to local and national sentiment – was that 'in their praiseworthy desire to give as much local employment as possible', the college authorities were having all the furniture, teak and pine made in the city, and 'more creditable still, the majority of it will be manufactured in the College workshops'.[114]

An editorial in *The Cork Examiner* on 28 December 1909 welcomed Windle's announcement that, as a consequence of the new university arrangements, Cork

7.5 Interior view, Aula Maxima, c1900. Conferrings began to take place here in 1910 when some students regarded conferring ceremonies as enjoyable indoor rags.

students would now be examined and conferred in Cork 'in the midst of their families and friends'. The first ceremony was held on 25 May 1910. Conferring day turned out to be a mixed blessing. It was, of course, and remains a happy day for graduates and their friends and relatives, and from the beginning presidents used the occasion for airing grievances and making policy pronouncements. During that first conferring speech ('the first Senate meeting of any university, at least since the times of St Finbarr [!], which has been held in Cork') Windle once again demanded 'our own independent university' or 'educational Home Rule for Cork',[115] and he outlined college achievements in various areas, notably in the Indian medical service, 'long considered a prize amongst the public medical services'.[116]

Some students regarded conferring ceremonies as enjoyable indoor rags. During the Windle and Merriman presidencies, degree day was an occasion of noise, high jinks and practical jokes. At the first conferring, students in the gallery indulged in good-humoured sallies, enjoining the mace-bearer[117] to 'take away that bauble' (at least they knew their English parliamentary history) and punctuating the president's address, especially when he called for an independent Munster university, with excessively hearty cheers.[118] The following year, degree day in the 'Large Hall' (consisting of a thirty-minute ceremony for sixty graduates) was once again marked by high-spirited demonstrations.[119] In 1912, the proceedings were 'almost decorous' but only because the 10 a.m. starting time was too early for those students who loved turning the ceremony into

> a wild display of boisterousness, and make it a moment of uneasiness for the President and the Professors, and of pantomimic delight for themselves. When they came into the gallery, the meeting was nearly over. They signalled their presence, however, by indulging in cat-calls, yelling and whistling, while a few fired off toy pistols and flung toy bombs.[120]

Archdeacon Tom Duggan of Cork (1890–1961) was among the first clerical students at UCC and he once recalled for the writer the hilarious conferring scenes he witnessed. He remembered in particular the rhythmic student chant that was raised whenever President Windle conferred a degree on a woman graduate (very much a novelty at that stage): 'Don't hold her hand, Bertie!' A railed gallery walkway (later removed)[121] extending around the Aula Maxima on either side facilitated the dropping of stink bombs, flour bags and similar missiles. Whether student antics were indulgently tolerated as pardonable middle-class high spirits or whether there was a lack of intent, or shortage of attendants, to enforce discipline is not clear.

A more serious outlet for student energy – or perhaps it was another variant of fun and games – was participation in politics. Political topics might be debarred from student societies, but there was a wider arena available. A large contingent of UCC students attended the great home rule demonstration in Dublin in March 1912. There were requests to wear 'the University colours' and a newspaper letter from 'A Student' pleaded for proper organisation and a banner with the slogan 'Cork Students want Home Rule'. A college that wanted home rule for itself, it was argued, should support the wider cause. Students were reminded that they were heirs to the college Fenian circle of 1867 and to those who had braved the hazards of rustication to present an address to Charles Stewart Parnell (an event long remembered in student political tradition).[122]

Scholarships: opportunities and difficulties

If the new University College, unlike its exclusive predecessor, was really 'the poor man's university' – the phrase most commonly bandied about in the pre-1908 agitation to suggest a new era of equality of opportunity – how did the citizens and their public representatives come to terms with it, and to what extent did they seize the opportunity? (It was pointed out, incidentally, that county councils felt they were in duty bound to support UCC through scholarships, if only as a quid pro quo for NUI adoption of compulsory Irish in matriculation![123]) The 1908 Act envisaged the provision of scholarships by local authorities and the scholarships issue became a matter of considerable argument, as at a meeting of Cork Corporation in March 1911. When Dr

Magner proposed striking a penny in the pound for scholarships for the children of ratepayers, he spoke about the benefits of 'a flourishing university in Cork' to the economy, and the opportunities which scholarships would provide for the children of post office clerks and low-grade civil servants. There was heated dissent from 'Land and Labour' representatives who claimed that only an already well-off minority class would benefit from the proposed scheme, that the great majority of children had no access to secondary education and therefore no access to scholarships, and that this showed up 'the poor man's university' for the cant it was.[124]

The lack of primary-to-secondary scholarships was raised again and again, particularly by national teachers who claimed that 'the poor man's son' was but a lever cynically used to have the NUI established, and now cast aside.[125] 'Was it fair or just that the parents of every thousand children attending the National Schools should be rated to give a university education free to two of that number . . .?'[126] The inequality of geographical opportunity was also raised: city privilege against country distance.[127] Various other aspects of the scholarships question were debated: could they be confined, under a means test, to the children of the deserving poor – or at least of artisans, labourers and small farmers?[128] Some scholarship results seemed to confirm the suspicion that the already relatively privileged were benefitting.[129] Indignation was reported in Waterford that scholarships had been 'collared' at the expense of 'the poor man's son' by those well able to pay.[130] Cork city councillor, J.J. Goggin, said that the poor man's son had as much chance of entering UCC as he had of jumping Shandon Steeple.[131]

Was it proper for county councils to stipulate that scholarships should be held only at UCC, or at least at NUI colleges? And should scholars be absolutely free to choose their faculty? If, for example, everybody opted for medicine, universities would be, more than ever, 'professional emigrant factories'.[132] There were innuendoes of nepotism[133] but there was also a soothing assurance from President Windle that 'suspense scholarships' could give national school pupils (many of whom stayed on at school in those days to reach a good standard of education) a year to study Latin and so matriculate, which proved, claimed Windle optimistically, that the scholarship system was 'successful in teaching the class of persons in need of them'.[134] However, the viewpoint was not uncommon that it was 'fraud' and 'gigantic humbug' to pretend that scholarships benefitted the talented poor.[135] As late as March 1916, Cork Corporation was still divided on the usefulness of awarding scholarships.[136]

Though South Tipperary scholarship aspirants got off to a surprisingly poor start (three candidates sat for four scholarships of £50 each but only two qualified!),[137] their county council was as agitated as any other body about the scholarship issue. The chairman's unabashedly racist sentiments – students should be stipulatedly of Irish birth since otherwise 'any German or Jew could get a scholarship after qualifying by residence in the county' – were endorsed by his patriotic colleagues. Even so, they felt the scholarship scheme would not really benefit 'the poor man's son' or the children of 'the ordinary farmer or shopkeeper or labourer'. The South Tipperary councillors had other worries about their young beneficiaries. One section of their adopted scheme read:

> To safeguard the morals of its scholars and to preserve them from the license and vice
> to which they would be exposed by lodging in the city under no proper supervision,
> the Co. Council shall require all its scholarship-holders to reside in a hostel duly
> recognised by the University . . .[138]

Decades later, county scholars were still expected as a matter of course to reside in the
Honan Hostel or in La Retraite, the residence for women students.

It may have been in reaction to the confusing and sometimes disappointing
scholarships situation that Professor T. Smiddy (economics, 1909–23) emphasised
adult education as an alternative approach to equality of opportunity. He suggested
that perhaps scholarships were poor value for public money.[139] Speaking at a prize-
giving ceremony in Tralee in 1914, he said the professors of 'Cork University' would
only be too glad to give lectures among the masses of the people if there was a
demand for it: 'The poor man's son should have as good an opportunity to have a
university training as a rich man's son'. Extension lectures for the masses would be
better than scholarships for the few.[140]

Critics of college

Letter-writers and members of public bodies often revealed attitudes of disenchantment, suspicion or class hostility where the college was concerned. Members of the
Technical Instruction Committee expressed such views at a meeting in March 1914 –
the poor man could not afford fees, lectures were in the daytime – and they were not
all reassured by the patronising and improbable assertion by A.F. Sharman Crawford (a
member of the Governing Body) that there was not a rich man's son in the college![141]
The *Free Press* championed the working man's cause – 'a national university for the
nation and not for any particular class'.[142]

At this time, the college proposed that its engineering students should be admitted –
for an agreed fee, of course – to the courses at the nearby Municipal Technical
Institute. In this connection, Windle was at pains to dispel the proletarian suspicions of
the college that had been voiced at a Technical Instruction Committee meeting, and
his enthusiasm led him to make extravagant claims for the egalitarian nature of the
student body:

> Those persons who state that the College is in any way closed to the children of the
> poorest worker speak in entire ignorance of the facts. I very much doubt whether
> there is a single student in this college whose parent does not earn his living by hard
> work, and many of them by manual labour . . . I may add that there is only one
> thing which will keep a child of the poorest person from entering this college, and
> that thing is want of brains.[143]

Such unconvincing exaggeration served only to harden the attitude of the college's
inveterate critics. Perhaps the foremost of these among public representatives at the
time were J.J. Goggin and John Dorgan. Their hostility to the college, and to college-

connected medicos in particular, surfaced during a debate at the board of guardians on Goggin's proposal that half of the fees received by the Union's medical staff from students attending the Union's hospital should be retained by the board on behalf of poor ratepayers. This fund would establish scholarships at UCC for the children of those financially unable 'to pay the enormous fees in that seat of learning', in order to enter the medical profession.[144]

In the course of the debate, Dorgan said he had no grudge against the college but it seemed there was no respect 'up there' for the man 'with the brogue'. He was thrown out once while attempting to enter 'but the big gate was opened wide to let three car-loads of magpie Yankees in'. 'There was a welcome for the fellow who spoke through his nose.' The college was charging so much – in soaring fees – for the theory of medicine that the guardians were justified in asking some return for the practical training they provided.[145] Though 'this hospital, dead and alive, supplies them with sources of information', there is 'no respect for a Corkman at University College'.[146] At another, and blackly humorous, debate on the supply of bodies to UCC for dissection, Dorgan maintained that only the corpses of the Catholic poor were supplied, and that college staff were haughty towards board of guardians members. The college paid no rates, its revenue was £23,000 per annum:

> and they wanted to use the Workhouse as a wing of the College. They had often used the phrase 'where Finbarr taught, let Munster learn'. Did Finbarr charge £23,000 a year for teaching what they taught, and taught in Irish?

The college contributed nothing to the coal fund, or to the upkeep of the workhouse. 'He wished there was some other industry that would give £23,000 p.a. that would be spent in the City, instead of giving it to people who spent it on the Riviera on their vacation (Laughter)'.[147]

No doubt, there was laughter of a well-bred kind in middle-class academic circles at the press report of a speech at a Cork United Trade and Labour Council meeting, when an enthusiastic vote of thanks was proposed to those responsible for building development under the Honan bequest, for using Cork labour and materials in the expenditure on the chapel and £5,000 'for the enlargement of the lavatories'. John Dorgan would not have joined in the patronising mirth at the malapropism.[148]

John Dorgan was an extreme, if not neurotically fixated, critic of the college. Other working-class and trade union representatives were also sensitive to perceived snubs from college quarters. At a June 1918 meeting of the Cork Trades Council, there was a complaint that the college bursar had been instructed not to reply to the council's queries about attendants' salaries. 'That was education as practised in the place where the youth of the country was looked after'. It was urged that the lord mayor, an *ex officio* governor, should demand a reason for this slight on the trade union movement.[149]

However, the college hardly impinged at all on the thinking or concerns of the mass of Cork workers. When socio-economic topics were being discussed at adult education conferences in UCC early in 1916, Mr Michael Egan TC hoped the workers of Cork who had not yet come to the conferences would soon lose their terror of the university precincts.[150] 'Terror' was hardly the word: it simply did not occur to many people (except for neighbourhood residents) to visit the college, though there may have been an element of nervousness there too. After all, the East Wing was a grand residential area, and with their gardener and distribution of plants, flowers and seeds to encourage labourers to beautify their cottages,[151] the Windles seemed at times to have a Big House lifestyle.

Windle himself made an observation (in Waterford in April 1913) that would hold true of some Cork citizens until quite recent times:

> I am often surprised to find how many people in the City of Cork, educated people, too, who have never been inside the walls of the University College, as it is now called, and have no idea of what kind of place it is.[152]

The conversazione sessions of the early 1920s were, in part, intended to remedy this state of affairs. Windle, however, believed that the constitutional transformation of 1908, despite the drawbacks of the federal connection, had really made UCC a people's college. That is why, in his president's report for 1911–12, he made the unusual proposal that the Governing Body should raise, by subscription, a fund

> to purchase the freehold of the various portions of land on which rent has at present to be paid. Considering the enormous benefits that the College confers upon the city – financial as well as educational benefits – it ought not to be too much to ask the citizens to do for this College what has been done in Belfast, and in many other places, for the local institutions of higher education.[153]

A reflective *Cork Examiner* leader philosophised in 1913 on the nature of the modern university, with particular reference to the changed condition of the Cork college since 1908. For long years, the people of Munster had no university they could conscientiously avail of: the problem now was to get people in every part of the province to use it. There was a good intake of students, and scholarships were liberally available but there was still a need to bring the people to the university. As Windle had noted, for Cork and the other Munster cities, the college must combine with its university function the attributes of a higher technical school, of an 'institute' devoted to the 'bread and butter' studies, now more onerous than ever they were.[154] The *Examiner* was to harp frequently on this utilitarian theme, and also to demand again and again that the Irish university system should emulate London University and provide facilities for extern degrees, or at least not place obstacles in the way of those Irish people who wished to sit the degree examinations of London University.

The Honan bequest

The press took a lively interest in the news of the Honan bequest and the subsequent working out of its provisions. The Honan Scholarships were instituted during Isabella (or Belle) Honan's lifetime, and the first awards made in 1910–11. The scholarship was intended for those who could not otherwise afford a university education and Munster, excluding Clare, was stipulated as the area of benefit. The scholarship was, and remains, unrestricted denominationally, unlike the Keliher Scholarships which are confined to Catholics.[155] The 'Honan' has always been *the* prestige undergraduate scholarship.

When Isabella Honan died in August 1913, the Honan trust funds, representing the residue of her late brother Robert's property, were bequeathed to the lawyer Sir John R. O'Connell (who was later ordained a Catholic priest) 'to be applied in my discretion for charitable purposes in Cork'. In a letter to President Windle on 4 April 1914, O'Connell stated that he had decided, in view of the previous Honan interest in UCC, to reconstitute St Anthony's Hall, then about to close, into a hostel for Catholic lay students, a development which 'would be of immense benefit to the Church and to the entire Catholic population of Munster'. O'Connell envisaged a married warden (Catholic, of course) chosen from the academic staff. There would also be 'a proper Chapel, suitable to the dignity of a University with a Chaplain resident in the Hostel . . . provided for by endowment'. The Munster bishops had expressed approval, and Windle himself had always dreamed of such a residential development. The hostel would have 'a thoroughly Catholic atmosphere', O'Connell promised, and it would be endowed to an extent that would ensure moderate fees. The Honan bequest would also bring secular benefits to the college. The biological institute would be completed, as would the hydraulic department of the engineering laboratories. The buildings would be renamed 'The Honan Hostel' and 'The Honan Biological Institute'. All work would be carried out in Ireland, as far as possible by Cork labour and with local materials, so as to maximise employment opportunities.

The issue of *The Cork Examiner* containing these glad tidings also carried a leading article expressing gratification at the news. This recalled the regret expressed at the time of the Irish Universities Act 1908 that the government had made no residential provisions. Accordingly, it was fortunate for the Catholic public of Munster that the Franciscans had converted the 'derelict but excellent' Berkeley Hall into St Anthony's Hall which had housed lay students as well as their own novices, and which would now become the Honan Hostel. The *Examiner* looked forward to seeing the new chapel in 'the Celtic Romanesque style', and expressed the hope that other wealthy people, 'and there are more such in Munster than perhaps would like to be known', would emulate the excellent Honan example.[156] Munster newspapers of 11 and 15 April carried advertisements for places in the Honan Hostel ('formerly St Anthony's Hall'), reopening on 20 April 1914, with Rev. D. Cohalan PhD as chaplain and Professor T. Smiddy as acting warden. The Governing Body expressed its appreciation of the Honan bequest on behalf of the people of Munster and gratefully accepted O'Connell's offer to defray half the expenses of taking down the high wall between the hostel and the college, and replacing it by a dwarf wall and railing to improve the general appearance of the area.[157]

The president's report for 1913–14 gave pride of place to the Honan bequest.[158] He mentioned that Sir John had purchased a house and lodge adjoining the hostel property and had assigned the house as the residence of the chaplain.[159] During the ensuing year, 'a very handsome chapel' of the Irish Romanesque order would be built in the hostel grounds. Windle announced the hostel would house forty or fifty students. When we consider that (as the report stated) the student body for 1913–14 was just over 400 (359 men, 76 women), the significance of the Hostel accommodation figures becomes clear, as does the delighted reaction of all concerned, especially the bishops. Forty to fifty constituted about 12 per cent of the men students or, allowing for city students living at home, well over 25 per cent of 'lodging' students. A substantial proportion of men students would now be housed in a Catholic milieu, in a college whose non-denominational terms of reference were otherwise tolerated rather than approved by the Catholic bishops.

The press carried details in January 1915 of the royal charter incorporating the governors of the Honan Hostel. The bishops, UCC staff members and representatives of the Catholic laity in Munster were all to be involved, with Sir John O'Connell as a life member of the board of governors, and the bishop of Cork as the 'visitor'. Their first meeting was marked by a big luncheon spread at the hostel, which was attended by the residents wearing academicals. Afterwards, the guests were shown through the hostel 'where the beautiful and numerous Arundel and Medici prints – so generously given by Sir John O'Connell – covering the walls of the corridors and bedrooms, were the particular objects of admiration'.[160]

By 1977, there were seven hostels or halls of residence in Cork housing a total of 254 students (more than half of whom were freshmen), amounting to 12 per cent of students living away from home. Most of these were run by religious orders and accommodated an average of twenty or so residents. By far the largest, and the big sister of the Honan Hostel (forty-one students), was the hall of residence run by the La Retraite sisters, a French order specialising in hostel accommodation for ladies. La Retraite was situated in spacious grounds just west of the Gaol Walk. It had formerly been the gaol governor's residence, was called Lee Cottage and had later been the home of the Murphy-O'Connor family. It had fallen into disrepair when, through the good offices of Bishop Daniel J. Cohalan, the La Retraite sisters took it over as a hall of residence for women students and opened it in October 1923. When a new wing was built in 1967, La Retraite housed ninety women students. (During vacations, the building was used for retreats.) In December 1977, it was acquired by UCC for normal college purposes – being renamed Áras na Laoi and greatly extended in 1991 – while La Retraite was transferred to Fernhurst House on nearby College Road. In its new home, La Retraite was able to accommodate a hundred women but, with the trend towards self-catering apartments, it went out of business in twelve years or so, selling the premises to the Bon Secours nuns to the considerable disappointment of the college, which had hoped to acquire it.[161]

The laying of the foundation stone of the Honan Chapel in October 1916 was well reported with good pictorial coverage.[162] In this and subsequent reports, the chapel was variously described as the Honan Hostel Chapel, the Collegiate Church (or Chapel) of

St Finbarr, or St Finbarr's Chapel. Whatever about the accuracy of title, the *Examiner* (though not necessarily the general student and graduate body) obviously understood the legal position – the chapel and hostel were technically and literally outside the grounds of the non-denominational college. As the paper well put it, they were 'intimately associated, though not officially connected, with University College'.

In his homily at the opening ceremony, Bishop Kelly of Ross made light of this fine distinction, thereby setting the future pattern. He deplored the divorce between school and Church in the 1908 Act, but rejoiced that they had linked together 'the Church and the College today'. And after all, did not the Protestants have St Fin Barre's Cathedral? The *Examiner* itself was hardly impartial in summing up the 1908 arrangement: one university was founded 'to meet the demands of the Catholics of the three provinces, one to appease the prejudices of the majority in the fourth province'.[163] There was understandable public enthusiasm for the Hiberno-Romanesque architectural gem on the eastern boundary of the college, midway on Donovan's Road. It was linked in customary fashion with St Finbarr's legendary foundation – 'in this very spot . . .' The 'real work of art' was described in great detail, with particular emphasis on the Harry Clarke and Sarah Purser windows, and the *opus sectile* stations of the cross. All involved in the 'handsome structure' were highly praised – architect James F. McMullen, builders John Sisk and Son, and the silversmiths, Egans, whose silver trowel had been used at the foundation ceremony and who supplied the beautiful vestments and sacred vessels. The opening ceremony was a splendid ecclesiastical, academic and civic occasion, with the sacred music celestially rendered by the much-lauded cathedral choir, conducted by Herr Aloys Fleischmann, father of the future professor of music.[164]

The Honan Chapel, where Catholic Action in its various forms was inculcated, was central to religious worship in the college but it also had an important social, not to say snobbish, role in the life of graduates. In a flowery and fulsome report of a wedding, *The Cork Examiner* commented cloyingly:

> The privilege of entering into the holy state of matrimony in the University Church is only extended to past students of the College and such occasions are therefore not only a source of joy to the contracting parties, their relatives and friends but are also occasions for the manifestation of a keen sense of pride and consolation by the President and professors under whose batons they studied for the various degrees of their chosen profession.[165]

A Protestant perception of incipient UCC Catholic triumphalism on such occasions as the red mass triggered off a lengthy correspondence in the letters page of *The Irish Times* between Canon J.W. Tristram of Dublin and Sir Bertram Windle, with Windle arguing his case as firmly (but not as aggressively) as O'Rahilly was to do a generation later.[166] Tristram had expressed Protestant fears and worries at the Church of Ireland synod when he asserted (developing his points in subsequent letters) that UCC had wilfully violated the non-denominational dividing line by celebrating the red mass in St Anthony's Hall, thus blurring the distinction between secular studies and religious worship. College employees had helped with arranging accommodation in church, and professors had lent prestige to the occasion by their presence at the mass. UCC was too 'close and intimate' with the Roman Catholic Church, and this in a college 'whose very title and *raison d'être* should make it entirely undenominational, especially when Protestant winners of County Council scholarships are told they must go there or go without'. Windle denied that the religion–education line had been blurred, and advised the Protestants to organise their own hostels and ceremonies, which was to be very much O'Rahilly's line of response in due course.

The Catholicising process: the beginnings

We tend to associate the intense and integralist Catholicising of Irish society with the early decades of independence but it had begun well before that. After all, James Joyce had proclaimed his *non serviam* very early in the century. Similarly, the Catholicising process at UCC which is generally attributed to the Merriman and O'Rahilly[167] regimes and which was certainly in full flower in the 1940s and 1950s was already under way during Windle's presidency. For example, the new Governing Body of the new UCC decided in 1909 to recognise Church holy days as college holidays.[168]

At the opening meeting of the UCC (Catholic) Students Union in 1910, the reverend preacher rang the changes on a theme that was to be familiar to students forty years later: Catholic students must blend secular knowledge and religious truth, since the NUI did not provide for the latter, and graduates must prepare themselves for their destiny as leading Catholic laymen.[169] A *Tablet* article in 1912 listed the measures UCC had taken to provide a religious dimension and thus remedy the defects of the neutral 1908 Act.[170] The red mass was celebrated in St Anthony's Hall to mark the opening of the academic year; the hall provided a Catholic milieu for clerical and lay students; the chapel there functioned as a parish church (outside college limits) for staff and students who wished to so regard it; and lectures were arranged in the hall on subjects of Catholic interest. There was a thriving confraternity for men students held in St Maries of the Isle school, with special preachers. The chaplain was full-time dean of residence for men students, appointed and paid by the Governing Body. Women students had their own officer of residence, sodality and special chaplain. All these developments were hailed as great advances but it was pointed out that 'non-Catholics' had their own opportunities, and that all religious organisations used the college notice-board, in an atmosphere free from rancour.

There was a triumphalist note in the *Examiner*'s coverage of the red mass in SS Peter and Paul's Church at the commencement of the academic years 1912–13 and 1913–14. The paper totally supported the involvement of Church, college and city in such a panoplied ceremonial. By their large attendance, UCC's Catholic students were bearing out Bishop Kelly's contention that the NUI colleges were the seedbed and nursery of Gaelic and Catholic Ireland. There was no opposition between science and religion, exulted the *Examiner*. It hoped that

these sentiments will be handed down from generation to generation and that our
University College will be a home of religion as well as learning, and thus provide
Ireland not only with men of brains but also with men of virtue and high moral
character.[171]

Three hundred students (out of a total of 430) were reported as being present at the
1912 red mass. This figure was miraculously surpassed the following year when a figure
of 600 students (out of a total of about 400) was claimed! The attendance probably
included many non-UCC students from various educational establishments around the
city. The preacher was Mgr O'Riordan of the Irish College at Rome,[172] and once again
the *Examiner* rejoiced that religion was not separated from education in Cork.[173]

Adult education: first steps

If Windle unexpectedly prefigures O'Rahilly in the context of Catholicising the
college, he also does so by taking early steps in the adult education area. Short courses
(generally, a fortnight) in many subjects including agriculture and archaeology (where
Windle lectured) were widely advertised[174] and just as extensively acclaimed[175] in the
autumn of 1911. A year later, Windle, lecturing in Limerick, said he would like to see
UCC as a centre for extension lectures throughout Munster. The idea had been tried
before but met with only partial success in Limerick.[176]

   The most exciting point of this early stage of UCC adult education was the so-called
economic conference series for workers, held in the college early in 1916. In particular,
a lecture on poverty in the city, given by a Dominican priest, Fr MacSweeney on 1
February 1916, together with a follow-up discussion a week later, caused quite a stir. It
was described as a real eye-opener for the people of Cork. The whole programme of
lectures had a radical tone with Professor Smiddy and the young Alfred O'Rahilly well
to the fore.[177] These first workers' economic classes were run on Workers' Educational
Association (WEA) lines, we are told, with great freedom of discussion.[178]

College and the Great War

The Great War increased wages and maintenance costs,[179] and boosted the number of
medical students but fired only a minority of the staff with anything like enthusiasm.
Windle praised John Redmond's stance and backed the war effort,[180] as did a number of
academic staff, notably Professors D.T. Barry[181] (physiology, 1907–42) and C.W.
Alexander.[182] 'I felt it my duty', Windle recorded, 'to place the College at the disposal
of the military and naval authorities as a Base Hospital with myself as its administrator
and my medical professors as surgeons.'[183] Some war hysteria was evident when there
were objections to the advertising of a chair of German at UCC at the end of 1914 –
there was no popular wish 'to use English taxes to spread German Kultur in Cork'.[184]
(Nor did the Crown wish to see Russian culture spread in Cork, apparently, disal-
lowing a statute for a lectureship in that language in 1917.) Professor Marcus Hartog, in

UNIVERSITY COLLEGE. CORK.

————

RECORD OF

STUDENTS PAST AND PRESENT ENGAGED
IN THE WAR.
DISTINCTIONS GAINED.
DEATHS.

————

RECORD OF

COLLEGE WAR GUILD.
SPHAGNUM DEPOT.
BOOKS FOR MUNSTER SOLDIERS' FUND.

————

1914-1919.

7.6 Cover from *List of War Dead*, which
records QCC/UCC graduates killed in
action in World War I.

a letter to the *Manchester Guardian*, advocated compulsory military training in peace-time: his references to England as 'our little island home' would hardly endear him even to readers of the *Cork Constitution* where the letter was reproduced.[185]

Something of a witch-hunt was raised by 'Loyalist' suggesting in the *Constitution* that UCC was a nest of pro-German sentiment, needing action by the authorities. 'Loyalist' asserted that some staff members were aliens, and the Irish wife of a certain professor declined to sign a petition demanding that aliens be interned.[186] Hartog denounced this as 'slanderous' nonsense but failed to convince 'Loyalist'.[187]

Sir Bertram and Lady Windle sponsored comfort-and-presents activities for soldiers at the front but a committee established in the college to supply books for the Royal Munster Fusiliers and the Royal Irish Regiment was not very successful. Professor D.T. Barry, the honorary secretary of the committee, pleaded in the *Examiner* for support for 'our poor fellows abroad' and this was endorsed by a leading article.[188] The deaths of students and relatives of staff killed in action were covered in the local press. So, too, was the loss of many UCC (QCC) graduates, and Governing Body sympathy was duly recorded. Capt. F.K. Cummins, son of Professor H. Ashley-Cummins (botany, 1909–31) was killed in action in France in March 1918.[189] In its review of the war for 1915 and 1916, the *Constitution* carried a long list of 'members of College' on active service.[190]

The nationalist resurgence

Windle's war enthusiasm met with mixed reactions from staff and students.[191] The 'home guard' 'Dads army' element of the staff were derided by nationalists as 'Methusaliers': the participation of students and former students in the war, and the inevitable fatalities, were recorded in the *UCC Official Gazette*. An attempt to launch an officers training corps seems to have been abortive.

As in the nation at large, the execution of the leaders of the 1916 Rising provoked strong nationalist reaction in UCC. The Union Jack (flown from the tower on royal family occasions) was removed by Flor O'Leary, a medical student, and replaced by the unfamiliar tricolour, to the hearty applause of a large crowd of students assembled in the Quadrangle. The sequel was the blocking up of the tower stairway by a military detachment from Victoria Barracks. In another post-1916 episode, the pro-British Professor Alexander (engineering) displayed, on the departmental notice-board, Bishop Kelly of Ross's condemnation of the Rising. When this was torn down by students, Alexander threatened to refuse them testimonials.

Though a company of the militantly nationalist Volunteers could not be formed in defiance of the college authorities, there were many student activists and sympathisers, particularly in the medical faculty. These included the brothers John and Patrick Kiely, afterwards prominent Cork surgeons – Patrick was to be professor of surgery from 1941 to 1967. Another medical student, Tadhg Murphy of Carrignavar, was wont to sit on a step on St Patrick's Hill, in between lectures, in the hope of getting a shot at General Strickland, the British commander in Munster. There is the doubtless apocryphal but delightful story of a medical student 'on the run' sneaking back to the college for an anatomy practical: unable to answer a particular question, he quietly placed a Webley on the table before his examiners, with the softly-spoken request, 'an easier bone, please, gentlemen'.

Seán Ó Faoláin recalled Republican students marching in the Terence MacSwiney funeral procession to St Finbarr's cemetery, with many more students lining the Western Road. John Griffin, the then head gardener, remembered snipers in the college grounds firing at gun posts in the adjoining gaol. Bombs were surreptitiously manufactured in the chemistry department. On one occasion, the strongly nationalist Professor William Stockley (English, 1909–31) was shot at, and on another, a party of students on a Cork harbour boat outing was attacked by a British patrol, with one girl being injured. Eamon de Valera, elected NUI chancellor in succession to Archbishop William Walsh in 1921, was greeted warmly by students during a visit to UCC, despite staff cold-shouldering.[192] Alfred O'Rahilly's role in the Anglo-Irish struggle is well known, but on 'the other side' Professor Charles Yelverton-Pearson (surgery, 1899–1928) received threats from the IRA early in 1921. So would have Windle, doubtless, had he still been in presidential office and not safely out of reach in Canada.

As on the occasion of the Parnell split,[193] the college was divided on the Anglo-Irish Treaty though O'Rahilly believed that, while Cork was Republican, most UCC graduates were pro-Treaty like himself.[194] However it should be kept in mind that, throughout all the 'revolutionary' period, a large number of students, if not the majority, were apolitical.

Agitation for independent university renewed

Windle's determination to achieve an independent university at Cork had never weakened despite the federal arrangement imposed by the Irish Universities Act 1908. Indeed, his experience of working that system over ten years renewed his resolve to revive the pre-1908 agitation for Cork autonomy. UCC could never realise its potential until it was independent. The NUI system, he argued, was cumbersome at every hand's turn. Changes in courses, for example, having been processed through the various college bodies, were further delayed pending approval by the NUI Board of Studies and Senate. In general, the large representation of UCD on the NUI Senate meant that Dublin consent was necessary for any proposal. By the same token, a unanimous Dublin bloc could carry the Senate on any matter even when opposed by Cork and Galway combined. (Such college vote formations have given way in our own day to something like consensus and to the tacit understanding that each college is facilitated by the others in the pursuit of its business, except in the rare case where there is a total conflict of interests.) For the presidents of UCC and (to a somewhat lesser extent) UCG, the most intolerable aspect of their involvement in the NUI system was the unconscionable waste of time in travelling to Dublin to transact NUI business (perhaps twenty to thirty days a year) and in dealing with related correspondence. It was further argued that securing external examiners, especially in medicine, for a three-college system presented difficulties. Various NUI meetings in Dublin involved not inconsiderable expenditure, and the travelling expenses of senators could be more beneficially diverted to the institution of badly-needed lectureships.[195]

Windle raised the topic of an independent university in his president's reports for 1909–10, 1911–12 and 1913–14 and he returned to it before the war ended. Even while he was still involved in the work of the Irish Convention 1917–18, he initiated his ill-fated Munster university campaign, the main outcome of which was his own departure from UCC and the consequent ascendancy of his Sinn Féin opponents in college politics. He was totally committed in his conduct of the campaign: 'This agitation for an independent university for Cork which I am now carrying on is just about enough of a job for any one man'.[196]

On 9 March 1918, the Governing Body gave official approval to the campaign for the establishment of a 'University of Munster'.[197] A subcommittee issued a supportive statement in pamphlet form arguing the merits of the case. Windle was the author of the pamphlet and there seemed to be strong public support for the cause. According to Windle's son-in-law, John J. Horgan, 'the desire for a university had long smouldered in the South, and Sir Bertram had now little difficulty in fanning it into a flame'.[198] The subcommittee statement pointed out that the ostensible reasons for refusing independence to Cork in 1908 no longer applied. At that time it had been argued that the college had no popular support in Munster, that student numbers were too low, and that the college lacked public or private financial support in the region. Now, ten years on (asserted the statement) the college was supported by all creeds and classes in Munster, it had 530 students (compared to 390 in Belfast when granted independence), and it was benefitting from scholarships from public bodies for its students, as well as private benefactions since 1908 to the tune of almost £105,000 (the reference here was particularly to Honan munificence). The teaching staff had been increased, the range of instruction expanded, and impressive additions made to the college buildings. The lifting of the 'Catholic ban' had been the great stimulus to progress which would have taken place in any university framework – a continuing Royal University context, for example. 'The success of the College has not been due to the foundation of the National University . . . It might even be said to have arisen in spite of that University'. (This argument seems both disingenuous and unconvincing.) The subcommittee further maintained that the NUI had discriminated against Cork through the built-in Dublin majority; that the federal system was expensive, and wasted money; and that its decision-making process was cumbersome.[199]

The Governing Body (many of whose members had served since 1908) also issued a resolution which was supported by churchmen, politicians, mayors, local representatives and numerous professional people – in all, over a thousand names. The resolution, proposed by Bishop Daniel J. Cohalan of Cork, rehearsed the defects of the federal system, which 'owing to the dissimilarity of local conditions limits the development of the College in directions which the Governing Body believes would be to the advantage and prosperity of Munster'. It therefore petitioned the government to legislate for an independent university

> and in making this request it desires specially to emphasise the great industrial developments which are now taking place in Cork; the further expansion which may be hoped for after the War; and the urgent necessity which exists that the College should be in a position to take the fullest advantage of these developments and to give them the maximum assistance.[200]

In March and April 1918, there was massive press coverage (no doubt orchestrated at least in part by Windle) of the 'independence' demand, and generally uncritical support was widespread. *The Cork Examiner* was a foremost advocate, of course,[201] supported, less enthusiastically, by its Protestant counterpart, *The Cork Constitution*.[202] Coverage was also extensive in the Irish and English Catholic press, the Dublin dailies, and educational and medical journals.[203] Archbishop William Walsh, chancellor of the NUI, was sympathetic but did not sign the petition for obvious reasons: if Cork ambitions were fulfilled, UCD and UCG would be left in a rump and impotent NUI.[204] Another dissenting voice was the distinguished Cork graduate Thomas Farrington who preferred the idea of one university for the whole of Ireland with as many autonomous colleges as necessary.

In early 1919, Windle stepped up his intensive campaign, lobbying vigorously in London and Dublin as well as at the Cork Chamber of Commerce.[205] Preparing for post-war regional economic expansion was repeatedly emphasised. He was asked by the government to draft a bill and charter for the proposed university. On 17 February 1919 he told Ian MacPherson MP, that:

The two Cork papers which rarely agree on any point have agreed on this one. *The Irish Times*, the *Irish Independent* both gave it their blessing, and as did the Educational Supplement to the London Times. The movement has the hearty approval of the Provost of Trinity College, Dublin.[206]

Windle expressed growing optimism in private correspondence at this time: 'I am making a gigantic struggle for my Cork University and am just beginning to see a glimmer of hope that it may be successful'. 'You know I am making every effort to get this place turned into an independent university, its present position being almost intolerable'.[207] It was also at this time that he wagered his own future in 'my College' on the outcome of the campaign.[208] This was in line with the over-riding importance he attached to the issue:

> If there is a chance of a University being set up here I would be prepared to remain . . . for some years in order to get it well rooted in the ground. If there is no chance . . . the probability is that I shall retire and take the modest pension which I can now claim.[209]

7.7 Alfred O'Rahilly as a young man. He and President Windle were often to disagree, to such an extent that Windle believed they could not co-exist in UCC.

He was encouraged by the support of such people as his friend Cardinal Gasquet ('if you were to give up, chaos would enter into the precincts of the University College').[210] In a private letter to Joseph McGrath, the first registrar of the NUI, on 5 March 1919, he was already regarding 'this university' as a 'foregone conclusion'. The important thing now was for Dublin and Galway to accept the inevitable change calmly and to make adjustments accordingly. 'No amount of resolutions passed by that august body of ineptitudes, Convocation, will have the slightest effect upon our action.'[211]

Windle's obsession blinded him to the formidable alignment of opponents determined to thwart his grand scheme. Resurgent Sinn Féin raised its voice inside and outside the college.[212] Alfred O'Rahilly, recently-appointed professor of mathematical physics (1917–43), mobilised anti-Windle opinion for both personal and political reasons. He owed his first appointment and initial advancement at UCC to Windle's influence but soon the two men were at daggers drawn, O'Rahilly belligerently objecting to Windle's allegedly dictatorial behaviour and attitudes. Despite a measure of common interests (for example in the relationship of science and religion), they were mutually antipathetic, temperamentally and culturally. They frequently clashed at Academic Council meetings, and Windle's camp tried to prevent O'Rahilly's appointment to the mathematical physics chair in June 1917.[213] It is not putting it too starkly to say that Windle eventually felt the two of them could not co-exist in UCC. However, it should be said that even Windle's admirers conceded 'he was intolerant of opposition and his judgement apt to be affected by his personal feelings'.[214]

Increasing Sinn Féin influence looked likely to result in a strongly nationalist presence sooner rather than later in the NUI Senate. The Governing Body, on the other hand, did not appear quite so amenable to the winds of change, with only four of the twenty-eight members being elected by graduates. His opponents claimed that this was the reason (though not explicitly admitted) why Windle was pushing the independence objective. O'Rahilly and Sinn Féin opposed what they regarded as an attempt to consolidate pro-British, pro-unionist control of UCC (there had already been opposition to the Windles' work in the college for the war effort). O'Rahilly had substantial support in the Academic Council which had not been privy to Windle's negotiations with the government.

In the wider political scene, for UCC to appeal for any reason to the British government in the spring of 1919 could be seen as disloyalty to the newly established Dáil Éireann. Accordingly, Sinn Féin declared its firm opposition to the independent university movement pending the settlement of the national question. Thus, the 'University of Munster' was caught up in, and became a victim of, the Anglo-Irish struggle.[215] It was in this context that Windle himself became a target of nationalist abuse in a student magazine. In its issue of March 1919 *An Mac Léighinn* assured its readers that UCC should no longer be thought of as the resort of 'shoneens and drunkards, swanks and idlers . . . We are on the high road towards a wee Irish-speaking Republic in University College Cork. The Professors had better look up or we shall soon not understand lectures delivered in a foreign tongue'. Windle was upbraided for his membership of the Irish Convention; Professors H. Ashley-Cummins, P.T. O'Sullivan (medical jurisprudence, 1909–23) and P.J. Merriman (history, 1909–19) were branded as being of similar political complexion while Professors Stockley and O'Rahilly were lauded for their nationalist stance.[216]

Michael Murphy, a lawyer friend of Windle, noted that the April issue of *An Mac Léighinn* clearly libelled the president when it offensively referred to him 'and the four other degenerates who run and ruin our university'. However, Murphy added: 'I implore you as a friend to take no notice of this thing'.[217] O'Rahilly, using a pseudonym, made a comprehensive statement in *New Ireland*, 15 April 1919, on the Munster university issue. This followed a joint meeting, arranged by him, of the Students Representative Council (SRC) and the University Graduates' Sinn Féin Club of which he was a founder member. O'Rahilly argued that the Governing Body had no mandate from the people of Munster to promote the independent university project, which needed to get a wide and representative airing throughout the province. No important step should be taken without NUI graduate approval by way of a Convocation referendum, and without the endorsement of the SRC of UCC. A further article by a still pseudonymous O'Rahilly in the following issue of *New Ireland* asserted that

> partly for reasons of personal ambition and partly out of anti-national spite, a small but dexterous caucus is making desperate efforts to rush this scheme before the next elections of the local bodies and of the Cork governing body, now that Irish representatives are not in Westminster to oppose the bill . . .
>
> On the present governing body of Cork there is not a single member whose national and educational ideals agree with those of the people of Munster as declared in the recent general election . . .

In the proposed bill, the NUI would be 'put into the melting pot' and Dublin Castle would take 'sole charge of the resultant operations'. All should take note that 'a handful of intriguers billing and cooing are trying to turn Cork University into a crown university'.[218]

The nineteen members of Sinn Féin recently elected to the first Dáil from the Munster constituencies also issued a statement in April denouncing the 'secret' negotiations with the British government concerning a separate Munster university, which they supported in principle but any movement on which should be deferred pending settlement of the national issue. The unrepresentative nature of the Governing Body was compounded by the fact that the triennial election had been deferred as a cost-cutting exercise and because the register of graduates had not yet returned to normal after the war. Conradh na Gaedhilge, Ard-Choiste Chorcaighe, also pledged its whole-hearted support against the 'intrigue'.[219] The NUI Senate was another powerful focus of opposition to Windle's plan. He was informed that Denis Coffey, UCD president, was 'bitterly – savagely – opposed to it and . . . his policy is procrastination'.[220] When the Irish Universities Bill was forwarded to the Senate, on 20 April 1919, the delaying strategy was applied under the direction of Professor Eoin MacNeill and Fr Timothy Corcoran SJ.[221] Convocation discussed the issue at length on

6 June 1919,[222] one sentiment being expressed that 'it would certainly be a great loss to the NU to lose the genius of the people of Cork'. There was also a strong rumour in Sinn Féin quarters that a Windle-influenced university in Cork would scrap compulsory Irish.[223]

O'Rahilly returned to the attack on Windle's policy in *New Ireland* on 26 April, 3 May and 10 May. This last piece, over the pseudonym 'Graduate', as well as illustrating O'Rahilly's considerable talent for personal invective, represented a significant assault on Windle's *ancien régime* in the college by the man who epitomised the new, native and robust brand of nationalism and who was to be Windle's *de facto*, and later *de jure*, successor as president of UCC. The old order was indeed changing fast. O'Rahilly's scathing article referred to a 'private and secret' Windle-led deputation being 'graciously received in the privy council chamber of Dublin Castle' by the viceroy, Lord French – and this at a time when 'our leaders were safely in jail for the French-Shortt plot'. To compound their offence, Windle and Sir Stanley Harrington 'dined and slept at the viceregal lodge'. O'Rahilly alleged that the members of the deputation represented nobody but themselves, and were opposed to the real aspirations of the people of Munster. He followed this by a personalised tirade, in which there is more than a hint of bigotry and xenophobia.

> Sir Bertram Windle is an Englishman . . . Sir Stanley [Harrington] is a privy councillor and crown nominee, a notoriously bad employer in Cork. Mr Bourke [the recorder of Cork] is official upholder of law and order in Cork. Mr Butterfield [lord mayor] is one of the present AOH [Ancient Order of Hibernians] nominees on Cork Corporation who will be retired at the next election. Professor Merriman[224] [registrar] is one of the high officials of the Ancient Order and has consistently opposed the national ideal in the university election and elsewhere. Sir John O'Connell[225] is a Trinity College graduate, lives in Killiney and has no right to interfere with the matter at all. Professor Pearson[226] is head of the Freemasons in Cork. Professor Marcus Hartog[227] is an elderly naturalised gentleman who cannot claim to represent even the Hebrew community in Cork. These gentlemen arranged the little bill with Viscount French . . .[228]

Even before this indictment was published, Windle was giving up the ghost. Writing to his friend John Humphreys on 7 May 1919, he described the future as 'black and uncertain':

> Desperate Sinn Féin opposition is on foot against the Munster University Scheme on the grounds – perfectly ridiculous – that nothing should be asked for from a British Parliament – which really means that the SF, not being able to do anything themselves, don't want anybody else to be allowed to do anything. If I do *not* get the University this year, I think I must resign; at present I see nothing else for it. I can't go on for ever standing the strain of low intrigue and the constant stream of abuse directed against me, as at anyone in this country who tries to do anything for it . . .[229]

Windle's son-in-law and great admirer, John J. Horgan, suggests that he was here exaggerating the extent of the intrigue and abuse directed against him.[230] Yet Windle's sense of unease must have been increased by reports of robust nationalist demagoguery at full pitch in 1919. The renowned Fr Christy O'Flynn, lecturing in Clonmel, referred to UCC as a show run by foreigners who did not care a halfpenny about Irish music, 'but, he added amidst laughter and applause, by the Lord Harry we will put them out'.[231]

Windle leaves college

Within some days, however, there was a development which Windle must have seen as providential intervention.[232] He received an invitation from St Michael's Catholic College in the University of Toronto to become a philosophy professor, specialising in the science– Christian philosophy relationship. This settled the matter of his future, since on 6 June the British government made it clear they were dropping the Irish Universities Bill in response to the formidable opposition it had provoked, especially in the NUI Senate.[233] 'A calamity for the South of Ireland, however it lets me out' was Windle's bitter response.[234] After that, with supporters pressing him to remain (the Governing Body later asked him to withdraw his resignation) there seemed to be some indecision but his mind was really made up – 'with what feelings of relief I am contemplating getting away from Cork and all its intrigues and worries'.

In mid-June 1919, Windle was fiercely attacked by J.L. O'Donovan, UCD, for an article he wrote in the English *Catholic Times* in which he said: 'We have a "sort of a university" but a very poor sort' not at all comparable with TCD or QUB – 'almost a *université pour rire*'. To write this in an English paper was to malign and insult his professorial colleagues, his university and his country, according to O'Donovan. Besides, it was 'a gross untruth', since a university could still exist despite inadequate facilities.[235] NUI Convocation similarly deplored the article.[236] Certainly, this was a considerable gaffe on Windle's part, even when one allows for his bitter feelings of frustration at the time. The disparaging phrase, *université pour rire*, became part of an anti-Windle tradition and wrongly came to be interpreted as bad-mouthing UCC rather than the NUI as a whole.

His final president's report (1918–1919) fired some parting shots at the NUI and the bonds of federalism. The Senate had refused the college's request for a deferral of examinations (the great flu had closed the college for a month, and five students died). It was also guilty of intolerable footdragging on the question of giving recognition to the Technical Institute, which had admitted UCC engineering students to its courses.

There were predictable tributes to Windle over the following months from individuals and groups in Cork and Munster.[237] Resolutions of appreciation and thanks were adopted by the Governing Body and Academic Council, the governors of the Honan Hostel (whom Windle had chaired) and various public bodies. Windle wrote what might be called a valedictory survey shortly before he left Cork. He brooded on the evils of the federal link: 'whatever Dublin desires, it can have; whatever Cork desires, it can only have if Dublin will permit it'. Though Cork must continue 'to inhabit the house of bondage', nevertheless the NUI 'is a mere incident' in the history of the Cork college, he reflected philosophically. The two things Cork needed most were freedom from outside domination, and sufficient funds. It is interesting that, given his bitterness and frustration, Windle should have bothered to write such a *committed* article on UCC at this time.[238]

During his last couple of weeks in Cork, he sat impatiently for a handsome portrait in oils (by Harry Scully) which at his wish was hung (and still hangs) in the Aula Maxima and a replica of which was presented to him and Lady Windle at a function in the Aula chaired by the famous Brother Connolly of Presentation College. The money for the portrait had been raised by subscriptions from colleagues and students.[239] Of the tributes paid to Windle on this occasion, two are particularly noteworthy. Professor Marcus Hartog, the most senior member of the academic staff, said Windle 'had not been merely their chief but their colleague'. And A.F. Sharman Crawford, thinking of previous 'administrations', said 'Sir Bertram was not a President who came and went: he was always there'. Interestingly, Windle's reply – his last public utterance in, and on, UCC – stressed that the citizens did not appreciate their university:

> He asked the people of Cork to think more of their College and he was astonished during the time he spent there how many residents of Cork had never been inside the College grounds. The people of Cork had got a College of which any city might be proud. It was thoroughly well equipped and did splendid work and deserved the financial support of the city of Cork.[240]

After two valedictory lectures in Glasgow, the Windles set sail on 20 December 1919 to begin a new life in Canada, and in Sir Bertram's case, another distinguished career.[241]

Windle was well advised to remove himself from Cork and the Irish scene when he did. Given his political views and his inflexibility of temperament, he would have found life increasingly uncomfortable in the 1920–21 period. He would have been seriously apprehensive – to the extent of fearing for his life – under a Sinn Féin administration. He might well have been fingered as an informer and collaborator, with the usual unpleasant consequences, if he had indeed supplied the British government 'with information on Sinn Féin activities within and without UCC in late 1918 and early 1919'.[242]

In July 1920, reflecting on the worsening situation in Ireland, Windle counted himself lucky:

> . . . if I hadn't left when I did but waited another year I could not have left in face of what is happening in Ireland. It would have been like resigning a commission when war broke out. Nothing of the kind was the case when I left, and no such comment could be made. Had I stayed, I should have been most certainly murdered. *I* could not, and would not, have put up with what my successor has put up with from the students. I should have expelled some of them with the inevitable result that I should have been shot or stabbed.[243]

His friend, Canon P.A. Roche, wrote Windle 'a parting word' in which he said: 'I meet no one *now* who does not deplore your loss and lament that no strong public movement was started to keep you in your old position'.[244] According to Cardinal

Gasquet, Prime Minister Lloyd George also regretted Windle's departure.[245] But in truth he was glad to be shut of Cork. Apart from the frustrating of his grand plan, he had often felt isolated,[246] depressed,[247] unhappy[248] and disenchanted[249] by feuding and intrigue. He suffered from bouts of ill-health, and 'I don't find this place too bracing'.[250] In this connection, his wife shrewdly remarked: 'He must try to realize that the atmosphere of Cork is not one in which a man can do the work of three'.[251] Many people who come to settle in Cork would readily agree with that observation. In any case, because of his later experiences there, 'he came to view Cork, its people and its college, with a somewhat jaundiced eye'.[252]

A jaundiced view of UCC

In Canada, where he spent the last ten years of his life, 1919–29, he seems to have virtually erased the Cork college from his memory, his considerable achievements as well as his final failure repressed rather than forgotten. When he talked about UCC at all, he saw his time there as a lamentable waste. When he visited Britain ('my native heath') and France in the summer of 1921, Ireland was not included in the itinerary though that was understandable at the period.[253] His references to Ireland sounded few positive notes. In 1928, he recalled Lough Ine nostalgically, 'one of the loveliest spots on God's earth'.[254] The lifestyle of the Windles in Toronto could hardly have been in sharper contrast to the manorial milieu of the East Wing, the president's garden and the college grounds. The couple had to look after themselves in their Toronto flat, 'a tiny place after the vast caravanserai we inhabited in Cork',[255] but at least they were 'avoiding all the bothers of servants'.[256]

Windle represented Cork Chamber of Commerce (of which he was an honorary member) at a conference in Toronto in September 1920: he had assented to their request to be their delegate 'as they always behaved well to me'.[257] When P.J. Merriman was elected president of UCC, Joe Downey, the bursar, cabled the news to Merriman's predecessor who was 'very glad' to hear it, but

> I do not envy him his task . . . I wanted nothing better than to serve the College, but when it was obvious that I was not going to be allowed to do so without unceasing friction and underhand cabals, I felt it was time for me to get out of it and, just at the right moment, God opened this door for me . . .[258]

In reminiscent mood in 1927, reflecting on the three universities in his life, he had nice things to say about Birmingham and Toronto but he maintained a significant silence about the third: 'as to Cork and the NUI which I helped to hatch . . .'[259] In June 1920, he deplored ever having got involved 'in the whirlpool of administration' and his 'wasted fifteen years in Cork, but I suppose God had some good reason for sending me there'.[260] In the same vein six months later, he brooded over the wrong turning in his life:

> I suppose we shall, if we get there, understand these things in heaven, and amongst

others, why I had to waste my time, as it seems to me, for fifteen years in Cork, and why Stensen was made a bishop, and Mendel an abbot, instead of their being kept at their scientific work.[261]

Cork, as well as Ireland in general, was not only wasteland but biblical exile and bondage. Windle thanked God who 'took me out of Egypt (I am only gradually beginning to realise what a dreadful time I had in Ireland, and how it has told on me)'.[262]

By any standards, Bertram Windle was a great president of Queen's/University College, if not indeed the greatest. Energetic, creative and visionary, he not only presided over, but was a primary contributor to, the transformation of Queen's College into University College, of the free-floating Royal into the co-ordinating federal framework of the National University of Ireland, and of elitist college governance into a more democratic and representative constitution. These were difficult changes which he handled with skill. Like O'Rahilly, his next-but-one successor, who epitomised and spearheaded the campaign against him, Windle was a polymath, making substantial contributions to various disciplines and therefore failing to achieve star quality in any of them. But (again like O'Rahilly), his versatile scholarship conferred eminence and distinction on his presidential office, and he never ceased to be productive during and after his administrative career. The combination of administrative competence and good scholarship has always marked outstanding presidencies of the college. It was an impressive measure of Windle's quality that during his time as president he held, at different points, the chairs of anatomy and archaeology. Through the Governing Body, he stressed the importance of research, and promised grants to departments undertaking it.[263]

Over the period of his presidency, and in large part because of his leadership, the 'derelict institution' of Tom Dillon's recollection[264] was restored and expanded, and new foundations were laid for its development in independent Ireland. From being little more than a glorified medical school, the college once again had the makings of a real university, not only because of the increase in student numbers and the improved quality of student life but because of the spread of new departments and courses (including journalism), the beginnings of the dental school[265] and the considerable physical expansion.[266] In this last respect, the college premises were substantially extended during Windle's presidency, particularly with the acquisition of the Athletic Grounds at the Mardyke in 1911, and of the Donovan's Land area (on which the dairy science institute was to be built) in 1918.[267] The physics and chemistry building was a long-awaited development, opening its doors in 1911. With Windle's encouragement, the derelict Berkeley Hall was refurbished and taken over as St Anthony's Hall and later as the Honan Hostel, catering for a residential need over the following seven or eight decades. The Honan Chapel (erected in 1916) could be described as the Hiberno-Romanesque gem in Windle's crown. The engineering and medical schools were reorganised, and the institution of the Students' Club showed a genuine college concern for student welfare. Windle was a strong supervisory presence in the college, observing the progress of new buildings and generally keeping a (p)residential eye on things. A diary entry in January 1916 depicts him as 'rooting out dirt and gloryholes in which porters delight'.[268]

A *sine qua non* of a successful college presidency, at least in a place like Cork, is a high community profile, which is much more than a matter of making witty after-dinner speeches. College activities were of great benefit to the local and regional economy[269] and Windle succeeded in conveying this fact to the community. He fulfilled the promise he made to the welcoming students in 1904 of identifying himself not only 'with your College, but also with the city' and indeed with the wider region. He fostered the first growth of adult education, and developed contacts with the Municipal Technical Institute (mechanical engineering classes for UCC students)[270] and the School of Commerce that were to flourish in the following decades. As president of the Cork Literary and Scientific Society, he eloquently personified the town–gown fraternity of learning. As a distinguished educationalist, he served on the General Council of Medical Education, he was a commissioner of intermediate education and he was president of the Irish Technical Instruction Association. (On his departure from UCC, he received a warmly appreciative letter from the committees of agricultural and technical instruction.[271]) He took a keen interest in the Irish industrial conference of 1905, of which he was president, making his inaugural address a clarion call for industrial self-reliance as an engine of national prosperity – ironically, the essence of Sinn Féin economic nationalism. It also appears that he must be given some credit for the idea of a distinctive Irish trade mark with its 'déanta in Éirinn' logo.[272]

At the meeting where the Governing Body recorded its 'appreciation of his invaluable services', a letter was read from James M. Burke which contained an understandably emotional and colourful description of Windle's achievements: 'He found Cork brick and he left it marble'.[273] Perhaps a more prosaic but not less generous assessment would be to say that, after Windle, UCC's future was assured. It is regrettable, then, that his departure was marked by rancorous controversy and that his memories of the college were so bitter and disenchanted. His pursuit of the will-o'-the-wisp of university independence smacked of hubris and locked him into a confrontation which spelled defeat and disillusion. He underestimated the obstacles in the path of an independent university for Cork, he did not really perceive the dissimilarities between Cork and Birmingham, and he did not understand the nature of the revolutionary forces Ireland was experiencing.[274]

It was his further misfortune that in the Ireland of 1919 his particular brand of politics was discredited. As a member of the Irish Convention, 1917–18, he strove enthusiastically to promote a North–South and Anglo-Irish *modus vivendi*, but compromise along Redmondite lines was out of fashion. Windle, in turn, regarded resurgent Sinn Féin with social and cultural distaste. He was unaware that the nationalist perception of UCC was of an institution still unacceptably anglophile, even if open to Catholics. Despite his earlier nationalist protestations, he was, as his son-in-law reminds us, 'by tradition and temperament, in sympathy with the outlook of the Anglo-Irish ascendancy class . . . he was . . . by blood and breeding more English than Irish'. His attitude towards Southern unionists is revealing in the extreme:

> These are the men who really appeal to me, and of course by birth and association I
> belong to them and understand them. They are gentlemen, and you know that their

7.8 Sir Bertram Windle sat impatiently for this portrait by Harry Scully during his last weeks in Cork.

word is their bond . . . These men acted in a most patriotic spirit, and if all the rest
had been like them the Convention would have been a great success.[275]

No wonder that Sinn Féin, within and without the walls of the college, disliked and
opposed him, and saw him as hopelessly out of touch. The favourite abusive epithets of
Irish-Ireland nationalism were hurled at him – West Brit, shoneen, toady. His representations to the British government on behalf of the college were distorted as
'toadying to England'.[276] He was swept away in the political turmoil of the times. His
resignation symbolised the ousting of the old order of which he was part. But his
prominent place in the history of the college is assured, as we might remind ourselves
whenever we look at his portrait in the Aula Maxima.

CHAPTER EIGHT

A 'NOMINAL' PRESIDENCY

Since God has given us the papacy, let us enjoy it.
Leo X

I have to run this place with a nominal president on my back.
Alfred O'Rahilly (registrar) in 1933, of President Merriman

IN THE PROCESS OF APPOINTING a president of a constituent college of the NUI, if the Governing Body of the college forwards three names from the list of applications, the NUI Senate *must* make the appointment from that shortlist. The GB therefore has the power of excluding from further consideration a candidate it does not favour. A special GB meeting on 29 November 1919 considered an effective field of five candidates, four of whom were UCC professors – David T. Barry (physiology), Patrick J. Merriman (registrar and professor of history), Patrick T. O'Sullivan (medical jurisprudence) and Timothy A. Smiddy (economics). The fifth candidate was Professor William Magennis (metaphysics) of UCD who had the backing of Sinn Féin which in effect had ousted Windle. Merriman had been on Windle's side as had D.T. Barry who was an unrepentant supporter of the British connection and a forthright opponent of Sinn Féin. The alignment of forces, therefore, was both an academic reflection of the wider tumult in revolutionary Ireland and a continuation of the power struggle which had previously centred on Windle.

The *Examiner* carried fine details of the successive polls at the GB election. (At that time, the press reported GB proceedings in considerable detail which was based on informed reporting, authorised or otherwise.) Magennis and Smiddy were eliminated and the names of Barry, Merriman and O'Sullivan were forwarded to the NUI Senate.[1] This meant, as everybody knew, that Merriman – a UCD man originally – was a certainty, since O'Sullivan and the pro-British Barry had little support outside Cork. So it proved three weeks later, when the Senate appointed Merriman by a large majority after only one ballot.[2]

Immediately after the GB meeting, Sinn Féin supporters of Magennis began to cry 'foul!'. They alleged the GB had used a particular voting system to enable the supporters of any two candidates to 'blanket' a third, and perhaps stronger, rival, thus thwarting the whole purpose of letting the Senate consider three favoured names. The exclusion of Magennis had been ensured, it was alleged, by two of the other candidates voting for themselves throughout, and against Magennis in the final ballot to determine a third name. A number of things enraged Magennis's supporters. They were angry that the GB (which had earlier attempted to rush Windle's university bill) had pro-longed its existence, was no longer representative, did not reflect the country's Sinn Féin complexion, and now had the audacity in indecent haste to 'fix' the presidency with its last gasp. (A new GB would take office on 1 February.) What compounded the 'offence' was that this was the first time in the history of the college that a president was supposed to be elected 'democratically' instead of being imposed from on high. Conversely, the recently instituted NUI Senate reflected the new national mood and very probably would have appointed Magennis if his name had got that far.

Writing to the *Irish Independent*, 'A Voter' (that is, a UCC governor) denounced the 'Tammany tactics' allegedly employed to keep out Magennis, 'incomparably the ablest and most distinguished candidate'.[3] 'An Old Graduate', writing in support, asked rhetorically where such skullduggery would end.[4] The writer pointed out that mayors did not vote for themselves where salaries were concerned. 'Such purity of election, it would seem, is not to be expected when the office sought is the presidency of a great University College from which the largest province in Ireland derives its higher education'.

'A Voter' followed up his first attack (Merriman had not been appointed by the NUI Senate at this stage) by saying that 'immediate publicity' was the only remedy against such 'scandals', 'political pull' and 'local prejudices'. He further claimed that those who had voted to keep out Magennis had been boasting of it in the interim. 'A nice example, indeed, to our corporations, councils and boards of guardians. What an insult to the NUI!'[5] Alfred O'Rahilly, the best-known Sinn Féin apologist in UCC, also denounced 'the Cork university scandal'.[6] He lavished praise on Magennis and belittled the other candidates as 'pass degree' men. Magennis had been active in sec-ondary and university education for thirty years and 'a strenuous defender of Catholic rights', as well as being a versatile and experienced university man.

'The lady doth protest too much, methinks'. The fulminations of the pro-Magennis camp were a measure of their fury at being outwitted, not a conclusive proof that the GB had acted scandalously. Nor was there anything substantial in the record to suggest that Magennis would have been any more impressive a president than Merriman. He might very well have been a more repressive one, given his enthusiastic involvement later on in state censorship policy. (Like others in the bright constellation of pre-independence Sinn Féin intellectuals, his focus became narrowed to authoritarian and censorship-fixated concerns in the new state.) At any rate, having been denied the glittering trophy, the Sinn Féin faction worked assiduously and successfully at getting the consolation prize. The registrarship was now vacant because of Merriman's eleva-tion to the presidency. O'Rahilly, proposed by Lord Mayor Tomás MacCurtain, was appointed to this post, defeating T.A. Smiddy, Merriman's nominee, by thirteen votes to eight.[7]

Now it was the turn of the *ancien régime* to fume, and complain of a vulgar new order. Professor D.T. Barry deplored the growing political violence in the country, attributing the blame to 'the lawless politician, right up – or down – to the new brand of university professor, the *soi-disant* modern democrat', at which caustic description of

8.1 Patrick J. Merriman, president UCC, 1919–43.

himself the new registrar would not have been amused.[8] Barry also criticised Lenten pastorals for allegedly citing the penal laws as a justification of the prevailing nationalist violence.[9]

But Barry really excelled himself (and no doubt was pleased with the storm he stirred up) when he contrasted standards of appointment in the old Queen's Colleges with those now in the NUI, the filling of the UCC registrarship being foremost in mind. The tone was one of inspired venom. Formerly

> teaching staff and other officials were chosen on account of their intelligence and status, academic acumen, business, etc. Now they are chosen for their patriotism – but no Englishman can fondly hope to grasp the full significance of this word – and the professors of twenty or thirty years' standing not only have nothing to say in the choice of their 'colleagues' but find their actions under the control of 'patriotic' pedagogues, bishops, 'Christian' Brothers and farmers.[10]

This elicited the predictable furious response from a Convocation meeting on 14 December 1920.[11] It rejected 'this libellous attack on our country, our university and Cork in particular' and endorsed a previous resolution by the SRC of UCC disclaiming Barry's attack 'in the pages of an obscure English periodical'.

Merriman as president

The bitter divisions over these appointments seemed inauspicious for the years ahead but there was, in fact, no sustained continuation of this particular conflict. Culturally and temperamentally, Merriman was a native, unlike Windle. The few survivors from the Windle camp were insignificant in the changed circumstances after independence, although D.T. Barry held the chair of physiology up to 1942. There was never any love lost between O'Rahilly and Merriman, they were in open conflict during the dairy science row from 1927 to 1936 and O'Rahilly fretted at Merriman's apparently endless tenure of office (1919–43).[12] However, O'Rahilly's forceful presence and influence often made him seem a *de facto* president, and Merriman's unassertive personality correspondingly dissolved into the background.

The news of Merriman's appointment was greeted with acclaim by the students who called enthusiastically in the Quadrangle for an appearance from the new president who duly obliged from his house in the East Wing. The students continued to celebrate (as they would cheerfully have done for any successful candidate) 'by parading the streets in various guises from about seven o'clock up to a late hour'. Cork County Board of the Gaelic Athletic Association congratulated 'a fine type of Irishman' who was a great supporter of the national games (Windle had been a patron of rugby). One of the first group pictures of the new president was taken in the college 'with Gaelic friends'. The *Examiner* duly published details of the 'brilliant career' of 'probably the youngest President ever'.[13] Though he was indubitably a first-class, first-place, medals-all-the-way graduate, his historical publications, such as they were, were run-of-the-mill stuff, and he remained thereafter undistinguished.

Significantly, contributors to the UCC Oral History Archives (UC/OHA) recalling their undergraduate days in the late 1920s or in the 1930s rarely mention Merriman but frequently refer to O'Rahilly as the dominant college personality. Only one former staff member speaks of Merriman in positive terms, saying that he did a good job, given the resources then available.[14] Otherwise, recollections are unfavourable and the general impression is that of a shadowy, retiring figure.[15] Professor Aloys Fleischmann remembered him as 'cantankerous' and 'negative', banning tennis in the Lower Grounds after 9 p.m. in the long summer evenings, because the sounds prevented him from sleeping.[16] When tributes had to be paid to him on such occasions as the conferring of an honorary degree by the NUI,[17] they were banal and clichéd. In time, the same was true of the numerous obituary eulogies, one such noting truthfully that he was 'unassuming'.[18] Cautious and conservative, he did not venture to change the structures inherited from Windle.

As president, he appeared at the usual college and public events, discharging the ceremonial functions of the presidency, uttering pleasantries at some length and attempting the occasional humorous sally. At a UCC Officers Training Corps dinner in Collins Barracks, he described himself as 'a man of peace amongst men of war'.[19] At a Graduate Club function, he recalled the bad old days when there were no food facilities in the college, and students had to bring sandwiches with them and go to the Western Star for a bottle of stout.[20] However, Merriman's efforts at being facetious generally ended in his being fatuous. When Fianna Fáil minister for education Tomás Derrig made the not uncommon charge that universities were not contributing adequately to the national life,[21] there was much reaction and comment from the other NUI colleges and TCD. However when Merriman was asked what was UCC's contribution to the Irish language movement and things national, he declined to comment, taking refuge in 'I am far too modest to tell'.[22] Typically, O'Rahilly attacked Derrig's statement head on.[23] Merriman once offered an implausibly ingenious explanation for his passivity, and permitted himself a simultaneous side-swipe at O'Rahilly: it was explained that 'he usually avoided taking any part in controversial matters lest, by virtue of his position, the College might be committed one way or another'.[24]

Merriman seemed at his best, if somewhat long-winded, when explaining college developments to the wider community, as at the annual conversaziones in the mid-1920s.[25] Whenever he and O'Rahilly appeared on the same platform, his remarks were general or cursory while the registrar tackled the substantive issue.[26] For the most part, however, it was O'Rahilly who dealt with the large questions of policy and strategy during Merriman's long presidency and who handled controversies as they arose. It was O'Rahilly, for example, who effectively answered the criticism of the president of the Cork Chamber of Commerce that the college was producing an 'undue multiplication' of Bachelors of Medicine and hardly any Bachelors of Agricultural Science.[27] That, it may be contended, was an appropriately academic topic for the registrar to pronounce on, but O'Rahilly frequently took over matters properly belonging to the sphere of presidential authority, as with the defacement of college crests in 1939.[28] It was O'Rahilly who angrily objected to legislation in 1933 reducing professorial salaries, as undermining university autonomy.[29] It was O'Rahilly who roundly castigated the management committee of Cork Fever Hospital for 'malignant' favouritism and local-ism in appointing a resident medical surgeon.[30] And it was O'Rahilly, never Merriman, who pontificated at the drop of a hat on every conceivable topic.

There were, no doubt, many aspects of the presidency Merriman found interesting and fulfilling, and not merely dining for college. He deftly manipulated the levers of power in the Governing Body and NUI Senate, on and from the occasion of his own election. He used his influence at the Senate to ensure the appointments of those he favoured,[31] and this was seen at the time as a proper exercise of academic power and in no way reprehensible. But much of his long presidential term was self-effacing to a negative degree. Was it that he was temperamentally indolent, or had little stomach for academic and political rough-and-tumble, or was he simply intimidated by O'Rahilly's whirlwind energy which must have seemed a daily reproach to him?

He must have found it difficult at times to accept with equanimity or even tolerance O'Rahilly's pre-eminent and much publicised position in the academic and civic life of Cork, and in national life generally. When the registrar was about to depart in September 1926 for a sabbatical year in Harvard, he was given a remarkable 'farewell dinner' attended by all kinds of notables, apparently not including Merriman. Various compliments, duly reported, were paid to O'Rahilly on this occasion. It was clear that all present regarded him, as early as 1926, only six years into Merriman's presidency, as the outstanding academic in Cork, if not in Ireland, and credited him, *inter alia*, with breaking down the hitherto prevailing UCC attitude of 'serene detachment' from the city.[32] Reading such fulsome tributes must have made Merriman even more conscious of the public perception of his do-nothing, near-nonentity status as president, impotent Merovingian king to O'Rahilly's mayor of the palace. Nor was he unaware of O'Rahilly's contempt for him as a 'nominal' president, nor perhaps of others' image of him as a mere lotus-eater.[33]

Inter-war academia

For many UCC professors in the inter-war years, life was leisurely and enriched by holidays and travel, with occasional participation in international conferences, such as the World Dairy Congress in Berlin in August 1937.[34] If there was a low level of research activity in some departments, it was due less to laziness than to lack of funding. The indomitable Professor D.T. Barry, voicing a complaint to be heard frequently in subsequent years, described as a national disgrace the prevailing attitude to medical research – a supine government and an apathetic people.[35] But Barry must have been heartened by the response from one citizen who promised him £1,000 for the medical research fund on condition that £4,000 more would be forthcoming from other private sources.[36] Perhaps the importance of research was not really borne in on a peripherally-situated college until post-World War II graduates got the opportunity of foreign study and returned with some experience of research progress elsewhere.[37] 'We are not aware of our problems until we are awakened to our wants', said Dr Johnson.

8.2 James Hogan, professor of history 1920-1963

Meanwhile, certain areas received press publicity for their research specialities, particularly dairy science, engineering (for the making of concrete) and most notably chemistry, a department which had a reputation for research stretching back to the foundation of Queen's College. The protectionist Ireland of the 1930s was especially interested in the potential of native resources, and considerable attention was aroused by the work of Professor J. ('Joss') Reilly and his associates in the practical applications of their research – developing oils from plants and extracting wax and other commercial substances from peat.[38] A significant event in this connection was an address by Seán Lemass on 'Industrial Possibilities' to the 1933–34 inaugural meeting of the Chemical Society.[39] Around this time also, UCC science graduates were finding jobs in the new sugar-beet factories.[40]

In the humanities, scholars like James Hogan (history, 1920–63), Daniel Corkery (English, 1931–47) and 'Tórna' (Tadhg Ó Donnchadha, Irish, 1916–44) were enhancing the reputation of their own disciplines as well as contributing to various areas of the public and national debate.[41] From the mid-1930s, a new star rose rapidly in the college firmament. Professor Aloys Fleischmann (music, 1936–80)[42] had won golden opinions from various eminences when as a student he founded the Art Society and delivered a brilliant inaugural address.[43] The college needed such a society because of 'philistine' attitudes at that time, he subsequently claimed.[44] Under its aegis, concerts, recitals and lectures were held, and impressive guest personalities were featured. The Art Society also sponsored sacred music in the Honan Chapel, and memorable painting and sculpture displays. From the beginning, Fleischmann was concerned to advance music and the arts in the wider community outside the walls, and over the next five decades his energetic contributions to the musical life of Cork probably constituted UCC's single most valuable service to the city. He promoted the professional interests of music teachers[45] and organised lively summer courses in the college, raising a storm when he condemned the use of tonic solfa![46] As founder of the Art Society and the Cork Orchestral Society, he was already being nationally acclaimed at thirty as a 'young and gifted live wire'.[47]

'He will become a musician with a European-wide reputation where King Jazz does not hold the sceptre', enthused an *Examiner* columnist in 1935.[48] Antipathy to jazz as 'jungle music' reflected the xenophobia of the period. Fleischmann opposed jazz on aesthetic grounds (and continued to do so) but he also shared the general mood of moral disap-

8.3 The Art Society's first meeting, November 1931. (L-R): Mr J. J. Horgan; Dr Thomas Bodkin; Mr Aloys Fleischmann (auditor); Professor W.F.P. Stockley; Professor D. Corkery.

proval: 'if jazz were turned into literature I do not think a page of it would be allowed by the Censorship Board'.[49] Abhorrence of perceived immoral and alien values was also being expressed by Fleishmann's colleagues. James Hogan denounced Hollywood and believed that the cinema should be taxed out of existence.[50] Éamon Ó Donnchadha of the Irish department argued that a fully developed national literature in Irish would be a bulwark against 'filthy foreignism'.[51] O'Rahilly himself could be uninhibited in the expression of xenophobic and (by later standards) racist opinions. Paying tribute to William Stockley (retiring professor of English) in 1931, O'Rahilly commented with characteristic flamboyance that Stockley was a gentleman of the old Newman school and belonged to a world 'where the lights of Broadway had not yet flashed, in which the raucous cacophony of black men had not drowned European music'.[52]

And yet this ostensible obscurantism was belied by the breadth of contacts indicated by the wide range of guests, lecturers and artists who spoke and performed in the college until the outbreak of war suspended such visits, and by the attendance of staff and students at international conferences. But visiting speakers and their chosen topics tended to be in harmony with the prevailing Catholic ethos, and there was little welcome for the liberals, the dissenters and the unorthodox.

In pre-specialist days, when embryonic academics were formed by a broad liberal schooling, versatility and erudition characterised many staff presentations. Thus, the learned and idiosyncratic Professor M.A. MacConaill (anatomy, 1942–73) held forth to the Academy of St Thomas on 'Thomism and Science'[53] and published a *rann* in memory of the historian Edmund Curtis;[54] Professor Frank Kane (physiology, 1942–54) talked to the Cork Historical and Archaeological Society on the history of Cork glass;[55] Professor J.C. Sperrin-Johnson (botany, 1932–48) discoursed on 'Shakespeare's Natural History' to the Philosoph;[56] and Professor Mícheál Ó Séaghdha (dairy technology, 1954–70) spoke to the same society about 'Ancient Irish Entertainments'.[57]

Dairy science

Much of public interest in UCC in the late 1920s was concentrated on the new dairy science institute. The inaugural meeting of the Dairy Science Society in the Aula Maxima in December 1926 was described as a 'memorable occasion'. President Merriman said the dairy science students had already made their mark in Gaelic games in the college and would benefit from meeting other students 'engaged in cultural studies'.[58] Some weeks later at a meeting in Mallow, chairman Edward MacLysaght (historian, genealogist, farmer, senator, UCC graduate and governor and man of many other parts) expressed thanks to Connell Boyle, professor of agriculture (1923–64)[59] and to UCC for its great work in connection with agriculture and its determined efforts to get more in touch with the farming community. The meeting broke into applause at the mention of the prospective faculty of dairy science. Boyle described plans for the erection of a dairy science institute, for an experimental creamery and for the running of a college dairy farm (of 135 acres, situated 2½ miles from the college).[60]

In accordance with the University Education (Agriculture and Dairy Science) Act 1926, UCC Statute XX established the new faculty with Professor Boyle as dean, and lectureships in dairy accounting and economics; dairy bacteriology; dairy chemistry; dairy engineering; and dairy technology.[61] The *Irish Independent* welcomed the prospect of 'degrees for farmers', the elevation of agriculture to the university level, the corresponding practical bent to an area of university education, and the general appropriateness of the development in a country 80 per cent dependent on agriculture.[62] Minister for agriculture Patrick Hogan hoped for the closest co-operation between the new Cork faculty and the country's dairy farmers. Scholarships would be provided for the creamery manager course.[63]

Some town politicking surfaced in connection with the building plans. Local TD Dick Anthony's part in 'securing' the ministerial go-ahead was highlighted at a meeting of the Cork and District Workers' Council, where the college authorities were alleged to be delaying matters, and a letter read from President Merriman was described as 'discourteous' and 'pert'.[64]

8.4 President Cosgrave lays the foundation stone for the Dairy Science Building, 20 July 1928.

The laying of the foundation stone of the new dairy science building on 20 July 1928 was a red-letter occasion for UCC. President W.T. Cosgrave and senior government ministers were present. Predictable references were made (and taken up in an *Examiner* editorial) to continuity with Cork's dairy and butter market tradition and with the Munster Institute founded on the initiative of President Sullivan. *The Irish Times* headline must have upset prickly Cork republicans – 'First Dairy College in the British Isles'. Merriman pointed out that the building would be in local limestone and roofed with West Cork slate: it would, moreover, be in harmony with the main college buildings.[65] Thereby hung a tale. The original intention had been to erect the building outside the college walls but neighbourhood householders objected, and threatened legal proceedings.[66] The result was a college decision to build within the walls (at the northern end of Donovan's Road) and there was a corresponding increase in the government grant to meet the extra cost of materials: the aesthetically correct limestone building was going to cost substantially more than the brick/concrete structure originally envisaged.[67] The increased grant was also intended to cover the 'absolutely necessary' lecture theatre which indeed became a centrally important debating forum, well known for decades to students and public alike.

In the following years considerable satisfaction, self-generated and otherwise, was expressed with the new project. Thomas Wibberley, Boyle's predecessor, claimed it was his pressure that eventually spurred the Department of Agriculture into action.[68] Professor A.J. Magennis reminded Cork Rotary of Bertram Windle's pioneering and precursory work in agriculture.[69] When the work of manufacturing butter and cheese was in full swing, *The Cork Examiner* was assured by the 'professor' in charge (Joseph Lyons) that the new model creamery had 'no equal in Europe'.[70] 'University Brand' creamery butter was being advertised under the moderately catchy slogan: 'Try it and you will always buy it'.[71] An *Irish Press* special feature noted that UCC researchers had discovered a method of reducing the bacterial content of cream without affecting its thickness, and that this was good news for the cream export trade.[72] In a society perennially preoccupied with class and professional distinctions, the *Irish Independent* remarked that the training of creamery managers, conducted only in Cork, would ultimately raise that occupation 'to the level and dignity of a profession in the true sense – a registered profession'. *The Irish Times* observed that 'Cork has become the centre of agricultural education in the Free State'[73] and that Northern Ireland students would be taking the dairy science courses. Indeed, such was the significance of the whole development (the *Irish Times* reporter noted, tongue-in-cheek) that the college motto might be changed to 'Where Finbarr taught, let Munster *churn*'. President Merriman was aware of the facetious suggestion but, he commented smilingly, 'we do not intend to make the desired alteration'.[74] Meanwhile, the incorrigible and ageless *enfant terrible* of the Fianna Fáil party, East Cork TD Martin Corry, raised a dissenting voice and articulated (as he often did) the unspoken thoughts of rural fundamentalists: how many university-trained farmers would go back to the land, and how many would be 'parasites' living on 'the unfortunate farmer'?[75] He might well have musically added another rhetorical question: 'How're you going to keep them down on the farm, after they've seen Paree?'

The dairy science row

Odium academicum would appear to be an inveterate, ubiquitous and incurable (if thankfully intermittent) malady. It can rage across the academic spectrum in any given grove, or among researchers in the same discipline in a wider academic fellowship. In some cases, the more arcane the discipline, the more intense the odium (as with nineteenth-century classicists). Personality clashes and such factors as envy and ambition are aggravated by the special climate of university life. The disagreements are fierce because, as has been famously said, there is so little at stake. Unlike the business world, there is no compelling sense of time being money. Academic activities are nowadays increasingly subject to the scrutiny of the public piper-payer, and a balance sheet must be struck, but there are no hard-faced investors demanding profits and dividends, or else! First-class minds are lured into a conflicting analysis of statutes and regulations, an analysis often exquisitely refined and seemingly interminable. Academics turned amateur administrators and lawyers stand excessively, self-righteously and intolerantly on their respective statutory rights. In some cases, the hard task of research and scholarship is put aside, perhaps with subconscious relief, to concentrate on internecine argument which (it is easy to delude oneself) can be construed as an issue of overriding importance to the academic community. In short, academic freedom and independence may degenerate into irresponsibility, lack of accountability and inordinate time wasting. This unfavourably drawn picture is a worst-case scenario, of course, but it helps to explain why the academic world is both resented and envied by, for example, public servants who have to operate in a very different environment.

As the reader will have gathered, the knives were frequently out in the college from the first decade of its existence. The most spectacular and prolonged dispute in the history of UCC – though hardly up to the standard of QCC battles royal – was 'the dairy science row', which darkened the favourable publicity on the faculty's beginnings, which went on from 1927 to 1936, and the effects of which persisted for many years thereafter. It began as a dispute about the structure of the faculty and this was inextricably linked with personality conflicts. Lines of battle were drawn up in the Governing Body, with the registrar opposing the president, and other bones of contention appearing, such as the registrar's rights and duties with regard to the conduct of academic correspondence. The intensity of the quarrel was proportionate to the number of persons and different levels involved, and to the variety of questions at issue. The seriousness of the affair is indicated by the fact that a visitation was involved, the only one in the history of UCC, though visitations were regular if not commonplace events during the Queen's College era.[76]

President Merriman and Professor Boyle had made no secret of their preference for a department, rather than a faculty, of dairy science. Though the legislation ignored their wishes, it seems that Boyle attempted from the outset to run dairy science as a department, asserting the professorial authority of a head over 'his' five lecturers, acting generally in an authoritarian manner and, moreover, directing dairy science as something of an independent republic in external association with the college. With the backing of President Merriman, he claimed overall authority as 'director' and had typewritten documents included in the minutes of the Governing Body to that effect.[77] Naturally enough, the five lecturers, severally and collectively, resented and resisted Boyle's claims. They regarded his position as faculty dean as one of honorary primacy and asserted their own rights as heads of five independent – and highly specialised – departments, with the status, though not the title, of professors. Moreover, they regarded agriculture (Boyle's area) as being the least important of the faculty disciplines.

Having appealed in vain to Merriman to uphold their position, they turned to the registrar in November 1932 to champion their cause. O'Rahilly was nothing loath. For one thing, he had long been unhappy with the wording of Statute XX: for another, this was the kind of battle he relished joining, with a gusto combining the Don Quixote and Sancho Panza aspects of his personality. It does not seem unfair to suggest that Alfie O'Rahilly entered no quarrel which he did not aggravate. Characteristically, he was to claim that he comported himself in the whole business with heroic self-restraint. Repeated attempts to get the Governing Body to deal with the matter in the autumn of 1933 only resulted in O'Rahilly being flung off the Finance Committee by the president and his supporters. The registrar was justifiably stung by this unprecedented and 'concentrated attack on my competence and honour'. In particular, the move put him (and kept him for the next two years) at loggerheads with Merriman.

Edward MacLysaght, who had been co-opted to the Governing Body in the mid-1920s 'perhaps as part of the effort then being made to de-anglicize' UCC, made some shrewd and frank observations in his diary before the crisis had reached its climax. At that stage his interpretation was understandably simplistic:

> A very bitter internal war has been in progress among the members of the staff for some time. The *casus belli* doesn't matter, it is really a preliminary contest in the anticipated struggle for the succession to that most ineffective of presidents, Professor Merriman, who is a rather pleasant prevaricator, adept at turning a deaf ear to awkward questions (usually mine) and gifted with a sense of humour which he manifests at the most unexpected times. The protagonists at any rate are on the one hand that brilliant and acerbic (then) lay theologian, Alfred O'Rahilly, the Registrar, and on the other the Professor of Agriculture, Boyle by name, who with his slow and ponderous good manners and bovine good humour is the very antithesis of the volatile 'Alfie' . . . Privately my view is that whoever is in the right as regards the actual dispute, O'Rahilly, for all his faults is with his brilliant intellect an asset to the College in a way Boyle could never be . . .[78]

Gradually, the Governing Body became sympathetic to the case presented by O'Rahilly, impressed no doubt by the force of his energetic and sustained arguments. However, when an internal committee failed to resolve the matter, the ultimate sanction of a visitation was invoked. By government order in February 1935, the Executive Council of the Irish Free State replaced the Crown as visitor of the NUI colleges.[79] Two High Court judges comprised the board of visitors and their brief was to investigate and settle the following main questions: the validity of the typewritten documents included in the Governing Body minutes purporting to regulate the conditions of the dairy science lectureships; the president's authority over the registrar in respect of academic correspondence; and the position of the dean of dairy science in this regard.

As things turned out, the visitation was confined to one preliminary session on 9 January 1936. A further meeting was fixed for 20 February but this never took place, being overtaken by the rapid progress of events. At a special meeting on 31 January, the Governing Body by a large majority decided, first, not to uphold the typewritten documents and, secondly, to support the registrar and the five lecturers.[80] The president and Professor Boyle backed down in the face of this rebuff, and tacitly conceded victory to their opponents.

O'Rahilly, in what could be construed as an olive branch gesture, now asked the press to refrain from giving the matter any further publicity, as 'a friendly settlement' had been reached.[81] Besides 'the case is of no interest whatever to the general public' and it 'could not easily be made intelligible to the ordinary reader'. The condescending tone of gown towards town was unintentional, no doubt, but nonetheless unfortunate and by no means confined to this particular occasion. Ironically, communications such as O'Rahilly's left the public with the impression that much dirty linen still needed washing. The press had shown a lively interest in the affair[82] but were excluded from the visitation inquiry, being told it was 'completely private and domestic'.[83] *The Irish Times* and *The Evening Echo* explained the significance of the outcome for the benefit of their readers (it may have been this piece of impertinence that provoked O'Rahilly's snooty rebuke). The visitation was described as unique and as the first in the NUI's history. The result was interpreted as a victory by default for the 'dons' against the president and the dean of dairy science.[84]

The dairy science row was now formally settled, the five lectureships became professorships within the next few years, the independence of their respective departments was upheld beyond doubt, and the faculty got on with its business. Yet sides had been intransigently taken in the college, attitudes of silent hostility were maintained even at a social and personal level, and the bad blood and the bitterness persisted long after the original issues had become a hazy memory.[85] In Belloc's lines,

> Some day when this is past, and all the arrows that we have are cast,
> We will ask each other why we hate, and fail to find a story to relate.

Perhaps the ghosts of the dairy science row were not well and truly laid until the faculty got a new 'habitation and a name' three decades or so later, thereafter going from strength to strength.

Seán Ó Faoláin

Seán Ó Faoláin's biographer has remarked, with reference to the contest between Ó Faoláin and Daniel Corkery for the UCC professorship of English in 1931, that 'the incident has always attracted more comment than it deserves'.[86] Perhaps so, but this is hardly surprising given the two personalities involved, the fact that the mentor–protégé relationship had long since turned sour, and that Ó Faoláin had become, in the wicked

8.5 Seán Ó Faoláin who described the UCC academic
appointments process as 'democracy gone dotty'.

Cork phrase, a Corkery glugger.[87] The contest for the chair has also been immortalised
by Ó Faoláin himself in his Gogol-like richly creative recollection of his campaign,
which vividly highlights the deficiencies ('democracy gone dotty') of the then appointment process.[88] Ó Faoláin's admirers see his rejection for the Cork professorship as
evidence of UCC's provincialism and obscurantism, in this period at least. The incident
has certainly been well recounted and analysed, and it is not proposed here to traverse
well-trodden ground except insofar as it has a bearing on Ó Faoláin's attitudes to UCC.[89]
Some comments on the episode, however, are difficult to understand. UCC was hardly
guilty of a philistine dereliction of duty because it favoured Corkery over the
young Ó Faoláin (a renowned graduate, certainly, but at that stage hardly 'the most

distinguished').[90] 'People say in retrospect that the wrong man was appointed.'[91] This is as dubiously speculative an opinion as Aloys Fleischmann's snobbish rumination that 'Cork would have been a better place because of the influence he would have exerted'.[92] Ó Faoláin himself believed that if appointed 'he would have been out of the place within three years, or else stayed on and gone to seed'.[93] In any case, it seems absurd to talk about UCC needing to make 'amends'[94] for having failed to appoint any given candidate!

Ó Faoláin was bitterly disappointed, of course, given his desire to come back from London to Ireland (though not, preferably, to Cork) to a regular salary not to be sneezed at; his conviction that he was the best man for the job; his hurt pride, and his rage at what he regarded as Alfred O'Rahilly's treachery. O'Rahilly had encouraged him several years before to set his sights on the chair[95] but was ambivalent when it came to the crunch.[96] Ó Faoláin suspected him of carrying out a devious Machiavellian ploy, but Patrick Maume (Corkery's biographer) is probably correct in suggesting a less malignant explanation – cock-up rather than conspiracy.[97]

In the course of his later distinguished career, Ó Faoláin was able to put the traumatic Cork affair in relieved perspective, and Maurice Harmon tells us it was not the crucial experience which turned him against his native city.[98] Yet it seems to have left an abiding bitterness and to have greatly influenced his bilious attitude to a mater he regarded as anything but alma (just like his own mother). When Aloys Fleischmann sounded him out in the 1950s, at O'Rahilly's request, about accepting an NUI honorary degree, the negative response was 'caustic'. On another occasion, he snubbed O'Rahilly when meeting him unexpectedly on a plane flight.[99] But it was his constant disparagement of UCC that proved he neither forgot nor forgave the mortal insult of his rejection in 1931.

His later strictures on the college were at odds with his student experience (undergraduate, 1918–21) which was enjoyable, liberating, fulfilling and maturing.[100] It is through the disenchanted and jaundiced prism of the intervening years that the college is viewed in *Vive Moi!*[101]

> I was happy for some five years in that cheating bridal bed. What riches of the sense, if not of the mind, of the emotions, if not of thought, its library alone gave me! I spent countless hours lounging in the club or outside on its grassy banks, arguing, dreaming, hoping, mocking, conspiring, flirting and, so, learning from my fellow students. And how constricted my whole subsequent life might have been in some dead-end, menial job if I had not for those years enclaved myself in this slightly absurd Lilliput.[102]

And there is the wryly affectionate reference:

> As an American friend once said to me when I talked to him about University College, Cork: 'Well, Seán, it may have been a bum joint, but it evidently suited you down to the ground'.[103]

Ó Faoláin recounts experiences of censorship in 'those battlements of unlearning'[104] that would have successive student generations up to the 1960s nodding in rueful recognition:

> We were not really all that free. I soon peeled off a few scraps of the illusion, which nevertheless persisted – I was no Joyce who saw through his college in Dublin within a matter of months. I peeled off one scrap the time I proposed that the Students' Club ought to have a small browsing library of modern Irish novels and other books of topical Irish interest. A local businessman, later a senator, James Dowdall, generously put up the money, I was appointed honorary librarian, and the books were duly installed. Within days the professor of education, a maiden lady of such highly genteel ways that we called her Feathery Ellen, observed among the novels Joyce's *Portrait of the Artist as a Young Man*. She at once had it removed. On another occasion I dropped in to the suggestion box of the main library the proposal that it ought to have some of the novels of Emile Zola. I got the astonished reply: 'But who on earth wants to read Zola at this date?' It was vain for me to answer that I was curious about Zola and wished to understand the course of the modern novel. Zola was not added to the library. Intellectually speaking we led the Simple Life in UCC.[105]

But the petty and restrictive cultural climate was not to be laid exclusively at the gate of the college. 'Lilliput' described town as well as gown. In a 'characteristically snooty manner' (his biographer's phrase), he observed that Cork was in no position to provide a balance to 'the college's simplicities', since it had no museums, art galleries, regional periodicals, publishing houses, and neither sister university nor a symphony orchestra.[106] The city's limitations were indicated

> by our common use of the definite, defining and confining singular article: the fountain, the Lough, the library, the college, the baths, the cricket field, the lower road, the top field, the regatta, the paper, the park, the statue.[107]

Ó Faoláin's vignette – lightly affectionate but essentially cruel – of his professor of English, W.F.P. Stockley, is doubtless influenced by his fury at Stockley's total support for Corkery's candidature in 1931, but it must be said that the picture he paints tallies with the impressions formed by others. As a student, he enjoyed Stockley's memorable 'at homes' in Tivoli, but not the professor's lectures:

> Alas, as a teacher he was a comical figure . . . His mind was like a lady's sewing basket after a kitten had been through it. His lectures were a host of bright scraps of quotations and casual references all jumbled colourfully together without order, sequence or evident purpose. It used to be said of him that he was the only man who ever spoke and wrote without using verbs.

Stockley's 'cloudy mystification' typified the mental confusion and disorder of UCC lecturers, as Ó Faoláin remembered them:

> When I left that college, I did not know what a bibliography was, how to compile a clear course of reading, how to attack any subject, ignorant of the difference between a conflation and a collation, a prime source and a secondary source, objective analysis and subjective feeling, how to compose a resumé, how properly to organise a theme.[108]

Ó Faoláin also recalled Sir Bertram Windle's alleged description of the college, 'when he left it in dudgeon, as a *université pour rire*'.[109]

Ó Faoláin's criticisms of UCC in *Vive Moi!* (in themselves a form of provincialism) are quite tame when compared with his scathing denunciations in correspondence with Aloys Fleischmann. (Fleischmann greatly admired Ó Faoláin and was hoping in 1968–69 to get UCC's 'most eminent graduate' to accept an honorary degree from the NUI, though Ó Faoláin was understandably 'rather bitter about the College in the past – he was banned on at least two occasions from lecturing here'.[110]) Late in 1948, Ó Faoláin's broadcast talk, 'Return to Cork', 'aroused intense resentment among Corkonians in general', according to Fleischmann, who mildly remonstrated with him, with particular reference to the description of UCC as 'fourth-rate'. After all, protested Fleischmann:

> A small college set in a relatively poor and uneducated agricultural community, lacking in grants and endowments, with a spoiled and twisted tradition (from religiosity), we cannot hope to be more than a little better than what we are nor are any of us under any delusions as to the deficiencies of our set-up.[111]

This apologetic attempt at defence provoked a splenetic outburst of excoriation from Ó Faoláin:

> Take your College. It's not 4th rate. It's useless . . . Your 'explanations' (which one knows so well) don't alter the fact. The place is USELESS. It's a fraud in fact. What good did Stockley do *me*? Endless harm. He did me great good about three times when he kindly invited me to tea in his lovely and gracious house. *That* was 'education'. But PROFESSOR Stockley . . . Holy God! Professor Tim O'Torna and his pigshead of a brother. That wet Treston! Old Porter was different: he was a gent and he had personality and that is all that matters after scholarship in a University. Mary Ryan – a monster as a professor: a sweet old lady no doubt. Do you know what she used to do? – She used to TEACH us. Sacred Heart – teaching in a University!!!! You know – grammar and syntax and this and that and . . . Oh! and Ah! and groans. And everybody said she was marvellous: because she *did* teach the little ducks, spoonfed them, breastfed them, predigested their pap for them. Aloys. A University is a University, as Gertrude Stein might say. Anything else is O.[112]

Obviously, the passing years hadn't sweetened the grapes. Ó Faoláin was still viciously snapping at the hand that had declined to feed him.

Daniel Corkery

Because of his writings, in particular *The Hidden Ireland*, Corkery has been central to the national debate about history and culture and he has been a seminal ideological and literary influence. Yet he did not loom large as a member of the college community. He gave public lectures and participated in debates under college society auspices but he was not an assiduous attender at Academic Council meetings and he stayed clear of college politics. He was not, so to speak, a college person.

By the time he settled into the professorship of English, his best creative and critical work was already done – *The Hidden Ireland* had appeared in 1924 and *Synge and Anglo-*

Irish Literature came out in 1931. As a university teacher, his impact on students was mixed. He did not suffer 'social' students gladly, he was better with small groups than with large classes and he was all too obviously less interested in some sections of the course than in others. On the other hand, he was an inspiration to kindred spirits, that is to say, to favoured students who shared his 'Irish-Ireland' views about Irish being the proper medium for Irish people to write in.[113]

A Catholic campus

Whatever the difference in their personalities and abilities, Merriman and O'Rahilly both operated in the same religious–cultural context, features of which were already to be observed in Windle's day but which became more fully developed after independence. In this respect, at least, UCC was a microcosm of the moral and religious ethos of the Irish Free State. Though the narrow and authoritarian religious

8.6 Daniel Corkery, professor of English, 1931–47, has been a seminal ideological and literary influence in Ireland.

culture of Merriman's presidency was intensified in O'Rahilly's reign, it was, at least, enlivened and made exciting by the latter's vibrant personality.[114]

The Catholicising of college, and the integralist attempt to harmonise religion and the secular curriculum, proceeded apace in the 1920s and the 1930s.[115] The process was marked by an extraordinary degree of smugness and self-congratulation, and an exaggerated sense of self-importance. This campus atmosphere persisted into the war years and the late 1950s. The academic calendar was marked by such religious occasions as the red mass marking the opening of the college year, the October and Lenten retreats and the annual Corpus Christi procession.[116] The centenary of Catholic Emancipation in 1929 was celebrated by a garden party in the Quadrangle hosted by the archbishop of Cashel and the bishop of Cork, and attended by 2,000 ring-kissing guests including the minister for education,[117] and by an open-air mass in the UCC Athletic Grounds before a massive congregation of 60,000, led by the head of government, W.T. Cosgrave.[118] The Patrician year of 1932 saw another great demonstration of faith with an equally large crowd in the same venue, led this time by Eamon de Valera, newly installed in power, with his defeated rival Cosgrave also in attendance.[119] The freedom of Cork was conferred on the papal nuncio in 1930, and the ceremony was conducted in the Quadrangle, a special dais being erected on the embankment.[120] All these Catholic public events made obvious nonsense of the non-denominational charter.

On one occasion the students at the red mass were told by Fr Finbarr Ryan OP that 'the university must progressively become Catholic'.[121] They were later reminded (in a purple-passage sermon that drew parallels between modern Cork and ancient Athens, the harbour being compared to Piraeus, and UCC to the Acropolis) that the college motto was about continuity not merely of location but of a harmonious concert of faith and learning.[122] A visiting English priest denounced Oxbridge and the Church of England ('the great pretender') and asked for the UCC students' prayers for the conversion of England.[123]

The replacement of the Queen Victoria statue in 1934 by one of St Finbarr, on the eastern pinnacle of the Aula Maxima, took place in the strongly nationalist atmosphere of the 1930s but the motivation was religious as well. There had been a general feeling for years that the alien symbol of an alien institution should be replaced by the patron saint of the diocese and the college. Modern research – ironically, by a UCC scholar[124] – may have undermined the reality of a historical Cork St Finbarr but the tradition of the college having a topographical and cultural continuity with the supposed founder of an early Christian monastery is a strong and deeply rooted one, respected even by nineteenth-century merchants and academics who had little rapport with the native culture.[125] The myth of St Finbarr has its own hallowed and enduring truth.

The statue of St Finbarr was the work of the young Séamus Murphy, then aged about thirty and just back from his studies in Paris. It was, no doubt, a very welcome commission. It was paid for by a fund raised by the Academy of St Thomas, of which Alfred O'Rahilly was the founder and, very probably in this instance, the chief financier. The statue was then presented to the Governing Body by the Academy. It was the first such religious object to be publicly accepted by a constituent college. Standing seven feet high and weighing one and a half tons, it is carved in durable Irish limestone to harmonise with the general architectural tone of the college. Interestingly, the saint is depicted austerely as a cowled monk rather than the conventional episcopal figure, and his right hand is raised in blessing. The contemporary report noted that the lines of the hair and beard appeared white in the light.[126]

The Victoria statue meanwhile was not destroyed but placed in an office in the East Wing where eventually its considerable weight proved too much for the floorboards. Accordingly, it was removed in 1946 and spared for the second time. On this occasion, it was buried in the president's garden[127] whence it was exhumed in late 1994 and displayed at the UCC 150 Universitas exhibition in the old council room. This college decision provoked some protests, but not, significantly, from the students. The simply designed, medieval style depiction of the young Victoria (executed by Cork

8.7 Statue of Queen Victoria, as exhibited
at the UCC 150 Anniversary Exhibition,
1995. Victoria was replaced by St Finbarr
on the pinnacle of the Aula Maxima in the
nationalist and religious atmosphere of the
college in 1934.

8.8 Students and staff outside Honan Chapel after mass for Pope Pius XI, 17 February 1939.

sculptor Paddy Scannell, and presented in 1849 as a gift to the college by the architect, Sir Thomas Deane) attracted much public attention.

The members of the academic staff were eager to show their credentials as pope's men and women. The professors, lecturers and assistants meeting in the council room on 30 June 1931, with President Merriman in the chair, offered their 'loyal homage to our Holy Father, Pius XI' in his various difficulties, and their gratitude for the authoritative guidance given by him on moral and social principles.[128] Similar sentiments were expressed by UCD and county councils,[129] and were very obviously orchestrated. In due course (five months) the pope's grateful acknowledgement was conveyed to President Merriman by Bishop Cohalan.[130] When Pius XI died in February 1939, many college functions were cancelled or postponed.[131] At an Inter-University Commerce Association dinner and dance in Birmingham University, Catholic delegates (including three from Cork) attended in dress mourning and refrained from dancing (though not presumably from drinking).[132] However, a photograph showing students leaving the Honan Chapel after a mass for the late pope does not project an image of inconsolable grief.[133]

On the local scene, Rev. D. Canon Cohalan, a former dean of residence, was presented with an episcopal ring by professors and students on his elevation to the see of Waterford: he spoke of the special rapport between Church and university.[134]

Student debate on Church power and influence was not encouraged, to put it mildly, during this neo-medieval period. The president's office operated as an effective thought-police control point, and both topics and speakers for college society meetings had to be approved in advance. Thus Merriman banned a proposed Philosophical Society debate on the greatly-daring theme, 'That this House deprecates the intrusion of Ecclesiastical Authorities in Political Matters'.[135] (What the organisers had in mind, very probably, was the attitude of bishops towards republicanism, a relatively more acceptable topic than a wide discussion of their political and social influence.)

However, it would be a serious misreading of the period to think of the students of those days as being coerced into a regimen of religious conformity. The great majority accepted without demur the religious culture in which they had grown up. When students attended the red mass and seasonal retreats in large numbers,[136] when they foregathered in the Quadrangle *en masse* to march in the annual Eucharistic procession, when they walked in the rain from the Honan Chapel to SS Peter and Paul and St Finbarr's South to gain the Jubilee Year indulgence,[137] they did so willingly because it was an age of faith. What degree of fervour and depth of conviction they felt is another matter. And there was always a dissident or unorthodox minority.

Relations between the sexes appeared to be guided by a strict code of propriety. The Ladies Club was an inviolable female sanctum, and it was out of bounds to men students. Women students were closely chaperoned, forbidden to smoke in public, and not allowed wear trousers. Displays of affection between courting couples – and many marriages originated in college courtships – were decorous in the extreme, and were a far cry from the primal embraces so much in evidence on campus at present. 'No canoodling in the Quad' was a catchphrase of the 1930s, and the caption of a celebrated *Kerryman* cartoon.[138] Loitering in the Lower Grounds was an occasion of sin and was discouraged. Lodgings were segregated by gender, and voluntary segregation was observed at lectures. Any female student who became pregnant (a very rare occurrence) simply went out of circulation. Homosexual activity was extremely covert though there was a notorious case in the 1930s of a medical student being caught *in flagrante* in a downtown public toilet and being expelled by resolution of the Governing Body: apparently, governors felt that it would be particularly unacceptable to allow a medical student of such proven propensities to qualify and practise. The student in question subsequently completed his studies in Edinburgh.[139] In general then, college attitudes to sexual behaviour mirrored those of the wider Irish society.

Students as a whole accepted the puritanical ethos as part of the prevailing moral–religious culture, though tradition has it that rugby-playing medical students enjoyed a robustly permissive sex life. In any case, it is impossible to guess at the real extent of

8.9 Picture-taking in the Quad after conferring ceremonies, 19 July 1937.

student sexual activity. Perhaps the relative licence extended to students in other areas (unruly conferrings, high-spirited rag days, heated political activism) was intended as a compensation for their docility in the moral–religious sphere, if not as a sublimation of repressed sexual urges.

In all this, we should remind ourselves that, from the 1920s to the 1960s, UCC was far from being a homogeneous society permeated by a single ethos. A whole academic community was not single-mindedly pursuing the goal of Catholicising the college or of integrating secular learning and Christian faith. Many students and staff members were preoccupied with quite different concerns. A worldly middle-class intention to further individual and family interests through professional careers was largely indifferent to religious – and nationalist – zeal. The medical school, its teachers and students, regarded itself as a more enduring phenomenon than fashionable trends in Catholic sociology. For example, such people would be proud of Alfred O'Rahilly's high national profile but at the same time they indulgently regarded him as an eccentric and refused to take him all that seriously. From another angle, the college was, of course, a community of learning (at both staff and student levels) where horizons were scholarly rather than ideological. But there were also Irish-Ireland ideologues among staff and students who felt more passionately about language revival and related values than they did about religious orthodoxy, and whose mission it was to cleanse the college culturally and rid it of 'West Brits' and 'shoneens'.[140] They saw themselves as conducting a *Kulturkampf* against the likes of eccentric Jersey-born, Oxford Eights,

Catholic convert, Professor Louis P.W. Renouf (zoology, 1922–54) who, blissfully insensitive to outraged indigenous feelings, proclaimed his opposition to compulsory Irish,[141] asserted that Irish children were fifty years behind their counterparts in the study of natural history,[142] and announced that practitioners of the great and manly game of rugby could never be guilty of a low trick![143]

In short, there was a mainstream ethos in the college of Merriman and O'Rahilly but there were also other small worlds, some of them oblivious to everything save their own existence, others mutually antagonistic, in all constituting quite a diverse community – a *universitas*, in fact.

Going to college

Aoibhinn beatha an scoláire . . . It is only in retrospect that student life in any given historical period can be described as idyllic. But UCC in Irish Free State days was a relaxed place, untroubled by the pressures that have been building up in recent decades. If a family could afford to sustain student status for their offspring (paying the fees was only part of the economic sacrifice demanded), then entrance to college did not present a scholastic challenge. The NUI matriculation examination – or the Leaving Certificate equivalent thereof – made no special demands on the average intelligence: whenever it did, friendly personators were available at a reasonable fee. A relaxed examination regimen continued within the college, which was convenient for the student who was content merely to pass. The facility of 'repeat' examinations allowed the idle rich at least to dawdle their way through an undergraduate career, thus giving rise to the phenomenon of the 'chronic' medical student. The term 'chronic' goes back at least to the beginning of the century but came to be especially associated with ex-soldiers after the Great War who received grants 'as long as they were students'. Later on, in one famous case, a chronic of over twenty years duration was passed out by a younger classmate, J.M. O'Donovan, who as professor of medicine, 1931–57, eventually became his examiner.[144] On the other hand, the motto of Professor D.P. Fitzgerald (anatomy, 1909–42) was reputedly that of Pétain at Verdun – 'they shall not pass'.

'Going to college' was the 'next thing to do' for the children of the urban well-off and it had considerable cachet. Snobbery characterised various aspects of college life, from the exclusion of 'outsiders' from weekly 'hops'[145] to the observation of well-bred idleness during the long vacation. Manual work was considered demeaning, but some modern languages students spent their summers on the Continent to good effect.

The socially elitist approach to a college education meant that the choice of faculties was often arbitrary. Even scholarship holders, for whom study was real and earnest, frequently made up their minds only at the last moment about what to do in college.[146] There was little in the way of advice or counsel available from the college staff who were, in general, remote from, and inaccessible to, their students.

A Cork graduate, in a contribution to the *Irish Statesman* in 1926, noted that the college had settled down to serious life after the disturbances caused by war and revolution. Despite the residue of political bitterness, student life was characterised by good humour and camaraderie. According to this account, students in general did not read which was an 'amazing admission'. This was one reason why enquiring minds were not in evidence at debates where opinions expressed were 'most orthodox'. The library 'doesn't stock even Shaw', probably considered subversive in an institution where the students looked like – and often were – mere children. This state of affairs, continued the graduate, suited the authorities very well, though it affected the standard of college education adversely. The university entrance age should be raised to nineteen, at least. This contributor finally remarked that the new weekly review *The Tribune* was largely written by professors like Busteed, Hogan and O'Donoghue [probably Tórna].[147]

Student numbers (male and female) increased fairly steadily throughout the interwar period but did so within a low (500–1,000) range, so that the modest amenities available – a comfortable ladies' club and a primitive men's one – made life pleasant on a beautiful and uncrowded campus. Daniel Corkery observed that it was more important for the students than the professors to have good leisure rooms.[148] Nevertheless, the early appearance of the work ethos was deplored in the mid-1930s:

8.10 'College unfair to us girls', from Quarryman, February 1942.

The freshmen show a definitely studious bent which has caused many a chronic to shake his head sadly and bemoan the passing of the good old days.[149]

'Twas ever thus. The New Year was marked by increased numbers reading in the library.[150] St Patrick's Day was a critical date in the student's progress. The tradition was already venerable that those who had not 'their course finished once' before the lawnmowers appeared in the Quadrangle would fail their examinations. 'The grass is now cut', warned a sombre UCC chronicler.[151] This was clearly a counsel of prudence, whereas refraining from walking through the middle of the Quadrangle to avoid examination failure was in the category of hallowed superstition.

Besides involving themselves in the turbulent politics of the 1920s and 1930s, hyperactive students had other opportunities for letting off steam. (Those in authority, in college and in society at large, smiled indulgently at the antics of privileged youth, though a sterner view was taken of similar activity on the part of a lower social class.) In a truly high-spirited class of their own were the statue-climbing exploits of an intrepid few who draped august eminences with incongruous souvenirs. Thus in the early 1930s the alcoved statue in the Honan Hostel was bedecked with a purple dressing gown and chamberpot, and Queen Victoria atop the Aula Maxima was clad in an undergraduate gown.[152]

Great fun was had by (nearly) all on the annual college rag days, which continued to flourish until they were abruptly terminated in 1944 by the new president, Alfred O'Rahilly. Participants (who were all male, women students acting only as costume makers, collectors and production assistants) prepared themselves in the Quadrangle for the procession down town, dressed in their 'picturesque and outlandish costumes'[153] while the preview was enjoyed by staff, students and porters.[154] Local, national and world celebrities of the day were impersonated, and mock degrees were sometimes conferred. The young Tomás MacCurtain was long remembered as a handsome Mae West. *The Cork Examiner* invariably praised the demeanour of the students, contrasting their behaviour with hooliganism elsewhere. Such a favourable view of their 'buffoonery' was not taken (on what transpired to be the last rag day) by a Circuit Court judge in 1943[155] nor by an outraged city sheriff eleven years earlier.[156] Female shop assistants who were the involuntary recipients of ardent embraces were not in all cases amused, nor were 'kidnapped' and 'blackmailed' motorists, nor college authorities hearing about twelve women students performing the cancan in the Palace Theatre. Of course, it was all in a good cause, as the newspapers and the civic authorities acknowledged when being presented with the proceeds (less unauthorised commission for drinking expenses) of rag day collections for charity – medical students, being most knowledgeable about these matters, always worked the best pitches. The 1943 rag seems to have breached the very generous permitted bounds of decorum (the St Vincent de Paul Society intimating that it would not accept in future any part of collection proceeds). This conveniently strengthened O'Rahilly's hand in banning rags altogether, not only for disciplinary reasons but because, as downtown events, they had not been amenable to college control.[157] The quid pro quo to the students for O'Rahilly's suppression of the rag and his reform of conferring day was the promise, duly fulfilled, of new amenities, especially a restaurant with a dance floor.

Youthful boisterousness was well in evidence on the campus itself. When President W.T. Cosgrave and colleagues visited the college in May 1928 and addressed the students in the Quadrangle, the reception was warm but hardly deferential. His speech, we are told, was 'punctuated by witty interjections' and he was saluted with shouts of 'Atta Boy, Liam' and 'Cheerio, Willie'. But Minister Paddy McGilligan, well seasoned in the school of tough parliamentary exchanges, returned the banter with interest, expressing the hope that the medical students would enjoy twenty-five years in such picturesque surroundings.[158]

Conferring ceremonies in the 1920s and 1930s continued to be marked, as in Windle's day, by scenes of extraordinary, at times chaotic, student rowdiness. When the popular Professor Timothy Smiddy attended conferrings – he left UCC in 1923 – there would be loud student calls for 'Tadhg'.[159] Sometimes the demonstrations were merely 'good humoured',[160] but more often than not dog-bombs and flour-bags were thrown, and a parody ('Poor Pad Joe') of a popular plantation song would be intoned in mock tribute to President Merriman. On one occasion a squib was thrown from the back of the Aula Maxima where the men students were assembled, causing the ladies to jump in consternation as the firework shot about the floor. The president, leaving the

8.11a Minister Patrick McGilligan (second from right) bantering with students in the Quad during government visit in May 1928. President W.T. Cosgrave is at far left.

8.11b Visit of President Cosgrave and Mr McGilligan to University College, Cork, 7 May 1928
Seated (L-R): Prof. Ó Donnchadha; E. P. M. McSweeney; Prof. Barry; Dr A. Patterson; Prof.
Fitzgerald; Dr J. C. Foley; W.T. Cosgrave; Prof. O'Sullivan; P. McGilligan; J. Downey; Prof. Conran;
Prof. Boyle; J.C. Dowdall; Dr Connolly; Mr Belas.
Second row: Mr Porter; Mr Ó Cadhlaigh; Prof. O'Donovan; Mr Leahy; Mr Hill; Mr Taylor; Fr Kieran;
Prof. O'Rahilly; Mr Conroy; Dr Edwin; Fr O'Brien; Mr Coffey; Mr Farrington; Prof. Dundon; Prof.
Bergin; Prof. Moore; Mr Cooke; Prof. O'Sullivan; Mr Hickey; Mr O'Donoghue; Mr Egan.
Third row: Miss Murphy; Mrs O'Neill; Dr McCarthy; Prof O'Donovan; Dr Grimes; Mrs O'Donovan;
Mr Buckley.
In doorway: Mr Magennis; Mr Egan; Prof. Pyne; Mr A. Barry.

platform and going in among the students, ordered the men to leave, which they
eventually did after causing the maximum commotion. They then proceeded to let off
their store of squibs in the Quadrangle. The year before, a dog-bomb narrowly missed
causing serious damage to the O'Sullivan Beare portrait.[161] However, a conferring held
in late July 1931 was reported as quiet, since the students were on holidays.[162] In 1933,
they amused themselves during the ceremony and the subsequent photography session
by heckling from a large and appreciative gallery such sallies as 'Is your hat straight?',
raising good-humoured laughter.[163] A picture of the Quadrangle on degree day in 1937
looks as if a riot had taken place at the south-west corner.[164] Some time later O'Rahilly
complained that 'hooliganism' had marred the photographing of graduates 'by means of
a discharge of sods of grass'.[165]

All this not-so-innocent fun suddenly came to an end with the accession of
O'Rahilly to the presidency. Henceforth dignity and good order would prevail on a
day that graduates would remember for its reverence and solemnity rather than for its
hilarity. The link between learning and religion would be underlined by mass and a
sermon in the Honan Chapel (and, of course, appropriate services by other denominations, if they so wished), after which there would be a procession to the Aula Maxima
where the president would give a post-conferring address, followed finally by a

reception for the new graduates and their families.[166] Observation of the new dispensation was ensured by packing the Aula with attendants and by threatening to meet any attempts at disruption with expulsion.[167] Soon, O'Rahilly's speeches on degree day included references to conferring as 'a kind of lay sacrament'[168] and as a transitional rite akin to ordination, medical emigrants-to-be being reminded that they could fill the role of lay apostles.[169] The days of humorous sallies, flour-bags and stink-bombs were well and truly dead. O'Rahilly's disciplinary clean-up also extended to other areas, so that there was an end, for example, to the merciless teasing of the distinguished lecturer in experimental physics whose students were addicted to throwing fistfuls of gravel at the blackboard. And the billiard table in the men's club was got rid of, as a distraction and a waste of time (which is precisely the point of billiards).

The post-civil war divide of the 1920s and the turbulent politics of the 1930s not surprisingly had an impact on the college, more particularly on those among staff and students who were politically minded to begin with. NUI Convocation deplored the existence of party alignments in governing bodies and Senate.[170] A branch of the Officers Training Corps established a link between the students and the army, which held annual dinners for the corps at Collins Barracks.[171] Though it was claimed that the organisation was non-political,[172] it was denounced at the 1933 Fianna Fáil ard-fheis as being anti-national and working hand in hand with the Blueshirts, and as attracting only the 'poorest type' of UCC student. President Merriman stoutly defended the corps against its detractors.[173] The Pearse Regiment of Volunteers in the late 1930s was a more acceptable outlet for student martial ardour,[174] and the Local Defence Force represented the reconciliatory spirit inspired by the Emergency.[175]

The Blueshirt movement had an obvious appeal for students coming from families of a particular political allegiance. In May 1934 some two hundred members of the College League of Youth in blue shirts and blouses, and carrying Fine Gael and college flags, marched to hear Professor James Hogan speak on 'The Corporate Society' at the Imperial Hotel, with W.T. Cosgrave in attendance.[176] For a time, Hogan was Blueshirtism's badly needed intellectual guru before he broke with the movement in protest against Eoin O'Duffy's irresponsible leadership.[177] In late May–early June 1935 he was drawn into acrimonious correspondence (given extensive space in all the dailies) over the charge, by the formidable Sinn Féin activist Mary McSwiney, that being a 'Republican' in 1920 had helped him secure his professorship. Peadar O'Donnell and, of course, Alfred O'Rahilly joined in the argument.

Republicanism in the college was a much more formidable and threatening movement than Blueshirtism, as was the case nationwide. Discoveries of explosives in the chemistry department indicated bomb-making there during the Civil War.[178] At the end of January 1939, republican activists left their destructive mark on the college for all to see to this day. Their escapade was widely reported and commented on, and led to a lively exchange of letters between the (more or less) anonymous perpetrators and Registrar O'Rahilly, President Merriman as usual remaining discreetly silent.

Between 2 and 4 a.m., on the morning of 31 January 1939, armed men broke into the room of the night porter, Denis O'Callaghan, near the Arch, marched him to an adjacent boiler room and there bound and gagged him. They then proceeded to place a ladder against the northern wall of the Arch and one of their number defaced the royal crest, smashing a large part of the crown and chipping the nose off the unicorn. They made good their escape, apparently exiting (as they had entered) over the College Road wall. The Barrack Street gardaí (the porter had freed himself and raised the alarm) searched the college grounds in vain.[179] *The Irish Times* (4 Feb. 1939) condemned the UCC defacement as the 'infantile' counterpart of IRA explosives at London tube stations. Asking rhetorically what offence had the 'inanimate unicorn' given, *The Irish Times* suggested that the mythical beast may have become in some way associated with the 'dream symbolism of callow youth'. The Council of the Guild of Students[180] issued a fence-sitting motion which condemned the mutilation of college property and expressed a reluctance to believe it was the work of students but also asserted that crests and insignia on college premises 'ought to have an Irish or religious significance'.[181]

In the press, O'Rahilly lambasted the 'petty vandalism' of 'some of our junior patriots', piling on heavy sarcasm and perhaps in the end indulging in overkill. Would they, he wondered, next start 'defacing the numerous small symbols of Lancaster and York in the College stonework' or were they prepared to start a subscription fund for replacing the carving? Why had not 'our young generalissimos' petitioned the Governing Body or discussed the matter with the college authorities before acting like 'bumptious, self-opinionated anarchists'? The Governing Body, he implied, would have acceded to a request to remove the crest.[182]

Unabashed, 'some of our junior patriots' adopted the sarcastic description of themselves and returned O'Rahilly's fire. The National University must be given a 'National' appearance, they proclaimed. They admitted they were in a minority but all students would come around to their view one day. They recalled comically that 'on the night of the dark deed, the Professor's contented snoring was clearly audible in the Quad . . .'[183] The episode of the 'superpatriots' caused O'Rahilly to reflect paternalistically that undergraduates, being 'mostly immature' and not 'overstudious', needed to be guided by the college authorities how to learn and equip themselves professionally. And there must be college discipline to deal with 'flagrant violation' of the rules as in the case of a meeting held without the president's consent by the so-called Cork University Republican Club which had not been given college recognition.[184] Obviously, the defacement episode rankled with O'Rahilly.

The Queen Victoria statue had figured in the exchanges between the 'superpatriot' students and O'Rahilly. Citing an example of peaceful nationalist action, O'Rahilly claimed that five years before, believing the statue to be inappropriate, 'we' had subscribed money for replacing it by one of St Finbarr.[185] The students retorted that 'the dear old lady is still tucked away intact!'[186] In fact, Professor Fleischmann maintained that what really led to Victoria's removal in 1934 was the threat of 'republican' students that they would blow her up unless she was taken down. Their threats also succeeded on another occasion when they warned they would cause trouble if Seán Ó Faoláin (regarded as an apostate by advanced nationalists) were allowed address the 'Philosoph': the registrar (O'Rahilly) reported on this to the Academic Council and the invitation was withdrawn.[187]

The only foreign policy debate that afforded some relief from the incestuous passions of cultural and political domestic argument in the Ireland of the 1930s was the Spanish Civil War. However, that struggle was seen through most Irish eyes as just a bloodier argument about being for or against the Catholic cause – 'God or no God'. At a rally in the Grand Parade, Alfred O'Rahilly and James Hogan were foremost in their condemnation of 'Red' atrocities in Spain.[188] Lecturer in Spanish, Joseph Healy (afterwards professor, 1961–63) wrote pro-Franco newspaper articles.[189] The debate about Spain seemed to bring out the abusive bullying side of O'Rahilly, and some intellectual arrogance as well. He declared that Irish workers must not align themselves with English workers on the issue. He demanded that local labour leaders clarify their stance, at which the Cork Workers Council took umbrage.[190] He denounced the National Union of Railwaymen for contributing to the alleviation of worker distress in Spain, and in subsequent correspondence an NUR protagonist accused him of pulling educational rank.[191] Towards the end of the Spanish war, O'Rahilly upbraided Cork Corporation for not passing a pro-Franco resolution.[192] In this as in other instances,[193] O'Rahilly's much-vaunted and self-proclaimed common man or 'Pat Murphy'[194] image was belied by his intellectually patronising and domineering approach and his lack of sensitivity to poorly educated opponents.

Irish–Ireland zealots

Another manifestation of passionate politics in the college derived from language revivalist policy and Irish-Ireland ideology. Governments expected the college to play its part in restoring Irish, and its contribution included the provision of oral Irish classes for students and the availability of lectures through Irish in certain departments. In the quaint phrase of one report, the college was responding to the 'readjusting of cultural conventions in this country'.[195] There was much support and publicity for the summer courses in Irish for teachers which were held successfully throughout the 1920s.[196] Professor Daniel Corkery was the most eloquent and influential advocate – through English – of the Irish-Ireland ideal. Reference has been made to Éamon Ó Donnchadha's attack on 'filthy foreignism'.[197] His brother, Tórna – Professor Tadhg Ó Donnchadha – equated the cinema with 'paganism and filth'.[198] The Irish-ising of the college had its enthusiastic advocates on the Governing Body. At Feis Phortláirge in 1935, 'An Fear Mór', well-known principal of the Irish college in Ring, said he and the mayor of Waterford would do their best in the Governing Body to Gaelicise UCC to such an extent that from the President down to the doormen no one would secure a position there without a knowledge of Irish.[199]

Yet the college, and the NUI in general, were fiercely criticised by outside revivalists for not doing enough for Irish. Tadhg Ó Tuama, of the Cork County executive of the

Gaelic League, complained that though UCC had been getting substantial annual grants for providing courses through Irish, only the minimum number of courses were being offered and only 5–10 per cent of students were taking such degree courses.[200] The Cork Ó Tuamas obviously felt very strongly about the matter, since Seán Ó Tuama stated at a Coiste Gnótha meeting of the Gaelic League that UCC was turning out men and women without Gaelic ideals, and these were the graduates people would look up to. '*Béarla* and *galldachas* were as strong in Cork University now as ever.'[201] Replacement, not bilingualism, was then the gospel of language revivalists.

Whatever the degree of UCC commitment to the national language policy, its efforts were largely ineffectual (again reflecting the situation in the wider community) and the attempts to promote the speaking of Irish in the student body failed miserably, after the initial enthusiasm subsided. The only saving grace was the popular Gaeltacht scholarship scheme which succeeded for reasons more social than cultural. Only when new oral Irish teaching methods were introduced in a more voluntary and less ideologically charged atmosphere, from the 1960s onwards, did a certain popular enthusiasm for Irish return to the college.

'An t-aos is aoirde léighinn do ghaolú, an gnó is tairbhthí don Ghaoluinn fé láthair' (Gaelicising those involved in higher learning is the most profitable task for the language at present), Tórna wrote to Ernest Blythe, finance minister and Irish language enthusiast, on 27 March 1925.[202] Conversely, the college was expected by governments – especially by the Fianna Fáil government coming to power in 1932 – to play its part in the national policy on the revival of the Irish language. Between 1933 and 1935, the GB discussed the matter extensively (in English) and on one occasion resolved that the posts of president, secretary, registrar and librarian should be filled only by Irish speakers. There was, at the very least, an expectation of a quid pro quo in respect of government funding for special projects. Lectures in the new dairy science courses, for example, were expected to have an Irish-language flavouring.[203]

One of the difficulties in the whole area of Irish language teaching – and it was a self-perpetuating problem – was a poor grasp of the language not only on the part of the students but frequently of their teachers as well. In 1943, it was estimated that in UCD

> one-third of the total number taking history took it through the medium of Irish but that only about half of this number had sufficient knowledge of Irish to do so profitably. . . . It was stated that there was a repugnance to taking lectures through Irish, except in the case of Nuns, Brothers and teachers to whom it was an advantage in their profession.[204]

It was these categories of students who had flocked enthusiastically to the well-attended summer schools in UCC in the 1920s, when the Honan Hostel was taken over by the nuns participating in the course.[205]

It was typical of O'Rahilly's pragmatic and extrovert approach that he should have warmly approved of, and helped to organise, the Gaeltacht holiday scheme.[206] His cultural background made him instinctively sympathetic to 'Irish-Ireland', and he was generally on the side of the 'Ireeshians' in the college as against those who were merely indifferent or who would have a 'rugby-club' hostility to Gaelic culture. Temperamentally, however, he was impatient with the ideologues who set unattainable targets for language revival and who denounced defaulters in lofty moral tones, using the condemnatory nationalist terminology which D.P. Moran had popularised in *The Leader*.

This ideological mentality is exemplified in the stance taken in the summer of 1936 by Cormac Ó Cuilleanáin, then a lecturer in Irish and a graduates' representative on the GB.[207] He was outraged by the appointment of Frances Vaughan to the professorship of education and by the connivance of her supporters who included President P.J. Merriman. Tórna and Ó Cuilleanáin had tested the 'nine serious candidates' for competence in Irish, and found only Vaughan unqualified: she had 'no Irish (seriously speaking)'. Yet Merriman, claimed Ó Cuilleanáin, had used his full influence as president to have her appointed, even maintaining – in the face of expert evidence to the contrary – that she had sufficient command of the language to lecture through it. For Ó Cuilleanáin, the appointment of a professor of education whose knowledge of Irish was 'practically nil' was tantamount to flouting 'the whole National Policy in Education' and this would forfeit the goodwill for the college of the Department of Education. For these reasons, as Ó Cuilleanáin wrote to Merriman, he could no longer serve with the president on the joint committee for the promotion of Irish, and he castigated

8.12 Cormac Ó Cuilleanáin, professor of history of modern Irish literature, 1950-66.

Merriman for his insincerity and for impugning the integrity of Tórna and Ó Cuilleanáin.[208]

Curiously, the republican diehard Mary MacSwiney (at the time, a member of the GB) also experienced the lash of Ó Cuilleanáin's wrath. She had apparently been 'sadly misinformed – or possibly grossly deceived' into supporting Frances Vaughan against all the Irish-Ireland elements of the faculty, Academic Council and Governing Body who had resolved that the professor of education must be well qualified in Irish – it was 'simply axiomatic'. Ó Cuilleanáin told MacSwiney:

> I am very, very busy counteracting the big last stand of the West Britons of UCC . . .
> When a fundamental all-important National Principle confronts me I can only take the side that Pearse and Terry would take.[209]

In another letter to a kindred spirit, Ó Cuilleanáin said that Vaughan was supported by 'everything, everybody that is anti-national, anti-Republican, anti-Gaelic . . . it is the last stand of the enemy here'. Denouncing 'the rottenness of the Anti-Irish' and the stupidity of their 'Irish' adherents, he affirmed support for the 'grand old cause', 'the sacred cause of Irish nationality'.[210]

The episode throws light on the *Kulturkampf* in the college in the 1930s, the uncompromising attitudes of the 'Irish-Ireland' camp and the seemingly insincere, if not deceptive and favouritistic, behaviour of Merriman. It is of interest that a lecturer should have denounced a president forthrightly to his face. But the incident also shows that O'Rahilly, against his natural instincts, could keep his head below the parapet on occasion. He 'held back throughout', according to Ó Cuilleanáin, 'possibly until he saw that the real Irish brigade meant business'.[211]

CHAPTER NINE

THE MANY SIDES OF TOWN
AND GOWN

College came down town and fraternised . . .
in fact, the College became a citizen . . .

businessman J.C. Foley, December 1928

THE INTER-WAR PERIOD saw a gradual strengthening of links between the college and the community, accompanied by an intermittent debate on the relationship. University extension lecturer Dominic Daly asserted in 1927 that the university must come to the people and that the new dairy science faculty must not be content with turning out 'academic farmers looking for soft jobs' or supplying creamery managers, but must help solve people's mundane problems.[1] On the other hand, Daly pleaded for bequests to aid the college and pointed out that its potential as a community resource remained largely untapped: he had heard Professor John Busteed (economics, 1924–64) complaining how seldom he was asked to lecture by local bodies![2] Prominent businessman J.C. Foley was more emphatic (though it should be said his remarks were made on the day he received an honorary degree in December 1928) that in the building up of civic–academic co-operation it was the college which had taken the initiative: 'College came down town and fraternised with the business associations, with the workers' associations, with the other educational schemes – in fact, the College became a citizen'.[3]

The Cork Examiner, while occasionally carping about 'bread-and-butter' issues and the university's failure to provide for extern students, had in general a positive attitude towards the college. By and large, that reflected the position of the interested public – supportive but occasionally critical. Letters to the editor had their own (generally anonymous) particular axes to grind: why weren't the citizens warmly encouraged to come to public lectures at the college?[4] Wouldn't it be a good idea if the college ('a closed borough to most of its citizens') held musical 'proms' for tourists and depressed citizens who might then feel they were getting some value from their taxes?[5] Why (asked a man who wanted to point out UCC from the Muskerry tram to an English visitor) were the college buildings 'kept carefully shrouded from the public gaze by an overgrowth of trees'?[6] Why was the college indulging in 'squandermania' at the public's expense, acquiring more agricultural land when the model farm was adequate, and purchasing a substantial house on the Western Road for demolition, at a time of a severe housing shortage?[7]

Come up and see us: the conversazione

The nativisation of the college, for long regarded by the Catholic and national majority as an alien institution, was a gradual process. The transformation to a constituent college of the new National University made UCC a more congenial place of learning to that majority (especially perhaps to Catholic women). Its scholarly disciplines were extended and its governance democratised. The various roles of O'Rahilly, Smiddy, Stockley and Hogan in the national revolution helped to bridge the long-standing alienation gap. Still, the instability of the 1914–23 era made further normalisation difficult. So it could be argued that the college was really not in a position to invite the citizens to view its educational amenities until the mid-1920s. That was the background to the imaginative idea of the conversazione, tried out in the Michaelmas term of 1925, and continued for some years. A conversazione (a word then commonly in use) was a soirée of a learned society, in this case an 'at home' or open day arranged by the college.

The Cork Examiner gave advance notice of the conversazione organised by the college's Scientific and Medical Society and held on 14 October 1925 and the following days. Now that the country had settled down, 'more or less', this would be 'a unique opportunity for the citizens of Cork to see for themselves the full scope of the work of the University' and the role it played in the life of the country.[8] The occasion was extensively covered (with detailed reports of lectures and demonstrations) in the press over the next several days.[9] President Merriman opened the proceedings with an address in the 'Examination Hall' at 3.30 p.m., giving a rather poor-mouthish account of the state of the college. Accepting that the town–gown connection had been 'slight' for obvious reasons, he pleaded for greater community interest and co-operation to 'bridge the gulf'. He implied that the lectureship in Irish music represented the sum total of the Corporation's interest in the college.

The *Examiner* thought the experiment an 'undoubted success' in bringing home the relevance of research. The citizens were amazed at the amount of interesting machinery, and were absorbed in the various processes demonstrated to them clearly and painstakingly by staff and students. Though 'the attendance was on the whole satisfactory', it was disappointing that some important sections of the city's commercial and industrial life, vitally affected by college work and research, were not fully represented.[10] (It should be added that one very popular area with rural visitors, from its inception in the late 1920s, was the dairy science institute. Groups were frequently shown around the creamery and the college farm.) Another opinion suggesting that the city was 'shy' of the college[11] was substantiated by the relatively small attendance[12] at the following year's two-day conversazione and by the press's repeated emphasis that a large proportion had never seen the college before: 'It is somewhat strange, though not inexplicable, that the people of Cork should be so unacquainted as to be almost indifferent to the existence of such beautiful buildings in which work of such outstanding importance is carried on'. (The *Examiner*'s coverage had, in part, a flippantly sexist slant: apparently the women were particularly interested in the chemical distillation of perfume.)[13]

An important (and balanced) editorial surveyed the college–community relationship in the mid-1920s.[14] It pondered the basic question: given the enthusiasm displayed twenty years before in canvassing for a popular university, and also given the assurances conveyed to the masses that the new institution would be for the 'poor man's son' as well as for the wealthy, how was the apparent apathy of the public now to be explained? There had been a disappointing lack of Scottish-type 'private benefaction' – Crawfords and Honans excepted – and of public subscription. Predicting that 'the university of the future will be a much more democratised institution than the university of the past', the editorial concluded that academic aloofness and public apathy were both to blame, but felt confident that the college would respond to public demands for its services.

Elsewhere, a report implied a gulf of credibility between citizens and the college. Saying that various experts were 'able and willing' to help the public, the report hoped 'that a great many of our citizens will take the opportunity of convincing themselves of this important though to many unbelievable fact'.[15] Welcoming the conversazione visitors in 1926, President Merriman struck the same notes: before 1909, the college was 'never very much in touch' with the city which 'had given the college the cold shoulder'. Since then, the college had made every effort to be of service to the community: to give only one example, the engineering laboratory carried out testing for public bodies and its latest customer was the Shannon hydroelectric scheme.[16] 'It was for the community to come forward.' The library was also at the disposal of the public.[17] Again at the 1927 conversazione, Merriman chattily drew the visitors (whose numbers were down from the previous year) into his confidence about college problems. Modernisation of the premises inevitably meant loss: steam heating of the examination hall meant spoiling the beautiful fireplace, and the consequence of the library overflow was the putting up of unsightly bookcases in the examination hall, and the erection of a wooden hoarding instead of a beautiful railing. Accommodation was at a premium all over the college.[18]

Registrar O'Rahilly addressed himself to the same theme of college–community relations, but did so with characteristic substance and vigour. He castigated 'public apathy' where UCC was concerned: for many, 'it went still by the old name of Queen's College'. There had been no sustained interest in extension lectures. Listing the strengths and weaknesses of the college and again emphasising its services to the community, the registrar said quality rather than quantity should be the goal – increased numbers were not necessarily valuable in themselves. O'Rahilly's audience rose enthusiastically, as always, to the anti-Dublin rhetoric which was a stock piece of his repertoire: the college should be liberated from Dublin control, the three NUI TDs[19] were all Dubliners and 'Cork University College' was subordinate to and hampered by the 'so-called' NUI.[20] What particularly ruffled Cork feathers was UCD's habit, copied by the press, of styling itself 'National'.[21]

It had been said at a Philosophical Society inaugural in 1926 that there was little or no town–gown rivalry in Cork, because town knew little of gown, and cared less.[22] The conversaziones represented an interesting attempt by the college to reach out eagerly to an apathetic community. One powerful motive for doing so was to seek financial support at the urging of the government, 'from local bodies and private benefactors'.[23] The conversazione initiative was a failure as a fund-raising drive but was moderately successful as a public relations exercise. The college was to score better in specific initiatives, such as establishing links with the School of Commerce and the Technical Institute.

UCC and the Examiner

If there was a 'want of understanding'[24] between the college and the community, it was certainly not the fault of 'de paper'. The *Examiner*, it was true, was intermittently critical of 'certain features of Irish university education'. Its editorials harped from time to time on a favourite theme – the NUI's failure, despite the 1908 Act's promises, to offer degree courses for extern students on the London University model, with the result that university education remained 'a closed preserve for the comparatively few who can afford to attend the Colleges'.[25] There was the occasional faintly sneering, anti-academic, anti-student sermon,[26] and a regular pattern of utilitarian, 'bread-and-butter' musings on education. (These leading articles were popularly attributed to a writer unrejoicing in the nickname of Pontius Pilate.) On the other hand, there was extraordinarily comprehensive coverage of college affairs, especially when measured by later standards. Public lectures by academics were covered in great detail even when the subject was more technical than popular.[27] (Such lectures were never less than 'interesting' and frequently 'brilliant'.) A controversial college 'story', which was widely reported and provoked much angry reaction, was Dr Michael Grimes's revelation that much of the milk sold in Cork city was dirty.[28] A 'notes and comments' feature regularly carried the activities of college clubs and societies.[29] The *Examiner*'s interest in the college was enthusiastically reciprocated. The local academics regularly wrote feature articles for the paper,[30] and joined in discussions in the correspondence columns with remarkable frequency and at considerable length. (Cork Chamber of Commerce and Rotary also gave Cork dons well-publicised platforms.) The *Examiner*–college relationship was mutually beneficial, since both parties in different ways had a product to sell. *The Irish Press* from its inception in 1931 took a considerable interest in UCC[31] and regularly featured such prominent professors as O'Rahilly and Busteed, whose views seemed to accord with the *Press*'s own philosophy of a sturdily self-sufficient, independent Ireland.

UCC and business

The college was particularly anxious to make better contact with the world of business in Cork and Munster. Three of the academic staff were involved in establishing Ideal Weatherproofs Ltd in 1933.[32] Businessmen traditionally had little respect for academic courses in commerce,[33] and there were pathetic pleas for the poorly regarded Bachelor of Commerce degree to be given a chance.[34] Some commerce students gained practical

9.1a Trade unionists attending a workers' course in social and economic science pictured with President Alfred O'Rahilly, Prof. Busteed, Fr O'Leary, Mr Weldon, Mr Parfrey and Mr Goggin.

9.1b Inauguration of the workers' diploma course in social and economic science at the Central Technical Institute, Waterford in November 1948. Second row (L-R): M. A. Coughlan; Patrick F. Parfrey; Fr Jerome O'Leary; A. K. Killeen (CEO Waterford VEC); President Alfred O'Rahilly; Fr John V. Fitzgerald; Professor John Busteed.

experience by being placed in Cork business houses during the long vacation.[35] But Cork business was particularly impressed by one remarkable academic who, almost single-handedly, was responsible for getting downtown commerce to adopt a much more favourable attitude to the college. This was the brilliant, unorthodox professor of economics, John Busteed who, next to O'Rahilly, was the city's most favoured academic, as well as a highly popular lecturer with the workers who attended extension courses and eventually studied for the adult education Diploma in Social and Economic Science. Busteed disarmed the commercial community at the outset by a Chamber of Commerce address which was brutally critical of Cork, its economic prospects and its 'bedraggled' appearance.[36] Things could only improve from that point. Four years later, he could say that, though he had been impatient with old fogeys when he came to Cork, he now knew no business community anywhere which would give the same support and understanding to a commerce faculty as Cork had given to UCC.[37]

Busteed was also instrumental in getting the Cork Chamber of Commerce to organise the setting up, through corporate and individual business subscriptions, of a bureau of economic research, modelled on similar units at Harvard and London, under his own directorship at UCC. This would gather statistical data relating to banks, agricultural credit, taxation, tariffs, trade balances and so on, providing a most useful guide for businessmen. Busteed subsequently defended the idea against dissidents in the Chamber of Commerce, and said the money subscribed had improved his departmental premises at UCC, as well as giving employment to carpenters, plumbers and fitters.[38]

UCC, the School of Comm. and the Tech.

The college's connection with the Cork Municipal School of Commerce and the Municipal Technical Institute in the 1930s and 1940s was a particularly fulfilling extramural relationship, involving practical and fruitful educational co-operation. The connection extended back to Windle's time and was not without its problems, since the junior partners in the relationship, so to speak, were inclined to be suspicious that they were being used by the college, whose facilities their own students were not in a position to avail of fully. There was disappointment, if not disenchantment, when the NUI declined to extend recognised status to the School of Commerce (which it had been led to expect), but this did not impair the long-term relationship.

In June 1940, O'Rahilly as registrar expressed the college's appreciation of the very valuable help its students were receiving from the School of Commerce where the shorthand and typing courses they attended enhanced the practical value of the BComm degree.[39] Similarly, those first year chemistry students in UCC who did not have a Leaving Certificate honours qualification in the subject were required to attend first year courses at the Municipal Technical Institute.[40] UCC and Cork City Vocational Education Committee (VEC) expressed mutual satisfaction at how well this arrangement worked out, and the head of physics and chemistry at the institute, J.C. Ahern, was made an honorary member of the UCC teaching staff.[41] The chairman of Cork City VEC expressed the hope in 1943 that a college of technology would soon be founded: in the meantime, however, the VEC was glad to harvest the fruits of its association with UCC.[42] The Diploma in Chemical Technology was first awarded at the July 1944 conferring ceremony, and the first recipient was Seán O'Leary, a brewer at Beamish and Crawford.[43] This was a popular mark of recognition of a productive town–gown relationship. A university Diploma in Commerce was another welcome development.

The ultimate flowering of this admirable co-operation with downtown educational institutions was the 1946 launch of the Diploma in Social and Economic Science. This imaginative initiative, the pioneering enterprise of Alfred O'Rahilly's adult education movement, would not have been possible without the collaboration of the trade unions and the Cork City VEC. The role of the School of Commerce was particularly indispensable, since the diploma students studied their practical subjects in the school.

Adult education

The story of the adult education movement in Cork and Munster is richly documented and well written up.[44] The writer will not retread the ground here, though he would like to note his own interest in the movement, as attested by the delivery of innumerable 'special lectures' over three decades in diploma-course centres all over Munster. *Quae regio in Momonia non est plena nostri laboris?* The whole development was a brilliant O'Rahilly inspiration, sustained by dedicated hard work on his part and on that of his associates, particularly Pádraig Parfrey and Rev. Jerome O'Leary. The Munster dimension fulfilled the province-wide remit of Queen's College Cork, and the declared objective of the UCC Governing Body in 1910 of extending 'the sphere of usefulness throughout Munster'.[45] The adult education courses were maintained after O'Rahilly's departure, though some college authorities regarded them as a marginal activity. The original ethos – to some extent formed by the crusading preoccupation of the time – became dated, and a certain ossification set in. Nevertheless, the radically transformed and expanded department of adult and continuing education of the 1990s, now in the college mainstream, is animated by the same spirit of community service that motivated the movement's founders.

The adult education movement of fifty years ago was firmly set in the contemporary dominant climate of Catholic sociology, of which Alfred O'Rahilly was the leading exponent. Accordingly, one powerful reason for founding the movement was to keep Catholic workers out of the clutches of the secular-minded Workers' Educational Association.[46] O'Rahilly also had to contend with a minority of disapproving academics who felt college energies should be reserved for 'real' students and whose reservations about adult education were partly derived from class prejudice and snobbishness. The writer recalls the brutally caustic comment, made only half in jest, of one of the college's professorial 'characters', long since dead: 'I'm not sure if I agree with this idea of O'Rahilly's. It's trying to make Jack as good as his master – and he isn't, damn him!' Finally, despite the understandable jubilation and euphoria marking the successful conclusion of the first diploma course for workers, the event was hardly a revolutionary breakthrough for the working class. The real educational and professional meat was still the prerogative of the privileged. The 'poor man's son' had still to inherit the college.

The diploma courses grew out of a number of earlier elements, the most popular and enduring of which was the university extension lecture. Though such lectures, under joint college–corporation auspices, were given in Windle's time (indeed, lectures open to the public date back to the early days of Queen's College), it was only in the early 1930s that the extension scheme was linked to tutorial classes and study circles for workers. It was understood that lecture courses would deal in particular with subjects of interest to the working class.[47] Topics covered in 1938, for example, included work, property, corporatism, vocational government, and Catholic social and economic thinking. The general thrust was that of Catholic sociology as an antidote to secularism and irreligion, and English Catholics of a conservative hue were prominent as guest lecturers.[48] Christopher Hollis, for example, packed out the dairy science theatre on an October Sunday night in 1938.[49] Such visitors spoke idyllically of Catholic Ireland as a model for the degenerate outside world. One lecturer developed his theme to melodramatic lengths, to the tumultuous applause of his audience. 'Will you serve God or Mammon?', Catholic convert, Commander H. Shove, asked rhetorically, asserting that he would rather see Ireland free and eating potatoes than eating bread and being the slaves of industrialists.[50]

A highlight of the extension courses in the early 1930s was the awarding of scholar-ships to a small group, enabling them to attend a summer school in Oxford for Catholic workers, organised by the Catholic Social Guild.[51] Selected working men would thus be inculcated with Catholic social principles, and the Cork Workers' Council subsequently heard glowing reports of the experiment.[52]

UCC and the museum question

From the 1920s to the 1940s, the museum question was intermittently debated. The basic issues were: the inadequacies and inaccessibility of college museums, and the need for a new museum building (possibly on college premises or on a handed-over gaol site), funded by the college or city or both, and serving as a regional centre for Munster.[53] There was the usual anti-metropolitan flavour about the discussion: why should all valuable antiquities (particulary Munster's) be housed in Dublin? The college was criticised for its alleged indifference to public needs in regard to the museum question. Rohu, the furriers, stated that widespread ignorance of natural history extended to the college itself: when they offered a specimen of rare shark many years before 'to a certain President of the Queen's College', his facetious suggestion that it be stuffed with sage and onions provoked a caustic response from the professor of natural history and caused the specimen to be lost to the National Museum in Dublin![54] Dick Anthony, the chairman of the Cork Workers' Council, believed a UCC-centred museum would help to bring the masses into closer contact with the university 'and tend to democratise that institution'.[55]

In 1931, there seemed to be moves afoot nationally to develop museum services, particularly with a view to training staff, and there was a report that UCC was preparing for a new forward effort.[56] The problem, as Professor Renouf (a committee member of the British Museum Association) pointed out, was that the collections – natural history exhibits, ogham stones and so on – were fine but the college had no space in which to show them to the public.[57] Many exhibits were still in packing cases, and meagre accommodation meant crammed showcases and inadequate classification. Could part of the new city hall be set aside for a museum, or would the college be uneasy about lending its collection if not assured of good care? (In retrospect, the college's concern seems ironic, given the dispersal, long since, of the natural history museum items.) Another possibility was the relocation of a museum in the Fitzgerald Park premises, taken over by the corporation after the burning of the city hall, but soon to be available again.[58] There was an absence of enthusiasm for that idea, mainly because of what was seen as a peripheral location.

The question dragged on. At an extension lecture in 1935, Seán Ó Ríordáin (soon to be professor of archaeology (1936–43)), advocated the setting up of a civic museum.[59] Two years later, President Merriman claimed that a public museum in Cork would stimulate interest in local history and archaeology, thereby enhancing civic spirit and morale.[60] Two years later again, Professor Ó Ríordáin declared that it was 'a slur on Cork that there is no public museum', adding that smaller cities in England and Germany had very fine museums.[61] After yet another two years, the *Examiner* editorially deplored the lack of a museum decade after decade, pointing out that the 'Park' museum was closed since 1924 and the college natural history museum was too crowded to accommodate visitors.[62]

When at last there was movement on the matter, the understanding was that the college, with a consultative committee, would have jurisdiction over the museum[63] while the corporation would be substantially responsible for its financial upkeep (striking a rate for the purpose) with the county council making a minor contribution. There was general disappointment that, with all the talk over the years of a specially designed building, the decision in the end was to use the Fitzgerald Park house. In June 1943, Ald. Sir John Fitzgerald, a trustee of the park, handed over the keys to the lord mayor for the purpose for which the building was donated to the city, namely, that of a municipal museum. In the course of subsequent publicity, it was stressed that the museum had to be a co-operative enterprise.[64] Professor John Busteed, a museum committee member, said that the project would help to counter 'Dublinitis' and that there had been a wonderful response to appeals for subscriptions.[65]

Finally, and with something of a flourish, the restored museum was opened by a government minister, P.J. Little, on 5 April 1945. Alfred O'Rahilly presided and had his usual tilt at Dublin which, he said, unfortunately had the monopoly of the word 'national'.[66] The curator, M.J. O'Kelly (professor of archaeology, 1946–81, and the outstanding field archaeologist of his day) and Professor Busteed appealed for funds.[67] Earlier, at a preview for the corporation, President O'Rahilly said the college was glad to spend money on the new civic enterprise (curator's salary, £350; property on loan worth £1,100), act as trustees for the citizens, and manage the museum during an experimental period. City manager, Philip Monahan, hoped that the museum would have a worthy location in the Grand Parade one day, with the Fitzgerald Park building being used as a storehouse.[68]

In January 1946, the Taoiseach, Eamon de Valera, visited the museum and was received by the curator, M.J. O'Kelly. An enraged President O'Rahilly explained that he had not been informed about the visit, declaring that since the institution was under UCC's and his jurisdiction '. . . we should have been honoured to receive him'.[69] Within a short time, there were complaints that college promises concerning the museum were not being kept. The powerful Monahan was never pleased that the institution was under the college's direction. 'Pat Freeman' in the *Examiner* asserted that it was being sought to reduce the temporary curator's salary to £100 per annum, and what could be expected for this nominal sum? The corporation should take over, and

9.2 M. J. O'Kelly, professor of archaeology, 1946–81.

make it a museum, not a mausoleum.[70] O'Rahilly quickly responded that the college would turn over the museum to the corporation at any time, while he regretted the circumstances that had forced the building to close for several months.[71]

The museum, now the Cork Public Museum, has had a cramped and limited life from its inception to this very day. In 1962 it became a part of Cork Corporation services, though the college continued to have representatives on its advisory committee.[72] Perhaps too much was expected over the decades from the college's limited resources. Notwithstanding the high quality and dedication of its successive curators, the museum continues to be the cinderella of municipal cinderellas – the least esteemed of city hall's cultural poor relations. Despite being a major tourist attraction, its location is still peripheral, and its budgeting and accommodation ludicrously inadequate by the standards of any comparably sized European city.

Even more culpably, the college's museum services are now non-existent, with its heritage – from the Bunnell Lewis plaster casts to the natural history exhibits and the O'Sullivan Beare portrait – dispersed, and thrown in obscure corners, a hidden testimony to a philistine scale of priorities. The history of the museum question in Cork, civic and academic, is one of sad neglect and broken promises.

Graduates associating

A number of impulses, in varying combinations, are involved in the formation of a graduates' association. These can be detected at different points in the history of the college. As early as 1859, a downtown philosophical society was formed to develop links between Cork-based graduates and those who had left the city.[73] Again, the Old Corkonians was an association of Queen's College graduates in England who wanted to maintain contact with one another and with the college. Nostalgia and loyalty to their alma mater made them protest against the change of the college's name in 1908–09. Sentiments of attachment and mutual solidarity are obviously stronger among emigrant graduates, and their large numbers in the greater London area and within the compact confines of England as a whole have made it relatively easy for them to associate. Hence the success of the NUI Graduates' Club. Apart from the social benefits of association, affection for the old college (rather than for the National University which, understandably, is a remote and nebulous abstraction for the average graduate, however important it may be in the acceptability of degree standards) expresses itself occasionally in funding the award of a graduates' medal or prize, perhaps to be competed for in specific areas of study. Left to themselves, however, graduates have not progressed beyond such gestures, and intermittent appeals to them to become substantial benefactors of their alma mater have in the past fallen on deaf ears.

Recent years have witnessed the new phenomenon of the college itself using its personnel and resources to organise an official, college-sponsored graduates' association on a global as well as an Irish basis. For example, faculty reunions on campus are encouraged and co-ordinated. The objective is to encourage, sustain and eventually cash in on graduate loyalty to an institution for services rendered. Previously, the college regarded graduates' associations with benign passivity: now it takes the initiative (as in the UCC Foundation) in bluntly asking graduates to put their money where their nostalgia is, at a period when money is badly needed for development plans, and is not forthcoming elsewhere. This new approach is proving to be slowly successful.

The formation of a graduates' association at local level – Cork or Munster – has its own rationale. A local association has social, cultural and continuing-educational purposes, it encourages promising students, and it welcomes home emigrant graduates on seasonal visits. But local graduates' associations may also be motivated by exclusiveness, snobbery or the spirit of faction, and the members sometimes fall out over political issues. Finally, women graduates, having their separate interests, have seen fit to form their own association.

Some of these elements are illustrated in the activities of UCC graduates over the decades. A preliminary meeting of graduates was held in a South Mall premises in October 1928, with a view to establishing a permanent organisation to 'conserve' the interests of UCC graduates resident in Munster, and to put forward representatives for the GB election. Dr E. Magner was in the chair, and the medical profession was strongly represented. It was stressed that any involvement in party politics would wreck the organisation.[74] There was an immediate protest in the press from Réamonn Ó Cinnéide (chemistry lecturer through Irish, and ardent Irish-Irelander) that the conveners had not issued many invitations and that they were either very shy or very exclusive![75] In response, Dr T.F. Hegarty with an address at St Patrick's Hill, Cork's Harley Street, honorary secretary of the newly formed Munster Graduates' Association, explained that the lack of a name-and-address register made it difficult to have a more representative gathering, which in any case was only the prelude to an imminent general meeting.[76] Though Ó Cinnéide was still suspicious that there had been a preemptive attempt to instal a caucus,[77] a potential split and the possible formation of two rival associations were averted. The provisional association put forward four independent candidates for the GB election.[78]

Ó Cinnéide continued to press for a more representative association to be formed,[79] and the Munster Graduates' Association finally emerged at a meeting in March 1929 where Ó Cinnéide was elected as a committee member, Dr Hegarty as honorary treasurer, and the medical presence was diluted overall. It was decided that a University Graduates' Club, Cork (or Cumann na gCéimithe i gCorcaigh) would promote social and intellectual relations among UCC graduates, as well as other university graduates in the Cork area.[80] The first annual dinner of the club (of which Professor P.T. O'Sullivan was president) was held on Hallowe'en 1929. President Merriman expressed the hope that some guestrooms could be provided for former students visiting the alma mater.[81] (This was a commendable idea which, alas, has remained only a notion.)

A few months later, during the Christmas season, the club held a reunion in the Victoria Hotel. About fifty attended and graduates home on holidays were welcomed. Dr J.C. Harte, the honorary secretary, said membership would have to be enlarged if they wanted to have a club premises. He listed lectures, recitals and excursions as club activities.[82] On two successive occasions at least, the club organised a successful and well-attended Gaelic celebrity concert in the Aula Maxima.[83] But the club's principal events came to be the reunion at Christmas time (which facilitated holidaying emigrant graduates) and an annual autumn-conferring dinner (held for many years at the Imperial Hotel) where the new graduates were among the guests.[84]

The locally based graduates' association did useful work in that it encouraged student endeavour, made new graduates feel at home, welcomed holidaying emigrant graduates, contributed to worthy causes and, through its cultural events, kept minds sharp that might otherwise have rusted. Yet an association of graduates had a certain exclusiveness and artificiality, and it existed less for the benefit of the college than for the enhancement of the graduates' status in society at large, especially at a time when the relative fewness of graduates served to emphasise their importance to themselves as an elite.

Anti-college snipings

The games/athletics side of college life came in for frequent public criticism. A.J. Beckett and E. Barrett of the UCC Athletic Club stoutly defended the position of athletics in the college against a Mr Dynan, NT, who had claimed that 'there seems to be nobody in that university who gives even an iota of attention to athletics'.[85] Much annoyance was expressed that an important soccer match in February 1926 could not be played in the UCC grounds because of the high fee demanded. The UCC Grounds Committee was described 'as a most autocratic personnel' which would not even make the grounds available the previous season for a St Vincent de Paul charity game. The college authorities, said the writer, should reflect on the fable of the greedy boy and the nuts.[86]

Outside sporting organisations felt that the college was unfairly privileged, in terms of resources and otherwise, when it came to competitive games: in short, the playing field was not level! There were arguments, for example, about date fixtures for GAA championship games, and assertions that the students had more time and better facilities at their disposal than clubs whose teams were full-time workers with little leisure time for training.[87] But there was also outside sympathy for those promoting the GAA in the college, because it was believed they were working in an environment hostile to Gaelic culture.[88] There was a perception of an institution allegedly inimical or indifferent to the Irish language revival. In 1937, the president of the Gaelic League referred to the 'British outlook' and 'studied reactionary attitude' of UCC and UCD.[89] However, the college authorities may have felt they were striking the right balance, considering they were also under attack for making extravagant provisions for teaching Irish. Cork county councillors felt it was wasteful to have four highly paid professors of Irish and various lecturers teaching through Irish.[90]

The college creamery seemed an unlikely target for criticism but there were complaints from Dick Anthony (a frequent proletarian critic of the college) and W.J. O'Sullivan HC, when UCC, subsidised by government, tendered to the North Infirmary Committee for butter supply. O'Sullivan sarcastically commented that the college

9.3 College club emblems from *Quarryman*, 1940s.

would be in the drapery business next![91] Joe Lyons, manager of the college creamery, made a prompt and spirited reply (as was usual for college staff at the time). There was no question, he said, of the government grant subsidising the college creamery, which was a commercial concern. Training students necessitated the large scale manufacture of butter. The system was that the college took the cream from the co-ops, churned it, sold the butter and returned to the co-ops all monies received less a fixed charge for manufacturing costs.[92]

A somewhat surprising anti-academic voice was that of Mgr Sexton, Catholic dean of Cork. At a Gaelic League public meeting in October 1928, Sexton spoke disparagingly, if facetiously, about the uselessness of universities in most pragmatic contexts. President Merriman made a mild, and Senator Dowdall (GB) a more robust, rebuttal on behalf of the college.[93] A few years later, at a public lecture given by Archbishop Downey of Liverpool in the presence of Bishop Cohalan of Cork, Sexton made further derogatory remarks, obviously playing for anti-intellectual laughs to a gallery which obligingly responded. Referring to the archbishop's lecture, he said they should be thankful they had someone to guide them and 'not be left at the mercy of the professors' who, he suggested, should confine themselves to looking after students.[94]

Was Sexton's a petulant maverick voice? More probably he spoke for the Cork Catholic clerical constituency, or at least a section of it. In that period, ecclesiastics tended to be resentful and suspicious of an independent lay intellectual world even where that world, UCC in this case, was so far from being secular that it was sincerely and quite safely inspired by the Catholic ethos. Moreover, Bishop Cohalan and his priests had not forgotten O'Rahilly's temerity, a decade or so before, in defending revolutionary nationalism against the bishop's condemnation. The description of O'Rahilly as a 'lay theologian' was still widely current in clerical circles, and was not used as a compliment.

The various anti-college barbs cited above, even when added up, do not amount to anything like a community rejection. On the contrary, the gradual public acceptance (or 'ownership', to use a modern term) of an erstwhile alien institution is unmistakable. And J.C. Foley was right: it was the college which 'came down town and fraternised' with the community. The courtship process, which had tentatively stirred in Windle's time but could not properly develop then for various reasons, really got under way with the conversaziones of the mid-1920s. Individual professors have to be given various degrees of credit for the successfully advancing relationship: Alfred O'Rahilly for his all-round involvement in community affairs, his co-operation with the School of Commerce and the Technical Institute under VEC auspices, and later in the 1940s the flowering of his adult education movement; John Busteed for charming the businessmen and helping to change their inherited blinkered attitude to UCC; and, increasingly, Aloys Fleischmann for his invaluable contribution to – indeed, his shaping of – the musical life of the city, extending over half a century.

The new entrance gates

The visual impact of the college on its neighbourhood became even more imposing with the erection of the new entrance gates on the Western Road in 1929. The entrance and new bridge had been eagerly awaited ever since the old bridge was swept away in the disastrous 1916 flood. Absence of funds and the high cost of labour and materials had been adduced as the main reasons for the delay, which met with much criticism.[95] But at the 1928 conversazione, President Merriman also mentioned the unprecedented deep pile drivings in the river bed because of soft foundations.[96] Apologising for the temporary entrance from Fernhurst Avenue, Merriman said a worthy new entrance would enable UCC to make a stronger case to government for a more impressive dairy science institute: it was now very important to have a fine building against the background of a new entrance and main avenue.[97]

Two years before the new entrance was completed, the *Examiner* described the plans in some detail, accompanied by a sketch. The entrance would not be at the former site (which had been a little farther west) but positioned across the Donovan's Road–

Western Road junction, and buildings acquired at the point would be demolished. The entrance, designed by Cork architects O'Connor and O'Flynn, was to be of two large cut-stone pieces (later described as of solid but graceful design) with ornamental wrought-iron gates and railings, and the college coat of arms in an overhead arch. Behind the gates would be a new avenue and a ferro-concrete bridge in one 60-foot arch, with ornamental side railings like those at the entrance. The new structures would open up an uninterrupted view of the college and the grounds, heretofore hidden away.[98]

The *Examiner* of 22 October 1929 published a photograph of the new entrance. The previous day's issue had described the imposing structure and stated it would be one of the city's principal landmarks. The paper noted that all the work was done in Ireland – the gates by Messrs McLaughlin, Dublin and the railings by John Buckley and Sons, Cork.[99]

Irish speakers were indignant that the inscription on the gates was not bilingual: surely, the 'galaxy of Irish professors' should be able to frame a suitable version of the 'Where Finbarr taught' motto in Finbarr's own language![100] In fact, a Gaelic League representative had an interview with President Merriman on the matter.[101] By the following July, at a UCC garden party marking the granting of the freedom of Cork to Apostolic Nuncio Paschal Robinson, the lord mayor, Cllr F.J. Daly, referred to the sacred precincts where St Finbarr had laboured as 'Ionad Bhairre Sgoil na Mumhan'.[102] It seems therefore that the present Irish version of the college motto was composed early in 1930, and that it owes its existence to the college's response to complaints about the monolingual English form on the new gates. Only the Irish motto now appears there.

Another important bridge over the river Lee (north channel) had been in use from 1927. This was the elegant suspension footbridge named Daly's Bridge and popularly known as 'the shaky bridge'. It spanned the north channel from Sunday's Well to Ferry Walk, and greatly facilitated the approach to the college for many staff and student pedestrians. But the new college entrance gates, through which the nuncio's entourage swept on that summer day in 1930, were artistically and symbolically impressive, openly ushering in, or so it seemed, the citizens' yearning to be educated. It is unfortunate, then, and also perhaps unhappily symbolic, that these splendid main gates have remained closed to traffic for many years now.

UCC and the Emergency

The Emergency period meant irritations, shortages and restrictions for UCC (as it did for the country at large) but it caused no major upheaval in the placid tenor of college life which remained essentially unchanged until the 1960s.[103] Perhaps the Catholic – and nationalist – ethos of the time was accentuated, as the state turned inward on itself. Foreign travel (on studentships, or to conferences) was obviously restricted, and international contacts were limited. At that stage of the college's development, however, only a minority of staff, and very few students,[104] were affected by the narrowing of these horizons. Musical activities appeared to be undiminished, and pianist Benno

Moseiwitch gave a recital under the auspices of the Art Society early on in the war.[105] The college also occasionally hosted scholars such as Ludwig Bieler who were war refugees. Guest lecturers and debaters from Dublin and elsewhere in the state continued to visit UCC and helped maintain a surprisingly vigorous level of debate on various topics. Life in Emergency Ireland was far from being the stagnant pool suggested in certain superficial surveys.

Various areas of college life had to adjust to Emergency conditions. Drays and wagonettes took the place of lorries and cars on rag day, and old sacks were adapted for costumes.[106] More seriously, students who joined the defence forces were granted certain examination exemptions by the NUI Senate.[107] As an economy-cum-convenience measure, the GBs of the constituent colleges had their term of office extended by special legislation (University Colleges Bill 1940).[108]

The extent of shortages and the degree of inconvenience were frequently determined by the foresight or lack of it shown by individual officers and departments. The Emergency had been anticipated, for example, by the department of chemistry which consequently did not lack for laboratory instruments and materials, but then chemistry had been an active research department all along.[109] Joseph Downey, the popular and efficient bursar and secretary, had stockpiled some coal which he got painted to identify it as college property and so give it some measure of protection against theft. But turf and timber soon took over as far from ideal sources of heat and energy. Former college attendants recall stacks of turf in the Quarry and the Medical Quadrangle whence it was drawn by horseload into bunkers near the Arch and thence conveyed by chute to the boiler room.[110] As warden of the Honan Hostel, Downey had prudently stocked up on chests of tea and sacks of sugar to supplement the meagre official rations. According to Eilís Dillon (who heard the story from Downey's successor as warden, Professor M.D. McCarthy), President O'Rahilly arranged a convenient interregnum in the wardenship when Downey died in office in 1944, and used it to remove Downey's store of tea and sugar to the president's house, greatly to the benefit of the college restaurant but sadly to the detriment of the hostel residents.[111]

Professor 'Joss' Reilly, the pragmatic bent of whose chemistry researches made him popular with government and press, offered some nutritious words of wisdom to the public, at this time of various dietary restrictions. Having written *Our Daily Bread*, he advised *Examiner* readers that wholemeal bread, which should not be stigmatised as 'black bread',[112] was an excellent foodstuff.[113] Mushrooms, he reminded *Irish Press* readers, had much nutritional value.[114] More ambitiously, he urged extensive cultivation of oil-producing plants for the production of oils and fats necessary for Irish industrial output.[115] Meanwhile, Professor Louis Renouf (zoology) in an interview in England, received with scant enthusiasm, helpfully listed seagulls, snails and seaweed as sources of food supply.[116] Professor Sperrin-Johnson (botany) was asked by the Cork Chamber of Commerce to help British manufacturing chemists whose overseas sources of dried medical plants had been cut off.[117] The *Examiner* recalled that Sir Bertram Windle had set up a clearing house for plants during the Great War.[118]

In contrast to that war, when there was an enthusiastic pro–British recruiting element among the staff (led by President Windle), increasingly opposed after 1916 by resurgent nationalists, the Emergency saw a virtual unity of patriotic purpose in the college, reflecting the national mood. A letter to the *Examiner* in December 1941 from the group leaders of the Local Defence Force (LDF) in the college stated that the eighty-strong force had been quietly in training since February, without benefit of military bands or patronage of public figures. It had undergone combat and engineering programmes in Collins Barracks and had been on manoeuvres, under its main director, Lt Mícheál Ó Séaghdha (afterwards professor of dairy technology). There was also a second-line ambulance unit of 100 members. The letter claimed that UCC was making a good contribution, proportionally, to 'the defence of Éire'.[119] At the close of the students' retreat in 1944, Bishop Cohalan inspected and blessed the LDF company.[120] Members wore their uniforms with pride, as is evident from the 1945 conferring picture of Lt Desmond M. Reilly with his father, Professor 'Joss'.[121] Students lacking in martial ardour had another practical outlet for their patriotism. President O'Rahilly and Professor Joseph Lyons (dairy technology, 1940–53) consulted with the County Cork Farmers' Association in June 1944 with a view to recruiting a land army of student volunteers to help save the harvest. It was emphasised that the students, who were to receive a modest sum in pocket money, would not displace the farm labour force![122]

The war had a greater impact on medical students and graduates than on any other section of the college community. Recently qualified Irish doctors availed of the vacancies created in Britain, both in general practice and junior hospital residencies, by their British colleagues on active service. Because of these opportunities, the number of medical students increased in UCC, and they were joined by British students whose own medical training schools were closed. At the end of the war, however, restrictions on Irish doctors in Britain were introduced, since preference would be given to demobilised British doctors. President O'Rahilly warned at the November 1945 conferring ceremony that the profession would experience overcrowding and that quality rather than high numbers would now be the rule in UCC. He suggested that, since there was a shortage of dentists in Britain, more students should consider that profession.[123]

The end of hostilities did not mean an immediate return to pre-war conditions. The Emergency lingered on, but gradually students began to travel again to take up postgraduate research, and to fulfil sporting engagements and debating commitments.[124] UCC delegates were part of an Irish team participating in an inter-varsity debate in Liverpool at Easter 1947. The topic was 'that there is no romance in modern life' and the Irish won.[125] Things were back to normal.

One unexpected, and not insignificant, consequence of the Emergency was a drastic reduction in the erstwhile generous press coverage of college affairs. Newsprint restrictions during the war meant smaller issues. When normality was eventually restored, much of wartime adaptation was there to stay. Newspaper styles changed, and college happenings never received the same spacious attention again.

CHAPTER TEN

O'RAHILLY ASCENDANT:
THE 1940S AND 1950S*

. . . a convent run by a mad reverend mother . . .
variously attributed

There but for the grace of God goes God.
Winston Churchill, of Stafford Cripps

IF THE IRISH UNIVERSITIES Act of 1908 was a reasonably satisfactory resolution of the protracted controversy about higher education for Irish Catholics, it invites historical comparison in some respects with the Emancipation Act of 1829. While the two measures had long-term significance and potential for the plain Catholics of Ireland, the immediate beneficiaries in both cases comprised a small and already relatively privileged elite. A generation after the 1908 Act, despite all the optimistic expectations of a 'poor man's university', inequality of educational opportunity was eloquently illustrated by the fact that the largest local authority in Ireland, Cork County Council, offered only three meagre UCC scholarships in competition to school-leavers. There is little evidence that the college establishment over the years was worried about class inequalities of access to its halls of learning. In this respect, Alfred O'Rahilly's Diploma in Social Science for workers was a sop to the academic conscience.

Access to college was partly a matter of geographical location. In pre-commuting days, students living at home in Cork with their parents enjoyed a considerable economic advantage over their country classmates coming from twenty or more miles away and seeking accommodation in lodgings. (During the Emergency and after, it was usual for students from as near as Midleton and Cobh to reside in Cork.) Thus, the accident of home location made all the difference to the fulfilment of aspirations cherished by those belonging to the same socio-economic stratum. Only in the city and in its immediate environs could the phrase 'the poor man's university' have any realisable meaning. In the 1944–45 university session (and for many a session before and after), half of the students at UCC came from the city area, and three-quarters of them hailed from Co. Cork, including the city.[1] This preponderant localism was

---

* This chapter is a revised and expanded version of two articles by the writer in *The Irish Review* (Cork University Press, no. 2, 1987 and no. 4, Spring 1988). The writer was an undergraduate in the late 1940s, and the personal, reminiscent tone of *The Irish Review* articles has been largely retained here.

a major reason for the consistently conservative political temperament of the student body.

But geographical advantage was not nearly as important as the financial position of the prospective student's parents. Fees had to be paid and a relatively leisurely existence subsidised: at that time, working one's way through college or taking a job during the long vacation incurred snobbish disapproval and was, to say the least, not a widespread practice. (Consequently, students other than the privileged had far less spending money than their successors today.) The earning loss to the family for several years had also to be absorbed. In these respects, the prospects of young people from artisan and lower middle class backgrounds (as distinct from those further down the social ladder) improved somewhat from the early 1930s to the late 1940s. But the steady job in the public service remained the most approved goal for the brightest secondary-school pupils.

As far as university education was concerned, it was a golden age for Cork's professional and commercial classes. This bourgeoisie was really an upper class. The *jeunesse dorée* made their presence felt in the upper reaches of the student body and they dominated the professional faculties, in particular the medical and dental schools. Their family dynasties were well represented on the teaching staff and, through part-time professorships, on the Academic Council. All in all, the medical and dental professions constituted, through the university system, a self-perpetuating class.[2] The first inter-university (QUB, TCD, the three NUI colleges) debate since pre-war days was on the motion, 'That the Irish Universities are creating a self-seeking professional aristocracy'.[3] The motion was lost but the case was hardly thereby disproved. The fact that the taxpayer at large shouldered a major burden of university financing was, curiously enough, never widely realised by the public. Needless to say, they were not assiduously enlightened by the benefitting minority.

If for no other than hard financial reasons, then, the university[4] was a remote and shadowy institution for most people in the far-flung regions of the county of Cork and throughout the province of Munster.[5] Yet, long before the fostering of personality cults by the media, certain UCC names had gained some popular prominence. At a time when Catholic apologetics were taken very seriously indeed, Alfred O'Rahilly's vigorous polemics in *The Standard* were avidly read and greatly admired. For cultural nationalists, Daniel Corkery's *The Hidden Ireland* had something of the character of a sacred text. The name of James Hogan (history) at that stage was as much associated with recent Blueshirt politics as with the historian's profession.

To be a UCC student, even of the lowly first arts variety (freshmen were called 'gybs' and 'gybesses'), and to sport the college scarf jauntily was to be at once the object of envious admiration and semi-malicious banter by outsiders. One learned to strike a balance between retaining the cherished friendships of one's home town and nurturing the new acquaintances of an exciting academic milieu. For, contrary perhaps to popular impression, the college in the immediate post-war years was an intellectually exhilarating place, inhabited by a bright run of students. The field of enquiry was not boundless, of course, and the parameters were electrified fences which emitted jolting reminders every so often. But it is historically wide of the mark to envisage Irish university life at that time as suffocatingly dull and provincial, just as F.S.L. Lyons in a rare lapse of historical imagination was mistaken in describing the atmosphere of neutral Ireland during the war in terms of the shadowy and unreal world of Plato's cave.[6] There were frustrations in college life arising from the fatuities of censorship – there was an X-rated section in the library, and one had to establish a bona fide reason for wanting to borrow James Joyce's works – but there was no overwhelming sense of claustrophobia. In fact, a Catholic ethos gave some people a feeling of belonging to a far wider world, in history as in the here and now, in the terrestrial as well as in the supernatural sense.

The forty or so residents of the Honan Hostel suffered the material deprivations of Emergency diet and indifferent cooking but were fortunate enough to experience something of the ambience of a residential university, the general absence of which was frequently deplored in university speeches. As a matter of policy, the hostel authorities gave precedence to applications from scholarship holders: indeed, residence in the hostel was usually a condition of local authority scholarships. Accordingly, Honan Hostel students comprised a sort of intellectual elite drawn from a range of faculties, and the discourse was stimulatingly boundless and free. Newman could have been talking about the hostel residents when he said: 'they are sure to learn one from another, even if there is no one to teach them: the conversation of all is a series of lectures to each'.[7] Ironically, despite the claims in hostel advertisements that the place fostered a climate of Christian study, its essential intellectual attraction was that of a (literally) freethinking fraternity.

In post-war Irish politics, there was an expectation of new beginnings. In college, as in the nation at large, such was the orthodox climate that only a daring few took their bearings from the welfare state across the Irish Sea. The Clann na Poblachta party hitched its wagon to Christian social principles rather than to a star of even moderately reddish hue. The promise of a new dawn at home was linked with something of an apocalyptic scenario in Europe where, in the self-righteous fervour of the first cold war, the Church and Western civilisation were believed to be locked in mortal and immortal combat with the satanic forces of materialistic, atheistic communism. Everywhere (students and public were told) the state, a miasmic monster, threatened. Domestically, it was alleged to take the form of creeping bureaucracy ('statolatry' was a favourite word of President O'Rahilly's) and it was to creep too far in 1951, with dramatic consequences. On the world stage, something could be done to stem the advancing red tide if our Christian (preferably Catholic) intellectuals, in sure possession of the truth, would ably expose the flawed philosophical premises on which Marxism insecurely rested. That impression was strongly conveyed, for example, to Professor James Hogan's history students.

Alfie

As we have seen, the dominant presence of Alfred O'Rahilly in UCC was by no means confined to the years of his presidency (1943–54). We have discussed his predecessor, P.J. Merriman, as a low-key unassertive president, during whose term of office (1919–43), O'Rahilly, the heir-presumptive, came to behave more and more as a *de facto* president.[8] In public utterances and in newspaper correspondence, O'Rahilly regularly spoke for the college, or rather put forward his views as representing the college. His influence derived more from his dynamic personality, national standing, and apparent multidisciplinary omniscience than from the admittedly powerful office of registrar. Such was his stature that he cast his shadow after as well as before. When he became a Holy Ghost priest in 1955 (his 'descent on the Holy Ghost' was the Cork description) his image still dominated the lacklustre reign of his successor, Henry St J. Atkins (1954–63) whose registrarship during the O'Rahilly presidency was a very subordinate office indeed. All in all, it is not fanciful to speak of a whirlwind age of O'Rahilly that lasted upward of forty years.[9]

'Personally, I hate the idea of the Presidency', confided Alfred O'Rahilly a week after he applied for the post and just as he commenced a vigorous canvassing campaign.[10] As president, he was the flesh-and-blood *genius loci* (the last living-in chief executive), the most colourful academic of his time, and the most vibrant president in the history of the college. A volatile and bustling polymath of inexhaustible energy and creativity, a Renaissance universal man who much preferred the Middle Ages, he threw himself with gusto into the great and petty debates of his day. He played an extraordinary number of extramural roles – social crusader, educationalist, political and social arbitrator, constitutional framer, Catholic Actionist, anti-communist polemicist, broadcaster, popular journalist. There were, and are, unflattering assessments of the man, in his own time and afterwards when he rapidly went out of fashion, and the folklore became cruelly unkind to him. He was not offended by the oft-quoted description 'a cross between Thomas Aquinas and Jimmy O'Dea',[11] since he was too big (figuratively speaking) to be concerned about conforming to conventional standards of stuffiness, so lamentably and so often confused with dignity. He knew, but did not care, that sedate colleagues regarded him as something of an academic clown-rogue. 'I never stand on dignity, I talk freely and expect to be talked to in the same way.'[12] He might also have relished a visiting English academic's description of UCC as 'a convent run by a mad reverend mother'. But he was not pleased by *The Irish Times* jibe that he had the best mind of the twelfth century, since he saw himself as a very modern man indeed.[13]

His vast range of scholarly interests – politics, sociology, finance, Christology, mathematical physics, history – aroused astonishment and envy, and it was inevitable that some of his publications should have provoked adverse criticism. One critique of his work on *Money* ended with the reflection that the book would enable people to relieve rural tedium by laughing the nights away.[14] O'Rahilly's contemplated multi-volume life of Christ prompted his NUI colleague, Mgr Pádraig de Brún, to observe that a life of O'Rahilly by Christ would be much more interesting.[15] The quip was neither kind nor original: Chesterton had made the remark in reference to Renan's *Vie de Jesus*, and the witticism doubtless had other purveyors. On a lighter and still mildly irreverent note, O'Rahilly's province-wide lectures on the Holy Shroud of Turin caused the subject to be waggishly dubbed 'Alfie's flying carpet'. But he also had legions of admirers, one of whom remarked that when O'Rahilly became president he left several vacancies to be filled (as the corpulent G.K. Chesterton did whenever he left his seat on a bus).[16]

In his relations with junior academic staff, O'Rahilly was reputed to be something of a bully and exploiter, and the portrait that emerges from the pages of Cormac Ó Cadhlaigh's unpublished memoirs is not a flattering one.[17] Neither is Eilís Dillon's

10.1 Lecturers, assistants and demonstrators, May 1944.
Front row (L–R): C.S. O'Connell; P.M. Quinlan; Miss O'Flaherty; Miss Moynihan; Miss Murphy; President A. O'Rahilly; Mlls. Y. Servais; Miss Walsh; Miss O'Donovan; Mrs Madden, Dr Paschal;
Second row (L–R): Dr O'Callaghan; S. Conlon; Dr Loughnan; S. Neeson; J.F. Buckley;
T. O'Mullane; P. Coffey; C. Ó Ceallaigh; S. Caomhánach; Dr M. E. Folan;
Third row (L–R): H.H. Hill; S.W. Farrington; C.P. McCarthy; E. Ó Donnchadha; R.F. Breathnach; F.A. McGrath; Dr B.F. Honan;
Back row (L–R): M.J. Ó Sé; D.T. McSweeney; S. Pender; P.J. Drumm; J.W. O'Byrne;
W.H. Porter.

recollection of the man.[18] In his residential quarters in the East Wing, his domestic life was hardly idyllic, and written notes conveyed through third parties did duty for marital dialogue over long periods. One reason why his Jesuit superiors turned him down for the priesthood in his younger days, we are told, was his 'extraordinary self-right-eousness'.[19] Students who watched him striding up the Honan Chapel, kneeling bolt upright in his prie-dieu[20] or loudly giving out the liturgical responses were inevitably reminded of Addison's Sir Roger de Coverley and perhaps of Winston Churchill's acid assessment (then very much quoted) of Sir Stafford Cripps: 'There but for the grace of God goes God'.

In the course of his early academic career in Cork, as he rapidly climbed up the *cursus honorum*, he displayed a marked propensity for biting hands that had earlier helped to feed him, and he brought to the academic disputes in which he became embroiled a truculent ruthlessness. Perhaps this was one reason why O'Rahilly's cantankerous and witty presence at academic meetings always held out an exciting prospect.[21] At a moment of disenchantment in his own career, he confided to Seán Ó Faoláin that 'any man under 35 ought to leave this country. No influence, no peace, no elbow room'.[22] In fact, O'Rahilly made plenty of elbow room for himself in UCC, bustling opponents out of the way. His admirers claimed he had no vindictiveness and never brooded over bitter controversies. George O'Brien, the economist, had an acidulous comment on this view: 'One does not forget being bitten by a mad dog. But the mad dog frequently forgets that he has bitten his victim'.[23] However, another facet of this extraordinarily complex man was his kindliness, helpfulness and generosity to staff and students in difficulties. He gave away substantial amounts of his own money to financially embarrassed colleagues and penurious students – and in total privacy.[24]

No other layman of his day so self-confidently assumed a central role in so many areas of Catholic life – philosophy, sociology, theology, scriptural studies. The reverend dean of residence and the reverend professor of philosophy, formidable personalities in their own right, were but Alfred's acolytes, Don Quixote's chaplains. But then O'Rahilly had never relinquished the priestly persona which dominated the beginning and the end of his career, and his sober attire was always paraclerical. He was a *prêtre* who had no intention of remaining for ever *manqué*. His religious arrogance, though quite innocuous, did not make him greatly beloved in high diocesan quarters: in particular, his post-1916 writings on the morality of revolution were resented, not only because they ran counter to the orthodox wisdom of the Ordinary but because his independent expertise offended the professional sensibilities of the clergy. It was at this time that the disparaging epithet 'lay theologian' was coined.[25]

In the 1930–31 session, while O'Rahilly was still registrar, he had clashed with the Catholic dean of residence, Fr James O'Brien, who had objected to a proposed lecture to the Philosoph on the topic of evolution, to be given by Professor Louis P. Renouf (zoology), himself a devout Catholic convert. Renouf withdrew, and a furious O'Rahilly (who had initiated the lecture invitation) co-ordinated protests to President Merriman and Bishop Cohalan of Cork. On successive Sundays in the Honan Chapel, O'Brien (whose sermons were normally unendurable) spoke strongly about intellectual pride and 'a wolf in sheep's clothing'. O'Rahilly had him arraigned before a diocesan court on defamation charges, and although O'Brien was acquitted, he was eventually transferred from his college post, in order to reduce tension.[26]

It is in the area of the petty and the absurd that otherwise outstanding people are liable to stick in the glue of their time. The college authorities in this period attempted to exercise a paternalism, comical in its consequences, over student life and morals. Alfred personally and solemnly advised individual students on the subjects they should choose (his formidable office secretary exercised powers of attorney in this regard); he gave or withheld permission for student debates; and he is reputed, on his grand surveillance prowls through the Quadrangle, to have chastely pinched the legs of seated female students in order to ensure that they were really wearing stockings (scarce and dear during the Emergency) and not the unauthorised lotion with which they were sometimes wont to decorate their nether limbs. However, the graduate-folk recollection is uncertain here: there is a variant memory that this tedious but necessary moral chore was performed by a clerical lieutenant. A related legend has it that a defiant young woman proved beyond doubt that she was wearing stockings by swiftly raising her skirt. There is a documentary basis for these doubtless exaggerated and embellished anecdotes, as the following letter to the women's club president shows:[27]

> University College
> Cork
> 14th May, 1947.
>
> Dear Miss Mitchell,
>
> I want to make it clear that I am not withdrawing my official request to the women students to wear stockings but I am willing not to press the case too much provided no abuses are made of it. Personally, if I were lecturing I would not allow girls to come in without stockings nor do I think they should attend Church without stockings.
>
> After enquiring, I have now ascertained that stockings are cheaper and plentiful at the moment. Therefore, it seems to me that there is no excuse for not wearing them. When the girls go hiking in the summer, etc. I do not mind what they do but we do want a certain amount of dignity and selfrespect here in the College.
>
> If I find any girls sitting down in the quadrangle with knees crossed, etc., and without stockings I shall have to take action.
> Meanwhile, understand that I am not going to be too meticulous unless the abuse becomes widespread.
>
> Yours sincerely
> A. O'Rahilly
> President

(However, we might recall that in his day the severe Bertram Windle insisted on a hair-up style for the women students, thereby causing instant *coiffure* transformations at the college gates.[28])

10.2 The author, John A. Murphy, being conferred
by President Alfred O'Rahilly, 30 October 1951.

O'Rahilly's foibles also included an artless vanity. One day in the new and ugly restaurant, which still stands as a useful, if architecturally repellent, monument to his building zeal,[29] he heard (indeed, was meant to hear) a group of students denouncing Myles na Gopaleen in whose *Irish Times* column O'Rahilly was just then being held up to splenetic ridicule in a parody of 'Kubla Khan': 'where Alph, the sacred raver ran'. He stopped to congratulate the students on their exquisite discrimination and great good sense, but tongues may have been firmly wedged in cheeks all round. It was during the joust between Myles and O'Rahilly that the Philosophical Society – which O'Rahilly regarded as his special forum – tried to have Myles elected a vice-president, hoping that his real name, Brian O'Nolan, would not be recognised by the president.[30]

Nonetheless, the serious point is that the controversies in which O'Rahilly became involved were a source of interest, and even pride, to the students, irrespective of the side they took in these debates. Their president was a pugnacious polemicist, a man of stature and a formidable Catholic intellectual, who brought prestige to UCC. Had he not claimed in 1933: 'I have not now the smallest doubt that I have Einstein refuted'?[31] He was also an exuberant and ubiquitous college presence, forever (or so it seemed) sweeping with flowing gown through Quadrangle, library and restaurant. A vivid (and characteristic) picture flashes into the writer's mind's eye of the president in the gallery of the Aula Maxima, one night in 1945, giving a one-man standing ovation, roaring 'bravo' and 'magnifique' at the conclusion of the dress rehearsal of Aloys Fleischmann's extravaganza, 'Clare's Dragoons', to the mixed embarrassment and amusement of that urbane academic.

More mundanely, O'Rahilly initiated many significant new departures – acquiring the gaol site, developing the library, starting the electrical engineering department, founding the Cork University Press,[32] providing satisfactory health[33] and restaurant services for students (including free meals for student waiters/waitresses) and establishing an adult education network.[34] He was popular with the students in whose welfare he took a paternalistic interest. He must be seen as one of the two great modernising presidents of UCC, the other – in a very different style – being M.D. McCarthy (1967–78). O'Rahilly fervently believed that the university man must serve the wider community outside the walls of academe, and he acted throughout his career on that belief. More than any other president since the foundation of the Queen's College, he personified the link between gown and town, gown and province, gown and nation. He liked to think that he had the common touch (the flat accent and 'Pat Murphy' persona could be seen as indicators) but its application was limited.

The development of adult education courses was an imaginative adaptation of the college motto: Finbarr was now to become a wandering scholar or itinerant schoolmaster throughout Munster. As for Cork itself, it really *was* O'Rahilly's adopted city and he preached the gospel of its economic and industrial expansion.[35] He had served on the corporation in the heroic age of MacCurtain and MacSwiney and he represented the city for a year in Dáil Éireann. (He had also been in jail and on the run!) His links with the local labour and trade union movement were long and close. In any given academic year, his crowded calendar of engagements always included 'downtown' speaking appearances.[36] But the most significant public manifestation of college–community co-operation during his time was the extension lecture system. In a period of sparse educational provision for the public and long before the electronic media were used for educational purposes, the regular lecture series provided a window for the interested people of Cork on the world of higher education. On Sunday nights, the dairy science lecture theatre gate on Donovan's Road was the only portal to the university – Alice's gate into the enchanted garden – through which most of the citizens would ever pass.[37]

In enunciating college policy in regard to the federal university link, O'Rahilly expressed satisfaction with the position obtaining since 1908 – and there was no dissenting voice. The later (and earlier) vogue for 'independence' would probably have been brusquely dismissed by O'Rahilly. Had not UCC virtual independence from the outset?

> This College is an autonomous academic institution and it means to retain its independence. It is the successor of the old Queen's College whose professors were appointed by the government and which sought to impose an alien ideology on our

people. Having won our cultural freedom we mean to keep it, for thereby we can best
serve the cause of liberty, truth and religion against the growing menace of Statolatry.[38]

College (i.e. O'Rahilly) thinking in this area was explained in unsigned 'comments' in
two early issues of the *Cork University Record*. In the first of these, after spirited side-
swipes at University College Dublin (for unjustifiably appropriating the title 'National',
a usurpation always keenly resented by Cork); all things metropolitan; *The Irish Times*
(for its patronising arrogance in wanting to bring Cork in out of the provincial cold
and into contact with the Protestant tradition); and Professor Michael Tierney of UCD
(for assuming the federal bond had outlived its purpose), 'we in UCC' go on to
'express a view'.

> Admittedly, the workings of the federal system could be improved upon but this
> College has full financial and disciplinary independence. It is in many ways a great
> advantage to us to have a central body for academic appointments and standards. And
> there is increasing recognition of the different needs and outlooks of the Colleges. It
> cannot be maintained that the functioning of a common Senate impedes our progress
> or individuality. On the contrary, the existence of such a joint body is of great help
> towards maintaining academic autonomy. This last point is the most important
> consideration which makes many of us soft-pedal local patriotism. The University
> which has a Charter (so has each of the Colleges) provides a practical (if not ideal)
> solution of a delicate and difficult religious problem. We are not anxious to put this
> again into the melting pot. Nor – with all due deference to our legislators – are we
> desirous of starting the habit of dissolving or establishing Universities by Act of
> Parliament. In this country we have no tradition or experience in such matters; few
> have such direct acquaintance with conditions elsewhere as to realise the importance of
> protecting academic autonomy against the subtle encroachments of the State. Anyway,
> it is well to draw attention to the fact that so far it is not from Cork that suggestions for
> breaking up the NUI have come.[39]

Shortly afterwards, the theme was re-stated, the context being the recent agitation for
new university institutions in Waterford and Limerick. This time the concern voiced
(about possible hazards of new university legislation) was not simply for academic
autonomy but for the Catholic ethos of UCC:

> It is not for selfish interests but solely to preserve our indispensable autonomy,
> especially in its religious aspect, that we are opposed to any interference with our
> existing rights guaranteed by our Charters. Especially in the Cork College, we have
> shown that our existing powers are ample for securing a thoroughly Catholic
> education for our co-religionists. We consider that our hardly won position would be
> completely jeopardised and endangered if we lost such guarantees and became subject
> to what would practically be a political majority in the Dail.[40]

An age of faith

The truth was that UCC, by charter non-denominational, by O'Rahilly's disingenuous claim multi-denominational, was in fact intensely Catholic in its ethos,

10.3 At the Eucharistic Procession, June 1948 (L–R): President Alfred O'Rahilly, Michael Sheehan, Lord Mayor and John A. Costello, Taoiseach.

probably a great deal more so than formally Catholic universities elsewhere, particularly in the United States. There were numerous explicit policy statements about the religious character of the college, of which the following is typical:

> But we know that we have a great function and a real mission: to produce leaders of thought and action. Nor in spite of the liberalistic bias of our foundation, do we believe in higher education divorced from sound philosophy and religion. Our students are over 97 per cent Catholic and we do not intend to ignore this fact. Negative undenominationalism does not appeal to us in Cork. We have always respected, and will always respect, the right of religious minorities among us. But it is no advantage to them that our Catholic students should be subjected to a purely secularist education. We therefore stand not only for a social philosophy such as is embodied in our Constitution – which we uphold, for example, in our courses in Philosophy, in Sociology, in Medical Ethics, in Economics, in our University Extension lectures; but we also maintain a specifically Catholic training for our Catholic Students – for instance in our courses of Apologetics, in the Legion of Mary, in the Sodality, in the College Retreats. We are desirous that the public should appreciate this.[41]

In any given year, the number of non-Catholic students at UCC was negligible. In the 1945–46 session, for example, out of 1,084 registered students, there were 13 Jews, 10 Church of Ireland members, 4 Presbyterians and, curiously, 1 Pilgrim.[42] Well-off Protestants could go to TCD and elsewhere, but there was no reason why Cork Jews, not all of whom were well-off, should go anywhere but to UCC. Before their numbers in Cork were seriously depleted in the 1960s and 1970s, Jews formed a distinctive element in the college, sprinkled around the humanities to an extent but making their own, in town and college, of the dental profession, despite occasional Judaephobia and some suggestion of opposition to the appointment of Jews to senior academic posts.[43] Although O'Rahilly was emphatic that provision was being made for the religious needs of non-Catholics, and although he promised that, if the demand was there, conferring day would be made as religiously significant for them as for Catholics, there was a certain measure of sophistry in this position, and nobody pretended that the handful of Jews and Protestants in any way diluted the Catholic ethos of the college.

The Catholicising of a nominally pluralist institution had been proceeding since Windle's time but intensified during O'Rahilly's presidency. It was not merely a matter of strategically displayed crucifixes[44] and of college observance of Church holy days (discontinued in 1987, partly because of an initiative undertaken by the present writer).[45] In many ways the college comported itself as it imagined a medieval university would in the high ages of faith. One of the year's highlights was the feast of St Thomas Aquinas on 7 March when the Dominicans on Pope's Quay were hosts to the academic community on the morning of this college holiday, which was rounded off by a eulogistic public lecture (sometimes given by O'Rahilly) on the 'angelic doctor'.

Various contributors to the UCC oral history project, recalling the era, are in agreement that the great majority of students, accustomed to religious compliance since childhood, simply never thought of *not* conforming.[46] Similarly, most students observed a sexual moral code which their latter-day successors would see as austerely celibate. Every student was obliged to choose an officer of residence, and a declaration of religious affiliation was, therefore, virtually obligatory. Facetious entries such as 'R.C. (retd)' where occasionally offered were not regarded as amusing. (Nowadays, students are no longer required to give their religious denomination, even for statistical purposes.)

There were college branches of such religious societies as the Legion of Mary and the St Vincent de Paul. Throngs assiduously attended the evening courses in Catholic apologetics (given by O'Rahilly; Rev. Professor James O'Mahony OFM Cap. [philosophy, 1937–62]; and Rev. Dr James Bastible, dean of residence) and subsequently sat examinations for a certificate in the subject. The great Catholic cry of the age was that students must equip themselves intellectually to expound and defend their religious heritage. Outside Ireland, the wider world for which many graduates were, perforce, destined was perceived to be in different ways hostile to the Faith of our Fathers: things worsened steadily along a west–east axis – pagan England, post-Christian Western Europe, communist Eastern Europe.

Students also packed the Honan Chapel (technically outside the technically non-denominational walls) for retreats at the beginning of each session and also during Lent, with separate times arranged for men and women. (On Sunday, the conclusion of the women's retreat was a gala occasion, with breakfast in the college restaurant, presided over by the bishop.) One recalls droves of students moving towards the chapel across the southern side of the Quadrangle on crisp October afternoons after lectures. The retreats were not at all as ferocious, lurid or sexually exciting as the parish missions of the period (perhaps the difference in nomenclature was significant). They were generally conducted by urbane Jesuits and Dominicans rather than by fiery Redemptorists and Passionists. The sermons were relatively genteel and upmarket, brimstone and hellfire being suitably transmuted for Catholics of intellectual and social class. After all, university students could be expected on graduation to experience a superior type of pleasure and pain and, even if condemned to suffer the latter eternally, would presumably inhabit their own select inferno.

Another feature of the age of faith was the presence of a seemingly large number of clerics and religious on campus. In fact, they constituted a small minority of students, with proportionately more women (52 nuns out of a total of 333 women in 1945–46) than men (66 male religious out of 751 men in the same session). The majority were concentrated in the humanities, with a small number in the sciences and only a sprinkling, and then for special reasons, in the professional schools. They were all in college but not of it. They sat at lectures in their serried ranks (self-arranged by gender and community – nuns, Capuchins, SMA students)[47] and they took no part in the activities of student clubs and societies. The ecclesiastical distrust of the 'godless' colleges died hard. Also, mixing with lay students in a relaxed environment had obvious dangers. Strict rules of residence in community houses made evening attendance at college difficult, whether for public lectures or debates, laboratory practicals or even choir rehearsals for sacred music. When Professor Aloys Fleischmann pleaded for some flexibility in the latter regard, he received a tersely negative reply from Bishop Cornelius Lucey of Cork.[48]

One professor who was spoken about in awed tones as having Lost His Faith treated the clerics with glacial politeness, referring to them when necessary as 'the gentlemen in brown' or 'the gentlemen in black'. Another arts lecturer persisted in being facetious or even mildly *risqué* in order to 'shock the nuns' but those independent-minded women merely extended to him the Christian charity of their Mona Lisa smiles. The professor who had Lost His Faith was regarded as an eccentric exception. The overwhelming majority of his colleagues were practising Catholics, and a few were exemplars of Catholic Action. The appointment of the occasional Protestant lecturer was hailed as proof of tolerance. A handful of agnostics remained in the closet. Only a distinguished senior academic could have indulged publicly in the witticism, on being asked by O'Rahilly whether he was enthusiastic about the recently proclaimed Dogma of the Assumption, that in his view every dogma was an assumption.[49]

The ethos of the college being Catholic, truth was pursued, in a large area of the humanities, in the direction of a destination already known. The parameters of knowledge were fixed rather than being 'beyond the utmost bounds of human thought' and the acquisition of learning was not an end in itself but part of the divine order of things. The broad contours of the landscape were already drawn: what remained to be filled in was topographical detail. In some disciplines, this exercise was not without scholarly excitement: in others, there were stultifying implications for the student with a restlessly searching intellect.

It is hardly an exaggeration to say that Catholic apologetics, as well as being an optional evening course, reigned in several lecture rooms under various disguises. The non-denominational intent of the charter was simply ignored. O'Rahilly admitted, or rather claimed, that Christian social principles animated the 'courses in Philosophy, in Sociology, in Medical Ethics, in Economics'. When he was discussing the proposed Diploma in Social and Economic Science course with the VEC and trade unions in Waterford in October 1948, he sounded the contemporary tocsin of the cold war:

> Do we think [a trade unionist] needs no course to become competent to discuss wages and profits, to decide a strike, to pass judgement on issues such as nationalisation, to resist the steady pressure of crypto-communists, to escape the subversive ideologies which are being trundled about? . . .
>
> Our course has also been described as 'sectarian'. I accept this opprobrious epithet since it comes from those who are trying to delude our workers – 98 per cent Catholic – with their humbug of neutrality. We can't be neutral today. We must make up our minds for or against communistic totalitarianism and secularist materialism. Issues such as private property, the family, the functions of the State, cannot be shirked. Our Constitution is not neutral; nor do we profess to be neutral. There is a grave danger lest a determined metropolitan[50] minority should mislead our workers with a scheme of undefined 'education' which may be used as a vehicle for alien propaganda. There is no ambiguity about the Cork College . . .[51]

10.4 Students and staff outside the Honan Chapel, 24 October 1938.

From the mid-1940s through the 1950s, there was a crusading urgency about this approach, which was applied extra- as well as intra-murally, to workers in diploma courses as well as to students. All must be equipped,[52] along prescribed lines, to fight against creeping statism at home and the spread of alien and subversive materialism, of the capitalist but more particularly of the communist variety. (The extraordinary reception given in Cork and other cities in February 1949 to Douglas Hyde's lectures on communism reflects the preoccupations of the time.[53]) In this connection, it was important to ensure that the personnel in such vital areas as sociology and adult education could be relied upon. In fact there was a significant clerical, paraclerical and clericalist elite in the college. The Governing Body in the late 1940s included a number of Catholic clerics who made their presence felt. The department of philosophy was headed by a member of the Capuchin order, which was also represented in economics, and later in applied psychology. Sociology (together with adult education) bore the signs of its orthodox birth for many years.

O'Rahilly was also anxious to have a chair of theology established but the experiment ran into many difficulties, since the Catholic bishops demanded the power of appointment and termination. (Of course, they had to fund the position, to conform to the NUI statutes.) A chair was established in UCC in 1955 and Fr James Good, lecturer in general philosophy – an NUI 'secular' post – was appointed professor of theology in 1958 during the Atkins presidency. But it never flourished as a full-time chair, and it lapsed after 1968 when Fr Good declared his public opposition to the *Humanae Vitae* encyclical letter on contraception, and suffered ecclesiastical censure accordingly.[54]

A perusal of examination papers illuminates the approach taken by examiners of the O'Rahilly period, and the kind of answers expected from the students. The line was obviously laid down in medical ethics where the lecturer was the Catholic dean of residence but other disciplines set the tone no less significantly. A philosophy question renowned in the folklore, 'Refute the pernicious errors of Kant' is apocryphal but the religious approach is evident elsewhere:

Pre-Medical Autumn 1943, Psychology and Sociology
Argue against the modern encroachments on the Family.
How would you establish the existence of the human soul as a spiritual reality?
BA, 1944, Logic
How would you refute Agnosticism?
BA, 1944, Psychology
How would you prove the immortality of the human soul?

Education as an academic discipline was regarded as being well within the Catholic sphere of influence. Though the UCC department of education was not run by clerics, it was in 'safe' hands during the 1940s and 1950s. Long after O'Rahilly's departure, when there was something of an interregnum in the professorship in the mid-1960s, the local bishop with the compliance of the UCC president tried to annex the department as a diocesan fief, pushing his own clerical choice for the chair. At a time of waning clericalism, it was one of the last assertions of episcopal political clout and it was as blatant as it was ineffectual. To the relief of most of the parties concerned, the attempt eventually came unstuck, and education as well as college posts in general soon passed out of the hands of political manipulators, clerical and lay. The case of philosophy was particularly revealing. Long a 'seminary' subject – only clerics took it at honours level, while lay students had to be content with an inferior general philosophy course – the department underwent a sea-change under Rev. Professor Brendan O'Mahony OFM Cap. (1965–). He freed the discipline from its Thomist straitjacket and brought it into the secular mainstream of the humanities, despite the objections of Bishop Cornelius Lucey, an influential member of the GB. Ironically, Fr Brendan was the nephew of his orthodox predecessor, Rev. Dr James O'Mahony – a clear case of nepotism gone wrong.

James Hogan

In the lengthy controversy about denominationalism in education, it was generally accepted that history, at every level, was pre-eminently a subject that lent itself to partisan interpretation. If one subscribed fervently to the idea of a Catholic education, then it was vital that the historians in school and university should be Catholic. For Catholic students, the historical view of the development and disintegration of European civilisation was one of the great ages of Catholic faith being followed by the disaster of the Reformation with all its ensuing evils. The most recommended exponent of this interpretation was Hilaire Belloc, whose idiosyncratic and dogmatic assertions UCC history students were encouraged to accept as scholarship. Belloc gradually lost favour but only to Daniel-Rops who was merely a more sophisticated propagandist.

In one way, James Hogan, professor of history at UCC from 1920 to 1963, defied and transcended all these general reflections. His association with the college was longer than O'Rahilly's, and like his more flamboyant colleague he was a part of the history of the revolutionary period and its aftermath. His contribution to national politics was neither as varied nor as positive as O'Rahilly's. Nonetheless, the careers of both UCC men support the interesting argument that it was in politics and ideology that Irish academics made their innovative and imaginative mark, and not in economics. That remained, if not a dismal, then certainly an extremely conservative science in which a dynamic initiative, when it finally came, was taken in the public service rather than in the groves of academe.[55] Perhaps this was because public debate had always, long before independence and up to the late 1940s, been about politics rather than economics.

A native of east Galway, Hogan, whose brother Patrick was well known as the first minister for agriculture in the infant Irish Free State, had taken an active part at an early age in the War of Independence and in the Civil War. Having already established a brilliant scholarly reputation, he was appointed professor of history in 1920 at the age of twenty-three. He was thus the youngest professor ever appointed in UCC, Aloys Fleischmann being slightly older on his appointment to the chair of music in 1936.

Hogan was also caught up in the exciting politics of the early 1930s, raising an early alert against the red peril with his *Can Ireland become Communist?* (Dublin, 1935). He was regarded as being on the (sparsely populated) intellectual wing of the Blueshirts but, disenchanted with Eoin O'Duffy's antics, he soon severed his connection with the movement. He also failed dismally in his attempt to get elected to Dáil Éireann in 1933 in the Fine Gael interest.

By the post-Emergency period, Hogan's days of military glamour and turbulent politics were long since over, though the aura of that exciting time still clung about him and enhanced his charisma for his students. A profound and distinguished scholar, he was now a senior academic (though still on the right side of fifty) with a record of publications as varied as they were original. He was an extremely influential figure in the college and in the wider community of the National University. Something of a kingmaker and an *éminence grise*, he was dominant behind the scenes during the rather passive presidency of Henry St J. Atkins.

In appearance and mannerisms, every bit the stereotype of the olympian professor, Hogan's appeal was really to his honours students while he was increasingly caviare to the general. On his better days, his was one of the most stimulating classes in the humanities, and a number of his students were to regard him as the formative intellectual influence on their lives, though they might come to disagree sharply with his worldview and its various expressions. His lectures at the general level dealt with broad historical themes and were unremarkable but his honours courses were odysseys in intellectual adventure leading to the exotic borderlands of philosophy and political theory – Aristotle, Luther, Machiavelli, Hobbes, Locke, Rousseau, Hegel and Marx. It was magnificent, but it was not history. Historical training proper came subsequently, in his direction of postgraduate research.

Hogan conformed in a highly nonconformist way to the Catholic ethos. In student folklore, he had also Lost His Faith but had Recovered It Again at a high intellectual level. His view of human nature and of history was pessimistic and his examination papers, it was once remarked (by the redoubtable and erudite Professor M.A. MacConaill of anatomy), resonated with melancholy echoes of the Fall. Hogan subscribed to the general cold war phobia of the late 1940s and the reason for his academic obsession with Hegel and Marx, so it was said, was that he was convinced a grave blow could be struck against Marxism-Leninism in its global political ramifications if only the underlying communist philosophy could be publicly shown to be thoroughly defective. If this was indeed his goal, he never arrived there but the travelling was a memorable experience for his students.

If the groves of Cork academe were Catholic, they were Gaelic and nationalist to a lesser extent. O'Rahilly himself exulted that the Gaels had taken over the college from the Anglo-Irish and the anglicized. (His amended form of the college crest – worked into the mosaic floor under the Arch in the late 1960s – attempted to excise an alien past by substituting a torch of learning for the royal lion.[56]) Had not his fellow-Kerryman, Tomás Rua Ó Súilleabháin, predicted *go mbeidh an dlí fúinn féin arís ar theacht*

Emancipation? The native ethos took shape in O'Rahilly's own robust Sinn Féin philosophy which succeeded Sir Bertram Windle's genteel parliamentarianism. In the significance of this transition, Merriman hardly counted. O'Rahilly strongly supported the national policy of neutrality and the anti-partition agitation which reached a climax in 1949 with the angry Irish reaction to the British-enacted Ireland Act of that year guaranteeing Northern Ireland its place in the UK. He also committed the college to the cause of the Irish language, in which however he was not particularly fluent.[57] He took various steps to encourage the use of Irish in the college, including oral Irish for first year students. In the first issue of the *Cork University Record*, he promised that Irish would be promoted under his leadership 'without lowering academic competence'. Textbooks would be published in different disciplines, and courses provided through the medium. The college, insisted its president, was a *pobal dhá-theangach* and it would have no effective influence on the national life until Irish played a lively and energetic part in the college's affairs.

There was vigorous Irish language activity in some student quarters. The Cuallacht was a very lively debating society in the 1940s and 1950s. The Cuallacht dress *céilí* was a popular and elegant annual social event. There was a surprising amount of Irish in the early issues of *The Quarryman*. Yet the response of the college at large to the official enthusiasm for the language was less than rapturous, and in this it largely reflected the wider national scene. Few of the academic staff shared the philosophy that adherence to the Faith necessarily meant devotion to a Gaelic Fatherland, and political alignments determined degrees of nationalist enthusiasm. For the anglicized bourgeois academics well represented in the professional schools, such enthusiasm was incomprehensible if not distasteful. O'Rahilly lived in a different world, or at least in different circles, from them. For some students the Irish language savoured unpleasantly of the classrooms from which they had just been liberated. Those were the days before an exciting cultural resurgence in the 1960s made Irish-Ireland something of a fashion once again among the student intelligentsia. In the 1940s and 1950s, preoccupation with things Irish – political or cultural – was seen by many students as stodgy and provincial: they preferred more universal subjects of discussion. (Daniel Corkery's inspirational force affected only his own students.) For that matter, the college also honoured other Irish traditions. One of the more interesting celebrations in the immediate post-Emergency period was the bicentenary of Dean Swift's death. On 30 November 1945, there were day-long events to mark the occasion, and the participants included Dr Edith Somerville (then eighty-seven years old), Elizabeth Bowen and the legendary Eoin (the Pope) O'Mahony.[58]

An impressive sprinkling of foreign students after World War II gave the college a rather illusory cosmopolitan flavour. In the 1948–49 session, out of a total student body of 974, there were 23 Poles, 10 Africans, 4 West Indians, 3 Canadians, 3 Americans, 2 Dutch and 14 'from Great Britain'.[59] At a time when Irish attitudes were shaped by a 'black baby' outlook, and before the winds of change blew over the Dark Continent, the African students attracted only facetious interest. Thus O'Rahilly flippantly warned a class not to call the first African student 'Snowball' – which they promptly did! But the Poles (former 'freedom fighters') were, in UCC eyes, an exotic presence, having about them the aura of exiles from another martyred Catholic nation. In the words of their supervisor, they had 'seen life at its most sombre',[60] they brought a fascinating European dimension to a sheltered Irish university college, and the Polish hostel in the Mardyke became for a time an exciting social and intellectual centre. The Poles were also reputed to have wreaked romantic havoc in UCC.

An authoritarian spirit prevailed in the college up to the early or mid-1960s, its small size being a facilitating factor. A 1940s picture of assistants and demonstrators, photographed with the president, evokes the atmosphere of a large public school, an image reinforced by the regular wearing of gowns by staff and students, the hourly ringing of the clock-tower bell, and the calling of class rolls.[61] The group picture also reminds us that the junior staff depended for their promotion on attitudes and behaviour acceptable to their superiors. It is noteworthy that those students who were successful in various student offices, and thereafter in the outside world, were frequently presidential favourites or protégés, there being no body of student dissent worth speaking of which might sustain anti-establishment challengers. It was significant that in 1946–47 the highly respectable president of the students' council felt obliged to argue that Irish students were not being dupes when they affiliated with the suspect International Union of Students: Cork students, he ritually added, were intellectually well equipped to take on communism.

The *Rules for Students* in force at that time must appear, in varying degrees, quaint, sexist, and irksome to today's liberated generation.[62] True, some of the rules could be circumvented, or ignored in practice in time-honoured Irish fashion, but read at their face value, they startle with their authoritarian ring. The tone is set in an opening section on 'Enforcement of Discipline' which begins with the stern and uncompromising statement:

> The President, as Executive Head, may inflict such punishment, by way of admonition, suspension, or fine, as may seem fit to him, in any case of breach of discipline which may come under his notice.

The staff were enjoined to repress 'by admonition and reproof, misconduct and disorder among the Students', though students could apply to the Academic Council for 'migitation or remission' of punishment. Attendance at lectures was regarded as compulsory, and gowns had to be worn in class. ('How can you expect to imbibe learning without a gown?', Daniel Corkery used to ask with ponderous irony.) The usual penalty for a breach of discipline was a stiff fine, payable at the head porter's office near the Arch.

A regulation causing hilarity whenever quoted was: 'It shall be a breach of College discipline for Students to frequent public houses or places of low resort'. The puritanical ban on taverns was unenforced and unenforceable, but what and where were the places of low resort, and what fervid imagination had shaped the phrase?

There was also temptation within the walls, and a beady eye kept watch for any sign of a drift towards free thought or free love.

> 10. No meeting of Students shall be held for the purpose of expressing any opinion or taking action in any matter unless the consent of the President shall have been previously obtained.
>
> 42. The College Restaurant, the Men's Club and Cloak Room and the Women's Club and Cloak Room are under the control of the President of the College.
>
> 43. All Dances and other social functions are under the control of the President of the College and cannot be arranged or held without his sanction.

If the rights of man were circumscribed, the rights of women were even more restricted. According to the college charter, women were entitled to hold any college office on a basis of equality with men (the NUI as a whole espoused the same principle from its foundation), and there was a good percentage of women lecturers by the late 1940s although non-statutory female staff retired on marriage. Women accounted for fewer than a third of the student body,[63] and some bourgeois parents were reluctant to undertake the expense of sending their daughters to college, since it seemed an unnecessarily extravagant method of finding them husbands. (However, strong farmers' daughters were well represented.) Women students found that the college authorities expected them to behave decorously in various ways. Since smoking in public was believed to be the hallmark of a 'fast' woman, women students were forbidden to smoke in the college grounds. Nor should they tempt young males beyond endurance: '17(b) Women Students shall not lie *about* on the grass'. Here, the innocuous adverb of place had a strong suggestion of lasciviousness. A 1962 *Quarryman* cartoon depicted women students on the march and demanding, straightfaced, 'why can't we smoke and lie about on the grass like the boys?' Students who were observed by the dean of residence or some similar worthy to be holding hands (then the ultimate in sexual experimentation) were liable to be severely reprimanded. Thus was the seemly republic of student virtue maintained. A male student in female disguise prankishly participated in a camogie game in the Quarry, and was delated to the puritanical authorities: only after strenuous representations was the threat of expulsion lifted and a brilliant career, as well as a future professorship, saved.

Students accepted all this as part of the only natural order they had ever known. (Indeed, for those who had just left harsh boarding schools, college meant exhilarating freedom.) *The Quarryman* plugged a pious, patriotic and docile line and its editorials (each heavily indebted to its predecessor for ideas and phrasing) pontificated on the burdens of leadership laid on the shoulders of graduates, and on the need to transmit the national heritage. There were only occasional murmurs about the prohibition, dating from O'Rahilly's accession, of the college rag. Gradually, however, a reaction to the bleak provincialism of the 1950s found bitter expression, as in these two extracts (significantly, the authors remained anonymous):

Irish universities are noted for their liberalism. To ensure that undergraduates are instructed in the right kind of liberalism all branches of philosophy are financed and staffed from Maynooth – the country's ecclesiastical centre. This is to ensure that Ireland's thinking must always remain in line with the other great Christian countries – America and Britain . . . Only when she sees clearly that her sole salvation can be American rocket sites on her soil as a deterrent against Communist aggression – only then can the epitaph of Mr Emmet be written.[64]

An earlier commentator was much more scathing:

Gaudeamus igitur . . . nearly 35 years of doctrinaire, conservative social and economic policies – grotesquely called our 'Gaelic, Christian way of life' . . . worst educational policy in Europe . . . this year as with every other since the foundation of the College, UCC will offer up in mellow Latin its batch of graduates in Ireland's unique export drive – the export in human beings . . .[65]

Conservatism and change

The college changed when Ireland changed, since the universities responded to, rather than significantly helped to create, the new influences in society, culture and the economy at the turn of the 1960s. At that stage the impulses for change were generated through television and by certain areas of the public service rather than by academics who, by and large, seemed to shrink from the spirited involvement in public life that had characterised the generation of O'Rahilly, Hogan, Smiddy, Busteed and Stockley. There was no eager anticipation by UCC academics of the more liberal and ecumenical climate of Vatican II. The writer recalls that as late as 1964, only four or five Catholic members of staff entered the heretical portals of St Finn Barre's Cathedral to pay their last respects to the genial and esteemed Professor F.J. Teago, who had come from Liverpool on retirement to help set up the electrical engineering department (1953–59).[66] The majority of the staff mourners, including the senior college officers, held up the wall outside while the service proceeded, because the Catholic chaplain had made plain the sinfulness of such fraternising.

But there was an inexorable change away from this moral infantilism as UCC moved into the heady years of social protest and the assertion of student rights. However, Cork was less affected by revolutionary winds than any other Irish campus. Radical student leaders and agitators emerged from the mid-1960s onwards, and new political societies were founded but the response of the mass of students ranged from the responsible to the phlegmatic. Even when the deepest emotional chords were struck, as in the reaction to Bloody Sunday in Derry in 1972, student wrath was kept well within orderly bounds. With regard to their more immediate concerns, students in the 1970s occasionally demonstrated in the Quadrangle and occupied administrative offices in protest against fee increases, and poor library and classroom accommodation. But there was never any cause for alarm, nor any serious threat to the normal workings of college and, significantly, to the running of examinations.

How should we account for the remarkable conservatism of Cork students over the decades? First of all the scions of the professional and merchant classes were unlikely to be active agents of social and economic unrest. The situation did not alter with the change in the nature of the dominant middle class – from old propertied to new urban, nor with the advent of a controlled meritocracy following on a partial grants system and the tightening up of entrance standards. A basic student gentility persisted. But apart from the class factor, the local base of the college community explains much of its conservatism. As has already been pointed out, there was a general pattern of half to three-quarters of the student body being natives of the city and county of Cork. This helped to ensure continuity of conservative values: students maintaining steady contact with family and community did not constitute easy prey for agitators. Irrespective of socio-economic class, such students tended to display consumer resistance to revolutionary sales talk, unlike, say, their fellows uprooted in the 1960s and 1970s from the western seaboard and lodged insecurely and often unsatisfactorily in metropolitan Dublin.

Other relevant sociological factors have been the size of the student body and the location of the campus. As late as 1959–60, there were only about 1,300 students in UCC, a very small academic community by any standards. The feeling of alienation was not at all as sharp as in larger and more impersonal institutions. The continuity of location on campus may have been an even more important psychological factor. Tradition, stability and convenience are all associated with a pleasant inner-suburb campus (albeit increasingly cramped), contrasting sharply with problems in other urban centres in adapting to a new, featureless and relatively remote location, with consequent commuting expense. The increasing pressures of modern student life have also effectively depressed the spirit of radicalism. The points system at entry sets the tone for high examination standards, though the real and earnest nature of student life is lightened by a varied recreational and social dimension.

Student radicals, then, have had a difficult time of it in UCC in arousing and mobilising opinion among their fellows on large political, social and economic issues. They have also experienced a chilling of their ardour when their clarion calls for student–worker solidarity, a cliché of socialist rhetoric, have repeatedly fallen on invariably deaf artisan ears. Whatever the experience elsewhere, there has never been the slightest evidence in Cork of student–worker rapport. On the contrary, the workers never had any reason to believe that they had anything in common with a privileged class whose hardships, like its youth and its radicalism, have been transient phenomena and whose extramural antics – college week, rag day, running joke candidates for municipal office – hardly betokened a high seriousness of social purpose.

This point raises the wider question of the perceptions that town and gown have had of each other in modern times. While the workers' jaundiced view of the students may not reflect the community's attitude towards the college as a whole, the academics and the citizens have never been mutually starry-eyed. Of course, modern Cork has always been aware that it is in so many ways a university city. The links between college and community are numerous and often obvious, and the contribution of some college departments, notably music, to the cultural life of the city and a wider region has been invaluable. The extension lecture system; adult education; the access of the citizens to the college's facilities; the college's role in the development of the municipal museum and more recently of the municipal archives; the college's medical links with the hospitals and the health boards; the availability of college expertise to business and industry – these are only some of the myriad points of contact. Staff and students (sociologists, for example) are now much more involved with the community than in the days when there was a touch of Victorian charity about college surveys of social conditions in Cork and of the diet of its citizens. Above all, the importance of the college to the economy of the region in terms of employment and purchase of goods and services has been repeatedly underlined by successive college presidents.

Despite all this, there is a sense in which town and gown have held each other at arm's length. The citizens have refused to be overawed by the collegians, since they are aware that the university of life provides its own rich experiences. Perhaps that is the sense of the enigmatic couplet in a popular local song:

> In the Courthouse and the College
> There are different sorts of knowledge

In the past, as has already been noted, the *Examiner* newspapers have not been enamoured of students and their political activities. Despite the provision of space for reports of UCC happenings, 'de paper' was intermittently critical of the college, repeatedly taking it to task for allegedly failing to fulfil the role of the 'poor man's university'. Local radio made insufficient use of academic activity as material of public interest, though international comings and goings of staff and students would seem to have been eminently newsworthy, to mention just one facet of modern college life. The public at large still nurtures grotesque misperceptions about the role of academics and the work-year of the college. There is some class-rooted resentment of what is seen as an enclave of the privileged elite, and a corresponding coolness at times between the college and the city hall. This was expressed in 1981, after a particularly unruly rag day, in the lord mayor's caustic reference to the offending students as 'subsidised brats'.[67]

College–community misunderstandings have been, to some extent, the fault of the college itself. Various efforts have been made from time to time by the college to maintain contact with its graduates but up to the relatively recent institution of an information office, there have been no channels of communication with the general public of the city and province. Historically, the college never felt the need nor the obligation to explain itself to the wider community, and its public relations activity has been notoriously hamfisted, as in the college's defence of its withdrawal from its Fota involvement. However, even with the smoothest PR machine imaginable, harmonious town–gown relations ultimately depend on the attitudes of the college body at large to the world beyond the ivory towers. *Trahison des clercs* is usually envisaged as a betrayal by academics of some lofty principle but the concept can be validly extended to describe attitudes of indifference to matters of community concern on the part of those from whom so much more is rightly expected.

Gaol acquisition

*We were hoping to take over this symbol of the British régime and to dedicate
it to the cause of culture and of peace.*

O'Rahilly to de Valera, 27 April 1945

The college pinned many hopes on government support for post-war developments.
New buildings were needed for various purposes, but this raised the danger of
encroachment on, and thus possible disfigurement of, the existing campus.[68] There
was little hope of expansion to the east, since Cork Corporation was adamant that
there would be no building on the Gillabbey site, in which the college had long
shown an interest. But a westward thrust was a definite possibility, and it was to be the
beginning of an expansion that culminated in the food science extension of the early
1990s which brought the college right up to the wall of the Bon Secours Maternity
Hospital. Such a development would have seemed sheer fantasy to the QCC
professors of 1874 who had sent a memorial to the lord lieutenant about their own
accommodation needs.[69] For them the grim county gaol was part of an unchanging
order, a place that now and then impinged unpleasantly, if unavoidably, on their own
college comings and goings. By 1945, the gaol was no longer a nuisance to the college
as it had been a century earlier but a potential asset. The neighbourhood population
had long since come to terms with an institution that was taken for granted as part of
the landscape. In any case, its associations were now more nationalist/ political than
criminal, and it was a declining and underused institution, being an enforced home to
no more than twenty or thirty borstal boys.

The college had had its eye on the gaol for a long time. Windle had suggested in
1908 that the city and county gaols should be amalgamated, and the county gaol given
to the college to round off its premises. Chief Secretary Birrell promised him it would
be kept in mind(!)[70] During the 1940s, the Governing Body made attempts to convince
the government that acquisition of at least part of the gaol was vital for the college's
development. In his memorandum on the state of the college submitted to the
Taoiseach on 27 April 1945, O'Rahilly appended a proposal for the transfer of the gaol
site to UCC, saying that 'some of us' had aspired to this ever since the struggle for
independence.[71] 'I often thought of it myself when I was a prisoner in the Gaol!'[72]

The college application to government in 1922 to cede the site had been, not surprisingly in the troubled circumstances of the period, turned down. It did not help that
the women's gaol across the valley in Sunday's Well became derelict and unusable.[73]
Now in 1945 O'Rahilly referred to accompanying diagrams to show how hemmed in
the medical building, in particular, was by the gaol boundary wall but also to indicate
how suitable the 3½ acre site was for any extension of the college. (He had hoped for
the erection of a hundred-bed hospital there run by the medical school next door 'but
I presume such a scheme has been superseded by the plan for a Regional Hospital at
Wilton'. *That* plan had to wait thirty years for implementation.) O'Rahilly went on to
tentatively suggest how the various gaol buildings could be converted to specific

purposes. 'The fine entrance [Pain's portico] would of course remain.' In fact, most of the buildings were to be demolished. For O'Rahilly, the gaol site would neatly circumvent

> the great difficulty in extending or erecting new buildings in our own grounds [which] is that it would be desecration and an eyesore not to have them in cut limestone to match our present beautiful Gothic buildings.[74] But if we have the Gaol site we could safely and aesthetically erect cheaper buildings (e.g. for Engineering).

Getting rid 'of the monstrous collection of cells, surrounded by an enormous ugly wall' and of other buildings 'would be an ideal public works scheme . . . and the recovered materials could be utilised'.

What O'Rahilly called a 'subsidiary' issue arose in connection with all of this – the Old IRA Men's Association campaign to have a fitting monument erected over the graves of those comrades who had died on hunger strike or were executed during the War of Independence. The association had collected £1,400 for the purpose. According to a later letter from O'Rahilly, it was the association which had taken the initiative in the pressure put on government to make over a portion of the gaol site.[75] In any case, it was clear that the college could not take over responsibility for the graves and proposed monument 'until the Gaol becomes part of College'. The public could hardly be allowed approach the graves through the gaol, and the college would not allow public access to its 'backyard' behind its buildings, even if portions of the high dividing gaol wall were to be broken down. The only sensible answer, it was argued, was college acquisition of part of the gaol site, the demolition of a derelict building and the construction of a new approach road from College Road through part of the gaol grounds.[76] One gathers the impression that the college played the graves card to acquire the site, though it was quite sincere about its role in commemorating the patriot dead. The college secretary, himself an IRA veteran, hoped the government did not think 'the College is endeavouring to extract the last ounce for having the graves in the College' and assured the government that it was a great honour.[77]

The Taoiseach, Eamon de Valera, could not but be sympathetic to an appeal that had such a strong nationalist dimension, especially in the prevailing post–neutrality patriotic atmosphere. The Old IRA Men's Association wrote in support of the college request,[78] and O'Rahilly's own memorandum to the Taoiseach struck an emotional chord:

> I am personally interested as I knew several of them and when, in March 1921, I was a prisoner in the 'cage' in Cork Barracks I actually heard the volleys which killed some of them and I led the prisoners in prayer for them.[79]

In the event, the college was initially given a one-acre portion fronting on College Road where a house and some unused old cells were demolished and the electrical engineering buildings were to be constructed.[80] In Dáil Éireann, James Dillon suggested (mischievously) that giving this area to UCC, as a result of college pressure on the

Taoiseach, had deprived borstal boys of their exercise grounds, as a result of which they had to be transferred to Clonmel. The minister for justice, Gerry Boland, denied this, saying that the accommodation at Clonmel was better and that Cork was wanted for short-term prisoners.[81] Dillon's allegations provoked an indignant response from O'Rahilly who claimed there was no encroachment on the exercise ground, and that the college had given film exhibitions to the boys and granted them use of the college athletic grounds,[82] for which they were thanked by the minister for justice.[83]

A decade later (24 May 1957), the remainder of the gaol site was made over to, and entirely incorporated in, the college and the dominant science building was built there in 1968–71. (Pain's classical portico, and the fine front wall in which it was set, were preserved.[84]) The founding professors of the Queen's College would have been astonished but gratified at such a development. They would hardly have been pleased however by the graves memorial to the executed 'rebels' or by the college president chairing its unveiling in 1948. The handsome monument, in ornamental if somewhat florid style, is well maintained and occasionally floodlit, and commemorative cere-monies take place every Easter. The monument bilingually records the names, among others, of thirteen Volunteers shot by firing squad in Victoria (now Collins) Barracks and buried here. The memorial is centrally located at the side of what it now the main traffic entrance into the college, where the gaol boundary wall used to be. Droves of students daily pass it by, unseeing it as part of a taken-for-granted landscape, perhaps not aware that it is not just a monument but a patriot grave, and in a post-nationalist age maybe not interested. In any case, the intentions of those who planned the monument fifty years ago were clear:

> It is confidently hoped it would be a reminder to those attending Munster's seat of learning, of the sacrifices made by the generation that achieved the country's freedom. It would act as an inspiration to the future generations to be always ready, if necessary, to defend that freedom.[85]

When O'Rahilly submitted another memorandum to the Taoiseach on 23 April 1946, he gratefully acknowledged the transfer of a portion of the adjoining gaol site, 'thanks to your personal interest and intervention'.

The Atkins presidency

By the time of O'Rahilly's retirement in 1954, a pattern had been established in the college, whereby there was a certain expectation that the registrar would succeed to the presidency. It was not of course that the registrar had the *ius successionis*, like a co-adjutor bishop, but that he was the heir presumptive, and cause would have to be shown why any other candidate should be seriously considered. The shaky but not widely challenged presumption was that the registrar, by virtue of his office, knew more about university matters, and in particular, about running the college, then anybody else. As a matter of practical politics, the registrar was positioned advanta-geously, over a period of years, to form alliances and nail down crucial votes in the

Governing Body. (The registrarship was a GB appointment.) The ingrowing provincialism inherent in this pattern of cosy succession was a cause of concern only to the few.

Alfred O'Rahilly's college career fitted in, and contributed, to the pattern but given
his unique standing, he had no need of the registrarship as a springboard to the chief
office. This was not necessarily true in other cases. Some good registrars made
disappointing presidents. Of them it could be said, as Tacitus said about Galba, *capax
imperii nisi imperasset* – he'd have been a great ruler if he'd never come to power. In
any event, of the seven presidents since 1920, five have succeeded to the office via the
registrarship, though one of those, Tadhg Ó Ciardha, had to serve as registrar from
1954 to 1978, becoming president only at his third attempt, having failed in his bids in
1963 and in 1967.

Henry St John Atkins – despite the patrician-sounding name, a Cork Catholic and a
'North Mon' boy – began his career as a secondary teacher, became an elegant rather
than an effective professor of mathematics and was never a distinguished mathematical
scholar. As registrar, he was the essence of benignity, affability and courtesy, qualities
with which neither his predecessor nor his successor was abundantly endowed. In those
days, the registrarship was an undemanding and very much a part-time position: a
notice on the office door (off the Stone Corridor in the North Wing) gave the
attendance hours as 12.00 to 1.00 daily.

10.5 President Henry St J. Aktins, 1954–63.

As UCC faced life after O'Rahilly in 1954, there was a feeling in some quarters that a vigorous (and perhaps tactful) new president from outside was required to grapple with such major problems as the overhaul of the medical school, the need to confront the strong vested interest of the region's hospital committees, and the future of dairy science in the context of the proposed new agricultural institute. Various 'big' names were improbably rumoured (Freddie Boland, Lord Pakenham, Lord Killanin, Sir David Kelly) but the actual field of candidates was considerably less exotic. The professor of philosophy, Rev. Dr James O'Mahony OFM Cap., was listed for a time but withdrew. In the words of Denis Gwynn (research professor of modern Irish history 1947–63, journalist, Catholic convert and arch-gossip on academic and political affairs),[86] 'it would have been deplorable to have a president who would always be obliged to consider his personal relations both with the bishop and with a religious order'.

Gwynn's comments were made in a letter to UCD president, Michael Tierney, and were intended for that influential man's information prior to the election process.[87] Gwynn continued:

> . . . we all wish there was some more exciting or distinguished candidate in the field . . . it looks to me as though there will be a clear contest between Atkins and McHenry,[88] and of the two I think that Atkins is far the more suitable. The whole college is torn with feuds and suspicions and there is no sort of social life. I can't feel that McHenry would be able to create a different atmosphere or would be even disposed to attempt it, whereas Atkins would devote his whole energies to creating a spirit of team work.

Gwynn did not take seriously the unexpected candidature of Myles Dillon, the distinguished Celtic studies scholar, and neither did the electors, apparently. As a figurehead and a scholar, Dillon would be fine but Gwynn felt that he would not have the competence or the local knowledge to deal with Cork's problems. (Of course, this was a stock objection to 'outside' candidates.) Dillon was supported by J.J. Horgan[89] (which was enough to rally support for Atkins) and by a small group of Cork professors who included Aloys Fleischmann, Risteárd Breatnach and Séamus Cavanagh, but not by the kingmaker James Hogan who kept his mind to himself and who was to be a much-deferred-to power behind Atkins's throne.

Dillon seems to have been very much the innocent abroad in the wildlife park of academic (and party) politics. Encouraged to run by the vice-chancellor, President Mgr Pádraig de Brún of UCG (who promised him he 'will do all he can') and by a small UCC clique, he deluded himself about the extent of his support and permitted himself the foolish expectation that Atkins would withdraw from the contest.[90] A Dillon – of renowned Fine Gael and Irish Party stock – could hardly expect to be backed by the Fianna Fáil mayors and councillors on the UCC Governing Body but he hoped the NUI Senate would have a friendlier complexion.[91] In the event, his support was derisory and he was considerably disillusioned. Though he wrote a note of congratulations to Atkins 'in the wholesome traditions of the football field',[92] he did not conceal from others his disappointment and his 'indignation qualified by a measure of relief . . . it is a serious matter that Governing Body and Senate have united in appointing a man whom they know to be unsuitable . . .'[93]

Unless he had an immense capacity for self-deception, Atkins could hardly have been unaware of a widely held negative view of his capabilities. However, his pleasant personality generated a certain goodwill, and the grace of a honeymoon period was enhanced by the college's general relief at being liberated from O'Rahilly's despotism.

One of the unresolved issues inherited by Atkins was that of higher-level agricultural education. There was much public debate about a proposed agricultural institute and the crucial question was whether it would supersede or co-ordinate agricultural education in the university colleges. UCC had difficulties about the issue, resenting the lack of consultation by government as well as financial pressure on the colleges to go along with the proposal so that the capital financing of the institute by the American Grant Counterpart fund could be expedited. In any case, UCC wanted its own faculty of agriculture, though the government would not provide any extra funds for this and believed it would cut across the setting up of the agricultural institute.[94]

Ignoring Thomas Paine's dictum that the 'most ridiculous and insolent' of all tyrannies is that of attempting to govern from beyond the grave[95] (in this case, Blackrock College), O'Rahilly in retirement joined in the institute debate with his usual gusto. In a long memorandum, he reviewed the government's attempt to 'transfer' dairy science to the proposed institute, and UCC's resistance to this proposal. Predictably, if not obsessively, O'Rahilly saw the sinister forces of the age at work – centralism, statism, bureaucracy. The institute would be no more than the Department of Agriculture, camouflaged and writ new: university professors, being too independent, would be replaced by 'disguised civil servants'. Interestingly, O'Rahilly took exception to the new-fangled American term 'campus', which had for him objectionable centralised and secular connotations. He also indignantly rejected the 'dirty deal' allegation that he had 'secured Electrical Engineering for Cork in return for abandoning Dairy Science'. Above all, he objected to the proposed removal of Catholic students from a university college where they were protected by 'religious and ideological guarantees' under the 1908 Act, to a neo-secular residential university:

> It is as if it were proposed to revive the Queen's Colleges . . . For, make no mistake, they have raised a religious issue. Fresh from celebrating Cardinal Newman, they have resurrected the banner of Sir Robert Peel.[96]

The old denominational animosities were part of the institute debate. UCD and UCC contended that the institute should be a recognised college of the NUI and not closely associated with Trinity College. The Catholic bishops supported the UCD–UCC stance and informed the government they would object if agriculture/ dairy science were to be diminished or impaired in the NUI, or if Trinity College were to dominate the teaching of agriculture in the new institute.[97] Whether or not the bishops saw agriculture as coming within their jurisdiction over faith and morals, they were now certainly identifying with the NUI as *their* university, whatever their reservations in 1908. Their priority now was to keep Catholics away from Trinity, and to ensure that generous governmental treatment would not make the 'Protestant' college too attractive.

In the end, there was government agreement that the institute would be concerned only with research and the colleges would continue to provide teaching facilities: however, UCC did not get its faculty of agriculture. During a visit to North America in the autumn of 1958 (a pioneering trip at that time – and not his only one – for an Irish university president), Atkins contacted the Rockefeller and Ford foundations but soon concentrated on the latter. He tried to interest it in financially assisting UCC to set up a food technology course in the dairy science faculty. In a subsequent extended application, Atkins pointed out that Ireland was making an outstanding contribution through its missionaries to social development in underdeveloped countries (a main concern of the Ford Foundation). But at home the university system badly needed funding, and UCC in particular was anxious to strengthen its dairy science faculty and thus improve its services to the agricultural community in Munster (Atkins made sure he reminded the Ford Foundation that Henry Ford's family had come from Co. Cork – whatever that sentimental item might be worth). Adult education also needed help, and the college's plans 'for the extension of this movement would be considerably helped if we had a Hall of Residence which would accommodate thirty students'.

Though the government promised the grants needed to staff and maintain the proposed development in dairy science, the Ford Foundation eventually turned down the UCC application. Since Atkins's charm and diplomacy were his chief card, he must have been very disappointed by the rejection. However, the consolation was that the government was now committed to financing a strengthened dairy science in Cork as an alternative to the establishment of a faculty of agriculture there.[98]

Atkins was interested in university developments elsewhere and had observed them in the course of his quite extensive travels. He had plenty of ideas for the development of the college but he lacked his predecessor's dynamism and in any case it was a period of conservatism and of debt containment rather than of expansion. In the end he found the external pressures and the internal frictions and frustrations wearisome, and prematurely retired in 1963 to enjoy *otium cum dignitate*. His persuasive powers cut no ice with multinationals like the Ford Foundation but they were more effective nearer home where he succeeded in staving off disaster for the dental school (a necessary exercise at frequent intervals) and in securing the continuing recognition by British and American registration bodies of Cork's medical school. Perhaps that was his most valuable service, but he also helped to lay the groundwork for the future development of food science.[99]

Otherwise, the presidency of Harry Atkins was colourless. He had a singular capacity for stating the obvious with intense earnestness. Dutiful and pious in his attitudes to the Catholic Church and almost comically deferential to ecclesiastics, he was prepared to see clericalism and censorship intensify in the dark years before Vatican II. Whatever the charter might say, he proclaimed at an honorary degrees conferring in 1959, UCC was a Christian, indeed a Catholic university.[100] The contract for the new science building was awarded during his presidency[101] but because of an influential ecclesiastical governor's vested interest, there was no open competition, and the result is an abominable monument to pedestrian architecture. Not to have seriously sought and considered alternative designs was a dereliction of duty.

10.6 Kathleen O'Flaherty,
professor of French, 1970–81.

Professor Kathleen O'Flaherty observed that although the cramped and narrow-minded culture of Merriman's presidency continued into O'Rahilly's day, life was considerably enlivened by the bustling vigour of a president whose polemical targets included churchmen as well as heretics and infidels.[102] With Atkins, the O'Rahilly religious ethos persisted but without a stimulating presence any longer at the top. It was a dull convent when the mad reverend mother had departed.

CHAPTER ELEVEN

ASPECTS OF COLLEGE
FINANCING, 1922–59

How can we possibly attain modern standards whilst labouring under such a handicap?
President Atkins, on the impoverished state of UCC,
14 September 1956

A NATIVE IRISH GOVERNMENT undertook the burden of university financing with a distinct lack of enthusiasm. Indeed, in the first months of the provisional government, Joseph Brennan (who was to be secretary, Department of Finance, 1923–27) writing to the British Treasury asked for confirmation that the forthcoming (1 April) instalment of grants to universities and colleges would be part of the 1921–22 vote and would be therefore paid by the British Treasury and 'not be a burden on the Irish Exchequer'. Mother England lost no time in calling the Irish bluff: the provisional government reluctantly had to accept that political independence had its financial obligations as well as its rights.[1]

A year later, finance officials felt some investigation was desirable into the financial needs of university institutions in the Saorstát, and into what means their governing bodies had been taking and might take to augment their financial resources as an alternative to looking to the government for assistance. The before-its-time suggestion of independent generation of funds was prompted, at least in part, by the fact that UCC and UCD had used grants of August 1922 to reduce their debts.[2]

In 1924–25, there were deputations from UCC to the executive council looking for a grant increase. Joe Downey, the bursar, wrote to the secretary of the Department of Education in August 1925 complaining of pressure from the banks because of the college overdraft. He also pointed out to the minister for finance (25 November 1925) that although fees were admittedly lower in the NUI than in English universities, the National University had been heralded, and was repeatedly proclaimed, as the 'poor man's University' – hence the difficulty in increasing fees. The college presented a lengthy financial memorandum in which the point of departure was the argument that the NUI had been underfunded to begin with and had never recovered from that initial handicap.[3] UCC, for example, was unable to pay the relatively moderate full-time salaries suggested by the Association of University Teachers – £1,100 per annum for professors, £650 per annum for lecturers and £500 per annum for assistants. UCC staff were unhappy in post-independence years that a lower scale of salaries obtained in Cork than in UCD and QUB, and they alleged, rather unconvincingly, that the discrepancy was gravely injurious to university education in Munster.[4] When the college sought to advertise in 1921 in the *British Medical Journal* for a full-time assistant in pathology at £300 per annum, publication was refused on the grounds that the minimum commencing salary recognised by the British Medical Association was £500.[5]

On 5 April 1927, President Merriman wrote to the minister for finance to point out that the latter's recent statement in the Dáil[6] had been misleading in that it gave the public the impression that Cork salaries were on the same level as those of Dublin and that recent legislation had cleared off the college debt. In fact, £5,000 was still undischarged which was approximately the cost of the proposed new bridge and entrance for which a loan was now being taken out. Provision had also to be made

> for a continuation of the splendid research work in the Chemistry Department . . . and for the establishment, with partial help from the local Chambers of Commerce, of a Bureau of Economic Research,[7] an attempt to collect statistical information; and for extending subjects taught through Irish from History, Geography, Mathematics, Education, Chemistry and Experimental Physics to Mathematical Physics, Botany and Rural Science and Commerce.[8]

In an interesting interlude in 1933, preoccupation with grants gave way to injured sensibilities on a point of principle, though one suspects that pocket, pride and snobbery were all involved. The academic staffs of the three constituent colleges protested at their inclusion in the Public Services (Temporary Economies) Bill which was intended to effect economies by reducing the remuneration of public servants.[9] The academics expressed amazement that a government led by the NUI chancellor (Eamon de Valera) should not have consulted the colleges' authorities before taking a step with such radical implications for 'Catholic University education in Ireland'. The colleges had always been self-governing in the matter of appointments, conditions of service and salaries. Now this unprecedented government interference was a grave threat to university autonomy, which had been won for 'Irish Catholic education' at such sacrifice, education for 'all classes of Irish Catholic boys and girls' at relatively low cost. The academic staffs claimed that their argument was supported by the standing committee of the bishops to whom they had submitted the matter.[10] The frankly (and somewhat menacingly) denominational tone of this rather hysterical document illustrates the fervent dogmatism of academics such as O'Rahilly and Tierney, and their cavalier identification of the non-denominational NUI as a Catholic university.

From the inception of the Queen's Colleges down to the present day, or at least down to the establishment of the Higher Education Authority (HEA) in 1968–71, there is a predictable pattern in the government–college dialogue on finance.[11] With the exception perhaps of the dismally depressed period at the turn of the century, the college is generally drawing attention to the lack of adequate accommodation for an increasing student population; the urgency of alleviating overcrowding in library, laboratory and lecture hall; the pressing need to implement this or that building project; the unsatisfactory level of salaries and wages; the need for more staff; and, to provide for all this, the imperative necessity of a substantially increased government grant, if indebtedness is to be cleared off and if academic standards are not to drift down to the level of a backwards provincial institution. For its part, the financial arm of government – and there is a marked continuity here between the approach of the Treasury and of its successor, the Department of Finance – has its own priorities. Of course, it recognises – grudgingly – the need for the college to be adequately aided out of the public purse but chides the academic authorities for not living within the state grant; reminds them to economise where possible and not to spend money on frivolities such as sports facilities; encourages them to look to increased student fees as an alternative source of revenue; and warns that the occasional *ex gratia* payment to wipe out an accumulated deficit will not be repeated. A not untypical comment occurs in the form of an undated, unsigned note on the 1925–26 estimates for university and college expenditure: 'I don't think the country gets value on this vote . . . of course, the majority of our students are trained for export'.[12]

The pattern described above is evident in the substance and tone of the correspondence on financial matters between government and UCC presidents in the 1930s and 1940s.[13] Merriman's memorandum to de Valera (referred to Finance) on 13 March 1934 points out that UCC never overcame the initial handicap of inadequate funding at the outset of the NUI in 1908. Salaries were fixed too low and there was never any margin for effecting economies in administration. The economic impact of the Great War aggravated this situation, and the destruction of the entrance bridge by a flood in 1916 was a 'catastrophe'.[14] (In the old Queen's College days, Merriman pointed out, the Board of Works would have carried out the restoration work.) 'For years, an unsatisfactory entry had to be used, available for pedestrians only', until the Governing Body, ashamed of the 'eyesore' which 'took very much from the prestige of the College', purchased the house in front of the entrance, and had a new entrance and bridge constructed in 1929 at a cost of £16,832, taking precautions against a repeat of the 1916 destruction, and planning for the avoidance of accidents on the road immediately outside the college, where the city trams and the Muskerry train ran. Merriman also claimed that despite the government grant for teaching certain subjects through Irish, the college was losing money on the scheme. Sounding a more positive note, the president pointed to the college's recent achievements – evening classes, extension lectures, a university press, an improved library, the marine biological station at Lough Ine. But 'the incubus of debt' and the payment of interest on the overdraft had prevented desirable developments. If the government would extinguish the debt (£24,726), the college staff would 'strain every nerve to render further service to the country'.[15]

The government's response to the Merriman memorandum was influenced by a lengthy comment on 26 June 1934 from the secretary of the department to Seán MacEntee, the minister for finance. This reveals the higher public servant's traditional attitude of impatience with, if not hostility to, academics, an attitude inspired perhaps by an inverted intellectual arrogance, as well as by a modicum of envy. In this case, the tone is caustic and the Downey–Merriman argument for state assistance is derided as 'very flimsy' and 'cluttered with irrelevant references to what might have happened' before the 1908 Act. The further snide comment is made 'that the main subject which the College Authorities were anxious about was the salaries of the Professors'. The government has no obligation, it is claimed, in respect of the bridge-entrance-avenue debt, the Athletics Grounds or the arts 'Classroom'. But if it is decided to help out the college authorities by way of special grant, care must be taken not to encourage them to 'believe they can run up debts, perhaps without due regard to economy, and then look to the State to extinguish them'.

Nevertheless, the government's response (de Valera concurred with the minister for finance's recommendations) was not unsympathetic but it reprimanded the college for running up debts and then looking to the state to bale it out; spoke of the necessity to exercise control of future building costs; and particularly deplored the financial losses on the Athletic Grounds (the cumulative deficit from 1932/33 was £6,095), asserting firmly that the government would accept no responsibility there. It was emphasised that these grounds were a municipal social amenity which raised the question of a grant from Cork Corporation. Over the previous two years £4,418 had been added to the debt through the erection of a pavilion and 'there appeared to be a strong case for obviating any deficiency on the Grounds by an increased students' subscription to the Club – these appear to be exceedingly light in the case of Cork . . .' As regards the inclusion of the cost of extra arts accommodation in the overall debt, MacEntee neatly stated that 'extra students means extra fees' and the cost should be met from the increased income from the additional students. And, if the government were to afford any financial assistance, then the college must do its national duty by the Irish language and extend its use in the curriculum.[16] MacEntee, it should be said, yielded little in respect of financial rectitude to his notoriously tight-fisted Cumann na nGaedheal predecessor, Ernest Blythe. In the event, a special additional grant of £15,000 was made to UCC in 1935–36 'towards extinction of College debt' (Merriman's application had been for £25,000) on condition that the college would be responsible in future for all running expenses and all capital expenditure save where exceptional circumstances called for a state grant which would have to have the minister's prior approval.

The college considered such circumstances existed in June 1940 when the bursar, Joe Downey, wrote to the Taoiseach applying for a grant of £11,000 from the special employment schemes vote to supplement the sum of £11,000 allotted to UCC from the National University funds, in order to erect a building for 'the cultural and recreational association of students and graduates'. (The idea of a 'union' building was very much in the news at the time, being enthusiastically promoted by meetings of the graduates' association.) Since no such building existed, it was necessary to hire halls for meetings, concerts and dances. Not only was this expensive but 'it is quite impossible for the College Authorities to superintend such functions adequately'. The dairy science lecture theatre was often inadequate for the crowds wishing to attend extension lectures. A hall was also needed for such diverse purposes as gymnasium classes and orchestral activities, all adding up to the expected amenities of university life.[17] The cost of the buildings now being proposed was estimated at £16,000, but a new biological building was also required at a cost of £6,000, thus making a total of £22,000.

However, the Office of Public Works did not consider it was appropriate to make a grant from the employment schemes vote for such purposes. The Public Accounts Committee, for its part, took exception to small grants made to UCC from this vote in 1934/35 and 1935/36 for improving the Athletic Grounds: any expenditure in this respect 'should be met from the resources of the College'.[18] The message was discouragingly clear. The proposed buildings did not fulfil the 'exceptional' criteria. Though the Taoiseach's office suggested that the matter be put before the Department of Finance for consideration under the vote for universities and colleges, and although the UCC bursar promised in July 1940 that he would do so, the college never did in fact put proposals before Finance, wisely concluding that it would be a waste of time, or worse. So the graduates' 'union' proposal quietly lapsed but it would have succumbed in any case to the financial freeze of the Emergency.

O'Rahilly's state-of-the-college memo, 1945

The most interesting and comprehensive financial statement of this period is that laid out in a memorandum submitted to the government by President O'Rahilly on 27 April 1945.[19] It not only surveys the financial position of the Emergency years but summarises the not inconsiderable college activities from 1939 to 1945 and makes it clear that the Emergency in UCC was far from being a period of just marking time. The memorandum also sketches the lines of possible post-war development and seeks some indication of government policy in this regard. There is a plea for some improvement in the static salaries of UCC staff. Finally, a cogent case is made for the acquisition by the college of the adjoining gaol site.

The preparation of the financial data in the memorandum was obviously the work of the college Finance Office where the formidable Jim Hurley had replaced Joe Downey, whose unexpected death had 'considerably put out' the president. The brisk, direct style and phrasing of the document are very much O'Rahilly's and sharply contrasts with the insipid flavour of Merriman's letter on finances ten years earlier. More than twenty years before the establishment of the HEA, O'Rahilly characteristically deplored the absence in Ireland of a university grants committee. There was 'no buffer body between us and the Government. I am, therefore, under the unpleasant necessity of appearing in the guise of an importunate mendicant'.

In surveying the financial position since 1938/39, the president pointed out that increased costs would have been even higher if instruments and materials had been available. As it was, overall costs had brought a 1938/39 deficit of £5,700 to £17,800 in 1943/44. O'Rahilly thought it 'a very creditable achievement' to have held increased expenditure reasonably down. This did not include salaries which remained 'stationary'. There was little room for manoeuvre in increasing college revenue. The government grant remained static at £40,000, and the only other source of income was students' fees (apart from the O'Kinealy bequest[20] which produced £1,300 per annum). In theory, fees were a flexible element – in practice, public opinion would tolerate only a limited increase. The college had increased fee income for the 1944/45 session by about £3,000. 'Moderate as this increase is relatively to our expenses', there was an outcry – including several editorials in *The Cork Examiner*.

Conscious that his ultimate plea would be for a wiping out of the deficit, O'Rahilly was at pains to show that the overspent money was well spent! First of all, he claimed that under his presidency, course and examination standards had been raised:

> We have abolished all exemptions, we have got rid of compensation in the Pre-Medical. We took the lead in the recently adopted regulation for getting rid of 'chronics'. For many years past, our rules for the renewal of Public Scholarships have been the highest in Ireland. We fully realise that a College such as ours must lay more stress on quality rather than on quantity.

Materially, the restaurant had been enlarged, and a new kitchen and women students' cloakroom had been built. The college had taken charge of the recently opened public museum and was paying the salary (£350 per annum) of the curator.[21] The college had not neglected its public obligations (film exhibitions for schoolchildren) nor its Irish language commitments – Gaeltacht scholarships for students, special Irish classes for trade unions, subsidies for Irish plays and the employment of 'a special Irish speaking attendant [Pádraig Ó Nuatáin[22]] who has been of great help to the Students'. More generally, the college had decided to establish a new department of biochemistry; to publish the results of a college-conducted social survey; and to extend the university press. In 1942, the pathological testing laboratory had been changed from a professional perquisite to a college-run enterprise, the profits of which helped to improve the departments of the medical school. A radical accommodation change had ensued on President Merriman's death. His house (henceforth the staff house) was taken over for offices, a music classroom, a room for board meetings and staff rooms – heretofore there were no staff common- rooms. A house ('Crossleigh') adjoining the college grounds on Donovan's Road was bought for the new registrar (Professor Atkins), at a cost of about £3,000.

> I consider that this arrangement has brought advantages and facilities worth the expenditure. Personally I abandoned all claims to the better house and garden; and I.hope in the near future that my present house will be available for offices and classrooms.[23]

O'Rahilly also mentioned (as was his wont) the government's favourable treatment of UCD, which had received an *ex gratia* grant of £70,000 in 1944 for liquidating its debt. UCC now appealed for similar action, but only to the tune of £18,000. It did so on the grounds of 'doing our job pretty well and fulfilling an important function in being a centre of thought and influence in the South of Ireland'. If the government agreed to wipe out the deficit, 'does this mean that we can guarantee to keep out of debt?' O'Rahilly's answer to his own question was a guarded 'yes'. 'After investigating the matter with Mr Hurley, I think I can answer that we can manage to keep within our income for the present' – provided there were no appreciable price increases or drastic reorganisation, and leaving aside the question of post-war reconstruction.

In fact, O'Rahilly devoted another section of his memorandum to post-war development, and he included a graph of the growth of student numbers at the college, 1849–1926.[24] The institution had been built for 250 students, now (in 1944–45) catered for 1,067, and urgently needed various improvements and facilities, even if, as seemed likely from the post-1918 situation, there was to be a post-war fall in student numbers, dropping to, say, 750. Again, O'Rahilly stressed how well the college, with all its limitations, had done, and he instanced the training of creamery managers; the development of chemistry courses along lines 'suitable for positions in our own country', with experiments on peat, oil-bearing plants, etc.; the introduction of diplomas in chemical technology and in commerce (in conjunction with the Municipal Technical Institute and the School of Commerce); and the active encouragement of students to consider career possibilities in the civil service.

The most urgent area of reform was the college's greatest resource, the library – 'the only first-class Library outside Dublin', and effectively a public one to boot. But accommodation was now at crisis point: 'the Library is all over the College' in various sections, the Aula Maxima had to become a reading room, and 'ideally we want a new Library and Reading Room to relieve the congestion'. The Honan biological building, built from a bequest, could no longer house botany, zoology, geology and geography! The botany and zoological laboratory was able to accommodate only about a fifth of the students at a time, and consequently 'our whole time-table is upset'. Engineering 'has had to invade the Medical Building' to provide an extra drawing office. Much equipment was obsolete, worn or simply non-existent. In medicine, alterations had been postponed because of the war, pathology had outgrown its space, and 'a new Department of Biochemistry is urgently required'.

Normally, Alfred O'Rahilly would be the last person to urge that things should be ordered on the British model, yet here for the purposes of argument he adverted to the provision being made across the Irish Sea for substantial increases in university financing in the post-war situation. Since UCC did not want to incur 'the heavy expenditure of preparing preliminary plans', could the government give 'some indication of policy as regards post-war development?'

> I assume that it is not desirable to have an out-of-date obscure provincial College here without reasonable facilities for functioning. Unlike many provincial cities in Great Britain – Oxford, Bristol, Reading, Hull, etc. – we have no wealthy manufacturers to act as founders or benefactors. In Ireland charitable bequests flow to the Church rather than to Universities or Hospitals.[25]

With regard to wages and salaries, the president pointed out that though Emergency bonuses had been paid to attendants, clerical staff and full-time assistants, there had been no advance whatever in the salaries of full-time professors and lecturers whose stipends were fixed mainly in 1927. These salaries (£900 for the highest paid professors, £550 for lecturers) compared unfavourably with the comparable civil service grades:

> I know for a fact that many of our staff – especially those with four or five children – are finding it difficult to make ends meet. Financial worries interfere with efficiency:

several of them have, with my permission, undertaken to spend their vacation in the prolonged drudgery of routine correction of examination papers.

However, as if realising that this *béal-bocht*ery would cause few tears to flow in Merrion Street, O'Rahilly admitted that the government could not legislate specially to raise 'our salaries'. ('I say "our" but there is no question whatever of raising my own'.) But if the debt were wiped out, the college could grant a small relief – 'say to the extent of £50' – to full-time staff, in recognition of the lack of a price-index bonus and of the extra lecturing and laboratory work of recent years: student numbers had increased from 441 in 1926–27 to 1,067 in 1944–45.

O'Rahilly, in a further memorandum to the Taoiseach on 23 April 1946 (partly prompted by the fact that 'in Limerick, at the consecration of Dr O'Neill you whispered to me that UCD had submitted a document much more detailed than mine'), argued a detailed case for an improved salary scale in the post-war situation.[26] He suggested that the higher-grade (£900) professorships – chemistry, experimental physics, engineering, anatomy and physiology – should be increased to £1,200, the 'ordinary' chairs from £800 to £1,100, and lectureships from £550 to £850. In general, the memorandum stressed 'the importance of having such an institution as ours outside the metropolis' but queried whether continuance should necessarily mean numerical expansion (a distinction which was to be lost sight of in the 1980s and 1990s): 'Personally, I would like our numbers to decrease from 1,000 to 700; our primary justification lies in quality, not quantity. In fact, we have of recent years been raising our standards'. But even without expansion, the college had pressing needs in respect of scientific and medical requirements, and library enlargement. 'We neglect no means of self-help', O'Rahilly claimed with pride, citing the use of the O'Kinealy bequest to meet current expenses; running and improving the Athletic Grounds 'through what we make in outside matches'; buying scientific equipment out of the profits from pathological testing ('not, as elsewhere, private property'); and the recent building of a kitchen at a cost of £3,000 to be paid out of increased fees.

Clearly, the government had no grand vision of a new university order in post-war Ireland. Matter-of-factly, the college's application for an £18,000 *ex gratia* payment was met with a government grant of £12,500.[27] This clearly was not enough and O'Rahilly, in consultation with the Finance Committee, applied on 15 October 1946 for an increase of £30,000 in the annual grant – for additional accommodation, library extension, new laboratories, dental and engineering expansion, more staff, and salary and wage increases.[28] Following discussions between the three NUI colleges and the Department of Finance in December 1946, the government decided to increase each college grant by 40 per cent provided fees would be increased by 50 per cent, to be phased in over a period. The increased annual grant of £16,000 was only half what UCC had sought, and linking the grant with an increased fee stipulation was a government strategy repeated in later times. Here was the major piper very definitely calling the minor tune, and in the process conveying an unpleasantly realistic reminder that in the last financial analysis university autonomy was illusory – a bitter pill for O'Rahilly to swallow, given his rhetorical bragging about the virtual independence of UCC, and his repeated warnings against state intervention.

College financing intermittently preoccupied O'Rahilly for the remainder of his presidency, and the pattern of periodic memoranda continued.[29] On 13 September 1950, he applied to the finance minister in the first coalition government, Patrick McGilligan, for an immediate increase of £39,000 to meet various costs, some of them due to inflation. The response in January 1951 was a rise in the annual grant from £60,500 to £96,500 and in the separate and independent dairy science grant from £19,500 to £23,500. Again this was not sufficient, and in March 1954 shortly before O'Rahilly's retirement there was a further application based on a rapid rise in the cost of living between 1950 and 1953. At this stage what depressed O'Rahilly was not only the inadequacy but the uncertainty and ad hoc-ery of government grants. His overall experience of university financing led him (in a memorandum dated 8 June 1954 outlining an expansion plan) to a cautious, if not downright pessimistic, reflection:

> I think we should very critically scrutinise any proposals for further expenditure. We have yet to ascertain what is the attitude of the Government towards paying for the commitments we have already incurred. Only such proposals as may fairly be regarded as *urgent* should be passed for immediate adoption.

Another presidential memorandum on 30 July 1951 was concerned to explain that there was much pressure on the college to restore electrical engineering, previously dropped.[30]

Jim Hurley

A college policy of financial conservatism had the enthusiastic support of James Hurley, bursar and secretary from 1944 to his death in 1965.[31] Hurley exercised a dominant influence in the direction of prudent housekeeping and staying within the budget. That was in any case the fiscal mood of the time, and it would have been his philosophy during his previous career at managerial level in local government. Jim Hurley was a homespun, larger-than-life, college 'character' for over twenty years. Burly, genial, inquisitive and given to colourful and robust colloquialisms, he was racy of the West Cork soil whence he was sprung.

As well as being an able administrator, he had been a hurling star and, during the War of Independence, a leading member of Tom Barry's flying column. He was reported to know the right answer to that perennially favourite Cork question, 'who shot Michael Collins?', but remained uncharacteristically reticent about it as long as he lived. As a Republican in the Civil War, he later had the reflective capability and largeness of mind to conclude – as he admitted to this writer – that the Treaty had best served the country's interest in 1922 and that he should have been on that side.

Hurley took a lively interest in academic appointments, which were frequently a matter of political and lobbying interest in the era of canvassing that preceded the institution of assessors' boards. An enthusiastic localist, Jim Hurley saw no reason why college positions should not be given (other things being equal) 'to our own', that is, to Irish graduates of Cork extraction. In this, he was far from being an embarrassing exception. In college government, he was a dominant member of the 'nationalist' or what was facetiously called the 'Fenian' faction, which was opposed to a real or imagined 'Blueshirt' or 'hibernian' group and which enthusiastically promoted the cause of the Irish language in the college. As an active and high-profile secretary and bursar, he claimed he should have been on the Governing Body *ex officio*. As has been indicated, he kept a tight hold of the purse-strings and it hurt him to have to part with college money. When autumnal love ripened into marriage for a female professor, he is reported to have remarked gratefully, in his colourful fashion, that a pay-out from the children's allowances fund seemed unlikely.

While his administrative expertise filled an otherwise incompetent vacuum from O'Rahilly's departure in 1954 to Hurley's own death in 1965, the policy of careful housekeeping deteriorated thereafter into grudging parsimony and penny-pinching. A retired professor of physics recalls that the secretary/typist to the arts faculty worked for him on some afternoons in the mid-1960s – a sufficiently weird arrangement in itself – and that on these occasions the typewriter had to be transported across the Quadrangle and back, since the then bursar considered it an extravagance to purchase a machine for the physics department![32] The ghost of that particular bursar, David Leo Whyte (1965–72), would doubtless retort, and with truth, that the college simply did not have any money. In 1959, Charles T.G. Dillon, the new professor of electrical engineering (1959–76), complained that his department was in a state of crisis.[33]

More supplication, 1956

The college was once again cast in the role of supplicant in March 1956 when President Atkins and Jim Hurley met the secretary and assistant secretary of the Department of Education to discuss additional grants to UCC for 1956–57.[34] For the college, as always, the trouble was that the grants were not additional enough. While Hurley seemed prepared to be relatively robust in pushing college demands, Atkins's natural politeness was uppermost and he expressed his sincere thanks, saying that 'if the Minister and the Department of Education were not sympathetic then he would despair of finding sympathy anywhere!' The memorandum notes: 'asked whether he thought the additional overall grant sufficient, Dr Atkins would not go further than to say that it "presented a problem"'. He also reiterated the opinion expressed by O'Rahilly in 1945 that a university grants committee was the only solution to the chronic problem of college financing.

Atkins also stated that if the college's request for the rest of the gaol site were granted (which it was), it would not automatically involve the state in provision of capital for building purposes. With regard to the application for a capital grant of £229,000 for the extension of the civil engineering school, the assistant secretary's response was unsympathetic – there were civil engineering schools in all four university institutions, and there seemed to be a relative sufficiency of civil engineers. Perhaps the sharpest point made by the departmental side – not for the only time in such negotiations – was that the college could substantially increase its revenues at a stroke by raising fees. After all, if UCC claimed equality with UCD in the matter of application for state assistance, Cork should equalise its fees with Dublin by raising them the requisite 30 – 40 per cent. The UCC representatives were clearly shocked by this suggestion, protesting that the Governing Body would not hear of an increase above 25 per cent.

However, as is clear from this meeting and elsewhere, Atkins was most intensely pre-occupied with the problematic future of the medical and dental schools. He was relieved that there was some, even if inadequate, provision in the increased state grants for these schools. He was particularly alarmed by the report on a recent inspection of the dental school and he intended sending a telegram immediately to a spokesman in London, so that the British dental authorities should be informed at once that it would now be possible for the college to appoint a director over the school. The sense of crisis over the medical and dental schools is evident in GB discussions in the autumn of 1953.[35] The college was much upset by Richard Gordon's *Doctor at Large* which referred to medical degrees being readily obtainable at the fictional 'College of Apothecaries of Cork'.[36]

It should be remarked here that the college's concern for the medical school has always been of a different order from its attitude to the dental school. If the Damoclean sword intermittently suspended over the dental school had suddenly and fatally fallen, there would have been professional, educational, and to some extent economic regret in Cork and Munster but there would also have been an understanding of the hard expensive facts of training dentists, and perhaps not a little relief. The medical school, however, for all its professional and social elitism, has always been an indispensable component of the college: it had a great deal to do with the foundation of, and for a long period virtually *was*, the college. Fear of its closure therefore was a nightmare rather than a nuisance. Atkins had the gravest doubts whether, after the next General Medical Council (GMC) in 1960, the medical and dental schools would continue to be recog-nised. In fact, the fate of all the NUI medical schools was interlinked, and unless considerable state money for staffing and equipment was forthcoming they were more likely to sink than to swim together. In that dire case, only the Trinity College medical school would survive (which would be a religious as well as an educational disaster, though Atkins did not actually say that).

In a letter to the Taoiseach, John A. Costello, on 14 September 1956, Atkins returned to the theme of 'the ultimate fate of our Medical School'.[37] The college's response to the adverse reports of the American Medical Association and the GMC had involved 'imperative increases in staffing etc' and thus had added to accumulated debt. The only reason that the college had not applied in recent months to govern-ment for a substantial grant increase, given 'the grossly inadequate provision proposed

11.1 President Eamon de Valera, chancellor of the NUI, in UCC
to open an INTO summer course, July 1959.

in the 1956/57 Estimates', was because it did not wish to embarrass the government at
a time of serious financial difficulties. Atkins then indulged himself in a piece of
what's-to-become-of-us-all handwringing, his pessimism doubtless taking its tone
from the black mood of the country in the mid-1950s:

> I wish to reiterate what I have frequently stated that University College, Cork is in a
> deplorable state financially and that we are subject to continuous criticism when we are
> compared with universities of comparable size in Great Britain. It is public knowledge
> that the Treasury Grant to Queen's University, Belfast, exceeds the total government
> grant to the three Constituent Colleges of the National University of Ireland together
> with Trinity College, Dublin. How can we possibly attain modern standards whilst
> labouring under such a handicap?

Nonetheless, ever the gentleman, he hastened to state in conclusion that he would
not add to the Taoiseach's worries and assured him that 'every avenue would be
explored with a view to improving the financial position in Cork'.

At a time in the 1940s and 1950s when the universities were desperate for more state
financing and when they were being advised, not so helpfully, to look to fee increases
for more revenue, there were some early indications of governmental encouragement
of private benefactors, or at least of those who wished to endow research. The 1946
Finance Act provided tax relief to persons making payments to Irish universities for the
purpose of undertaking research related to the business or trade of such persons. The
1957 Finance Act provided similar relief to those who contributed financially to

research without any limitation on the type of research.[38] The idea was good but research was not flourishing and university benefactors were traditionally few. Research funding as a significant part of university revenue lay far in the future.

Accommodation: 1959 commission

Given a chronically bad college financial situation, the prospects of meeting accommodation needs in the late 1950s were not encouraging. The Commission on Accommodation Needs of the Constituent Colleges of the National University of Ireland was set up on 26 September 1957 and its report was published on 1 May 1959.[39] The submissions of President Atkins and the Governing Body referred to steadily increasing student numbers since the foundation of the state (apart from a decline in the 1920–26 period). A traditional pattern was evident in the geographical spread of students – 90 per cent from Munster, with over 50 per cent being born within thirty miles of the college. College policy was to make UCC 'part of the city and of the province, and to forge strong links with the industry and agriculture of the province'. President Atkins stated that about 75 per cent of Cork graduates were employed in Ireland. Although Irish universities had been comparable with those in America and Britain in the 1930s (was this retrospective wishful thinking?), they had fallen behind through lack of investment and the failure to recognise the existence of an 'academic revolution'.

Accommodation in UCC was pathetically inadequate everywhere but particularly in botany (where a leaky wooden hut was used as a junior laboratory), zoology, dairy technology and civil engineering (with army huts being used as drawing offices). If UCC was to be effectively modernised, claimed the president, it would need 89,000 square feet of new accommodation at a cost of about £550,000. With regard to student recreational facilities, fifteen additional acres of playing fields – and concomitant pavillions – were needed, as the Athletic Grounds were 'extremely congested'.

There was a sympathetic response from the commission which believed that the college's case was not exaggerated. Some of the conditions were of a subfactory standard. There was a 'virtual absence of private rooms for members of the staff' in the arts faculty. The report also deplored the poor working conditions in physiology where 'corridor space had been converted into rooms without windows'. While the commission was pleased with the restaurant ('a valuable community centre'), it found the facilities of the men's club to be meagre and the two small rooms for the three hundred women students to be hopelessly inadequate.

It took another decade for substantial improvement to be made in departmental accommodation, and students had to wait until the mid-1990s to enjoy the amenities which Joe Downey had described in 1940 as 'usually associated with university life' when he was urging the building of a student hall.[40] Meanwhile, the commission on accommodation solemnly endorsed the presidential promise, approved by the GB, that no matter how bad things were, there would be no building in the Quadrangle, the gardens or the 'open southern end'![41] Some years later, there was a rumour circulating in the college that only the alertness of the secretary had made the Governing Body aware of a proposal to create two storeys out of the Aula Maxima.

CHAPTER TWELVE

THE RESPONSIBLE REVOLUTION: THE 1960s AND AFTER

It is an age of revolution in which everything may be looked for.
Thomas Paine, 1737–1809

THE STOLID CONSERVATISM of UCC students was confirmed by their relatively mild response to the shock of student revolution worldwide in the 1960s. If
the revolution mood of UCD was 'gentle', then that of UCC was workmanlike and
constructive. Nevertheless, the scent of complex change in the Irish air was eagerly
sniffed by a ginger group of Cork students in the first half of the decade.[1] As elsewhere,
the pace of change was set by radical-minded individuals while the masses passively
adapted and the establishment slumbered on in its cosy world. Both President Atkins and
President McHenry were unimpressed and relatively uninfluenced by the winds of
change blowing through the Arch and the student body. In the early 1960s, the conservatism of staff attitudes is reflected in their submissions to the UCC Consultative Group,
set up in connection with the Commission on Higher Education.[2] Even for subsequent
presidents, change was constitutional rather than revolutionary, rarely offering a
disruptive threat to the serene tenor of academic existence. The Cork phase of the
student revolution was belated and therefore muted, and for the staff it was a transient
irritation rather than a challenge. Student demands were reasonable and sometimes symbolic, such as the opening up of the president's garden. All too soon, in the late 1980s,
the new conservatism set in, and students became absorbed in the bleakly mundane concerns of responding to higher examination standards, problems of finance and overcrowding, and the beckoning demands of the market economy outside. Forgotten were
the heady days of the Maoists and the red-flag waving on the fall of Saigon (1975). The
noisiest 'demo' of the early 1990s was against a cut in postgraduate grants (GB meeting,
18 October 1994). But if student power was only a rapidly retreating 1960s slogan, gains
had been made and there was no return to the deferential and hierarchical modes of a
former age.

The change in student ethos was linked to the rapid growth in student numbers.
There was a 65 per cent increase in the number of full-time students between
1959–60 and 1964–65.[3] The growth was particularly notable in the 1960–63 period,
especially in the sciences.[4] Cork student leaders of the early 1960s had the new
confidence of their age. Medical students (male) traditionally had a swaggering self-
assurance based on a cocky view of their own importance in Cork society which

311

entitled them to range freely in the pastures of sex and drink. Coolly disregarding authoritarianism, convinced of their superiority, and aided by the snobbery and inferiority complex of other students, they dominated, one might say overbalanced, college society. They were disproportionately prominent in running student societies, when they were interested, and they were particularly to the fore in the Philosophical Society, where they could provide impressive speakers. All this imbalance was levelled out in the process of student change. Non-medical students took up the running, emulated the sexual mores and general confidence of the meds (using that confidence politically rather than socially), integrated them into the swell of change, and ended their hegemony without at all eclipsing their distinctive lifestyle.

Student change was effected through student societies, new and old, and through Comhairle Teachta na Macléinn (CTM) itself.[5] The Political Discussion Group radicalised thinking generally, and the Markievicz Society was an early influence in promoting feminist consciousness among women and men students. Various kinds of Catholic activism – Christus Rex, Pax Romana, the Academy of St Thomas, the Legion of Mary – lost support and gradually faded away. Lively debate polarised around domestic and international issues in a way difficult to imagine ten years previously. Gradually, the college authorities changed their traditional opposition to allowing political party activity on campus.

In the repressive climate of 1951, the Mother and Child Scheme crisis generated little discussion in the college, though O'Rahilly made a right-wing meal out of it in the *Catholic Standard*. In contrast, the Congo crisis of 1961, and Ireland's part therein, provoked a lectures-and-discussion clash between those who deplored the Irish-supported 'violation' of Catholic Katanga by secular UN forces, and those who championed the agency of a new international order against neocolonial and reactionary interests. There are other ways of describing the issues, of course. Established conservative staff and radical students (plus a handful of junior lecturers) formed the opposing battle lines. It was the first modern and modernising international argument the college had known, and it was an enlivening experience for a new generation of students.[6]

Nationalism and the Irish language (still inextricably linked) were inherited contexts which even radical students saw no incongruity in espousing. A student republican group joined forces with the veteran IRA guerrilla leader, Tom Barry, to stage an absurd protest against the Earl of Rosse opening the 1964 Choral Festival, much to the annoyance of the festival's founding father, Professor Aloys Fleischmann. When he castigated the CTM for their immaturity in supporting the protest, thus proving their unfitness to participate in college government (which they had been claiming), their saucy reply ('commending your interest in student affairs'), confirmed once again that the age of student deference was over.[7]

Student activism took a more mature and progressive form in the shape of the 1967 'Teach-In', a major debate on the state and direction of the nation. It was held in multiple sessions in the Aula Maxima, various national figures participated, and the whole event was well publicised by John Healy, Ireland's leading journalist. It was typical of the UCC student tradition that for them the mainstream event of 1960s activism was a highly responsible, if exciting, 'teach-in' rather than Quadrangle or street rioting.

Adjustment in staff–student relations

From the mid-1960s, the deference of authoritarian days was replaced by a new independent-mindedness, a new questioning. Increased fees (a 25 per cent jump in 1971–73, for example) and crowded accommodation were no longer fatalistically accepted. Protest took the form of office occupation, picketing of Governing Body meetings, and even a lectures boycott but none of these ever caused unpleasantness or serious disruption, however fearful the more conservative staff might be that once the students began to reason (to adapt Voltaire) all was lost. Staff–student relations underwent an adjustment rather than a radical egalitarian change. While still according them the respect that was their due, students no longer revered their lecturers as olympian untouchables, and staff could no longer afford to treat students with what had been in some cases a cavalier disdain, as in being late for lectures, or simply not turning up without explanation. Classroom regimentation was dealt a blow with the disappearance of roll-calling in most lectures. The new lecturer–student relationship was marked by mutual respect and a welcome measure of informality. This was reflected, for example, in the gradual discarding, from the mid-1960s, of student and staff gowns. This did not happen without some regret on the part of the traditionalists, a handful of whom still accoutred themselves for teaching, thus establishing a reputation for old-world quaintness.[8] Sartorial change greatly enhanced informality and the end of the old stiffness which had assumed that correct attire would be observed all round. Twenty years earlier, even the most threadbare male student had been expected to wear a tie, and 'sports' jackets were frowned upon in the staff common-room.[9] From the 1960s, the informalising or Americanising of student lifestyle appeared to gather pace. And by the 1970s, so the joke went, the only way to tell academic from attendant staff was that the latter wore ties. Women students were also more sartorially relaxed. It is hard to speculate whether O'Rahilly would have been more scandalised by miniskirts than by slacks: in comparison, the unstockinged leg of his prurient day would have been the epitome of modesty.

Lecture-hall seating no longer conformed to lay–clerical and male–female segregation lines. With the reduction in, and later the near collapse of, religious vocations, the serried ranks of nuns, and of Capuchins and Kiltegan priestlings were no more.[10] Religious who still came to the college did so as individuals (though continuing to be based for the most part in community houses) whose habits – in both senses – now made them indistinguishable from lay students, who in turn were taking up seats according to personal inclination rather than by gender. Another straw in the more benign wind was a greater humanity in the way students were addressed by lecturers, the severe 'Mr' and 'Miss' giving way to more familiar vocatives.

But though lecturers and students might be more relaxed in one another's company (even to the hitherto unheard of extent of having a drink together after a society debate, for example), the rapid growth in student numbers paradoxically made mutual acquaintanceship more difficult than in the days of the socially unapproachable professor. The massive numbers at first year lectures in certain subjects meant a generally one-way communication, and called for histrionic rather than lecturing skills. The proliferation of 'junior' staff to deal with student population expansion, and the increasing specialisation and mushrooming of options, meant that many students had little contact with their professor until their honours degree year or even the postgraduate stage. In general, the huge numbers together with work burdens caused disorientation problems for some students, and lecturing was supplemented by counselling, the new secular age counterpart of spiritual advice. On the other hand, staff availability to students was facilitated by the fact that even junior lecturers now had offices.

It should be said that the lecturing staff has always enjoyed a particularly close relationship with students in the night classes for arts, commerce and law degrees. While standards are not lowered nor a 'simplified' approach adopted, lecturers are conscious of the sacrifices made by mature and highly motivated students, and are aware that a more direct and less speculative line is the appropriate one to take. Night

12.1 Seán Ó Riada, who lectured in UCC from 1963
until his premature death in 1971.

12.2 The poet Seán Ó Ríordáin.

students are understandably anxious to get to the heart of the matter: moreover, they know where that heart lies. The hard work involved for a lecturer in taking a night class through to degree stage results in a deep satisfaction with a task successfully achieved. These remarks apply at a more individual level to the 'mature' students who account for a steadily increasing percentage of student numbers in the day classes.

Intoxicating milieu

The various liberating forces of the carefree 1960s produced a literary and musical flowering in the nation at large and in a particular form at UCC. While it would be absurd to generalise about a 'sex, drugs and rock-'n-roll' culture, there was a new sexual exhilaration, intensified by a nodding acquaintanceship with mild drugs, while poetry (in English and Irish) and traditional music supplied the third component. Irish culture, escaping at last from the shackles of nationalism, stimulated a young school of poets writing in an intoxicating bilingual milieu. Composer and musician Seán Ó Riada lectured from 1963 to his premature death in 1971, and his all too brief association with UCC glitteringly symbolised the vibrancy of the 1960s in (certain areas of) college life. Three other 'Seáns' were similarly influential in the period – Ó Tuama (Irish), Lucy (English) and Ó Ríordáin, as visiting lecturer (Irish).[11] Things have long since returned to a more prosaic level but the gains of the sexual revolution have been consolidated. Amorous entanglements in the lower grounds and even in the president's garden no longer raise eyebrows, and gay and lesbian groups have been recognised as student societies, with only a lone ecclesiastical voice mildly raised in dissent at the Governing Body.

The decline of college authoritarianism and of clerical influence brought about self-determination in student affairs, and the college authorities tacitly conceded as much. The process gained pace from the 1960s to the 1980s. Student societies selected their own topics for debate without having to seek staff or presidential approval, and they were also at liberty to invite unvetted speakers. The right to publish student magazines without censorship was gradually established, or more accurately, accepted. In this connection, the controversy surrounding the publication of *The Red Rag* in 1973 was a turning point. It contained politically 'objectionable' material and sexually explicit cartoons, which the student editors claimed were send-ups of sleazy English magazines but which scandalised some academics. Against the better judgement of others who felt the best way to deal with such effusions in the modern age was simply to ignore them, the Academic Council set up a subcommittee to investigate the matter. The students enjoyed themselves enormously in ably defending their position and producing 'expert' legal opinion. The process turned out to be embarrassing for the Academic Council, which realised it had overreached itself. It was a maturing experience in dealing with the new confident student breed.

The conservative older professors continued to bemoan the collapse of moral standards, and the dean of the arts faculty solemnly announced he could not 'present' the editor of the magazine for a degree at the forthcoming conferring, since he could not truthfully affirm that the young man was suitable, in the presentation formula phrase, *tam in moribus quam in doctrina*! The gentleman in question went on in due course to become a pillar of the administrative establishment in another university. The college authorities thereafter left the students to their own publishing devices. Official eyes are today studiously averted from the pages of the weekly *Gazette*, which regularly offers a rough diet of sexual explicitness and anti-religious effusions, and makes extensive use of a rich scatological vocabulary. A scurrilous production in the Irish language, *Cocascáil: Irisleabhar Seachtain na Gaeilge, 1987*, attracted even less attention.

Men and women students of the 1990s take all this in their stride. Similarly, official recognition of the Gay and Lesbian Society did not, as some conservative governors feared, herald the arrival of a Cork Gomorrah, the mainstream sexual orientation continuing to prove durably attractive. Nor did religion disappear from the campus. Its adherents had every opportunity to express their beliefs and practices in a variety of liturgical, charitable and socially conscious forms. Yet they now constitute – for the moment, at least – a low-profile minority on campus. Ecclesiastics were still prominent on the Governing Body – but their contributions were offered democratically and were generally secular in content. Moving with the times, they rarely brought any specific clerical or denominational interest to bear on the proceedings.

Student liberation, such as it was in UCC, was looked on sympathetically by junior staff, who were being recruited from the late 1960s in considerable numbers to deal with the increase in students. There was a certain near-generational community of view with students and a corresponding gulf between younger and older staff. Like students, junior staff also had their grievances. Professors and statutory lecturers were first-class members of the academic community, with independent powers of examining; the automatic right to sit in, and deliberate at, faculty meetings; and, as full members of the university, the privilege of attending conferring ceremonies. Assistant lecturers (or college lecturers as they were to become) were college employees not university lecturers, were formally categorised as assistants to the professors, and resented their exclusion from faculty meetings and conferrings. Since they did not have a statutory obligation to examine, they were well paid for the extra duties of invigilating at examinations and marking scripts. But in an academic community sensitively preoccupied with pecking order, title and prestige, the subordinate status rankled. For reasons of elitism, inertia and the complexity of the college– university relationship, it took time for the grievances of junior staff to be examined, let alone resolved. Participation in faculty meetings satisfied a basic academic-community aspiration: levelling out a difference of title proved a much more difficult matter. Meanwhile, the Academic Staff Association (deriving much of its strength from its affiliation with the Irish Federation of University Teachers) played a vital role in focusing staff problems and making sure they stayed on the agenda of the college authorities. Some of the senior professors, as well as deploring the change in student mores, were inclined to think that trade unionism was an inappropriate activity for the academic staff.

Was general change in UCC from the 1960s facilitated by change in the class composition of students and staff over the same period? UCC students (and *a fortiori* staff) have come historically from an urban and rural class that ranges from the affluent to the frugally self-sufficient. Educationally and socially ambitious sections of the lower middle classes – teachers and law clerks, for example – traditionally made sacrifices to send their sons and (less commonly) daughters to college. But a university education was entirely beyond the means of children of artisans and unskilled labourers, except for the occasional scholarship holder. There was no post-war revolution in social intake, as there was in the UK, because the privileged fee-paying system remained unchanged. But there seems to have been a shift – difficult to chart statistically – within the 'middle class' student body from the children of old propertied or opulent professional families to those of a new urban middle class, more favourably disposed to cultural and social change, and slightly better endowed with social conscience.

The growth in student numbers from the 1960s was in itself a democratising tendency since it helped to dilute elitism. But it was the introduction of student grants, grudging and ungenerous though they might be in amount, together with the raising of entrance standards, that achieved a substantial measure of equality of opportunity, broadening and lowering the class intake, and sharpening if not radicalising student concerns – though leaving the college still a world away from the utopian goal of 'the poor man's university', the visionary meritocracy which was optimistically expected with the passing of the Irish Universities Act of 1908.

The McHenry presidency

The college administration of the 1960s neither initiated nor responded to the groundswell of change in the student body and in a section of the academic staff. Administratively and physically, the college had difficulty in merely ticking over, and it deteriorated throughout the mid-1960s. Perhaps this was due to a chronic shortage of money rather that to managerial ineptitude. A cautious and conservative president, Henry St J. Atkins, who retired in 1963, was a relic of the O'Rahilly era and it is understandable that he should not have been innovative. The academic community, who surely should have been able to sniff the bracing winds of change, might at this point have looked for an appropriate leader to respond to the challenge. The sixty-seven-year-old Professor John J. McHenry who now became president (1964–67) could not reasonably hope to transcend his caretaker status. A distinguished professor

12.3 President John J. McHenry, 1964–67.

of experimental physics (who had unsuccessfully contested the presidency in 1954), McHenry was a man of considerable presence, dignified and courteous (if a little glacial), with considerable *gravitas*. But, quite simply, he was too old, all the more so at a time of radical change.

The extremely capable college secretary, Jim Hurley, kept the college functioning till his lengthy illness and premature death in February 1965. His successor, D.L. (Leo) Whyte, was a dominant bureaucratic figure during the remainder of the McHenry presidency. When McHenry was about to reach his seventieth birthday, there was an outlandish move to keep him in office. The proposer of this non-starter cited historical and contemporary examples of geriatric energy and innovativeness (GBM, 24 Jan. 1967), but the Governing Body was unimpressed and signalled the start of a new presidential contest. McHenry's presidency had been the shortest in the history of the college.

Ó Ciardha opposed

It was not so much that an influential academic caucus ardently desired a prolongation of McHenry's presidency but that his probable successor provoked strong opposition. The extension proposal was in reality a ploy to prevent Tadhg Ó Ciardha (Carey) from becoming president. The majority vote of the Governing Body, where he had established a power base, was a show of support for Ó Ciardha, registrar since 1954 and therefore heir presumptive to the presidency. He had already unsuccessfully contested the presidency against McHenry (more than twenty years his senior) in 1963. He was opposed by a significant group of academics for their different reasons. One of his opponents, a contemporary and rival young(ish) bull, may have had his own sights set on the presidency next time round. Ó Ciardha had one of the sharpest minds in Irish university circles and an unrivalled knowledge of how the university system worked but his seemingly arrogant and brusque manner in office, classroom and council chamber had alienated some of his colleagues as well as future graduates. On the other hand, his familiarity with and keen knowledge of local affairs, as well as his fluency in vernacular discourse made him popular with lay (i.e. non-academic) members of the Governing Body. In turn, his popularity with lay governors confirmed the opposition of those academics (not usually members of the GB) who superciliously resented lay influence in academic appointments and believed that the Governing Body was largely composed of ignoramuses as well as being a hotbed of localism, favouritism and nepotism.

Another reason for the opposition to Ó Ciardha was good, old-fashioned Cork snobbery. He was a scholarship boy of working-class background who was a product of the North Monastery school, an all-Irish Christian Brothers educationally-brilliant but socially-downmarket institution. Though Ó Ciardha was ideologically conservative and conventionally religious, he made no secret of his robust contempt for the refined sensitivities of the Cork bourgeoisie, and the sentiment was thoroughly reciprocated. (As president, he was to discontinue the traditional strawberries-and-cream garden parties.) Moreover, his political camp was unreconstructed Fenian Irish-

Irelandism. To some extent, the Irish language was still a litmus test of where one 'stood' in college on related issues. At a more disinterested level, some of Ó Ciardha's opponents believed that being registrar did not confer an automatic right of succession and that he lacked presidential quality. He was undistinguished as an academic and virtually unpublished, and his administrative experience was largely local. Some felt that a person of wider experience was needed to reform and reconstruct UCC.

A round robin now mobilised the opposition.[12] The ringleaders, having selected the man to stand against Ó Ciardha, undertook the difficult task of persuading him to enter the fray against a former student and a fellow-statistician, with a similar cultural background. Professor Michael Donald McCarthy, popularly known as 'Donal Mac', had been a highly successful and popular professor of mathematical physics (1944–49) who had left UCC in 1949 to become assistant director (later director) of the Central Statistics Office. His relationships with O'Rahilly and with Atkins were, for different reasons, cool to chilly. He had moved in the mid-1960s to the newly established Economic (later 'and Social') Research Institute where he was approached by his crown-bearing former Cork colleagues.[13] The decision to contest the vacant presidency was not taken lightly and was influenced (according to an intimate source) by his concern at the condition of UCC, as was evident particularly in the neglected state of its buildings.[14] The prolonged use of army huts as drawing offices for engineering students seemed particularly symbolic of dereliction.

Ó Ciardha was solidly supported by the Governing Body (by eighteen votes to seven for McCarthy) but his opponents had worked hard on the more academically influential university Senate in Dublin. The result here was dramatically close, McCarthy being appointed president by a margin of just one vote. Ó Ciardha did not participate in the election, feeling it was improper to vote for himself: if he had done so, the result would have been a tie (since McCarthy was not a Senate member) and the chairman's casting vote would have ensured the registrar's election.[15] (While the voting proceeded, Ó Ciardha's walk around Merrion Square could be considered to be the most important perambulation in college history.) As things turned out, Ó Ciardha accepted his defeat gracefully, and during the years of McCarthy's presidency (1967–78) he co-operated loyally in the work of reform and reconstruction. Given the registrar's expertise and influence, McCarthy's reforms could not have been successfully implemented if Ó Ciardha had sulked in his tent (or rather, in his gloomy office). Conversely, it was in McCarthy's enlightened self-interest to recognise Ó Ciardha's strength in the GB and accord him proportionate influence in the administration. This was a formidable governing duo at a time when college power was still concentrated in the top two offices, though the committee system was now being introduced.

The McCarthy presidency

McCarthy was a native of Midleton, a former Cork hurler and in some ways as local and as racy of the soil as Ó Ciardha. But one of the significant differences was that he had outside experience as a public servant and administrator which he could now bring back

12.4 President Michael D. McCarthy, 1967–78.

to the college. People also believed, as they generally do in Ireland, that the personal contacts he had made in high places would be very useful. Cork academics felt their Dublin colleagues had the great advantage of frequently rubbing shoulders on the social circuit with government ministers and heads of civil service departments. McCarthy, it was thought in a vague way, had access to this magic circle and Cork would now benefit accordingly. His objective was to reform and modernise UCC after a long period in the doldrums and at a time of imminent expansion. He brought to this task a remarkable combination of qualities – formidable intelligence, flinty integrity, tough courage, mature and varied experience (he was aged sixty years when he took over) and an extraordinary capacity for sustained hard work. In addition, he had an overriding sense of purpose.

Six college officers were now to constitute the top management: the president, registrar, bursar (from 1974 entitled finance officer and secretary), librarian, college engineer (later called the planning officer), and dean of student affairs (regrettably a short-lived office, being replaced after the retirement of its first occupant, Professor Seán Teegan, by the less prestigious part-time office of ombudsman). McCarthy's reform of the administration included the appointment of a new finance officer and secretary (Michael F. Kelleher, 1974–), who was to be one of UCC's most valuable assets. The direction of the library was also put on a more professional basis though the librarianship was to lack continuity and sustained purpose for many years.

Canvassing and reform

> *Canvassing is forbidden but candidates may interview governors*
> appointments regulation

Canvassing by, and on behalf of, candidates for academic posts was a feature of college life from its foundation up to the institution in the mid-1970s of the assessors board system. In Queen's College days, testimonials were hawked around and various pressures put on Dublin Castle, which made the appointments. With the institution of the National University, the hydra of democracy (of a sort) took over that role. Today, there tends to be a selective recollection that the only practitioners of what is seen as a dubious process were non-academic or 'political' members of the Governing Body. It is conveniently forgotten that hectic canvassing went on at faculty and Academic Council levels; that meetings to consider appointments were looked forward to as enjoyable and exciting, ensuring attendance by otherwise infrequently seen members; and that few academics dissented from the system, recriminations arising only when there were allegations of violations of the unwritten rules of the game. In the academic bodies, at least, the appointments process was perceived as judgement by one's peers, and it was not so much the canvassing itself that in the end aroused opprobrium and discredited the system as the concomitant secrecy, skullduggery and double-crossing.

Because of its critical role in the appointments process, the Governing Body was a forum of intense canvassing. Unfortunately, local authority representation meant that the GB could also be a centre of competing party politics. In theory, canvassing was forbidden but by virtue of a fine distinction, candidates were permitted to interview governors. Governors, both academic and lay, enjoyed the feeling of power, real or illusory, that derived from being lobbied and from casting votes. This was not necessarily incompatible with the performance of duty according to one's conscience. Despite condescending academic folklore to the contrary, lay governors were not notoriously more amenable to influence than others, simply less informed and more susceptible to political pressures in favour of local candidates. An academic (significantly) tells the story[16] of a bewildered county councillor sitting next to him at a Governing Body meeting, complaining that he had been told to vote for 'a fellow called Lucy' and being unable to find that name in the list of candidates. To his great relief, the mystery was solved when he was told that 'Lucy' was not a male surname but a female Christian name! The episode more than any other that has given lay governors a bad name is Seán Ó Faoláin's canvassing odyssey for the UCC chair of English in 1931, as recounted in his *Vive Moi!*[17] However, it should be remembered that his offensive depiction of county councillors as bucolic ignoramuses owes as much to the wounded *amour propre* of a rejected candidate as to his caustic pen. Nonetheless it is true that under the system applicants from outside the college, or at least outside the NUI, stood little chance of being appointed.

The Senate of the National University has traditionally been regarded as the ulti-mate guarantor of academic integrity, the assembly that has transcended the sordid politics of governing bodies, reversed their sometimes dubious decisions, and upheld the high-minded recommendations of the Academic Council. Disregarding the ingenuous assumptions here, the basic fact is that senators – whether academics, convocation representatives or government nominees – were (and are) the final arbiters of statutory appointments and could therefore themselves be subjected to heavy pressures. Heads had to be counted in the Senate as well as in the subordinate bodies and there was no divine guarantee that every senator would rigorously exclude all non-academic considerations. For example, there was for years a dominant Cumann na nGaedheal/Fine Gael faction in that august body.

Professor Aloys Fleischmann recalls that he and Professor James Hogan attempted at an early stage to break the bonds of localism and favouritism, by suggesting to the Academic Council that a selection committee including external assessors should be set up to 'vet' candidates for academic positions.[18] For some years, the idea was opposed 'with might and main' particularly in the Governing Body where, according to Fleischmann, there was a xenophobic objection to external assessors as alien, with all the sinister connotations of that term. This obscurantism was eventually faced up to, and faced down, by President McCarthy under whom the assessors-based appoint-ments process, with external representation, was established. Perhaps Fleischmann had too pessimistic a view of the role of the GB, of which he himself had never been a member. In retirement, and shortly before his death, he expressed renewed (though quite unfounded) fears that the old localism might creep back under a new and more autonomous status for the constituent colleges.[19]

The 'assessors board' process, though occasionally in need of refinements, has worked well, raising the standards of appointments and consequently college prestige, and effectively ending canvassing, party politics, nepotism and localism. The recommending (faculties, Academic Council) and appointing (Governing Body, Senate) bodies still retain their powers, since the assessors boards have no statutory standing, but the appointment process in the overwhelming majority of cases now simply consists of unanimous endorsements of the assessors' recommendations. The occasional refusal of automatic endorsement reflects either a rare flaw in the working of the system or a notorious lapse into the old politicking. The exceptions only serve to demonstrate the well-nigh universal acceptance of the process. It is difficult to exaggerate the importance of its introduction at a time when the college was about to undergo unprecedented staff expansion.

Interestingly, the process does not apply to the appointment of college presidents. (Fleischmann recalls that Academic Council support for reform was conditional on the exclusion of presidential candidates from any assessors system: many members had a potential interest in the office.[20]) And so the Governing Body and university Senate exercise their appointing powers in presidential elections in the old-fashioned way.

But canvassing by presidential candidates now takes place in open democratic forum – judgement by peers in the best sense – and while intermediate bodies like faculties, the Academic Council and the Academic Staff Association have no structural or formal part in the appointment proceedings, their recommendations in an increasingly democratised university community are unlikely to be ignored. Even so, a presidential election can leave festering wounds.

One case that illustrates the infirmities of the old system concerns a vacant lectureship in medical jurisprudence in the college in 1933. (Part-time posts in the medical school were eagerly sought after: they carried social prestige, they represented an entrée into a charmed medical circle, and they boosted professional practice.[21]) The candidates included Dr John Kiely and Dr Noel O'Donovan, both of whom were to make their names in surgery, and Dr Michael Riordan, President P.J. Merriman's brother-in-law. According to Kiely, O'Donovan was the firm choice of the Governing Body but Merriman's influence with the NUI Senate secured Riordan the job.[22] Merriman, however, was most indignant at the Governing Body vote:

> Friends of two of the candidates got political influence at work and members attended the Governing Body whom I hardly knew . . . None of the candidates has ever been prominent in politics, but a prominent Cumann na nGaedheal officer regarded the result as a victory. And yet I know Riordan lent his motor car to Cumann na nGaedheal at the last election.[23]

As a footnote, the Governing Body discussion afforded a lurid sidelight on Alfred O'Rahilly's personality, as James Hogan revealed to Michael Tierney:

> O'Rahilly who was supporting Donovan changed over to Kiely at the last moment, proposing him in a speech which did more harm than good . . . It is very like O'Rahilly to put his foot in it. He is a very dangerous friend. The Jesuits must have infected some fatal virus in his blood, for otherwise he can be very brilliant.[24]

It is not surprising that Hogan, witnessing these shenannigans, should have favoured a reform of the appointments system. It is also evident that Merriman's objection was to unfair tactics rather than to the system itself.

A related reform was the abolition in 1973 of Statute XXXIV (1937), the so-called 'Irish statute', a cultural purity test which had required candidates for statutory posts in a number of departments to establish their competence in the Irish language. If they failed to do so, in the judgement of the professor of Irish who was assigned this unpleasant and invidious task by statute,[25] they were excluded from further consideration. The statute was widely perceived as unjustly excluding possibly superior candidates (to the college's detriment) and as hypocritical to boot, since the Irish language was rarely used as a teaching medium in the stipulated departments. However, as a compensation for the abolition of Statute XXXIV the Irish language was accorded special status in the college, with the establishment of an important statutory supervisory board, Bord na Gaeilge (Statute XCV 1973).

The 'administrative revolution'

In the McCarthy years and after, some academics did not take kindly to what they saw as the mushroom growth of professional college administration, and some administrative–academic tension has persisted. The 'them and us' attitude is a common feature of modern university development. In the first place, UCC academics had been accustomed, pre-McCarthy, to having virtually no administration at all. Now, it seemed, administrators were proliferating everywhere (contemporaneous staff and student expansion was overlooked!) but most objectionably in the hallowed wings of the Quadrangle, where lecturing had proceeded from the foundation of the Queen's College. The well-equipped and richly carpeted offices of some administrators was contrasted with the academics' austere accommodation (with serviceable floor matting). Academics saw themselves as more and more pushed out to the periphery of the campus. Besides, some of these new administrative jobs seemed to have little justification for existence. And, of course, in terms of funding, the creation of every new administrative post was held to be at the expense of library development or of an additional lectureship!

One can understand how some of these neurotic (and perhaps intellectually snobbish) academic attitudes developed, and there was some substance in the complaints. There was an ill-defined but real perception that the balance between academics and administration had altered, making it difficult to locate where the real decisions were being made.[26] Besides, it cannot be gainsaid that professional university administrators and librarians sometimes forget that their sole purpose is to serve academic needs, and instead behave as if their offices were ends in themselves. But in UCC at least, the administration has served the academic community well, and at its highest level has shown itself sensitively attuned to academic concerns and values.

The administrative takeover of Quadrangle offices made sense in terms of the need for a central service to academic departments, few of which in any case are more than a few minutes' walk from the Quadrangle, in what is still a remarkably compact campus. In this connection, it was really the arts departments (or *some* arts departments), rather than the academic community at large, that resented the loss of Quadrangle lecture rooms, which they also would have grudged to their fellow-academics. It is interesting that when the administrative revolution had been accomplished a number of lecture rooms were retained in the West Wing. This was a concessionary gesture to nostalgia but it was also a proper acknowledgement of the academic desire to maintain teaching continuity in the heart of the college, even though many faculties had no share in this continuity.

Greatly improved facilities for the academic staff were a welcome feature of the McCarthy administration. A properly equipped office for each staff member was soon taken for granted, though a satisfactory telephone service had to await telecommunications advances at large. (A much recounted incident featured an enraged professor who finally gave up on the frustrations of the college telephone service, pulled his office phone from its moorings, parcelled it up, stormed his way to the college secretary's office, and there deposited the offending item.) The privacy of individual rooms – and this was the presidential intention – now encouraged staff to stay on campus during (and indeed after) office hours, in contrast to the general tendency, say, thirty years earlier, to come to the college only to give lectures. At that period, so-called staff 'private' rooms were few and far between, and were anything but private, being little more than points of call for collecting or depositing books and gowns, or exchanging guarded pleasantries with colleagues. Interviews with students or supervision of postgraduates had to take place while standing at a window-sill in the corridor of the West Wing, or in a corner of the history library. The new arrangements were obviously beneficial all round – to staff, students, and teaching and research standards. The academics who most appreciated the new facilities were those who had experienced the skeletal servicing of the old penny-pinching days.

From the late 1960s departments were assigned secretary/typists on a regular basis, with the larger departments having a gradually expanding secretariat. Throughout the college, the secretariat was structured into hierarchies or grades so that limited opportunities for promotion came to exist in this area. Management structures and industrial relations were the new catchwords and the new order of the day. Technicians, tradesmen, gardeners and 'general operatives' (formerly labourers) made up the essential infrastructure of the college. One retired academic rather cynically reflected that the efficiency with which the college functioned was proportionate to the degree of descent in the pyramid: where things really worked was, literally, on the ground. A new college sub-empire, the origins of which date from McCarthy's time, comprises the network of attendants and security personnel, a far cry from the handful of porters fifty years ago.

Vice-presidency revived

At the foundation of the Queen's Colleges, the office of vice-president was one of prestige and influence as is evident from the inclusion of vice-presidents in the Colleges Board of 1845, and from the significant part played by Vice-President John Ryall in the early history of QCC. However, the office did not survive Ryall. The long ascendancy of Professor Alexander Jack as registrar (1876–1906) and his prominent part in keeping things going during the turn-of-the-century decline gave the registrarship an importance which it maintained thereafter. With the expansion of the 1960s and 1970s, such was the burden of presidential work that it was deemed necessary in 1973 to revive the office of vice-president, albeit in a role of lesser importance than in the 1845 arrangement. (Deputy or acting presidents were in a different category, being appointed in an ad hoc capacity to function during presidential absences or illnesses, or during an interregnum.) Under the new dispensation, the vice-president would be available to help out the president generally, to chair faculties and committees, and to represent the college extramurally. Some initial GB opposition seemed to be based on the fear that the new post might encroach on, or tend to undermine, the registrar's jurisdiction. The job specifications were rather vague. College wags said that President McCarthy created the office so that he could get on with the work while the vice-president attended dinners, but that these roles were reversed post-McCarthy. The vice-president would be appointed by the Governing Body, on the president's nomination, from the senior professorial staff and would serve on a part-time basis. The post was not envisaged as being at all on the same exalted level as that of registrar or secretary, the two top officials who together with the president formed the college troika. Nevertheless, the vice-presidency became imperceptibly more significant when the office was put on a statutory basis in 1976. The first vice-president (1974–76) of the modern era was Professor Patrick D. Barry (mathematics, 1965–) who did notable work in handling relations between UCC and Limerick third-level colleges which were put for a time, with varying degrees of enthusiasm, under the general umbrella of the NUI and the particular supervision of UCC. By far the happiest and longest-lasting relationship was the association between UCC and Mary Immaculate College of Education, Limerick.

The succession of vice-presidents proceeded smoothly and efficiently on a three-year tenure basis until 1989, when a new president appointed two vice-presidents (one of them being the first woman to hold the office) whose assigned tasks gave rise to an apparent conflict of jurisdictions with the registrar and the secretary. A com-

12.5 Professor Máire Mulcahy became the first woman vice-president in 1989.

mittee of the Governing Body investigated the issues involved, and the GB on 23 October 1990 confirmed that:

> within the central administrative structure, executive responsibility for the non-
> academic business of the College is, under the President, assigned to the Finance
> Officer and Secretary [and] . . . executive responsibility for the academic business of
> the College (including the role related primarily to academic planning, the formulation
> of academic policy and the continuous review and monitoring of its implementation)
> is, under the President, assigned to the Registrar.

Thus, the primacy of the registrar and of the finance officer and secretary in their respective areas was confirmed. The inference was that the vice-presidents occupied relatively subordinate offices which must not encroach on the areas of the two senior college officers. In particular, the GB decision was regarded as vindicating the position of the registrar in the academic community. As frequently happened in college history, the dispute about issues had been compounded by a personality clash, but fortunately that resolved itself with one change of personnel. However, there remained an undercurrent of tension which resurfaced some years later.

Physical development

Si monumentum requiris, circumspice. As well as the administrative revolution, and the reform in the appointments system, the principal McCarthy legacy was the college development plan of 1972.[27] This was a twenty-year programme of physical develop-ment around the original buildings: the college was to stay where it always had been, there would be no Cork Belfield, only an extended campus. The plan not only provided for future buildings and land acquisition in the vicinity but for a student population expanding from its 1972 base of about 4,000 to a maximum of 7,000 twenty years ahead. McCarthy felt that the distinctive character of the UCC campus could not be maintained if the student body were to exceed 7,000. The development plan received the approval of the Cork Corporation and the financial support of the government. Understandably, the plan has had to be adapted in the intervening years, because of changing priorities, financial cutbacks and so on. Indeed, the plan itself provided for periodic reviews. Basically, however, the 1993 revision is firmly grounded on the original 1972 plan.

Of the two major buildings associated with McCarthy's presidency, one gave him little joy and the other he did not live to see. We have already referred to the circumstances in which the contract for the science building was awarded. The building was to provide spacious accommodation (though the design of the chemistry laboratories was too inflexible for modern trends) and two splendid lecture theatres, which also became favourite centres for debating societies. But the exterior was, by any aesthetic standards, an 'abomination', to use the description of former President Tadhg Ó Ciardha who admitted he could hardly bear to look at it![28] Fortunately, it does not impair the view of the Quadrangle, though its towering bulk dominates the skyline when the college is viewed externally from certain directions.

The building had commenced before McCarthy's appointment as president, but he had to deal with its development and outcome (1967–71). The cladding proved to be defective and much of it needed to be replaced. Perhaps the general annoyance with the science building explains why there was never any official opening ceremony. The allocation of space within the building was another headache for McCarthy and his successor. The original intention was that the science building would replace the old physical and chemistry laboratory built in Windle's time (and today occupied by civil engineering), and that physics and chemistry would share the new accommodation equally. In the event, chemistry, with an increased professorial staff and an active and varied research programme, took by far the larger space while the physics area was much reduced. The physics department was very unhappy about this arrangement. Other disciplines such as computer science (and the computer centre) were also accommodated. One of the important issues involved in all of this was McCarthy's insistence that allocation of space was not a matter of individual departments' rights but the business of the general college administration. It is a matter that has never been quite resolved to everybody's satisfaction.

The new library was planned in McCarthy's time but because of unconscionable delays was not completed until 1982. From the foundation of Queen's College Cork, the library was regarded as the very heart of its activities, not alone for its students and staff but as a research centre for the scholars of Munster. This was a recurring theme over the decades, with particular reference to the humanities. Recurring, too, were the complaints about library overcrowding, and inadequate shelving and storage space. There was a great leap forward during O'Rahilly's time, with much of the development attributable to his own direct and energetic involvement – a commemorative tablet outside the old library in the North Wing referred to him as '*bibliothecae curator diligentissimus*'.[29]

Despite extended opening hours, the hiving off of sectional or faculty libraries and the use of the Lee Maltings for storage, the rapid expansion of student numbers in the 1960s and 1970s made the provision of a new library building imperative. President McCarthy set up a special committee to consider all aspects of library planning. The committee travelled extensively to view university libraries in various countries. The decision (part of the college plan) to build the new library in the Quarry may fairly be described as a stroke of genius. Not only did it exemplify the already proven ingenuity of college planners in resourcefully finding locations in a restricted area and maximising the use of space but the Quadrangle was at last gracefully completed in a harmonious and unobtrusive blend of old and new, with the ancient trees on the embankment acting very effectively as an aesthetically pleasing screen.

Some graduates and a few staff sentimentally regretted the demise of the old Quarry. It was of the very essence of the college experience, they protested, nostalgically recalling muddily titanic inter-faculty sporting battles long ago, and conveniently forgetting the hazards presented by a dangerously thin pitch surface and the inconvenience caused by noise levels to neighbouring lectures. While nostalgia is understandable and touching – and pays its own tribute to the college – it has little to do with here-and-now imperatives, and is strongest, significantly, in graduates no longer in touch with the needs of an ever-developing institution. They wanted the college they knew to remain just as they remembered it in their golden student days.

It was agreed that the splendid modern five-storey structure should be called the Boole Library, after the great mathematician who is the most renowned professor in the history of the college. It was an unusual and very welcome development in UCC to have a building (or a lecture hall or a laboratory) called after a prominent personage associated with the college. The Boole appellation was applied, not only to the library but also to the whole new underground complex of associated build-ings – four spacious lecture halls, a student centre and assorted offices and shops. An arresting pedestrian entrance on College Road provided a novel view of the college. The extensive tiled plaza ('Red Square') over the underground area, situated between the library and the restaurant, quickly became the new focus of student activity, providing not only a social meeting place but an open-air forum for art exhibitions and musical performances. Thus there was a historic student-grouping shift away from the Stone Corridor (the area adjacent to the old library) just about the time when the pressure of increased student numbers on restricted central-campus space began to be palpable.

A Cork university yet again?

McCarthy's presidency coincided with a period of much discussion at national level about the future structure of the Irish university system, though the outcome was to be inconclusive and change was deferred to another day. McCarthy and most of the Cork academic community favoured independent university status for the college, an intermittently flickering aspiration going back through Windle's time to the early years of QCC. That aspiration was modified by the sober reflection that new government legislation might well put the existing measure of autonomy, as represented by the charter, at risk. That was O'Rahilly's attitude in the 1940s and 1950s when a neurotic distrust of state action prevailed. In the more buoyant atmosphere of the late 1960s and early 1970s, there was an eager expectation of change for the better in university structures – more, not less, autonomy for Cork. Of the other two NUI colleges, Galway, being the smallest and naturally worried by its viability, was more fearful of change while the attitude of the giant UCD, generally in favour of independence, would always be the crucial factor in deciding the eventual outcome. In UCC, special committees devoted much time and research to investigating all potential aspects of a new Cork university structure, and extensive reports were prepared.

University issues, however, have never loomed large on government agendas, and the proposal made by Richard Burke, minister for education 1973–76, seemed particu-larly egregious. It was that UCD and TCD should each be independent universities, while Cork and Galway, 130 miles apart, should comprise what would in effect be a rump NUI. Limerick, which had long been clamouring for a university institution, was not even mentioned! The existing state of affairs was infinitely preferable to this worst of all possible Irish university worlds. UCC and UCG co-operated to oppose the Burke plan, which was dropped after the minister met representatives of the two colleges. Such a ministerial change of mind was a very rare event.[30] However, by the end of McCarthy's presidency, an independent Cork university was nowhere in sight, and the failure to realise one of his cherished hopes was a major disappointment to him.

Being a hard worker himself and insisting on high standards generally, Donal McCarthy did not suffer fools, laggards or sots gladly. Far from genial by disposition and exhibiting at best a very dry sense of humour, he seemed impersonal, if not dour, to many of his colleagues. In fact, he was an extraordinarily kind man, as is attested alike by students and staff whose personal problems were greatly eased by his understanding and generosity. He felt no particular sense of obligation to those who had campaigned for his appointment as president (or perhaps against the appointment of another), and had no hesitation in 'scorning the base degrees by which he did ascend'. Within months, some of his erstwhile supporters were accusing him of being stubborn and authoritarian, and the nickname 'Papa Doc', half-critical, half-humorous, was bandied around. One department head has claimed that McCarthy used the phrase 'it is my will' when pressed to say why he wanted a particular course terminated.[31] His critics complained that he acted as one who 'always knew better' than his colleagues about their business. He was indifferent to the need for good public relations, but that was an old college deficiency, in his case probably aggravated by his public service career. He was allegedly stubborn in, for example, instructing that lectures should go ahead at a time of student boycotts, and pedantically insisting on the observance, to an absurdly rigid degree, by holders of full-time statutory posts of the rule that they should not engage in any extramural activity involving payment of a fee no matter how nominal. When he expressed the view that the registrarship should not necessarily be reserved for academics, he was regarded as having been adversely affected during his years in Dublin by the civil service mentality. Above all, his opponents resented his attack on the 'god' professors, that is, his belief that it was high time to reduce or delimit the customary powers, status, privileges, prerogatives and absolutist attitudes associated with holding a chair. These powers, he believed, should be reduced or shared, or transferred to the administration. However, professorial power continued to be protected by statute and by mutual interest and solidarity. At the same time, the president was accused of being unable or unwilling to delegate any of his own power. The office of the vice-presidency was forced on McCarthy, like an auxiliary on an unenthusiastic bishop. The first vice-president was told by McCarthy that his main duty was 'to stop bandwagons rolling' at faculty level.

Yet no one could deny the president's intellectual capabilities and few could equal his ability to grasp the essence of any college problem. His integrity and courage commanded respect, whether in confronting and winning over a hostile student audience packing the restaurant at a time of considerable unrest or in stoically reacting to unpleasant scenes in Limerick when a National Institute of Higher Education graduand contemptuously flung back at him, as conferrer, the gown and NUI-accredited degree parchment.

In assessing his presidency, it has to be said that he enjoyed the good fortune of being in office at a period when funding was relatively *fliúrseach*. On various occasions, as when considerable expense was incurred in an abortive pile-driving operation on the old dairy science site, he was able to use his influential Dublin connections to excellent effect. In general, he benefitted from the years of plenty, in contrast to his successor, Tadhg Ó Ciardha, who was to be adversely affected towards the end of his tenure by recruitment embargoes and crippling cutbacks. And if the McCarthy presidency was a period of expansion and administrative development, then one could argue that this was an inevitable response to unprecedented student growth, and to expanding and expansive times. All that being said and conceded, M.D. McCarthy was one of the great presidents of the college, taking his place in the pantheon with Kane, Sullivan, Windle and O'Rahilly.[32] 'Here was a Caesar: when comes such another?'

The end of (p)residency

McCarthy's term of office marked the final end of the residential presidency, for which specific provision had been made in the original QCC plan. Merriman was the last president to die in the East Wing, O'Rahilly the last to live there.

After his departure, O'Rahilly's house became part of 'office' college. Professor Henry St J. Atkins both as registrar and as president lived in a college-acquired residence on Donovan's Road, and so did President McHenry. Professor Ó Ciardha as registrar was never housed in the college environs because of the ever-pressing need for further office and classroom space. When President McCarthy was appointed, the college purchased a house on the Rochestown Road as a presidential residence. After McCarthy's retirement, this house was eventually sold.

While presidents no longer lived on the college grounds, one or two porters' lodges were still inhabited, the West Lodge being the last college dwelling to be converted to office use in 1986. The last remaining residential personality in the college was the warden of the Honan Hostel, the La Retraite nuns having taken themselves off campus. Technically speaking, the warden lived outside the college grounds, since the hall of residence he supervised was denominational in character. This arrangement ended in 1991, when the hostel went out of business and the premises were purchased by the college for future development.

For some academics, the ending of the residential presidency was a matter for satisfaction, a necessary sign of modernisation – apart altogether from space require-ments – and a development in keeping with the spirit of the 1960s. A president on the premises, it was argued, symbolised an authoritarian and institutional age now thank-fully departed. (The memory of O'Rahilly's dominating and ubiquitous presence in his East Wing base powerfully conditioned this viewpoint.) Others regretted the break with tradition which they had seen in healthy continuity in English and American universities. They felt that the college now lacked a certain presence, a collegial atmosphere, a lived-in feel. Eilís Dillon's view was that 'the College lost something that had given it character and style. The value of the living presence of the President was too subtle for O'Rahilly's comprehension . . .'[33] If true, that would be richly ironical, given that the residential O'Rahilly was the most high-profile on-campus president in the college's history. At any rate, the days of gracious living – and of cheap and plentiful domestic service – in the East Wing were well and truly over.

Ó Ciardha at last

Tadhg Ó Ciardha was appointed president of UCC by the NUI Senate on 13 July 1978. (McCarthy had vacated the office on reaching the retirement age of seventy.) Ó Ciardha had not grown 'tired of knocking on Preferment's door'. It was his third application for the post, and this time there was no attempt to stop him, nor were there any other serious contenders. He went in cardinal and easily came out pope. He was then in his late fifties.

Ó Ciardha's personality and qualities have already been described. His loyal co-operation with McCarthy in running the college during the previous ten years had dissipated residual academic hostility and further consolidated the goodwill which he had long enjoyed in the Governing Body. What also helped to end any opposition was his magnanimous, ungrudging nature, as well as an increasing mellowness. His satisfaction on obtaining the long-coveted presidency was obvious, and over the next decade he found the office enjoyable and fulfilling. However, as he aged, he lacked the energy the job demanded. Soon after his accession, there was a short but unpleasant college workers' strike on a trivial issue. It was the first all-out, official dispute in college history, though there was no suggestion that the new president was in any way responsible.

Ó Ciardha had served twenty-four years as registrar (as O'Rahilly had done), and university administration was his whole career since he had never seriously pursued his research interests. He brought to his new position an unrivalled knowledge and under-standing of the workings both of the college and of the NUI, and he enjoyed genial relations with other university heads. In UCC, some academics were still irritated by what they perceived to be his domineering if not intimidating approach, particularly when he chaired their deliberations. His pragmatic, no-nonsense attitude grated on the more preciously academic of his colleagues. By the same token, he had a genuine rapport with the Governing Body, the lay members of which, at least, generally ate out of his hand. They also enjoyed the post-meeting hospitality, a new development which, he claimed, served a very useful social function.[34] His popularity with local authority representatives and officials was further enhanced by his unaffected hail-fellow-well-met egalitarianism, his convivial habits and his undiminished enthusiasm for Gaelic games, bowl playing and things generally racy of the soil. His strong interest in the Irish language helped its status on campus and he encouraged and supported the work of the statutory Bord na Gaeilge.

Ó Ciardha's critics alleged that his was a tick-over leisurely presidency, that he coasted on his predecessor's achievements, that his move across the Quadrangle from registrar's to president's office was just a location shift, and that being president meant little more than mechanically applying college and university regulations with which his long apprenticeship uniquely familiarised him. This view does him less than justice. He was no radical innovator, he was inexperienced outside the NUI context at a period when new horizons were beckoning, and he presided over UCC rather than setting the pace for future progress. Yet his presidency was benign (perhaps because he pushed no new ideas) and free from factionalism, and a broadly united college was no mean legacy for him to leave. As registrar, he had the name of chaining himself inflexibly to regulations yet he used the presidency subtly and flexibly, informally exploiting his *de facto* power rather than rigidly invoking his statutory prerogatives. He was far less bureaucratic in his approach than his predecessor.

At the least, he presided efficiently over an ever-growing college and over the development of a number of important buildings. (The sound of construction, he once remarked, was music to his ears since it signified the burgeoning life of the college.) Foremost of these was the Boole Library and lecture complex, already referred to and opened by Dr Patrick Hillery, president of Ireland, in 1984. Here was a splendid resource, yet it experienced considerable growing pains, ranging from changes in the classification system to problems of personality and morale. Some of the latter landed on the president's desk, and they were compounded by the failure to secure the services of an efficient librarian prepared to give a substantial period of service to the job. There were arguments between the faculties about an equitable distribution of resources for the acquisition of books and journals, and there was a notable lack of discipline in student behaviour on the premises.

The commemoration stone of the new dairy and food science building had been laid during his final months in office by President McCarthy, on 18 May 1978. The plan to locate this new development on the demolished creamery site at Donovan's Road had been an expensive failure because of piling difficulties on a soft foundation, and the location then chosen was immediately south of (the old) La Retraite, fronting the Gaol Walk on the western side, across from the science building. (A catwalk, part of the pedestrian spine of the 1972 development plan, eventually connected both areas.) The opening by President Ó Ciardha of the new dairy and food science building was doubly significant: it was the first stage in a new westward expansion, and it marked a great and continuing success story of the 1980s, that of food science as an area of excellence and of fund-generating capacity. (Where Finbarr taught, let Munster churn, and *earn!*) The building also provided additional lecture rooms for general use.

In terms of physical expansion, there was also a *drang nach osten*. The college had long wished to build on the Gillabbey Rock site. While a development there might be in accordance with legend and tradition, it was finally and firmly ruled out on environmental grounds by Cork Corporation to which the college eventually relinquished the site. But the Lee Maltings premises was a valuable acquisition in 1969. It was offered to the college by Beamish and Crawford who no longer needed it, and the deal was quickly clinched with characteristic informality over a pint by Ó Ciardha (still registrar at that stage) and a representative of the brewery firm who happened to be a friend of his.[35] Acquiring such a premises for conversion was unusual at that time, but it was a successful move, providing the college with desperately needed book storage, a recreational complex, more lecture halls and a new home for the department of zoology. It was acquired primarily to meet the short-term needs of physics and chemistry but it became an exciting experimental area for developments. A nearby building housed what was to be a spectacularly successful enterprise – the National Microelectronics Research Centre (NMRC), under the leadership of Professor Gerry Wrixon. Though existing under a general college aegis, it functioned independently as a fund-generating research unit in an area of vital interest to the national economy, and created substantial employment in its own right.

Ó Ciardha's informal approach to doing business was again evident in the agreement he and Michael Kelleher (finance officer and secretary) concluded with Joe McHugh (Cork city manager) whereby the Munster Institute was transferred to UCC for a nominal rent, despite the reservations of city hall officials.[36] The rapport established with McHugh was important: Ó Ciardha could shrewdly sense a certain town hostility (at both elected and official level) to gown, and possessed the astuteness to handle it skilfully. The hostility was the local expression of a general public service coolness towards academics and was the product of a number of attitudes – insecurity, envy, resentment of a different lifestyle, inverted snobbery. Ó Ciardha believed – and with some justification – that college – community relations considerably improved under his presidency. O'Rahilly, for example, had courted trade union leaders with passionate enthusiasm, and was a renowned disputes arbitrator but his 'town' approaches were selective. McCarthy had been largely indifferent to public relations and in any case his (very fruitful) contacts were with Dublin government centres rather than with Cork businessmen. Ó Ciardha prided himself on his awareness of the college's need to embrace the whole business and professional community, to proclaim that it had services to sell and that it needed other things. The consequence was the further development of links between business firms and individual college departments – for example, the Allied Irish Banks chair of management, one of a number of new departments that began to proliferate from McCarthy's day.

For all his vaunted plebian manner and lifestyle, Ó Ciardha was much too dauntingly formidable a presence – forever dominating an argument, it would seem – to be accepted as the common man's president. He was also a product of the authoritarian tradition of college government. Though he tried to be open to students, he was a remote and unapproachable figure as far as they were concerned.[37] In any case, perhaps approachability was a myth in the anonymous atmosphere of a greatly enlarged college.

On the other hand, the president was a very real presence to the academic staff. In his one-to-one relations with his colleagues, his apparent gruffness belied an attentive and concerned approach. In the compendious persona – counsellor, confessor, director, *primus inter pares* – of the presidency, Ó Ciardha's human relations skills were far ahead of his predecessor. Such skills were desperately necessary towards the end of his term when a deteriorating national financial situation and a consequent regimen of national fiscal austerity ushered in a depressing era of cutbacks, recruitment embargoes and early retirements. An important facet of all this was a new rigidity in governmental and Higher Education Authority attitudes. The college was not allowed flexibility with its reduced revenues in deciding where to apply the cuts – in being allowed to choose, for example, between a building and a job. In other words, university autonomy was further impaired: indeed, the very existence of the HEA was itself a limitation of that autonomy. It was a significant sign of the times that whereas formerly new statutes were formally processed as a matter of course and never questioned, it was now considered politic to let the HEA see draft statutes, to obviate objections at a later stage.

The over-65 professors were victims of the cutbacks regimen, and it was Ó Ciardha's painful duty to apply the axe, with little advance notice, in four or five cases in UCC. In the more leisurely times then ending, the Senate could and almost invariably did extend annually the appointment of 65-year-olds, on the recommendation of the Governing Body with the approval of the president. Whether any efficient institution should, even in the best of circumstances, continue to employ geriatrics up to the age of 70 is another question. Certainly, the case for making space for new-blood appointments was undeniable, and the retention of 65 to 69-year-olds was unjustifiable when their younger colleagues were being invited to retire. Yet the relatively sudden enforced departure of the elderly professors seemed harsh, and Ó Ciardha found his role as executioner particularly distressing in the case of one victim who had built up an excellent department, who had not completed full pensionable service, and who was an old and close friend to boot. It was, of course, highly anomalous (though Ó Ciardha did not seem to have been aware of this) that the president thus reluctantly stoning his colleagues should have shared the same geriatric glasshouse, except that his statute was surrounded by unbreakable glass.

Fota: vision and delusion

The most traumatic episode of Ó Ciardha's presidency was the 1987 Fota débâcle, which was also a public relations disaster for the college. On 4 March 1974 Professor Tom Raftery (agriculture, 1964–) proposed that the college should acquire the magnificent 780-acre Smith-Barry estate at Fota in east Cork which had come on the market. He argued that the college farms to the west of the city should be sold, and replaced by the farmland (500 acres) on the estate which, as one block, would more appropriately cater for UCC's present and future needs. It would generate £30,000 per annum profit, he confidently predicted. The Fota estate was also renowned for its internationally famous arboretum, and was otherwise remarkable in its flora and fauna so that, Raftery claimed, the estate had great potential for promoting research in such areas as botany and zoology. In short, it would be a multidisciplinary resource and 'a rare asset for this College . . . which would be the envy of every other College and

University in this country and many outside this country . . .'[38] It was also suggested that a college takeover of Fota would be excellent for community relations.

President McCarthy and the Finance Committee were less than impressed, and believed the proposal had a number of difficult implications. Did the college need such a large area of farmland? What business had it maintaining woodlands, arboretum and gardens? The committee presciently warned against the college's succumbing to the 'public demand for Fota Estate to be purchased as a public amenity'.[39] The president maintained that the college's 'only academic requirement' in respect of farms was to 'provide an adequate "laboratory" for our existing Department of Agriculture'.[40] Indeed, there were those who questioned whether the college needed to have a farm at all for 'laboratory' purposes. Despite this early scepticism, the Governing Body soon succumbed to the pressures of the pro-Fota lobby. Only two governors, the president and Professor Seán Teegan, dissented. In June 1975, the GB decided to acquire the Fota estate in the belief that the sale of the Maglin and Cooleen farms (at Ballincollig) would generate more money than the purchase price of Fota, and that careful husbandry would make the Fota farm viable.[41] In a confident-sounding statement of 21 October 1975, the GB announced its new acquisition and its intention 'not to dispose of any of the land on the estate'.[42]

For some time, the roseate optimism surrounding the purchase seemed justified. Fota became an enjoyable public amenity. The college maintained the arboretum; it upgraded the structure of the impressive Fota House to accommodate the splendid collection of paintings owned by the director of the house, local businessman, Mr Richard Wood (some, but not enough, use was made of the house during the 'college years' for meetings and social events); it provided and managed car parks; and, of course, it operated the farm. The most imaginative project at Fota was the wildlife park, run by the Royal Zoological Society in conjunction with the college. The park reflected the progressive trend in animal exhibition and conservation whereby a spacious natural habitat was provided, rather than the cramped surroundings of the conventional zoo. Fota House and the wildlife park were open to the public, and so were, in season, the arboretum and gardens which were under the direct management of the college.[43]

But all this cost more money than the college had bargained for, or could afford. It was estimated in March 1987 that the total investment was £1.1 million. There was nothing like an adequate sum from any source to set against this. Various difficulties had been experienced in disposing of the college farmland west of the city at the maximum prices predicted and expected. The college farm at Fota was losing money, the substantial sand and gravel pits there were not providing the expected revenue, Fota as a whole was being run at a loss, and the annual deficit was steadily increasing. In fact, Fota was being substantially subsidised from the college general account, and not surprisingly the auditor-general's office was expressing grave concern. There was diminishing enthusiasm within the college for Fota. As with many affairs, the ardour cooled when the early intoxication abated.

Far from being the enviable asset predicted in 1974, Fota had become an albatross for the college by the mid-1980s. Accordingly, when an English company expressed an interest in January 1986 in purchasing parts of Fota with a view to its commercial development, the Finance Committee's response was positive, and negotiations continued over the following twelve months. The 331 acres to be purchased for stg £1.4 million included Fota House, the arboretum, the gardens, and areas of the parkland and woodland. The development would include a hotel, leisure and conference facilities, time-share lodges and a golf course, but would not involve the wildlife park, or the college farming activities. The public would still have access to the park, as well as to the house and arboretum. Indeed, the college convinced itself that these public amenities would prosper under the new arrangement since they 'would form part of a much larger and better endowed leisure complex'. But there was no doubt about the main attraction of the agreement: 'It would remove from the College the responsibility, for which it is not geared either financially or otherwise, to promote an activity clearly outside the purely academic domain'.[44] The deal was approved by the Governing Body at a special meeting on 10 April 1987,[45] and that was the first stage in the eventual disengagement of the college from Fota, though there were to be many other complications along that road.

The deal with the developers brought public wrath down upon the head of the college, and provoked fierce media controversy in the spring of 1987.[46] UCC's promise to guarantee continued public access to Fota's amenities did not save it from accusations of philistinism and betrayal of public trust. Within the college itself, some governors resented the fact that the Finance Committee's negotiations with the developers between January 1986 and March 1987 had not been brought before the GB (arguably in violation of the statutes) until a very late stage when the gun was put to the GB's head.[47] It was then informed that unless there was immediate approval, the developers would withdraw from the deal. Such unseemly haste suggested complicity in a *fait accompli* and aggravated the public odium which the college was incurring. Richard Wood, the director of Fota House, was particularly angry that he had been kept totally out of the picture: thenceforth, his relations with the college, like the condition of the house itself, further deteriorated until he eventually (in 1993) removed his collection of paintings to the welcoming young arms of the University of Limerick.

Throughout the affair, the UCC authorities acted in what they believed to be the best interests of the college, and they were genuinely concerned with safeguarding continuing public enjoyment of Fota's unique amenities. The deal seemed the only practical way out of a parlous financial situation, and the suggested alternative – that a voluntary public trust, given time, could take over the estate – was in reality only a fantasy. Given the college's considerable and costly investment in developing Fota's amenities, many of the charges levelled against it were unfair, if not malicious. As far as the average citizen was concerned, it was a case of eaten bread being soon forgotten. The Cork public were very pleased when UCC took over Fota and came to expect the amenities provided as a right: the same public turned correspondingly nasty when this agreeable state of affairs was threatened. On more reasoned reflection, the citizens might well have enquired why UCC had been let carry the Fota burden virtually single-handed for so long without any help from the Cork civic authorities.

The whole episode offered some valuable lessons to the college. First, it needed to be on its guard in future against being seduced by glamorous propositions into flamboyant extramural adventures to the detriment of its vital concerns. Secondly, dealing at length behind closed doors, indeed behind the interior doors of an inner sanctum, was not acceptable either within or without the groves of academe.[48] The episode intensified the lecturing staff's demand for greater participation in decision making. Finally, the college's embarrassingly inept handling of the media throughout suggested it was high time it paid proper attention to public relations.[49]

CHAPTER THIRTEEN

THE COLLEGE IN THE 1990s

'An alma mater, knowing her children one by one, not a foundry or a mint or a treadmill'
(Newman, *Idea of a University*): UCC 1990s ??

The students are the life of the place.
retired attendant's comment

President Mortell

THE ACCESSION OF Michael P. Mortell to the presidency (appointed by the NUI Senate on 26 January 1989) was notable for a number of reasons. At forty-seven, he was the youngest president since Merriman's election in 1919. Like four of his six UCC predecessors, he had served as registrar and obviously found that office to be a useful power base, springboard and apprenticeship for the presidency. He was the first president not to be appointed for life, his term of office being confined to ten years: limited but generous tenure provides both an incentive and an edge to a presidency. Remarkably, Mortell was the third mathematician in turn to become president (with a statistician succeeding him in the registrarship). He also maintained the broader pattern of presidents coming from the science/mathematics 'side of the house' since 1943. 'What! will the line stretch out to the crack of doom?'

The presidential campaign which saw the successful emergence of Mortell was another sign of the changing times. (In the past a vacant presidency was not even advertised.) Though the formal appointment process was still limited to the Governing Body and NUI Senate, the impressively strong candidates in 1988 had to respond to the democratic demands of their colleagues that they should present themselves to various academic and administrative groupings for informal assessment. Thus the candidates had to make their respective cases to gatherings of the different faculties, to the Academic Staff Association and to the Academic Council, and they were exposed to searching questions at each meeting. The informal votes taken on these occasions reflected a broad range of opinion throughout the college and provided a democratic consensus on the relative merits of the candidates. The formal appointing bodies were guided by this exercise in democracy: they would have ignored it at their peril. They could not, for example, entertain the idea of appointing a candidate who had not submitted himself or herself to the rigours of peer assessment. The NUI Senate, in turn, was morally bound to respect consensus, which it duly did. There could be no lobbying or caucusing in favour of a dark horse. Conversely, for the first time a new president could claim, at the outset of his term, the substantial support of the academic community. The same community, however, remains a highly critical monitor of presidential performance, and the honeymoon predictably was of short duration, since (apart from any other considerations) no president can hope to promote the interests of different, if not competing, individuals and factions.

The unpretentious personality and egalitarian style of President Mortell made a considerable impression on all sections of the college 'family' at the beginning of his term of office. In the Cork manner, his performances as a county hurling star were fondly recalled. His popularity was increased by the enjoyably extravagant parties he threw at intervals during the opening years (they were to cease gradually and mysteriously). Invitations were open to all grades of college staff – from professors to general operatives – but not (understandably, and to their chagrin) to students. On these memorable gala occasions, various tastes in dancing and musical entertainment were catered for at different gaily decorated venues throughout the college. The festive atmosphere was enhanced by generous provision of food and copious liquid refreshment. (It was a pleasing paradox that a teetotaller president should be such a *flaithiúil* host.) Such convivial evenings contrasted sharply with the staid garden parties of the

13.1 President Michael Mortell with his immediate predecessor,
Tadhg Ó Ciardha, 1978–88, at the unveiling of President Ó Ciardha's portrait.

College income by source, 1980–94 (%)

State	Grant	Fees	Research	Other
1980–81	81.8	12.3	5.2	–
1990–91	54.2	23.5	19.4	–
1991–92	52.3	25.0	20.3	2.4
1992–93	49.3	26.8	21.2	2.7
1993–94	49.0	27.5	21.8	1.7

past, dropped after the McCarthy presidency. In the elegant new Mortell regime, more select hospitality was lavishly offered on special occasions, in such imaginatively unusual locations as the Aula Maxima, the new council room and the splendidly extended and refurbished presidential office. The new broom had luxurious floors to sweep. There was also something of an artistic renaissance in the college under Mortell, with a strong contemporary emphasis on the visual arts. Adventurous nude sculptures were seen to decorate the president's garden, a development which doubtless triggered off sepulchral rotations among his predecessors.

Changes in funding

However, in the best leadership tradition, occasional bread and circuses enhanced the work performance rather than interfered with it. The early 1990s were years of expansion despite the restrictive effects of the new funding mechanism which determined the size of the college budget by unit costs. In effect, this meant that though student numbers continued to climb, overall funding did not increase in proportion. Under government pressure, fees rose inexorably and the fees component continued to increase as a percentage of the total college revenue.[1] Research funding, insignificant in the early 1980s, also played an important role as the state grant dramatically fell to below the half-way mark in college income. Research income, whether from 'Europe' or private industry, had to be generated by academics themselves, since the state was notoriously penny-pinching in this area.

It was being made clear by governments that universities were expected, more and more, to generate their own funds. There was a government attitude, supported or perhaps prompted by a slightly hostile non-academic public service and unopposed by an uninterested and uninformed public, that academic institutions had been spoonfed in the past and were not really cost effective or efficient. University funding was also a political issue, as well as an item of political rhetoric. The 1992 'Rainbow' coalition had included 'free university education' on its programme, and when the minister for education announced her intention rather suddenly in July 1994 to abolish university fees, the superficiality of the approach soon became apparent. Fees abolition might well increase rather than diminish privileged middle-class access to third-level education; it was pointed out that a much greater obstacle to equality of opportunity was presented by student maintenance costs; and educational inequality was in any case a symptom of a profound socio-economic and cultural imbalance in Irish society.

This debate intensified with the definite announcement in the 1995 Budget that fees for full-time undergraduates would be halved in 1995–96 and abolished in 1996–97. This was a dramatic reversal of the policy of previous governments, which had steadily reduced the central block grant while forcing the colleges to increase their fees. The new, radical decision had many implications which needed to be carefully studied. The provision of university places would not be made easier: indeed, fees abolition was likely to lead to an increased demand for places. Suddenly, the college administrators felt apprehensive about what the future might hold for both university autonomy and university financing. At the least, they hoped the historic government decision would mean there would be no overall loss of income and that the unit of resource per student would be maintained. Meanwhile, university chiefs, desperate at the prospect of intolerable overcrowding (partly the consequence of government pressure on universities to accommodate more and more students, thus helping the cosmetics of the unemployment figures) pleaded for more government aid to alleviate the impact of further hordes of students on cramped campuses.

President Ó Ciardha had begun the drive to tap the potential of college graduates as a source of revenue but it took his successor's youthful energy to get it going properly. There was only a sprinkling of private and commercial patrons available. They contributed to a development fund which was applied to selected projects. The college had never succeeded in attracting any spectacular 'sugardaddy' benefactor. Perhaps it never seriously tried. Singularly failing to locate a latter-day Crawford or Honan, UCC set about attempting to loosen the purse-strings, modest or affluent, of its legions of graduates. Successive graduates' associations had intermittently existed, but their *raison d'être* had been mainly social and recreational. Now it was time to call in the chips of their loyalty to the alma mater, wherever they lived, at home or abroad, but particularly perhaps if they had 'made good' in Britain or in the United States. After all, it was only fair that Irish men and women who had been professionally trained at little cost to themselves but largely at the expense of the taxpayer, whose careers had prospered, who waxed sentimental at references to Quad and Quarry, and who flaunted the college colours with pride should now be expected to make a contribution in return.

The Graduates Association was put on a serious footing for the first time, with a back-up college-based organisation. Branches were set up in Dublin and other centres in Ireland. Members involved themselves in social, sporting and cultural activities, and while the association offered valuable 'networking' opportunities to recent graduates, fund-raising was never very far off the agenda. Branches were organised abroad, particularly in the United States, and a quarterly publication, *The Graduate*, kept the UCC diaspora informed of the association's proceedings and of developments in the college.[2] The UCC

Foundation was established to enable graduates to play their part in the development of several key projects (business school and languages centre, outreach programme in adult and continuing education, indoor sports complex) by making one of a number of tax-efficient donations. The figure of the president was a lynchpin in this ambitious expansion of the graduate network. He travelled abroad extensively on its behalf, founding branches, appealing for support, and keeping in touch with various key figures.

Numbers explosion

Graduates returning to the college in the early 1990s after many years, whether for an in-service course or for one of the increasingly popular class reunions, were doubtless reassured to discover that the heart of UCC was beating strongly and that the Quadrangle was as attractive as they had remembered it. But they would have been alarmed, particularly if they visited during term and had memories of the 1940s when the student body was around the 1,000 mark, by the palpable evidence of congestion. Total student numbers virtually doubled between 1980–81 and 1993–94.

Our returning nostalgic graduate would be in a position to observe interesting patterns within those global figures. For instance, over the decade from 1980–81 to 1990–91, the greatest growth in full-time undergraduate students occurred in the arts faculty, with an increase of 112 per cent; law, science, food science and commerce also increased by significant amounts (38 per cent to 56 per cent); and engineering and medicine remained constant. Postgraduate numbers continued their upward climb (e.g. 1,263 postgraduates. out of a total of 7,386 students in 1990–91; 1,919 out of 9,907 in 1993–94) while there was a competitive demand for places by 'mature' students, reflecting heightened awareness of education as personal fulfilment, greater scope for leisure activities, and the absence of employment opportunities.

Total student numbers, 1980–94

Year	Total
1980–81	5,361
1988–89	6,492
1989–90	6,932
1990–91	7,386
1991–92	8,519[3]
1992–93	9,418
1993–94	9,907

In 1990–91 statistics on student accommodation showed that, as always, a substantial majority of UCC students were from the Cork area, with men students (62 per cent) having a greater home dependency than women (51 per cent). Self-catering accommodation – including the new student apartments – continued to be popular

(38 per cent of women students; 28 per cent of men), while traditional lodgings were a declining option (7 per cent of men; 6 per cent of women).

UCC had always been conscious of its perception (by condescending metropolitans) as smugly insular and provincial, and in recent times at least had striven to counter this by aiming at a minimum 5 per cent non-Irish student quota. (For various modern reasons, the Irish non-Munster element is also on the increase.) European Union-sponsored schemes under programmes such as ERASMUS and TEMPUS helped to achieve this desired quota. The somewhat misleadingly described exchange programmes with American colleges (in fact, few Irish students returned the visit) brought more foreign students on to the Cork campus, and medical students paying hefty 'economic' fees (to the considerable financial benefit of the college) came from Malaysia, Singapore and the Middle East. Thus, in 1990–91 there were over 400 foreign students registered (out of 7,386 students in all) from 41 different countries: these included 182 ERASMUS students, while 100 UCC ERASMUS students went to EU centres. In 1991–92, the increase in ERASMUS and American students accounted for over one-quarter of the increase (548) in full-time undergraduate numbers. Overall, the number of overseas students rose from 324 in 1989–90 to 732 in 1992–93. The latter figure represented an 8 per cent non-Irish presence in the student body. It was a far cry from the 1940s when Alfred O'Rahilly rather condescendingly instructed his class how to behave towards the handful of African students then coming to UCC. Now there was a cosmopolitan flavour in lecture halls, and exotic snatches of foreign languages and accents around the college and the city.

Expansion in courses

The traditional evening BA, once extremely restricted in scope and largely availed of by national teachers in pursuit of a quick and financially beneficial degree, now attracted a variety of takers. It underwent complete restructuring with the emphasis on integrated studies. The doubling of part-time undergraduate students from 331 in 1990–91 to 679 in 1991–92 reflected the attraction of the new evening degree courses, and places in evening law were much in demand. Degrees and diplomas proliferated across the college – after all there were now sixty departments spread across eight faculties – and a greatly extended adult and continuing education department provided a variegated and updated service both on campus and extramurally. An ever-expanding commerce faculty, and greatly sought-after business and management courses, represented a far cry from the poor-relation days of the BComm. In the humanities, a phenomenal range of post-graduate courses was on offer, dealing with everything from counselling psychology to women's studies. In the post-Fleischmann era, the department of music continued to sound harmonious chords between town and gown.

One of the dismal clouds in this otherwise bright firmament was the virtual collapse of ancient classics as the premier academic discipline. The last professor of the subject, John P. Fogarty (1959–83) died suddenly in office, and was not replaced. For a dwindling handful, Latin and Greek were still available but for the great majority the study of 'the glory that was Greece and the grandeur that was Rome' no longer required a knowledge of the matrix languages of Western civilisation. The ancient world was now studied in translation, in a pallid Readers Digest-type shadow of the real thing.

Women and change

It's still a man's world at the top in UCC. In some contrast to the situation forty years ago (four women out of a total of forty professors in 1954–55), there are now only six women professors out of a total professorial body of nearly a hundred. Two members of the twenty-eight strong Governing Body (1995–98) are female. Women appear in much larger numbers in subprofessorial (that is, lower-paid) grades. For a number of years, one of the women professors also doubled, at the President's invitation, as one of the two vice-presidents. While this was an eminently satisfactory appointment, it was nonetheless a transparently token gesture to the politically correct principle of gender balance. Otherwise, there is still an all-male college hierarchy, and the presidency has remained firmly male, the only female challenge – in 1988–89 – being ineffectual.

In terms of the women's movement generally, staff and student life in college is a microcosm of the national scene – a purposeful pushing forward of objectives with the minimum of zealotry. Though there are women's committees of various sorts, and women's studies are successfully promoted in the curriculum, the general thrust is towards integration – a common students' club, for example – rather than the old segregation in some new form. The election of the first woman president of the students' union (Anne O'Connor in 1968–69) was obviously a milestone in college history, and women have long since taken a full place as auditors and chairs of college societies. Of even more significance was the emergence of articulate and eloquent women speakers at society meetings. Oral history informants who recall student debates of the 1930s remember in particular the passively silent presence of women students at meetings of the college's premier debating society, the Philosoph.

In an overwhelmingly male-dominated college at upper staff levels, the gender balance has tilted the other way in the student body. From the smallest beginnings in President Sullivan's time in the 1880s, women students constituted 60 per cent of the total by 1993–94. They had always been strong in the arts faculty, where they now outnumbered men by over two to one. Women were also in the majority by various margins in food science, law and medicine. Science was evenly balanced, and only in engineering, traditionally a male bastion, were women a small minority.[4]

The growth of godlessness

Changes in the religious ethos of the college since the mid-1960s have been profound, and they mirror post-Vatican II changes in Church and nation. It is true that, with the expansion of student numbers, the number of Catholic chaplains has been increased to three (including a nun) and it is to be noted that while their appointments are made by the local bishop, their salaries are paid by the college. This arrangement is anomalous, to say the least, in terms of the charter. But it is one of those tacit Irish compromises which are in nobody's interest to challenge directly and which make for a quiet life. (A diploma in the teaching of religious education – formerly Catechetics – is another example.)

The Catholic chaplaincy is a self-effacing preserve on campus. The chaplains are not known to the general body of students but diffidently wait to be sought out, in contrast to the dominant role exercised by the diocesan *apparatchiks* who ruled the spiritual roost in the ages of faith. College Catholicism is of the post-Vatican II à la carte kind, and the Honan Chapel now resounds to guitar strumming and choral pop rather than to the rich austerities of sacred music. Choice, not group pressure or social ritual, is the prerogative of men and women students who mingle freely at the still frequent religious services, in contrast to the rigid segregation of former years. It is significant however that a grossly overcrowded campus has heard no complaints about inadequate chapel accommodation, unless it be at society weddings. The reduction of the religious dimension in college life is further attested by the merely token attendance of staff and students at the annual Eucharistic procession through the streets of Cork. Numerous staff members and droves of students once marched in academicals in the procession, and stood and knelt devoutly at benediction in the Grand Parade.

Deanships of residence, created at the institution of the Queens' Colleges to supervise student accommodation, have now been abolished. Students no longer needed to have their 'digs' approved and in any case had recourse in ever-increasing numbers to (unsupervisable) accommodation in houses and apartments. This development, in turn, enhanced an independent mentality. Deans of residence became redundant, but retained their role as chaplains. The women's dean of residence also became obsolete, the position being allowed to lapse after the retirement in the early 1970s of Mrs Kitty Madden. Her function of chaperone is long since irrelevant. New student residences in the shape of self-catering apartments have come into existence. Castlewhite, ingeniously built in precious space between the river and the Western Road, was a college undertaking which opened in 1991, while Brookfield, a little distance away on College Road, was a private enterprise development. And there were other, smaller apartment buildings in the vicinity of the college. Between them all, they provided some 1,250 places by 1991, a not insignificant proportion of the accommodation needs of out-of-town students. They also double as accommodation centres for campus conferences, summer schools and related trade. In 1993–94, 3,772 students were housed in self-catering accommodation and a further 598 in lodgings. A residential dimension to College was a long-cherished dream from the beginning but the independent, unisex and decidedly secular form it took in the 1990s would have surprised, not to say shocked, the shades of Sullivan, Windle and O'Rahilly.

As the Castlewhite complex opened, the Honan Hostel closed, and this coincidence neatly symbolised the transition from supervised residential accommodation informed by a denominational ethos to an independent, largely unrestricted mode of student life where discipline was necessarily self-imposed. The Honan Hostel went out of business not only because it was decrepit and uneconomic but because its original rationale and ethos were out of joint with the new times. The demise of the new La Retraite for women students was another instance of the same process. Broadly speaking, the change marked the final end of the age of faith and the college's acceptance of the secular ethos. UCC in the mid-1990s was 'godless' beyond Cardinal Cullen's wildest nightmares. Had he foreseen such a development, he would surely have settled gladly for what Presidents Kane, Sullivan and Windle had to offer!

Physical development revised

Back in the 1970s, President McCarthy had envisaged a student ceiling of 7,000, believing that any larger number was incompatible with the character of the campus. But plans are made to be adjusted or scrapped, as he was well aware, and circumstances and thinking had changed radically by the 1990s. *Tempora mutantur et nos mutamur in illis.* The review of the 1972 development plan, approved and adopted by the Governing Body in July 1993, took into account the 1992 government green paper, *Education for a Changing World*. The review provided 'a basis for recommending alternative student population targets of 10,500 and 13,500 over the next ten years'. Obviously, this would require rapid and extensive physical development, bearing in mind that for the existing student population of 9,418 in 1992–93, only two-thirds of the necessary accommodation was available.

The review envisaged a twofold process – completing the physical development of the main campus site within the framework of the 1972 plan, and providing for further expansion 'in a series of proximate satellite locations', within an acceptable walking distance of the main campus in order to avail of existing established 'core' facilities. Still, the president insisted, the college would remain essentially where it was: 'Our revised Plan, when fully implemented, will result in a compact unified campus based on the existing College grounds and in continued harmony with its urban location'. (It was ruefully recalled that the college had turned down the Jury's Hotel site in the 1930s, then on offer for £600!) This guiding principle was to be dramatically challenged in the spring of 1994 when a proposal to acquire the vacant Our Lady's Hospital was unconventionally sprung on an unsuspecting Governing Body.

Already by the end of the 1980s, office accommodation in the Quadrangle area had been radically adapted and transformed, many of the changes being made possible by the availability of the vacated library space. Thus, in the North Wing, the old library ground floor (once the senior reading room) was metamorphosed into a comfortable and well-serviced staff common-room. This change gave particular satisfaction to the more senior academics who had long felt embarrassed by having to introduce visiting lecturers and examiners to the shabby staff house premises in the East Wing where hospitality was limited to biscuits, teabags and ersatz coffee. The upper reaches of the old library, long floored in as a separate storey, now became a handsome new council room, the old council room (an ante-room to the Aula Maxima) being much too small for a greatly expanded academic staff. The impressive stone stairway now gave access on the right to the new council room and on the left to a complex of finance offices, such as the fees and accounts section, in the area once housing the natural history museum.

13.2 Boole Library (1982).

Further along the North Wing to the west, where the old history library used to be, was the oddly-named case study room (the Irish version, Seomra Pléite na gCás, conveyed a much clearer description of its purpose). The archway tower room itself, for long the seat of the librarian and the repository of various reference volumes, and commanding splendid views across the river valley to the heights of Sunday's Well, has remained unaccountably vacant for years.

Once upon a time, the troika of president, registrar and secretary all had their modest offices on the ground floor of the North Wing. That space now served more mundane purposes while the college officers and their staffs occupied extensive premises elsewhere. The president's domain extended along most of the East Wing ground floor while the offices of the secretary and finance officer, the greatest bene- ficiary of the administrative revolution, sprawled over the upper floor of the East and North wings. In the corresponding level of the West Wing, the registrar presided over a complex of offices dealing with student admission, registration, records, examinations and other aspects of academic administration. The style of these offices, including his own, was workaday and far from grandiose. Also in the West Wing, a third or 'attic' storey was constructed (exemplifying once again college ingenuity in creating accom- modation where before there had been no obvious space) to provide further offices. As has already been noted, some lecture rooms were retained or restored on the ground floor of the West Wing, so that a sense of teaching continuity in the college core was observed in both symbolic and practical terms. In the same spirit, a clutter of makeshift offices was cleared away to provide once again that pleasant L-shaped promenade (and sensible shelter in the all-too-frequent inclement weather) from the south tip of the West Wing to the Aula Maxima which was an amenity of Sir Thomas Deane's original plan.

The Aula Maxima, where town and gown had excitedly assembled on opening day in 1849; which had witnessed such student exuberance at conferrings before O'Rahilly restored discipline; and which had served variously as reading room, examination centre, reception area, concert hall, dance hall and banquet centre, still remained, in impressive continuity, the ceremonial heart of the college, largely unchanged in appearance since its construction. It was still, in the mid-1990s, a hallowed setting for the pageantry of graduation day and though overcrowding (despite multiple conferring sessions) meant increasing discomfort for relatives and friends of the graduands, any suggestion that the ceremonies might be held elsewhere in the college would verge on the sacrilegious. Besides, there was no 'elsewhere'.

Overcrowding in the early 1990s was such an intensifying phenomenon that the college had to run very hard with extensions, new buildings and property acquisitions in order to stay in the same place. The pressure of students on food service outlets had

13.3 Castlewhite Apartments (1991).

been partly relieved years before by the provision of cafe services in the 'Mini-Rest' (the upper floor of the main restaurant), in the Lee Maltings and in the 'Kampus Kitchen', a basement area of the science building. Now, in 1990–91, the situation improved further with the building of an extension to the main restaurant. The staff dining room also served as a convenient centre for various receptions and functions.

Extensions to Áras na Laoi (the old La Retraite), the electrical engineering building and the food science building provided further office and lecturing accommodation. In accordance with the revised 1972 development plan, two new building projects were advanced within the old campus block just to the west of the Donovan's Road houses – an applied business/humanities building on the site of the closed Honan Hostel which the college had purchased and demolished; and a student centre, funded from a special levy on students' fees, which commenced construction near the walled garden area in the summer of 1994, and which would replace the cramped premises in the Boole basement, as well as providing other amenities. Viewed from the Lower Grounds in the early summer of 1995, this nearly completed building looked very impressive. The arts faculty had a keen interest in the proposed building (to be funded out of EU structural funds) on the Honan Hostel site, fervently hoping that it would serve as a long-awaited humanities building. In terms of accommodation, the largest faculty was very much the poor relation, having no home to call its own, long resident in numerous college-acquired houses on the campus periphery, and its lecturers often forced to teach and conduct seminars in unsuitable and ill-adapted rooms in these houses.

The initial location suggested for the students' centre caused disagreement between the college and some local residents. In 1991–92, it was proposed to develop Mackesy's Field car park, across College Road from the southeastern corner of the campus, to provide the new student centre and relocate the Granary Theatre there. The theatre's original premises had been absorbed in the redevelopment of the Lee Maltings complex after the NMRC fire in February 1991, and it needed a new location as quickly as possible. Householders in the vicinity of the main campus vigorously expressed their concern about probable noise levels and other nuisance aspects of the proposed Mackesy's Field development. Because of these objections and consequent planning permission difficulties, the Mackesy's Field project was abandoned. It was then decided to build the student centre inside the walls, as it were, and to relocate the theatre (hardly a bone of contention in itself) to the Presentation College area. The residents' lobby was still opposed to what it believed would be the unfavourable environmental impact of new buildings just inside Donovan's Road. The college authorities, backed by the Governing Body, while having no desire to confront their residential neighbours, were nonetheless insistent that they had both the right and the duty to provide for a rapidly expanding student population on the college premises generally and certainly within their own walls, and this time the students' centre went rapidly ahead.

The neighbourhood residents had formed an effective and articulate lobby which made representations to the city hall, to the president and individual members of the Governing Body. This was the town–gown relationship at its nearest and most

13.4 Food Science Extension (1993).

sensitive point. On the one hand, the presence of the college had made the whole neighbourhood a very desirable area, to use the auctioneers' catchphrase. Indeed, to a large extent, the development of the area was due to the college, which supplied an elegant ambience that was socially upmarket. Though the college was a private corporation rather than public property, its attractive grounds were freely available to local residents (and their dogs) for exercise and social strolling. Since the neighbourhood was generally middle class, it supplied a fair sprinkling of college students, and from the residents' standpoint this was another convenient and pleasant link. In the 1950s the incorporation of the gaol in the college had dealt with a feature which had been a problem, if only marginally so, for the college and the community from the early days.

The general serenity of neighbourhood–college relations had been occasionally disturbed long before the early 1990s. The site of the dairy science building in the late 1920s was switched to an intramural location as a result of residents' representations.[5] Even so, residents complained about noise and smoke emissions from the building at the bottom of Donovan's Road, and there were successful court applications for the reduction of rateable valuations in respect of houses on Fernhurst Avenue.[6] However, the grievances expressed sixty years later were of a different nature and much more serious. They were a consequence of student growth, changing social manners and a rapidly deteriorating environment.

In the course of the organised opposition to the development of the Mackesy's Field site, the various complaints came to a head. Many related to traffic flow problems and to obstructive car parking by students, and more focused on obnoxious nocturnal behaviour, particularly noisy carry-ons after socials and dances. These activities were especially distressing to elderly residents who formed a high proportion of the local population. It was felt that a students' centre in their midst, as it were, would aggravate these nuisances, particularly the noise levels which seem to be an integral part of much popular entertainment nowadays. Some of the leading lobbyists were of the opinion that the only cure for the root problem of overcrowding in a restricted suburban area was the opening of a second campus, the first having reached saturation point.

The college obviously would not accept the validity of all the arguments made by the residents' representatives, but promised to help abate some of the worst nuisances. In the last analysis, however, the more students, the more bustling the campus, and the college would have to agree that the key to the problem in large measure was more accommodation, which at this stage was bound to be located more and more off-campus. Across the valley in Sunday's Well, the capacious Good Shepherd Convent was purchased. Other premises which were leased or bought by the college included the former Eye, Ear and Throat Hospital, the Presentation College building on Western Road, and the Cooperage and fine Georgian Distillery House (across the north channel from the Lee Maltings). This eastward development was in line with President Mortell's philosophy of bridging the gap in different senses between the college and the city. This represented a continuity of aspiration in that the founding fathers felt the college was too far, again in different senses, from the city and would have welcomed eastward links.

During 1994, however, there was increasing interest in what might turn out to be a dramatic westward leap. There were combined initiatives, incentives and political pressures to get UCC to acquire Our Lady's Hospital (formerly Cork District Lunatic Asylum) a mile to the north-west of the college on the Lee Road. This vast building, dating from 1852, had been vacated for some years by the Southern Health Board. It was argued, particularly by the medical faculty, that acquisition of the building and grounds (fifty-one acres, compared with an existing campus of forty-four acres) would

13.5 New Granary Theatre (1994).

offer the college a spectacular opportunity to develop a national medical and health sciences complex, to relieve chronic overcrowding, to be part of an important Northside development and, most historic of all, to open a second campus, linked to the mother campus by (*inter alia*) a shuttle service, American-style. Throughout the second half of 1994, a GB-commissioned feasibility study considered the vital questions: how could the acquisition and development of Our Lady's be reconciled with the concept of UCC as 'a compact unified campus'? How much money was needed to develop the derelict building and grounds for the college's purposes? What would be those purposes? Who would provide the money (perhaps £30 million)? The answers would determine whether the proposed acquisition would be rejected as an unsustainable albatross, or be proceeded with in the most imaginative and ambitious decision made by the college since its foundation. In the end, the GB approved the proposal[7] which was then considered by the Higher Education Authority. By the summer of 1995, the indications were that neither the HEA nor the government favoured the allocation of the considerable capital required, and that the second campus was vanishing like a mirage.

To match the physical expansion of the development plan, a five-year academic plan, prepared by the Academic Planning and Development Committee (APDC), was being considered in 1994 by the Academic Council and by the Governing Body. The APDC, comprising college officers, faculty deans and representatives of Academic Council and Governing Body, attempts to integrate academic planning with the key issue of resources, and is an important initiative of the Mortell presidency. Its draft five-year plan led to fierce debate at the Academic Council, focussing particularly on the primacy of the council in academic policy making, as opposed to the enhanced role for faculty deans envisaged in the draft plan. The upshot has been the production of an alternative Academic Council plan, *A framework for planning to the year 2000*, and the setting up of a powerful committee system by the council. Both plans, together with the Devlin Report on governance (referred to below) constitute a major resource for the Governing Body.

The college itself and its component parts are faced by perennial challenge and opportunity. The University Dental School and Hospital is one such area. Located in the North Infirmary since the initiation of the BDS degree in 1913–14, the dental school was translated to the new purpose-built University Dental School and Hospital, linked to the Regional Hospital (later named the Cork University Hospital), in Wilton in 1982–83. The future of the dental school was problematic for a number of years: since the state required only a limited number of dental graduates, the fundamental question was whether a dental school in Cork was really necessary. The Cork answer was that a school located in Cork was a necessary health service for the area. This, rather than any argument about what quota of dental graduates was needed, was the crucial – and in the end the convincing – point. In 1994, the government guaranteed that there was no threat to dentistry in UCC.[8] The dental hospital is an important community health facility, treatment being given to scores of patients daily, and continuing education

13.6 University Hospital and Dental School.

courses are regularly provided for dentists in the Southern and Mid-Western Health Board areas. It has to be said that the dental school has been beset by exceptional problems of departmental restructuring and difficult staff relations, and overcoming these is a considerable challenge. But the opportunity for remarkable progress is there also, as is evident from the success of the Oral Health Research Unit in attracting projects in the areas of health services research, epidemiology and clinical trials.

The illustrated and attractively-presented annual president's reports for the early 1990s give an informative account of the multifarious research activities which characterise UCC in the last decade of the century and millennium but which so obviously set the pattern for the future. Even to list some of these is to realise what a remarkable spread of disciplines UCC has and what an *iolscoil* it truly is. The aquaculture development centre encompasses postgraduate aquaculture-related teaching and research and is of national importance in the context of the rapidly expanding fish farming industry. The microwave laboratory at UCC plays a central role in the Programme in Advanced Technology (PAT) in the area of telecommunications. In other departments there are new and exciting interdisciplinary departures. The department of history and the computer bureau have joined with the Royal Irish Academy in a ten-year programme to produce a *Thesaurus Linguarum Hiberniae*, an on-line marked-up text base of all Irish literary and historical materials in the five literary languages of Ireland – Irish, Hiberno-

Latin, Old Norse, Anglo-Norman French and Hiberno-English. The executive systems research centre is the national centre for research into the design and development of information systems for managers. All these centres illustrate the basic truths at the heart of academic research. Research is a fundamental human activity: 'all men, by their very nature, feel the urge to know', in Aristotle's famous phrase.

There was a notable switch of overseas direction in the 1980s and 1990s as far as postgraduate and postdoctoral research was concerned. Previously, UCC researchers, particularly in the food and mathematical sciences, had availed of the strong links established with universities in the US. The good offices of Professor Patrick M. Quinlan (mathematical physics, 1951–87) were important here. Quinlan (a significant presence over the decades in the UCC corridors of power) was able to 'place' postgraduate students in those American academic circles where he had considerable influence. Gradually, however, the lure of European network funding powerfully attracted American-based UCC researchers back to the teaching and research staff of their alma mater. Without the incentive of EU research funding, abandoning their American careers for an otherwise meagrely-endowed Irish scene would have been an unrewarding prospect.

Apart from student growth and physical development, what also distinguishes today's college is its ceaseless, bustling multifaceted activity. Like the deathless boast of London's Windmill Theatre, the modern college never closes. While the academic year

13.7 Good Shepherd Convent, a capacious college acquisition of the 1990s.

is still formally divided into the traditional three terms, and the two-semester division is increasingly the reality, much goes on outside this framework. Lectures stop and term finishes, it is true, but in a way that did not happen a generation ago, many students remain on campus, read in the library, and socialise in the restaurant. During vacation, and especially during the Long Vacation, the college appears to be as busy as in the height of term, the yardstick here being the chronic difficulty in finding a parking place. Only the most churlish civil servant, for years complaining that university accommodation was underused for half the time, would not now graciously admit that UCC at least makes use of its facilities from early till late, all the year round. In-service courses, various refresher programmes, miscellaneous conferences, adult education sessions, and teaching-English-to-foreigners classes keep the classrooms occupied, the college coffers topped up and the college contract caterers smiling. The flagship of the impressively growing fleet of summer schools is the UCC International Summer School in Irish Studies, sailing since 1979 and offering credits to European, American and other foreign students. In turn, the contacts made in and through this school led to the institution of the Colby College and Boston College exchange programmes. And there were many other examples of the new age of academic tourism.

How many in town are aware of this transformed and hyperactive gown? The old myths die hard and the populace at large still tends to have an image of UCC as a leisurely 1930-ish kind of place which 'closes' for five months of the year.[9] It is obviously in the best interest of the college that these and related myths should be dispelled to the extent that it is possible to do so. This has been one of the many tasks of the Information Office set up in 1986 in the Ó Ciardha presidency. It was a welcome new departure for an institution which up to recent times seemed largely indifferent to extramural opinion. The minimally staffed Information Office has been concerned with much more than correcting negative images. Positively, it has kept the general community informed of events in the college, and to this end it has maintained a constant liaison with the media. Students and staff of all kinds are kept in touch with happenings through the weekly calendar *Eolas*; the quarterly *Graduate* maintains vital information links between the college and its alumni; the office organises a weekly half-page article in *The Cork Examiner* on aspects of college life; and daily walking tours offer a first-hand introduction to the college to large numbers of citizens and visitors. Finally, the Information Office has been at hand to help handle the publicity projection of issues like fee increases. The office had been established but not perhaps sufficiently experienced when the Fota crisis broke in the spring of 1987. As we have seen, there were aspects of the college's handling of the episode that clearly demonstrated the need for smoother and more sophisticated public relations, an area to which the Information Office was to make an invaluable contribution in the following years. It was notable, for example, that the college's approach to the neighbourhood residents in 1991–92 was much smoother, more diplomatic, and more assured than its handling of the Fota controversy five years earlier.

13.8 Student Centre, almost completed, September 1995.

It is arguable that if a university is to have a publishing unit it should be a real arm of excellence, or else it should be dispensed with entirely. Perhaps that was the challenge facing the Cork University Press as the 1990s dawned. In the event, the press was wholly reorganised during the first half of 1992. Its publishing list was radically broadened, it contributed to public debate by producing a booklet series on current affairs, and, while maintaining the highest standards in its impressive output of academic titles, it also ventured into the non-academic area with the launching of the imaginative *The Cork Anthology* in 1993. Under a new publisher, the Cork University Press faced the competitive world of academic publishing with confidence, and it has already become a distinguished and culturally vital expression of the academic community.

A perusal of any issue of *Eolas*, the weekly calendar of college events, will confirm that there is on offer to the students of UCC in the 1990s a rich and wide range of recreational and cultural activities, probably unrivalled in Ireland. There is a bewildering array of sporting and athletic clubs to choose from, with corresponding facilities available in the Lee Maltings and the college sports ground in its traditional Mardyke home, with provision for future developments in the Curraheen Road area. Music, drama and the arts flourish in their various forms, with lunchtime and evening concerts arranged during term, enriching the community as well as the students. The internationally celebrated Vanbrugh String Quartet are artists in residence and, as well as giving concerts, make their contribution to the work of the music department. A novel development has been the institution of a writer in residence (in association with the Arts Council), who also makes an extramural contribution by directing a series of community workshops. By 1995 communications were enhanced by the introduction of a student radio station.

Staff matters

Staff aspirations to career advancement were provided for by the promotions scheme, which however did not satisfy everyone. It was natural that academics should hope to have their career achievements recognised in terms of prestige and remuneration, and that they should feel disappointed and frustrated when their hopes were dashed, especially if that happened, as it could and did, more than once. The trouble was that the college authorities had no power to create what it might regard as an adequate number of promotional outlets for college lecturers aspiring to be statutory lecturers, and for statutory lecturers wishing to become associate professors. Mainly for financial reasons the HEA was prepared to sanction only a limited number of promotional posts. The great majority of candidates were well qualified and suitable for promotion but in such a severely competitive situation the promotions boards had to make excruciatingly fine and difficult decisions. Eventually in 1994, the academic promotions scheme was amended in a number of procedural respects and it was hoped that the improved working of the scheme would help to make the boards' decisions more acceptable all round. There is, of course, no such thing as a wholly satisfactory promotions system, and it should be remembered that on the administration side of the college there was in some areas what might be described as a tolerable level of frustration at the lack of adequate opportunities for career advancement. With reference to academics, however, the prospect of promotion (based, above all, on scholarship) was a powerful incentive to research. The promotions scheme is one important explanation of the flourishing state of research in UCC.

Meanwhile the 'god (or godless)' professor's divine right to rule a department was being circumscribed on the one hand by the growth of the college administration and, on the other, by the democratic resolve of the departmental staff to have their say and, perhaps, take their turn at leadership. This development, like so many others, was the consequence of growth: after all, for a long time, a professor was a one-person department. Apart altogether from the antiquated assumption that the professor was the boss, there was the question of an academic's (more accurately, some academics') capacity and suitability (leaving aside inclination) to deal with the increasingly complex administration of even a moderately large university department. Furthermore, what was coming increasingly under scrutiny in UCC was the proliferation of departments. This development had come about not only through specialisation but because of the National University custom of creating a new department for every professor in a new subject.

Other departments had been established because of personality factions, or in a power-building process. UCC was now realising that merging departments where possible (one history department replaced three in 1992, and the mathematical departments agreed on a common school in 1995) made for efficiency and economies, and hopefully harmony, though vested interests would inevitably retard the process. A judicious balancing of carrot and stick was called for, while mild knocking of heads together might also be necessary on occasion.

In 1994, knocking of heads together was also needed, it seemed, at the very top. Strained relations between the president and the registrar (Professor M.A. Moran, 1989–) made the administration of college affairs extremely difficult; wasted the time, absorbed the energies and divided the loyalties of academics and governors; scandalised students and the general public; and threatened to mar the UCC 150 celebrations in 1995. In the end, however, polarisation seemed to yield to a mediation and recon-ciliatory process, and members of the college community soon began to ask one another in bewilderment what it had been all about. Students of college history could console themselves by philosophically reflecting that the institution, more than once before, had survived palace quarrels that had developed from personality clashes, policy differences and jurisdictional arguments.

A Cork university, at last?

With regard to the federal university framework, the constituent colleges of Cork, Dublin and Galway went on sharing the same NUI bed in recent decades, more or less amicably. Whatever suited Dublin had perforce to suit the rest, and in the end UCD decided it could and would be independent without altogether severing the NUI link. And so in the early 1990s the National University of Ireland put its ingenious proposals for a new structure before government, which accepted them in principle in its green paper on education in 1992 and agreed to enact them in the commemorative year of 1995.[10]

The three constituent colleges would now become constituent *universities* of the National University of Ireland, a constitutional arrangement akin to the mystery of the Trinity. Thus University College Cork would be retitled 'The National University of Ireland, Cork'. St Patrick's College, Maynooth, heretofore having the somewhat second-class status of a 'recognised college' of the NUI, would now enjoy full con-stituent university status, like the other three. Its acceptability was facilitated by a radical internal reorganisation, whereby the 'secular' college, with its own master, was clearly distinguished from the pontifical college. In this connection, an interesting con-sensus emerged in the NUI Senate that, in all the changed circumstances, the ban in the 1908 Act on public funding for 'any theological or religious teaching or study' was no longer tenable and should be repealed.

Provision would be made in legislation for the amendment of the Irish Universities Act 1908 and associated charters so as to effect the transfer of powers and functions from the NUI Senate to the constituent universities. Each constituent university would have the power to appoint its own staff, including the president, in accordance with the appointments procedure approved by the NUI Senate (in effect, the assessors board system). Lecturers appointed by each governing body in the former constituent college would now become lecturers of the relevant constituent university. The enhanced powers of the new constituent universities would include establishing their own degree and diploma courses, setting their own marks and standards and, in consultation with the external examiner, setting their own examinations. The NUI Senate would continue to appoint external examiners on the agreed recommendation of the constituent universities. The Senate's other residual responsibilities would be co-ordinatory and generally supervisory in the area of appointment procedures. And it would continue to be concerned with maintaining appropriate entrance standards and the highest international standards for degrees and diplomas. The NUI would also be a forum for consideration of developmental policies in education in Ireland and in the evolving European Union. For their part, the constituent universities would consider what internal reorganisation might be necessary in the new context of independence. Irrespective of university restructuring, was it not time to reconsider the composition of governing bodies whose membership had been fixed nearly a century ago in a very different Ireland? A modernised governing body, with much greater power and responsibility, would also have to reform its *modus operandi*. In UCC's case, a Joint (Governing Body–Academic Council) Committee on Governance and Management – the Devlin Committee – extensively investigated the workings of the college, and made many recommendations in a comprehensive report in the summer of 1994.

Obviously, its new constitutional status would mean change, challenge and opportunity for 'the National University of Ireland, Cork', as the president observed in his annual report for 1991–92. But he also noted that institutional restraints had not hindered 'the development of UCC from its original position as a small Constituent College of the National University to its present position as a de facto independent vibrant University'. Indeed, it could be argued that the college had enjoyed quasi-university status all along; that, while the federal structure might delay the implementation of UCC proposals, this was no bad thing; that the NUI generally respected decisions made in Cork; and that it had monitored and guaranteed standards in appointments and in degrees. At any rate, to the extent that Cork had pursued the holy grail (or the will-o'-the-wisp) of an independent university from the outset, it seemed to have been found at last in 1995.

The proposed change would not greatly affect the attitudes of students and graduates who identified with the living reality of the college and for whom the university has always been an abstraction or just an office in Dublin where certain correspondence having to do with examination forms and fees, had to be transacted. Graduates might appreciate the international recognition secured by an NUI degree (and this would continue into the new structure) but their affectionate loyalty was to the college. Would they now get their tongues and their hearts around the cumbersome NUIC acronym or would they nostalgically bemoan the phasing out of the euphonious UCC, just as their predecessors had lamented the filling in of the Quarry and, long before that, the eclipse of the name 'Queen's College Cork'? Whatever about new structures and titles, 'the college' would endure in the hearts and minds of its alumni and alumnae.

In a sense, the changing relationship between college and university was unimportant – certainly less important than the college's relations with the government or the HEA. Despite the government's apparent malleability on the proposed changes in the structure of the NUI, there persisted a certain anti-academic coolness on the part of some public servants at least. They had no great enthusiasm for guaranteeing traditional university autonomy, believing rather that third-level institutions, old and new, should be organised along common, government-suggested lines. As the green paper on education put it: 'the legislative framework for universities, which has grown up on an ad hoc basis, needs to be rationalised'. The Department of Education was also interested in 'rationalising the composition and functions of governing bodies and strengthening the executive role of college presidents'.[11] In all this wider context, perhaps the college had not given enough thought to what its relationship should be with the new University of Limerick (which it rather feared as a competitor) and with the Cork Regional Technical College (with which it did not co-operate sufficiently in the interest of maximising use of common resources).

Governments in the 1990s looked like being increasingly interventionist, pressuring universities to generate more and more of their own funding and at the same time expecting more accountability for diminishing state grants. The interventionist mentality also expected learning and research to have measurable practical applications. The concept of 'useful knowledge', so prominent in the educational philosophy of the Queen's College in the 1840s, was underlined afresh in the 'enterprise culture' of the 1990s. Given the state's poor record in funding research, it was hardly surprising to find it displaying a philistine attitude to pure research in Irish universities, suggesting that results of research in other countries could be 'bought in' for application! Such a mind-set is basically in conflict with the *raison d'être* of any institution of learning.

Teaching and research are the priorities of a university. However, the modern university is drawn into a host of other laudable activities:

> consultancy work for industry, providing professional services to the local community in disciplines from Archaeology or Social Studies to Medicine and Dentistry, co-operating in regional development and facilitating the development of international links for the region. In short, the university is an integral part of the cultural, scientific and developmental infrastructure of the region and should be seen in this wider context by those involved in planning its future development.

The description is President Mortell's, and the diverse functions mentioned are clearly evident in the case of UCC. Its service to Cork city and county, and to the southern region generally – to the Munster area in which it was set from the beginning – is an integral part of its personality, now more than ever, according as its services become more diversified. All traces of the ivory tower, still visible twenty years ago, have now vanished.

But the president also reminds us of the dangers of this situation, citing an OECD 1984 report. If a university takes on too much, if there is a 'functional overload', the prime functions of teaching and research may be performed inadequately, particularly if the resources do not grow to match the increasing social demands:

> If we do not focus clearly on the central mission of a university, we are in danger of dissipating our energies and compromising our integrity so that we risk losing sight of our raison d'être. If that were to happen, it would undermine everything else we might hope to achieve.[12]

The oral history project

Oral history, so-called, has its limitations and dangers, and the quality and importance of contributions obviously vary from one deponent to the next. That being said, personal recollections over a long period can illuminate and enliven the impersonal written record. In 1990–91, some 130 depositions were taken from a wide range of individuals connected with UCC, the great majority of them former employees from the academic, administrative, technician, attendant and general operative spheres. In some cases, memories went back to the early 1920s. A number of deponents have died since the project was undertaken and it is desirable that fresh contributions should be sought at regular intervals.

Some of the most interesting tapes in the Oral History Archives (UC/OHA) are those recorded from retired college technicians, tradesmen, attendants and general workers, many with a lifetime of service to their credit. Their observations, of a kind not to be found otherwise, throw light on the relationships between different layers of the total college community at a time – say, up to the end of the Atkins presidency in 1963 – when that community was much smaller and more intimate. The reflections of some of these deponents would have surprised the academics whom they served and who probably took them very much for granted. There are individual variations, of course, and specific references cannot be given here for obvious reasons but the interested researcher can easily locate a particular OHA source.[13]

A common note struck in these depositions is that of loyalty to the college. In one case, this is frankly stated as 'love', expressing itself, for example, in supporting UCC hurlers in championship games and consequently being taunted by fellow-workers with charges of treachery to the parish club. One general operative regarded the college as his 'second home'. Loyalty in another case meant behaving oneself off duty so as not to 'let down' the college. There are recollections of much unpaid work ('when service sweat for duty, not for meed'), and the complaint in this respect was less about lack of remuneration than about the college's failure to distinguish between dedicated workers and those who simply did the minimum necessary to stay in a job. Frequently, technicians performed all kinds of services for 'their' professors without pausing to consider whether these were remotely consonant with their terms of employment. One man recalls that at spring-cleaning time, he would 'air' the O'Rahilly marital mattress and he somehow connected that unusual service with the time when, nearing the age of eighteen and fearing dismissal as a gardening hand because the college would not or could not afford to pay him a man's wages, he daringly bearded President O'Rahilly leaving the Honan Chapel after mass and (successfully) pleaded to be kept on!

A variant of this personal patronage was the close relationship between a professor and the porter assigned to his department. A porter was often the professor's 'man', combining general supervision of the department with a personal valet/minder approach. Such a relationship was noted in the department of chemistry, for example, where the porter would grandly respond, on being pressed for information by students after examinations, '*we* have no results yet'. Professor William Bergin sometimes neglected to attend to a critical area of his attire and would, on such occasions, have his lecture interrupted by a porter called Foley (one of two notable brothers) with the urgent message, 'you're wanted on the phone'. This was the pre-arranged code for undone flies to be buttoned outside the door (a slow routine in pre-zip days) and so avert further student levity.[14] Pat O'Flaherty, porter to the West Wing, was a Jeeves-like figure, deferential and diplomatic, affectionately remembered by many, including the present writer.

Not all the recollections have a romantic afterglow. There is general agreement that the college was a pleasant environment to work in, but hours were long (in the time before the five-day week) and wages low, the college being then a parsimonious master, perhaps of necessity. It did not always practise the high principles of social justice it preached in adult education lectures. Security of tenure could sometimes depend on student numbers. Attendants aspiring to degree courses were discouraged. However, one of the unusual advantages of living in a more-or-less benevolent feudal community was that, in some cases, at least, family health problems were dealt with free of charge by one or other of the Cork dynastic medical families associated with the college. And it was college policy, uniquely egalitarian, to extend fee remission to children of all full-time staff, irrespective of rank. At a time when the provision of scholarships was extremely meagre, this was welcomed as a substantial perquisite – in effect, a mechanism for transcending class barriers. A worker chosen to occupy one of the college's three residential lodges – at the main, west and south entrances – regarded himself as especially fortunate: the benefit meant free family housing and an idyllic playing ground for the children.[15]

According to one deponent, a departing worker (who apparently had time to rehearse spontaneous witticisms) on being asked by the genial 'Paaks' Coffey what struck him most about college, replied 'the incompetence of the professors and the presumptions of the porters'.[16] Whatever about the truth of the former, most porters were very far from presumptuous. But some of them, and their technician and general-worker brothers and handful of sisters, silently resented the prevailing assumption of the college authorities that the lower orders had no contribution to make to running the place and that in any case it was none of their business. (The enthusiastic co-option of a union representative to the GB lay far in the fantastic future.) It was only the rare eccentric radical among the workers who had the temerity to wonder about the gap between his £150 per annum

13.9 Jack Foley, retired physics technician.

and the professor's £900. What rankled with not a few was the lordly patronising attitude of, admittedly, a small minority of professors. In any case, professors lived in a different world and the only social mingling with the infrastructural personnel was at certain overlapping boundary levels, and then only on rare occasions.

When President O'Rahilly ostentatiously poured tea for workers at adult education socials, that was part of another agenda. In the real, everyday college attendants and technicians were allowed into the restaurant for a cup of tea only during the Emergency. Fifty years later, the common-room, at last living up to its name, admitted all to its amenities, irrespective of their grade in the college community.

Loyalty to the college

As one of three Governing Body nominees, the writer was privileged to serve on the Devlin Committee which carried out an extensive series of interviews in the first half of 1994 with representatives of the entire college community – different levels of academic, administrative and library staff; directors of research and service units; technicians, maintenance staff and general services personnel; and, certainly not least, the president of the Students' Union.[17] In the course of this unusual exercise, the committee was impressed by the spirit of collegiality that animated the interviewees. If some of them were critical of various aspects of college management, it was because they wished to see the college keeping pace with change and effectively responding to the challenging demands of teaching and research. 'Loyalty' (doubtless an embarrassingly old-fashioned concept for some readers) is the only term to describe their common attitude, and it is the reflection of *their* regard for a hallowed academic institution.

This sense of identification with the college family is found at all levels but is expressed most strongly and frankly, perhaps, by those who dwell far from the topmost reaches inhabited by a charmed academic circle. The picture is not always idyllic, of course, but what is impressive is the widespread sense of belonging. However, perhaps the college is less one family than a series of families occupying the same territory. A domestic garden is home to various forms of life, all of whom separately regard it as their exclusive property – insects, birds, dogs and cats, and *homo* more or less *sapiens*. Thus the college is subconsciously viewed, to some extent, as *their* particular territorial realm by academics, administrators, technicians, general workmen and women, attendant/security personnel – and students.

Students first and last

From pursuers of one-year diplomas, through the undergraduate masses, to post-graduates, 'the students are the life of the place' to quote the OHA comment of a now retired attendant.[18] This may seem a trite observation at first glance, but the essential vitality of students is sometimes better appreciated at close quarters (because it is more vibrantly expressed) by technicians and attendants than by academics. Students have always been 'the life of the place', in spiritedly defending their rights at visitations, in nationalist demonstrations in Sullivan's day, in the excitement of the Parnellite decade, in riotous downtown protests against a visitation decision in 1899, in boisterous con-ferring antics down to the 1940s, and in rag-day mayhem of the pre-O'Rahilly and post-McCarthy years. Even if student behaviour of this kind is dismissed as 'under-graduate' in the pejorative sense, vitality still abounds meritoriously at more disciplined levels in a rich profusion of clubs and societies.

The writer is inevitably drawn to reflect on changes in the nature of the student body since his own student days fifty years ago, and indeed since he began to lecture in UCC in the early 1960s. There are such obvious differences as a tenfold increase in numbers since the early 1940s, and the fact that women now comprise a clear majority. The students of the 1990s experience a more relaxed college lifestyle. In spite of small class numbers, yesterday's professors kept their students at arm's length. Formality – social, sartorial, appellative – was the order of the day. While students nowadays will find a large and overcrowded college impersonal in some respects, paradoxically they enjoy easier access, through contact hours and tutorials, to their lecturers, if not to their head of department. (College has also an excellent record in providing facilities for disabled students.) Moreover, such is the (relatively) informal and egalitarian spirit of the age that academics are more approachable and give themselves fewer authoritarian airs than their predecessors.

But in another sense the age can never be egalitarian enough. The student body has been considerably democratised since the introduction of the grants system. If the term 'middle class' is loosely used of the students' background, then it must be interpreted as embracing a much wider section of society than it did in 1960 or 1945, or *a fortiori*, in 1849. Equality of opportunity is pushing out new frontiers but UCC is still far from being that 'poor man's university' which was expected with the passing of the Irish Universities Act in 1908.[19] The admission to college of the children of the poorest social classes, stigmatised by ghetto addresses, must await a more radical change in our society than we have yet seen. The day of justice will not be advanced by token courses, nor even by college buildings located in the Northside.

It is their middle class interests, their geographical rootedness and the remarkable continuity of the catchment areas that have made Cork university students such conservative creatures over the 150-year period of the college's existence. Conservatism in this sense means an absence of radical activism rather than social indifference. The students of the 1960s who participated in the famous 'teach-in' and whose immediate successors were involved in office 'sit-ins' were expressing various degrees of social concern. These periods were short lived, however, and the high-standard, examination-orientated, competitive pressure for good results that increasingly characterised the 1980s left little space for radical agitation, and indicated a return to traditional conservative patterns. Life was real, life was earnest and a good degree was the goal. It has to be said, however, that though the leisurely, pressure-free students of the 1940s were not excessively worried about examinations, radical activism was not on their agenda either, because their political–social consciousness had not yet been sharpened.

The ultimate continuity in the college is the perennial nature of the student temperament and character. Allowing for individual variations – from laziness and vice to assiduity and virtue – there is a valid generalisation to be made. Underneath all the changes since 1849 the eternal student persists, creating the charming illusion of changelessness and of youthful immortality, and sharing some of the elixir with the academics. Then and now, in the Queen's College of the past, in the University College of today and in tomorrow's National University of Ireland, Cork, students are eager, stimulating, idealistic (even at their most cynical) and vulnerable (even at their toughest). They are the perpetually shining hour. They are indeed the life of the place. *Semper sint in flore.*

Appendix A

Officers and Professors

(Queen's College Cork, 1845–1908; University College Cork, 1908–95)

These lists are compiled from the Staff Roll Books (President's Office), the Secretary's Office, *Sessional Lists*, the College Calendars, *President's Reports*, the *Cork University Record* and the *UCC Record*. Because of inconsistencies in the information available, the lists may not be entirely free from inaccuracies.

President

Sir Robert Kane	1845–73
William K. Sullivan	1873–90
James W. Slattery	1890–96
Sir Rowland Blennerhassett	1897–1904
Sir Bertram Windle	1904–19
Patrick J. Merriman	1919–43
Alfred O'Rahilly	1943–54
Henry St J. Atkins	1954–63
John J. McHenry	1964–67
Michael D. McCarthy	1967–78
Tadhg Ó Ciardha	1978–88
Michael P. Mortell	1989–

Registrar

Francis Albani	1849–54
Robert J. Kenny	1854–76
Alexander Jack	1876–1906
William F. Butler	1906–09
John P. Molohan	1910–15
Patrick J. Merriman	1915–19
Alfred O'Rahilly	1920–43
Henry St John Atkins	1944–54
Tadhg Ó Ciardha[1]	1955–78

From the time the registrarship became a full-time office under the reforms of the 1970s, the holder has held a nominal professorship (no duties, no salary) to ensure his academic standing. Thus Ó Ciardha as registrar was professor of mathematical statistics; Mortell, of applied mathematics; and Moran, of applied statistics.

Michael P. Mortell	1979–89
Michael A. Moran	1989–

Secretary and Bursar[1]

Edward M. Fitzgerald	1849–71
John England	1871–86
Lt Col. W.R. Jenny[2]	1888–1902
Denis C. Newsom	1902–08
Samuel Hollins	1909–10
H.C. Clifton	1910–12
Joseph Downey	1912–44
James Hurley	1944–65
David L. Whyte	1965–72
Michael F. Kelleher	1974–

Vice-President[3]

John Ryall	1845–75
Patrick D. Barry	1974–76
Edward F. Fahy	1976–79
Thomas F. Raftery	1979–82
John J. Lee	1982–85
Shawn Doonan	1985–89
Desmond M. Clarke	1989–92
Máire F. Mulcahy	1989–94
John F. O'Connor	1992–95
Rev. Brendan E. O'Mahony	1994–

Librarian

Henry Hennessy	1849–55
Matthias O'Keeffe	1856–75
Richard Caulfield	1875–87
Owen O'Ryan	1888–95
William F. Butler	1896–1900
John Fawcett	1910–30

---

[1] Title of office changed in 1974 to Finance Officer and Secretary.
[2] Remembered as rude and overbearing – 'be sure you bang the damn door'. He shouted at freshmen as though they were privates on a barrack square, in the memory of D.P. Fitzgerald (afterwards professor of anatomy), *CUR*, no. 4, Summer 1945.
[3] From 1989 there were two vice-presidents.

T.A. Conroy[1]	1932–52
Daniel O'Keeffe	1959–72
Patrick J. Quigg	1973–86
Thomas J.A. Crawshaw	1991–94
John Fitzgerald	1995–

Planning Officer[2]

| Edward McCarthy | 1971– |

Dean of Student Affairs

| John P. Teegan | 1974–83 |

Professors[3]

Accounting
(Accountancy until 1949)

A.J. Magennis	1927–34
C.P. McCarthy	1946–49
Edward P. Cahill	1988–

Agriculture

Edmund Murphy	1849–68 (Agriculture and Botany)
Thomas Wibberley	1920–22 (Howard Harrington Professor of Agriculture)
Connell Boyle	1923–64
Thomas F. Raftery	1964–

---

[1]   Conroy, however, had no statutory authority and acted under the vigorous 'honorary directorship' of Alfred O'Rahilly whose legacy was an impressively improved library and an idiosyncratic classification system. In the list of librarians above, gaps at a number of points were filled by acting librarians.

[2]   Formerly College Engineer and Planning Officer.

[3]   Apart from mainstream chairs – and a number of departments have more than one – some professorships, particularly in law and medicine, have been part-time. Moreover, before promotional associate professorships became available under the modern scheme dating from the 1970s, a 'personal' professorship would be established from time to time, for one of a number of reasons.

Anatomy and Physiology
(a single chair before 1907)

Benjamin Alcock	1849–54
J. Henry Corbett	1855–75
J.J. Charles	1875–1907

Anatomy
(see Anatomy and Physiology)

Bertram Windle	1907–09
D.P. Fitzgerald	1909–42
Micheal A. MacConaill	1942–73
Gerald N.C. Crawford	1973–77
John P. Fraher	1977–

Ancient Classics
(separate chairs of Latin and Greek until 1915)

Hubert J. Treston	1915–58	
John P. Fogarty	1959–83	
William H. Porter	1946–50	(Ancient History)

Applied Psychology

Rev. Peter Dempsey OFM Cap.	1964–82
Maxwell Taylor	1983–

Archaeology

Bertram Windle	1910–15
Rev. Patrick Power	1915–32
Seán P. Ó Ríordáin	1936–43
Michael J. O'Kelly	1946–81
Peter C. Woodman	1983–

Biochemistry

P.J. Drumm	1946–52
Thomas G. Brady	1952–77
Shawn Doonan	1978–93
T.G. Cotter	1995–

Botany
(Plant Science from 1985)

Edmund Murphy	1849–68
(Agriculture and Botany)	
H. Ashley-Cummins	1909–31
J.C. Sperrin-Johnson	1932–48
Oliver M. Roberts	1949–78
Alan C. Cassells	1979–

Celtic Languages and Literature

Owen Connellan	1849–63

Celtic Languages and Philology

Séamus Caomhánach	1945–70

Chemistry

John Blyth	1849–72	
Maxwell Simpson	1872–91	
Augustus E. Dixon	1891–1924	
Joseph Reilly	1924–59	
Francis L. Scott	1960–73	
John P. Teegan	1962–83	(Spectroscopy)
Joseph Cunningham	1970–	(Physical)
Brian J. Hathaway	1970–94	(Inorganic)
Michael A. McKervey	1975–90	(Organic)
William B. Jennings	1992–	(Organic)
G.G. Guilbault	1995–	(Analytical)

Civil Engineering

Christopher B. Lane	1849–53	
John England	1853–55	
Alexander Jack	1855–1906	
Connell W. O'D. Alexander	1906–20	
Henry N. Walsh	1921–57	
James C.I. Dooge	1958–70	
Edmund C. Dillon	1962–70	(Concrete Technology)
Edmund C. Dillon	1970–87	
James P.J. O'Kane	1990–	

Computer Science

Patrick G. O'Regan	1975–	
James A. Bowen	1992–	(Software Engineering)

Dairy
(see Food)

Dental Prosthetics
(now subsumed in Dentistry, Restorative)

M.A. Roche	1950–59
Leslie B. Scher	1960–63
William T. MacCulloch	1969–92

Dental Surgery

J.R. Hackett	1946–48
Norman P. Butler	1950–64
John G. Russell	1964–93
Duncan Sleeman	1995–

Dentistry, Conservative
(now subsumed in Dentistry, Restorative)

Brian Barrett	1964–95

Dentistry, Preventative and Paediatric

Denis M. O'Mullane	1984–

Dentistry, Restorative
(subsuming Dental Prosthetics and Dentistry, Conservative)

R.J. McConnell	1995–

Dentistry
(see Orthodontics)

Early and Medieval Irish Language and Literature

Pádraig S. Ó Riain	1973–

Economics

Timothy A. Smiddy	1909–23	
John Busteed	1924–64	
Rev. W. Paschal Larkin	1956–64	(Economic Theory)
David P. O'Mahony	1966–87	
Connell M. Fanning	1990–	

Education

Elizabeth M. O'Sullivan	1910–35
Frances Vaughan	1936–48
Lucy M. Duggan	1949–62
Vincent A. McClelland	1969–77
Daniel G. Mulcahy	1978–91
Áine Hyland	1993–

Electrical Engineering (and Microelectronics)

F.J. Teago	1953–59	(College Professor)
Charles T.G. Dillon	1959–76	
Michael C. Sexton	1976–94	
Robert Yacamini	1996–	
Gerard T. Wrixon	1984–	(Microelectronics)

English
(see also History and English Literature)

William F.P. Stockley	1909–31	
Daniel Corkery	1931–47	
Bridget G. McCarthy	1948–66	
Seán Lucy	1967–87	(Modern)
Riobárd P. Breathnach	1967–72	(Old and Middle)
Éamonn Ó Carragáin	1975–	(Old and Middle)
Colbert J. Kearney	1989–	(Modern)

Food Chemistry
(Dairy Chemistry until 1969; Dairy and Food Chemistry until 1988)

Gerald T. Pyne	1940–69
Patrick F. Fox	1969–

Food Economics
(Dairy Accounting and Dairy Economics until 1973; Dairy and Food Economics until 1978)

Michael Murphy	1946–69
Denis I.F. Lucey	1978–

Food Engineering
(Dairy Engineering until 1968; Dairy and Food Engineering until 1988)

Francis A. McGrath	1946–67
Edward C. Synnott	1969–

Food Microbiology
(Dairy Bacteriology until 1961; Dairy and Food Microbiology until 1988)

Michael Grimes	1940–61
Timothy O'Mullane	1961–87
John J. Condon	1989–

Food
(see Nutrition)

Food Technology
(Dairy Technology until 1971; Dairy and Food Technology until 1988)

Joseph Lyons	1940–53
Michael J. O'Shea	1954–70
John Foley	1971–

French
(in Modern Languages until 1909; in Romance Languages until 1969)

Kathleen O'Flaherty	1970–81
Robert J.E. Pickering	1983–93
Patrick T. O'Donovan	1994–

Gaelic Languages
(Research professorship)

T.F. O'Rahilly	1929–35

Geography
(also see Geology and Geography)

Charles S. O'Connell	1959–76
William J. Smyth	1978–

Geology
(also see Mineralogy)

Peter M. Brück	1979–

Geology and Geography

Isaac Swain	1909–44

German
(in Modern Languages until 1909)

Wally Swertz	1909–15
Bridget Lyndsay	1915–21
Mary Boyle	1922–68
Peter Schäublin	1968–92
Mary P. Howard	1993–

Greek
(in Ancient Classics from 1915)

John Ryall	1849–75
Vaughan Boulger	1875–83
William Ridgeway	1883–94
Charles H. Keene	1895–1914

History
(in History and English Literature until 1909)

P.J. Merriman	1909–19	
James Hogan	1920–63	
Denis Gwynn	1947–63	(Research Professor of Modern Irish History)
Séamus Pender	1955–71	(Irish)
John G. Barry	1965–89	(Medieval)
Oliver MacDonagh	1967–73	(Modern)

John A. Murphy	1971–90	(Irish)
John J. Lee	1974–93	(Modern)
Kennedy F. Roche	1976–81	(History of Political Ideas)
Dermot F. Keogh	1991–95	(Jean Monnet Professor)

(again one department from 1993)

John J. Lee	1993–
Dermot F. Keogh	1995–

History and English Literature

Rev. Charles F. Darley	1849–57
William Rushton	1858–71
George F. Savage Armstrong	1871–1905
William F.P. Stockley	1905–09

Hygiene and Public Health
(Hygiene until 1928; also see Social Medicine)

Denis D. Donovan	1909–27
John C. Saunders	1928–62

Irish
(also see Celtic Languages; Gaelic Languages; Early and Medieval Irish)

Rev. R.H. Henebry	1909–16	
Tadhg Ó Donnchadha (Tórna)	1916–44	
Risteárd Breatnach	1945–81	
Cormac Ó Cuilleanáin	1950–66	(History of Modern Irish Literature)
Seán Ó Tuama	1982–91	(Modern Irish Literature)
Seán Ó Coileáin	1983–	(Modern Irish Language)

Italian
(in Modern Languages until 1909; in Romance Languages until 1969)

Piero Cali	1979–91
Eduardo Saccone	1994–

Jurisprudence and Political Economy
(also see Law; Medical Jurisprudence; Philosophy)

R. Horner Mills	1849–93

Latin
(in Ancient Classics from 1915)

Bunnell Lewis	1849–1905
John P. Molohan	1905–1915

Law

G. Lawrence	1910–13	(Real Property)
W.J. Dunlea	1910–27	(Jurisprudence)
Henry J. Maloney	1912–25	(Common)
George J. Daly	1925–41	(Common)
C.K. Murphy	1927–56	(Jurisprudence)
Denis P. O'Donovan	1942–47	(Common)
Edward F. Ryan	1950–82	(Common)
Bryan J. Murphy	1957–86	(Jurisprudence)
Bryan E. MacMahon	1977–87	
John F. O'Connor	1989–95	
Brian A. Carroll	1994–	

Law
(English)

Francis A. Walsh	1849–52
Michael Barry	1852–70
Mark J. O'Shaughnessy	1870–84
Ralph W.B. Barry	1884–1902
George C. Green	1902–08

Logic and Metaphysics
(see also Philosophy)

George Sidney Read	1849–83
George J. Stokes	1884–94

Management
(and Marketing)

Leonard Wrigley	1981–88
Sebastian Green	1990–

Materia Medica

Alexander Fleming	1849–58
Purcell O'Leary	1858–74
Matthias O'Keeffe	1875–84
C. Yelverton-Pearson	1884–99
John Dundon	1899–1927

Mathematical Physics

Matthew J. Conran	1910–13
E.H. Harper	1913–16
Alfred O'Rahilly	1917–43
Michael D. McCarthy	1944–49
Patrick M. Quinlan	1951–87

Mathematics

George Boole	1849–64
Robert Romer	1865–67
Charles Niven	1867–80
John C. Malet	1880–86
Arthur H. Anglin	1887–1913
Matthew J. Conran	1913–35
Henry St J. Atkins	1936–54
Patrick B. Kennedy	1956–63
Patrick D. Barry	1965–

Medical Jurisprudence

P.T. O'Sullivan	1909–23
C.K. Murphy	1924–27

Medicine

D.C. O'Connor	1849–88
Edward R. Townshend	1889–97
W.E. Ashley-Cummins	1897–1923
P.T. O'Sullivan	1924–31
James M. O'Donovan	1931–57
Denis J. O'Sullivan	1961–91
Fergus L.J. Shanahan	1992–

Mental and Moral Science
(also see Logic and Metaphysics; Philosophy)

George J. Stokes   1894–1909

Midwifery
(see Obstetrics and Gynaecology)

Mineralogy and Geology

James Nicol   1849–53
Robert Harkness   1853–78

Modern Languages
(Romance Languages and German after 1909)

Raymond de Vericour   1849–79
Owen O'Ryan   1879–95
William F. Butler   1895–1909

Music

Frederick St John Lacy   1909–34
Carl Hardebeck   1922–23   (Irish Music)
Aloys G. Fleischmann   1936–80
David Wulstan   1980–83
Nicholas Sandon   1986–93
David H. Cox   1994–

Natural History
(see Zoology)

Natural Philosophy
(see Physics)

Nutrition

Patrick A. Morrissey   1986–

Obstetrics and Gynaecology
(Midwifery to 1909)

J.R. Harvey	1849–78
Henry Macnaughton-Jones	1878–83
Henry Corby	1883–1924
J.J. Kearney	1926–48
William Kearney	1949–77
David M. Jenkins	1979–

Ophthalmology

Arthur W. Sandford	1910–26
Vernon O'Hea-Cussen	1946–63

Orthodontics

Mary Hegarty	1964–

Paediatrics

Richard G. Barry	1970–77	
Peter J. Kearney	1980–	
Gerald H. Cussen	1981–92	(Neonatal Paediatrics)

Pathology

A.E. Moore	1909–40
William J. O'Donovan	1941–65
Colin J.E. Wright	1967–78
Cuimín T. Doyle	1979–

Pharmacology and Therapeutics

Michael B. Murphy	1992–

Philosophy
(Mental and Moral Science to 1909)

George J. Stokes	1909–10
Rev. T.E. Fitzgibbon	1910–37
Very Rev. James E. O'Mahony	1937–62
Rev. Brendan E. O'Mahony	1965–

Philosophy and Jurisprudence

George J. Stokes   1910–24

Physics
(Natural Philosophy to 1909)

George F. Shaw   1849–55
John England   1855–94
William Bergin   1895–1931
John J. McHenry   1932–64
Edward F. Fahy   1961–64   (Nuclear and Theoretical Physics)
Edward F. Fahy   1964–88
John G. McInerney   1992–

Physiology
(see Anatomy and Physiology)

David T. Barry   1907–42
Francis Kane   1942–54
Paul J. Cannon   1954–58
John D. Sheehan   1959–87
William J. Hall   1987–

Plant Science
(see Botany)

Psychiatry

Robert J. Daly   1971–

Romance Languages
(Modern Languages to 1909)

Mary Ryan   1910–38
Eithne Byrne-Costigan   1939–69

Social Medicine
(see Hygiene and Public Health)

John P. Corridan   1973–85

Social Theory and Institutions
(see Sociology)

Sociology
(formerly Social Theory and Institutions)

Damian F. Hannan	1971–76
John M. Maguire	1978–

Spanish
(formerly in Romance Languages)

Joseph G. Healy	1961–63
Niall J. Ware	1964–78
Terence T. Folley	1978–

Statistics

Tadhg Ó Ciardha	1952–78
Michael A. Moran	1975–89

Theology

Rev. James Good	1958–70

Surgery

Denis B. Bullen	1849–64
William K. Tanner	1864–80
Stephen O'Sullivan	1880–99
Charles Yelverton-Pearson	1899–1928
John Dundon	1928–40
Patrick Kiely	1941–67
Michael P. Brady	1968–

Zoology
(Natural History to 1909)

Rev. William Hincks	1849–53
Wyville Thompson	1853–54
William Smith	1854–57
J. Reay Greene	1858–77

A. Leith-Adams	1878–81
Marcus Hartog	1882–1921
Louis P.W. Renouf	1922–54
Fergus J. O'Rourke	1955–81
Máire F. Mulcahy	1983–

Associate Professors

Ted O'Leary	Accounting	1991–
Frederick W. Powell	Applied Social Studies	1990–
Walter A. Lorenz	Applied Social Studies	1995–
James J.A. Heffron	Biochemistry	1985–
Eric R. Tully	Biochemistry	1981–88
Louis A. Buckley	Conservative Dentistry	1981–
Daniel G. O'Donovan	Chemistry	1975–92
William S. Murphy	Chemistry	1983–
Laurence D. Burke	Chemistry	1984–
Trevor R. Spalding	Chemistry	1994–
R. Paul Brint	Chemistry	1995–
Patrick Coffey	Civil Engineering	1957–64
David M.F. Orr	Civil Engineering	1987–
John S. Campbell	Civil Engineering	1990–
Mary R.M. Herbert	Early and Medieval Irish	1993–
Denis O'Sullivan	Education	1995–
Michael C. Sexton	Electrical Engineering	1975–76
John M.D. Murphy	Electrical Engineering	1980–
Gerard T. Wrixon	Electrical Engineering	1981–84
William M. Kelly	Electrical Engineering	1992–
John Montague	English	1986–88
David M. Mulvihill	Food Chemistry	1994–
Patrick A. Morrissey	Dairy and Food Chemistry	1981–86
John J. Condon	Food Microbiology	1980–89
Charles Daly	Food Microbiology	1984–
Thomas J.F. O'Gara	Food Microbiology	1989–
John K. Collins	Food Microbiology	1992–
Denis J. Buckley	Food Technology	1991–
Matthew M. MacNamara	French	1990–
T. Patrick O'Flanagan	Geography	1990–
Kennedy F. Roche	History	1976–79
Donnchadh Ó Corráin	History	1980–
Thomas J. Dunne	History	1993–
David G. Morgan	Law	1991–
Deirdre A.M. Hunt	Marketing and Management	1991–

Robert E. Harte	Mathematics	1983–89
John B. Twomey	Mathematics	1983–
Patrick D. MacHale	Mathematics	1990–
Finbarr Holland	Mathematics	1980–
Gerard Murphy	Mathematics	1995–
Martin J.A. Stynes	Mathematics	1996–
John B. Ferriss	Medicine	1983–
Patrick F. Duggan	Medicine	1988–
John K. Collins	Medicine	1994–
Seán Ó Tuama	Modern Irish	1967–82
Desmond M. Clarke	Philosophy	1986–
Robert G.L. Barden	Philosophy	1990–
Michael M.D. Mansfield	Physics	1988–
Niall S. Ó Murchadha	Physics	1989–
William J. Hall	Physiology	1976–87
Brian J. Harvey	Physiology	1992–
Terence W. O'Reilly	Spanish	1989–
Patrick D. Bourke	Statistics	1990–
William O. Kirwan	Surgery	1983–
Máire F. Mulcahy	Zoology	1980–83
Alan A. Myers	Zoology	1987–
Paul S. Giller	Zoology	1995–

APPENDIX B

CREST AND MOTTO

At the planning stages of the Queen's Colleges, Dublin Castle brushed aside the matter of a distinctive seal for each college, in effect taking the line that expense must be avoided and that any old seal would do.[1] However in 1889, President W.K. Sullivan, out of his concern for the status of the college, pressed for the granting of a distinctive and authentic coat of arms.[2] The Ulster King of Arms duly obliged on 20 March 1889,[3] authorising the college to use

> the Arms following, that is to say, Per pale gules and azure, on the dexter side a lion statant gardant imperially crowned or, on the sinister side three eastern crowns ppr. on a chief of the third an ancient ship between two castles in fess of the first in centre chief point of achievement an open book garnished of the third, for Motto Where Findbarr taught Let Munster learn.

In lay terms, the crest comprises the royal lion; the three ancient sub-divisions of Munster (the kingdoms of Desmond, Ormond and Thomond); the arms of the city of Cork; and the open book of learning. Because of the abolition of the office of vice-presidency and the consequent redefinition of 'the Body Politic and Corporate', there later appears to have been some doubt about the continuing correctness of the armorial bearings.[4] Any such doubt was resolved by a reaffirmation of the original 1889 grant on 2 July 1894.[5]

The motto has remained unchanged[6] over the century, apart from variations of the spelling 'Findbarr': the Irish language version was devised in 1930, in circumstances already related.[7] In contrast, many changes have been rung on the crest over the years, and a perusal of successive presidential letterheads would make an interesting study. Even in Queen's College days, various unauthorised embellishments appeared, including a harp and a shamrock: for a time, the lion raised its paw, as if ready for a friendly greeting.[8] At all stages, liberties were taken with the design of the three crowns, and even more so with the ship and castles.

[1] See pp. 17–18.
[2] See p. 137 above.
[3] Letter Patent Declaring Armorial Bearings, in UCC Archives.
[4] See correspondence between President Slattery (1890–91) and Ulster King of Arms, UC Archives.
[5] Letter Patent as above n. 3, verso.
[6] When the historical foundation of the Finbarrian tradition appeared to have been undermined by Professor Ó Riain's researches, a tongue-in-cheek letter-writer suggested a new motto: 'Where Munster thought that Finbarr taught': *IT*, 14 Oct. 1994.
[7] See p. 264 above.
[8] See letterheads of President Slattery's day (1890–96), UC Archives.

Official crest, 1889 (left) and variant crest, 1950s (see pp. 137, 283)

However, the most radical changes in the crest took place during O'Rahilly's presidency (1943–54), and should be understood in the context of the strongly Catholic–nationalist climate of that period. Thus, in 1950 the artist Robert Gibbings engraved a new coat of arms for Cork University Press which for over two decades had general, if spurious, currency as a college crest. In the Gibbings version[1] the lion was eliminated (after all, Ireland had just recently proclaimed itself a Republic) and a torch of learning now flamed over a book emblazoned with the Jesuit (O'Rahilly's formative influence) acronym AMDG (Ad Maiorem Dei Gloriam – For the greater Glory of God). It is this post-British shield – without the AMDG legend – that was worked into the mosaic flooring under the arch in the late 1960s.[2]

It was under President M.D. McCarthy (1967–78) that the process of restoring the original crest was begun.

---

[1] See *CUR*, no. 19, 1950.

[2] This crest is surrounded by the grand neo-medieval description: *Studium Generale Corcagiense* AD 1845.

APPENDIX C

A COLLEGE ANTHEM

That most sentimental and nostalgic of Cork Queensmen, Henry Macnaughton-Jones (professor of midwifery, 1878–83) composed a number of QCC-related verses around the turn of the century, for the delectation of the Old Corkonians, the London-based graduates' club. His effusions included 'Where Finbarr taught let Munster learn',[1] (composed in the college jubilee year of 1895) and 'There's an old College',[2] which was set to the air of 'The Bells of Shandon' and one verse of which, at least, would have amused 'Father Prout' himself:

> In architecture, or hall of lecture/There's nought more pleasing appeals to me
> And its exterior has no superior/In Oxford, Cambridge or TCD
> Its limestone fretting, and greensward setting/In contrast letting our fancy free
> That green quadrangle doth oft entangle/In happy moments my thoughts of thee.

Macnaughton-Jones, incidentally, was the donor of the handsome Mahoney painting of the college which hangs today in the president's office and which illustrates the cover of this book. (He was particularly concerned about the future of the college under the 1908 Act: see *CE*, 7 May 1908.)

In the mid-1940s, Professor Aloys Fleischmann made a more credible and serious attempt to provide a college anthem, words and music, in English and Irish. This was 'Scoil Bharra Fhinn' or 'Where Finbarr taught' and it was announced as 'a new College song'.[3] It was given at least two rousing renditions (lustily abetted by the writer) after performances of Handel's *Saul* in the Aula Maxima on 2 and 3 March 1946[4] but thereafter met with the same indifferent fate, for whatever reasons (student embarrassment or self-consciousness about singing a college anthem?), as Macnaughton-Jones's composition. The *Cork University Record* praised Fleischmann's anthem as 'well-written' but presciently wondered whether it would 'take' in the long run.[5]

---

[1] Macnaughton Jones, H., *A Piece of Delf and Other Fragments* (London, 1905), pp. 60–62. There is a signed copy by 'The Author' in the Boole Library, UCC.

[2] ibid., pp. 63–4. For a synopsis of his career, see Ronan O'Rahilly, 'Henry Macnaughton Jones', *CUR*, no. 14, Christmas 1948, pp. 34–35.

[3] *CUR*, no. 4, Summer 1945, pp. 43–8.

[4] *CUR*, no. 6, Easter 1946, p. 3.

[5] *CUR*, no. 9, Easter 1947, pp. 2–3.

APPENDIX D

ENTRANCES, BRIDGES AND GATES

Readers will be aware from earlier chapters of the anxiety of the college authorities in the first thirty years (1849–79) to secure a suitable entrance from the Western Road reasonably near to town (see, in particular, pp. 62–4, 107–8, 111–12). The college's concern had to do with convenience, prestige, psychology and security. The western entrance was seen as at once too near the insalubrious gaol and too far from town, with a consequent loss of public interest in the college.

From the beginning, there was a right of way to the college on the southern side (see pp. 24, 26, ch. 1. n.59). O'Dwyer, in his *Architecture of Deane and Woodward*, refers to a 'gateway . . . built . . . to the south-east of the quadrangle, at the entrance to the grounds from the access laneway. It was moved to its present location, on College Road, in 1864 after additional land had been acquired, the date 1849 on its plaque being somewhat confusing in referring to its original construction'. (The south lodge also dates from 1864.) Is this the same 'large and handsome gateway', in its original position, referred to by *The Cork Examiner* (7 Nov. 1849) in its opening-day description of the college? This also must be the 'upper' or 'principal' gateway which the QCC professors, in their 1874 memorial, complained of as being surrounded by human and animal squalor. This southern entrance did not become acceptable until the area became gentrified some time later.

Meanwhile, a long-cherished aspiration was realised with the opening of a Western Road entrance in 1879 (see p. 112) at a point some yards to the east of the present main gates. Participants in the BMA conference of 1879 entered through this new gate and exited via the western avenue. The head porter's lodge ('a very inartistic building', in Professor Yelverton-Pearson's recollection), surmounted this arched entrance, with a bridge behind leading to the eastern avenue. A bridge of Oregon pine was replaced in 1910 by a ferro-, or reinforced, concrete structure. Professor Alexander (civil engineering) whose demonstrator, James Waller, designed it was also involved in the project and, according to tradition, was greatly shocked and depressed when the much-vaunted bridge collapsed in the severe flooding of November 1916. However, it was recognised that this entrance would in any case have become increasingly subject to the hazards of modern traffic, not to speak of the Muskerry Railway.

The task of building a new entrance and bridge was long delayed, mainly because of war-induced shortage of finance and material. The present Western Road entrance was finally opened in 1929 (see p. 264). Meanwhile, the old lodge was demolished but the splendid wrought-iron gates, together with their limestone archway, were salvaged. As a fine example of Cork craftsmanship, they were exhibited in London before being re-erected (with the archway), in their present location, at the western or 'Gaol' gate.

See: 'Changes in the College buildings', *CUR*, no. 2, Summer 1954; P. Coffey, 'The Arches of the Years', *UCCR*, no. 42, 1967, pp. 21–40; H. Glavin, 'A Half-Century of Memories of UCC', *UCCR*, no. 43, 1968, pp. 49–50; C. Yelverton Pearson, 'A review of medical education in Cork', *The Lancet*, 31 Dec. 1927, pp. 1377–80.

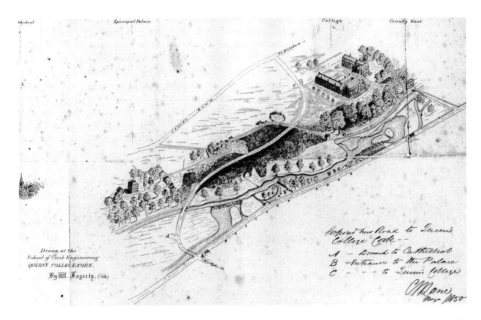

Above: proposed new road to college, 1850. For the background to this interesting sketch map, see p. 64. The signature in the bottom right-hand corner is that of C.B. Lane, professor of civil engineering, 1849–53. The cathedral shown was demolished in 1865, and replaced by the present St Fin Barre's Cathedral (1867–70).

Below: new main entrance completed in 1929 (see pp. 263–4). In the background, and constructed in the same period, are the main (east) lodge and dairy science (now geography) building (see p. 224). Note Muskerry rail tracks.

Collapsed ferro-concrete bridge, 1916 (see p. 389).

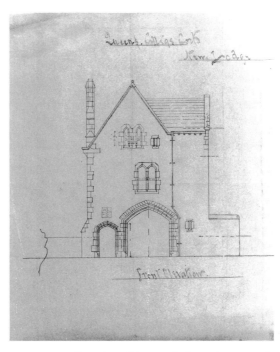

Drawing of the new lodge and entrance from the
Western Road, 1879 (see pp. 111–12).

THE UNIVERSITY FRAMEWORK

Queen's College Cork functioned within the federal framework of *The Queen's University in Ireland* from 1850 (incorporated 3 September 1850) to 1882 (dissolved 3 February 1882).

The Queen's University was replaced under the University Education (Ireland) Act 1879 by *The Royal University of Ireland* (1882–1909; first matriculations in 1881), an examining and degree-conferring body which did not require college residence or lecture attendance and with which, accordingly, QCC had no federal or organic connection.

The Royal University in turn was replaced by *The National University of Ireland* (Irish Universities Act 1908), which restored the federal framework under a more representative constitution and which began to function on the same day its predecessor was dissolved, 31 October 1909. Meanwhile a new charter, 2 December 1908, had changed the Queen's College Cork to University College Cork.

DUBLIN CASTLE OFFICIALS IN CORRESPONDENCE WITH QCC

Sir Maziere Brady

Served successively as solicitor-general, attorney-general, chief baron of the court of exchequer before becoming lord chancellor of Ireland, 1846–66. Vice-chancellor (and enthusiastic supporter) of the QUI, 1850–71.

Thomas H. Burke

Under-secretary, 1869–82. Murdered, together with the newly arrived Chief Secretary Lord Frederick Cavendish, by the Invincibles in the Phoenix Park, Dublin on 6 May 1882.

Sir Thomas Larcom

Served in the Ordnance Survey in the 1830s, and afterwards in famine relief administration and on the Board of Works. Commissioner on colleges (1845), promoted the development of the Queen's Colleges, member of QUI Senate. Under-secretary, 1853–68 and reported to be the real administrator of Ireland, while the lord lieutenant danced and the chief secretary hunted. The Larcom Papers in the NLI are an important source for the administrative history of the period. For his seminal role in the history of the Irish census, see *Irish Historical Statistics: Population 1821–1971*, ed. W.E. Vaughan and A.J. Fitzpatrick (Dublin 1978), pp. xii–xiii.

Sir Thomas N. Redington

Member of Devon Commission. Under-secretary 1846–52, the first Catholic to hold the office. One of the four-member commission that investigated the state of the Queen's Colleges in 1857–58.

Sir John Young

Chief secretary, 1852–55.

Augustine Birrell

Chief Secretary, 1907–16

NOTES

Chapter 1

1. See R.D. Anderson, 'Universities and Elites in Modern Britain', *History of Universities* (Oxford, 1991), vol. X, pp. 225ff.
2. *Royal Commission of Enquiry into Primary Education (Ireland)*, vol. iv, Minutes of Evidence 27150–1.
3. Quoted T.W. Moody and J.C. Beckett, *Queen's, Belfast 1845–1949* (London, 1959), vol. I, p. lviii (hereinafter *Belfast*).
4. Sir James Graham, home secretary, speaking on the Colleges Bill 1845, quoted ibid., vol. I, p.8.
5. At a QCC prize-giving ceremony on 27 Nov. 1857, *President's Report* (hereinafter *PR*), 1856–57, p. 44.
6. T.W. Moody, 'The Irish University Question in the Nineteenth Century', *History*, xlii, 148 (1958)
7. *The Cork Examiner* (hereinafter *CE*) was to claim that the agitation 'commenced in Cork and was almost exclusively confined to Cork'(26 Sept. 1849).
8. *Belfast*, vol. I, pp. lxii, lxiii.
9. See Denis Gwynn, 'The Origins of Queen's College, Cork', *Cork University Record* (hereinafter *CUR*), no. 10, Summer 1947, p. 30.
10. See Denis Gwynn, 'James Roche, "father" of QCC', *CUR*, no. 13, Summer 1948. The portrait is on permanent loan to the college archives (UC Archives): see Governing Body Minutes (hereinafter GBM), Dec. 1992.
11. See Denis Gwynn, 'The Munster College Petitions in 1838', *CUR*, no. 11, Christmas 1947, p. 33. See O'Connell to James Roche, 19 Oct. 1838, *Correspondence of Daniel O'Connell*, ed. W.J. Fitzpatrick (London, 1888), vol. II, p.153.
12. Denis Gwynn, 'Sir Thomas Wyse and the Cork College', *CUR*, no. 16, Summer 1948; Denis Gwynn, 'Major N.L. Beamish and QCC', *CUR*, no. 24, Easter 1952.
13. Gwynn, 'Wyse', p. 28.
14. UCC has a copy of Partridge's portrait of Thomas Wyse in the National Gallery. The copy is the work of Wyse's grandson, T. Bonaparte Wyse. Coincidentally, Smith O'Brien's portrait in UCC was painted by *his* grandson, Dermot O'Brien: see Gwynn, 'Wyse', p. 29.
15. This is a reference to the so-called Canova casts, given by Pope Pius VII to the prince regent (afterwards George IV) as a gesture of gratitude for British help in restoring Vatican art treasures at the end of the Napoleonic wars. It appears the prince regent was not enthusiastic about them and they wound up in Cork in 1818, where some of them are to be seen in the Crawford School of Art. They should not be confused (though they are) with the classical casts acquired from the British Museum by Professor Bunnell Lewis (Latin, 1849–1905). Some of these casts used to grace the corridor and lecture rooms of the West Wing, but the collection is now widely dispersed. Dr Patrick A.J. Cronin, Ancient Classics, has investigated the history of these casts.
16. Gwynn, 'Origins', and Gwynn, 'Wyse'.
17. S.F. Pettit, 'The Queen's College Cork: Its Origins and Early History, 1803–58' (PhD thesis, NUI, 1973), pp. 86ff. I am much indebted to Dr Pettit's researches. For Denny Lane, see Maura Cronin, 'Denny Lane', *Journal of the Cork Historical and Archaeolgical Society* (hereinafter *JCHAS*), vol. 100, 1995 and vol. 101, 1996.

18. Bullen's evidence is cited in Pettit, 'QCC'.
19. See Ronan O'Rahilly, *A History of the Cork Medical School* (Cork, 1949).
20. Chief Secretary's Office Registered Papers (hereinafter CSORP) 1845 6766.
21. Pettit, 'QCC', pp. 74ff., 128, 137–55.
22. J. Windele, *Notices of the City of Cork and its vicinity* (Cork, 1839), pp. 112–16, 122.
23. Auspiciously, Fleming's Christian name was Alexander.
24. Pettit, 'QCC', pp. 137–55.
25. D. Gwynn, 'Cork Cuvierian Society, 1849–51', *CUR*, no. 23, Christmas 1951, pp. 27–34. For the distinguished career of Joseph E. Portlock (1794–1864) in the Irish public service, see *DNB*.
26. *Belfast*, vol. I, pp. lx, 3–6; Pettit, 'QCC', pp. 223, 227, 229.
27. *An act to enable her majesty to endow new colleges for the advancement of learning in Ireland* (8&9 Vict. c. 66, 31 July 1845).
28. *Belfast*, vol. I, pp. 5–7, 19.
29. See ibid., vol. I, pp. lxvi–lxvii.
30. Quoted ibid., vol. I, p.10.
31. ibid., vol. I, pp. 32–9; charter in UC Archives.
32. Deasmhumhan Ó Raghallaigh, *Sir Robert Kane* (Cork, 1942); T.S. Wheeler, 'Sir Robert Kane, His Life and Work', *National Resources of Ireland* (Dublin, 1944); T.S. Wheeler, 'Sir Robert Kane, First President of Queen's College, Cork', *CUR*, no. 3, Easter 1945, pp. 29–38. Kane's prophetic advocacy of growing beet in Ireland for sugar production was hailed by later disciples of self-sufficiency: see generous tributes (e.g. from Eamon de Valera) on the occasion of the RDS centenary symposium, *CE*, 17 Apr., *II*, 13 Apr. 1944 and in particular, *Irish Press* (hereinafter *IP*), 13, 14, 15 Apr. 1944.

    Twenty years after Kane's death, his nephew, Fr Robert Kane S.J., delivered the Lenten sermons which provoked James Connolly's celebrated *Labour, Nationality and Religion* (Dublin, 1910).
33. See *Belfast*, vol. I, p. 36.
34. Quoted Emmet Larkin, *The Making of the Roman Catholic Church in Ireland 1850–60* (Chapel Hill, 1980), p. 186.
35. For salaries of presidents and professors, see *Belfast*, vol. I, pp. 9, 54.
36. ibid., vol. I, pp. 40–50.
37. Reporting the proceedings of opening day, *The Cork Examiner* (9 Nov. 1849) asserted that opposition to the Queen's Colleges had compelled the drafters of the statutes to 'adopt many precautions and guards which . . . are calculated to remove grave doubts and objections which existed in the public mind'.
38. CSORP 1846 01676.
39. CSORP 1846 0302.
40. CSORP 1846 0988.
41. CSORP 1846 03238.
42. CSORP 1846 01052.
43. Report of Board of Colleges, UC/PR/K/10. 19 January 1846.
44. 28 February 1847, ibid.
45. *Belfast*, vol. I, pp. 7, 9, 71–6. This section draws heavily on the admirably researched Moody and Beckett work.
46. The fear that local autonomy in academic appointments would mean favouritism and nepotism echoed down the decades. It was a particular concern of Professor Aloys Fleischmann.
47. *Belfast*, vol. I, pp. 71–2.
48. ibid., pp. 73–6, 225–6.
49. ibid., pp. 225–6.

50. ibid., pp. 207, 226, 228, 230.

51. ibid., vol. II, p. 540.

52. *The Queen's University in Ireland and the Queen's Colleges* (Dublin, 1856). Kane claimed that Cork graduates did better than those of the other two colleges in securing positions at Woolwich and in the Indian Civil Service.

53. Emmet Larkin, *The Consolidation of the Roman Catholic Church in Ireland, 1860–1870* (Chapel Hill, 1987), pp. 493 ff.

54. *Belfast*, vol. I, p. 281.

55. CSORP 1846 03144.

56. Board of Works Letter Book (hereinafter BWLB) 1/13/1/1, 1845.

57. UC/PR/1 (1–15).

58. UC/PO/OPW/2.

59. UC/PR/1 (1–15). Deane's 'rough' sketch showing Leslie's house is reproduced in this book, p. 24. The 'three Colleges sites' mentioned by Deane include two others briefly considered – at Victoria Road and at Blackrock Road. 'The Road leading at the rear to the back entrance . . . to be widened to 30 feet' was a right-of-way access from what is now College Road.

60. Al. Stewart of Board of Works, note to Treasury, 5 May 1846 [OPW 5951]; 14 Mar. 1873, no. 423.

61. For deed of conveyance and plan, see UC/PR/1 (36), (37). The twentieth-century conveyances (in the UC Archives) concerning the legendary Gillabbey site are of particular interest. One is a conveyance from the Cork Diocesan Trustees (Roman Catholic) to UCC on 14 May 1949 and relates to a lot of 1 acre, 3 roods, 10 perches 'known as the Cell of St Finbarr and commonly known by the name of Gillabbey' (Reg. of deeds 20 July 1949, Book 35 no. 75). The other is the 2 May 1978 conveyance (999 years lease at £100 per annum) from UCC to Cork Corporation of the Gillabbey Rock site (1.3 acres). This marked the formal end of a long-cherished college ambition to extend the campus eastward to this location. Building permission was never forthcoming, with good reason, and the site is now preserved as a park amenity for the convenience of staff, students and general public (Reg. of deeds 25 September 1978, Book 111 no. 174).

62. The Shanakiel site for the lunatic asylum was also selected in 1846 but purchase difficulties meant delays in construction which was not completed until 1852. See Hanora M. Henry, *Our Lady's Psychiatric Hospital, Cork* (Cork, 1989).

63. Sir Thomas Deane was reputed to be ruthless in handling competition from his rivals.

64. CSORP 1846 0 14032.

65. CSORP 1846 0 14334.

66. See Samuel Lewis, *A Topographical Dictionary of Ireland* (London, 1846), vol. I, pp. 405–6, 412.

67. Denis Gwynn, 'Sir Thomas Deane and the College Buildings', *CUR*, no. 18, Easter 1950, pp. 26–30, and no. 19, Summer 1950, pp. 25–31.

68. See Joseph Walker, secretary Board of Works, to John Butler, 28 July 1847, BWLB 1/13/1/1.

69. BWLB 1/13/1/1.

70. There is a (post-factum) nationalist tradition that disaffected workmen allowed the statue to dangle momentarily with a rope around its neck. The statue was the work of a Cork sculptor Edward Ambrose and represents the young Victoria in medieval garb, to accord with the Gothic style of the building. For the statute's subsequent dethronement, burial, exhumation and exhibition, see p. 233–5.

71. *CE*, 3 Aug. 1849.

72. *CE*, 26 Sept. 1849. To sort out the *Examiner's* confused 'Gilleda' reference, see Pádraig Ó Riain's comment on Gilla Áeda Ua Muigin in his *Beatha Bharra* (London, 1994), pp. 25–6.

73. E. Blau, *Ruskinian Gothic*, quoted *Oidhreacht Chorcaí* (Newsletter of the Cork Civic Trust), June 1992.

74. 'The Quad at UCC', *Oidhreacht Chorcaí*, June 1992. Also, see Ralph Sutton's interesting but rather fanciful 'Significant Details of the College Buildings', *CUR*, no. 12, Easter 1948, pp. 22ff. A full architectural context will be provided by a forthcoming publication: Frederick O' Dwyer, *The Architecture of Deane and Woodward* (Cork, 1996). Discussing the 'missing' fourth side, O'Dwyer reminds us that enclosed quadrangles were then regarded as unhealthy, and suggests that a wall intended by Deane for the south side of the quadrangle was never built. O'Dwyer also deals with the Oxford inspiration, for which see in addition, Henry H. Hill, 'Cork Architecture', JCHAS, vol. 48, 1943, p. 97.

75. T.B. Macaulay, *The History of England from the Accession of James II* (Everyman edn, London, 1906), vol. II, p. 344. Various nineteenth-century guides and histories refer to the building in glowing terms, e.g. 'this beautiful and chaste building . . . noble tower . . .': G.B. Gibson, *The History of the County and City of Cork*, II, 362 (London, 1861).

76. *Belfast*, vol. I, p. 109n.

77. *Dublin Opinion*, June 1924, reproduced in *Thirty Years of Dublin Opinion* (Dublin, 1952), p. 64.

78. *Belfast*, vol. I, p. 62.

79. *CE*, 29 Sept. 1849.

80. CSORP 1846 014164. Today, the library and associated lecture-theatre complex are named after Boole, and a fine memorial window in the Aula Maxima also commemorates him.

81. See Pettit, 'QCC', p. 278.

82. CSO UNREG 1845 65.

83. Pettit, 'QCC', p. 286.

84. CSO UNREG 1845 65.

85. CSORP 1849 65.

86. ibid.

87. CSO UNREG 1845 88, quoted *Belfast,* vol. I, p. 62.

88. CSO UNREG 1845 158, quoted *Belfast*, vol. I, p. 63.

89. *Belfast*, vol. I, p. 65.

90. Quoted Monica Taylor, *Sir Bertram Windle: A Memoir* (London, 1932).

91. B.A. Cody, *The River Lee, Cork and the Corkonians* (first published 1859, republished Cork, 1974), p. 54. Advertising a vacant chair, says Cody, was 'a mere farce'.

92. *Belfast*, vol. I, p. 66.

93. ibid., p.65, n. 5.

94. ibid., p. 60.

95. Socinians, a sixteenth-century Italian sect, did not believe in Christ's divinity, though conceding his greatness as a prophet.

96. See *Belfast*, vol. I, pp. 64-6.

97. Pettit, 'QCC', p. 291.

98. For example, in 1853 a medical student had to pay three guineas for every three months of practical anatomy: Kane Correspondence, UC/PO/45.

99. CSORP 1850 07155.

100. CSORP 1849 65. See pp. 95–6, for Fitzgerald's absconding with college funds. In this connection, it is interesting that one of his backers in 1849 was Sadleir who swindled a large sum in 1856 and who, besides, is excoriated in the nationalist tradition for accepting government office in violation of his pledge as an Independent MP.

101. CSORP 1853 58. For Harkness, see *DNB*, and Ronan O'Rahilly, 'Stained Glass Windows in the Aula Maxima', *CUR*, no. 18, Easter 1950, pp. 25–26.

102. See p. 65-7.

103. CSORP 1854 61.

104. ibid.; Kane Correspondence, UC/PO/49, 2 Mar. 1854.

105. CSORP 1864 61.

106. See below, ch. 4.

107. CSORP 1864 68.
108. CSORP 1875 20, 21.
109. CSORP 1864 58.

Chapter 2

1. Apart from newspapers and other sources mentioned in the following pages, see Pettit's informative and interesting account, 'QCC' pp. 5–26; also S.F. Pettit, 'The First Session, 1849–50, *UCC Record* (hereinafter *UCCR*) no. 49, 1974, pp. 5–14. On 7 November 1849, *The Cork Examiner* had a piece on the opening day ceremony, as well as an extensive article, repeated from its issue of 26 September, on the building, its various rooms and their function. The accounts in *The Freeman's Journal* (9 November) and the *Illustrated London News* (17 November) essentially reproduced the *Examiner*'s coverage of 7 November. On 9 November the *Examiner* reported the speeches of Sir Robert Kane and others in detail.

2. *The Cork Examiner* (7 November 1849) gave an unrealistically large estimate of 1,000–1,200. The *Illustrated London News* figure was 900, including a considerable number of ladies.

4. See Larkin, *Roman Catholic Church 1850–60*, p. 9.

5. Corrigan was to be a very active member of the Queen's University Senate, 1850–80: *Belfast*, vol. I, p. 226.

6. The two prime movers, Wyse and Smith O'Brien, were notable absentees on the great day. Both, it could be said, were detained on her majesty's service in their different ways. Wyse was now British minister in Athens (referred to floridly by Kane as being 'under that azure sky of Hellas') and Smith O'Brien (referred to by nobody at the ceremony), having been transported as a felon, was languishing in Van Diemen's Land at the Queen's pleasure.

7. *Inaugural address delivered at the opening of the Queen's College Cork by the President of the College, Sir Robert Kane. With an account of the general proceedings at the public inauguration of the College, November 7 1849* (Dublin: Hodges and Smith, Publisher to the University, 1849). See also *CE*, 9 Nov. 1849.

8. *CE*, 20 July 1949.

9. References to Finbarr touched local pride and drew applause at the Kane banquet some months later. Public reaction would be much the same today despite a UCC professor's iconoclastic conclusion that the eponymous Cork saint was not a Cork man at all and never set foot in the place: Ó Riain, *Beatha Bharra*. Also see Pádraig Ó Riain, 'Another Cork Charter: The Life of St. Finbarr', *JCHAS*, vol. 90, 1985, pp. 1–13.

10. Cody, *River Lee*, pp. 51–2; Ó Raghallaigh, *Kane*, pp. 31–2; Desmond MacHale, *George Boole* (London, 1985) p. 89.

11. MacHale, *Boole*, p. 114.

12. *CE*, 27 Mar. 1850.

13. Sir Robert Kane, *Address delivered at the Public Distribution of Prizes on October 25, 1850* (Dublin, 1850).

14. *Cork Southern Reporter*, 9 Apr. 1850: published separately as *Banquet to Sir Robert Kane, Knt, FRS, MRIA, President of Queen's College Cork, given at the Imperial Hotel Cork, April 8, 1850* (Cork, 1850). For a 'centenary' commentary on the event, see Denis Gwynn, 'The College's First Year', *CUR*, no. 21, Easter 1951, pp. 20–7.

     The arrangements for the banquet were made by a special mayor's committee: Notice from Mayor's office, Paradise Place, 30 Mar. 1850, U 140/D, Cork Archives Institute.

15. For Delany, see Evelyn Bolster, *A History of the Diocese of Cork: The Episcopate of William Delany 1847–1886* (Cork, 1993).

16. Push-ha'penny and billiards were the mid-twentieth-century equivalent, as this writer recalls.

17. Davis's statement of 17 May 1845 is a particularly striking formulation of his national philosophy applied to education: 'The objections to separate education are immense. The reasons for it are reasons for separate life, for mutual animosity, for penal laws, and for religious wars', quoted Bolster, *Delany*, p. 163.

18. *Cork Southern Reporter*, 9 Apr. 1850.
19. They attended to their spiritual duties in the oratory of Castlewhite where modern (and secular) student residences now stand.
20. Even before Delany's time, there were complaints in January 1847 that Bishop John Murphy was tolerating priests writing in the *Examiner* on behalf of the new colleges: see Desmond Bowen, *Paul Cardinal Cullen and the Shaping of Modern Irish Catholicism* (Dublin, 1983), p. 47.
21. Larkin, *Roman Catholic Church 1850–60*, p. 20.
22. See ibid. in general, and Larkin's chapter on 'The Synod of Thurles' in particular. Also, for the bishops and the Queen's Colleges, see Fergal McGrath, *Newman's University, Idea and Reality* (London, 1951), ch. 2; and *Belfast*, vol. I, ch. 1–2. Delany was being referred to in Cullenite circles in September 1853 as 'of Godless College notoriety': see Bowen, *Cullen*, p. 121.

    One bishop is reputed to have suggested that being on the Queen's Colleges side was not good for one's health. Bishop Higgins of Ardagh informed Cullen in September 1849 that Fr J.W. Kirwan, PP, Oughterard who had accepted appointment as president of Queen's College Galway 'has had a third attack of paralysis and his life is despaired of. One of his curates, an ardent admirer of the Infidel Colleges, has also been attacked by paralysis whilst a second curate of his who detests these establishments is quite well! Is it a judgement from God?': quoted Bowen, *Cullen*, p. 67. Kirwan died on 24 December 1849: *Belfast*, vol. I, p. 77.
23. Of the south Munster bishops whose flock might have an interest in attending QCC, Timothy Murphy of Cloyne and William Keane of Ross were Cullenites, while Cornelius Egan of Kerry was pro-colleges. Murphy, however, was reluctant to oppose QCC: see Bowen, *Cullen*, p. 212; also Larkin, *Roman Catholic Church 1850–60*.
24. CSORP 1850 05825, 05513.
25. CSORP 1850 06116.
26. *CE*, 1 November 1850.
27. *CE*, 6 December 1850.
28. Quoted Larkin, *Roman Catholic Church 1850–60*, p. 118; see also Bolster, *Delany*, ch. VI.
29. Bolster, *Delany*, p. 172.
30. See Larkin, *Roman Catholic Church 1850–60*, pp. 46–47.
31. Emmet Larkin, *The Consolidation of the Roman Catholic Church in Ireland 1860–70* p. 503.
32. Emmet Larkin, *The Roman Catholic Church and the Home Rule Movement in Ireland, 1870–74* (Chapel Hill, 1990), p. 275.
33. Emmet Larkin, *The Roman Catholic Church and the Creation of the Modern Irish State, 1878–86* (Philadelphia, 1975), pp. 207–12.
34. For a general account, see MacHale, *Boole*, pp. 92ff. See also Kathleen O'Flaherty, 'Politics in QCC', *CUR*, no. 22, Summer 1951.
35. College Council Minutes (hereinafter CCM), 24 July 1850; *Royal Commission to inquire into the progress and conditions of the Queen's Colleges at Belfast, Cork and Galway: Report, Minutes of Evidence, Documents, Tables and Returns, 1857–58* [2413], pp. 7–8.
36. *CE*, 12, 14 Aug. 1850.
37. CCM, 10 Sept. 1850.
38. *1857–58 Comm. Rep.* p. 8. Also see MacHale, *Boole*, pp. 92–3.
39. *Pastoral letters and other writings of Cardinal Cullen*, ed. P.F. Moran (Dublin, 1882), vol. I, p. 67.
40. See Larkin, *Roman Catholic Church and Home Rule 1870–74*, p. 164. François Guizot (1787–1874) was the French historian and statesman.

Chapter 3

1. Pettit, 'QCC', especially pp. 293–352. See also Pettit, 'The First Session'; and *Belfast*, vol. I, pp. 47–54.
2. *PR*, 1852–53.

3. *Prospectus QCC: By order of the President, 22 August 1849* (Dublin, 1849). Introductory public lectures inaugurated the Arts, Medicine and Law courses (*CE*, 9, 12 Nov. 1849).

4. *PR*, 1849–50.

5. ibid.; Registrar's Roll Book, 1849 (UC Archives). An early medical student of later nationalist note was the Fenian, John O'Leary: see J. Hurley, 'The College Record Books', *CUR*, no. 27, Easter 1953. Later on, the Presbyterian home ruler, J.B. Armour of Ballymoney, took an honours MA in classics at QCC: *CE*, 16 Oct. 1865. While his Cork sojourn broadened his mind, the atmosphere there 'was an atmosphere of tobacco smoke': J.R.B. McMinn, *Against the Tide: A Calendar of the Papers of Rev. J.B. Armour* (Belfast, 1985), pp. xiv, xv.

6. The western gate, then the main college entrance.

7. Albani to Deane, 13 May 1850, Registrar's Letter Book.

8. The western avenue

9. CCM, 15 Jan. 1850.

10. Registrar's Letter Book.

11. Minute Book, February 1850. The tower clock, made by Mangans the jewellers, was installed in 1851.The wheezy ringing of the clock-tower bell at five to, and on the hour (approximately) echoes down the decades in many a nostalgic graduate's memory. The practice has long since been discontinued.

12. CCM, 19 Mar. 1850.

13. Registrar Albani to Board of Works, 18 May 1850, Registrar's Letter Book, quoted Pettit, 'QCC', p. 320.

14. But how much had changed a century later? See Professor John Busteed's complaint about his working conditions: see ch. 9, n.38.

15. CCM, 26 Mar. 1850.

16. *PR*, 1849–50; CCM, 26 Mar., 14 Oct. 1850; Medical Faculty Minutes, 6 July 1850.

17. Medical Faculty Minutes, 1 Mar. 1850.

18. CCM, 4 Dec. 1849, 15 Jan. 1850. A student was required to raise his cap in salute if he chanced to meet the president or vice-president in academic costume: CCM, 11 Sept. 1850.

19. Science Division (Arts Faculty) Minutes, February 1850.

20. Cunningham had been employed at the Royal Cork Institution where he had been warned about his addiction. Kane reported to the 1857–58 commissioners that Cunningham had again fallen from grace.

21. This is apparently the first mention of sporting activity in the College Council Minutes, 12 Mar. 1850.

22. Science Division (Arts Faculty) Minutes, 20 Mar. 1850.

23. Pettit, 'QCC', pp. 337–40. A century later, President O'Rahilly did not scorn to order from second-hand book catalogues to build up the library: UC/OHA, Kathleen O'Flaherty, 28 Nov. 1990.

24. See section on the Farm Committee, pp. 27ff.

25. The new railway age should have greatly facilitated Kane in the matter of travel. The Cork–Dublin line started business on 29 October 1849, coinciding virtually with the opening of Queen's College Cork. Initially, travelling time was six to seven hours (compared to seventeen hours for the pre-rail stage coach) but the opening of the tunnel into Cork in 1855 meant a shorter journey overall. Kane's successors for the rest of the nineteenth century and up to the end of the Great War enjoyed a travel time of four hours or less: see R.N. Clements, 'A Century of Main Line Trains', *Cuisle: Ireland's Transport Magazine*, November 1949, pp. 11–16.

26. Kane Correspondence in UC Archives, as detailed below.

27. UC/PO/OPW/17.

28. UC/PO/OPW/75.

29. UC/PO/OPW/51, 53, 55, 82–9.
30. For examples, see UC/PO/OPW/3, 5, 17.
31. UC/PO/OPW/14.
32. For example, there were two in King (now MacCurtain) Street in the 1850s, a distance of perhaps a mile and a half.
33. UC/PO/3
34. UC/PO/92: also see 104, 110.
35. Barry (1813–80) was born in Ballyclough, Co. Cork. Distinguished legal career in Melbourne; solicitor general of Victoria; judge; first chancellor of new Melbourne University; knighted 1860; regarded in Victoria as a founding father.
36. UC/PO 35, 36, 42, 47. See also *PR*, 1850–51. For O'Leary, who was a grandnephew of the well-known Capuchin, Fr Arthur O'Leary, see Eric Lambert, 'General O'Leary and South America', *The Irish Sword*, vol. XI, 1973–74, pp. 58–74. A Venezuelan postage stamp commemorating him is reproduced, *The Irish Sword,* vol. XIV, 1980–81, p. 69. See also *UCCR*, no. 49, 1974, pp. 15–17. There is a commemorative plaque at his birthplace, 89–90 Barrack Street, Cork.
37. UC/PO/48, 113.
38. UC/PO/51.
39. UC/PO/62, 63.
40. UC/PO/8.
41. UC/PO/30.
42. UC/PO/73.
43. UC/PO/114.
44. UC/PO/44.
45. UC/PO/126.
46. UC/PO/10.
47. UC/PO/85, 87.
48. UC/PO/138.
49. *PR*, 1849–50.
50. *Minutes of the proceedings of the Committee for establishing a Botanic Garden and experimental Farm in connection with Queen's College, Cork appointed at the suggestion of William Fagan Esq. M.P. seconded by Thomas R. Sarsfield Esq. High Sheriff of the City, on the day of inauguration of Queen's College. Thomas S. Dunscombe, Secretary.* UC/GB/12(1).
51. Balance of the Reproductive Loan Fund. It could be appropriated only to supplement local contributions – hence the importance of subscriptions.
52. A mile or so west of college, between the 'Straight Road' and the Model Farm Road (at that time the 'New Road' and the 'Old Road', respectively, to Ballincollig).
53. See pp. 42ff.
54. U 140/D, Cork Archives Institute.
55. Dated October 1850, at the Royal Cork Institution: UC/PO/15. As the letter makes clear, the arrangements made by the college for free public lectures (CCM, 22 Oct. 1850) did not suit the society's members.
56. *The Memorial of the President and Professors of Queen's College Cork to the Lord Lieutenant,* 13 March 1874, p. 10: CSORP 1875 4629.
57. The last public execution in the UK took place in Newgate, London 26 May 1868: Pieter Spierenburg, *The Spectacle of Suffering* (Cambridge, 1984), p. 198.
58. CSORP 1850 0 3117; CCM, 7 May 1850.
59. CSORP 1850 0 3874; UC/PO/OPW/6. As early as 1846, the *Cork Constitution* (2 May 1846) referred to a proposed road and bridge to the college from Western Road and a proposed bridge 'crossing the Lee to Sunday's Well to enable students to procure convenient lodgings'. Obviously, these were not built. O'Dwyer, *The Architecture of Deane and Wood-*

ward (forthcoming) quotes a contemporary commentator who felt 'the College is at sufficient distance, without compelling students and professors to go beyond it, by the circuitous approach to the County Gaol, unless they choose the dirty back lanes in the neighbourhood of St. Finn-Barrs'.

60. Memorials were sent in April to the lord lieutenant and the gaol board of management 'praying that the place of public execution be changed' (CCM, 1 Apr. 1851). Some weeks after, college activities were cancelled on Sat. 10 May 1851 because of an execution (CCM, 9 May 1851). Saturday was a working half-day until the 1950s.
61. CSORP 1851 0 2138.
62. UC/PO/OPW/106.
63. UC/PO/9.
64. CSORP 1855 4513.
65. CSORP 1864 14473.
66. CSORP 1868 613.
67. CSORP 1868 702.
68. CSORP 1868 942.

Chapter 4

1. CSORP 1853 10148.
2. See MacHale, *Boole*, p. 142. To Professor MacHale, man and book, I am much indebted.
3. The de Vericour affair was even earlier (July 1850) and it left its own aftermath of tension, but it is treated elsewhere in the context of the 'godless' colleges discussion: see pp. 46–8.
4. For the background of Celtic languages in the Queen's Colleges, of Connellan's appointment to QCC and of the course of his professorship there, see Cornelius G. Buttimer, 'Celtic and Irish in College, 1849–1944', *JCHAS*, vol. 94, 1989, pp. 88–107; and 'An Ghaeilge i gColáiste na hOllscoile, Corcaigh, 1845–1995', *The Irish Review*, no. 17, Summer 1995.

   Buttimer suggests that the appointment of a Protestant from the north-west to the Cork college was a deliberate move to counteract any nationalist impact the teaching of Celtic (i.e. Irish) might have on the students. But was not the association of language with nationalist feeling and ideology a later nineteenth-century development? Buttimer also thinks that Celtic was included in the curriculum for symbolic and political reasons, ostensibly to make the colleges more palatable to national opinion, but was then rendered ineffective by restrictions.

   Connellan's colleagues in QCC requested the lord lieutenant to raise the status of Irish, and to raise the salary to that 'of the Professor of the most favoured language': RIA 1117. For Connellan, also see Denis O'Leary, 'The first Professor of Irish in QCC', *CUR*, no. 9, Easter 1947.
5. *PR*, 1855–56, Professors' Reports. Cody, *River Lee*, giving a robust, nationalist contemporary opinion, felt that setting up such a chair, and then giving it no encouragement, meant that it was bound to be a sham and a sinecure (p. 473).
6. *1857–58 Comm. Rep.*, pp. 21–2.
7. See Buttimer, 'An Ghaeilge' and 'Celtic and Irish'.
8. CSORP 1851 01216.
9. CSORP 1851 01217.
10. CSORP 1851 01266.
11. CSORP 1851 01608.
12. CSORP 1851 01609, 01671.
13. In a council resolution of 14 February 1851 (CCM), there was indecision on the question of whether the President had the power of compelling the delivery of public lectures, though such was probably the spirit of the statutes.
14. CSORP 1852 01059.
15. Faculty Minutes, 15 March 1851.

16. MacHale, *Boole*, pp. 96–7.
17. CSORP 1852 01059.
18. CSORP 1852 02965.
19. CSORP 1852 02439.
20. CSORP 1852 02669.
21. CSORP 1852 02965.
22. CSORP 1853 3310.
23. *PR*, 1851–52, Triennial Visitation, 11–12 May 1852.
24. UC/PO/24, 25, 32, 46.
25. CSORP 1852 96.
26. CSORP 1853 9400.
27. UC/PO/33.
28. CSORP 1852 96.
29. *PR*, 1851–52, Triennial Visitation, 11–12 May 1852.
30. Bullen to Young, 20 Oct. 1853, CSORP 1853 9452.
31. CSORP 1852 11950, 9400, 9546, 17206.
32. CSORP 1853 9546.
33. CSORP 1854 11930.
34. CSORP 1853 9546.
35. CSORP 1853 no file number.
36. CSORP 1854, 11930, 12812, 17228.
37. MacHale, *Boole*, p. 142. For further details on Alcock, and his continuing protests in 1855, see Ronan O'Rahilly, *Benjamin Alcock* (Cork, Oxford, 1948).
38. *PR*, 1855–56.
39. *1857–58 Comm. Rep.*
40. ibid., p. 31.
41. CSORP 1853 4335.
42. CSORP 1853 11494.
43. CSORP 1853 10635.
44. CSORP 1853 7482, 3291, 3310, respectively. Lane added that he had been anxious for some time to sever his connection with QCC.
45. MacHale, *Boole*, p. 92. Of course, Boole may not have been much interested in the political purpose of the banquet.
46. Quoted MacHale, *Boole*, p. 137. The influence of 'faculty wives' (*recte* 'partners'?) has been immense but largely unquantifiable.
47. ibid., pp. 143–4.
48. Wheeler, 'Kane'.
49. For the above paragraphs, see MacHale, *Boole*, pp. 144–52.
50. *Report, Minutes of Evidence, Documents Tables and Return* 1857–1858 [2413] XXI 53. What follows is largely based on this document, (in particular *Report*, pp. 31–3; App. A, pp. 103ff, 347–60) and also on references to it in MacHale, *Boole*; Pettit, 'QCC'; and Moody and Beckett, *Belfast*.
51. CSORP 1858 17500; Correspondence between Presidents of Queen's Colleges . . . and Irish government on Residence . . . *Parliamentary Papers 1859 Session I* (197) XXI Pt. II 411 [mf 64.170].
52. Paper cutting in Larcom Papers, NLI, Ms 7667.
53. CSORP 1860 20659.
54. Quoted Wheeler, 'Kane', pp. 35–6.
55. Quoted Larkin, *Roman Catholic Church 1850–60*, p. 465.
56. For what follows see *1857–58 Comm. Rep.*, particularly *Report*, pp. 33–5; App. A pp. 103ff; also *Belfast*, vol. I, pp. 140–49, 268–70.

57. See Joseph Lee, *The Modernisation of Irish Society, 1848–1918* (Dublin, 1973), pp. 31–2.
58. Murphy had an active profile in the opening years of the college: see above p. 57–8.
59. See *Belfast*, vol. I, p. 305.
60. A symbol claimed exclusively by the rugby club (virtually synonymous with medical students) and dating to a QCC/TCD game on 2 Dec. 1886 when, the colours of both teams being identical, Cork assumed the historic distinguishing mark.
61. *Belfast*, vol. I, p. 253.
62. See Sir Robert Kane, *The Queen's University in Ireland and the Queen's Colleges: an Address delivered at the Distribution of Prizes in Queen's College, Cork, 27 November 1856* (Dublin, 1856).
63. *Belfast*, vol. I, p. 233.
64. ibid., p. 269.
65. CSORP 1849 01077.
66. CSORP 1849 01412.
67. See D. Gwynn, 'Sir Thomas Deane and the College Buildings', *CUR*, no. 19, Summer 1950, p. 28; CCM, 14 Oct. 1850.
68. The proposed link-up of the two 'Quads' is shown in an interesting 1879 sketch plan: UC/BU/DWG. For the then fashionable E-shaped plan, see *Belfast*, vol. 1, pp. 109–10.
69. CSORP 1865 4615.
70. CSORP 1865 4980.
71. CSORP 1865 4987.
72. CSORP 1865 7237.
73. *PR*, 1862–63, pp. 134, 135; CSORP 1862 1995, 2415; *Illustrated London News* (hereinafter *ILN*), 24 May 1862.
74. For what follows, see Kane to Larcom, 15 May 1862, *PR*, 1861–62, pp. 120–21; ibid., pp. 9–10; CSORP 1862 14077; *ILN*, 24 May 1862.
75. The scene was graphically pictured in two sketches (see illustrations p. 83) in the *ILN*, 24 May 1862, reproduced *Quarryman*, Feb. 1942. The throng of young and old observing the scene suggests that such a display of pyrotechnics remained unrivalled as a civic spectacle until the Courthouse (1891) and Opera House (1955) fires.
76. Peter Goulden report, 21 July, CSORP 1862 2415.
77. There were to be recriminations from the city about college negligence concerning hydrants. By the time the water was brought to bear on the fire, the West Wing was presumably beyond saving, and efforts were concentrated on preventing the flames from reaching the library: CSORP 1862 1824.
78. A poster dated 19 May 1862 and signed 'Robert J. Kenny, Registrar' offered a reward (in the name of the president, vice-president, professors, officers, graduates and students) of £150 for information, in addition to the £100 offered by the government: CSORP 1862 14077. See p. 84.
79. *PR*, 1861–62, pp. 97–106, 117.
80. CSORP 1862 16200; *PR*, 1862–63, pp. 98–109, esp. 103.
81. *PR*, 1863–64, extended to 31 Mar. 1865.
82. *PR* ending 31 Mar. 1866, pp. 92, 99. Professor O'Leary was a grandson of Art Ó Laoghaire, the 'outlaw'. He was a son of the 'Conchubhar Beag an cheana' mentioned in the famous *Caoineadh*. Together with his father and grandfather, he lies buried in the well-known tomb at Kilcrea Abbey: Seán Ó Tuama, *Caoineadh Airt Uí Laoghaire* (Baile Átha Cliath, 1961), p. 12.
83. *PR*, 1874–75, p. 60.
84. *The Times*, 6 June 1863.
85. *PR*, 1862–63, pp. 10, 126–9; CSORP 1863 5982.
86. *PR*, 1862–63, App. pp. 130, 134–5; Kane to Larcom, 23 Oct. 1863, enclosing Bullen's deposition, CSORP 1863 9078.
87. Double-jobbing in Dublin would be the ideal solution to Kane's bilocational problem.

88. In the contemporary sense of a book or journal in which notable events or sayings are recorded.
89. Dean of Cork, influential cleric, confidant of Bishop Delany: Bolster, *Delany*, has numerous references to Murphy.
90. CSORP 1862 9078.
91. For above paragraphs, see *PR*, 1862–63, App. pp. 130–38; CSORP 1863 7479.
92. Steward of the college: for speculation on his involvement, see pp. 91–2.
93. CSORP 1864 13643.
94. *The Ulster Observer*, 14 Apr. 1864.
95. Visitation, *PR*, 1863–64, pp. 114–16.
96. Sir George Grey (1799–1882).
97. CSORP 1864 14473.
98. CSORP 1864 15137.
99. In 1860, over 1,000 Irish volunteers constituted as the Battalion of St Patrick, formed part of a brigade in defence of the Papal States. In their (futile) resistance to the invading Piedmontese, they suffered some casualties (perhaps forty or so), and were acclaimed as heroes by Irish nationalist opinion. Most of them landed at Queenstown in November 1860, and there were extensive homecoming celebrations: see R.V. Comerford, *The Fenians in Context* (Dublin 1985) pp. 60–2. Also see Emmet Larkin, *Roman Catholic Church in Ireland 1860–70*.
100. CSORP 1864 14473.
101. CSORP 1862 2415.
102. CSORP 1863 7479.
103. CSORP 1863 6852.
104. CSORP 1864 13643.
105. According to one recollection, Bullen accused Kane of causing the fire in order to divert attention from his continuing absence: Richardson Evans, *Evening Echo* (hereinafter *EE*), 11 Feb. 1982.
106. *PR*, 1862–63, pp. 138ff.
107. *1857–58 Comm. Rep.*, App. A, p. 222, para. 3122.
108. Bullen to Carlisle, 14 May 1862, *PR*, 1862–63, p. 137.
109. CSORP 1862 14733.
110. Reported *CE*, 29 May 1862.
111. CSORP 1862 14733. John Blyth was professor of chemistry, 1849–72.
112. (London, n.d.), vol. I, pp. 15–16.
113. e.g. D. Ó Raghallaigh, 'The College in Flames', *Quarryman*, Feb. 1942.
114. One of the last public hangings in the United Kingdom: see ch. 3, n. 57.
115. CSORP 1862 14733.
116. CSORP 1862 151180.
117. Goulden reports, 7 June (CSORP 1862 1995) and 21 June (CSORP 1862 2092).
118. CSORP 1862 2148.
119. CSORP 1862 2415.
120. CSORP 1862 2537.
121. CSORP 1862 2437.
122. CSORP 1862 10102.
123. CSORP 1862 2415.
124. CSORP 1862 16646.
125. CSORP 1864 14099.
126. CSORP 1862 2836.
127. CSORP 1862 2573.
128. Kane to Larcom, enclosing Bullen's deposition, 23 Oct. 1863, CSORP 1863 9078.
129. UC/PO/80–83.
130. CSORP 1862 15180.

131. CSORP 1862 14733.
132. Quoted *CE*, 29 May 1862.
133. CSORP 1862 2415.
134. CSORP 1862 2573.
135. *CE*, 16 May 1862.
136. CSORP 1862 1824.
137. CSORP 1862 14189.
138. *CE*, 16 May 1862.
139. *CE*, 13 Oct. 1866.
140. *CE*, 8 Apr. 1870.
141. CSORP 1862 14894.
142. CSORP 1862 17350.
143. CSORP 1862 2608.
144. CSORP 1862 3704.
145. UC/PO/OPW/69.
146. CSORP 1862 14733.
147. *PR, to year ending 31 March 1872*, pp. 105–7.
148. It is of interest that this sentence is underlined in red ink by President James Slattery (1890–96) whose copy of this particular president's report is in the Boole Library, UCC.
149. *PR, to . . . 1872*, p. 108.
150. CSORP 1871 5786.
151. CSORP 1871 115678. Also see *PR*, 1871–72.
152. CSORP 1871 5018, 10137, 13427, 16658, 22164.
153. The longest presidential term in the college's history – though his twenty-four years since the *opening* of the college was almost equalled by President P.J. Merriman (1919–43).
154. CSORP 1873 10706.
155. CSORP 1873 11109, 11738, 12398.
156. See Deasmhumhan Ó Raghallaigh, *Sir Robert Kane*, (Cork 1942) ch. V; Wheeler,'Sir Robert Kane', *CUR*, no. 3, Easter 1945, p. 38.
157. CSORP 1873 7147.
158. Ó Raghallaigh, *Kane*, pp. 30–31.

Chapter 5

1. This work has been described by the late Professor John Kelleher of Harvard (in a letter to Professor Seán Ó Coileán, UCC) as 'the morning sun of Celtic scholarship'.
2. The above summary of O'Sullivan's career is based on an account in 'Mss papers of Issac Nash Notter', U.53, UCC, later published, apparently without acknowledgement by 'J.C.' [James Coleman?] in *JCHAS*, 2ⁿᵈ ser., vol. X, 1904, pp. 236–41; T.S. Wheeler, 'Life and work of William K. Sullivan', *Studies*, vol. XXXIV, 1945, pp. 21–36; and T.S. Wheeler, 'William Kirby Sullivan', *CUR*, no. 4, Summer 1945, pp. 31–8. George Stephenson and his son Robert, pioneers of railway locomotion, visited J.B. Sullivan's paper mill in 1824 to carry out a commission.
3. See ch. 1, n. 2.
4. Quoted Bolster, *Delany*, p. 173.
5. The following account of Sullivan's departure from the Catholic University is indebted to the researches of Emmet Larkin, *Roman Catholic Church and Home Rule 1870–74*, pp. 379–83.
6. MP for Co. Limerick, 1847–74, and under-secretary for the Colonies. Other applicants for the vacant presidency included Vice-President Ryall, professors Corbett (anatomy and physiology) and England (natural philosophy): see CSORP 1873 6963, 8602 and 9477, respectively
7. W.K. Sullivan, *University Education in Ireland: a letter to Sir John Dalberg Acton* (Dublin and London, 1866). This is Lord Acton, the historian.

8. See *Belfast*, vol. I, p. 60. Clarendon was lord lieutenant at the time of the Colleges Bill.
9. Larkin, *Roman Catholic Church and Home Rule 1870–74*, p. 389n.
10. Cullen, who rather grudgingly described Sullivan as 'very good at teaching', assessed his probable salary gains as 'something more' than the £300 p.a. salary and equal sum in students' fees he had been getting in the Catholic University.
11. T.H. Burke, under-secretary for Ireland, 1869–82 murdered, together with Chief Secretary Lord Frederick Cavendish, by the Invincibles in the Phoenix Park, Dublin, on 6 May 1882.
12. CSORP 1873 14246.
13. CSORP 1874 2338; Wheeler, 'Sullivan' *CUR* and *Studies*.
14. CSORP 1875 221.
15. CSORP 1875 3229, 3546.
16. CSORP 1875 4629.
17. 'The Rousseaux Price Indices, 1800–1913, Sauerbeck–*Statist* Price Indices, 1846–1966', Br. Mitchell, *British Historical Statistics* (Cambridge, 1988).
18. See ch. 4, n. 68.
19. The memorial is accompanied and illustrated by a copy of the ordnance map, with the relevant properties marked. The Property Register acquisition map (UCC Archives) should also be consulted in conjunction with this.
20. Italics in original. See Appendix D.
21. This was before the south channel flowing through the college was simplified into one stream in the 1960s.
22. As is evident from the detailed acquisitions map (UCC Archives).
23. The breakdown of students by origin in 1875–76 was similar to the pattern a century later: 93.8% came from Munster and 75.2% from Cork city and county. Sullivan expected a higher proportion from adjoining counties as the college 'became better known and understood there'.
24. *PR*, 1874–75, 1880–81.
25. *PR*, 1879–80, 1883–84.
26. *PR*, 1885–86.
27. *PR*, 1875–76.
28. *PR*, 1884–85.
29. *PR*, 1886–87.
30. *PR*, 1880–81.
31. *PR*, 1873–74. During the college working day, museums were used for teaching purposes.
32. *PR*, 1874–75.
33. *PR*, 1877–78.
34. *PR*, 1885–86.
35. See overview campus map on back endpaper.
36. *PR*, 1873–74.
37. See correspondence between Sullivan and Under-Secretary Burke in September 1877, CSORP 1877 14238.
38. *PR*, 1877–78.
39. See Ronan O'Rahilly, 'The BMA in QCC, 1879', *CUR*, no. 11, Christmas 1947, pp. 27–31. Conference participants arrived at the college by the new entrance and left by the western or gaol gate.
40. *PR*, 1877–78, 1878–79, 1879–80.
41. *PR*, 1885–86.
42. In the College Archives, there survive over 200 letters relating to the construction of the observatory and the telescope. The principal correspondents are Sir Howard Grubb and Professor John England (natural philosophy, 1855–94).
43. *PR*, 1877–78, 1878–79.

44. Drawn up for the college archivist, UCC, by John Butler, Armagh Observatory, dated 27 January 1994, and entitled 'The Crawford Observatory of University College, Cork'.

45. See Visitation Report, 16–17 May 1894 in *PR*, 1895–96.

46. *CE*, 22 Feb. 1943, editorial.

47. Notably in our own day by Dr Colm O'Sullivan.

48. UC/OHA, Aloys Fleischmann, 5 Dec. 1990.

49. 'How a fly staggered scientists', *John Bull* (n.d. but probably Apr. 1913), p. 208.

50. *PR*, 1874–75.

51. *PR*, 1874–75, 1879–80.

52. George Berkeley, renowned eighteenth-century churchman and philosopher, bishop of Cloyne, 1734–52.

53. Richard Whately, prominent Protestant churchman and theologian, archbishop of Dublin, 1831–63.

54. *PR*, 1883–84, 1885–86.

55. CSORP 1898 4802.

56. CSORP 1907 10552.

57. CSORP 1907 10918.

58. CSORP 1907 11458.

59. CSORP 1907 15543.

60. For an overview, see Patrick Conlan OFM, 'Berkeley Hall – St Anthony's Hall – Honan Hostel (UCC)', *JCHAS*, vol. 100, 1995, pp. 16–28.

61. Alfred G. Dann, *George Webster, D.D.* (Dublin, 1892). Rev. H.H. Dickson, in his preface, believed it was regrettable that Webster, a Dublinman, ever went to Cork, a place swamped by 'provincialism and parochialism'.

62. *PR*, 1873–74, 1875–76, 1878–79. See also Kane Correspondence UC/PO where Webster is constantly making complaints and representations, while disarmingly apologising to Kane – 'you will say that I am troublesome': 101, 24 Mar. 1860. See also UC/PO 67, 77, 111, 112, 121, 124.

63. *Belfast*, vol. I, p. 284.

64. ibid., 285–6; Larkin, *Roman Catholic Church and Home Rule 1870–74*, pp. 159–76.

65. The buildings were centred in Earlsfort Terrace, Dublin. All examinations were conducted in Dublin except matriculation and, from 1884, first university examinations.

66. Apart from other issues, alumni of an institution they accept as familiar feel uncomfortable with changes in title and nomenclature, as many QCC graduates did in 1908–10.

67. *Belfast*, vol. I, pp. 286–9.

68. ibid., pp. 293–8, 302, 309, 355.

69. *PR*, 1878–79.

70. CCM, 10 Feb. 1882; *CE*, 9 Feb. 1882.

71. Assuming he was the same S.E. Moxley who unavailingly appealed his rustication sentence to an extraordinary visitation, 7–8 Dec. 1880: see *PR*, 1880–81.

72. *PR*, 1879–80; *Cork Constitution* (hereinafter *CC*), 20, 22 Mar. 1880; *Cork Daily Herald*, 22 Mar. 1880; *CE* 27 Mar. 1880; CCM, 6 Apr., 10 May 1880. See K[athleen] O'F[laherty], 'Politics in QCC', *CUR*, no. 22, Summer 1951, pp. 22–6.

73. *PR*, 1883–84.

74. *CE*, 24 Jan. 1885; Wheeler, 'Sullivan', *CUR*. The College Council Minutes ignore the visit.

75. *PR*, 1883–84.

76. *PR*, 1883–84, pp. 9–23.

77. *Parliamentary Election Results in Ireland, 1801–1922*, ed. B.M. Walker (Dublin, 1978), p. 129.

78. Emigrant to US, Fenian, meteorologist, journalist, explorer, died on Arctic expedition, October 1881. Remains were brought from Yakutsk via Hamburg to New York, and thence

back to Cork (15,000 miles). See accounts by John T. Collins (*EE*, 30 Apr. 1953) and Walter McGrath (*EE,* 24 June, 9 July 1979). I am indebted to Mr McGrath for these references.

For Magner (who also complained of exorbitant fee-charging by Professor Charles of anatomy and physiology, of professors abusing the library system and of spying porters) see *CC* , 7 Apr. 1884; *Cork Daily Herald*, 7 Apr. 1884; *CE*, 28 Jan., 5 Feb. 1885.

79.   *CE*, 17 May 1884, editorial.
80.   *CE*, 18 May 1884.
81.   See below, p. 130.
82.   *Corporation of Cork: Reports and Returns of Committees and Officers for the years 1884 and 1885,* pp. 61–77 (Cork Archives Institute).
83.   e.g. Proceedings, Triennial Visitation, 12 Apr. 1867, *PR* 1866–67, p. 113.
84.   For much of the information in this section, I am indebted, as ever, to Virginia Teehan, the college archivist; and to Deirdre Mortell for letting me read her unpublished paper, 'Women in Queen's College, Cork, 1883–1912'.
85.   See *Belfast*, vol. I, pp. 231–2.
86.   CCM, 10 Jan. 1882.
87.   *PR*, 1886–87.
88.   See below, p. 173.
89.   Mortell, 'Women in College'.
90.   Letters laid before CC, 1888–92.
91.   *QCC*, vol. IV, no. 1, Dec. 1907, p. 15.
92.   Kathleen O'Flaherty, 'Admission of Women Students to QCC', *CUR*, no. 15, Easter 1949, pp. 16–21.
93.   Letters laid before CC, 1888–89; CCM, 26 Feb., 20 Mar., 9 Apr. 1889.
94.   CCM, 11 June 1908.
95.   For interesting anecdotal reminiscences of Ryall, Bunnell Lewis, George Boole and other QCC luminaries, see *EE* articles by Joy Rathbone, 7 Jan. to 18 Feb. 1982.
96.   See *Belfast*, vol. I, p. 40.
97.   i.e., end.
98.   Emeritus Professor E.C. Dillon (civil engineering), in the course of his researches in the history of the engineering department, has become an authority on Jack. See also Michael Cahill, 'Memories of Queen's College Cork', *CUR*, no. 29, Summer 1954, pp. 24ff.
99.   CSORP 1875 13694, Chair of Greek, Sullivan to CSO, 26 Aug. 1875.
100.   CSORP 1875 unnumbered letter, Under-Secretary to Sullivan, 31 Aug. 1875.
101.   CSORP 1875 13421.
102.   CSORP 1875 13772.
103.   CSORP 1889 1108.
104.   *CE*, 6 Apr. 1895.
105.   *PR*, 1880–81, 1884–85.
106.   Probably *The Freeman's Journal*, which had shown a keen interest in the student events of February–March 1884.
107.   CSORP 1885 12390. In his 1884–85 president's report, Sullivan also raised the danger of losing Crawford's 'splendid gift' and, incidentally, made it clear that the 'arts professors' who might hope to benefit from it included the science as well as the literature division of the then arts faculty.
108.   Larkin, *Roman Catholic Church and the Modern Irish State 1878–86*, p. 241.
109.   CSORP 1885 2905.
110.   UC/PR/9.
111.   'Rough-hewn with a broad chisel' (Oxford English Dictionary).
112.   CSORP 1889 2374.
113.   CSORP 1889 3923. See Appendix B.
114.   Wheeler, 'W.K. Sullivan', *Studies*.

115. For properties acquired under Sullivan, see UC/PR/4, 5, 6, 7, 8, 9, and map.
116. The Sullivans had two sons and three daughters. Sullivan's wife, Frances, was a sister of Sir John Pope-Hennessy, MP and Henry Hennessy, the college's first librarian. Among Sullivan's descendants were his grandson Professor Thomas Dillon of UCG (who has left us his student impressions of QCC at the end of the century: *CUR*, no. 3, Easter 1945) and the latter's daughter, the writer, Eilís Dillon.
117. *CE,* 26 June 1894.

Chapter 6
1. See p. 155.
2. The college archivist, Virginia Teehan, was successfully persistent in unearthing the relevant Slattery files in the National Archives. Professor David Slattery (Department of Public Health, University of Liverpool) has been actively researching his great-uncle's career, completing a short biographical essay in April 1995. He has kindly donated to the college a portrait of Slattery (a small man of unprepossessing visage) by John B. Yeats, father of W.B. and Jack, with whom Slattery was acquainted at TCD. The portrait has been refurbished – and its subject moderately rehabilitated – and it hangs at last on the Aula Maxima gallery wall, so that amends have been made all round. That just leaves one rogue president to be accounted for. For memories of, and folkore concerning Slattery and Blennerhassett, see 'John Griffin looks back', *CUR*, no. 2, Christmas 1944.
3. For career testimonials, and correspondence concerning his appointment, see CSORP 1890 10892.
4. There were other QCC applicants – Professors Corby (midwifery), England (natural philosophy), O'Ryan (modern languages) and Ridgeway (Greek – his rather esoteric research speciality was the small stature of the Homeric horse). Henry Hennessy (librarian, QCC, 1849–55; later, professor at the College of Science; W.K. Sullivan's brother-in-law) also applied. His influential brother, Sir John Pope-Hennessy, tried to have an influential word put in the chief secretary's ear.
5. Slattery's emphasis.
6. Professor David Slattery speculates that Chief Secretary A.J. Balfour, at the suggestion of Chief Baron Palles, chose Slattery as the safest man in such seditious times: 'James W. Slattery, 1831–97', unpublished 1995, p. 25.
7. In *PR*, 1895–96, pp. 29–90; also in CSORP 1896 19451. For details of the confrontations between Slattery and the council, see College Council Minutes. Extensive correspondence has also come to light on the controversy surrounding Professor John England's attempt to have his services extended well beyond the age of sixty-five. At one point, reacting to the council's opposition to his (Slattery's) wishes, the president noted: 'Another instance of the attempt of the elected members of the Council to encroach on the President's duties and powers': extract from the Council Book, 17 May 1892, Professor England's case, Slattery correspondence, UC/PO.
8. Hartog (natural history, later zoology, 1882–1921) was of French-Jewish descent. See J.C. Sperrin-Johnson, 'Professor Marcus M. Hartog', *CUR*, no. 7, summer 1946, pp. 14–16.
9. The mark on the wall was pointed out by Bill Porter, classics lecturer, to his student Bryan Murphy: UC/OHA, Bryan Murphy, 15 Jan. 1991.
10. CSORP 1894 14857. For the Perrott's Inch transaction, as well as the sources in the text, see CSORP, 30 Oct, 1893 13489.
11. CSORP 1893 12189, 12752, 14246.
12. CSORP 1896 7864.
13. *Dublin Gazette*, 14 Aug. 1896.
14. CSORP 1896 14823.
15. CSORP 1896 14056.
16. CSORP 1896 19175, 19451.

17. CSORP 1896 19451.
18. CSORP 1896 20639.
19. CSORP 1896 20992.
20. ibid.
21. CSORP 1896 21730.
22. CSORP 1897 6560.
23. ibid.
24. The others were Sullivan and Merriman. Of course Slattery was no longer president when he died.
25. Information from Professor David Slattery.
26. Professor David Slattery ('Slattery', unpublished) details his great-uncle's illnesses. (pp. 32ff.). He also rightly comments that the Slattery saga, with its climax of bankruptcy, dismissal and death is 'worthy of any good Victorian plot' (p. 41).
27. D.J. Hickey and J.E. Doherty, *A Dictionary of Irish History since 1800* (Dublin, 1980), which erroneously puts him in the home rule camp. See also *Burke's Peerage and Baronetage* (London, 1875), p. 282; and *CE*, 3 Jan. 1939.
28. *CC*, 25 Sept. 1904.
29. *Parliamentary Election Results*, ed. B.M. Walker, pp. 102, 109, 125, 132.
30. I am indebted to Dr Timothy P. Foley, 'Thomas Maguire and the Parnell Forgeries', *Journal of the Galway Archaeological and Historical Society*, vol. 46, 1994, p. 185, for drawing my attention to Blennerhassett's involvement. See *The Special Commission 1888: Report of the Proceedings* etc., 4 vols, reprinted from *The Times* (London, 1890), vol. iii, p. 718.
31. CSORP 1897 160, 5406, 5756.
32. CCM, 26 Mar. 1897.
33. UC: Misc. Letters 1897–1908.
34. *PR*, 1896–97. *The Freemans Journal* (8 Oct. 1897) was infuriated by what it saw as the grandiose vapourings of a political placeman. It asserted that QCC was already overstaffed and too lavishly endowed, with ridiculously few and mediocre students. The whole situation was 'a little farcical and could scarcely occur, in any country of the world, but Ireland'.
     Blennerhassett's ideas are elaborated in his inaugural address, *University Education in England, France and Germany with special reference to the needs of Ireland* (London, 1898). Also see Buttimer, 'Celtic and Irish in College', pp. 92–3.
35. *PR*, 1902–03, also *PR*, 1899–1900.
36. *PR*, 1897–98.
37. *PR*, 1896–97.
38. *PR*, 1899–1900.
39. *PR*, 1896–97.
40. CSORP 1902 25790.
41. *PR*, 1896–97.
42. *PR*, 1897–98.
43. A couplet in a nostalgic tribute in verse composed in 1895 recalls titanic struggles in the Quarry: 'We pledge the sunken field where oft in friendly wrangle/Arts and medicine vied, and our green quadrangle', *Old Memories of the QCC*, read at the 'Old Corkonians' Dinner, London, 30 Mar. 1895 (UCC MP 886).
44. Statement prepared by President Blennerhassett for government consideration, placed before council, CCM, 8 June 1899. See also *PR*, 1898–99, 1899–1900.
45. CCM, 20 Oct. 1897.
46. *PR*, 1902–03.
47. ibid. A cynic might observe that one effective way for a president to ensure harmony with the professors is to absent himself from proceedings as often as possible.
48. 6 Sept. 1904, CSORP 1904 17902.

49. Michael Cahill, 'Memories of Queen's College, Cork', *CUR*, no. 29, Summer 1954, pp. 24ff.
50. Larry O'Leary, UC/OHA, 6 Dec. 1990. Perhaps Blennerhassett used the mounting block, now at the north-west corner of the walled garden.
51. CCM, 29 Nov. 1899.
52. 16 Jan. 1901, CSORP 1901 1066: he assures Dublin Castle that 'the public interest will not suffer' because of his absence.
53. 3 Mar. 1901, CSORP 1901 4645.
54. CSO minutes, 6, 7 Mar. 1901, CSORP 1901 4645.
55. CSORP 1904 3390.
56. CSORP 1904 17902.
57. CSORP 1905 1747.
58. CCM, 19 Oct. 1911; *CE*, 20 Oct. 1911.
59. UC/OHA, James Murphy, 16 Jan. 1991, citing Jim Hurley (secretary and bursar, 1944–65). Blennerhassett, attending an RUI Senate meeting in Dublin in 1905, was singled out by nationalist students for special hissing: 8 Nov. 1905, CSORP 1905 23551.
60. *CE*, 30 Mar. 1875.
61. Ryall was professor of Greek.
62. CCM, 25 Jan. 1870.
63. *CE*, 28 Jan. 1870.
64. See Professor. D.T. Barry, 'The Cork Medical School', *CUR*, no. 15, Easter 1949, p. 15.
65. *CE*, 27 Mar. 1895.
66. *CE*, 15 Mar. 1872; *The Irish Daily Telegraph*, 15 Mar. 1872. The medical students had objected to the temporary appointment of 'a Dublin medical gentleman' as a deplorable indication of the tendency 'to appoint strangers in preference to alumni of the College and graduates of our University': *The Irish Daily Telegraph*, 29 Feb. 1872. The same issue of the *Telegraph* carries a *Dublin Evening Mail* opinion piece welcoming the appointment of Dr Maxwell Simpson to the chair of chemistry in QCC, not only because he was a distinguished scientist, but because 'the vicious rule of appointing strangers to the Queen's Colleges, to the disadvantages of Irishmen generally of equal and sometimes superior merit, had been broken'. Simpson, it appears, had been a Young Irelander: *CE*, 7 Dec. 1939.
67. UC: Letters laid before Council, 1888–92.
68. UC: Misc. Letters, 1897–1908.
69. UC: Misc. Letters, 1907–08.
70. UC: Letters laid before Council, 1903.
71. CCM, 11 Dec. 1903.
72. UC: Misc. Letters, 1897–1908.
73. Hartog to College Council, 8 Jan. 1906, ibid.
74. UC: Misc. Letters, 1897–1908; CCM, 8 June 1899, Blennerhassett statement. When the writer was an undergraduate in the late 1940s, the 'professors' private rooms' in the West Wing (really ante-rooms) closely corresponded to the above description.
75. PR, 1899–1900.
76. *CC*, 27 Nov. 1899. Also see *The Quarryman*, 1930.
77. CCM, 29 Nov. 1899.
78. CCM, 29 Nov., 1 Dec. and 13 Dec. 1899.
79. *Reports of the commissioners appointed by His Excellency John Poyntz, Earl Spencer, K.G., Lord Lieutenant of Ireland, to inquire into certain matters affecting the well-being and efficiency of the Queen's Colleges in Ireland* (Dublin, 1885). The report is summarised in *Belfast*, vol. I, pp. 310–11.
80. *Belfast*, vol. I, p. 305.
81. ibid., pp. 315, 320; *PR*, 1877–78, 1878–79.
82. For the Better Equipment Fund, see *Belfast*, vol. I, pp. 349ff.

83. *Royal Commission on University Education in Ireland, Final Report* (1903), p. 3, cited in *Belfast*, vol. I, pp. 353–4.
84. *Belfast*, vol. I, p. 359.
85. ibid., p. 365.
86. ibid., pp. 364, 381ff.

Chapter 7

1. Much of this chapter is indebted to Monica Taylor, *Sir Bertram Windle: A Memoir* (London, 1932). Taylor's book, about one-third of which deals with the Cork phase of Windle's career, is generally uncritical, exasperatingly fails to document sources and is not particularly knowledgeable about the Cork context. Yet it is a mine of information and it quotes copiously from Windle's diary (which seems to be no longer available) and from his extensive personal correspondence. See also John J. Horgan, 'Sir Bertram Windle', *Studies*, vol. XXI, December 1932, pp. 611–26. Horgan was Windle's son-in-law: see n. 18, below.
2. Once introduced facetiously as having the first three letters of the alphabet before his name and all the rest after it: Horgan, 'Windle', p. 623; Taylor, p. 1.
3. See Edith Somerville and Martin Ross, *Irish Memories* (London, 1917); Sir Bertram A.C. Windle, 'Genealogical Notes on the Family of Cramer or Coghill', *JCHAS*, vol. XVI, 1910, pp. 66–81.
4. Taylor, p. 20.
5. ibid., p. 386.
6. ibid., p. 37.
7. ibid. pp. 37–8.
8. ibid., p. 146.
9. ibid., p. 288.
10. ibid., p. 155.
11. CSORP 1906 11625.
12. CSORP 1906 856.
13. CSORP 1909 14630.
14. Taylor, p. 289.
15. For what follows, see ibid., Ch. XIII.
16. ibid., p. 21.
17. ibid., pp. 147–9; *CE*, 9 Nov. 1904.
18. Horgan, son of a leading Parnellite, was a solicitor, coroner (inquest on *Lusitania* sinking in 1917 returned verdict of wilful murder against the Kaiser), well-known figure in civic and university life, author of *From Parnell to Pearse*. He was to marry Windle's daughter, Mary, though the courtship did not at first meet with Windle's approval. He thought Horgan 'an estimable young man' but 'she is much too young and immature for anything of the kind, so I stamped on it and sent Mary off for a couple of months' rambling' (June 1906). But true love withstood the test, and the couple were married on 16 September 1908, Windle wryly noting in his diary that he had lost a daughter and gained a university settlement: see Taylor, pp. 181, 198.
19. There were only five women students in 1902–03 (*PR*). D.L. Kelleher, who read the address of welcome, knew that things could only improve under Windle. He later recalled (CUR, no. 2, Christmas 1944, p. 32) that there was 'nothing of a university' about QCC, in Blennerhassett's time.
20. Taylor, p. 149.
21. By subscription, though the college tried to get money from the Treasury as well: Registrar to CSO, 5 Mar. 1907, CSORP 1907 4859.
22. Ultimate control of the purse-strings by a staff member was for long a feature of student societies. A QCC graduate in the Far East, Lt-Col. M.J. Sexton, MD, RAMC, hoped graduates could be members. Sexton was fulsome in his praise of Windle's presidency at this early

stage: Sexton to Windle, 1 Aug. 1906, 1 May 1907, 22 July 1912, UC Special Collections, Anglo-Indian Collection.

23. CCM, 23 May 1906.
24. UC: Misc. Letters 1897–1908, H. Barter to College Council, February 1908.
25. Taylor, pp. 162ff.; see also *PR*, 1904–05.
26. Taylor, p. 177.
27. Windle to Lord Lieutenant, 8 July 1906, CSORP 1906 23186.
28. Taylor, p. 198.
29. ibid., pp. 164, 167. For Lewis, see Thomas Dillon, 'Reminiscences', *CUR*, no. 3, Easter 1945.
30. Windle to CSO, 9 Jan. 1906, CSORP 1906 615.
31. 20 Jan. 1905, Taylor p. 165.
32. CCM, 27 April 1898
33. UC: Misc. Letters, 1897–1908.
34. GBM, 15 June, 15 Dec. 1910.
35. CCM, 29 Mar. 1905.
36. CCM, 18 May 1908. The college authorities continued to be conservative in this regard for a long time.
37. GBM, 19 Oct. 1911.
38. Taylor, pp. 163–4: Ep[iscopus] = Bishop (O'Callaghan).
39. ibid., p. 177.
40. 12 Jan. 1906, CSORP 1906 856.
41. Mary Rose Lynch, Rosebank, Old Blackrock Road, Cork to Michael Davitt, 1 Mar. 1906, TCD, Ms 9659 (B) (no. 82). I am indebted to Áine Ní Chonaill for this reference. See also Terence O'Brien to Davitt, 22 Jan. 1906, TCD, Ms 9653 (no. 59). Mary Aherne, one of the handful of Catholic women in QCC at this time, was forced to withdraw (having performed brilliantly) because of ecclesiastical pressure: see her obituary, *CUR*, no. 11, 1947, p. 18.
42. Windle to Sir James Dougherty, Under-Sec., 9 Mar. 1905, CSORP; Windle diary, 17 Feb. 1905, Taylor p. 168; See also *PR*, 1904–05, p. 7. Eugene MacSweeney and Harriet Martin were appointed jointly to the lectureship in education, for the institution of which see CCM, 23 Feb., 8 Mar., 10 May 1905.
43. Windle to John Humphreys, 14 Jan. 1908, in Taylor, p. 191. The material in these paragraphs is based on *PR*, 1903–04, 1904–05, 1905–06.
44. Aloys Fleischmann, 'The Music Department', unpublished; Aloys Fleischmann, UC/ OHA, 5 Dec. 1990; W.F. Butler (Registrar) to Chief Sec., 12 Nov. 1906, CSORP 1906 24745; CCM, 7, 22 Nov. 1906. 'He was not musical, much to Lady Windle's sorrow': Taylor, p. 289; see also Horgan, 'Windle', p. 626.
45. Taylor, p. 206.
46. *PR*, 1913–14.
47. *PR*, 1906–07.
48. Windle to Chief Sec., 12 Jan. 1906, CSORP 1906 856; *PR*, 1905–06.
49. Chief Sec. to Treasury, 20 Jan. 1906, CSORP 1906 857.
50. CSORP 1906 2309.
51. *PR*, 1906–07, p. 16, App. A, pp. 18–19.
52. *PR*, 1906–07, pp 16, 20–21.
53. *PR*, 1906–07, pp. 15–16, 20; Taylor, pp. 184–5.
54. Letter to *CE*, quoted Taylor, pp. 186–7.
55. Taylor, pp. 188–9.
56. ibid., p. 192.
57. *CE*, 27 Apr. 1908.
58. Texts in *PR*, 1907–08, App. A, p. 10.
59. Taylor, p. 193. *CE*, 9 May 1910 had an editorial on the draft charter.

60. ibid., p. 195.
61. ibid., p. 196.
62. *Charter of UCC* (Cork, 1912), V (p. 7).
63. *Irish Universities Act 1908: A Statute for UCC* (Dublin, 1909), ch. XIV, 8, pp. 21–2.
64. Taylor, p. 198.
65. ibid., p. 199.
66. ibid., p. 208.
67. Windle's capital letters, ibid., p. 201.
68. ibid., p. 205.
69. GBM, 15 Dec. 1908.
70. CCM, 27 May 1908.
71. Taylor, p. 199.
72. GBM, 15 Dec. 1908.
73. Taylor, p. 204.
74. ibid., p. 198.
75. UC/PR/10 and map. The sports side of college was 'a very necessary thing with so many ramping young men about': Windle to Chief Secretary, 22 Apr. 1911, CSORP 1911 8163. The new all-weather track and pitch, opened on 15 June 1979, affords enhanced opportunities for the sublimation of 'ramping' proclivities.
76. GBM, 5 Nov. 1909.
77. CSORP 1911 8163.
78. *PR*, 1908–09, pp. 7–8.
79. Taylor, p. 210. The ceremony went off with a flourish, even though there was only a handful of (medical) graduates, and one higher-degree recipient, J.J. Kearney.
80. ibid., p. 207.
81. GBM, 2, 10 May 1913.
82. See UC/OHA, 29 Jan. 1991, President Tadhg Ó Ciardha.
83. Taylor, p. 162.
84. CSORP 1909 2876.
85. Diary, 3 Dec. 1908, quoted Taylor, p. 199.
86. Michael Tierney, *Eoin MacNeill*, ed. F.X. Martin (Oxford, 1980), p. 87.
87. Windle to Joseph McGrath (first NUI registrar), 24 Mar. 1910, NUI Archives, quoted Donal McCartney, *The National University of Ireland and Eamon de Valera* (Dublin, 1983), p. 16.
88. Windle to Attn. Gen., 23 Apr. 1919, Munster University Papers (hereinafter MUP), Box 175, Special Collections UCC.
89. Memo for Chief Sec., 23 Apr. 1919, MUP.
90. *CE*, 21 Oct. 1913.
91. *CE*, 18 Nov. 1913.
92. *CE*, 19 Nov. 1913.
93. *CE*, various letters throughout November 1913.
94. *CE*, 25 Nov. 1913.
95. *Cork Free Press*, (hereinafter *FP*), 2 Dec. 1913.
96. *FP*, 24 Jan. 1914.
97. *CE*, 18 Oct. 1912.
98. *CE*, 19–20 Dec., 1912.
99. *CE*, 17 Jan. 1913.
100. *CE*, 20–24 Jan., 5 and 8 Feb. 1913.
101. *CE*, 6 Aug. 1911.
102. e.g. F. St John Lacy, lecturer in music (*CE*, 12 Jan. 1911) pointing out that UCC was the only NUI College in which music degrees could be taken; Professor C.W.O'D. Alexander (*CE*, 28 Oct. 1912) explaining the cement testing process in the engineering laboratory, 'the only laboratory of its kind in Ireland'.

103. *CE*, 6 Feb. 1912.
104. *CE*, Sept. 1912. The original phrase was Edward Bulwer-Lytton's.
105. *CE*, 25 Mar. 1911.
106. *The Freeman's Journal* (hereinafter *FJ*), Nov. 1912.
107. *CE*, 6, 10, 11 May, 30 June 1911, 20 Apr. 1912; *CC*, 20 Apr. 1912.
108. *CE*, 20 Nov. 1909, 6 Feb. 1911.
109. *CC*, 14 May 1912.
110. See his first conferring speech, *CE*, 26 May 1910.
111. *CE*, 6 Nov. 1909.
112. *CE*, 1 Nov. 1911.
113. *CE*, 14 Sept. 1911.
114. *CE*, n.d., p. 19, Newspaper Cuttings, UC Archives; *CE*, 14 Sept. 1911.
115. He surely meant a Republic!
116. *CE*, 26 May 1910, and editorial.
117. This was the splendid new (and present) silver mace. The cost was met by subscriptions from staff and friends in 1910. It was exhibited in the window of Egans, the silversmiths, in Patrick Street in March 1914, and readers were reminded that the mace was the first important order issued in Cork since the old school of silversmiths died out nearly a century before, Cork needs being supplied in the interim, 1825–1910, from England (*CE*, 14 Mar. 1914). The mace, draped in crepe, was carried at the obsequies of those associated with the college: *CE*, 27 Feb. 1912. Such a college funeral was that of Professor Molohan (Latin), registrar, early in 1915.
118. *CE*, 26 May 1910.
119. *CE*, 1 Nov. 1911.
120. *CE*, 4 Nov. 1912.
121. See *PR*, 1913–14.
122. *CE*, 30 Mar. 1912.
123. *CE*, 30 Aug. 1911.
124. *CE*, 25 Mar. 1911.
125. *CE*, 25 Feb. 1912; see Cork Co. Co. discussion, *CE*, 4 Aug. 1911. Also see *CE*, 30 Aug. 1911, 15 July 1912.
126. *CE*, 4 May 1911.
127. *CE*, 23 Feb. 1911.
128. *CE*, 30 Aug. 1911; *CE*, 20 Feb. 1912.
129. Letter from J. Cummins, *CE*, 16 Aug. 1912.
130. *CC*, 28 Oct. 1915.
131. *EE*, 26 Feb. 1916. See also *CC*, 1 Mar. 1916; *CE*, 2 Mar. 1916.
132. *CE*, 2 Aug. 1911.
133. See discussion on award of scholarship to Dr Magner jnr., *CE*, 30 Nov., 2 Dec. 1911.
134. *CE*, 18 Oct 1912. *CC*, 23 Oct. 1913, provides a useful review of the workings of the scholarship schemes to that point.
135. Letter of Jeremiah Cummins, *CE*, 9 Mar. 1916.
136. *CC*, 9, 13 Mar. 1916.
137. *Tipperary Star*, 4 Nov. 1911.
138. *CE*, 2 July 1911.
139. *CE*, 13 June 1926.
140. *Kerry News*, 9 Mar. 1914.
141. *CC*, 10 Mar. 1914.
142. *FP*, 12 Mar. 1914.
143. *CE*, 17 Mar. 1914.
144. *CC*, 20 Mar. 1914.
145. *FP*, 3 Apr. 1914.

146. *FP*, 8 Apr. 1914.
147. *FP*, 31 July 1914. Much later, a tablet in Curraghkippane cemetery, overlooking Cork city, commemorated all those whose bodies were used in research – *in rebus humanis* – at UCC.
148. *FP*, 2 May 1914.
149. *CE*, 15 June 1918.
150. *CC*, 25 Mar. 1916.
151. *CE*, 28 Feb. 1912.
152. *CE*, 19 Apr. 1913.
153. *CE*, 18 Oct. 1912.
154. *CE*, 23 Apr. 1913.
155. *Calendar UCC, 1994–1995*, pp. 846–8.
156. *CE*, 6 Apr. 1914. See Patrick Conlan, OFM, 'Berkeley Hall – St Anthony's Hall – Honan Hostel (UCC)', *JCHAS*, vol. 100, 1995, pp. 16–28.
157. *FP*, 12 May 1914.
158. Also reported *CC*, 19 Oct. 1914. A bequest of a very different kind was noted around this time. Peter O'Kinealy (late of the Indian civil service) left a substantial residue of estate to UCC 'for the furtherance of secular and scientific instructions . . . provided none of the income is to be used for the support or maintenance of religious instruction': *CC*, 10 Nov. 1914. The college file is: O'Kinealy Fund, 1679, Secretary's Office. Surprisingly – or perhaps not – the fund has received little publicity, considering it was as financially substantial as the Honan bequest.
159. The house is situated on College Road, between the south lodge and hostel gates, and is now occupied by college departments.
160. *The Irish Times* (hereinafter *IT*), 19 Jan. 1915.
161. *UCCR*, no. 53, 1978, pp. 49ff.; no. 54, 1979, pp. 15–16.
162. *CE*, 23 Oct. 1916. The lengthy inscription on the right-hand side of the door may still be read.
163. *CE*, 23 Oct., 6 Nov. 1916.
164. ibid.; Michael J. O'Kelly's comprehensive guide to *The Honan Chapel, University College Cork* (Cork, 3rd edn, 1966). There were earlier guides by Rev. Professor Power and Rev. Sir John O'Connell. Jeanne Sheehy, *The Rediscovery of Ireland's Past: The Celtic Revival 1830–1930* (London, 1980) describes the chapel design as 'not very distinguished' (p. 142) but has a detailed account of the furnishings (pp. 163–7) of this 'great monument of Celtic Revival art'.
165. *CE*, 24 Feb, 1926.
166. *IT*, 21–26 Apr. 1913. The red mass is the votive mass of the Holy Ghost, inaugurating the college year.
167. See J. Anthony Gaughan, *Alfred O'Rahilly: I, Academic* (Dublin, 1986), pp. 126–9.
168. GBM, 2 June 1909.
169. *CE*, 30 Jan. 1910.
170. Reproduced, *CE*, 14 Aug. 1912.
171. *CE*, 9 Nov. 1912.
172. Author of *Catholicity and Progress in Ireland* (London 1905), an extensive rebuttal of Sir Horace Plunkett's attack on Irish Catholicism as a reactionary force in his *Ireland in the New Century* (London 1904).
173. *CE*, 28 Oct. 1913.
174. See *CE*, *FP* and many Munster papers on 28 Oct. 1911.
175. e.g. *Waterford Star* and *Kerry Sentinel*, 28 Oct. 1911.
176. *CE*, 7 Oct. 1912.
177. *CE*, 8 Jan., 1, 8 Feb. 1916; *CC*, 21, 26 Feb., 25 Mar. 1916. See also Mícheál Ó Murchú, 'Alfred O'Rahilly and the provision of Adult Education at University College Cork', *Social Commitment and Adult Education,* ed. Denis O'Sullivan (Cork, 1989).

178. *CE*, Sept. 1919.
179. Windle article in *Times Special Irish Number*, 4 Nov. 1919.
180. Taylor, pp. 237ff.
181. *CE*, 18 Aug. 1914.
182. *FP*, 11 Sept. 1914. Alexander was to stipulate in his will that none of his estate was to go to any institution 'under clerical domination': *Morning Post*, 7 Mar. 1921. It is of interest that when he was in the process of applying for the vacant chair of engineering in 1906, he had enquired (setting a trap, perhaps) if the college, in making appointments gave 'some consideration to the candidate's religious beliefs' and 'if it is desirable that the Professor of Civil Engineering should, in addition to other professional qualifications, be a member of the Roman Catholic Church': 5 June 1906, Alexander to Jack, UC/unspecified.
183. Taylor, p. 237.
184. *IT*, Dec. 1914. Bridget Lyndsay (nee Danaher) was appointed in 1915 (professor, 1915–21).
185. *CC*, 22 May 1915.
186. *CC*, 26 May 1915.
187. ibid.
188. *CE*, 18 Apr. 1916.
189. *CE*, 4 Apr. 1918.
190. *CC*, 16 Oct. 1916. See *PR*, 1918–19 for details.
191. For what follows see: 'John Griffin looks back', *CUR*, no. 2, Christmas 1944, p. 28; H. Glavin, 'A half-century of memories of UCC', *UCCR*, no. 43, 1968, p. 48; Maurice Harmon, *Seán Ó Faoláin* (Dublin, 1994), pp. 51–5; UC/OHA, John Kiely, 25 June 1991; UC/OHA, Una Riordan, 20 Mar. 1991; J. Anthony Gaughan, *Alfred O'Rahilly, II: Public Figure* (Dublin 1989) p. 96. (for the threats on Yelverton-Pearson); Cormac Ó Cuilleanáin, 'Gaelachas i dtosach Ré an Choláiste', *CUR*, no. 30, Summer 1955, pp. 39–40 (for the attempt to form an officers training corps). For the Alexander incident, see *UCCR*, no. 42, 1967, pp. 21–40.
192. For de Valera's application for the chair of mathematical physics in UCC in 1913, see McCartney, *Eamon de Valera*.
193. K[athleen] O'F[laherty], 'Politics in QCC', *CUR*, no. 22, Summer 1951, pp. 25–6. A pro-Parnell letter to the paper (*CE*, 4 Dec. 1890) was disowned by other students (*CE*, 13 Dec. 1890).
194. O'Rahilly to Michael Hayes, 2 Jan. 1922, Michael Hayes Papers, UCD Archives, p. 53/440.
195. For above, see Taylor, pp. 276–7.
196. ibid., p. 267.
197. See Munster University Pamphlets, Special Collections, Boole Library, UCC; GBM 9 Mar. 1918.
198. Taylor, p. 262.
199. *Statement of the Governing Body in support of the claim for the establishment of a separate university for Munster* (Cork, 1918), in MUP.
200. MUP; GBM, 9 Mar. 1918.
201. See its opinion column on 26 Mar. 1918, where the case is argued at length.
202. *CC*, 27 Mar. 1918.
203. See Newspaper Cuttings File, UC Archives, for these months.
204. *CE*, 26 Mar. 1918.
205. Taylor, p. 274.
206. MUP. The two Cork papers are, of course, the *Examiner* and the *Constitution*.
207. Taylor, p. 274.
208. ibid., p. 275.
209. Windle to Arthur W. Samuels, Irish Attn.Gen, 21 Feb. 1919, MUP. See also Taylor, pp. 274–5.
210. Taylor, p. 274.

211. in MUP.
212. It was at this time when academics were becoming increasingly *engagé*, that the secretary of the college, Joseph Downey, sent a letter on the president's instruction to all staff on 22 October 1917, deploring the use by staff members of the college address in public communications (especially in letters to the press) on current affairs, and hoping that in future such communications would be sent from private addresses (copy of Downey's letter in the writer's possession). This counsel of perfection was to be repeated *ad nauseam* over the years with no discernible effect. After all, the president's office could hardly impose any sanctions without incurring damaging accusations of censorship in the groves of academe. The use of the college address was calculated to make the maximum impression on the reading public, though whether it achieved this effect was doubtful.
213. Gaughan, *O'Rahilly*, vol. I, pp. 58, 62, 63.
214. This is part of an assessment of Windle by his friend and UCC colleague, Dr Magner, in Taylor, pp. 286–90.
215. *O'Rahilly*, vol. I, pp. 66–9. See also letters of UCC Sinn Féin Club, *CE*, 28 Apr. 1919, and of Liam de Róiste, *CE*, 23 Apr. 1919.
216. *An Mac Léighinn: The Student*, produced by the National Students' Club, Cork, vol. 2, no. 3, Mar. 1919.
217. MUP.
218. *O'Rahilly*, vol. I, pp. 69–70.
219. ibid.; MUP. For Sinn Féin objections to the election deferral, see GBM, 5 Feb. 1919. For Munster TDs' statement, see GBM, 24 Apr. 1919.
220. Sir Plunket Waldron to Windle, 27 Mar. 1919, MUP.
221. *O'Rahilly*, vol. I, p. 70. For NUI opposition, see *Irish Independent* (hereinafter *II*), 6 Mar., 24 May 1919.
222. *FJ, II, IT, CE*, 7 June 1919.
223. *II*, 26 Apr. 1919.
224. O'Rahilly, as registrar 1920–43, was to quarrel with P.J. Merriman (president, 1919–43). The relationship plummetted during 'the dairy science row' in the early 1930s (see pp. 225–7). O'Rahilly had ill-concealed contempt for Merriman: see *O'Rahilly*, vol. I, pp. 151–2 and UC/OHA, Declan McSweeney, 4 Feb. 1991.
225. The lawyer (afterwards priest) through whose good offices as executor, UCC benefitted from the Honan bequest.
226. C. Yelverton-Pearson, professor of surgery.
227. of zoology.
228. Gaughan, *O'Rahilly*, vol. I, p. 71.
229. Taylor, p. 277.
230. Horgan, 'Windle', pp. 621–2.
231. *II*, May 1919.
232. For what follows, see Taylor, pp. 277–92.
233. Windle's report to the GB makes it clear that he thought the government was never really in earnest all along (MUP). The GB pointed out that NUI opposition proved the UCD camp dominated the Senate: GBM, 13 June 1919.
234. 'Calamity' was surely a gross exaggeration. The writer's opinion is that the federal link, now being attenuated in the 1990s, has on balance been beneficial to the college and that the pursuit of 'independence' has been, at times, an obsessive distraction.
235. Letter to editor, *II*, 16 June 1919.
236. *CE*, 12 Nov. 1919.
237. See, especially, *CE*, 4, 11 Oct. 1919, but also *Morning Post*, 4 Oct. 1919; *The Times*, 6 Oct. 1919, *Manchester Guardian*, 7 Oct. 1919, *Times Education Supplement*, 9 Oct. 1919, *Tablet*, 11 Oct. 1919.

238. *Times Special Irish Number*, 4 Nov. 1919.
239. *II*, 21 Oct. 1919; *CE*, 30 Oct. 1919; *Irish News*, 3 Nov. 1919.
240. The function was reported in detail in *CE* and *CC*, 15 Nov. 1919. Windle's term as president ended on 21 Nov. 1919: GBM, 9 Oct. 1919.
241. Taylor, Part. III, 'Toronto'; Horgan, 'Windle', pp. 662ff.
242. *O'Rahilly*, vol. I, p. 73.
243. Taylor, p. 311.
244. ibid., p. 292.
245. ibid., p. 312.
246. ibid., p. 208.
247. ibid., p. 176.
248. ibid., p. 191.
249. ibid., p. 190.
250. ibid., p. 181.
251. ibid., p. 186.
252. Dr Magner in ibid., p. 289.
253. ibid., p. 324.
254. ibid., p. 409. The college had a marine station at Lough Ine, (near Baltimore, Co. Cork).
255. ibid., p. 313.
256. ibid., p. 297.
257. ibid., p. 316.
258. ibid., p. 298.
259. ibid., p. 386. A portrait of Windle was hung in the Birmingham Medical School during its centenary celebrations: *CE*, 4 Jan. 1926. There is also a portrait, and a Windle House, in St Michael's College, Toronto.
260. Taylor, p. 310.
261. ibid., p. 321. Niels Stensen (1638–86) was the Danish scientist of whom Windle wrote a short biography. Windle was also interested in Gregor Johann Mendel (1822–84), the Austrian biologist who pioneered the study of genetics. See *Cambridge Biographical Dictionary*, 1990 edition.
262. Taylor, p. 301.
263. See GBM, 26 Oct. 1910, 8 Feb. 1918.
264. Dillon, 'Reminiscences', p. 19.
265. See *CC*, 11 June 1913.
266. For Windle's own summary of faculty developments between 1907 and 1918, see Taylor, p. 207.
267. For details of these two large property acquisitions, see UC/PR/10 and UC/PR/11, respectively; also see 'The University Athletic Grounds', *UCC Official Gazette*, Jan. 1912, pp. 1–2, and pictures.
268. Taylor, p. 251.
269. See *PR*, 1913–14.
270. *CE*, 17 Mar. 1914.
271. Text in Taylor, pp. 282–3.
272. See ibid., pp. 171–176; Horgan, 'Windle'. Windle's ideas for the economic development of Cork are outlined in the preface he wrote for *Cork: Its Trade and Commerce* (Cork, 1919). College, he says, is only waiting to help Cork businessmen.
273. GBM, 9 Oct. 1919.
274. See Denis Gwynn's comments on Windle, UCC, Mss U 52, Item no. 58, Misc. Box.
275. Horgan, 'Windle', p. 619.
276. The observation about distortion was made by a former student: Taylor, p. 304.

Chapter 8

1. GBM, 29 Nov. 1919; *CE*, 1 Dec. 1919.
2. Minute book of Senate, NUI, 16 Dec. 1919; *CE*, *II*, 17 Dec. 1919.
3. *II*, 4 Dec. 1919. This was the Professor William Magennis (d. 1946) who was to make an egregiously conservative contribution to the notorious debate on censorship (the 'Tailor and Ansty' debate) in Seanad Éireann: see *Parliamentary Debates Seanad Éireann*, vol. 27, Nov.–Dec. 1942.
4. *II*, 5 Dec. 1919. Pseudonymous letters (names with the editor) were then commonly published.
5. *II*, 8 Dec. 1919.
6. *Old Ireland*, 6 Dec. 1919: quoted *O'Rahilly*, vol. I, pp. 74–5.
7. GBM, 19 Mar. 1920. Lord Mayor MacCurtain was murdered early the following morning, 20 Mar. 1920, his thirty-sixth birthday.
8. *CC*, 19 Mar. 1920.
9. *CC*, 19 Feb. 1920.
10. Quoted *O'Rahilly*, vol. I, p. 77.
11. Minute book of Convocation, NUI, 14 Dec. 1920.
12. Next to Kane (1845–73), he was the longest-serving president in the college's history. O'Rahilly made no secret of his contempt for Merriman – 'I have to run this place with a nominal president on my back', he wrote in 1933. When O'Rahilly's portrait was painted by James Sleator, president of the Royal Hibernian Academy, the subject complained that Sleator had failed to show him as intelligent and resolute as the Merriman portrait which the artist had executed from a photograph. Both portraits hang on the gallery wall in the Aula Maxima. See *O'Rahilly*, vol. I, pp. 152, 243.
13. *CE*, 17 Dec. 1919. Picture, *CE*, 22 Dec. 1919. Kane was thirty-six at appointment, Merriman forty-one.
14. UC/OHA, Declan McSweeney, 4 Feb. 1991.
15. UC/OHA, John Mullane, 17 Dec. 1990, Bryan Murphy, 15 Jan. 1991.
16. UC/OHA, Aloys Fleischmann, 5 Dec. 1990: see, similarly, Larry O'Leary, 6 Dec. 1990. O'Leary says the college grounds were usually closed at teatime, leaving only the president to stroll in his domain and causing Bill Porter (ancient classics) to fume – on failing to gain access to collect a book from a 'private room' – 'He must have been a storekeeper's son'.
17. *IT*, 2 June 1928.
18. *CE*, 14 Sept. 1943. He was the last president to die in residence and have a college funeral. The coffin was borne to the Honan Chapel by 'employees': *CE*, 15 Sept. 1943.
19. *CE*, 8 Nov. 1933.
20. *CE*, 31 Oct. 1929. Though several licensed premises in the vicinity of the college as well as in town have been, and are, associated with student social life and though an on-campus bar has existed since 1974, the Western Star ('Starry's') with its unpretentious and unchanging basic decor is the UCC pub, *par excellence*. In the writer's student days, the solemn maxim *per ardua ad astra* was waggishly translated as 'after work to the Star'.
21. *IT*, 10 Mar. 1934.
22. *IP*, 12 Mar. 1934.
23. *CE*, *IP*, 17 Mar. 1934.
24. *CE*, 23 Nov. 1936.
25. See, e.g., *EE*, 12 Oct. 1927.
26. When the renowned Brother Connolly was returning thanks for his honorary degree, he referred to Merriman's 'unobtrusive but persuasive manner' and O'Rahilly's 'Napoleonic strength and decision of character'. The remarks, intended to be diplomatic and complimentary to both, were quite telling. *CE*, 12 Dec. 1927.
27. *CE*, 28 Aug. 1925.
28. See below, pp. 243–5.

29. *IP*, April 1933.
30. *CE*, 22, 23 Feb. 1939; *IP*, 24 Feb. 1939.
31. See observations (p. 324) of John Kiely (UC/OHA, 25 June 1991) concerning Merriman's promotion of his brother-in-law's candidacy for a medical post in UCC. See also (pp. 247–8) Cormac Ó Cuilleanáin's condemnation of Merriman for ensuring the appointment, in controversial circumstances, of Frances Vaughan as UCC professor of education in 1936.
32. *CE*, 14 Sept. 1926.
33. See *O'Rahilly*, vol. I, p. 152.
34. *II*, 23 Aug. 1937.
35. *CE*, 22 Oct. 1936.
36. *CE*, 16 Jan. 1937.
37. UC/OHA, Seán Teegan, 23 Apr. 1991.
38. See, e.g., *IT*, 15 May 1926; Weekly *IT*, 16 June 1928; *II*, 27 Mar. 1929; *Manchester Guardian*, 11 June 1935; *CE*, 7 May 1936; *II*, 5 May 1937; *IP*, 2 Feb. 1939; *IP*, 3 Aug. 1939.
39. *CE*, 29 Jan. 1934.
40. *CE*, 15 Oct. 1934.
41. Hogan is discussed below, pp. 282–3. For Corkery, see below, p. 231–2, and Patrick Maume, *Life that is Exile: Daniel Corkery and the Search for Irish-Ireland* (Belfast 1993).
    For the fluctuating fortunes of the Department of Irish in QCC and UCC, see Cornelius G. Buttimer, 'An Ghaeilge i gColáiste na hOllscoile, Corcaigh, 1845–1995', and 'Celtic and Irish in College'.
42. UC/OHA, Aloys Fleischmann, 5 Dec. 1990; see his unpublished overview of 'The Music Department, UCC' and interview by Tomás Ó Canainn, published posthumously, *CE*, 22 July 1992.
43. *CE*, 2 Nov. 1931; *IT*, 16 Nov. 1931.
44. UC/OHA, 5 Dec. 1990.
45. *CE*, 13 Oct. 1936; *II*, 12 Oct. 1936.
46. The courses were held in mid-June, 1938 and 1939, and the proceedings and debates were well covered in *CE* and other papers.
47. *II*, 11 Dec. 1940.
48. *CE*, 18 Mar. 1935.
49. *II*, 14 May 1936; also *IP*, 14 May 1936, *CE*, 15 May 1936.
50. *IP*, 11 Jan. 1940.
51. *CE*, 18 Oct. 1927.
52. *CE*, 27 July 1931.
53. *CE*, 8 Mar. 1943. MacConaill, an enthusiastic member of the FCA (local defence force), was given to wearing his academic garb over his officer's uniform.
54. *IT*, 3 Apr. 1943.
55. *CE*, 16 Dec. 1944.
56. *CE*, 25 Jan. 1943. Sperrin-Johnson's exotic reputation was guaranteed by his residence in Blackrock Castle.
57. *CE*, 1 Nov. 1945. Ó Séaghdha also debated the history of the Irish dance with colleagues Fleischmann and R.A. Breatnach (professor of Irish, 1945–81): see *JCHAS*, LXl (1956) 58–65.
58. *CE*, 6 Dec. 1926. The writer recalls a remark made to him in the early 1970s by President McCarthy to the effect that the dairy science people still constituted an extramural ghetto. There was also, in earlier decades, a general college attitude of snobbishness towards the 'cowpunchers'. The dairy science building was seen as peripheral, and this compounded the ghetto image.
59. Prof. T. Wibberley had held a privately endowed (by Mr Howard Harrington), £500 per annum chair of agriculture at UCC, 1920–22: for appointment, see GBM, 9 Oct. 1919; *CE*, 11 Oct. 1919.

60. *CE*, 30 Dec. 1926. For the complicated background to the establishment of the dairy science faculty, see *O'Rahilly*, vol. I, pp. 109–11.

61. GBM 4 Mar. 1927; *CE*, 2 July 1927. The posts were widely advertised in April–May 1927 in professional journals in Britain, USA, Europe and South Africa: see Ledger of Advertisement Cuttings, Finance Office, UC Archives.

62. *II*, 18 July 1927.

63. *IT*, 29 Dec. 1927.

64. *CE*, 23 June 1928.

65. *CE* and *IT*, 21 July 1928.

66. GBM 15 Oct. 1926.

67. *CE*, 23 June 1928, letter from Minister Hogan to Dick Anthony TD; Vote, Universities and Colleges, Parliamentary Debates Dáil Éireann (hereinafter *DÉ*), vol. XXVI, cols. 1776–96, 8 Nov. 1928, where Hogan referred to the 'handsome building'.

68. *CE*, 29 Apr. 1929.

69. *CE*, 5 Dec. 1928.

70. *CE*, 10 May 1930.

71. *CE*, 17 May 1930.

72. *IP*, 8 Dec. 1931.

73. *IT*, 11 Jan. 1932.

74. *IT*, 28 Sept. 1929.

75. *DÉ*, vol. XXVI, col. 1788, 8 Nov. 1928. See remarks of chairman, South Tipperary County Council, in 1911 when he ridiculed the notion of an agricultural faculty at a university, quoting an English agriculturalist to the effect that 'an academic or literary environment tends to spoil a student for agricultural life': *CE*, 2 July 1911. A similar sentiment was expressed by 'Husbandman' in a letter, *CE*, 10 Dec. 1918.

76. *O'Rahilly*, vol. I, pp. 111–19, summarises the dispute, and also includes, by way of appendices, O'Rahilly's various statements on the matter (pp. 266–327). My account here is indebted to Gaughan. Also see National Archives file, S7172A.

77. GBM, 3 June 1927.

78. Edward MacLysaght, *Changing Times: Ireland since 1898* (Gerrards Cross, 1978), p. 153, 9 Oct. 1929.

79. *IP*, 22 Mar. 1935.

80. GBM, 31 Jan. 1936.

81. *CE*, 21 Apr. 1936.

82. See *CE*, 16 Sept. 1935; *II*, 13 Sept. 1935; *The Times*, *IT*, 10 Dec. 1935; *IP*, 14 Dec. 1935.

83. *CE*, *IP*, 10 Jan. 1936.

84. *IT*, *EE*, 17 Apr. 1936.

85. See UC/OHA, Declan McSweeney, 4 Feb. 1991, G.T. Pyne, 28 Nov. 1990. It was suggested to a newly appointed junior lecturer by a usually mild-mannered and tolerant colleague that he should not accept an invitation to play bridge in the 'enemy's house'!

86. Maurice Harmon, 'The Chair at UCC', *The Cork Review 1991*, ed. Seán Dunne.

87. *gliogar*, 'an addled egg' (Dineen's Irish-English Dictionary): colloquially, one who fails to produce despite careful incubation.

88. Seán Ó Faoláin, *Vive Moi!* (London, 1965), pp. 257–61.

89. As well as Ó Faoláin's own account, see the articles by Maurice Harmon and Dermot Keogh in *The Cork Review 1991*; and Maurice Harmon, *Seán Ó Faoláin* (London, 1994), pp. 90–95.

90. Dermot Keogh, 'Democracy Gone Dotty', *The Cork Review 1991*.

91. Harmon, 'The Chair'.

92. Aloys Fleischmann, 'Seán Ó Faoláin: A Personal Memoir', *The Cork Review 1991*, pp. 92–4.

93. Ó Faoláin, *Vive Moi!*, p. 261.

94. Keogh, 'Democracy'.

95.   In September 1926, when O'Rahilly and Ó Faoláin were both passengers on a liner to the US: Ó Faoláin, *Vive Moi!*, p. 209; Harmon, *Ó Faoláin*, p. 73.

96.   Ó Faoláin, *Vive Moi!*, pp. 257–8, 261; Harmon, *Ó Faoláin*, p. 95. See also *O'Rahilly*, vol. I, pp. 104–6.

97.   Maume, *Life that is Exile*, pp. 118–20.

98.   Harmon, 'The Chair'.

99.   Fleischmann, 'Ó Faoláin', p. 93; Harmon, *Ó Faoláin*, pp. 161–2.

100. Harmon, *Ó Faoláin*, p. 49.

101. Ó Faoláin, *Vive Moi!*, chapter 9, 'College Days'.

102. ibid., p. 127.

103. ibid., p. 131.

104. ibid., p. 138.

105. ibid., pp. 128–9. 'Feathery Ellen' was Elizabeth M. O'Sullivan, professor of education, 1910–35.

106. Harmon, *Ó Faoláin*, p. 49.

107. Ó Faoláin, *Vive Moi!*, p. 129.

108. ibid., pp. 129–31.

109. ibid., p. 127. This is a distorted version of what Windle said: see p. 207.

110. UC/Fleischmann Papers: Fleischmann to President M.D. McCarthy, 22 Dec. 1968 and 2 Jan. 1969. However, Ó Faoláin gave a lecture in the college in October 1957 (see Harmon, *Ó Faoláin*, p. 213).

111. UC/Fleischmann Papers: Fleischmann to Ó Faoláin, 27 Dec. 1948.

112. UC/Fleischmann Papers: Ó Faoláin to Fleischmann, n.d. but Jan. 1949. Tadhg Ó Donnchadha (Tórna) was professor of Irish, and his brother Éamon lectured in modern Irish. See also Harmon, *Ó Faoláin*, p. 48. Hubert Treston was professor of ancient classics, and William (Bill) Porter was the popular, learned and amiably eccentric lecturer in the same department. Mary Ryan was professor of romance languages.

113. See Maume, *Life that is Exile*, pp. 21ff. For a student recollection of Corkery, see Tom McElligott, *Six o'clock all over Cork* (Dublin, 1992), pp. 80–81.

114. This point was made by Kathleen O'Flaherty in her contribution to the oral history project: UC/OHA, 28 Nov. 1990.

115. Lip service, at least, was widely paid to the integralist ideal. Thus the Cork branch of the Irish Guild of SS Cosmas and Damian, meeting in the CYMS Hall, was unanimous in its wish to integrate Catholicism with professional practice: *CE*, 8 Nov. 1935.

116. Each year, the newspaper photographs showed a strong and prominent college contingent.

117. *CE*, 10 July 1929. The accompanying photographs are of particular interest.

118. *CE*, 8 July 1929.

119. *II*, 11 July 1932.

120. *CE*, 17 July 1930; *II*, 18 July 1930.

121. *CE*, 20 Oct 1925. Fr Ryan who later became archbishop of Trinidad was a member of a well-known Cork business and academic family. His sister was Mary Ryan, professor of romance languages, 1910–38, who, as has been mentioned already, was the first woman professor in the UK.

122. *CE*, 19 Oct. 1926.

123. *CE*, 18 Oct. 1927.

124. Professor Pádraig Ó Riain (early and medieval Irish, 1973–). See ch. 2, n.9.

125. See various speeches in 1849–50, for example, Sir Robert Kane's address on opening day, p. 41.

126. *CE*, 5 June 1934.

127. See H. Glavin, 'A Half-Century of Memories at UCC', *UCCR*, no. 43, 1968, pp. 53–4; Larry O' Leary, 'A Royal Burial at UCC', *UCCR*, no. 49, 1974, pp. 68–80; Ralph Sutton, 'Significant Details of the College Buildings', *CUR*, no. 12, Easter 1948, p. 25.

128. *CE*, 1 July 1931.
129. *CE*, 29 June 1931.
130. *CE*, 20 Nov., *II*, 21 Nov. 1931.
131. *CE*, 15 Feb. 1939.
132. *CE*, 23 Feb. 1939.
133. *CE*, 18 Feb. 1939.
134. *CE*, 27 Mar. 1943.
135. The 'Philosoph' was the oldest and, as now, the premier student debating society. It appears that Professor George F. Savage Armstrong (history and English literature, 1871–1905) named it the University Philosophical Society and that Alfred O'Rahilly, who took a paternally proprietorial interest in its activities, was responsible for calling it the Literary and Philosophical Society: see *CE*, 18 June 1936. It was patronised (and monitored?) by prominent staff members, and attracted outstanding speakers from the city and province, and from much further afield.
136. See the edifying scenes at the close of the 1935 men's Lenten retreat, and the remarks of Rev. Ed. P. Treacy CSSR: 'in no university in the world could there be found a greater demonstration of Catholic fervour and love of God': *CE*, 4 Mar. 1935.
137. *CE*, 23 Nov. 1926.
138. UC/OHA, Victor and Margaret J. O'Connor Constant, 4 Mar. 1991.
139. ibid.; UC/OHA, B.J. Murphy, 15 Jan. 1991.
140. See below, p. 248.
141. *CE*, 11 June 1924.
142. *Morning Post*, 7 Jan. 1928.
143. *CE*, 22 Oct. 1926. See Cork County Board GAA response to Renouf's praise of rugby, *CE*, 29 Oct. 1925.
144. See 'Paaks' Coffey in *UCCR*, no. 42, 1967, p. 28.
145. University notes, *CE*, 31 Nov. 1931.
146. UC/OHA, Seán Teegan, 30 Apr. 1991.
147. *Irish Statesman*, 3 Apr. 1926. Also see *The Tablet*, 3 Apr. 1926.
148. Letter to editor, *II*, 13 Nov. 1940.
149. *EE*, 23 Dec. 1935.
150. *CE*, 11 Jan. 1939.
151. *CE*, 24 May 1939.
152. UC/OHA, Victor and Margaret J. O'Connor Constant, 24 May 1991; Seán Teegan, 30 Apr. 1991. The adventurer supreme in such episodes was 'Joey' Kerrigan, mountaineer and potholer *extraordinaire*, and sometime owner of a popular college second-hand bookshop in Washington Street. Another form of student prankishness was running 'joke' candidates for the Corporation: see indignant reference by Labour TD J. Hurley in Dáil debate, *CE*, 6 Dec. 1939.
153. *CE*, 11, 16 May 1931.
154. UC/OHA, Larry O'Leary, 6 Dec. 1990.
155. *CE*, 29 Apr. 1943.
156. *CE*, 18, 22 Apr. 1932.
157. For the rags of the Merriman period, frequently described in detail, with illustrations, see (in addition to newspaper references above) *EE*, 8, 10 May 1929; *Cork Weekly Examiner*, 18 May 1929; *EE*, 23, 27, 28 Apr. 1932; *IP*, 25 Apr., 19 May 1932; *CE*, 3 and (editorial) 4 May 1933; *CE*, 8, 12, 15 May 1933; *CE*, 30 Apr. 1934; *CE*, 6 May 1935; *CE*, 4 May 1936; *IP*, 3, 4 May 1936; *Sunday Independent*, 20 Mar. 1938. Also see UC/OHA, Larry O'Leary, Victor and Margaret J. O'Connor Constant, Seán Teegan.
158. *CE*, *II*, 8 May 1928.
159. *Manchester Guardian*, 22 Nov. 1928.
160. *CE*, 30 Dec. 1929.

161. *CE*, 8 Nov. 1930. The O'Sullivan Beare picture dominated the portrait wall for decades. Its presentation to the college in 1914 was seen as a significant occasion: *CE, CC, FP*, 22 Jan. 1914; *UCC Official Gazette*, Mar. 1914, pp. 93–4; D. Gwynn, 'The Donal O'Sullivan Beare Portrait', *CUR*, no. 20, Christmas 1950, pp. 32–6. Where is it now?

162. *CE*, 20 July 1931.

163. *CE*, 1 Nov. 1933.

164. *CE*, 3 Nov. 1937; see report *IT*, 3 Nov. 1937.

165. *IP*, 9 Feb. 1939.

166. *CE*, 1 Nov. 1943; *II, IP*, 5 Nov. 1943.

167. UC/OHA, Aloys Fleischmann, 5 Dec. 1990.

168. *CE*, 20 July 1945.

169. *CE*, 17 Jan. 1945.

170. *CE, IT*, 12 Dec. 1934.

171. On one such occasion (*CE*, 9 Dec. 1931) the national anthem was followed by the 'College Yell', presumably the rugby chant, Ta-Rax-Rum. See also *CE*, 9 Dec. 1930 and 6 Dec. 1932.

172. *CE*, 22 Feb. 1930.

173. *CE*, 9, 10, 13, 14, 18 Nov. 1933.

174. *CE*, 13 July 1937, 8 Feb., 6 Mar. 1939.

175. *CE*, 5 Dec. 1941.

176. *CE*, 3 May 1934.

177. *CE*, 1 Sept. 1934. See Maurice Manning, *The Blueshirts* (Dublin 1970) pp. 147ff.

178. *CE*, 3 Oct. 1934, 5 Jan. 1935.

179. *Daily Express*, 31 Jan. 1939; *CE*, 3 Feb. 1939.

180. The elected ruling council of students has had various names from time to time – the Guild Council (abbreviation), the SRC (Students' Representative Council), and the Students Union. There has also been a bewildering succession of student constitutions.

181. *CE*, 18 Feb. 1939.

182. *CE*, 4, 6 Feb. 1939; *IP*, 7, 9 Feb. 1939.

183. *CE*, 6, 8 Feb. 1939.

184. *CE*, 11, 13 Mar. 1939; also see *IP*, 30 Mar. 1939.

185. *CE*, 4 Feb. 1939.

186. *CE*, 6 Feb. 1939.

187. UC/OHA, Aloys Fleischmann, 22 May 1991.

188. *CE*, 21 Sept. 1936.

189. *CE*, 11, 18, 23 Nov. 1937.

190. *CE*, 25 Sept. 1936.

191. *CE, EE*, mid-Oct. 1936.

192. *CE*, 29 Apr. 1939.

193. In an argument about the milling industry, Patrick Bourke, denigrated by O'Rahilly as a Rank (flour company) mouthpiece, *IP*, 29 Mar. 1932, resentfully retorted that the registrar was unfairly pulling intellectual and educational weight and rank on one who had to leave school early because of poverty. Similarly, in a dispute over a Cork Fever Hospital appointment, O'Rahilly was accused of displaying snobbery towards working-class members of the committee, the kind of people who 'employ and handsomely award professors'. *CE*, 6 Nov. 1929.

194. Pseudonym used by O'Rahilly in his *Standard* articles.

195. *CE*, 4 Oct. 1926.

196. See, e.g., *II*, 20 May 1922; *CE*, 29 May 1922; *Irish School Weekly*, 8 May 1926; *CE*, 5 Aug. 1926; *CE*, 10 July 1929.

197. *CE*, 18 Oct. 1927.

198. *II*, 22 Feb. 1935.

199. *CE*, 3 June 1935.
200. *CE*, 2 Jan. 1930: see also Coiste Gnótha criticism, *CE*, *II*, 15 July 1931.
201. *CE*, *IP*, 7 Sept. 1932.
202. S 018/0001/25. This file has much material on proposals to teach through Irish at UCC. Blythe was advised (28 Aug. 1925) that Cork was afraid it would lose 'out students, etc.' to Galway.
203. GBM, 1 Mar. 1935; UC/OHA, Gerald Pyne, 28 Nov. 1990.
204. Report of the committee appointed by the Academic Council May 1943 to consider what steps may be taken by the college [UCD] in the interests of the Irish language: UCD Archives, Blythe Papers, P24/998.
205. See contemporary newspaper reports and July 1924 prospectus in Department of Education files.
206. The Gaeltacht scholarships – granted, in practice, to all reasonably serious applicants – were held in Ring, Co. Waterford in O'Rahilly's day (see a glowing account of their success in *CUR*, no. 2, Christmas 1944, pp. 4–5), and subsequently in west Kerry.
207. Subsequently professor of the history of modern Irish literature (1950–66). He was warden of the Honan Hostel in the 1950s and was the husband of writer Eilís Dillon, great-grand-daughter of President W.K. Sullivan: see her 'In the Honan Hostel', *The Cork Anthology*, ed. Seán Dunne (Cork 1993). Writing in *CUR*, no. 4, Summer 1945 ('Nótaí Gaedhilge'), p. 19, Ó Cuilleanáin pessimistically speculates whether the poor health of Irish in the college is not due to the 'two camps' which never mixed. Eilís Dillon is also the author of *Death in the Quadrangle* (London, 1956), an academic whodunnit, which some see as having a disguised UCC setting. It shows Dillon to have had a jaundiced view of professors, even though (or perhaps because) she married two in succession.
208. Ó Cuilleanáin to Merriman, 6 July 1936, Ó Cuilleanáin Correspondence, Special Collections, UCC.
209. Ó Cuilleanáin to Máire Nic Shuibhne, 27 June 1936.
210. Ó Cuilleanáin to (not named), 26 June 1936.
211. ibid.

Chapter 9

1. *CE*, 13 June 1927.
2. *CE*, 25 Oct. 1927.
3. *CE*, 17 Dec. 1928.
4. *CE*, 9 Feb. 1926.
5. *CE*, 30 June 1926.
6. *CE*, 6 Oct. 1928.
7. *CE*, 21 Feb. 1928. The demolition was in connection with the new entrance, presumably: see pp. 263ff.
8. *CE*, 14 Oct. 1925.
9. *CE*, 15, 16, 17, 19 Oct. 1925; *II*, 15 Oct. 1925.
10. *CE*, 15 Oct. 1925.
11. Letter to editor, *Irish Statesman*, 7 Nov. 1925.
12. Directed around the college (including the restaurant of the student's club for light refreshments) by stewards with flashlamps: *CE*, 13 Oct. 1926.
13. *CE*, 13, 14, 15 Oct. 1926.
14. *CE*, 14 Oct. 1926.
15. *CE*, 13 Oct. 1926.
16. An earlier example of college service was the report from Professors Isaac Swain (geology and geography) and H.N. Walsh (civil engineering, 1921–57) on the possibility of an urban water supply 'from the gravels in the Lee Valley near the present waterworks'. This prompted Cllr Barry Egan to observe that the University College was 'at last taking its rightful place in works of civic importance': *CE*, 7 May 1923.

17. *CE*, 14 Oct. 1926.

18. *EE*, 12 Oct. 1927. Merriman again held forth on college problems when welcoming visitors to the 1928 conversazione: see *CE*, 11 Oct. 1928; *IT*, 15 Oct. 1928.

19. NUI graduates' representatives sat in the Dáil under the Free State constitution: thereafter (Bunreacht na hÉireann, 1937) they were translated to the Seanad.

20. *CE*, 14 Oct. 1927.

21. e.g., *IP*, 2 Dec. 1931, 29 Mar. 1933; *IT*, 15 July 1937; *CE*, 7 Oct. 1946.

22. *CE*, 5 Nov. 1926. See also *CE*, 23 Oct. 1927, where a leading article, 'Universities and the Public', suggested the public did not appreciate the amenities offered by UCC – for example, access to the botanical garden, plant houses and the natural history museum where conducted tours were available. (Extensive finance offices now occupy the former museum space in the North Wing.)

23. President Merriman, as reported *CE*, 14 Oct. 1926.

24. Merriman, *CE*, 11 Oct. 1928.

25. *CE*, 20 May 1924: see also *CE*, 30 Mar. 1926, 8 June 1926, 14 Apr. 1927, 2, 5 Apr. 1938, 24 Jul. 1939, 17 Oct. 1944. O'Rahilly (14 Apr. 1938) robustly attacked the proposition that the NUI should facilitate extern students of London University, and condemned the alleged irreligious ethos of that institution.

26. *CE*, 15 Feb. 1933.

27. e.g., a report of a specialised archaeological paper by Rev. Patrick Power (professor of archaeology, 1915–32).

28. *CE*, 9 July 1925, 4 Mar. 1933, 7, 8 Apr. 1933.

29. e.g., *CE*, 20 Dec. 1929, 7 Feb. 1930.

30. e.g., Professor H.N. Walsh on the Shannon scheme, *CE*, 2 May 1924.

31. Reporting in precise detail, for example, how President Merriman broke his leg: *IP*, 11 Feb. 1935.

32. Information from Mr Bill Nolan who has researched this topic.

33. See *CE*, 5 Nov. 1926, 'Philosoph' inaugural report. A character in Compton MacKenzie's novel *Sinister Street* (1913) says 'going to Oxford comes against you in the City, you know. Waste of time, really.'

34. *CC*, 7 July 1921; *CE*, 4 Dec. 1933.

35. *Times Educational Supplement*, 31 Dec. 1921.

36. *CE*, 24 May 1924.

37. *CE*, 28 May 1928.

38. *CE*, 5 June 1926, 26 Nov. 1926. For Busteed, see obituary by Paschal Larkin in *UCCR*, no. 40, 1965; UC/OHA, David O'Mahony, 24 Jan. 1991. In a letter to Merriman, 4 Jan. 1928, (in writer's possession), Busteed referred to the 'real Western Front conditions' in his office – 'overcoats, gloves and leg wrappings on all day'. He was a successful investor of college funds, and he was largely instrumental in healing the rift in the Irish trade union movement in 1959. He was famous, *inter alia*, for walking heroic distances and for lecturing to his classes at unpredictably infrequent intervals. I am indebted to Professor David O'Mahony, Busteed's successor, for sharing his reminiscences with me.

39. *CE*, 18 June 1940.

40. *CE*, 12 Sept. 1939.

41. *CE*, 28 May 1940.

42. *CE*, 13 July 1943.

43. *CE*, 19 July 1944.

44. See Mícheál W. Ó Murchú, 'Alfred O'Rahilly and the Provision of Adult Education at UCC', and list of references therein, in Denis O'Sullivan, ed., *Social Commitment and Adult Education* (Cork, 1989), pp. 25–39; Gaughan, *O'Rahilly*, vol. 1, pp. 93–102. The department of adult and continuing education, UCC, has extensive files going back to the

beginning of the development. Also of interest is Con Murphy (UCC adult education organiser in the early 1950s and life-long friend of O'Rahilly's) UC/OHA, 1 Feb. 1991.

45. *University Extension Lectures*, UCC 1910.
46. See *CE*, 18 Nov. 1930, 31 Jan. 1931; letter to editor, 3 Feb. 1931.
47. *CE*, 23 Apr. 1930.
48. *CE*, 18 Feb. 1931, 22 Oct. 1938, 19 Apr. 1932. The lectures were reported in detail. Attendances were generally large: *CE*, 4 Dec. 1931; *Catholic Herald*, 4 Dec. 1936.
49. *CE*, 25 Oct. 1938.
50. *CE*, 17 Jan. 1931.
51. *CE*, 18, 20 June 1931.
52. *CE*, 17 Oct. 1931.
53. *CE*, letter to editor, 15 May 1926; editorial, 17 May 1926; 18, 22 May 1926.
54. *CE*, 20 May 1926.
55. *CE*, 31 July 1926.
56. *CE*, 3 Aug. 1931; *IT*, 24 July 1931.
57. *CE*, 23 Oct. 1931.
58. *IT*, 26 Oct. 1931, 16 Nov. 1931; *CE*, 15 May 1935.
59. *CE, IP*, 19 Nov. 1935.
60. *II, IP*, 9 Apr. 1937.
61. *CE*, 30 Mar. 1939.
62. *CE*, 5 June 1941.
63. *CE*, 7 Dec. 1943.
64. *CE*, 4, 5 June 1943.
65. *CE*, 1 Sept. 1943.
66. *CE*, 5 Apr. 1945.
67. *CE, II*, 23 Apr. 1945.
68. *CE*, 19 Feb. 1945.
69. *CE*, 28 Jan. 1946 (picture); O'Rahilly letter to editor, 29 Jan. 1946.
70. *CE*, 18 Jan. 1947.
71. *CE*, 20 Jan. 1947.
72. At present (1995) the writer has the honour of chairing that committee.
73. *CC*, 5 Feb. 1859; *Southern Reporter*, 16 Feb. 1859.
74. *CE*, 27 Oct. 1928.
75. Letter to editor, *CE*, 30 Oct. 1928.
76. *CE*, 31 Oct. 1928.
77. *CE*, 5 Nov. 1928.
78. *CE*, 19 Nov. 1928; *IT*, 17 Nov. 1928.
79. *CE*, 21 Dec. 1928.
80. *CE*, 7 Mar. 1929.
81. *CE, II*, 31 Oct. 1929.
82. *Cork Weekly Examiner*, 4 Jan. 1930.
83. *CE*, 2 Apr. 1940; *EE*, 24 Feb. 1941.
84. *CE*, 8, 27 Dec. 1939, 30 Oct. 1939, 31 Oct. 1940.
85. *CE*, 8 Nov. 1937. Were A.J. Beckett and Derry Beckett (of the victorious Cork 1945 All-Ireland football team) one and the same?
86. Letter to editor, *CE*, 13 Feb. 1926; *Football Sports Weekly*, 20 Feb. 1926.
87. *CE*, 21 Oct. 1929.
88. See report on Cork County GAA convention, *CE*, 28 Jan. 1929. At that convention, the UCC delegates supported – forty years too early! – the deletion of the ban on 'foreign' games. Also see *CE*, 17, 21 Oct. 1929; *CE*, 7 Feb. 1930 (university notes). When O'Rahilly was appointed president, the UCC delegate to the Cork County Board GAA rejoiced that the Gaelic flag would now be raised aloft: *CE*, 2 Feb. 1944.

89.   *II*, 2 June 1937. Also see *CE*, 2 Jan. 1930 (meeting of Cork County Executive, Gaelic League).
90.   *IT*, 1 Apr. 1929.
91.   *II*, 14 Oct. 1936.
92.   *CE*, 16 Oct. 1936.
93.   *CE*, 29 Oct. 1928.
94.   *CE*, 18 Apr. 1932.
95.   e.g., corporation meeting, *CE*, 22 Feb. 1923.
96.   Decades later, similar foundation problems in this area caused the transfer of the new food science building to its present site west of the Gaol Walk.
97.   *CE*, 11 Oct. 1928. The dairy science foundation stone had been laid two months before.
98.   *CE*, 18 Nov. 1927.
99.   *CE*, 21 Oct. 1929.
100. *CE*, 25 Oct. 1929, 13 Nov. 1929 (letters to editor).
101. *CE*, 15 Nov. 1929.
102. *CE*, 17 July 1930; *II*, 18 July 1930.
103. According to *The Lancet*, 29 Aug. 1942, the war had no serious effect on the NUI colleges.
104. One of these, just then ready to take off on a studentship, was Kathleen O'Flaherty, subsequently lecturer in the French department (professor, 1970–81): see her contribution to UC/OHA, 28 Nov. 1990.
105. *CE*, 1 Jan. 1940.
106. *CE*, 29 Apr. 1943.
107. *CE*, 9 Apr. 1940.
108. *CE*, 17 Oct. 1940.
109. UC/OHA, Seán Teegan, 30 Apr. 1991.
110. UC/OHA, John Mullane, 17 Dec. 1990; Larry O'Leary, 6 Dec. 1990.
111. Dillon, 'In the Honan Hostel', p. 111. See above, ch. 8, n. 207. The present writer was a hostel resident, 1945–48, and well recalls the austere cuisine of the immediate post-war years.
112. *CE*, 8 Jan. 1941. See leader of same issue, and subsequent (10 Jan. 1941) letter.
113. *CE*, 24. Apr. 1941.
114. *IP*, 26 May 1941. A leader (*IP*, 20 Jan. 1942) suggested greater milk consumption, quoting Reilly.
115. *IT*, 25 Oct. 1941.
116. *II*, 26 Feb. 1940.
117. *CE*, 16 Nov. 1940.
118. *CE*, 25 Nov. 1940.
119. *CE*, 5 Dec. 1941.
120. *CE*, 13 Mar. 1944.
121. *SI*, 21 Jan. 1945.
122. *CE*, 19 June 1944; *II*, 20 June 1944.
123. *CE*, *IP*, 7 Nov. 1945.
124. Dr Desmond Reilly's account of life at Notre Dame University (*CUR*, Easter 1947) had an attractive novelty at that time.
125. *EE*, 22 Apr. 1947.

Chapter 10

1.   M.D. McCarthy, 'Some University Statistics', *CUR,* no. 4, Summer 1945, p. 12. The picture had changed somewhat by 1959–60 when there were 431 Cork city students and a further 234 from within thirty miles radius out of a total of 1,304: *PR*, 1959–60.

   McCarthy's wide-ranging *CUR* article, setting contemporary statistics in historical perspective, is of exceptional interest. It was partly intended to bolster O'Rahilly's argument (*CUR*, same issue) that the Waterford and Limerick agitations for a university were unsustainable.

2. The proportion of medical students decreased from 35% of the student body in 1943–44 (*CUR*, no.1, Summer 1944, p. 7) to 12% in 1959–60 (*PR*, 1959–60).

3. *CUR*, no. 6, Easter 1946, pp. 10–11.

4. 'University' was the usual term outside the Cork city area, the institution was generally called 'the college' in the city itself, and urban school pupils preferred the casual abbreviation, 'the uni'.

5. The minority of non-Cork students tended to come from counties Waterford (traditionally orientated towards UCC) Limerick and South Tipperary rather than from Kerry and Clare.

6. *Ireland since the Famine* (London, 1971), p. 551.

7. J.H. Newman, *The Idea of A University*, ed. I.T. Ker (Oxford, 1976), p. 130. Eilís Dillon's memoir 'In the Honan Hostel' vividly evokes the place and the time.

8. Letter to P.J. Connolly SJ, quoted *O'Rahilly*, vol. I, p. 152.

9. The man's multifaceted career has been comprehensively covered by J. Anthony Gaughan in four volumes: *Alfred O'Rahilly, I Academic* (Dublin, 1986); *II, Public Figure* (Dublin, 1989) *III, Part 1, Controversialist* (Dublin, 1992); *III Part 2 Controversialist* (Dublin, 1993). While Fr Gaughan tends to diagnose O'Rahilly's warts as benign, his work is exhaustive and admirably lucid, and I am greatly indebted to it. Various personal recollections and assessments of O'Rahilly are to be found in the College Oral History Archives (UC/OHA).

10. Alfred O'Rahilly to Michael Tierney, 20 October 1943, Tierney Papers, UCD, LA 30/104; see also *O'Rahilly*, vol. I, pp. 123–4.

11. *O'Rahilly*, vol. I, pp. 149–50.

12. O'Rahilly to Cormac Ó Cuilleanáin, 25 January 1939, Ó Cuilleanáin Correspondence, Special Collections, UCC.

13. According to Eilís Dillon, 'In the Honan Hostel', p. 112, the 'convent' description was by a newly appointed Dubliner to the UCC science faculty, but it has also been attributed to an intrigued extern examiner. See also *O'Rahilly*, vol. I, p. 202.

14. C.D. Ahearne, *Professor O'Rahilly's Pig* (Cork 1941), p. 14. This is a pamphlet of 14 pp., a copy of which is in UCC.

15. *O'Rahilly*, vol. I, p. 200.

16. *The Standard*, 5 November 1943.

17. 1959. Ó Cadhlaigh's daughter, Mrs Essie O'Donoghue, kindly permitted me to consult her father's manuscript.

18. Dillon, 'In the Honan Hostel' pp. 112–13.

19. *O'Rahilly*, vol. I, p. 54.

20. On the 'epistle' side. He is said to have resented the fact that the corresponding chair across the aisle on the more liturgically important 'gospel' side was by tradition assigned to the warden of the Honan Hostel.

21. UC/OHA, Aloys Fleischmann, 5 Dec. 1990.

22. *O'Rahilly*, vol. I, p. 104.

23. George Meenan, *George O'Brien: A Biographical Memoir* (Dublin, 1980), p. 138.

24. See UC/OHA, Kathleen O'Flaherty, 28 Nov. 1990. Other reliable information on this aspect has been conveyed to the writer.

25. Bishop Daniel Cohalan caustically referred to 'the Corporation and their lay theologian' when they disagreed with his excommunication of the IRA in December 1920, because of their ambushes. Cohalan's gibe reflected clerical professional jealousy. O'Rahilly, protesting at the 'nickname', said it had first been used by 'the Protestant *Cork Consititution*'. *O'Rahilly*, vol. II, pp. 91–2.

26. *O'Rahilly*, vol. I, p. 102; UC/OHA, Aloys Fleischmann, 5 Dec. 1990, Seán Teegan, 6 May 1991.

27. Copy in writer's possession. This should be considered in the context of the times, e.g. the Modest Dress and Deportment Crusade (see *Catholic Times*, 6 Jan., 1928).

28. See Professor 'Paaks' Coffey's reminiscences, *UCCR*, no. 42, 1967, p. 60.

29. Bernard MacDonagh's mural, commissioned by O'Rahilly, still looks down on the dining students. The professors and students of fifty years ago served as models for some of the figures. See description of the new restaurant in *CUR*, no. 17, Christmas 1949, pp. 10–11.

30. During the 'Mother and Child Scheme' controversy in April-May 1951, O'Rahilly in his *Standard* articles berated *The Irish Times* and its 'hired humourist', 'professional jester', 'phraseological gunman', viz. Myles na Gopaleen. The latter responded in similar scurrilous (and moderately funny) vein, dubbing the UCC president a 'self-licensed demagogue' (*IT*, 2 May), referring to the 'labyrinth of intrigue and backstairs work' of university appointments (16 May) and dismissing 'this diminutive lyceum known as UCC' which cost the taxpayer £99,000 p.a. (23 May).

31. *O'Rahilly*, vol. I, p. 171.

32. In her Oral History Archives contribution (28 Nov. 1990), Professor Kathleen O'Flaherty has much of interest to say about O'Rahilly and his work for – and semi-proprietorial interest in – the CUP. She asserts that the library under his direction became the best university library in Ireland.

33. For the setting up of the student health service, see GBM, 23 Mar. 1946.

34. See above, pp. 255–6 and notes.

35. See his response at a civic luncheon, St Patrick's Day 1948, to the toast of 'the City': *CUR*, no. 10, Summer 1947, p. 7.

36. See the 'Chronicle' in any issue of the *CUR* from 1944.

37. Still in use in what is now the geography building. Before large lecture theatres became available in the science building and the Boole basement, the accessible 'dairy science' was the popular venue for public and 'showpiece' lectures and debates.

38. Conferring address, reported *CUR*, no. 11, Christmas 1947, p. 23.

39. *CUR*, no. 2, Christmas 1944, pp. 2–3. Towards the end of his presidency, O'Rahilly reminded Archbishop J.C. MacQuaid of Dublin (26 January 1954) that 'I have always sacrificed Cork interests (separate university for Cork) to what I believe to be the Catholic interest (Charter: protected autonomy)': see *O'Rahilly*, vol. III, Pt 2, p. 180.

40. *CUR*, no. 4, Summer 1945, pp. 2–3.

41. *CUR*. no. 1, Summer 1944, p. 3.

42. *CUR*, no. 5, Christmas 1945, p. 2.

43. As a student in the early 1930s, Gerald Y. Goldberg (contributor UC/OHA, 25 Jan. 1991) experienced only isolated instances of anti-Semitism. O'Rahilly (then registrar), though straightforward in his dealings with Goldberg, would not allow the dozen or so Jews to form their own students association.

44. The crucifixes, O'Rahilly could claim (tongue-in-cheek) were aesthetic rather than denominational in intent: see *The Standard*, 6 Dec. 1946.

45. Cessation of college activities on holy days had become increasingly inconvenient, particularly in the Trinity term. Resistance to their discontinuance was a trade union issue, and had little to do with religious sensibilities.

46. The point is convincingly well made by President Tadhg Ó Ciardha (UC/OHA, 5 Jan. 1991) and also by Mr and Mrs V. O'Connor-Constant (UC/OHA, 4 Mar. 1991).

47. Well into the 1960s, lay students also observed a quasi-voluntary segregation with women sitting behind the nuns who were in the front rows.

48. Fleischmann Papers, UCC.

49. Attributed to Professor John Busteed.

50. For the Cork Catholic intellectual, there was a statist, not to say a secular, whiff about Dublin *tout court*.

51. *CUR*, no. 14, Christmas 1948, pp. 32–3.

52. The writer so equipped himself, when selecting books as a prize, with some of the works of Jacques Maritain and Fulton Sheen.

53. *CUR*, no. 16, Summer 1949, p. 1. There was a Mindszenty scholarship, intended to support a Hungarian refugee student, but there was a disappointing response to appeals to fund it: UC/OHA, Con Murphy, 1 Feb. 1991 and subsequent dates.

54. See Rev. J. Good, 'Theology in UCC', *UCCR*, no. 46, 1971, pp. 12–17. Some support for Fr Good was mobilised among his UCC colleagues, and an ineffectual *démarche* made to Bishop Lucy. The writer was a member of that UCC delegation.

55. See Ronan Fanning, 'Economists and governments: Ireland, 1922–52', *Hermathena*, vol. CXXXV, Winter 1983, pp. 138–55. Professor John Busteed was the exception to this general observation and, by the same token, was regarded as something of a maverick by the gnomes of Finance, as Fanning reminds us.

56. See Appendix B.

57. Though he was linguistically skilled, according to Professor Kathleen O'Flaherty (UC/OHA, 28 Nov. 1990).

58. *CUR*, no. 6, Easter 1946, p. 2.

59. *CUR*, no. 15, Easter 1949, p. 2. Surprisingly for those days, this represented a non-Irish presence of over six per cent. The foreign students frequented the Philosoph, and a Gold Coast man, K.A. Sekyi, discoursed impressively on the Lee hydroelectric scheme: *II*, 25 Oct. 1948.

60. K. Michalski, 'The Polish Students at UCC', *CUR*, no. 8, Christmas 1946, p. 5. For the opening of the Polish Hostel ('Little Poland'), see *CE*, 21 Oct, and (leading article) 22 Oct. 1948; *II*, 26 Oct. 1948.

61. Gowns were discarded from the 1960s, only the occasional traditionalist among the staff now observing sartorial correctness at lectures and academic meetings.

62. References here are to *UCC Rules for Students*, October 1944. The letter of the rules remained substantially unchanged up to the early 1960s.

63. 31% in the 1940s (see *CUR* issues from no. 1, Summer 1944, onwards); about one-quarter in the late 1950s (*PR*, 1958–59, 1959–60).

64. 'How green is the Emerald Isle?', *The Quarryman*, 1963, p. 40.

65. *The Quarryman*, 1958, pp. 7–9.

66. Professor Teago died on 4 October 1964: see Obituary, *UCCR*, no. 40, 1965, pp. 53–4.

67. *CE*, 16 Dec. 1981.

68. See P. Coffey, 'The College and the Gaol', *CUR*, no. 7, Summer 1946, pp. 17–18.

69. See above pp. 102ff.

70. Correspondence 25 and 27 May 1908, CSORP 1908 11161.

71. D/T S13258A.

72. Was he, ever? He spent periods in 1921 in Collins (then Victoria) Barracks, Spike Island and Bere Island: see *O'Rahilly,* vol. II, pp. 106–27. College folklore has it that he marked examination scripts in the county gaol. In fact, this would have been in Victoria Barracks.

73. See O'Rahilly to editor, *CE*, 18 Nov. 1946.

74. In the late 1920s the dairy science building plan had been changed from brick to limestone, for this aesthetic reason: see above, p. 224.

75. *CE*, 18 Nov. 1946.

76. See J.R. Boyd-Barrett, architect, to President O'Rahilly, 25 Feb. 1946, S13258A.

77. UCC secretary, J. Hurley to Seán McCarthy, TD, 12 Mar. 1946, S13258A.

78. Mr McCarthy, rúnaí, to Taoiseach, 28 Apr. 1945, S13258A.

79. Their bodies were taken from Victoria Barracks to the county gaol for burial: the graves are in a portion of the former exercise yard.

80. Coffey, 'The College and the Gaol'; O'Rahilly, *CE*, 18 Nov. 1946; *EE*, 10 June 1946.

81. *CE*, 15 Nov. 1946.

82. *CE*, 18 Nov. 1946; *II*, 20 Nov. 1946.

83. *CE*, 15 Mar. 1947.

84.   There still remains a portion of the outside gaol wall at the north-western corner as well as a section of the boundary wall running down from the medical building to the western gate. On the front wall, to the west of the portico, are two plaques: the larger, executed in 1947 by Séamus Murphy and framed in bronze, commemorates the patriot dead of the 1919–23 period while a small marble plaque was erected in 1990 (in defiance of GB disapproval) and recalls the shooting of an IRA escaper in 1940.

      For the incorporation of the remainder (and larger portion) of the gaol site in the college grounds, see *UCCR*, no. 33, Easter 1958.

85.   S13258A. *The Irish Press* (9 July 1948) had an article on the monument and the Murphy plaque.

86.   Gwynn had a regular column, 'Now and Then', in *The Cork Examiner*, in which he frequently discussed college affairs in a fairly cosmetic manner. The column also included boringly extended obituary comments about which it was (not very originally) observed that they added a further dimension to the terrors of dying.

87.   1 Oct. 1954, Tierney Papers, UCD, LA 30/163.

88.   John J. McHenry, then professor of experimental physics and Atkins's successor as president.

89.   Cork solicitor, public figure, conservative nationalist in the Redmondite tradition, Sir Bertram Windle's son-in-law. See ch. 7, n. 18.

90.   Dillon to Fleischmann, 17 Oct. 1954, Fleischmann Papers, UCC.

91.   ibid. Dillon to Tierney, 17 Oct. 1954, Tierney Papers, UCD, LA 30/163.

92.   Dillon to Fleischmann, 4 Nov. 1954, Fleischmann Papers, UCC.

93.   Dillon to Tierney, 15 Nov. 1954, Tierney Papers, UCD, LA 30/163.

94.   McGilligan Papers, UCD, P 35/d 96, 97, 98; secretary, Department of Agriculture to president, UCC, 20 Mar. 1953, S15677A.

95.   Paine, *The Rights of Man* (Dublin, 1972 edn), p. 7.

96.   For the above, see: GBM, 18 Sept. 1954; secretary, Department of Agriculture to president, UCC, 20 Mar. 1953, S15677A; O'Rahilly memo, 13 July 1955, O'Rahilly statement, 15 July 1955; O'Rahilly letter to *II*, 21 July 1955; *II* report on institute, 20 July 1955; Minister (James Dillon) for Agriculture's reply to O'Rahilly, 27 July 1955; O'Rahilly's rejoinder, 4 Aug. 1955. (Copies of the above documents are in the writer's possession.) See also Connell Boyle and Patrick M. Quinlan, 'Agriculture and the University', *University Review*, vol. I, no. 2, Autumn 1954.

97.   Bishops to Taoiseach, 1 Oct. 1957, S16289, S13258; McGilligan Papers, UCD, P 35/d97.

98.   S16704A.

99.   Atkins to Minister for Agriculture, 1 May 1959, on importance of food technology, S16704A.

100.   *UCCR*, no. 34, Easter 1959, p. 34.

101.   See appointment of architect, GBM, 29 Nov. 1960. Also see GBM, 25 Oct. 1960.

102.   UC/OHA, 28 Nov. 1990.

Chapter 11

1.   F 087/0005/25: Joseph Brennan to Treasury, 14 Mar. 1922; A.P. Waterfield to secretary of Finance, 22 Mar. 1922. For Waterfield, see Ronan Fanning, *The Irish Department of Finance 1922–58* (Dublin, 1978).

2.   Fin. 1. 596/54, note initialled ADC, 7 Mar. 1923.

3.   F 087/0002/25.

4.   Mathew Conran, dean of science, and Annraoi Breathnach (H.N. Walsh), dean of engineering to finance minister, 15 Dec. 1925: F 087/0002/25.

5.   F 087/0002/25, F 087/0007/25.

6.   *DÉ*, vol. XVIII, cols. 369–70, 8 Feb. 1927. In this vote on universities and colleges the minister for finance, Ernest Blythe, also said the government had urged UCC and UCD to raise fees in order to increase revenue but gave the opposite advice to UCG because it should

encourage student intake as it was doing 'national work'. This kind of approach infuriated O'Rahilly: see S 018/0001/25.

7. See p. 254.

8. F 087/0002/25.

9. See debate in *DÉ*, vol. XLVI, cols. 1881–2038, 31 Mar. 1933.

10. McGilligan Papers, UCD, P 35 d/75.

11. However, Queen's College had been much more at the mercy of the government than was UCC. Dublin Castle's tight supervision of the Queen's Colleges, in particular the very real power to dismiss, or threaten to dismiss, fractious or negligent professors, was closely related to its control of the purse-strings. The Board of Works dealt with buildings, maintenance and repairs but it was the government which exercised the ultimate sanction of withholding or releasing funds. Salaries were the direct responsibility of the Treasury, through the Castle officials. The system was very different from the modern one of the block grant. The bursars operated under strict government supervision.

12. F 152/50/24.

13. For what follows see D/T S13258A.

14. Prices rocketed from 1914: see the 'Sauerbeck–*Statist* Price Indices, 1846–1966', Br. Mitchell, *British Historical Statistics* (Cambridge, 1988), p. 726. On the other hand, prices fell between the wars and the pound increased in value, which militated against the *béal bocht* approach.

15. F 68/1/34.

16. See GBM, 29 Mar. 1935, 14 Feb 1936 .

17. Downey to de Valera, 19 June 1940, S13258A.

18. Department of Finance to Department of Taoiseach, 10 July 1940, S13258A.

19. S13258A.

20. See ch. 7, n. 158.

21. See above, pp. 257–8. For subsequent difficulties, see *O'Rahilly*, vol. I, pp. 134–5.

22. A genial figure in the Men's Club. He was a great admirer of an tAthair Peadar Ó Laoghaire, whose driver he had been. He played the accordion at student *céilí* 'hops', and ceased playing any set only when the dancers applauded!

23. The president's house, where Merriman had been living was the northern half of the East Wing. The rather smaller registrar's house took up the remainder of the wing. O'Rahilly remained on here after becoming president and when he retired this, too, was converted into offices. According to Eilís Dillon, 'In the Honan Hostel', p. 110, 'he could not bear the thought of being succeeded by an inferior within the very walls of his house'.

24. The work of M.D. McCarthy, afterwards president: see ch. 10, n. 1.

25. This is an interesting observation from someone of O'Rahilly's quasi-ecclesiastical bent. He may have ruefully reflected that the money donated by the Cork industrialist, William O'Dwyer, for the building of Blackpool Church (colloquially dubbed 'O'Dwyer's fire escape') could have done a great deal for the college.

    T.A. Conroy in the library was also deploring the absence of a benefactor : 'When will a Bodley, a Marsh or a Carnegie knock on the doors of UCC?' (*CUR*, no. 4, Summer 1945, p. 58).

26. S14018A & B.

27. GBM, 22 Jan. 1946.

28. GBM, 22 Jan. 1947.

29. For what follows, see *O'Rahilly*, vol. I, pp. 135–7.

30. S13258B.

31. His residence was 6 Elderwood, College Road, across from the southern gate. A number of college staff members lived in the spacious Elderwood houses and in the adjoining Carrig Side terrace. The proximity gave them a special sense of identification with the college. This was especially true of the popular lecturer in civil engineering (afterwards – 1957–64 – associate

professor), 'Paaks' Coffey, who, wearing his hat (back on his head) as 'college engineer', and puffing at his cigarette, proprietorially inspected the college on his evening strolls. Most of these terraced houses are now college property, being used as departmental offices and seminar rooms.

32. UC/OHA, Francis Fahy, 26 Feb. 1991.
33. GBM, 12 Nov. 1959.
34. S13258A.
35. GBM, 27 Oct., 30 Nov. 1953.
36. GBM, 2 Apr., 18 June 1957, 24 Mar. 1958.
37. S14402B, copy in S13258B.
38. S16335.
39. Filed in McGilligan Papers, UCD, P 35 d/84. Government Publications Pr 5089. Also in S16289. For UCC's submissions, see pp. 53–72.
40. Downey to de Valera, 19 June 1940, S13258A.
41. *UCCR*, no. 35, Easter 1960, p. 30.

Chapter 12

1. UC/OHA, Eoghan Harris, 23 Apr. 1991.
2. UC/PO/254.
3. *Commission on Higher Education 1960–67* (Dublin, 1960–67), vol. I, pp. 35–7.
4. See GBM, 21 Jan. 1964.
5. Students' Representative Council.
6. As a young lecturer, the writer was one of the protagonists.
7. UC/OHA, Eoghan Harris, 23 Apr. 1991; letters exchanged between Aloys Fleischmann and CTM, 8, 19 May 1964, Fleischmann Papers, UCC.
8. Academic costume was obligatory from early QCC days, and Windle had insisted that men students should wear mortar boards as well.
9. UC/OHA, Declan McSweeney, 4 Feb. 1991.
10. In their heyday, the Capuchin students could be matutinally observed proceeding in crocodile from St Bonaventure's at Victoria Cross (now a hotel) to the college. Other religious were less regimented, and mingled a little more with students. All, however, ever-mindful of the virus of modernism, tended to keep to themselves.
11. A recent collection commemorates the period: *Jumping Off Shadows: Selected Contemporary Irish Poets*, ed. Greg Delanty and Nuala Ní Dhomhnaill (Cork, 1995).
12. Understandably resented by Ó Ciardha: UC/OHA, Tadhg Ó Ciardha, 21 May 1991. This is an exceptionally interesting deposition.
13. Professors Fleischmann, Pyne and Quinlan: UC/OHA, Aloys Fleischmann, 5 Dec. 1990.
14. UC/OHA, Mrs McCarthy (the president's widow), 23 Jan. 1991.
15. UC/OHA, Tadhg Ó Ciardha 21 May 1991.
16. To the writer.
17. Ó Faoláin, *Vive Moi!*, pp. 257–61.
18. UC/OHA, 5 Dec. 1990.
19. In letter to Nuala Ó Faoláin (copy to writer), 6 July 1992. See also his 'University Appointments', *University Review*, vol. 1, no.11 (n.d.).
20. UC/OHA, 5 Dec. 1990.
21. Curiously, part-time posts in law did not have a similar cachet, being seen as a distraction from serious professional practice, if not indeed as evidence of eccentricity: UC/OHA, Bryan Murphy, 15 Jan. 1991.
22. UC/OHA, 25 June 1991.
23. Merriman to Michael Tierney, 4 July 1933, Tierney Papers, UCD, LA 30/111.
24. Hogan to Tierney, 13 July 1933, Tierney Papers, UCD, LA 30/111.

25. See Professor R.A. Breatnach's objections to the arrangement: memo, GBM, 25 Jan. 1955.
26. UC/OHA, Bryan Murphy, 15 Jan. 1991.
27. See *PR*, 1971–72; *UCCR*, no. 48, 1973.
28. UC/OHA, 29 Jan. 1991. For the awarding of the contract, see above p. 296.
29. For his library role, see *O'Rahilly*, vol. I, pp. 85–91; UC/OHA, Kathleen O'Flaherty, 28 Nov. 1990.
30. UC/OHA, Tadhg Ó Ciardha, 21 May 1991.
31. UC/OHA, Rev. Peter Dempsey, 7 Dec. 1990.
32. For an assessment of his presidency, see J.P.T. (Professor John P. Teegan), *UCCR*, no. 53, 1978, pp. 11–17.
33. Dillon,'In the Honan Hostel'.
34. UC/OHA, Tadhg Ó Ciardha, 5 Feb. 1991.
35. UC/OHA, Tadhg Ó Ciardha, 29 Jan. 1991.
36. UC/OHA, Tadhg Ó Ciardha, 21 May 1991.
37. He was not, however, remotely as paternalistic as a professorial colleague who, when asked if he would take student views into account when planning courses, replied he would readily do so as soon as it was established that birds were knowledgeable about ornithology.
38. Memo, T. Raftery, 4 Mar. 1974, Item 16 Finance Committee Minutes. The Finance Committee and Governing Body minutes quoted in these and the following notes are in the Secretary's Office.
39. Finance Committee response to Raftery memo.
40. Memo, M.D. McCarthy, GBM, 2 July 1974.
41. GBM, 24 June 1975.
42. GBM, 21 Oct. 1975.
43. See description of development in *UCCR*, no. 51, 1976, pp. 5–14, and UCCR no. 55, 1980, pp. 19ff.
44. Finance Committee Minutes, 7 Apr. 1987.
45. GBM, 10, 28 Apr. 1987.
46. See press coverage, Mar.–Apr. 1987.
47. GBM, 28 Apr. 1987.
48. This lesson was learned. It was arranged (GB, May 1987) that henceforth the Finance Committee would inform the GB annually of the issues currently engaging its attention.
49. The Information Office had only just been established at his time. See below, p. 357.

Chapter 13

1. Statistics on funding, student numbers, etc. for the early 1990s are given in convenient form in the successive annual *President's Reports* (*PR*) from 1990–91 to 1993–94 (including *PR*, Nov. 1994), from which the statistical material and presidential quotations in this chapter are drawn.
2. However, the demise of the informative and substantial *Cork University/UCC Record* (1944–80) is regrettable.
3. Including a government-sponsored additional student intake. The figure of 8,519 represented an increase of 1,133 on 1990–91, the largest year-on-year increase ever experienced in the college.
4. See figures in *Annual Accounts for year ending 30 Sept. 1994* (UCC), p. 26.
5. Department of Agriculture files, AG 1 E1 2577/1926.
6. *CE*, 20 Nov. 1935.
7. 'Our Lady's Hospital Feasibility Study: Final Report', October 1994. Presented by Deloitte and Touche, Management Consultants to the Governing Body.
8. Orally conveyed by the minister for health to the president who reported to the Governing Body accordingly: see Special Governing Body Minutes July 1994.

9. Even from the mouths of babes . . . . a colleague's small daughter, on being asked where her daddy worked, replied: 'he doesn't work, he's up at UCC'.

10. See various NUI documents, 1991–94, on the future structure of the NUI.

11. *Education for a Changing World* (Dublin, 1992), pp. 203, 196.

12. *PR*, 1990–91.

13. UC/OHA, e.g. Tim Humphreys, 17 Jan. 1991; John Mullane, 17 Dec. 1990; Jimmy Murphy, 16 Jan. 1991; Larry O'Leary, 6 Dec. 1990; Jerry Scannell, 25 Jan. 1991; Tom Twohig, 13 Dec. 1990.

14. UC/OHA, W.D. O'Connell, 18 Jan. 1991.

15. A fourth lodge was Honan Hostel property. Its occupant, in addition to his secular college duties, acted as sexton to the Honan Chapel.

16. UC/OHA, Larry O'Leary, 6 Dec. 1990.

17. 'Report of Joint Committee on Governance and Management' (chaired by Mr Liam St J. Devlin), submitted to the president on 22 July 1994 and initially discussed by the Academic Council and Governing Body, September 1994.

18. In contrast, the denizens of the old common-room, surveying the tranquillity of the near-deserted Quadrangle in early autumn, would murmur to one another, not entirely in jest: 'Ah, wouldn't it be a grand place without the students'.

19. Despite increased government spending on education, social inequalities persist: see *White Paper on Education* (1995) pp. 97ff. Projects such as the BITE programme, under Dublin City University auspices, show how third-level institutions may help. A number of studies have demonstrated the low level of working class representation in Irish universities. See Patrick Clancy, *Participation in Higher Education: A National Survey* (Dublin, 1982) and *Who goes to College: A Second National Survey* (Dublin, 1988). Clancy notes the low representation of students from less privileged backgrounds in such high status faculties as law and medicine. Teresa Dowling's research had similar results for UCC specifically, and further established that students from privileged backgrounds tended to have longer second-level careers and more opportunities for individual coaching: Teresa Dowling, 'Inequalities in Preparation for University Entrance: An Examination of the Educational Histories of Entrants to UCC', *Irish Journal of Sociology*, vol. I (1991), pp. 18–30.

    I am indebted to Teresa Dowling of the Department of Sociology for these references.

BIBLIOGRAPHY

The bibliography deals with the sources used in writing the book, but it is also intended as a general guide to materials for further study of particular aspects and phases of the college's history.

Archival Sources

National Archives of Ireland, Dublin

Chief Secretary's Office Registered Papers, 1845–1908 (CSORP). (This vast collection is of central importance for the history of Queen's College Cork. Cited by year and reference number.)
Chief Secretary's Office Miscellaneous Letters and Papers
Board of Works Provincial Colleges Letter Books

For the post-independence history of UCC, there is much source material in the files of the Department of the Taoiseach and the Department of Finance in particular, but also in the Department of Education, Department of Agriculture and Department of the Gaeltacht.

UCC Archives

A progressive archival policy is reflected in the appointment of a full-time college archivist, Virginia Teehan, and in the consequently flourishing state of the archives. These include:

Charters and Statutes for QCC and UCC
Queen's College Council Minutes
UCC Governing Body Minutes
UCC Finance Committee Minutes
UCC Academic Council Minutes
Faculty Minutes
Miscellaneous letters and Letter Books. (The preserved correspondence is both external – with governments and other outside bodies – and internal e.g. letters laid before council by students and others.)
Files on individual chairs and on special issues
Title deeds, property registers, architectural plans and drawings, photographs, general memorabilia

Registrar's Letter-books
Staff Roll Books of Professors and Lecturers
Class Rolls etc.
Proceedings of Student Societies
Collections of papers and letters of individuals associated with the college
Oral History Archives (OHA). Between November 1990 and June 1991, some 130
    individuals associated with the college – retired or long-serving staff members of all
    grades, and a selection of graduates – were interviewed on tape. The result is a
    kaleidoscopic impression of the college since the 1920s, ranging from the richly
    anecdotal to the academically reflective.

In general, the College Archives (identified by the generic description UC, followed by
the particular creating office) reflect the functioning, society and character of the college in
its two successive incarnations. The archives are an evolving collection.
    The office of the finance officer and secretary retains contemporary files. To protect
the interests of both staff and students, the house policy is observed that records are closed
to the research public for thirty years from the last citation date.

Cork Archives Institute

Dowden Papers
Corporation of Cork: Reports and Returns of Committees etc.

Special Collections, Boole Library, UCC

Papers of such professors as George Boole, Tórna (Tadhg Ó Donnchadha), Cormac Ó
Cuilleanáin and Daniel Corkery
Munster Pamphlets (MP)
Munster University Papers (MUP)
Anglo-Indian Collection

There is material of considerable college relevance in the Munster Pamphlets (MP)
collection.

University College, Dublin: Archives

Papers of Ernest Blythe, Michael Hayes, Patrick McGilligan, Eoin MacNeill, Michael
    Tierney

National Library of Ireland

Letters and papers (largely press-cuttings) collected by Sir Thomas A. Larcom, under-
    secretary 1853–68, member of QUI Senate

Monteagle Papers: correspondence of Lord Monteagle, 1790–1866, particularly letters from Lord Clarendon (lord lieutenant), 1850–51

Trinity College Dublin: Archives

Papers of Michael Davitt

Office of Public Works (OPW): Archives

Annual Reports of the Commissioners of Public Works

National University of Ireland: Archives

NUI Senate and Convocation Minutes

Published Material

Parliamentary proceedings (in particular: Hansard, Dáil Éireann, Seanad Éireann)
Bills and Statutes, in particular:
    Colleges (Ireland) Act 1845. 8 & 9 Vict., c.66, 31 July 1845
    Royal University of Ireland Act 1881. 44 & 45 Vict., c.52, 22 Aug. 1881
    Irish Universities Act 1908. 8 Edw. VII, c.38, 1 Aug. 1908
President's Reports, (PR), Queen's College Cork, 1849–1909: the college president was bound by law to make an annual report, published as a parliamentary paper. Each *President's Report* contains information of greatly varying substance and importance: during the Slattery (1890–96) and Blennerhassett (1897–1904) presidencies, for example, some of the reports are skimpy in the extreme. Generally, however, the reports are mines of information on building development, student statistics (including denominational breakdown), and the conditions of the individual departments, the library and museums. They reflect changing concerns from one presidency to the next. They incorporate the reports of departmental heads and of deans of residence, and include lists of staff publications and examination papers as well as statements of presidential policy and aspirations. Finally, they carry the texts of visitation proceedings, extraordinary as well as triennial. Copies are available for consultation in the Boole Library.
President's Reports (PR) University College Cork, 1909–
Reports from the Select Committees on Foundation Schools and Education in Ireland: part I – 1835; part II – 1836. H.C. 1835 (630), 1836 (586), in H.C. 1836, xiii. I to 1822 [Evidence taken before Wyse Committee]
Report from the Select Committee on Foundation Schools and Education in Ireland (9 Aug. 1838). H.C. 1837–38 (701), vii, 345–436 [Report of Wyse Committee]
Reports of Her Majesty's Commissioners appointed to inquire into the progress and condition of the Queen's Colleges at Belfast, Cork and Galway. H.C. 1857–8 [2413], xxi, 53–572 [Commission dated 6 Feb. 1857; report 30 June 1858]

Report of the Treasury Commissioners appointed to inquire into certain matters connected with the Queen's Colleges at Belfast, Cork and Galway. Dublin 1876
[prepared for use of the government and not presented to parliament. Copy in National Archives Registered Papers 1907, 6333]

Reports of the Commissioners appointed by His Excellency John Poyntz, Earl Spenser, Lord Lieutenant of Ireland, to inquire into certain matters affecting the well-being and efficiency of the Queen's Colleges in Ireland. H.C. 1884–5 (C. 4313), xxv. 1–658
[Commission dated 6 May 1884; report of majority (pp. 1–62) dated 18 Feb. 1885, of minority (pp. 63–104), 23 Feb. 1885]

Other Relevant Parliamentary Papers:

Returns of Number of Days since opening of Queen's Colleges at Belfast, Galway and Cork that Presidents and Members of Council were in Residence 1852–53 (515) XCIV.515 [mf. 57.690]

Correspondence between Presidents of Queen's Colleges in Ireland and the Irish Government on Residence of their Presidents in their Colleges 1859 Session 1 (197) XXI Pt. II. 411 [mf. 64. 170]

Return of Depositions before Justices of Peace in case of Burning of Queen's College Cork 1864 (194) XLVI.437 [mf. 70.373]

Correspondence relative to Burning of Queen's College, Cork 1864 (210) XLVI 449 [mf. 70.373]

Return of Number of Days during which President attended Queen's College Cork 1867–68 (12) LIII. 773 [mf. 74.635]

Post-independence Commissions

Report of Commission on Accommodation Needs of the Constituent Colleges of the National University, 1959 PR 5089

Commission on Higher Education 1960–67 (Dublin, 1967): submissions by members of UCC staff in UC/PO/254

College Publications

QCC Calendars
UCC Calendars
Prospectus, Queen's College Cork. By order of the President. 22nd August 1849. (Alex Thom, Dublin)
UCC Official Gazette (1911–20)
Sessional Lists (1926–43: examination results, lists of graduates, staff publications, etc.)
The College Courier (UCC staff newsletter, 1976–84)
The Graduate (1990–)
A Handbook of UCC (Cork, 1912), Munster Pamphlets (MP) 902 Box 4. (This is an informative and well-illustrated publication at a time of transition. A clear sketch-map of the campus reflects developments in Windle's early presidency. The prospectus

highlights the BA degree in journalism as unique in Ireland, or perhaps in the British Isles.)

Cork University Record (CUR): from April 1956 *UCC Record (UCCR)* Appearing from 1944 to 1980, initially three times a year and then annually, the *Record* was a substantial publication serving a variety of purposes. It chronicled the year's events; carried examination results, statements of college policy, and news of staff appointments and obituaries; and included articles on college history as well as personal reminiscences. These latter were particularly important, since some of the contributors in the early issues represented a link with the origins of the college: thus John Griffin, retired head gardener, recalled (*CUR*, no. 2, Christmas 1944) talking in 1882 to an older gardener who witnessed 'the first sod being turned' for the college foundations. While the discontinuance of the *Record* in 1980 was regrettable, the published issues constitute an important source for the history of the college. The *Record* has a simple index and it has not been thought necessary to detail its voluminous contents in this bibliography.)

Student Magazines:

The Quarryman	*An Síol*
The Locker	*Aire*
QCC	*The Gazette*

These files are in Special Collections, Boole Library.

Contemporary Publications

Banquet to Sir Robert Kane, President of Queen's College Cork, given at the Imperial Hotel, Cork, April 8, 1850 (Nash: Cork, 1850) [MP 902, Box 4]

Blennerhassett, Sir Rowland, *University Education in England, France and Germany with a special reference to the needs of Ireland, being the inaugural Address delivered at Queen's College Cork* (John Murray: London, 1898)

Blennerhassett, Sir Rowland, 'University Education in Ireland', *Nineteenth Century*, Apr. 1904.

Kane, Sir Robert, *Inaugural Address delivered at the opening of Queen's College Cork* . . . 7 November 1849 (Dublin, 1849) [MP 902, Box 4]

Kane, Sir Robert, *Address delivered at the Public distribution of Prizes, Queen's College, Cork, 25 October 1850* (Hodges and Smith: Dublin, 1850).

Kane, Sir Robert, *The Queen's University in Ireland and the Queen's Colleges, their progress and present state: An Address delivered at the distribution of prizes in Queen's College Cork, 27 November 1856* (Dublin, 1856)

Sullivan, W.K., *University Education in Ireland: a letter to Sir John Dalberg Acton* (Dublin and London, 1866)

Visit of Her Most Gracious Majesty, Queen Victoria, to the City of Cork (Purcell: Cork, 1849) [MP 902, Box 4]. Refers to her procession, on the afternoon of 3 August 1849, 'passing the Queen's College where H.M.'s statue, presented by Sir Thomas Deane, was inaugurated with great enthusiasm'.

Windle, Bertram C.A., 'The Irish University Question', *Fortnightly Review*, May 1905

Windle, Bertram C.A., 'The City and the University' (Presidential Address, Cork Literary and Scientific Society), *University Review*, February 1907

Windle, Bertram C.A., 'The Irish Universities Bill, 1908', *Dublin University Review*, Apr. 1908.

Windle, Bertram C.A., 'The Future Universities of Ireland', *Dublin University Review*, Oct. 1908

Wyse, Thomas, MP, *Speech on the extension and improvement of academical, collegiate and university education in Ireland at the meeting held for that purpose at Cork, 13 November 1844, with notes documentary and illustrative* (London, 1845) [TCD, M. p.52 and RIA, Haliday 1930]

Newspapers

Catholic Herald
Cork Constitution (CC)
Cork Evening Echo (EE)
The Cork Examiner (CE)
Cork Free Press (FP)
Cork Southern Reporter
Cork Weekly Examiner (CWE)
The Freeman's Journal (FJ)
Illustrated London News (ILN)
Irish Builder and Engineer
Irish Independent (II)
The Irish Press (IP)
Irish Statesman
The Irish Times (IT)
Kerry News
Kerry Sentinel
Manchester Guardian (MG)
Morning Post
The Standard
The Times (T)
Times Educational Supplement (TES)
Tipperary Star
Waterford Star

Other Works

Ahearne, C.D., *Professor O'Rahilly's Pig* (Cork, n.d.)

Anon., 'The Three Year Plan', *CUR*, no. 4, Summer 1945

Anon., 'Recent Gifts to the College', *CUR*, no. 19, Summer 1950 (includes 'new' coat-of-arms)

Anon., 'Dr. O'Rahilly and UCC: An Appreciation', *CUR*, no. 30, Summer 1955

Anon., 'The University and the Business Community', *UCCR*, no. 32, Easter 1957

Anon., 'La Retraite, College Road', *UCCR*, no. 54, 1979

Anon., 'The Crawford Donations', *UCC Official Gazette,* VI, 16 December 1915

Barry, P.D., ed., *George Boole: A Miscellany* (Cork, 1969)

Bolster, E., *A History of the Diocese of Cork: The Episcopate of William Delany 1847–86* (Cork, 1993)

Buttimer, C.G., 'Celtic and Irish in College, 1849–1944', *JCHAS*, vol. 94, 1989

Buttimer, C.G., 'An Ghaeilge i gColáiste na hOllscoile, Corcaigh, 1845–1995', *The Irish Review*, no. 17, Summer 1995

Bowen, D., *Paul Cardinal Cullen and the Shaping of Modern Irish Catholicism* (Dublin, 1983)

Boyle, Connell and Patrick M. Quinlan, 'Agriculture and the University', *University Review*, Autumn 1954

Cahill, M., 'Memories of Queen's College Cork', *CUR*, no. 29, Summer 1954

Coakley, D., and M. Horgan, *Through the Eyes of the Quarryman* (Cork, n.d.)

Cody, Bryan A., *The River Lee, Cork and the Corkonians* (first published 1859; republished Cork, 1974)

Coffey, P., 'The College and the Gaol', *CUR*, no. 7, Summer 1946

Cohen, Yvonne, 'New Light on George Boole: An Analysis of the Boole Papers of UCC', MA, 1989, UCC (Ch. 4, Queen's College Cork)

Conlan, Patrick, OFM, 'Berkeley Hall – St Anthony's Hall – Honan Hostel (UCC)', *JCHAS*, vol. 100, 1995, pp. 16–28

Conroy, T.A., 'The Library', *CUR*, no. 4, Summer 1945

Cooke, Richard T., *The Mardyke: Cork City's Country Walk in History* (Cork, 1990)

Cummins, N. Marshall, *Some Chapters of Cork Medical History* (Cork, 1957)

Cronin, Maura, 'Denny Lane', *JCHAS*, vol. 100, 1995, and vol. 101, 1996

Dann, Alfred G., *George Webster DD* (Dublin, 1892)

Dann, Alfred G., *The Story of Berkeley Hall . . . now St Anthony's Hall, Cork* (Ennis, 1909)

Delanty, Greg and Nuala Ní Dhomhnaill (eds), *Jumping Off Shadows: Selected Contemporary Irish Poets* (Cork, 1995)

De Vericour, R., *An Historical Analysis of Christian Civilisation* (London, 1851)

Dillon, Eilís, 'In the Honan Hostel', *The Cork Anthology*, ed. Seán Dunne (Cork, 1993)

Dillon, Thomas, 'Bunnell Lewis: Reminiscences', *CUR*, no. 3, Easter 1945

Dillon, Thomas, 'Further Reminiscences', *CUR*, no. 4, Summer 1945

Dowling, Teresa, 'Inequalities in Preparation for University Entrance: An Examination of The Educational Histories of Entrants to UCC', *Irish Journal of Sociology,* vol. I, 1991

Dunne, Seán (ed.), *The Cork Review* (Cork, 1991)

Dunne, Seán (ed.), *The College: A Photographic History of University College Cork* (Cork, 1995)

Egan, Bartholomew, OFM, 'The Friars Minor and the Honan Hostel UCC', *Archivium Franciscanum Historicum* An. 73, 1980

England, John, *The Catholic University and the Queen's Colleges* (Cork, 1865). England was professor of natural philosophy at QCC

Fanning, Ronan, *The Irish Department of Finance 1922–58* (Dublin, 1978)

Fanning, Ronan, 'Economists and Governments: Ireland 1922–52', *Hermathena*, no. cxxxv, Winter 1983

Fitzgerald, D.P., 'The Cork Schools of Medicine', *CUR*, no. 4, Summer 1945

Fleischmann, Aloys, 'Music in UCC', *CUR*, no. 4, Summer 1945

Fleischmann, Aloys, 'The Music Department, UCC', unpublished

Fleischmann, Aloys, 'University Appointments', *University Review,* vol. 1, no. 11 (n.d.)

Fleischmann, Aloys, 'Seán Ó Faoláin: A Personal Memoir', in Seán Dunne (ed.) *The Cork Review* (Cork, 1991)

Gaughan, J. Anthony, *Alfred O'Rahilly*, 4 vols. but particularly *I: Academic* (Dublin, 1986) and *II: Public Figure* (Dublin, 1989)

Girvin, Brian, 'The Evolution and Consolidation of University Education in Cork, 1849–1967', unpublished

Glavin, Harry, 'A half-century of memories of UCC', *UCCR*, no. 42, 1967

Good, James, 'Theology in UCC', *UCCR*, no. 46, 1971

Griffin, 'John Griffin Looks Back', *CUR*, no. 2, Christmas 1944

Grubb, Howard, 'On the Equatorial Telescope and on the New Observatory of the Queen's College, Cork', paper read 21 April 1879, Scientific Proceedings of the RDS, II, part v, pp. 347–69 [MP 902, Box 6]

Gwynn, Denis (research professor of modern Irish history, UCC, 1947–63) is the author of a large number of articles in *CUR/UCCR* from 1947 to 1960, dealing with the origins of the Queen's College, the Crawford benefactions, and Windle's presidency. They are too numerous to detail here, but are easily locatable

Gwynn, Denis, 'Monsignor Alfred O'Rahilly 1884–1969', *Studies*, vol. LVIII, Winter 1969

Harmon, Maurice, 'The Chair at UCC', in Seán Dunne (ed.) *The Cork Review* (Cork, 1991)

Harmon, Maurice, *Seán Ó Faoláin* (London, 1994)

Hegarty, W.J., 'The Irish Hierarchy and the Queen's Colleges (1845–50)', *CUR*, no. 5, Christmas 1945

Hennessy, J. Pope, *The Failure of the Queen's Colleges and of Mixed Education in Ireland* (London, 1859). Hennessy was a Catholic graduate of QCC

Horgan, John J., 'Sir Bertram Windle', *Studies*, vol. XXI, December 1932

Joint Committee on Governance and Management: Report to Governing Body UCC, 1994

Keogh, Dermot, 'Democracy gone dotty', in Seán Dunne (ed.) *The Cork Review* (Cork, 1991)

Keogh, Dermot, 'The Catholic Church and the Godless Colleges, 1845–1995', in Long and Corkery (eds), *Theology in the Universities* (forthcoming)

Larkin, Emmet. In Larkin's monumental work in several volumes on the 'making' of the nineteenth-century Irish Catholic Church, there are informative references to ecclesiastical attitudes to the Queen's Colleges and to Cork in particular. See references in text and notes to individual volumes.

McCarthy, J.P., 'In Search of Cork's Collecting Traditions: from Kilcrea's Library to the Boole Library of Today', *JCHAS*, vol. 100, 1995

McCarthy, M.D., 'The Cork University Social Survey', *CUR*, no. 3, Easter 1945

McCarthy, M.D., 'Some University Statistics', *CUR*, no. 4, Summer 1945

McCartney, Donal, *The National University of Ireland and Eamon de Valera* (Dublin, 1983). Deals in detail with de Valera's application for the chair of mathematical physics in UCC in 1913

McElligott, (Tom) T.J., *This Teaching Life: A Memoir of Schooldays in Ireland* (Mullingar, 1986)

McElligott, Tom, *Six o'clock all over Cork* (Dublin, 1992)

McElligott, T.J., 'West Wing Days', *CE*, 30 Dec. 1994 [Reminiscences of the 1930s in UCC]

McGrath, Fergal, *Newman's University: Idea and Reality* (London, 1951)

MacHale, Des, *George Boole: His Life and Work* (Dublin, 1985)

MacLysaght, Edward, *Changing Times: Ireland since 1898* (Gerrards Cross, 1978)

Macnaughton Jones, H., 'Old Memories of the QCC'. Poem read at the Old Corkonians Dinner, 30 Mar. 1895. [MP 886]. [Nostalgically-charged rhyming couplets, with informative notes]

McNaughton Jones, H., *A Piece of Delf and Other Fragments* (London, 1905)

Maume, Patrick, *Life that is Exile: Daniel Corkery and the Search for Irish–Ireland* (Belfast, 1993)

Michalski, K., 'The Polish Students at UCC', *CUR*, no. 8, Christmas 1950

Moody, T.W., 'The Irish University Question in the Nineteenth Century', *History*, vol. xlii, no. 148, 1958

Moody, T.W. and J.C. Beckett, *Queen's Belfast 1845–1949. The History of a University* 2 vols. (London, 1959)

Mortell, Deirdre, 'Women in Queen's College, Cork, 1883–1912', unpublished paper

Murphy, John A., 'Post-war Society: The Ambience of a College', *The Irish Review*, no. 2, 1987, and 'A Catholic College: UCC in the 1940s and 1950s', *The Irish Review*, no. 4, 1988

Murphy, John A., 'A Godless College?', in Long and Corkery (eds) *Theology in the Universities* (forthcoming)

Ó Cadhlaigh, Cormac, 'Scoláire bocht: mar is fearr is cuimhin liom', ch. 4, (unpublished memoirs)

Ó Ciardha, T., 'Town and Gown in Closer Liaison: Future Plans for UCC outlined', *UCCR*, no. 54, 1979

Ó Cuilleanáin, Cormac, 'Gaelachas i dtosach Ré an Choláiste', *CUR*, no. 30, Summer 1955

O'Dwyer, Frederick, *The Architecture of Deane and Woodward* (Cork, forthcoming)

Ó Faoláin, Seán, 'Daniel Corkery', *Dublin University Magazine*, April–June 1936

O'F[laherty], K[athleen], 'Monsignor Alfred O'Rahilly', *UCCR*, no. 45, 1970

O'F[laherty], K[athleen], 'Random Notes on QCC in the Fifties', *CUR*, no. 10, Summer 1947

O'F[laherty], K[athleen], 'Politics in QCC', *CUR*, no. 22, Summer 1951

Ó Glaisne, Risteárd, *Dubhghlas de h-Íde: Ceannrodaí Cultúrtha, 1860–1910* (Baile Átha Cliath, 1991)

O'Kelly, M.J., *The Honan Chapel UCC* (Cork, 1966)

O'Leary, Denis, 'The First Professor of Irish in QCC' (Owen Connellan), *CUR*, no. 9, Easter 1947

O'Leary, Larry, 'A Royal Burial at UCC', *UCCR*, no. 49, 1974

Ó Murchú, Mícheál W., 'Alfred O'Rahilly: Pathfinder in Adult Education', *Irish Ecclesiastical Record,* vol. 7, no. 2, 1988

Ó Murchú, Mícheál W., 'Alfred O'Rahilly and the Provision of Adult Education at University College, Cork', *Social Commitment and Adult Education*, ed. Denis O'Sullivan (Cork, 1989)

O'Neill, Mary, 'The Herbarium of University College, Cork', *UCCR*, no. 44, 1969

Ó Raghallaigh, Deasmhumhan, *Sir Robert Kane, First President of QCC* (Cork, 1942)

Ó Raghallaigh, Deasmhumhan, 'The College in Flames' in D. Coakley and M. Horgan (eds) *Through the Eyes of the Quarryman* (Cork, n.d.; reprinted from *Quarryman* 1942)

O'Rahilly, Alfred, 'The Irish University Question', *Studies*, vol. L, 1961 and vol. LI, 1962

O'Rahilly, Ronan, 'Henry Macnaughton-Jones', *CUR*, no. 14, Christmas 1948

O'Rahilly, Ronan, 'The BMA in QCC' [1879], *CUR*, no. 11, Christmas 1947

O'Rahilly, Ronan, 'Stained Glass Windows in the Aula Maxima', *CUR*, no. 18, Easter 1950

O'Rahilly, Ronan, *Benjamin Alcock: The First Professor of Anatomy and Physiology in Queen's College, Cork* (Cork, 1948)

O'Rahilly, Ronan, *A History of Cork Medical School* (Cork, 1949)

Ó Riain, Pádraig, *Beatha Bharra* (London, 1994)

Ó Riain, Pádraig, 'Another Cork Charter: the life of St Finbarr', *JCHAS*, vol. 90, 1985

Oldham, Alice, 'Women and the Irish University Question', *New Ireland Review*, vol. VI, Feb. 1897

Pearson, C. Yelverton, 'A review of medical education in Cork', *The Lancet*, 31 Dec. 1927

Pettit, Seán F., 'The Queen's College Cork: Its Origins and Early History 1803–58', PhD thesis, NUI, 1973

Pettit, Seán F., 'The Queen's College Cork: The First Session, 1849–50', *UCCR*, no. 49, 1974

Pettit, Seán F., 'The Queen's College Cork: Archival Sources, 1849–50', *UCCR*, no. 51, 1976

Pettit, Seán F., *This City of Cork 1700–1900* (Cork, 1977), especially chs. X and XI

Power, Rev. Patrick, *The Chapel of St Finbarr, UCC* (Cork, n.d.)

Power, Rev. Patrick, *The Ogham Stones UCC* (Cork, 1931)

Quinlan, P.M., 'UCC and the Agricultural Institute', *CUR,* no. 31, Easter 1956: see also
  Boyle, Connell

Ryan, Mary, 'Professor E.M. O'Sullivan: Memories of a Colleague', *UCCR,* no. 32,
  Easter 1957

Slattery, David, 'James W. Slattery, 1831–97', unpublished paper, 1995
Sperrin-Johnson J.C., 'Professor Marcus Hartog', *CUR,* no. 7, Summer 1946
Sutton, Ralph, 'Significant Details of the College Buildings', *CUR,* no. 12, Easter 1948

Taylor, Monica, *Sir Bertram Windle* (London, 1932)
Tierney, Myles, *Eoin MacNeill, 1867–1945* (Oxford, 1980)

Vaughan, W.E., *A New History of Ireland, v: Ireland under the Union, I 1801–70* (Oxford,
  1989)

Wheeler, T.S., 'Sir Robert Kane, His Life and Work', *Studies,* vol. XXXIII, 1944
Wheeler, T.S., 'Sir Robert Kane: His Life and Work', *National Resources of Ireland* (RDS,
  1944)
Wheeler, T.S., 'Sir Robert Kane; First President of QCC', *CUR,* no. 3, Easter 1945
Wheeler, T.S., 'William Kirby Sullivan: His Work as Second President of QCC', *CUR,*
  no. 4, Summer 1945
Wheeler, T.S., 'Life and Work of William K. Sullivan', *Studies,* vol. XXXIV, 1945
White Paper on Education 1995 (Government Publication: Dublin)
Wibberley, T., 'Agricultural Education', *Studies,* vol. VIII, 1919
Windle, Bertram C.A. In addition to speeches noted above under Contemporary
  Publications, note Windle's address to *6th All-Ireland Industrial Conference* (Cork, 1910,
  MP 417), and his speech to *14th Annual Report of the Cork Industrial Development
  Association 1916* (Cork, 1917, MP 352)

INDEX